THE WORLD CUP
THE COMPLETE HISTORY

THE WORLD CUP
THE COMPLETE HISTORY

TERRY CROUCH

with JAMES CORBETT

First published in Great Britain
2002 by Aurum Press Ltd
7 Greenland Street, London NW1 0ND
www.aurumpress.co.uk

This revised edition published 2010

A catalogue record for this book is
available from the British Library.

ISBN 978 1 84513 527 0

10 9 8 7 6 5 4 3 2 1
2014 2013 2012 2011 2010

Printed and bound in the UK by Thomson Litho Ltd

Contents

The Authors

TERRY CROUCH was educated in Barnet, where he played in amateur football leagues. He managed to continue supporting Queens Park Rangers while living in Garstang, Lancashire, with his wife and five children, where he coached with Garstang Juniors and Imperial Football Club.

He compiled and wrote two editions of this book, dedicated them to his uncle, Laurie Crouch; his cousin, friend and team-mate Michael 'Martin' Lannon; and, with love, to his father, Barry Crouch. He died in 2008.

This 2010 edition has been completed by James Corbett, who is the author of *Everton: School of Science* and *England Expects*, a history of the England football team. He is European Correspondent of *World Football Insider* and lives in London.

Introduction

THE **WORLD CUP** is the greatest sporting event on Earth, a competition that evokes memories so vivid, so breathtaking, of the heroes of yesteryear: Pelé, whose genius embellished four, three times a winner, Cruyff of Holland and Puskás of Hungary, gallant losers both, for teams whose failure was glorious. Beckenbauer, West Germany's immaculate, marvellous captain who saw the heartbreak of 1966 and suffered agony in 1970 before finally triumphing in front of an ecstatic nation four years later. Kempes of Argentina and the Italian Rossi, who in 1982 and 1978 respectively scored the goals that earned their teams the glory. Schiaffino, brilliant Uruguayan, outstanding in victory in 1950 and again in defeat in 1954. Then there was England, Champions in 1966, for whom their accomplished, assured captain, the fair-haired Bobby Moore, was a wonderful example of spirit, sportsmanship and dignity; his untimely death left a nation in mourning.

Of all these great players who have thrilled us, none surely have so thoroughly dominated a tournament as did Maradona in 1986, mesmerizing opponents with his powerful running and trickery, and leading Argentina inevitably to a second title. Tragically, the stocky little striker also became embroiled in controversy and then disgraced himself in a drugs scandal, demonstrating once again the frailties of many great players in the cauldron of the modern game.

Great matches are also remembered fondly: France and Brazil in 1986, Italy and Brazil in 1982, both absorbing contests tactically, from very different footballing cultures. France and West Germany's unbearably exciting semi-final match in Spain, and of course Hungary's victory over Uruguay in 1954, when two genuinely great teams fought out an unforgettable encounter.

The competition, however, is not just for the great and the good: it is, and should always remain, a celebration, an opportunity for the

Davids to mix with the Goliaths, and do battle beneath the floodlights of football's greatest stage. Who would forget the plucky little Koreans of 1966; Roger Milla and his indomitable lions of Cameroon in 1990, so close to a semi-final place; Haiti, who almost unbelievably led the Italians in 1974; and Cuba, who back in 1938 eliminated a strong Romanian side. The beauty of the World Cup is that it embraces all, giving us the pleasure of watching El Salvador, Zaire, New Zealand, Israel, Japan and Jamaica embark, no matter how brief the experience, on their great adventure.

With such a prize on offer, it is little wonder that on occasion frayed tempers spark violent and chaotic confrontation, none more so than the notorious 'battle of Santiago', when ill-judged remarks by the Italian press infuriated the Chileans into retribution. From the start it was claimed that Chile were abusive and spitting, though the trouble erupted after an off-the-ball incident left an Italian with a broken nose. Thereafter what had begun as ugly and ill-tempered degenerated into anarchy, with the ball often incidental to proceedings. Chile won but few cared.

Through seventy-six years of absorbing drama, however, it is memories of sportsmanship and skill that quite rightly dominate our recollections, and it might be that the forever endearing image of the competition be that of a smiling Pelé and Bobby Moore exchanging shirts after the epic encounter in Leon 1970, each showing great mutual respect to a fellow giant of this most beautiful of games.

I sincerely hope that this book does justice to those to whom it is dedicated, the players who have entertained us so royally in this, the world's most prestigious sporting event.

CHAPTER 1

URUGUAY

1930

In 1904 an association designed to represent the interests of international football was founded in Paris. The Federation of International Football Associations, or FIFA, as it was known, initially consisted of seven countries: Belgium, Denmark, France, Holland, Spain, Switzerland and Sweden. One of its goals was to arrange a World Championship.

By World War I, membership had increased substantially; Argentina, Brazil, Chile and the United States truly gave FIFA world representation. The four 'Home' Associations, England, Northern Ireland, Scotland and Wales, had also joined, but for them problems lay ahead. On resumption of sporting links after the war England, supported by Scotland, Wales, Ireland, France and Belgium, expressed a reluctance to compete with their recent enemies, Germany, Austria and Hungary. Furthermore, and crucially, at a conference in Brussels in 1919 delegates agreed on a policy 'not to meet Neutral Associations nor neutral clubs who had played against the Association or the clubs of the Central Empires', and in so doing cast themselves adrift from world football. Belgium swiftly reneged, their stance inappropriate for a nation about to host the Olympic Games of 1920, but for Britain it was to be the first of many spats that would condemn their Associations ultimately into the international wilderness.

At their meeting in 1926 Henri Delauny, secretary of the French Federation, addressed FIFA delegates. 'An International Football Competition,' he said, 'could no longer be the preserve of the Olympic Games, an amateur event. Professionalism had arrived.'

But what was a professional footballer? The British Associations, having rejoined, had no doubts and submitted their definition. FIFA, with so many varying attitudes amongst its membership, could not agree, and this time the split was irreparable. Britain for many years would play no part in the World Championships, spending their time in the words of FIFA secretary Dr Schricher in 'splendid isolation'.

For the rest, however, the World Cup would shortly become reality.

In 1928 FIFA proposed at its congress that 'plans should be prepared for the staging of the World Championship', and twenty-five nations cast their votes in favour. Only Scandinavia, Sweden, Norway, Denmark, Finland and Estonia dissented. Hugo Meisl, a leading figure in Central European Football, whose recent successes had included the Mitropa Cup for club sides and then the Nations Cup contested by Czechoslovakia, Austria, Switzerland, Italy and Hungary, was given the task of organizing the event, which would need to embrace the footballing nations of South America.

Those wishing to act as hosts for the inaugural competition included Sweden (rather surprisingly, since it had opposed its inception), Holland, Hungary and Spain, but the honour was bestowed on Uruguay, Olympic Champions, who had offered to meet all entrants' travelling costs and expenses. Sculptor Abel Lafleur designed a trophy, and the title of 'The Jules Rimet Cup' was bestowed upon it in recognition of the contribution of the President of FIFA.

1930 URUGUAY 13 July–30 July

ENTRIES

Argentina	Paraguay
Belgium	Peru
Bolivia	Romania
Brazil	United States
Chile	Uruguay
France	Yugoslavia
Mexico	

GROUP STAGES

Uruguay, whose football team had impressively won gold at the 1928 Olympic Games, secured the right to host the inaugural competition for the Jules Rimet Trophy. Having emphasized that this was the year the country would celebrate its centenary, one hundred years of independence, an International Football Tournament would fit in with the celebrations. Indeed, a brand new Stadium in Montevideo, 'The Centenario', would be built in order to stage the matches. Inevitably, however, the decision to stage so prestigious an occasion on the South American continent led to the withdrawal of the cream of European football. Italy, Holland, Spain and Sweden, all of whom had declared an interest in hosting the tournament, sulkily pulled out. Austria, Germany, Hungary, Switzerland and Czechoslovakia also said no to so long a journey – despite Uruguay's generous offer to pay all expenses – and Britain, no longer a member of FIFA, maintained their splendid isolation.

The draw pitted teams in four groups of three or four, with only the winners progressing to the semi-finals. Group One featured Argentina, who, along with Uruguay from Group Three, was one of the joint favourites. Indeed, Argentina was runner-up to Uruguay at the Amsterdam Olympics. Stábile and Monti were key players for a team renowned for its virtuoso performances. France, also in the group, were one of four European teams to make the arduous journey south. However, theirs was a respectable rather than exceptional side, with Pinel their towering centre half, and Alex Thepot a goalkeeper of repute. Chile had been playing the game for many years, the South Americans benefiting from a vibrant British community in the nineteenth century. For them, Subiabre, a fine inside forward, represented the greatest danger to their opponents. Mexico, new to the game (their federation had been founded just three years earlier), was the fourth member of an interesting quartet.

In Group Two were Brazil, Bolivia and a fine Yugoslavian team. Football in Brazil, South America's largest nation, was flourishing, though as an international force they were yet to make a mark, largely, it was suggested, as a result of flagrant prejudice operated against their best black players by the country's authorities. Yugoslavia had surprisingly disappointed during the Olympics, failing miserably against Portugal; still, they were here and not without hope. In Stefanovic and Beck, Cup winners in France with Sete and Sekulic at Montpelier, they had a trio of professional mercenaries. Marjanovic, too, was a splendid forward, and Tirnanic a tricky right winger.

In Group Three, Uruguay, four weeks in training, had separated from society. Their preparation had been serious, their intention to win. Mazáli, their celebrated goalkeeper, was discarded when he dared to break an imposed curfew. Amongst their many excellent players were Ballesteros (Mazáli's replacement), Andrade, Scarone and Nasazzi (right back and captain). Peru also arrived courtesy of the recent founding of a National Football Federation. Theirs was an inexperienced team of whom there were few expectations. The Romanians, like all the European entrants, were from the middle order of the continent's footballing powers, though their monarch, King Carol, had gone to extraordinary lengths to ensure their participation, granting amnesty to suspended players, picking the team personally and negotiating their release from employers.

Group Four featured the United States, Belgium and Paraguay, none of whom were highly regarded; indeed, many of the better players in the United States had joined Britons imported into the country in the American soccer league that had subsequently been outlawed by the United States Association. However, they were fit, and with their impressive physiques they had been dubbed by the French 'The Shot Putters'.

All matches at Montevideo

Group 1	Group 3

Group 1

Argentina
Chile
France
Mexico

Group 3

Peru
Romania
Uruguay

Group 2

Bolivia
Brazil
Yugoslavia

Group 4

Belgium
Paraguay
United States

It was France from Group One who opened the Tournament, easily beating Mexico by racing to a 3–0 lead. Though the Mexicans fought back bravely, it was a lost cause, and they finally suffered a 4–1 defeat, Carreño's goal earning the team some small consolation. On the same day, America provided an immediate shock by pounding their more experienced Belgian opponents 3–0. Packed with British ex-patriots, they proved surprisingly fast and powerful – Belgium, in truth, were a disappointment.

The next day Yugoslavia allayed fears that the South American teams would be totally dominant, deservedly beating Brazil 2–1. Tirnanic and Marjanovic gave them an interval advantage, and Brazil, who replied through Preguinho, floundered against Stefanovic and his defensive colleagues as they sought in vain for an equalizing goal. Meanwhile, Romania's 'King's Men' beat the inexperienced Peruvians 3–1, Staucin scoring three and Vogl excelling. For the most part, though, football proved a secondary consideration in a rough ill-tempered affair: De Las Casas, capping a miserable day, was sent off – the first player ever dismissed in a World Cup fixture.

Argentina now came into the competition, winning 1–0 against France, the goal provided by the tough-tackling Monti, though they were unimpressive and given an uncomfortable time by their opponents. A distraction caused by referee Sr. Rego blowing the half-time whistle too soon provoked a pitch invasion which considerably delayed the re-start of the match. France suffered further when a problem that would plague future tournaments surfaced for the very first time: one of eccentric organisation. France, the losers, had been asked to play a second game in two days and were clearly disadvantaged, whilst Chile had not yet played at all!

The following day Chile got their opportunity and swept aside the naive

Mexicans, Subiabre twice finding the net, and Vidal, the Chileans' other inside forward, also rewarding enterprising play.

Yugoslavia in their three-way Group confirmed a place in the semi-finals against Bolivia, though their victory celebrations – considered inevitable – were delayed by their hopelessly outplayed opponents, whose luck and desperate tackling worried them for an hour. Bolivia, however, soon tired and finally collapsed, going down 4–0. Beck scored two, Marjanovic and Vujadinovic one each, as Yugoslavia finally feasted on Bolivia's frailties.

To general surprise America also qualified, beating Paraguay in the same overpowering manner in which they had disposed of Belgium. Patenaude, America's centre forward, added two to his total, while Florie, their captain and star player, made it a third.

Curiously Uruguay, hosts and favourites, started poorly, the waiting and expectation clearly upsetting their concentration as Peru, so ineffective against Romania, pushed them hard. Castro finally relieved their anxiety with a well taken goal, though their opponents, with Pardon, playing in goal in place of Valdiviso, and left back Maquillon, performed heroics in stemming the steady tide of attacks launched at their goal.

On the following day Chile beat France, the goal-scoring inside forward Subiabre whipping his shot beyond the excellent Thepot, thus condemning the French to an early exit. Meanwhile, Argentina flowed over Mexico, scoring six times. Stábile, a thorn in the side of the Mexican defenders, lead the goal glut, while Zumelzu, making his first appearance, converted two penalties gained from ill-judged tackling. At least poor Mexico could be consoled by their three goals.

In Group Four a match rendered academic by America's previous success saw Paraguay edge out Belgium. Peña, a clever outside left, supplied a goal to decide a moderate game between two disappointing teams. Brazil, too, already eliminated by Yugoslavia, won their final Group Two fixture 4–0 against Bolivia, though again the Bolivians gave an obstinate, gritty performance, refusing to yield until finally, as in their first match, their stamina and luck dissolved.

Uruguay confirmed their predictable progress from Group One by bewildering the 'King's Men' from Romania with faster movement and rapid passing, Dorado, Scarone, Cea and the young star Anselmo giving them an easy win. In Group One, however, the final fixture in the qualifying round saw Argentina defeating Chile amidst controversy and ugliness. An unpleasant kick by the tempestuous Monti on Chile's Torres as he stooped to head the ball led to a brief reign of chaos as a brawl ensued. When referee M. Langenus had finally regained control, Argentina reasserted their dominance and Chile succumbed 3–1.

Final Tournament – Uruguay

Group 1

France (3) **4, Mexico** (0) **1**
13.7.30 MONTEVIDEO
France: Thepot, Mattler, Capelle, Villaplane, Pinel, Chantrel, Liberati, Delfour, Maschinot (2), Laurent (1), Langiller (1)
Mexico: Bonfiglio, Gutierrez R, Rosas M, Rosas F, Sanchez, Amezcua, Perez, Carreño (1), Mejia, Ruiz, Lopez
Referee: Lombardi (Uruguay)

Argentina (0) **1, France** (0) **0**
15.7.30 MONTEVIDEO
Argentina: Bossio, Della Torre, Muttis, Suarez, Monti (1), Evaristo J, Perinetti, Varallo, Ferreyra, Gierro, Evaristo M
France: Thepot, Mattler, Capelle, Villaplane, Pinel, Chantrel, Liberati, Delfour, Maschinot, Laurent, Langiller
Referee: Rego (Brazil)

Chile (1) **3, Mexico** (0) **0**
16.7.30 MONTEVIDEO
Chile: Cortes, Morales, Porier, Torres A, Saavedra, Helgueta, Ojeda, Subiabre (2), Villalobos, Vidal, Scheuerberger
Mexico: Sota, Gutierrez R, Rosas M, Rosas F, Sanchez, Amezcua, Perez, Carreño, Ruiz, Gayon, Lopez
Referee: Christophe (Belgium)

Chile (0) **1, France** (0) **0**
19.7.30 MONTEVIDEO
Chile: Cortes, Ciaparro, Morales, Torres A, Saavedra, Torres C, Ojeda, Subiabre (1), Villalobos, Vidal, Scheuerberger
France: Thepot, Mattler, Capelle, Chantrel, Delmer, Villaplane, Liberati, Delfour, Pinel, Veinante, Langiller
Referee: Tejada (Uruguay)

Argentina (3) **6, Mexico** (1) **3**
19.7.30 MONTEVIDEO
Argentina: Bossio, Della Torre, Paternoster, Cividini, Zumelzu (2 pens), Orlandini, Peucelle, Varallo (1), Stábile (3), Demaria, Spadaro
Mexico: Bonfiglio, Gutierrez R, Gutierrez F, Rosas M (2 pens), Sanchez, Rodriguez, Rosas F, Lopez (1), Gayon, Carreño, Olivares
Referee: Saucedo (Bolivia)

Argentina (2) **3, Chile** (1) **1**
22.7.30 MONTEVIDEO
Argentina: Bossio, Della Torre, Paternoster, Evaristo J, Monti, Orlandini, Peucelle, Varallo, Stábile (2), Ferreyra, Evaristo M (1)
Chile: Cortes, Ciaparro, Morales, Torres A, Saavedra, Torres C, Avellane, Subiabre (1), Villalobos, Vidal, Aquilera
Referee: Langenus (Belgium)

	P	W	D	L	F	A	Pts
Argentina	3	3	0	0	10	4	6
Chile	3	2	0	1	5	3	4
France	3	1	0	2	4	3	2
Mexico	3	0	0	3	4	13	0

Group 2

Yugoslavia (2) **2, Brazil** (0) **1**
14.7.30 MONTEVIDEO
Yugoslavia: Jaksic, Ivkovic, Mihailovic, Arsenijevic, Stefanovic, Dokic, Tirnanic (1), Marjanovic (1), Beck, Vujadinovic, Sekulic
Brazil: Joel, Brilhante, Italia, Hermogenes, Fausto, Fernando, Poly, Nilo, Araken, Preguinho (1), Moderato
Referee: Tejada (Uruguay)

Yugoslavia (0) **4, Bolivia** (0) **0**
17.3.30 MONTEVIDEO
Yugoslavia: Jaksic, Ivkovic, Mihailovic, Arsenijevic, Stefanovic, Dokic, Tirnanic, Marjanovic (1), Beck (2), Vujadinovic (1), Najdanovic
Bolivia: Bermudez, Durandal, Ciavarria, Argote, Lara, Valderrama, Gomez, Bustamante, Mendez, Alborta, Fernández
Referee: Mateucci (Mexico)

Brazil (1) **4, Bolivia** (0) **0**
20.7.30 MONTEVIDEO
Brazil: Velloso, Ze Lulz, Italia, Hermogenes, Fausto, Fernando, Benedito, Russinho, Leite, Preguinho (2), Moderato (2)
Bolivia: Bermudez, Durandal, Ciavarria, Sainz, Lara, Valderrama, Ortiz, Bustamante, Mendez, Alborta, Fernández
Referee: Balway (France)

	P	W	D	L	F	A	Pts
Yugoslavia	2	2	0	0	6	1	4
Brazil	2	1	0	1	5	2	2
Bolivia	2	0	0	2	0	8	0

Group 3

Romania (1) **3, Peru** (0) **1**
14.7.30 MONTEVIDEO
Romania: Lapusneanu, Steiner, Bürger, Rafinski, Vogl, Fieraru, Covaci, Desu, Wetzer, Staucin (2), Barbu (1)
Peru: Valdiviso, De Las Casas, Soria, Galindo, Garcia, Valle, Flores, Villanueva, Denegri, Neira, Souza (1)
Referee: Warken (Chile)

Uruguay (0) **1, Peru** (0) **0**
18.7.30 MONTEVIDEO
Uruguay: Ballesteros, Nasazzi, Tejera, Andrade, Fernández, Gestido, Urdináran, Castro (1), Petrone, Cea, Iriarte
Peru: Pardon, De Las Casas, Maquillon, Denegri, Galindo, Astengo, Lavalle, Flores, Villanueva, Neira, Souza
Referee: Langenus (Belgium)

Uruguay (3) **4, Romania** (0) **0**
21.7.30 MONTEVIDEO
Uruguay: Ballesteros, Nasazzi, Mascheroni, Andrade, Fernández, Gestido, Dorado (1), Scarone (1), Anselmo (1), Cea (1), Iriarte
Romania: Lapusneanu, Bürger, Tacu, Robi, Vogl, Fieraru, Covaci, Desu, Wetzer, Rafinski, Barbu
Referee: Rego (Brazil)

	P	W	D	L	F	A	Pts
Uruguay	2	2	0	0	5	0	4
Romania	2	1	0	1	3	5	2
Peru	2	0	0	2	1	4	0

Group 4

USA (2) **3, Belgium** (0) **0**
13.7.30 MONTEVIDEO
USA: Douglas, Wood, Moorhouse, Gallacher, Tracey, Brown, Gonsalvez, Florie, Patenaude (1), Auld, McGhee (2)
Belgium: Badjou, Nouwens, Hoydonckx, Braine, Hellemans, Declercq, Diddens, Moeschal, Adams, Voorhoof, Versijp
Referee: Macias (Argentina)

USA (2) **3, Paraguay** (0) **0**
17.3.30 MONTEVIDEO
USA: Douglas, Wood, Moorhouse, Gallacher, Tracey, Brown, Gonsalvez, Florie (1), Patenaude (2), Auld, McGhee
Paraguay: Denis, Olmedo, Miracca, Etcheverri, Diaz, Aguirre, Nessi, Dominguez, Gonzales, Caceres, Peña
Referee: Macias (Argentina)

Paraguay (1) **1, Belgium** (0) **0**
20.7.30 MONTEVIDEO
Paraguay: Benitez P, Olmedo, Flores, Benitez S, Diaz, Garcete, Nessi, Romero, Gonzales, Caceres, Peña (1)
Belgium: Badjou, De Deken, Hoydonckx, Braine, Hellemans, Moeschal, Versijp, Delbeke, Adams, Nouwens, Diddens
Referee: Vallarino (Uruguay)

	P	W	D	L	F	A	Pts
USA	2	2	0	0	6	0	4
Paraguay	2	1	0	1	1	3	2
Belgium	2	0	0	2	0	4	0

THE SEMI-FINALS

Pitting Uruguay against Yugoslavia, and Argentina against USA, sadly the semi-finals were hopelessly one-sided. Argentina first contemptuously overwhelmed the Americans, their lead, thanks in the main to heroic defending, restricted at half-time to 1–0; thereafter it became a procession as the South Americans ambled to the first ever World Cup final by 6–1.

Yugoslavia also found to their chagrin that they were no match for Uruguay, and were themselves ground down by a team infinitely more talented than their own. Cea fired a hat-trick, Anselimo a brace and Iriarte finally dispatched them. Sekulic's goal in response was a mere blip in the mounting celebrations.

Semi-Finals

Argentina (1) **6, USA** (0) **1**
26.7.30 MONTEVIDEO
Argentina: Botasso, Della Torre, Paternoster, Evaristo J, Monti (2), Orlandini, Peucelle, Scopelli (2), Stábile (2), Ferreyra, Evaristo M
USA: Douglas, Wood, Moorhouse, Gallacher, Tracey, Brown (1), Gonsalvez, Florie, Patenaude, Auld, McGhee
Referee: Langenus (Belgium)

Uruguay (3) **6, Yugoslavia** (1) **1**
27.3.30 MONTEVIDEO
Uruguay: Ballesteros, Nasazzi, Mascheroni, Andrade, Fernández, Gestido, Dorado, Scarone, Anselmo (2), Cea (3), Iriarte (1)
Yugoslavia: Jaksic, Ivkovic, Mihailovic, Arsenijevic, Stefanovic, Dokic, Tirnanic, Marjanovic, Beck, Vujadinovic, Sekulic (1)
Referee: Rego (Brazil)

THE FINAL

As had been anticipated, it was Uruguay and Argentina, obviously the best teams, who would renew their bitter rivalry in a final contest for the Trophy of Jules Rimet and the title 'World Champions'.

For the final, Uruguay were forced to recall Castro in place of the injured Anselmo. The home team consequently began nervously, conceding the initiative. A goal by Dorado failed to galvanize them, and the persistence of Argentina was rewarded as first Peucelle and then the prolific Stábile put them ahead at the end of the first half. However, Uruguay began to find their form, with Cea ending a Nasazzi run firing past Botasso for 2–2, and hard though Argentina tried, they could not resist. Iriarte made it 3–2 and then Castro crowned his good fortune with a fourth. To the cacophonic symphony of their delirious supporters, Uruguay were acknowledged Champions.

Final

Uruguay (1) **4, Argentina** (2) **2**
30.7.30 MONTEVIDEO
Uruguay: Ballesteros, Nasazzi, Mascheroni, Andrade, Gestido, Fernández, Dorado (1), Scarone, Castro (1), Cea (1), Iriarte (1)
Argentina: Botasso, Della Torre, Paternoster, Evaristo J, Monti, Suarez, Peucelle (1), Varallo, Stábile (1), Ferreyra, Evaristo M
Referee: Langenus (Belgium)

The Tournament itself had been a great success, ensuring its own future. Moreover, the best teams by far had contested an exciting final. Still, with so many of Europe's finest declining to compete, there had been a predictability about proceedings which somewhat diminished Uruguay's achievement. The champions would remember, and in 1934 when Europe, specifically Italy, hosted the competition, Uruguay would tartly but understandably refuse to travel to defend their crown.

CHAPTER 2

ITALY

1934

Qualifying Tournament
32 entries

Argentina, Austria, Belgium, Brazil, Bulgaria, Chile, Cuba, Czechoslovakia, Egypt, Estonia, France, Germany, Greece, Haiti, Holland, Hungary, Republic of Ireland, Italy, Lithuania, Luxembourg, Mexico, Palestine, Peru, Poland, Portugal, Romania, Spain, Sweden, Switzerland, Turkey, USA, Yugoslavia

Group 1 (USA, Cuba, Mexico, Haiti)
Haiti v Cuba 1–3, Haiti v Cuba 1–1, Haiti v Cuba 0–6, Mexico v Cuba 3–2, Mexico v Cuba 5–0, Mexico v Cuba 4–1
Extra qualifying match (in Rome)
USA v Mexico 4–2
USA qualified

Group 2 (Brazil, Peru)
Brazil qualified (Peru withdrew)

Group 3 (Argentina, Chile)
Argentina qualified (Chile withdrew)

Group 4 (Egypt, Palestine, Turkey withdrew)
Egypt v Palestine 7–1, Egypt v Palestine 4–1
Egypt qualified

Group 5 (Sweden, Estonia, Lithuania)
Sweden v Estonia 6–2, Lithuania v Sweden 0–2
Sweden qualified

Group 6 (Spain, Portugal)
Spain v Portugal 9–0, Spain v Portugal 2–1
Spain qualified

Group 7 (Italy, Greece)
Italy v Greece 4–0
Italy qualified

Group 8 (Austria, Hungary, Bulgaria)
Bulgaria v Hungary 1–4, Austria v Bulgaria 6–1, Hungary v Bulgaria 4–1
Austria and Hungary qualified

Group 9 (Czechoslovakia, Poland)
Poland v Czechoslovakia 1–2
Poland withdrew before return match
Czechoslovakia qualified

Group 10 (Yugoslavia, Switzerland, Romania)
Yugoslavia v Switzerland 2–2, Switzerland v Romania 2–2, Romania v Yugoslavia 2–1
Switzerland and Romania qualified

Group 11 (Holland, Belgium, Rep of Ireland)
Rep of Ireland v Belgium 4–4, Holland v Rep of Ireland 5–2, Belgium v Holland 2–4
Holland and Belgium qualified (Belgium on goal average)

Group 12 (Germany, France, Luxembourg)
Luxembourg v Germany 1–9, Luxembourg v France 1–6
Germany and France qualified

1934 ITALY 27 May–10 June

QUALIFIERS

Argentina	Holland
Austria	Hungary
Belgium	Italy
Brazil	Romania
Czechoslovakia	Spain
Egypt	Sweden
France	Switzerland
Germany	United States

It was Italy who emerged from numerous FIFA conferences with the nomination as Europe's first host nation. Eager to impress, Mussolini's fascist government relished the opportunity to espouse their virtues, their fine team offering them plentiful scope for propaganda. General Vacaro, appointed as a political representative and President of their Federation, later declared, 'The ultimate purpose of the Tournament was to show that fascist sport partakes of a great quality of the ideal.'

Once again Britain was in 'isolation', and Uruguay, still angry at the European snub of 1930, declined the invitation. Undoubtedly, though, the field was stronger this year and constituted most of the world's footballing powers of the time. Interestingly, too, the group format incorporated by FIFA for the Montevideo Tournament was dispensed with in favour of a more traditional sixteen-team knockout competition.

Italy were the favourites, with Louis Monti, the roving centre half, one of three Argentineans of Italian origin selected. Pozzo, their coach, justified the Argentineans' inclusion on the grounds that they would have been called to the flag during the Great War: 'if they were able to die for Italy they could certainly play for Italy'. Guisseppe Meazza would also play for the Italians, a goal-scoring inside forward and darling of the Internazionale fans. Austria were a major challenger – their 'Wunder Team' inspired by Hugo Meisl had annihilated Bulgaria to qualify and had defeated Italy in a friendly match in Turin. Smistik was an adventurous centre half, and the tall blond Matthias Sindelar their sinewy centre forward. Argentina had entered but, tired of losing their best players to the Italian League, they cautiously left many of the team at home. Brazil had also come without the necessity of qualifying. Peru withdrew. Hungary and Spain came as dark horses: the Spanish had demolished poor Portugal 11–1 on aggregate (and included their legendary goalkeeper Ricardo Zamora), and Hungary had a talented team aided by the extraordinary centre forward Dr Georges Sarosi. As for the rest, Czechoslovakia had beaten England earlier in May and appeared to be an emerging nation, while Germany, Sweden, Switzerland, Romania, Belgium, France and Holland completed Europe's entrants. The USA, with a much changed team, and mysterious Egypt, conquerors of Hungary in the Olympic Tournament of 1924, represented the North American and African continents. Coincidentally, Egypt had drawn… Hungary!

The Draw

Italy v United States	**Rome**
Czechoslovakia v Romania	**Trieste**
Austria v France	**Turin**
Belgium v Germany	**Florence**
Brazil v Spain	**Genoa**
Argentina v Sweden	**Bologna**
Egypt v Hungary	**Naples**
Holland v Switzerland	**Milan**

THE PRELIMINARY ROUND

Italy opened their World Cup in devastating style in Florence, sweeping a disappointing America aside by Schiavio scoring a hat-trick. Egypt brought back to Hungary painful memories of Paris 1924. Troubling them repeatedly and with Fawzi snatching two goals, they were level at half-time 2–2. There the similarity ended, as Hungary finally raised their game to eliminate the brave Africans 4–2.

A lethargic Germany were promptly punished by Belgium, whose goals from Voorhoof gave them a surprising early lead. However, the Germans responded, and Conen, scorer of three goals, inspired a comeback from behind for a 5–2 victory, Szepan for Germany proving to be a huge influence. At Bologna an Argentinean team shorn of its class of 1930 by the depredations of Italian clubs went out at once by 3–2 to Sweden, for whom Jonasson, excellent at centre forward, scored twice. There was disappointment for the South Americans that their own aspirations could not have matched the achievements of Stábile and company in the 1930 World Cup. Sweden for their part demonstrated sound technique and unflappable temperament. Brazil were also beaten easily, 3–1, by Spain. Iraragorri and Langara twice netted before the interval, and for Brazil, despite their centre forward Leonidas managing a goal, there was no way back. Switzerland beat Holland in Milan, though it was surprisingly close. Abegglen (one of three brothers to play for the Swiss) scored once and Kielholz twice, with Holland's reply coming from Vente and Smit. It was at Trieste that Romania, with just Covaci remaining from their Uruguayan enterprise, went out rather unluckily to the Czechs. Dobai put them ahead before Nejedly and then Puc put Czechoslovakia into a 2–1 lead. They held this courtesy of their redoubtable goalkeeper, Planicka, who twice denied the clever and spirited Romanians at the death. Finally, Austria's 'Wunder Team' played France in the last game of the series. France threatened immediately and thereafter matched their more illustrious opponents throughout, despite the loss of their captain, Nicholas, to injury, which left them with only ten fit men. The game ended 2–2. For France the extra-time defeat was cruel: Schall was offside when he received the ball but was allowed to go on and score. Later, much later, Schall would admit that he was indeed offside, but by then France had gone home.

Final Tournament – Italy
Preliminary Round

Italy (3) **7, USA** (0) **1**
27.5.34 ROME
Italy: Combi, Rosetta, Allemandi, Pizziolo, Monti, Bertolini, Guaita, Meazza (1), Schiavio (3), Ferrari (1), Orsi (2)
USA: Hjulian, Czerkiewicz, Moorhouse, Pietras, Gonsalvez, Florie, Ryan, Nilson, Donelli (1), Dick, MacLean
Referee: Mercet (Switzerland)

Czechoslovakia (0) **2, Romania** (1) **1**
27.5.34 TRIESTE
Czechoslovakia: Planicka, Zenizek, Ctyroky, Kostalek, Cambal, Krcil, Junek, Silny, Sobotka, Nejedly (1), Puc (1)
Romania: Zambori, Vogl, Albu, Deheleanu, Cotormani, Moravet, Bindea, Covaci, Sepi, Bodola, Dobai (1)
Referee: Langenus (Belgium)

Spain (3) **3, Brazil** (0) **1**
27.5.34 GENOA
Spain: Zamora, Ciriaco, Quincoces, Cillaurren, Muquerza, Marculeta, Lafuente, Iraragorri (1 pen), Langara (2), Lecue, Gorostiza
Brazil: Pedrosa, Sylvio Hoffmann, Luz, Tinoco, Martim Silveira, Armandinho, Canalli, Luizinho, Waldemar, Patesko, Leonidas (1)
Referee: Birlem (Germany)

Switzerland (2) **3, Holland** (1)
27.5.34 2 MILAN
Switzerland: Sechehaye, Minelli, Weiler, Guinchard, Jaccard, Hufschmid, Von Känel, Passello, Kielholz (2), Abegglen III (1), Bossi
Netherlands: Van der Meulen, Weber, Van Run, Pellikaan, Anderiesen, Van Heel, Wels, Vente (1), Bakhuijs, Smit (1), Van Nellen
Referee: Eklind (Sweden)

Sweden (1) **3, Argentina** (1) **2**
27.5.34 BOLOGNA
Sweden: Rydberg, Axelsson, Andersson S, Carlsson, Rosen, Andersson E, Dunker, Gustavsson, Jonasson (2), Keller, Kroon (1)
Argentina: Freschi, Pedevilla, Belis (1), Nehin, Sosa-Ubrieta, Lopez, Rua, Wilde, De Vincenzi, Galateo (1), Irañeta
Referee: Braun (Austria)

Germany (1) **5, Belgium** (2) **2**
27.5.34 FLORENCE
Germany: Kress, Haringer, Schwartz, Janes, Szepan, Zielinski, Lehner, Hohmann, Conen (3), Siffling, Kobierski (2)
Belgium: Van De Weyer, Smellinckx, Joachim, Peeraer, Welkenhuyzen, Klaessens, Devries, Voorhoof (2), Capelle, Gimmonprez, Herremans
Referee: Mattea (Italy)

Austria (1) **3, France** (1) **2** (aet, 1–1 at 90 mins)
27.5.34 TURIN
Austria: Platzer, Cisar, Sesta, Wagner, Smistik, Urbanek, Zischek, Bican (1), Sindelar (1), Schall (1), Viertel
France: Thepot, Mairesse, Mattler, Delfour, Verriest (1 pen), Llense, Keller, Alcazar, Nicolas (1), Rio, Aston
Referee: Van Moorsel (Netherlands)

Hungary (2) 4, Egypt (2) 2
27.5.34 NAPLES
Hungary: Szabo A, Futo, Sternberg, Palotas, Szücs, Lazar, Markos, Vincze (1), Teleki (1), Toldi (2), Szabo F
Egypt: Moustafa Kemal, Ali Caf, Hamitu, El Far, Refaat, Rayab, Latif, Fawzi (2), Muktar, Masoud Kemal, Hassan
Referee: Barlassina (Italy)

Quarter-Finals

Italy v Spain	**Florence**
Austria v Hungary	**Bologna**
Czechoslovakia v Switzerland	**Turin**
Sweden v Germany	**Milan**

THE QUARTER-FINALS

Performing stoically in Florence and with great distinction, the Spanish, unfortunate in drawing rampant Italy, went out in a replay. Regueiro put them ahead in the first tie but though the magnificent Zamora produced heroics in goal, Italy's bombardment finally paid dividends when Ferrari grabbed their equalizer. Extra time brought no goals but several bruises as the spirit of the game degenerated. Significantly Zamora, a casualty, did not recover for the replay just 48 hours later. This time Italy prevailed as two tired teams battled out another dour physical struggle officiated with astonishing ineptitude by the myopic refereeing of M. Mercet of Switzerland, Meazza firing past Nogues, Spain's replacement goalkeeper, for a deserved win. Quincoces, however, was hugely impressive in the Spaniards' defence.

Czechoslovakia again squeezed through in Turin against Switzerland in a lively encounter, Svoboda and Sobotka scoring for the Czechs, and Kielholz and Abegglen III for the Swiss. It was 2–2 and the game appeared to be drifting towards extra time when Nejedly struck an 85th minute winner past the despairing Sechehaye.

Austria, too, progressed at the expense of their Danubian rivals Hungary by 2–1, though instead of the anticipated football exhibition, an ugly, ill-tempered affair saw a series of niggling spiteful challenges, one of which resulted in Hungary's Markos being dismissed. 'It was a brawl,' said Hugo Meisl afterwards.

Germany were the final entrants to the semi-finals, removing a Swedish team reduced to ten men for most of the game, with a result of 2–1. Hohmann scored two goals against the gallant Swedes, though they clung on, scoring through Dunker, and harried the Germans vainly to the final whistle.

Quarter-Finals

Germany (0) **2, Sweden** (0) **1**
31.5.34 MILAN
Germany: Kress, Haringer, Busch, Gramlich, Szepan, Zielinski, Lehner, Hohmann (2), Conen, Siffling, Kobierski
Sweden: Rydberg, Axelsson, Andersson S, Carlsson, Rosen, Andersson E, Dunker (1), Gustavsson, Jonasson, Keller, Kroon
Referee: Barlassina (Italy)

Czechoslovakia (1) **3, Switzerland** (1) **2**
31.5.34 TURIN
Czechoslovakia: Planicka, Zenizek, Ctyroky, Kostalek, Cambal, Krcil, Junek, Svoboda (1), Sobotka (1), Nejedly (1), Puc
Switzerland: Sechehaye, Minelli, Weiler, Guinchard, Jaccard, Hufschmid, Von Känel, Jaeggi IV, Kielholz (1), Abegglen III (1), Jack
Referee: Beranek (Austria)

Austria (1) 2, **Hungary (0)** 1
31.5.34 BOLOGNA
Austria: Platzer, Cisar, Sesta, Wagner, Smistik, Urbanek, Zischek (1), Bican, Sindelar, Horvath (1), Viertel
Hungary: Szabo A, Vago, Sternberg, Palotas, Szücs, Szalay, Markos, Avar, Sarosi (1 pen), Toldi, Kemeny
Referee: Mattea (Italy)

Italy (0) **1, Spain** (1) **1** (aet, 1–1 at 90 mins)
31.5.34 FLORENCE
Italy: Combi, Monzeglio, Allemandi, Pizziolo, Monti, Castellazzi, Guaita, Meazza, Schiavio, Ferrari (1), Orsi
Spain: Zamora, Ciriaco, Quincoces, Cillaurren, Muquerza, Lecue, Lafuente, Iraragorri, Langara, Regueiro (1), Gorostiza
Referee: Baert (Belgium)

Quarter-Final Replay

Italy (1) **1, Spain** (0) **0**
1.6.34 FLORENCE
Italy: Combi, Monzeglio, Allemandi, Ferraris IV, Monti, Bertolini, Guaita, Meazza (1), Borel II, Demaria, Orsi
Spain: Nogues, Zabalo, Quincoces, Cillaurren, Muquerza, Lecue, Ventoira, Regueiro, Campanal, Chacha, Bosch
Referee: Mercet (Switzerland)

THE SEMI-FINALS

At Milan, with the benefit of just two days to recover and prepare, Italy showed remarkable resolve in outworking the Austrians. Guaita, one of the Argentineans, gave them an early lead as they dominated the first half, so that Austria's revival proved too little too late and they went out lamely 1–0. In

Rome it was again the free-scoring Nejedly who proved to be the decisive factor. Taking the lead, the Czechs appeared on course, and though Noack scored comically for the Germans when the reliable Planicka inexplicably watched the shot fly into his goal, they were not distracted, winning easily 3–1.

Semi-Finals

Czechoslovakia (1) **3, Germany** (0) **1**
3.6.34 ROME
Czechoslovakia: Planicka, Ctyroky, Bürger, Kostalek, Cambal, Krcil (1), Junek, Svoboda, Sobotka, Nejedly (2), Puc
Germany: Kress, Busch, Haringer, Zielinski, Szepan, Bender, Lehner, Siffling, Conen, Noack (1), Kobierski
Referee: Barlassina (Italy)

Italy (1) **1, Austria** (0) **0**
3.6.34 MILAN
Italy: Combi, Monzeglio, Allemandi, Ferraris IV, Monti, Bertolini, Guaita (1), Meazza, Schiavio, Ferrari, Orsi
Austria: Platzer, Cisar, Sesta, Wagner, Smistik, Urbanek, Zischek, Bican, Sindelar, Schall, Viertel
Referee: Carraro (Italy)

PLAY-OFF FOR THIRD PLACE

In the third and fourth place play-off, Austria, so disappointing against Italy, could not lift their spirits sufficiently to beat the technically inferior but tough Germans and went down 3–2 in an indifferent match in Naples.

Match for Third Place

Germany (3) **3, Austria** (1) **2**
6.6.34 NAPLES
Germany: Jakob, Janes, Busch, Zielinski, Münzenberg, Bender, Lehner (2), Siffling, Conen (1), Szepan, Heidemann
Austria: Platzer, Cisar, Sesta (1), Wagner, Smistik, Urbanek, Zischek, Braun, Bican, Horvath (1), Viertel
Referee: Carraro (Italy)

THE FINAL

The final took place in Rome as the Italian Government milked the moment for yet more fascist propaganda. With a strong will and high expectations, Italy attacked. Czechoslovakia, underrated throughout, defended calmly; the excellent Planicka instilled confidence, and gradually through their neat passing and the presence on the left wing of the speedy Puc, the Czechs gained control. Indisputably the better team, they finally took the lead. Taking a corner, Puc saw the ball returned to him and this time drove it fiercely across Combi and into the Italian net. Now with twenty minutes left and their opponents in apparent disarray, the Czechs went for a clincher. However, Sobotka missed when he might have scored, then Svoboda struck a post mightily. Italy, stunned and outplayed, shook themselves and responded, miraculously, with an unrepeatable freak of a shot: Orsi bent an outrageous right foot past Planicka. Worse was still to follow for the bold Czechs, as the Italians, marginally stronger in extra time and encouraged by their home crowd, pressed. Finally it was Schiavio collecting Guaita's pass who thumped their second goal home: a winner. Italy, to delirious acclaim, had won – but they had been more than a little lucky.

Final

Italy (0) **2, Czechoslovakia** (0) **1** (aet, 1–1 at 90 mins)
10.6.34 ROME
Italy: Combi, Monzeglio, Allemandi, Ferraris IV, Monti, Bertolini, Guaita, Meazza, Schiavio (1), Ferrari, Orsi (1)
Czechoslovakia: Planicka, Zenizek, Ctyroky, Kostalek, Cambal, Krcil, Junek, Svoboda, Sobotka, Nejedly, Puc (1)
Referee: Eklind (Sweden)

The Tournament of 1934 held in Europe had been dominated by the Europeans in much the same way as Uruguay had been the preserve of the South Americans. Middle Europe, quite the most powerful football region in the world, had supplied the serious challengers and made the Tournament truly competitive, its outcome uncertain to the very end. Austria, the 'Wunder Team', appeared strangely weary by the semi-final and were beaten and outworked by a team clearly disadvantaged by a demanding schedule that included a replay. Czechoslovakia ultimately proved themselves an exceptional team, though when the opportunity came to crown themselves World Champions, they were wasteful, and Italy – tired, dishevelled Italy – gathered themselves and stormed to courageous triumph. In truth, Italy, despite their opportunist government's unpleasant undertones, deserved to win. They were hard working, skilful and resourceful, and few begrudged their success. Of course, the politics were something else. The Belgian referee John Langenus, who watched the game, later remarked, 'Italy wanted to win, it was natural, they just allowed it to be seen too clearly.'

CHAPTER 3

FRANCE

1938

Qualifying Tournament
36 Entries
Italy qualify as holders, France qualify as hosts

Argentina, Austria, Belgium, Brazil, Bulgaria, Colombia, Costa Rica, Cuba, Czechoslovakia, Dutch East Indies, Egypt, El Salvador, Estonia, Finland, France, Germany, Greece, Holland, Hungary, Republic of Ireland, Italy, Japan, Latvia, Lithuania, Luxembourg, Mexico, Norway, Palestine, Poland, Portugal, Romania, Surinam, Sweden, Switzerland, USA, Yugoslavia

Group 1 (Germany, Sweden, Estonia, Finland)
Sweden v Finland 4–0, Sweden v Estonia 7–2, Finland v Germany 0–2, Finland v Estonia 0–1, Germany v Estonia 4–1, Germany v Sweden 5–0

	P	W	D	L	F	A	Pts
Germany	3	3	0	0	11	1	6
Sweden	3	2	0	1	11	7	4
Estonia	3	1	0	2	4	11	2
Finland	3	0	0	3	0	7	0

Germany and Sweden qualified

Group 2 (Poland, Norway, Yugoslavia, Rep of Ireland)
Poland v Yugoslavia 4–0, Yugoslavia v Poland 1–0, Norway v Rep of Ireland 3–2, Rep of Ireland v Norway 3–3

	P	W	D	L	F	A	Pts
Norway	2	1	1	0	6	5	3
Poland	2	1	0	1	4	1	2
Yugoslavia	2	1	0	1	1	4	2
Rep of Ireland	2	0	1	1	5	6	1

Poland and Norway qualified

Group 3 (Romania, Egypt)
Romania qualified (Egypt withdrew)

Group 4 (Switzerland, Portugal)
Switzerland v Portugal 2–1 (in Milan)
Switzerland qualified

Group 5 (Hungary, Greece, Palestine)
Palestine v Greece 1–3, Greece v Palestine 1–0, Hungary v Greece 11–1
Hungary qualified

Group 6 (Czechoslovakia, Bulgaria)
Bulgaria v Czechoslovakia 1–1, 0–6
Czechoslovakia qualified

Group 7 (Austria, Latvia, Lithuania)
Latvia v Lithuania 4–2, Lithuania v Latvia 1–5, Austria v Latvia 2–1
Austria qualified

Group 8 (Belgium, Holland, Luxembourg)
Holland v Luxembourg 4–0, Luxembourg v Belgium 2–3, Belgium v Holland
1–1
Holland and Belgium qualified

Group 9 (Dutch East Indies, Japan)
Dutch East Indies qualified (Japan withdrew)

Group 10 (Brazil, Argentina)
Brazil qualified (Argentina withdrew)

Group 11 (USA)
USA withdrew

Group 12 (Colombia, Costa Rica, Cuba, Mexico, El Salvador, Surinam)
Cuba qualified (all teams except Cuba withdrew)

It was 1938 and as the world of football descended on France, the dark clouds
of war gathered menacingly over Europe. Austria, annexed by Germany, had
been forced to withdraw, their best players conscripted into the German team;
Spain were absent, plunged into bloody Civil War at home; and Argentina, failing in their quest to host the Tournament, rather snootily pulled out. Britain
still remained on the outside looking in, and Uruguay disappointingly chose
not to compete, increasingly concerned with professionalism and its debilitating effects on their national game.

Once more, however, the field was an impressive one, and though there
were only fifteen entrants without Austria, the format remained as a straight
knockout, with Sweden receiving a first round bye.

Italy were the favourites again, their amiable coach Pozzo declaring his
team better than that of 1934. Olympic Champions two years earlier in
Germany, Italy now included Ferrari and Rava from that fine team. The Czech
side were also strong, retaining such key men as Planicka, Nejedly and Puc
from the previous Tournament, though prior to the competition they had suffered the shocking trauma of an 8–3 defeat by Hungary, clearly indicating that

the Hungarians, too, demanded respect. Likewise, Switzerland had improved, surprising England in a pre-Tournament friendly in Zurich. For the rest there were France, the hosts; Germany fortified by the Austrian contingent; and Brazil, now a force on their own continent, with Leonidas, a small acrobatic centre forward, to lead them. Poland and Norway, having qualified at the expense of the Republic of Ireland and Yugoslavia, would play in their first competition, Holland in their second, and Belgium, Sweden and Romania in their third. Cuba, having entered for their second attempt at qualification, had watched as one by one their rivals, Colombia, Costa Rica, Mexico, El Salvador and Surinam, had withdrawn for various reasons; so it was that in such peculiar circumstances they were in France without playing a single match! Dutch East Indies had similarly arrived at the Finals by default through Japan's withdrawal. Like Cuba, little was known of these mysterious men from the Indian Ocean.

1938 FRANCE 4 June–19 June

QUALIFIERS

Austria (withdrawn)	Holland
Belgium	Hungary
Brazil	Italy
Cuba	Norway
Czechoslovakia	Poland
Dutch East Indies	Romania
France	Sweden
Germany	Switzerland

The Draw

Belgium v France
Brazil v Poland
Cuba v Romania
Czechoslovakia v Holland
Dutch East Indies v Hungary
Germany v Switzerland
Italy v Norway
Sweden – Bye

PRELIMINARY ROUND

The Tournament began with a stark contrast in the quality of the teams and matches. Hungary, seizing on the weaknesses of the team from the Dutch East Indies, rampaged through them, threatening a huge total. With a score of 4–0 at half time, however, it was a merciful 6–0 at the end, Sarosi and Zsengeller with two goals each, Toldi with one and Kohut with one, the outclassed Asians going out at Reims. Switzerland and Germany meeting in Paris served up a tense, close affair. The Germans fielding four Austrians took the lead, a cross from one of them, Presser, met emphatically by Gauchel for 1–0. Switzerland, undeterred, responded swiftly, and Abegglen III rose to head an equalizer to finish 1–1. Extra time brought drama, Presser being banished for a foul, but no goals. The replay provided more excitement still as the Swiss, 2–0 behind and heading towards the exit door, recovered, exhibiting a remarkable strength of character to score, survive an onslaught and a period playing with ten men to ultimately surge to a handsome victory over their broken, weary opponents 4–2. Romania, too, were forced to an unlikely replay by the minnows from Cuba. Trailing, Cuba made a mighty effort, upsetting the Europeans with their pacey forwards and scoring an equalizer. Extra time saw them take the lead before Romania composed themselves, went on the offensive and levelled at 3–3. Shockingly, Romania in Toulouse, learning nothing from the first match, went out controversially. They only had themselves to blame: again the first goal, scored by Dobai, was theirs; again the persistent Cubans fought back through Sosa and Maquina for 2–1, and this time it proved enough. Italy, given the relatively simple task of removing Norway, made horribly hard work of it in Marseilles. The Norwegians, revelling in the role of no-hopers, fell behind at once but thereafter tore into the Italians with relish, Olivieri, the brilliant goalkeeper, denying them aided by his goal frame – which was hit three times. But even his inspired acrobatics could not prevent Brustad's equalizer. With extra time the sleeping giant awakened from its slumbers and struck down. Finally the game outsider who had had the temerity to challenge them succumbed, Piola stabbing home a loose ball for 2–1. Italy had been fortunate indeed.

Czechoslovakia also needed extra time to dismiss their resolute opponents, though Holland's resistance crumbled after they fell behind. It was 3–0 at the end, and the Dutch left to rue the absence of their most prolific goal-scorer, Bakhuijs.

France also came through, but more comfortably against a desperately moderate Belgian team 3–1. Nicolas, their captain, so unlucky in Italy four years earlier, scored twice and created uncertainty in the minds of Belgium's brittle defenders.

So to Strasbourg and an absorbing, pulsating contest between two uninhibited teams, Poland and Brazil intent only on attack. Brazil began the better, taking control and the half-time lead; Poland, undeterred, hit back in sensational fashion to leave the score 4–4 at the end, Leonidas and his Polish counterpart Willimowski each with a hat-trick, though neither had slaked their thirst for goals as extra time proceeded. Another for both left the game extraordinarily poised at 5–5. But it was Brazil who found a winner: Romeo allowed space and thumped the ball home for 6–5. Dejection for the Poles but delirium for Brazil.

Final Tournament – France Preliminary Round

Switzerland (1) **1, Germany** (1) **1** (aet, 1–1 at 90 mins)
4.6.38 PARIS
Switzerland: Huber, Minelli, Lehmann, Springer, Vernati, Lörtscher, Amado, Walaschek, Bickel, Abegglen III (1), Aeby
Germany: Raftl, Janes, Schmaus, Kupfer, Mock, Ritzinger, Lehner, Gellesch, Gauchel (1), Hahnemann, Pesser
Referee: Langenus (Belgium)

Hungary (4) **6, Dutch East Indies** (0) **0**
4.6.38 REIMS
Hungary: Hada, Koranyi, Biro, Lazar, Turai, Balogh, Sas, Zsengeller (2), Sarosi (2), Toldi (1), Kohut (1)
Dutch East Indies: Mo Heng, Hu Kon, Samuels, Nawir, Meng, Anwar, Hang Djin, Soedarmadji, Sommers, Pattiwael, Taihutti
Referee: Conrie (France)

France (2) **3, Belgium** (1) **1**
5.6.38 PARIS
France: Dilorto, Cazenave, Mattler, Bastien, Jordan, Diagne, Aston, Nicolas (2), Delfour, Vienante (1), Heisserer
Belgium: Badjou, Paverick, Sayes, Van Alphen, Stynen, De Winter, Van de Wouwer, Voorhoof, Isemborghs (1), Braine, Byle
Referee: Wuthrich (Switzerland)

Brazil (2) **6, Poland** (1) **5** (aet, 4–4 at 90 mins)
5.6.38 STRASBOURG
Brazil: Batatais, Domingos, Machado, Procopio, Martim Silveira, Afonsinho, Lopes, Romeo (1), Leonidas (4), Peracio (1), Hercules
Poland: Madesjski, Szcepaniak, Galecki, Gora, Nyc, Dytko, Piece L, Piontek (1), Szerfke, Willimowski (4), Wodarz
Referee: Eklind (Sweden)

Czechoslovakia (0) **3, Holland** (0) **0** (aet, 0–0 at 90 mins)
5.6.38 LE HAVRE
Czechoslovakia: Planicka, Burger, Daucik, Kostalek (1), Boucek (1), Kopecky, Riha, Simunek, Zeman, Nejedly (1), Puc
Holland: Van Male, Weber, Caldenhove, Paauwe, Anderiesen, Van Heel, Wels, Van de Veen, Smit, Vente, De Harder
Referee: Leclerq (France)

Italy (1) **2, Norway** (0) **1** (aet, 1–1 at 90 mins)
5.6.38 MARSEILLES
Italy: Olivieri, Monzeglio, Rava, Serantoni, Andreolo, Locatelli, Pasinati, Meazza, Piola (1), Ferrari (1), Ferraris II
Norway: Johansen H, Johannesen R, Holmsen, Henriksen, Eriksen, Homberg, Frantzen, Kvammen, Brunyldsen, Isaksen, Brustad (1)
Referee: Beranek (Austria)

Cuba (1) **3, Romania** (1) **3** (aet, 2–2 at 90 mins)
5.6.38 TOULOUSE
Cuba: Carvajales, Barquin, Chorens, Arias, Rodriguez, Berges, Maquina (1), Fernandez, Socorro, Tunas (1), Sosa (1)
Romania: Pavlovici, Burger, Chiroiu, Vintila, Rasinaru, Rafinski, Bindea, Covaci (1), Baratki (1), Bodola, Dobai (1)
Referee: Scarpi (Italy)

Replays

Switzerland (1) **4, Germany** (2) **2**
9.6.38 PARIS
Switzerland: Huber, Minelli, Lehmann, Springer, Vernati, Lörtscher (o.g.), Amado, Abegglen III (2), Bickel (1), Walaschek (1), Aeby
Germany: Raftl, Janes, Streitle, Kupfer, Goldbrunner, Skoumal, Lehner, Stroh, Hahnemann (1), Szepan, Neumer
Referee: Eklind (Sweden)

Cuba (1) **2, Romania** (1) **1**
9.6.38 TOULOUSE
Cuba: Ayra, Barquin, Chorens, Arias, Rodriguez, Berges, Maquina (1), Fernandez, Socorro (1), Tunas, Sosa
Romania: Sadowski, Burger, Felecan, Barbulescu, Rasinaru, Rafinski, Bogden, Moldoveanu, Baratki, Pranzler, Dobai (1)
Referee: Birlem (Germany)

THE QUARTER-FINALS

At this point Sweden belatedly entered the Tournament, lucky in receiving a bye extended with a quarter-final against tiny Cuba. Exhausted by their Herculean effort against Romania, it was predictably a no contest, the powerful Scandinavians winning at a canter, Wetterström, their speedy winger, providing four of their eight goals.

In Paris, Italy recovered from their indifferent form to account comprehensively for French hopes. Colaussi for Italy and Heisserer for France scored before the interval for 1–1, but thereafter the French, encouraged by vociferous support, tried to seize the initiative, allowing Italy to capitalize on the counterattack, Piola their executioner with two goals to win the game 3–1. Hungary, rampant and then oddly lethargic against the feeble Dutch East Indies, met the Swiss, their far fresher team winning the day 2–0 with quicker, cleverer football, Zsengeller providing the goals.

In Bordeaux a promising match between Czechoslovakia and Brazil was absolutely ruined by sickening violence and undisciplined retaliation as both teams sought to take the law into their own hands. Brazil started the trouble but Czechoslovakia suffered the more severe injuries – Planicka had an arm broken, and the immensely gifted Nejedly a leg – though they were hardly blameless themselves. Brazil had two sent off, the Czechs one, and in extra time the eight remaining Europeans defied nine South Americans. The result of this shambles was a final score of 1–1, the consequence a replay… and FIFA prayed for cool heads.

In the event the teams collectively made a remarkable fifteen changes and the result two days later was a relatively calm affair. Czechoslovakia, while missing the influence of Nejedly, scored first through Kopecky – who later limped off injured – and should have won; but they didn't. Brazil equalized through Leonidas and then Roberto fired them into the semi-finals. They had been more than a little lucky.

QUARTER-FINALS

Sweden (4) **8, Cuba** (0) **0**
12.6.38 ANTIBES
Sweden: Abrahamsson, Eriksson, Källgren, Almgren, Jacobsson, Svanström, Wetterström (4), Keller (1), Andersson H (1), Jonasson (1), Nyberg (1)
Cuba: Carvajales, Barquin, Chorens, Arias, Rodriguez, Berges, Ferrer, Fernandez, Socorro, Tunas, Alonzo
Referee: Krist (Czechoslovakia)

Hungary (1) **2, Switzerland** (0) **0**
12.6.38 LILLE
Hungary: Szabo, Koranyi, Biro, Szalay, Turai, Lazar, Sas, Vincze, Sarosi, Zsengeller (2), Kohut
Switzerland: Huber, Stelzer, Lehmann, Springer, Vernati, Lörtscher, Amado, Walaschek, Bickel, Abegglen III, Grassi
Referee: Barlassina (Italy)

Italy (1) **3, France** (1) **1**
12.6.38 PARIS
Italy: Olivieri, Foni, Rava, Serantoni, Andreolo, Locatelli, Biavati, Meazza, Piola (2), Ferrari, Colaussi (1)
France: Dilorto, Cazenave, Mattler, Bastien, Jordan, Diagne, Aston, Heisserer (1), Nicolas, Delfour, Veinante
Referee: Baert (Belgium)

Brazil (1) **1, Czechoslovakia** (1) **1** (aet, 1–1 at 90 mins)
12.6.38 BORDEAUX
Brazil: Walter, Domingos, Machado, Procopio, Martim Silveira, Afonsinho, Lopes, Romeo, Leonidas (1), Peracio, Hercules
Czechoslovakia: Planicka, Bürger, Daucik, Kostalek, Boucek, Kopecky, Riha, Simunek, Ludl, Nejedly (1 pen), Puc
Referee: Hertzka (Hungary)

Replay

Brazil (0) **2, Czechoslovakia** (1) **1**
14.6.38 BORDEAUX
Brazil: Walter, Jau, Nariz, Brito, Brandao, Argemiro, Roberto (1), Luizinho, Leonidas (1), Tim, Patesko
Czechoslovakia: Burkert, Burger, Daucik, Kostalek, Boucek, Ludl, Horak, Senecky, Kreutz, Kopecky (1), Rulc
Referee: Capdeville (France)

THE SEMI-FINALS

Brazil, tired after their traumas, were beaten with some comfort by the more fluent Italians in Marseilles. Forced into changes, they resisted bravely through until Colaussi fired home and Meazza added a second by converting a penalty kick resulting from an untimely challenge by Domingos on Piola, for 2–0. A late goal by Romeo could not save them. The Champions were through and would defend their title in Paris.

Hungary earned the right to face them, dismissing Sweden with contemptuous ease. The Swedes took the lead when Nyberg astonished the Hungarians with a shot after just 35 seconds; but then their luck ran out. Hungary began to dominate absolutely. Szengeller, prolific throughout the competition, added three more goals, Sarosi and Titkos, the left winger, joining the party as they ran out 5–1 winners at the end. It was a score which without argument flattered the outclassed Scandinavians.

Semi-Finals

Italy (0) **2, Brazil** (0) **1**
16.6.38 MARSEILLES
Italy: Olivieri, Foni, Rava, Serantoni, Andreolo, Locatelli, Biavati, Meazza (1 pen), Piola, Ferrari, Colaussi (1)
Brazil: Walter, Domingos, Machado, Procopio, Martim Silveira, Afonsinho, Lopes, Luizinho, Peracio, Romeo (1), Patesko
Referee: Wuthrich (Switzerland)

Hungary (3) **5, Sweden** (1) **1**
16.6.38 PARIS
Hungary: Szabo, Koranyi, Biro, Szalay, Turai, Lazar, Sas, Zsengeller (3), Sarosi (1), Toldi, Titkos (1)
Sweden: Abrahamsson, Eriksson, Källgren, Almgren, Jacobsson, Svanström, Wetterström, Keller, Andersson H, Jonasson, Nyberg (1)
Referee: Leclerq (France)

PLAY-OFF FOR THIRD PLACE

On the day of the final, Sweden and Brazil contested third place in Bordeaux. Brazil, still appearing weary, surprisingly went behind, and at half time seemed destined for defeat. It was then that Leonidas, the little centre forward notably absent from their semi-final defeat, struck twice. Consequently, Brazil deservedly raced to a 4–2 victory – theirs had been an exciting though controversial adventure.

Match for Third Place

Brazil (1) **4, Sweden** (2) **2**
19.6.38 BORDEAUX
Brazil: Batatais, Domingos, Machado, Procopio, Brandao, Afonsinho, Roberto, Romeo (1), Leonidas (2), Peracio (1), Patesho
Sweden: Abrahamsson, Eriksson, Nilsson, Almgren, Linderholm, Svanström, Persson, Andersson H, Jonasson (1), Anderson A, Nyberg (1)
Referee: Langenus (Belgium)

THE FINAL

So to the third World Cup final in Paris, and this time the quicker, more incisive Italian team left no one in any doubt as to who was the world's finest team. Collaussi, a constant threat, scored first, and despite Titkos's reply within two minutes, Meazza seized on Piola's inviting pass to regain the lead. Hungary, slick and patient going forward, allowed Italy far too much room to attack them. Meazza scored again for 3–1 and while Sarosi scored from close range for 3–2, the masterful Italian defence held sway and Piola capped a fine performance with an excellent goal, driving home Biavati's inventive reverse pass for 4–2. Italy were Champions again.

Final

Italy (3) **4, Hungary** (1) **2**
19.6.38 PARIS
Italy: Olivieri, Foni, Rava, Serantoni, Andreolo, Locatelli, Biavati, Meazza, Piola (2), Ferrari, Colaussi (2)
Hungary: Szabo, Polgar, Biro, Szalay, Szücs, Lazar, Sas, Vincze, Sarosi (1), Zsengeller, Titkos (1)
Referee: Capdeville (France)

So Italy were crowned kings of football again. True, they had been shaken by the valiant Norwegians, but had learned and prospered from their experience. Czechoslovakia and Brazil, both fine teams, had indulged in an ugly, brutal encounter, which ultimately accounted for the survivor, Brazil, unlikely to recover from so physical a contest so soon. Hungary had improved immensely, their progress, amidst all of the shenanigans seen elsewhere, largely unnoticed – but they would return with a vengeance.

Whilst all departed, the triumphant and the vanquished, perhaps all cast an anxious glance skyward at those bleakest of storm clouds. Bearing with them war, tragedy and sadness, they would plunge the world into a protracted conflict, and football would be rendered meaningless.

As war raged, what of the Jules Rimet Trophy? Deeply distrustful of their own Mussolini-led government, Italy's Sports Ministry conspired to remove it from its storage in the vaults of a Rome Bank and delivered it to their secretary, Otto Barassi, who, fearful of its discovery and confiscation, hid it in a shoe box stowed under his bed! There it remained in safety, waiting patiently for hostilities to cease so that once again it could ignite and inflame the passions of football lovers the world over in its own unique way.

CHAPTER 4

BRAZIL

1950

Qualifying Tournament
33 entries
Italy qualify as holders, Brazil qualify as hosts

Europe and Near East (19): Austria, Belgium, England, Finland, France, Northern Ireland, Republic of Ireland, Israel, Italy, Luxembourg, Portugal, Scotland, Spain, Sweden, Switzerland, Syria, Turkey, Wales, Yugoslavia

South America (8): Argentina, Bolivia, Brazil, Chile, Ecuador, Paraguay, Peru, Uruguay

North and Central America (3): Cuba, Mexico, USA

Asia (3): Burma, India, Philippines

Europe and Near East

Group 1 (Austria, Turkey, Syria)
Turkey v Syria 7–0
Austria withdrew; Syria refused to play the return game with Turkey, who withdrew. Portugal were offered a place in the final but declined.

Group 2 (Yugoslavia, Israel, France)
Yugoslavia v Israel 6–0, Israel v Yugoslavia 2–5, France v Yugoslavia 1–1, Yugoslavia v France 1–1
Play-off (in Florence): Yugoslavia v France 3–2
Yugoslavia qualified

Group 3 (Switzerland, Luxembourg, Belgium)
Belgium withdrew
Switzerland v Luxembourg 5–2, 3–2
Switzerland qualified

Group 4 (Sweden, Rep of Ireland, Finland)
Sweden v Rep of Ireland 3–1, Rep of Ireland v Finland 3–0, Finland v Rep of Ireland 1–1, Rep of Ireland v Sweden 1–3
Sweden qualified

Group 5 (England, Scotland, Northern Ireland, Wales)
Northern Ireland v Scotland 2–8, Wales v England 1–4, Scotland v Wales 2–0, England v Northern Ireland 9–2, Wales v Northern Ireland 0–0, Scotland v England 0–1

	P	W	D	L	F	A	Pts
England	3	3	0	0	14	3	6
Scotland	3	2	0	1	10	3	4
Wales	3	0	1	2	1	6	1
Northern Ireland	3	0	1	2	4	17	1

England qualified with Scotland, who refused a final place, as did France, who were invited to replace them.

Group 6 (Spain, Portugal)
Spain v Portugal 5–1, 2–2
Spain qualified

South America

Group 7 (Chile, Bolivia, Argentina)
Argentina withdrew
Chile and Bolivia qualified

Group 8 (Uruguay, Paraguay, Ecuador, Peru)
Ecuador and Peru withdrew
Uruguay and Paraguay qualified

North and Central America

Group 10 (USA, Mexico, Cuba)
USA v Mexico 0–6, Mexico v USA 6–2, Cuba v USA 1–1, USA v Cuba 5–2, Cuba v Mexico 0–3, Mexico v Cuba 2–0

	P	W	D	L	F	A	Pts
Mexico	4	4	0	0	17	2	8
USA	4	1	1	2	8	15	3
Cuba	4	0	1	3	3	11	1

USA and Mexico qualified

Asia

Group 9 (Burma, India, Philippines)
All withdrew

1950 BRAZIL 24 June–16 July

QUALIFIERS

Bolivia
Brazil
Chile
England
Italy
Mexico
Paraguay

Spain
Sweden
Switzerland
United States
Uruguay
Yugoslavia

As hosts in 1950, Brazil, a nation consumed with football passion, had a massive task to perform in satisfying the organizational demands of the Tournament in so huge a country. Indeed, Portugal, previously eliminated, were offered a place in the draw vacated by Turkey, but on seeing their itinerary, which involved fixtures against Uruguay and Bolivia taking place some 2000 miles apart, declined. There were other withdrawals and some noticeable absentees: Argentina, in a spat with the Brazilian Federation, refused to play; Hungary and the Soviet Union were in self-imposed isolation; and both Czechoslovakia and Austria felt themselves ill-equipped for so competitive a Tournament. Britain, however, at last had a representative: England (Scotland, who had also qualified, elected to stay at home). Germany, another not attending, were still in exile, excluded following World War II.

So it was that another South American competition relied heavily on nations from its own continent; coincidentally, again there were a meagre thirteen entrants. Bizarrely, FIFA did not rearrange the draw that farcically allowed Uruguay and Bolivia alone to contest Group Four. It seemed that twenty years had not improved chaotic organization.

In Group One, Brazil were the clear favourites, scandalously given the added advantage of playing all their matches in Rio de Janeiro whilst the rest would be forced to travel thousands of miles up to Belo Horizonte, west to São Paulo, or far down in the south to Porto Alegre – nearer to the borders of Uruguay, Argentina and Paraguay than to Brazil's own capital.

The immensely talented Yugoslavia would keep them company; with Mitic, Bobek and Cajkovski, they had taken the silver medal two years earlier at the Olympic Games. Mexico had again qualified from the feeble North and Central America Group. Asked only to finish first or second in a competition containing the USA and Cuba, they duly obliged, scoring seventeen goals in the process. The fourth competitor was Switzerland, their team including Neury, Antenen and Falten, though significantly Steffen, their huge blond left back, would be absent.

England would be in Group Two with Chile, the USA and their anticipated rivals Spain. A fine team, the English were still revered by most in world football, and with Finney and Matthews on the wings, and the goal-scoring talents of Jackie Milburn and Stanley Mortensen at their disposal, they were expected to offer a strong challenge. Chile, playing their second Tournament, qualified somewhat absurdly, along with Bolivia, without playing a match, courtesy of sulky Argentina. Interestingly, one of Milburn's team-mates at Newcastle United, George Robledo, would oppose him at Rio, having been born at Iquique of a Chilean father and English mother. The USA struggled to gain any credibility, having suffered two humiliating defeats by unsung Mexico; moreover, their captain Eddie McIlvaney, a Scot, had been released on a free transfer by little Wrexham F.C. just eighteen months earlier. Spain, emphatic winners over Portugal, offered England the greatest threat, with Ramallets, an accomplished goalkeeper, and Basora and Zarra, lively, inventive strikers.

Mercifully for Italy, Sweden and Paraguay, contesting Group Three, the fixtures would be played at the neighbouring towns of Cuntiba and São Paulo, thus at least minimizing the travel problems others would experience. Italy had been willing to compete, shaming those who stayed away. Torino, their champions of four consecutive seasons, had been wiped out a year earlier in the Superga air disaster when their plane travelling home from Portugal plunged into a hillside. Despite the Italian team being so utterly decimated, eight of their players killed in an instant and their chances of successful defence all but gone, to their great credit they had still come. Sweden, too, had seen a great side devastated, though happily not through disaster but the lure of the lira. Olympic champions in 1948, four of their squad had absconded to the Italian League and would not be present. Skoglund, however, was a new and promising discovery, Jeppsson a hard and forceful centre forward, and Nordahl a commanding defender – making them rightly optimistic. Paraguay, back again after twenty years in the wilderness, had Unzain, a tricky left winger bound for Lazio in Rome, to call on, and had the previous year finished second in the South American Championship. Unfortunately, this achievement was somewhat diminished by the insistence of the professional players in Uruguay not to compete but instead to leave their country hopelessly weakened.

What of Uruguay? The 1930 Champions and back to contest the finals for the first time since, their chances had been enhanced by their Group Four draw, leaving them with the relatively straightforward-looking task of disposing of one solitary opponent: Bolivia. Juan Schiaffino, their tall, athletic inside forward from Penarol, was exceptional, Obdulio Varela, a ball-playing centre half, and Rodriguez Andrade, a powerful half back whose uncle José had played in that final in Montevideo, were recent victors over Brazil and thus highly regarded. Bolivia for their part had been particularly unfortunate in drawing as opposition one so familiar and, on evidence of past matches, so infinitely superior.

Venues for all matches

Rio de Janeiro, Belo Horizonte, São Paulo, Porto Allegre, Curitiba, Recife

Group 1

Brazil
Mexico
Switzerland
Yugoslavia

Group 3

Italy
Sweden
Paraguay

Group 2

Chile
England
Spain
United States

Group 4

Bolivia
Uruguay

THE FIRST SERIES

The honour of the opening match fell to Brazil and Mexico. The Mexicans were immediately seen to be impostors on the world stage, and Brazil, needing to win to satisfy the huge crowd at the Maracana stadium, duly obliged without extending themselves, Jair and Baltazar supplying a goal each. Ademir, both speedy and extravagantly gifted, scored two more for a final result of 4–0. Mexico had been lucky to escape a far worse mauling.

A very different story took place in São Paulo as Sweden and Italy in Group Two did battle in a tense and competitive encounter. Poor Italy, already weakened in playing strength, debilitated and ill-prepared after a lengthy and troublesome journey – their players, hardly surprisingly, refused to fly – now had to contend with eccentric team selections made not by a coach but by Torino's Travelling Club President, Feruccio Novo! Still, they led through Carapellese before losing their grip: Jeppson, Andersson and then Jeppson again on seventy minutes appeared to put matters beyond them, but Mussinelli scored to cause the Swedes anxiety, and at 2–3 Carapellese crashed the ball mightily off the bar. Sweden had won but it had been a close-run affair.

England in Group Two had no such difficulty against Chile. Able to dispense with the services of Stanley Matthews and win as comfortably as they wished against outplayed and increasingly dispirited opponents, they managed two goals through Mortenson and Mullen. The climate and the altitude, it was agreed, had been far harder to overcome than the Chileans.

Also in Group Two, the USA at Curitiba had the audacity to awaken Spain from the slumber of their siesta. John Souza powered his effort past the unconvincing Eizaquirre, and the USA shockingly held the lead into the last ten minutes. They clung on, demonstrating considerable fortitude and a little luck, but Spain predictably overcame them at the last, Basora, a dynamic winger, scoring twice in a minute. As the gallant Americans contemplated the probability of imminent defeat, Zarra, Spain's centre forward, confirmed it, arriving late to bullet a header home for 3–1. In Group One, Yugoslavia at Belo Horizonte demolished Switzerland with remarkable ease and efficiency, the first 45 minutes being enough time for them to impose themselves and establish an unassailable 3–0 lead. This they held without difficulty to the end, Tomasevik with two and Ognanov with one, but it was Rajko Mitic who caught the eye with an outstanding performance.

THE SECOND SERIES

Back again in Group One, just three days later Yugoslavia routinely dispatched poor Mexico 4–1 in Porto Allegre. A storming start deflated opponents low on confidence, the younger Cajkowski scoring twice, Tomasevic and Bobek completing Mexican misery, though Casarin at least provided them with some small consolation. Brazil, fielding a much-changed team in São Paulo, failed to the dismay of their enthusiastic supporters to beat Switzerland, despite prolonged encampment in the Swiss half and twice holding the lead. Alfredo scored first but Jacques Fatton capitalized on hesitant defending to power Bickel's cross past Barbosa for 1–1. Baltazar, Brazil's muscular centre forward, thumped home a second, but Switzerland, constantly under siege, denied them another and then at the very end stole into Brazil's penalty area in the form of Tamini for a 2–2 draw.

In Group Two, Spain won against Chile, though without the dramatic finish needed against the USA. Having Zarra and Basaro scoring in the first half, they dominated with their sharper, more imaginative play. England, to the disbelief of all, were horribly embarrassed by the gritty Americans at Belo Horizonte and lost 1–0. True, the USA were almost comically lucky, but what they had almost achieved against Spain they completed here. England took command from the start, forcing America back on their heels, struck a post, shot wide, were defied by the athleticism of Borghi the goalkeeper and last-ditch tackling. It wasn't until after 37 minutes on a rare sortie out of massed defence that the Haitian-born Gaetjens stumbled on to Bahr's cross to deflect the ball past Bert Williams. England, undeterred, pounded away for an hour, saving, hitting woodwork, hacked of the line or too high or too wide as the fates conspired along with the heroic efforts of their gallant opponents to deny them. Finally, painfully it was over, England had been beaten and the USA team, which had ridiculed its chances, had triumphed gloriously. Group Three saw Paraguay enter the fray at Curitiba against Sweden and force a creditable draw that eliminated the watching Italians. The Swedes took the game to the South Americans, gaining a 2–0 advantage through Palmer and Sundqvist, but Paraguay, lifted by the occasion and a sense of pride, fought back courageously in the sunshine, earning an unlikely share of the spoils.

THE THIRD SERIES

From Group One came Brazil, who finally overcame the very fine Yugoslavian team in Rio. Tired from their long hauls up and down the country and further hampered by a head injury to Mitic before the game, which forced them to begin with ten men, Yugoslavia fell behind immediately to Ademir's shot. Regrouped and galvanized by Mitic, who returned swathed in bandages, they worried Brazil with their neat and thoughtful passing. Chances came and went but for them it was not to be: Zizinho latching on to Bauer's pass ran and shot past the goalkeeper and the Brazilians were through to the rapturous acclaim of their vociferous supporters. In the other tie played at Porto Allegre, Switzerland, victory now rendered meaningless, raced to a 2–0 lead against Mexico, but allowed their opponents a goal from a Tournament which for them had been an unmitigated failure. At Recife the exhausted USA team could not conjure another miracle, and Chile, after two consecutive defeats without scoring, took full advantage to gain a convincing 5–2 victory, Cremaschi snatching the Tournament's first hat-trick. In Rio, England, needing to win, went out, beaten in desperately unfortunate circumstances by Spain. Matthews and Finney operating in tandem raked the flanks while Mortenson and Milburn proved troublesome to the Spanish defence, though Ramallets, a reserve goalkeeper, played an inspired game and enjoyed one moment of outrageous luck when the roaming Milburn thumped a header into his net. It was quite erroneously ruled offside. Zarra finally confirmed English failure, rising to meet Basara's firm cross to beat Williams from close range 1–0. For England their first World Cup had been a wholly forgettable experience.

Group Three saw Paraguay given the highly improbable task of defeating Italy to progress. They failed – allowing Sweden to advance. Carapellese and Pandolfini scored for Italy, but for their disappointed team this was a low-key occasion, their chances ruined by acrimony and dissent.

Astonishingly, it was on this day, 2 July, when eight teams were making their preparations to go home, that Uruguay and Bolivia entered the competition and opened and indeed closed 'Group' Four. Entirely predictably, the Bolivians were quickly overwhelmed. Uruguay's new and brightest star, Schiaffino, toying with his bemused opponents, provided four goals as his team ran in eight without reply. The ludicrous 'disorganization' had handed Uruguay a huge advantage, for while other teams had journeyed thousands of miles playing three competitive fixtures, they, at Belo Horizonte, were in an unassailable position after 45 minutes!

Final Tournament – Brazil

Group 1

Brazil (1) **4, Mexico** (0) **0**
24.6.50 RIO DE JANEIRO
Brazil: Barbosa, Augusto, Juvenal, Ely, Danilo, Bigode, Maneca, Ademir (2), Baltazar (1), Jair (1), Friaca
Mexico: Cabajal, Zetter, Montemajor, Ruiz, Ochoa, Roca, Septien, Ortiz, Casarin, Perez, Velasquez
Referee: Reader (England)

Yugoslavia (3) **3, Switzerland** (0) **0**
25.6.50 BELO HORIZONTE
Yugoslavia: Mrkusic, Horvat, Stankovic, Cajkovski I, Jovanovic, Djajic, Ognanov (1), Mitic, Tomasevic (2), Bobek, Vukas
Switzerland: Stuber, Lusenti, Quinche, Bocquet, Eggimann, Neury, Bickel, Antenen, Tamini, Bader, Fatton
Referee: Galeati (Italy)

Brazil (2) **2, Switzerland** (1) **2**
28.6.50 SÃO PAULO
Brazil: Barbosa, Augusto, Juvenal, Bauer, Rui, Noronha, Alfredo II (1), Maneca, Baltazar (1), Ademir, Friaca
Switzerland: Stuber, Neury, Bocquet, Lusenti, Eggimann, Quinche, Tamini, Bickel, Freidländer, Bader, Fatton (2)
Referee: Azon (Spain)

Yugoslavia (2) **4, Mexico** (0) **1**
28.6.50 PORTO ALEGRE
Yugoslavia: Mrkusic, Horvat, Stankovic, Cajkovski I, Jovanovic, Djajic, Mihailovic, Mitic, Tomasevic (1), Bobek (1), Cajovski II (2)
Mexico: Carbajal, Gutierrez, Ruiz, Gomez, Ochoa, Ortiz, Flores, Naranjo, Casarin (1), Perez, Velasquez
Referee: Leafe (England)

Brazil (1) **2, Yugoslavia** (0) **0**
1.7.50 RIO DE JANEIRO
Brazil: Barbosa, Augusto, Juvenal, Bauer, Danilo, Bigode, Maneca, Zizinho (1), Ademir (1), Jair, Chico
Yugoslavia: Mrkusic, Horvat, Brokela, Cajkovski I, Jovanovic, Djajic, Vukes, Mitic, Tomasevic, Bobek, Cajkovski II
Referee: Griffiths (Wales)

Switzerland (2) **2, Mexico** (0) **1**
2.7.50 PORTO ALEGRE
Switzerland: Hug, Neury, Bocquet, Lusenti, Eggimann, Quinche, Tamini, Antenen, Freidländer, Bader (1), Fatton (1)
Mexico: Carbajal, Gutierrez, Gomez, Roca, Ortiz, Guevara, Flores, Ochoa, Casarin, Barbolla, Velasquez (1)
Referee: Eklind (Sweden)

	P	W	D	L	F	A	Pts
Brazil	3	2	1	0	8	2	5
Yugoslavia	3	2	0	1	7	3	4
Switzerland	3	1	1	1	4	6	3
Mexico	3	0	0	3	2	10	0

Group 2

England (1) **2, Chile** (0) **0**
24.6.50 RIO DE JANEIRO
England: Williams, Ramsey, Aston, Wright, Hughes, Dickinson, Finney, Mortensen (1), Bentley, Mannion (1), Mullen
Chile: Livingstone, Farias, Roldon, Alvarez, Busquets, Carvalho, Prieto, Cremaschi, Robledo, Muñoz, Diaz
Referee: Van de Meer (Netherlands)

Spain (0) **3, USA** (1) **1**
25.6.50 CURITIBA
Spain: Eizaguirre, Antuñez, Alonso, Gonzalvo J, Gonzalvo M, Puchades, Basora (2), Hernandez, Zarra (1), Igoa, Gainza
USA: Borghi, Keough, Marca, McIlvenny, Colombo, Bahr, Craddock, Souza J (1), Gaetjens, Pariani, Valentini
Referee: Viana (Brazil)

USA (1) **1**, **England** (0) **0**
29.6.50 BELO HORIZONTE
USA: Borghi, Keough, Marca, McIlvenny, Colombo, Bahr, Wallace, Pariani, Gaetjens (1), Souza J, Souza E
England: Williams, Ramsey, Aston, Wright, Hughes, Dickinson, Finney, Mortensen, Bentley, Mannion, Mullen
Referee: Dattilo (Italy)

Spain (2) **2**, **Chile** (0) **0**
29.6.50 RIO DE JANEIRO
Spain: Ramallets, Alonso, Parra, Gonzalvo J, Gonzalvo M, Puchades, Basora (1), Igoa, Zarra (1), Panizo, Gainza
Chile: Livingstone, Farias, Roldon, Alvarez, Busquets, Carvalho, Prieto, Cremaschi, Robledo, Muñoz, Diaz
Referee: De Gama (Brazil)

Spain (0) **1**, **England** (0) **0**
2.7.50 RIO DE JANEIRO
Spain: Ramallets, Alonso, Parra, Gonzalvo J, Gonzalvo M, Puchades, Basora, Igoa, Zarra (1), Panizo, Gainza
England: Williams, Ramsey, Eckersley, Wright, Hughes, Dickinson, Matthews, Mortensen, Milburn, Baily, Finney
Referee: Galeati (Italy)

Chile (2) **5**, **USA** (0) **2**
2.7.50 RECIFE
Chile: Livingstone, Machuca, Roldon, Alvarez, Busquets, Farias, Muñoz, Cremaschi (3), Robledo (1), Prieto (1), Ibañez
USA: Borghi, Keough, Marca, McIlvenny, Colombo, Bahr, Wallace, Pariani (1), Gaetjens, Souza J (1 pen), Souza E
Referee: Gardelli (Brazil)

	P	W	D	L	F	A	Pts
Spain	3	3	0	0	6	1	6
England	3	1	0	2	2	2	2
Chile	3	1	0	2	5	6	2
USA	3	1	0	2	4	8	2

Group 3

Sweden (2) **3, Italy** (1) **2**
25.6.50 SÃO PAULO
Sweden: Svensson, Samuelsson, Nilsson E, Andersson (1), Nordahl K, Gaerd, Sundqvist, Palmer, Jeppson (2), Skoglund, Nilsson S
Italy: Sentimenti IV, Giovannini, Furiassi, Annovazzi, Parola, Magli, Muccinelli (1), Boniperti, Capello, Campatelli, Carapellese (1)
Referee: Lutz (Switzerland)

Sweden (2) **2, Paraguay** (0) **2**
29.6.50 CURITIBA
Sweden: Svensson, Samuelsson, Nilsson E, Andersson, Nordahl K, Gaerd, Jönsson, Palmer (1), Jeppson, Skoglund, Sundqvist (1)
Paraguay: Vargas, Gonzales, Cespedes, Gavilan, Lequizamon, Cantero, Avalos, Lopez A (1), Saquir, Lopez F (1), Unzain
Referee: Mitchell (Scotland)

Italy (1) **2, Paraguay** (0) **0**
2.7.50 SÃO PAULO
Italy: Moro, Blason, Furiassi, Fattori, Remondini, Mari, Muccinelli, Pandolfini (1), Amadei, Capello, Carapellese (1)
Paraguay: Vargas, Gonzales, Cespedes, Gavilan, Lequizamon, Cantero, Avalos, Lopez A, Saquir, Lopez F, Unzain
Referee: Ellis (England)

	P	W	D	L	F	A	Pts
Sweden	2	1	1	0	5	4	3
Italy	2	1	0	1	4	3	2
Paraguay	2	0	1	1	2	4	1

Group 4

Uruguay (4) **8, Bolivia** (0) **0**
2.7.50 BELO HORIZONTE
Uruguay: Maspoli, Gonzales M, Tejera, Gonzales J, Varela, Andrade, Ghiggia (1), Perez, Miguez (2), Schiaffino (4), Vidal (1)
Bolivia: Gutierrez B, Acha, Bustamante, Greco, Valencia, Ferrel, Algrañez, Ugarte, Caparelli, Gutierrez E, Maldonado
Referee: Reader (England)

Final Group

Venues: São Paulo, Rio de Janeiro
Brazil
Spain
Sweden
Uruguay

The Final Group

THE FIRST SERIES

The meeting between Brazil and Sweden in Rio began nervously. The Swedes' English manager, George Raynor, would later complain, 'we had two chances before they even moved'; they did and they missed them. Brazil through Ademir took the first opportunity that came their way, relaxed, and thereafter Sweden looked increasingly bewitched, chasing the shadows of a confident team far too fast in thought and movement to be resisted. Ademir imposed himself thoroughly over poor Nordahl and scored again. Chico made it three at half-time, and aided by little Maneca the hosts compounded the Scandinavians' misery, with their ruthless finishing embellishing the team's sumptuous play 7–1. The Olympic Champions were emphatically put to a Brazilian sword.

Uruguay in São Paulo found Spain an entirely different proposition to their hapless Group Four opponents. Trailing to an early goal from Ghiggia, the Spaniards staged a determined fightback, inspired by their clever winger Basora, which threatened to sweep Uruguay away. Twice Basora created himself time and space to shoot unerringly for 2–1 at the interval. Now Uruguay responded, but Ramallets, forced again to ply his trade with acrobatic verve, denied them, assisted by courageous defending until the 73rd minute when the rampaging centre half Varela – at the heart of Uruguay's revival – saved them with a thunderous shot for 2–2.

THE SECOND SERIES

At this point Brazil met Spain and again proved irresistible, their blend of powerful running and bewildering movement altogether too much for the Spaniards at Rio. Eizaquirre, strangely returned to goal in place of Ramallets, was a busy man as Spain collapsed to a 6–1 defeat. Curiously for Brazil, however, the rapacious Aldemir did not score. Uruguay also managed a win at São Paulo against Sweden, and in doing so kept the competition alive to the final matches, though again it was a desperately close-run thing, their skill being largely negated by Sweden's organization. Despite Ghiggia equalizing Palmer's opener for the Swedes, the Uruguayans promptly fell behind again when they allowed Sundqvist to shoot past Paz. As in their first match, Uruguay fought back furiously, and the Swedes, weary from their efforts and reduced through injury to ten fit men, could not hold them. Miguez, with two second-half goals, finally confirmed the South Americans' victory.

THE THIRD SERIES

In São Paulo, Spain and Sweden fielding unfamiliar teams competed in a match rendered meaningless by previous results. It was Sweden, the fresher of two exhausted teams, who took third place courtesy of goals by Sundqvist, Palmer and Mellberg (belatedly making his Tournament debut). Spain through Zarra gained only one goal.

For Uruguay in the throbbing Maracana Stadium replete with almost 200,000 people, the opportunity to again become World Champions still existed. Unfortunately, the task, in such a distinctly hostile theatre against distinguished and awe-inspiring hosts, appeared immense. They had to win. Anything less and Brazil would be crowned Champions. The hosts, therefore, were naturally the favourites, but Uruguay were no less confident. They had already beaten Brazil earlier that year. Clavia Costa, Brazil's philosophical coach, warned against complacency in the days preceding this deciding fixture, recognizing the danger Uruguay presented.

The game itself proved a marvellous and stirring contest. Brazil predictably tore into their old rivals ferociously, Maspoli leaping about his goal to defy them as the pressure increased. Jour Friaca and then Ademir thwarted in turn, Uruguay, however, were not confined to desperate defending. Schiaffino was invited to shoot by a Miguez pass hammered goalwards but denied by the diving Barbosa. Brazil again attacked: Jair struck a post, Maspoli frustrated Ademir and Zizinho, and as half-time beckoned Brazil drew breath and Uruguay, showing remarkable fortitude, finished the half threateningly. The second half began and at once the match seemed decided – Friaca streaking through received Zizinho's pass and beat the Herculean Maspoli in one movement. Bedlam ensued. Surely now Brazil would be Champions? But Uruguay persisted, would not be intimidated, and encouraged by earlier counter-attacks they carried on. The fresher legs their schedule had allowed them slowly but surely grew stronger at wrestling control away from the Brazilians. Schiaffino, elegant and precise, bore down on them menacingly, while Varela, a largely destructive force in the first half, powered through tackles, demanding still greater efforts of his team-mates. It was Schiaffino who brought them parity, exploiting oceans of space to drive Ghiggia's cross past Barbosa, 1–1. Visibly crumbling, Brazil found themselves in the unfamiliar role of defending. They could not hold on. Ghiggia running them ragged on the right wing played a one-two with Perez and steered the ball past Barbosa, 2–1 for Uruguay, and they held their lead to the end for a famous and remarkable victory and the Jules Rimet Trophy.

The 1950 Tournament played in so huge a country had, it must be said, been a logistical nightmare. Nevertheless, the absurdity of Uruguay playing one qualifying match while most played three clearly gave them an advantage the organizers must have foreseen. In the end, though, they played with admirable resilience and refused to be intimidated – as others had been – by Brazil. This single factor may have been critical. Brazil, devastated by so bitter a defeat, would have to wait. However, they had played easily the best football, a revelation, with short and long passing, fast and then pedestrian movement designed to upset the rhythm and concentration of their opposition. For Europe there was much to do. True, Yugoslavia had been unlucky and England had suffered an unthinkable aberration, but Sweden and Spain, the continent's representatives in the last four, had been simply outclassed in embarrassing fashion, at least by Brazil.

Final Pool

Brazil (3) **7, Sweden** (0) **1**
9.7.50 RIO DE JANEIRO
Brazil: Barbosa, Augusto, Juvenal, Bauer, Danilo, Bigode, Maneca (1), Zizinho, Ademir (4), Jair, Chico (2)
Sweden: Svensson, Samuelsson, Nilsson E, Andersson (1 pen), Nordahl K, Gaerd, Sundqvist, Palmer, Jeppson, Skoglund, Nilsson S
Referee: Ellis (England)

Uruguay (1) **2, Spain** (2) **2**
9.7.50 SÃO PAULO
Uruguay: Maspoli, Gonzales M, Tejera, Gonzales J, Varela (1), Andrade, Ghiggia (1), Perez, Miguez, Schiaffino, Vidal
Spain: Ramallets, Alonso, Gonzalvo M, Gonzalvo J, Parra, Puchades, Basora (2), Igoa, Zarra, Molowny, Gainza
Referee: Griffiths (Wales)

Brazil (3) **6, Spain** (0) **1**
13.7.50 RIO DE JANEIRO
Brazil: Barbosa, Augusto, Juvenal, Bauer, Danilo, Bigode, Friaca, Zizinho (1), Ademir (2), Jair (1), Chico (2)
Spain: Ramallets, Alonso, Gonzalvo M, Gonzalvo J, Parra, Puchades, Basora, Igoa (1), Zarra, Panizo, Gainza
Referee: Leafe (England)

Uruguay (1) **3, Sweden** (2) **2**
13.7.50 SÃO PAULO
Uruguay: Paz, Gonzales M, Tejera, Gambetta, Varela, Andrade, Ghiggia, Perez (1), Miguez, Schiaffino (2), Vidal
Sweden: Svensson, Nilsson E, Andersson, Johansson, Gaerd, Sunqvist, Palmer (1), Jeppson (1), Jönsson, Nilsson S
Referee: Galeati (Italy)

Sweden (2) **3, Spain** (0) **1**
16.7.50 SÃO PAULO
Sweden: Svensson, Samuelsson, Nilsson E, Andersson, Johansson, Gaerd, Jönsson, Mellberg (1), Rydell, Palmer (1), Sundqvist (1)
Spain: Eizaguirre, Alonso, Asensi, Silva, Parra, Puchades, Basora, Hernandez, Zarra (1), Panizo, Juncosa
Referee: Van de Meer (Netherlands)

Uruguay (0) **2, Brazil** (0) **1**
16.7.50 RIO DE JANEIRO
Uruguay: Maspoli, Gonzales M, Tejera, Gambetta, Varela, Andrade, Ghiggia (1) Perez, Miguez, Schiaffino (1), Moran
Brazil: Barbosa, Augusto, Juvenal, Bauer, Danilo, Bigode, Friaca (1), Zizinho, Ademir, Jair, Chico
Referee: Reader (England)

	P	W	D	L	F	A	Pts
Uruguay	3	2	1	0	7	5	5
Brazil	3	2	0	1	14	4	4
Sweden	3	1	0	2	6	11	2
Spain	3	0	1	2	4	11	1

CHAPTER 5

SWITZERLAND

1954

Qualifying Tournament
38 entries
Uruguay qualify as holders, Switzerland qualify as hosts

Europe and Near East (28): Austria, Belgium, Bulgaria, Czechoslovakia, Egypt, England, Finland, France, West Germany, Greece, Hungary, Republic of Ireland, Northern Ireland, Israel, Italy, Luxembourg, Norway, Poland, Portugal, Romania, Saar (now part of Germany), Scotland, Spain, Sweden, Switzerland, Turkey, Wales, Yugoslavia

South America (4): Brazil, Chile, Paraguay, Uruguay

North and Central America (3): Haiti, Mexico, USA

Asia (3): China, Japan, South Korea

Europe and Near East

Group 1 (West Germany, Saar, Norway)
Norway v Saar 2–3, Saar v Norway 0–0, West Germany v Saar 3–0, Saar v West Germany 1–3, Norway v West Germany 1–1, West Germany v Norway 5–1

	P	W	D	L	F	A	Pts
West Germany	4	3	1	0	12	3	7
Saar	4	1	1	2	4	8	3
Norway	4	0	2	2	4	9	2

West Germany qualified

Group 2 (Belgium, Sweden, Finland)
Finland v Belgium 2–4, Belgium v Finland 2–2, Sweden v Belgium 2–3, Belgium v Sweden 2–0, Finland v Sweden 3–3, Sweden v Finland 4–0

	P	W	D	L	F	A	Pts
Belgium	4	3	1	0	11	6	7
Sweden	4	1	1	2	9	8	3
Finland	4	0	2	2	7	13	2

Belgium qualified

Group 3 (England, Scotland, Northern Ireland, Wales)
Northern Ireland v Scotland 1–3, Wales v England 1–4, Scotland v Wales 3–3, England v Northern Ireland 3–1, Wales v Northern Ireland 1–2, Scotland v England 2–4

	P	W	D	L	F	A	Pts
England	3	3	0	0	11	4	6
Scotland	3	1	1	1	8	8	3
Northern Ireland	3	1	0	2	4	7	2
Wales	3	0	1	2	5	9	1

England and Scotland qualified

Group 4 (France, Rep of Ireland, Luxembourg)

Luxembourg v France 1–6, France v Luxembourg 8–0, Rep of Ireland v Luxembourg 4–0, Luxembourg v Rep of Ireland 0–1, Rep of Ireland v France 3–5, France v Rep of Ireland 1–0

	P	W	D	L	F	A	Pts
France	4	4	0	0	20	4	8
Rep of Ireland	4	2	0	2	8	6	4
Luxembourg	4	0	0	4	1	19	0

France qualified

Group 5 (Austria, Portugal)

Austria v Portugal 9–1, 0–0
Austria qualified

Group 6 (Turkey, Spain)

Spain v Turkey 4–1, 0–1
Play-off (In Rome): Turkey v Spain 2–2 (Turkey won toss up)
Turkey qualified

Group 7 (Hungary, Poland)

Poland withdrew
Hungary qualified

Group 8 (Czechoslovakia, Romania, Bulgaria)

Czechoslovakia v Romania 2–0, Romania v Czechoslovakia 0–1, Bulgaria v Czechoslovakia 1–2, Czechoslovakia v Bulgaria 0–0, Romania v Bulgaria 3–1, Bulgaria v Romania 1–2

	P	W	D	L	F	A	Pts
Czechoslovakia	4	3	1	0	5	1	7
Romania	4	2	0	2	5	5	4
Bulgaria	4	0	1	3	3	7	1

Czechoslovakia qualified

Group 9 (Italy, Egypt)
Egypt v Italy 1–2, 1–5
Italy qualified

Group 10 (Yugoslavia, Greece, Israel)
Israel v Yugoslavia 0–1, Yugoslavia v Israel 1–0, Yugoslavia v Greece 1–0,
Greece v Yugoslavia 0–1, Israel v Greece 0–2, Greece v Israel 1–0

	P	W	D	L	F	A	Pts
Yugoslavia	4	4	0	0	4	0	8
Greece	4	2	0	2	3	2	4
Israel	4	0	0	4	0	5	0

Yugoslavia qualified

South America

Group 12 (Brazil, Paraguay, Chile)
Paraguay v Chile 4–0, Chile v Paraguay 1–3, Chile v Brazil 0–2, Brazil v Chile
1–0, Brazil v Paraguay 4–1, Paraguay v Brazil 0–1

	P	W	D	L	F	A	Pts
Brazil	4	4	0	0	8	1	8
Paraguay	4	2	0	2	8	6	4
Chile	4	0	0	4	1	10	0

Brazil qualified

North and Central America

Group 11 (Mexico, USA, Haiti)
Mexico v Haiti 8–0, Haiti v Mexico 0–4, Mexico v USA 3–1, USA v Mexico 0–4,
USA v Haiti 3–0, Haiti v USA 2–3

	P	W	D	L	F	A	Pts
Mexico	4	4	0	0	19	1	8
USA	4	2	0	2	7	9	4
Haiti	4	0	0	4	2	18	0

Mexico qualified

Asia

Group 13 (South Korea, Japan, China)
China withdrew
Japan v South Korea (in Tokyo) 1–5, 2–2
South Korea qualified

1954 SWITZERLAND 16 June–4 July

QUALIFIERS

Austria	Mexico
Belgium	Scotland
Brazil	South Korea
Czechoslovakia	Switzerland
England	Turkey
France	Uruguay
Hungary	West Germany
Italy	Yugoslavia

In 1954 the circus rolled into Switzerland, a country fortunate to escape the ravages of war suffered by most of their European counterparts. Despite the close proximity of all stadia to Berne, the nation's capital, the organization left much to be desired and was at times chaotic. Interestingly, it was here for the very first time that images would be beamed direct into the homes of those with television sets – technology had arrived.

The Tournament itself, having dispensed with the 'Final Pool' and returned again to its original semi-final and final format, had sixteen nations competing in four groups of four, with two seeded teams in each. Curiously, FIFA insisted that these 'seeds' would not meet each other, and consequently only two rather than three matches would be played. Other extraordinary decisions led to extra time in all drawn matches, play-offs rather than goal average to decide who would go through, and, most farcical of all, the seeds being identified before qualification had been determined. Turkey, therefore, in eliminating Spain on the toss of a coin, claimed without merit the Spaniards' privileged seeding, a decision that would have serious ramifications for the Tournament as a whole.

In Group One France, without any notable achievement in previous Tournaments, had been seeded, though their qualification form against weak opposition had been remarkable. Brazil, so unlucky four years earlier, were also seeded and had replaced their previously unsuccessful squad with a new and more youthful team. Qualification for them, too, had proven little more than a formality, but undoubtedly Argentina's self-imposed exile eased their passage considerably. Yugoslavia, a gifted team boasting Vukas and Zebec, both additions to their Olympic Games silver medal winners, had a record in qualifying that was astonishingly consistent – four successive 1–0 victories. Mexico, lastly, had won the right to compete with emphatic victories over Haiti and USA. Carbajal, their goalkeeper, and Cardenas, their right half, were fine players, but the draw inspired little confidence for them.

Group Two saw the all-conquering Hungarians, Olympic Champions, begin a campaign many viewed as an inevitable procession. With such talent they had twice destroyed England, and had in Puskás a colossus capable of wreaking havoc on any defence, with Czibor, Toth, Kocsis and the marvellous Nandor Hidegkuti as his attacking accomplices; they were hugely favoured. Turkey, the other 'seed', had been surprising in holding Spain to a 2–2 draw in Rome. Their chance came virtue of a coin toss. Yet in Turgay and Lefter they possessed talent. Germany, back now competing in world sport, had eliminated Saar and Norway comfortably. With Fritz Walter, the crafty veteran, they had a formidable and influential forward. Korea, the fourth of the group, were the mystery team, Asia's first entrant due to a qualification win over the equally diminutive Japanese in Tokyo.

In Group Three Uruguay participated to defend their crown, playing in a European competition for the first time. They remained unbeaten in the history of the Tournament and Schiaffino, the lithe lanky marksman of 1950, returned with them. Scotland, second again in the British championship, finally assented to play, their reward this toughest of groups. Czechoslovakia, too, was unseeded, with a new team primarily drawn from Army side U.D.A., and their presence a result of victory in both Romania and Bulgaria. The Austrians seeded with Uruguay had an elegant and exceptional side, though recently eclipsed by Hungary as Central Europe's dominant team. They presented a considerable obstacle to the ambitions of others, with Ocwirk, a magnificent centre half, and a potentially destructive forward line.

In Group Four England, with brilliant wingmen Finney and Matthews, muscular centre forward Lofthouse and the forceful leadership of Wright, had had their confidence shattered after the two debacles with Hungary. Belgium, through at the expense of Sweden, posed little threat to the Tournament elite, though Coppens of Beerschot was a highly regarded forward. Italy, for so long the dominant force in world football, had still not fully recovered from the aircrash that robbed them of the services of the entire Torino side – their very best – and in spite of qualification being secured by virtue of two wins over Egypt, theirs was a team in transit. Finally came Switzerland, the host, with the dangerous attackers Antenen and Fatton, Neury splendid at full back and a defence reliant on a revolutionary 'sweeper-up' system. They were not without a chance.

Venues for all matches:

Basle, Lausanne, Berne, Lugano, Geneva, Zurich

Group 1

Brazil*
France*
Mexico
Yugoslavia

Group 3

Austria*
Czechoslovakia
Scotland
Uruguay*

Group 2

Hungary*
South Korea
Turkey*
West Germany

Group 4

Belgium
England*
Italy*
Switzerland

* denotes seeded teams

THE FIRST SERIES

In Group One at Lausanne the talented Yugoslavians squeezed by the French 1–0, Milutinovic providing the goal. Brazil, playing the plainly inferior Mexicans in Geneva, dispatched them mercilessly, Didi and Julinho playing starring roles. Poor Mexico, already 4–0 at the interval, rallied bravely in the second half as Brazil, satisfied, relaxed their efforts, scoring just once more.

In Group Two Hungary crushed the disadvantaged Koreans in an embarrassingly one-sided encounter in Zurich. They, too, led 4–0 at half-time, though Korea's inadequacies and Hungary's steamroller attack saw the massacre continue unabated thereafter, 9–0 at the end, and for Kocsis an easy hat trick. 'Seeded' Turkey, to no one's surprise, were beaten by Sepp Herberger's German team. Level through Suat going into the second half, the Turks could not sustain their effort, and Germany, as was widely expected, ran away with it 4–1.

In Group Three the Scots, finally making their debut against the talented Austrians, fell behind to a goal from Probst and responded forcefully, rocking the Austrians back on their heels, Mochan denied at the end by Schmied confirming them as unfortunate losers 1–0. Uruguay, the Champions, faced with a muddy pitch and heavy, unfamiliar conditions, still made little of defeating a Czech side playing with limited ambition, their splendid little winger Abbadie rampant, Miguez and the brilliant Schiaffino, veterans of 1950, scoring the goals in Berne.

In Group Four England played Belgium in Basle. Bizarrely, after falling behind at the very beginning, the English restored order, dominated, scored three times, then threw away the initiative and their advantage, allowing Anoul a second goal and Coppens one to take the Belgians undeservedly into extra time. In those thirty extra minutes England again raised themselves and took what should have been a decisive lead through Lofthouse, but with Matthews limping on the field injured, they allowed their gallant opponents an unlikely equalizer, Dickinson misplacing his defensive header disastrously beyond Merrick and into the English goal, 4–4. Also in Group Four, at Lausanne, the Swiss hosts prevailed over Italy in an ill-tempered, ugly game that bordered on the unruly. Italy, threatened with defeat by an incisive team whom they had largely outplayed, showed their dark side, with two Swiss players being kicked in the stomach and the weak referee, Sr. Viana, being pursued and remonstrated with by irate Italians at full time. The Swiss, meanwhile, in spite of provocation, sensibly kept their heads, and Hügi rewarded them with a late winner.

THE SECOND SERIES

Back in Group One, France made changes against the Mexicans and remained uninspired, their 3–2 victory in Geneva courtesy only of generous and inept defending. At Lausanne clearly the better of the Group rivals met in an absorbing contest, Yugoslavia, cleverly organized by Cajkovski and Boskov, enjoying much the better of an entertaining first half, and Zebec shooting their goal past Castilho. Brazil responded, Didi earning them the draw their industry deserved with a magnificent half volley. Extra time came and went, for a score of 1–1.

In Group Two, Hungary played a Germany weakened considerably by changes, devastating them 8–3 in Basle. Kocsis again benefited most from their rampaging forward play, scoring four times, though significantly Puskás was injured by a clumsy kick from Liebrich. Germany without argument was overwhelmed by the most irresistible force. Turkey, beaten so comprehensively by Germany, underlined Korea's inferiority with a 7–0 win, the Asians' abject failure demonstrating the colossal difference in standards at the Tournament.

Scotland, too, now without a manager after protracted squabbles at Basle, experienced humiliation as they fell prey to a rampant Uruguayan team full of craft and invention. Led by the exquisite touch of Schiaffino and their pacey, vibrant wingers, Abbadie and Borges, the Scots fell apart in a depressingly undisciplined manner, Uruguay 7–0 winners at the end. Austria confirmed their progress into the quarter-finals with an equally emphatic 5–0 defeat of Czechoslovakia. Clever though their attacking play undoubtedly was, the Czechs were a disappointing team. Shorn of combative instincts and four goals down at half-time, the margin at the end owed more to good fortune and wasteful finishing from the Austrians than a Czech revival.

In Group Four England ground out a 2–0 victory over Switzerland. The Swiss, curiously pedantic after their rigorous performance against Italy, allowed the English to dominate and exorcise from their mind the traumatic experience of Belgium in Basle. Italy, for their part, exposed the Belgians at Lugano, 4–1. Switzerland in Basle and a play-off awaited them.

Final Tournament – Switzerland

Group 1

Yugoslavia (1) **1, France** (0) **0**
16.6.54 LAUSANNE
Yugoslavia: Beara, Stankovic, Crnkovic, Cajkovski, Horvat, Boskov, Milutinovic (1), Mitic, Vukas, Bobek, Zebec
France: Remetter, Gianessi, Kaelbel, Penverne, Jonquet, Marcel, Kopa, Glovacki, Strappe, Dereuddre, Vincent
Referee: Griffiths (Wales)

Brazil (4) **5, Mexico** (0) **0**
16.6.54 GENEVA
Brazil: Castilho, Santos D, Santos N, Brandaozinho, Pinheiro, Bauer, Julinho (1), Didi (1), Baltazar (1), Pinga (2), Rodriguez
Mexico: Mota, Lopez, Gomez, Cardenas, Romo, Avalos, Torres, Naranjo, Lamadrid, Balcazar, Arellano
Referee: Wyssling (Switzerland)

France (1) **3, Mexico** (0) **2**
19.6.54 GENEVA
France: Remetter, Gianessi, Marche, Marcel, Kaelbel, Mahjoub, Kopa (1 pen), Dereuddre, Strappe, Ben Tifour, Vincent (1)
Mexico: Carbajal, Lopez, Romo, Cardenas (o.g.), Avalos, Martinez, Torres, Naranjo (1), Lamadrid, Balcazar (1), Arellano
Referee: Asensi (Spain)

Brazil (0) **1, Yugoslavia** (0) **1** (aet, 1–1 at 90 mins)
19.6.54 LAUSANNE
Brazil: Castilho, Santos D, Santos N, Brandaozinho, Pinheiro, Bauer, Julinho, Didi (1), Baltazar, Pinga, Rodriguez
Yugoslavia: Beara, Stankovic, Crnkovic, Cajkovski, Horvat, Boskov, Milutinovic, Mitic, Zebec (1), Vukas, Dvornik
Referee: Faultless (Scotland)

	P	W	D	L	F	A	Pts
Brazil	2	1	1	0	6	1	3
Yugoslavia	2	1	1	1	2	1	3
France	2	1	0	1	3	3	2
Mexico	2	0	0	2	2	8	0

Group 2

Hungary (4) **9, South Korea** (0) **0**
17.6.54 ZURICH
Hungary: Grosics, Buzánszky, Lantos (1), Bozsik, Lorant, Szojka, Budai, Kocsis (3), Palotás (2), Puskás (2), Czibor (1)
South Korea: Hong, Kyu Park, Kang, Min, Yae Seung Park, Chu, Chung, Kap Park, Sung, Woo, Yung Keun Choi
Referee: Vincenti (France)

West Germany (1) **4, Turkey** (1) **1**
17.6.54 BERNE
West Germany: Turek, Laband, Kohlmeyer, Eckel, Posipal, Mai, Klodt (1), Morlock (1), Walter O (1), Walter F, Schäfer (1)
Turkey: Turgay, Ridvan, Basri, Mustafa, Cetin, Rober, Erol, Suat (1), Feridun, Burhan, Lefter
Referee: Da Costa (Portugal)

Hungary (3) **8, West Germany** (1) **3**
20.6.54 BASLE
Hungary: Grosics, Buzánszky, Lantos, Bozsik, Lorant, Zakarias, Toth J (1), Kocsis (4), Hidegkuti (2), Puskás (1), Czibor
West Germany: Kwaitkowski, Bauer, Kohlmeyer, Posipal, Liebrich, Mebus, Rahn (1), Eckel, Walter F, Pfaff (1), Hermann (1)
Referee: Ling (England)

Turkey (4) **7, South Korea** (0) **0**
20.6.54 GENEVA
Turkey: Turgay, Ridvan, Basri, Mustafa, Cetin, Rober, Erol (1), Suat (2), Necmettin, Lefter (1), Burhan (3)
South Korea: Hong, Kyu Park, Kang, Han, Chong Kap Lee, Kim, Yung Keun Choi, Soo Nam Lee, Gi Choo Lee, Woo, Chung
Referee: Marino (Uruguay)

	P	W	D	L	F	A	Pts
Hungary	2	2	0	0	17	3	4
West Germany	2	1	0	1	7	9	2
Turkey	2	1	0	1	8	4	2
South Korea	2	0	0	2	0	16	0

Group 3

Austria (1) **1, Scotland** (0) **0**
16.6.54 ZURICH
Austria: Schmied, Hanappi, Barschandt, Ocwirk, Happel, Koller, Körner R, Schleger, Dienst, Probst (1), Körner A
Scotland: Martin, Cunningham, Aird, Docherty, Davidson, Cowie, McKenzie, Fernie, Mochan, Brown, Ormond
Referee: Franken (Belgium)

Uruguay (0) **2, Czechoslovakia** (0) **0**
16.6.54 BERNE
Uruguay: Maspoli, Santamaria, Martinez, Andrade, Varela, Cruz, Abbadie, Ambrois, Miguez (1), Schiaffino (1), Borges
Czechoslovakia: Reimann, Safranek, Novak, Trnka, Hledlik, Hertl, Hlavecek, Hemele, Kacany, Pazicky, Peser
Referee: Ellis (England)

Austria (4) **5, Czechoslovakia** (0) **0**
19.6.54 ZURICH
Austria: Schmied, Hanappi, Barschandt, Ocwirk, Happel, Koller, Körner R, Wagner, Stojaspal (2), Probst (3), Körner A
Czechoslovakia: Stacho, Safranek, Novak, Trnka, Pluskal, Hertl, Hlavacek, Hemele, Kacany, Pazicky, Krauss
Referee: Stafanovic (Yugoslavia)

Uruguay (2) **7, Scotland** (0) **0**
19.6.54 BASLE
Uruguay: Maspoli, Santamaria, Martinez, Andrade, Varela, Cruz, Abbadie (2), Ambrois, Miguez (2), Schiaffino, Borges (3)
Scotland: Martin, Cunningham, Aird, Docherty, Davidson, Cowie, McKenzie, Fernie, Mochan, Brown, Ormond
Referee: Orlandini (Italy)

	P	W	D	L	F	A	Pts
Uruguay	2	2	0	0	9	0	4
Austria	2	2	0	0	6	0	4
Czechoslovakia	2	0	0	2	0	7	0
Scotland	2	0	0	2	0	8	0

Group 4

England (2) **4, Belgium** (1) **4** (aet, 3–3 at 90 mins)
17.6.54 BASLE
England: Merrick, Staniforth, Byrne, Wright, Owen, Dickinson (o.g.), Matthews, Broadis (2), Lofthouse (2), Taylor, Finney
Belgium: Gernaey, Dries, Van Brandt, Huysmans, Carre, Mees, Van den Bosch P, Houf, Coppens (1), Anoul (2), Mermans
Referee: Schmetzer (West Germany)

Switzerland (1) **2, Italy** (1) **1**
17.6.54 LAUSANNE
Switzerland: Parlier, Neury, Kernen, Flückiger, Bocquet, Casali I, Ballaman (1), Vonlanthen, Hügi II (1), Meier, Fatton
Italy: Ghezzi, Vincenzi, Giacomazzi, Neri, Tognon, Nesti, Muccinelli, Boniperti (1), Galli, Pandolfini, Lorenzi
Referee: Viana (Brazil)

England (1) **2, Switzerland** (0) **0**
20.6.54 BERNE
England: Merrick, Staniforth, Byrne, McGarry, Wright, Dickinson, Finney, Broadis, Wilshaw (1), Taylor, Mullen (1)
Switzerland: Parlier, Neury, Kernen, Eggimann, Bocquet, Bigler, Antenen, Vonlanthen, Meier, Ballaman, Fatton
Referee: Zsolt (Hungary)

Italy (1) **4, Belgium** (0) **1**
26.6.54 LUGANO
Italy: Ghezzi, Magnini, Giacomazzi, Neri, Tognon, Nesti, Frignani (1), Cappello, Galli (1), Pandolfini (1 pen), Lorenzi (1)
Belgium: Gernaey, Dries, Van Brandt, Huysmans, Carre, Mees, Mermans, Van den Bosch H, Coppens, Anoul (1), Van Den Bosch P
Referee: Steiner (Austria)

	P	W	D	L	F	A	Pts
England	2	1	1	0	6	4	3
Switzerland	2	1	0	1	2	3	2
Italy	2	1	0	1	5	3	2
Belgium	2	0	1	1	5	8	1

In Zurich in a play-off for a quarter-final place, Germany confirmed their obvious superiority over the Turks, crushing them again, 7–2. Morlock, one of a number 'hidden' against Hungary, reappeared to score a hat-trick.

Switzerland somewhat surprisingly also confirmed an earlier win and eliminated debilitated Italy 4–1, this time with less difficulty and in a match with considerably fewer violent challenges. Italy went home, their undistinguished challenge over.

Group Play-Offs for Second Place

West Germany (2) **7, Turkey** (1) **2**
23.6.54 ZURICH
West Germany: Turek, Laband, Bauer, Eckel, Posipal, Mai, Klodt, Morlock (3), Walter O (1), Walter F (1), Schäfer (2)
Turkey: Sükrü, Ridvan, Basri, Naci, Cetin, Rober, Erol, Mustafa (1), Necmettin, Coskun, Lefter (1)
Referee: Vincenti (France)

Switzerland (1) **4, Italy** (0) **1**
23.6.54 BASLE
Switzerland: Parlier, Neury, Kernen, Eggimann, Bocquet, Casali, Antenen, Vonlanthen, Hügi II (2), Ballaman (1), Fatton (1)
Italy: Viola, Magnini, Giacomazzi, Neri, Tognon, Nesti (1), Muccinelli, Pandolfini, Lorenzi, Segato, Frignani
Referee: Griffiths (Wales)

THE QUARTER-FINALS

The hosts, Switzerland, went out at Lausanne in a remarkable match with their Austrian neighbours. Going 3–0 up in twenty minutes, the Swiss allowed Austria back as the Körner brothers, at first unsettled, ultimately tore ragged holes in Switzerland's famed 'Catenaccio' defence. After five astonishing goals in seven minutes and a missed penalty to boot, Austria led 5–3 in the most dramatic circumstances imaginable, and all this in the first half. There were more twists before the interval, as the shell-shocked Swiss hauled themselves back into contention, Ballaman thumping their fourth. Predictably the frenzied activity calmed as the two teams sparred, a semi-final place at stake. Wagner completed a hat-trick to go 6–4; Hügi, tough and mobile, shot; Schmied, the Austrian's custodian, was deceived by the unfortunate deflection by Hanappi to go 6–5; and finally Probst, running at tired Swiss defenders, eluded desperate tackles before unleashing a shot into the net: 7–5.

In Geneva the heavily favoured Yugoslavians were beaten by the less sophisticated but tenacious Germany. Horvat, the stout centre half, gave the Germans a gift in the opening moment, flicking an optimistic through ball past his own goalkeeper. Greatly encouraged by their lead, though largely outplayed by imaginative opponents, Germany resisted with grim determination. For Yugoslavia, driven inevitably by Zebec and Milutinovic, chances came and went, frustration increased and then the diminutive Rahn settled matters. Receiving the ball in what many believed to be an offside position, he ran on and shot past Beara for a contentious decisive second goal. Four minutes from the end the score was 2–0 and Yugoslavia were out.

At this stage England also departed, though against the irresistible Uruguayan forwards their effort was commendably pugnacious. Borges opened the scoring at five minutes, seizing Abbadie's pass to drive past Merrick in England's goal. The English responded with greater endeavour. Matthews, thirty-nine, still mesmerizing, taunted the Uruguayans to set up an equalizer, with Lofthouse the beneficiary. Now they pressed hard. Wilshaw was culpable from a gilt-edged opportunity when he saw his wastefulness punished and Varela's tame effort unforgivably beat Merrick. The brilliant Schiaffino reaching Varela's free kick, taken illegally, shot the South Americans 3–1 ahead after the interval, and in spite of bewildered protests, it was crucially allowed to stand. While England bravely continued their fight, the Uruguayans, with several carrying injuries, began to wilt. Finney's shot, too good for Maspoli, put the score at 2–3. Matthews struck a post and was then denied by athletic goalkeeping, but hard as they tried, there was no way back, Ambrois sealing their fate at the end with a shot past the unfortunate Merrick. Despite playing with great distinction, England had lost. Indeed, they might have won in the end had their efforts not been undone by clumsy and uncertain goalkeeping.

To Berne and notoriety as arguably the two finest teams in the Tournament, Hungary and Brazil, indulged wilfully in an orgy of violent tactics, brutal challenges and spiteful petulance. Hungary, quicker in thought and movement in the early stages, rapidly established a two-goal advantage. After three minutes Hidegkuti drove the ball home in a scramble, and then Kocsis, fed by Hidegkuti, made it 2–0 in less then ten minutes. Brazil fought back, warming to their task, probing constantly, frustrated by niggling sly fouls designed to slow them down and break their rhythm. However, from one such challenge Indio earned Brazil a penalty; Santos converted it for 2–1. The pattern of the contest continued and worsened, the mood of the players blackening, the undercurrent one of simmering ugliness. Hungary, with Toth reduced to a limping passenger, earned a penalty and scored. The menacing Julinho on a meandering run brought the Brazilians to 2–3. And the game erupted. Bozsik, tackled unfairly by Santos, punched him, and the pair, after a protracted boxing match, were dismissed. Didi struck the bar for Brazil, whilst Djalmo Santos gave up all pretence of playing football and pursued Czibor about the field, enraged and without thought of the consequences. Then in a flash the game was over – in the very last minute Kocsis guided Czibor's cross into the Brazilian goal, to give Hungary a 4–2 victory. Still, Tozzi at the death managed to get himself sent off for a pointless kick at Hungary's Lorant, and then at the final whistle pandemonium ensued. Puskás, still injured and a spectator, allegedly struck Pinheiro with a bottle, causing a three-inch cut. The incensed Brazilians invaded the Hungarian dressing room. A pitched battle ensued, fists, boots and bottles being used in extended and chaotic savagery that left Toth unconscious and most bruised or bleeding. For both of these great teams it was a sad day indeed.

Quarter-Finals

Austria (5) **7, Switzerland** (4) **5**
26.6.54 LAUSANNE
Austria: Schmied, Hanappi (o.g.), Barschandt, Ocwirk (1), Happel, Koller, Körner R, Wagner (3), Stojaspal, Probst (1), Körner A (2)
Switzerland: Parlier, Neury, Kernen, Eggimann, Bocquet, Casali, Antenen, Vonlanthen, Hügi II (2), Ballaman (2), Fatton
Referee: Faultless (Scotland)

Uruguay (2) **4, England** (1) **2**
26.6.54 BASLE
Uruguay: Maspoli, Santamaria, Martinez, Andrade, Varela (1), Cruz, Abbadie, Ambrois (1), Miguez, Schiaffino (1), Borges (1)
England: Merrick, Staniforth, Byrne, McGarry, Wright, Dickinson, Matthews, Broadis, Lofthouse (1), Wilshaw, Finney (1)
Referee: Steiner (Austria)

West Germany (1) **2, Yugoslavia** (0) **0**
27.6.54 GENEVA
West Germany: Turek, Laband, Kohlmeyer, Eckel, Liebrich, Mai, Rahn (1), Morlock, Walter O, Walter F, Schäfer
Yugoslavia: Beara, Stankovic, Crnkovic, Cajkovski, Horvat (o.g.), Boskov, Milutinovic, Mitic, Vukas, Bobek, Zebec
Referee: Zsolt (Hungary)

Hungary (2) **4, Brazil** (1) **2**
27.6.54 BERNE
Hungary: Grosics, Buzánszky, Lantos (1 pen), Bozsik, Lorant, Zakarias, Toth M, Kocsis (2), Hidegkuti (1), Czibor, Toth J
Brazil: Castilho, Santos D (1 pen), Santos N, Brandaozinho, Pinheiro, Bauer, Julinho (1), Didi, Indio, Humberto, Maurinho
Referee: Ellis (England)

THE SEMI-FINALS

In Basle the West Germans, thus far perceived as gritty artisans amongst high-calibre artists, shocked the pundits again by demolishing a confused Austrian team made vulnerable through the introduction in goal of Zeman, reputedly their finest, at the expense of the dependable Schmied. The consequences proved disastrous as the 'inferior' team put them to the sword, Schäfer deflecting Fritz Walter's cross to open their account, then Morlock, offered a similar proposition by the crafty Walter, making it 2–0. Probst briefly brought Austria hope, capitalizing on Turek's fumble, but Walter, aided by his brother Otmar, finished them with Teutonic efficiency, a penalty by Fritz making it 3–1. The Austrians slowly, visibly, lost their collective will and crumbled. Otmar headed a fourth, Fritz a fifth and then gloriously, to the general disbelief of 58,000 witnesses, Otmar headed powerfully again past the horribly indecisive Zeman for 6–1. The Germans would contest one more game and again be a long outsider.

In Lausanne, Uruguay finally, after twenty-four years, lost a World Cup match, though this keenly contested semi-final, absorbing throughout, was arguably the finest yet in the competition's history. Hungary, fast and fluent, earned some redemption from the deplorable scenes of Berne three days earlier. Puskás, still struggling to shake off the effects of Liebrich's tackle, was again absent; Varela, too, an inspiration throughout for the Uruguayans, was sadly missed, as both teams made a number of enforced and significant changes. Competitive early on, Uruguay nonetheless were unable to prevent Hungary taking their customary fast start, as Czibor scored early and Hidegkuti added a second from an emphatic header. Losing 2–0 at half-time, Uruguay demonstrated their marvellous spirit and technique, lifted as they were by the indomitable wizardry of Schiaffino: unlucky twice himself, he continued to wield the greatest influence on proceedings. Hohberg finally accepted an opportunity on 75 minutes, and then three minutes from the end he ran on to another Schiaffino pass. To the mortification of the Hungarians, he fired Uruguay level before being engulfed by his jubilant colleagues, 2–2 and into extra time. Uruguay might have taken the initiative but the hero became the villain, Hohberg striking another Schiaffino through-ball on to the goal post before, at the other end, the powerful Kocsis condemned them to defeat with two late and unstoppable headers, 4–2. 'We beat the best team we ever met,' said Hungarian coach Mandi.

Semi-Finals

West Germany (1) **6, Austria** (0) **1**
30.6.54 BASLE
West Germany: Turek, Posipal, Kohlmeyer, Eckel, Liebrich, Mai, Rahn, Morlock (1), Walter O (2), Walter F (2 pens), Schäfer (1)
Austria: Zeman, Hanappi, Schleger, Ocwirk, Happel, Koller, Körner R, Wagner, Stojaspal, Probst (1), Körner A
Referee: Orlandini (Italy)

Hungary (1) **4, Uruguay** (0) **2** (aet, 2–2 at 90 mins)
30.6.54 LAUSANNE
Hungary: Grosics, Buzánszky, Lantos, Bozsik, Lorant, Zakarias, Budai, Kocsis (2), Palotás, Hidegkuti (1), Czibor (1)
Uruguay: Maspoli, Santamaria, Martinez, Andrade, Carballo, Cruz, Souto, Ambrois, Schiaffino, Hohberg (2), Borges
Referee: Griffiths (Wales)

Before the final, Austria and Uruguay at Zurich played out a miserable third and fourth place game. Austria, the better side, won with some ease – they had more to prove after their shocking aberration against Germany. Uruguay, tired after their Herculean semi-final effort, lacked motivation, and unable to galvanize themselves they went down 3–1, though their first ever European adventure had been a memorable one.

Match for Third Place

Austria (1) **3, Uruguay** (1) **1**
3.7.54 ZURICH
Austria: Schmied, Hanappi, Barschandt, Ocwirk (1), Kollmann, Koller, Körner R, Wagner, Dienst, Stojaspal (1 pen), Probst
Uruguay: Maspoli, Santamaria, Martinez, Andrade, Carballo, Cruz (o.g.), Abbadie, Hohberg (1), Mendez, Schiaffino, Borges
Referee: Wyssling (Switzerland)

In the final at Berne, the great Puskás was recalled for Hungary, despite remaining doubts over his fitness. The Germans, for their part, revelled in their role as the underdog, hoping to be carried to triumph on a tide of partisan support from a crowd predominantly behind them. So it began on 4 July 1954, and within eight minutes the extraordinary Hungarians had again secured a two-goal lead, Puskás first driving in Kocsis' deflected attempt and then, before Germany could compose themselves, Czibor seizing on a misunderstanding between Kohlmeyer and Turek for a second. Germany, bewildered, managed an immediate and significant response, thus saving themselves from ignominy, Morlock stretching fully to divert Rahn's cross past Grosics for 2–1. Astonishingly, within 16 minutes it was 2–2, Walter curling a tantalizing cross over from a corner, eluding all but Rahn who drove it gratefully home. Hungary attacked remorselessly, although Puskás laboured, already showing ill effects from his earlier injury. Turek, in Germany's goal, performed heroics to deny in turn Puskás and Kocsis, Hidegkuti's shot crashing back off the post. In the second half the all-out assault by the imperious Hungarians continued unabated. Puskás was frustrated twice by Turek, Toth grazed the West German bar, then Hidegkuti, so reliable, fired wide with the goal agape. It was Rahn who punished their wasteful shooting: grabbing a rare loose ball in Hungary's penalty area after Otmar Walter had distracted defenders, he flashed his shot into the groping Grosics' net. Germany led 3–2 and now they had but five minutes to defend. Puskás had other ideas – less agile than before, instinct eased him on to Toth's incisive pass and he beat Turek with aplomb to go 3–3. However, Welsh linesman Mr Griffiths flagged for offside and Germany retained their slender, fragile lead. Yet there was still time for more drama as Czibor let fly and Turek miraculously turned away. Germany, with grit, courage and no little luck, had defied the odds and their more illustrious opponents to win an unlikely and famous victory.

Final

West Germany (2) **3, Hungary** (2) **2**
4.7.54 BERNE
West Germany: Turek, Posipal, Kohlmeyer, Eckel, Liebrich, Mai, Rahn (2), Morlock (1), Walter O, Walter F, Schäfer
Hungary: Grosics, Buzánszky, Lantos, Bozsik, Lorant, Zakarias, Czibor (1), Kocsis, Hidegkuti, Puskás (1), Toth J
Referee: Ling (England)

The Tournament had been an enormous success. Goals had been plentiful throughout and marvellous spectacles were played out before enthusiastic crowds: Austria's remarkable defeat of the Swiss, Brazil's contest with the Yugoslavs, Hungary's demolition of all-comers, including the infamous 'Battle of Berne' with Brazil, and the exhibition in Lausanne with Uruguay. Yet Hungary, unquestionably the best team with their marvellous flowing football, had been denied the ultimate prize by a German team whom they had destroyed in the early rounds. Germany, shrewdly managed and resilient, had earned their place in the history books; for them obstinacy, organization, good fortune and a clever forward line had prevailed.

CHAPTER 6

SWEDEN

1958

Qualifying Tournament
53 entries
West Germany qualify as holders, Sweden qualify as hosts

Europe (29): Austria, Belgium, Bulgaria, Czechoslovakia, Denmark, England, Finland, France, East Germany, West Germany, Greece, Holland, Hungary, Iceland, Republic of Ireland, Northern Ireland, Italy, Luxembourg, Norway, Poland, Portugal, Romania, Scotland, Spain, Sweden, Switzerland, USSR, Wales, Yugoslavia

South America (9): Argentina, Bolivia, Brazil, Chile, Colombia, Paraguay, Peru, Uruguay, Venezuela

North and Central America (6): Canada, Costa Rica, Curaçao, Guatemala, Mexico, USA

Asia/Africa (9): China, Cyprus, Egypt, Indonesia, Israel, Sudan, Syria, Taiwan, Turkey

Europe

Group 1 (England, Rep of Ireland, Denmark)
Rep of Ireland v Denmark 2–1, England v Denmark 5–2, England v Rep of Ireland 5–1, Denmark v England 1–4, Rep of Ireland v England 1–1, Denmark v Rep of Ireland 0–2

	P	W	D	L	F	A	Pts
England	4	3	1	0	15	5	7
Rep of Ireland	4	2	1	1	6	7	5
Denmark	4	0	0	4	4	13	0

England qualified

Group 2 (France, Belgium, Iceland)
France v Belgium 6–3, France v Iceland 8–0, Belgium v Iceland 8–3, Iceland v France 1–5, Iceland v Belgium 2–5, Belgium v France 0–0

	P	W	D	L	F	A	Pts
France	4	3	1	0	19	4	7
Belgium	4	2	1	1	16	11	5
Iceland	4	0	0	4	6	26	0

France qualified

Group 3 (Hungary, Bulgaria, Norway)

Norway v Bulgaria 1–2, Norway v Hungary 2–1, Hungary v Bulgaria 4–1, Bulgaria v Hungary 1–2, Bulgaria v Norway 7–0, Hungary v Norway 5–0

	P	W	D	L	F	A	Pts
Hungary	4	3	0	1	12	4	6
Bulgaria	4	2	0	2	11	7	4
Norway	4	1	0	3	3	15	2

Hungary qualified

Group 4 (Czechoslovakia, Wales, East Germany)

Wales v Czechoslovakia 1–0, East Germany v Wales 2–1, Czechoslovakia v Wales 2–0, Czechoslovakia v East Germany 3–1, Wales v East Germany 4–1, East Germany v Czechoslovakia 1–4

	P	W	D	L	F	A	Pts
Czechoslovakia	4	3	0	1	9	3	6
Wales	4	2	0	2	6	5	4
East Germany	4	1	0	3	5	12	2

Czechoslovakia qualified

Group 5 (Austria, Holland, Luxembourg)

Austria v Luxembourg 7–0, Holland v Luxembourg 4–1, Austria v Holland 3–2, Luxembourg v Holland (in Rotterdam) 2–5, Holland v Austria 1–1, Luxembourg v Austria 0–3

	P	W	D	L	F	A	Pts
Austria	4	3	1	0	14	3	7
Holland	4	2	1	1	12	7	5
Luxembourg	4	0	0	4	3	19	0

Austria qualified

Group 6 (USSR, Poland, Finland)

USSR v Poland 3–0, Finland v Poland 1–3, USSR v Finland 2–1, Finland v USSR 0–10, Poland v USSR 2–1, Poland v Finland 4–0

	P	W	D	L	F	A	Pts
USSR	4	3	0	1	16	3	6
Poland	4	3	0	1	9	5	6
Finland	4	0	0	4	2	19	0

Play-off (in Leipzig): USSR v Poland 2–0
USSR qualified

Group 7 (Yugoslavia, Romania, Greece)
Greece v Yugoslavia 0–0, Greece v Romania 1–2, Romania v Yugoslavia 1–1, Romania v Greece 3–0, Yugoslavia v Greece 4–1, Yugoslavia v Romania 2–0

	P	W	D	L	F	A	Pts
Yugoslavia	4	2	2	0	7	2	6
Romania	4	2	1	1	6	4	5
Greece	4	0	1	3	2	9	1

Yugoslavia qualified

Group 8 (Northern Ireland, Italy, Portugal)
Portugal v Northern Ireland 1–1, Italy v Northern Ireland 1–0, Northern Ireland v Portugal 3–0, Portugal v Italy 3–0, Italy v Portugal 3–0, Northern Ireland v Italy 2–1

	P	W	D	L	F	A	Pts
Northern Ireland	4	2	1	1	6	3	5
Italy	4	2	0	2	5	5	4
Portugal	4	1	1	2	4	7	3

Northern Ireland qualified

Group 9 (Scotland, Spain, Switzerland)
Spain v Switzerland 2–2, Scotland v Spain 4–2, Switzerland v Scotland 1–2, Spain v Scotland 4–1, Scotland v Switzerland 3–2, Switzerland v Spain 1–4

	P	W	D	L	F	A	Pts
Scotland	4	3	0	1	10	9	6
Spain	4	2	1	1	12	8	5
Switzerland	4	0	1	3	6	11	1

Scotland qualified

South America

Group 1 (Brazil, Peru, Venezuela)
Venezuela withdrew
Peru v Brazil 1–1, 0–1
Brazil qualified

Group 2 (Argentina, Bolivia, Chile)
Chile v Bolivia 2–1, Bolivia v Chile 3–0, Bolivia v Argentina 2–0, Chile v Argentina 0–2, Argentina v Chile 4–0, Argentina v Bolivia 4–0

	P	W	D	L	F	A	Pts
Argentina	4	3	0	1	10	2	6
Bolivia	4	2	0	2	6	6	4
Chile	4	1	0	3	2	10	2

Argentina qualified

Group 3 (Paraguay, Uruguay, Colombia)
Colombia v Uruguay 1–1, Colombia v Paraguay 2–3, Uruguay v Colombia 1–0, Paraguay v Colombia 3–0, Paraguay v Uruguay 5–0, Uruguay v Paraguay 2–0

	P	W	D	L	F	A	Pts
Paraguay	4	3	0	1	11	4	6
Uruguay	4	2	1	1	4	6	5
Colombia	4	0	1	3	3	8	1

Paraguay qualified

North and Central America

Sub-Group 1 (Costa Rica, Curaçao, Guatemala)
Guatemala v Costa Rica 2–6, Costa Rica v Guatemala 3–1 (match abandoned, awarded to Costa Rica), Costa Rica v Curaçao 4–0, Guatemala v Curaçao 1–3, Curaçao v Costa Rica 1–2, Curaçao v Guatemala not played

	P	W	D	L	F	A	Pts
Costa Rica	4	4	0	0	15	4	8
Curaçao	3	1	0	2	4	7	2
Guatemala	3	0	0	3	4	12	0

Sub-Group 2 (Mexico, Canada, USA)
Mexico v USA 6–0, USA v Mexico 2–7, Canada v USA 5–1, Mexico v Canada 3–0, Canada v Mexico 0–2 (in Mexico City), USA v Canada 2–3

	P	W	D	L	F	A	Pts
Mexico	4	4	0	0	18	2	8
Canada	4	2	0	2	8	8	4
USA	4	0	0	4	5	21	0

Final round
Mexico v Costa Rica 2–0, 1–1
Mexico qualified

Asia/Africa

Sub-Group 1 (Indonesia, China, Taiwan)
Taiwan withdrew
Indonesia v China 2–0, 3–4
Play-off (in Rangoon): Indonesia v China 0–0
Indonesia won on scoring more goals in previous matches

Sub-Group 2 (Israel, Turkey)
Turkey withdrew

Sub-Group 3 (Egypt, Cyprus)
Cyprus withdrew

Sub-Group 4 (Sudan, Syria)
Sudan v Syria 1–0, 1–1

Second Round
Israel walked over (Indonesia withdrew); Sudan walked over (Egypt withdrew)

Final Round
Israel walked over (Sudan withdrew); Wales won draw among all second-placed teams to play Israel; Belgium and Uruguay declined
Israel v Wales 0–2, 0–2
Wales qualified

1958 SWEDEN 8 June–29 June

QUALIFIERS

Argentina	Mexico
Austria	Northern Ireland
Brazil	Paraguay
Czechoslovakia	Russia
England	Scotland
France	Sweden
Germany	Wales
Hungary	Yugoslavia

Sweden and the twelve nominated venues would host the sixth World Cup and the country, delighted in the return of its own stars from abroad, awaited its beginning with eager anticipation. Fifty-three entrants had been reduced to sixteen finalists, and on this occasion, unlike the 1954 Tournament, the Group rivals would all play each other. Quite remarkably all four home nations were represented, though Wales had been the recipients of huge good fortune. Apparently eliminated by Czechoslovakia, they were offered another opportunity against Israel; this they seized, and with such greats as Allchurch and the mighty John Charles in their midst, they were not overawed by their grouping with Sweden in the nation's capital at Stockholm and at Sandviken. The Swedes were formidable, and having been Olympic Champions in 1948 they constructed their team of veterans around Gustavsson and Hamrin, who were playing their club football in Italy. Hungary, too, were drawn here, though they were hardly recognizable now from the brilliant team of four years earlier: the country invaded by its Soviet neighbours had consequently lost the services of many of its greatest players, Puskás included. Mexico again had qualified, eliminating Costa Rica, but their overall record in the competition did not bode well for their chances of advancement from the Group.

Scotland had excelled themselves in ousting Spain and their reward was Group Two, their games to be played at a succession of small towns west of Stockholm, the largest of which was Norrköping. France were also there, assisted by Kopa, the Real Madrid star, and a number of players from their finest club Reims, one of Europe's very best. Paraguay, undeniably deserving qualifiers, had met and annihilated Uruguay in a truly shocking upset in Ascension by 5–0. Yugoslavia were the fourth team, whose qualification was only assured in their last game, a 2–0 winner-take-all affair with Romania.

In the south, Malmö, Halmstad and Hälsingborg welcomed Group One with Northern Ireland led by Danny Blanchflower, these conquerors of Italy facing tough opposition in the World Champions, Germany, the South American champions, Argentina, and the Czechs with a significantly altered team following their disappointment in Switzerland.

The final Group at Gothenburg would prove a difficult prospect for all those involved. Brazil, travelling with a young and largely experimental team, had narrowly edged Peru out but nevertheless had established a reputation that had seen them installed as favourites. England, though weakened by the tragic loss of their Manchester United trio, Edwards, Taylor and Byrne in the Munich Air disaster, were still capable and dangerous opponents. The last teams involved were Austria, third in the Swiss Tournament, and the Russians, whose first ever qualification by virtue of a 2–0 play-off in Leipzig over Poland had been achieved at the first attempt. Two years earlier, at the Melbourne Games the Soviet Union had been Olympic Champions.

Group 1

Venues: Malmö, Halmstad, Hälsingborg
Argentinat
Czechoslovakia
Germany
Northern Ireland

Group 2

Venues: Örebro, Norrköping, Västerås, Eskistuna
France
Paraguay
Scotland
Yugoslavia

Group 3

Venues: Stockholm, Sandviken
Hungary
Mexico
Sweden
Wales

Group 4

Venues: Gothenburg, Borås, Uddevalla
Austria
Brazil
England
USSR

THE FIRST SERIES

With each group beginning its first round fixtures on 8 June, local interest focused sharply in on the Swedes playing in Stockholm against Mexico. As they had hoped, Sweden won against accommodating opponents who barely threatened to score and ultimately were lucky to lose only by 3–0.

In Group Three at Sandviken, Wales were making their Tournament debut, performing with great credit against Hungary. Fighting back from Bozsik's early strike, Wales replied through the towering John Charles, whose header flew past Grosics, again keeping goal for the Magyars.

The Germans in Group One swept aside a sadly depleted Argentina, whose best players had stayed with their Italian clubs, though Corbatta, a tricky little winger, did give them a single goal of consolation in a 3–1 defeat. Northern Ireland, close by in Halmstad, continued to prove themselves worthy finalists, Cush providing their goal against a disappointing Czechoslovakia.

In Group Two a remarkable opening fixture between France and Paraguay took place. The South Americans, considered dark horses, were level against France at half-time. Thereafter, however, they fell apart under pressure from quite irresistible French attacking; Fontaine (with a hat-trick), Vincent and Piantoni all from the exciting Reims club were among the scorers as they won 7–3. Up the road at Västerås, Scotland, playing with great spirit, recovered from going a goal behind to the very dangerous Yugoslavians after seven minutes, finally gaining parity with Murray's second half shot.

England opened their competition in Gothenburg against Russia, Olympic Champions and a team of the highest quality. Inevitably England struggled before rescuing an unlikely draw after Simonian's early goal. Defeat appeared inevitable when Ivanov netted a second on the hour. Yet the English recovered their composure and Kevan, their centre forward, stretched to divert a free kick beyond Yashin before Tom Finney, the mercurial Preston North End winger, connected a late, though deserved, penalty kick to go 2–2. But Russia had certainly been the better side. Brazil, nominal favourites, with eight changes from Switzerland faced a similarly changed Austria at Borås and beat them with consummate ease, 3–0, Mazzola, their centre forward, claiming two of the goals; Austria were unable to reply.

THE SECOND SERIES

Wales, now in Stockholm, faced Mexico in their second Group Two encounter. Taking a first half lead through Allchurch, they failed to capitalize on it, and their meek opponents salvaged an undeserved draw with Belmonte's drive.

With great difficulty Sweden overcame Hungary the next day on the same ground. Hamrin, their spectacular but unpredictable winger, scored twice, once gloriously. Tichy in between insisted he had equalized when his shot struck the bar and came down behind Svenssen in goal for the Swedes. Mr Mowat, the referee, thought otherwise, and despite Tichy having his moment late on to make it 2–1, it was a case of too little too late.

In Group One the Czechs, so uninspired against the Irish, made changes in their forward line for their Hälsingborg appointment with Germany, consequently surprising the champions. A goal behind to a Dvorak penalty, the Germans' situation became dire when Zikan beat Herkenrath for 2–0. They rallied bravely and were saved by the tigerish and robust little Rahn with two late goals. Northern Ireland, given to causing shocks, were stunned themselves by an Argentinean team determined, resolute and supplemented astonishingly by Labruna, a forward making his competition debut at the age of forty! Though Peter McFarland managed to equalize Corbatta's first goal, when Corbatta scored again, followed by Menendez, the game became out of the reach of the dejected Irishmen in the second half.

Paraguay, back at the scene of their aberration against free scoring France, played the Scots and confirmed themselves strong in attack but vulnerable in defence. Still, for Scotland they proved just too much, winning an open and entertaining game by 3–2. The other Group Two match ended with precisely the same score, Yugoslavia prevailing with a goal three minutes from time, the Yugoslavs organized and dangerous on the counter-attack absorbing the best efforts of the French and exposing with a surgeon's precision their frailties.

Brazil, devastating at half steam against the unfortunate Austrians, ran into a rather better prepared, more obstinate England team in Gothenburg and struggled. The English, growing in confidence, were denied a penalty after Kevan eluded Bellini, and the game ended goal-less. The other Group Four fixture at Borås saw Russia ease past Austria in a dull and strangely passionless affair, a goal either side of the interval deciding the outcome, 2–0.

THE THIRD SERIES

Sweden, in their final group match with two victories under their belt, made changes in Stockholm. Hamrin, Gren and the veteran Neils Leidholm were among those rested. Wales were the beneficiaries of such generosity, grinding out a deserved draw in a largely uneventful match free of goals. Hungary in the same group blasted out the dismal Mexicans with four goals, shattering their increasingly fragile opponents.

Down in Malmö, Germany received a second successive surprise against the gallant Irish. McFarland put the underdogs ahead, Rahn scored to level at half-time, and though McFarland arrived to shoot Ireland ahead at 2–1, the squat young German centre forward Seeler grabbed a point for the Germans ten minutes from time. Gregg and Blanchflower had been hugely influential in Ireland's performance, and Germany were seen to be lucky with their 2–2 draw.

Remarkably, the hitherto unimpressive Czechs astonished Argentina at Hälsingborg and in so doing extended their Tournament and eliminated their opponents. With a score of 3–0 at half-time, it ended 6–1 as the disconsolate South Americans fell apart in embarrassing fashion.

In a tight Group Two, Scotland went out, their brave effort against France being undermined by two first-half strikes by the formidable partnership established by Kopa and Fontaine. Scotland, needing to win, fought back, but a solitary goal from Baird in his first appearance proved no more than a consolation for their endeavour. Paraguay also went home despite another goal glut, a 3–3 draw with Yugoslavia proving not quite enough for the royally entertaining South Americans. They had endeared themselves to spectators, and regardless of their elimination, they had distinguished themselves as worthy finalists

Finally to the west coast and Gothenburg where Brazil burst the Soviet bubble. Fielding the seventeen-year-old Pelé in place of Mazzola and with the mesmerizing Garrincha at work, they pulled Russia's defence apart. Vava scored both early and late in the match, but the 2–0 score didn't adequately represent Brazil's total domination of proceedings. England, in the other Group Four game against twice beaten Austria, stoically stuck to their line-up that had proved so effective in securing a draw with Brazil. They promptly fell behind when Austria, through Koller, scored their first goal of the competition. England responded first through Fulham's Johnny Haynes and then Kevan, but a second Austrian goal through Körner ensured a 2–2 draw, and for England the prospect of a play-off match.

But four days before the quarter-final ties, FIFA had a problem: without any provision for separating teams tied on points, they had three inconclusive Groups. Thus Czechoslovakia and Ireland in Malmö, Hungary and Wales in Stockholm, and Russia and England in Gothenburg would meet for a second time, just two days before the quarter-final, to decide who would be going through.

Final Tournament – Sweden First round

Group 1

West Germany (2) **3, Argentina** (1) **1**
8.6.58 MALMÖ
West Germany: Herkenrath, Stollenwerk, Juskowiak, Eckel, Erhardt, Szymaniak, Rahn (2), Walter F, Seeler (1), Schmidt, Schäfer
Argentina: Carrizo, Dellacha, Vairo, Lombardo, Rossi, Varacka, Corbatta (1), Prado, Menendez, Rojas, Cruz
Referee: Leafe (England)

Northern Ireland (1) **1, Czechoslovakia** (0) **0**
8.6.58 HALMSTAD
Northern Ireland: Gregg, Keith, McMichael, Blanchflower, Cunningham, Peacock, Bingham, Cush (1), Dougan, McIlroy, McParland
Czechoslovakia: Dolejsi, Mraz, Novak, Pluskal, Cadek, Masopust, Hovorka, Dvorak, Borovicka, Hertl, Krauss
Referee: Seipelt (Austria)

West Germany (0) **2, Czechoslovakia** (2) **2**
11.6.58 HÄLSINGBORG
West Germany: Herkenrath, Stollenwerk, Juskowiak, Schnellinger, Erhardt, Szymaniak, Rahn (1), Walter F, Seeler, Schäfer (1), Klodt
Czechoslovakia: Dolejsi, Mraz, Novak, Pluskal, Popluhar, Masopust, Hovorka, Dvorak (1 pen), Molnar, Farajsl, Zikan (1)
Referee: Ellis (England)

Argentina (1) **3, Northern Ireland** (1) **1**
11.6.58 HALMSTAD
Argentina: Carrizo, Dellacha, Vairo, Lombardo, Rossi, Varacka, Corbatta (1 pen), Avio (1), Menendez (1), Labruna, Boggio
Northern Ireland: Gregg, Keith, McMichael, Blanchflower, Cunningham, Peacock, Bingham, Cush, Coyle, McIlroy, McParland (1)
Referee: Ahiner (Sweden)

West Germany (1) **2, Northern Ireland** (1) **2**
15.6.58 MALMÖ
West Germany: Herkenrath, Stollenwerk, Juskowiak, Eckel, Erhardt, Szymaniak, Rahn (1), Walter F, Seeler (1), Schäfer, Klodt
Northern Ireland: Gregg, Keith, McMichael, Blanchflower, Cunningham, Peacock, Bingham, Cush, Casey, McIlroy, McParland (2)
Referee: Campos (Portugal)

Czechoslovakia (3) **6, Argentina** (0) **1**
15.6.58 HÄLSINGBORG
Czechoslovakia: Dolejsi, Mraz, Novak, Dvorak (1), Popluhar, Masopust, Hovorka (1), Borovicka, Molnar, Farajsl (2), Zikan (2)
Argentina: Carrizo, Dellacha, Vairo, Lombardo, Rossi, Varacka, Corbatta (1), Avio, Menendez, Labruna, Cruz
Referee: Ellis (England)

	P	W	D	L	F	A	Pts
West Germany	3	1	2	0	7	5	4
Northern Ireland	3	1	1	1	4	5	3
Czechoslovakia	3	1	1	1	8	4	3
Argentina	3	1	0	2	5	10	2

Group 2

Yugoslavia (1) **1, Scotland** (0) **1**
8.6.58 VÄSTERÅS
Yugoslavia: Beara, Sijakovic, Cmkovic, Krstic, Zebec, Boskov, Petakovic (1), Veselinovic, Milutinovic, Sekularac, Rajkov
Scotland: Younger, Caldow, Hewie, Turnbull, Evans, Cowie, Leggat, Murray (1), Mudie, Collins, Imlach
Referee: Wysling (Switzerland)

France (2) **7, Paraguay** (2) **3**
8.6.58 NORRKÖPING
France: Remetter, Kaelbel, Lerond, Penverne, Jonquet, Marcel, Wisnieski (1), Fontaine (3), Kopa (1), Piantoni (1), Vincent (1)
Paraguay: Mageregger, Miranda, Arevalo, Villalba, Lezcano, Achucarro, Aguero, Parodi, Romero (1), Re, Amarilla (2, 1 pen)
Referee: Gardeazabal (Spain)

Paraguay (2) **3, Scotland** (1) **2**
11.6.58 NORRKÖPING
Paraguay: Mageregger, Miranda, Arevalo, Villalba, Lezcano, Achucarro, Aguero, Parodi, Romero (1), Re, Amarilla (2, 1 pen)
Scotland: Younger, Parker, Caldow, Turnbull, Evans, Cowie, Leggat, Collins (1), Mudie (1), Robertson, Fernie
Referee: Orlandini (Italy)

Yugoslavia (1) **3, France** (1) **2**
11.6.58 VÄSTERÅS
Yugoslavia: Beara, Tomic, Cmkovic, Krstic, Zebec, Boskov, Petakovic (1), Veselinovic (2), Milutinovic, Sekularac, Rajkov
France: Remetter, Kaelbel, Marche, Penverne, Jonquet, Lerond, Wisnieski, Fontaine (2), Kopa, Piantoni, Vincent
Referee: Griffiths (Wales)

France (2) **2, Scotland** (0) **1**
15.6.58 ÖREBRO
France: Abbes, Kaelbel, Lerond, Penverne, Jonquet, Marcel, Wisnieski, Fontaine (1), Kopa (1), Piantoni, Vincent
Scotland: Brown, Caldow, Hewie, Turnbull, Evans, Mackay, Collins, Murray, Mudie, Baird (1), Imlach
Referee: Brozzi (Argentina)

Paraguay (1) **3, Yugoslavia** (2) **3**
15.6.58 ESKISTUNA
Paraguay: Aguilar, Arevalo, Echague, Villalba, Lezcano, Achucarro, Aguero (1), Parodi (1), Romero (1), Re, Amarilla
Yugoslavia: Beara, Tomic, Cmkovic, Krstic, Zebec, Boskov, Petakovic, Veselinovic (1), Ogjanovic (2), Sekularac, Rajkov
Referee: Macko (Czechoslovakia)

	P	W	D	L	F	A	Pts
France	3	2	0	1	11	7	4
Yugoslavia	3	1	2	0	7	6	4
Paraguay	3	1	1	1	9	12	3
Scotland	3	0	1	2	4	6	1

Group 3

Sweden (1) **3, Mexico** (0) **0**
8.6.58 STOCKHOLM
Sweden: Svensson, Bergmark, Axbom, Liedholm (1 pen), Gustavsson, Parling, Hamrin, Mellberg, Simonsson (2), Gren, Skoglund
Mexico: Carbajal, Del Muro, Villegas, Portugal, Romo, Flores, Hernandez, Reyes, Calderon, Gutierrez, Sesma
Referee: Latyschev (USSR)

Hungary (1) **1, Wales** (1) **1**
8.6.58 SANDVIKEN
Hungary: Grosics, Matrai, Sarosi, Bozsik (1), Sipos, Berendi, Sandor, Hidegkuti, Tichy, Bundzsak, Fenyvesi
Wales: Kelsey, Williams, Hopkins, Sullivan, Charles M, Bowen, Webster, Medwin, Charles J (1), Allchurch, Jones.
Referee: Codesal (Uruguay)

Mexico (1) **1, Wales** (1) **1**
11.6.58 STOCKHOLM
Mexico: Carbajal, Del Muro, Gutierrez, Cardenas, Romo, Flores, Belmonte (1), Reyes, Blanco, Gonzalez, Sesma
Wales: Kelsey, Williams, Hopkins, Baker, Charles M, Bowen, Webster, Medwin, Charles J, Allchurch (1), Jones
Referee: Lemesic (Yugoslavia)

Sweden (2) **2, Hungary** (0) **1**
12.6.58 STOCKHOLM
Sweden: Svensson, Bergmark, Axbom, Liedholm, Gustavsson, Parling, Hamrin (2), Mellberg, Simonsson, Gren, Skoglund
Hungary: Grosics, Matrai, Sarosi, Szojka, Sipos, Berendi, Sandor, Bundzsak, Bozsik, Tichy (1), Fenyvesi
Referee: Mowat (Scotland)

Sweden (0) **0, Wales** (0) **0**
15.6.58 STOCKHOLM
Sweden: Svensson, Bergmark, Axbom, Borjesson, Gustavsson, Parling, Berndtsson, Selmosson, Kallgren, Lofgren, Skoglund
Wales: Kelsey, Williams, Hopkins, Sullivan, Charles M, Bowen, Vernon, Hewitt, Charles J, Allchurch, Jones
Referee: Van Nuffel (Belgium)

Hungary (1) **4, Mexico** (0) **0**
15.6.58 SANDVIKEN
Hungary: Ilku, Matrai, Sarosi, Szojka, Sipos, Kotasz, Budai, Bencsics, Hidegkuti, Tichy (2), Sandor (1)
Mexico: Carbajal, Del Muro, Gutierrez, Cardenas, Sepulveda, Flores, Belmonte, Reyes, Blanco, Gonzalez (o.g.), Sesma
Referee: Eriksson (Finland)

	P	W	D	L	F	A	Pts
Sweden	3	2	1	0	5	1	5
Wales	3	0	3	0	2	2	3
Hungary	3	1	1	1	6	3	3
Mexico	3	0	1	2	1	8	1

Group 4

USSR (1) **2, England** (0) **2**
8.6.58 GOTHENBURG
USSR: Yashin, Kessarov, Kusnezov, Voinov, Krischevsky, Zarev, Ivanov A, Ivanov V (1), Simonian (1), Salnikov, Iljin
England: McDonald, Howe, Banks, Clamp, Wright, Slater, Douglas, Robson, Kevan (1), Haynes. Finney (1 pen)
Referee: Zsolt (Hungary)

Brazil (1) **3, Austria** (0) **0**
8.6.58 UDDEVALLA
Brazil: Gylmar, De Sordi, Santos N (1), Dino, Bellini, Orlando, Joel, Didi, Mazzola (2), Dida, Zagalo
Austria: Szanwald, Halla, Svoboda, Hanappi, Happel, Koller, Horak, Senekowitsch, Buzek, Körner A, Schleger
Referee: Guigue (France)

Brazil (0) **0, England** (0) **0**
11.6.58 GOTHENBURG
Brazil: Gylmar, De Sordi, Santos N, Dino, Bellini, Orlando, Joel, Didi, Mazzola, Vava, Zagalo
England: McDonald, Howe, Banks, Clamp, Wright, Slater, Douglas, Robson, Kevan, Haynes, A'Court
Referee: Dusch (West Germany)

USSR (1) **2, Austria** (0) **0**
11.6.58 BORÅS
USSR: Yashin, Kessarov, Kusnezov, Voinov, Krischevsky, Zarev, Ivanov A, Ivanov V (1), Simonian, Salnikov, Iljin (1)
Austria: Schmied, Kozliczek E, Svoboda, Hanappi, Stotz, Koller, Horak, Kozliczek P, Buzek, Körner A, Senekowitsch
Referee: Jorgensen (Denmark)

Brazil (1) **2, USSR** (0) **0**
15.6.58 GOTHENBURG
Brazil: Gylmar, De Sordi, Santos N, Zito, Bellini, Orlando, Garrincha, Didi, Vava (2), Pelé, Zagalo
USSR: Yashin, Kessarov, Kusnezov, Voinov, Krischevsky, Zarev, Ivanov A, Ivanov V, Simonian, Netto, Iljin
Referee: Guigue (France)

England (0) **2, Austria** (1) **2**
15.6.58 BORÅS
England: McDonald, Howe, Banks, Clamp, Wright, Slater, Douglas, Robson, Kevan (1), Haynes (1), A'Court
Austria: Szanwald, Kollmann, Svoboda, Hanappi, Happel, Koller (1), Kozliczek E, Kozliczek P, Buzek, Körner A (1), Senekowitsch
Referee: Asmussen (Denmark)

	P	W	D	L	F	A	Pts
Brazil	3	2	1	0	5	0	5
USSR	3	1	1	1	4	4	3
England	3	0	3	0	4	4	3
Austria	3	0	1	2	2	7	1

THE PLAY-OFFS

England, who had struggled to contain Russia during their drawn encounter, this time had much the better of it. Unfortunately, they lost to Iljin's second half shot, Brabrook (replacing Brian Douglas) twice thumping Yashin's goal frame.

Behind to Tichy's goal for Hungary, Wales pulled themselves level with a drive from distance by Allchurch and then led when Medwin took full advantage of a misunderstanding between Grosics and his defender to rifle home a second. Hungary lost their heads, Sipos aimed a kick at Hewitt and was dismissed, and for the ten men there was no way back.

Northern Ireland, without regular goalkeeper Harry Greg, managed once again to overcome the Czechs with an inspired performance owing as much to courage as to skill. Zikan scored first but McParland saved the Irish with an equalizer and ensured extra time. Ten minutes of that had gone when the Aston Villa striker McParland flashed the winner beyond Dolejsi, his fifth goal in three matches.

Group Play-Off for Second Place

Northern Ireland (1) **2, Czechoslovakia** (1) **1** (aet, 1–1 at 90 mins)
17.6.58 MALMÖ
Northern Ireland: Uprichard, Keith, McMichael, Blanchflower, Cunningham, Peacock, Bingham, Cush, Scott, McIlroy, McParland (2)
Czechoslovakia: Dolejsi, Mraz, Novak, Bubernik, Popluhar, Masopust, Dvorak, Molnar, Farajsl, Borovicka, Zikan (1)
Referee: Guigue (France)

USSR (0) **1, England** (0) **0**
17.6.58 GOTHENBURG
USSR: Yashin, Kessarov, Kusnezov, Voinov, Krischevsky, Zarev, Apuchtin, Ivanov V, Simonian, Falin, Iljin (1)
England: McDonald, Howe, Banks, Clayton, Wright, Slater, Brabrook, Broadbent, Kevan, Haynes, A'Court
Referee: Dusch (West Germany)

Wales (0) **2, Hungary** (1) **1**
17.6.58 STOCKHOLM
Wales: Kelsey, Williams, Hopkins, Sullivan, Charles M, Bowen, Medwin (1), Hewitt, Charles J, Allchurch (1), Jones
Hungary: Grosics, Matrai, Sarosi, Bozsik, Sipos, Kostasz, Budai, Bencsics, Tichy (1), Bundzsak, Fenyvesi
Referee: Latyschev (USSR)

THE QUARTER-FINALS

So to the quarter-finals and Stockholm, where Sweden inevitably beat Russia, tired after their play-off exploits two days earlier. Defending stoutly, they resisted for an hour until the dazzling Kurre Hamrin demoralized them with a close range header, Simonsson adding a late second amidst the mounting excitement.

Ireland were also plainly exhausted, playing their third match in five days. They found the fast attacking flair of a relatively fresh French team altogether too much. Down 1–0 at half-time, the game deteriorated for Ireland to end at 4–0: a sad though predictable end for a brave team.

Wales, facing the now rampant Brazilians without the imposing presence of the injured John Charles, fought a magnificent rearguard action. Shrugging off fatigue, they clung on up to half-time until Pelé's shot was deflected past Kelsey. Although there was no way back, their efforts in defeat earned Wales the admiration of the football world.

Germany in Malmö completed the semi-finalists, though somewhat luckily. Yugoslavia, much the better side despite the absence of Sekularac and the introduction of a new goalkeeper, Krivokuca, lacked the incisiveness to take full advantage, and Rahn exploited their generosity fully with a solitary goal.

Quarter-Finals

West Germany (1) **1, Yugoslavia** (0) **0**
19.6.58 MALMÖ
West Germany: Herkenrath, Stollenwerk, Juskowiak, Eckel, Erhardt, Szymaniak, Rahn (1), Walter F, Seeler, Schmidt, Schäfer
Yugoslavia: Krivokuca, Sijakovic, Cmkovic, Boskov, Zebec, Krstic, Petakovic, Ogjanovic, Milutinovic, Veselinovic, Rajkov
Referee: Wyssling (Switzerland)

France (1) **4, Northern Ireland** (0) **0**
19.6.58 NORRKÖPING
France: Abbes, Kaelbel, Lerond, Penverne, Jonquet, Marcel, Wisnieski (1), Fontaine (2), Kopa, Piantoni (1), Vincent
Northern Ireland: Gregg, Keith, McMichael, Blanchflower, Cunningham, Cush, Bingham, Casey, Scott, McIlroy, McParland
Referee: Gardeazabal (Spain)

Sweden (0) **2**, **USSR** (0) **0**
19.6.58 STOCKHOLM
Sweden: Svensson, Bergmark, Axbom, Borjesson, Gustavsson, Parling, Hamrin (1), Gren, Simonsson (1), Liedholm, Skoglund
USSR: Yashin, Kessarov, Kuznezov, Voinov, Krischevsky, Zarev, Ivanov A, Ivanov V, Simonian, Salnikov, Iljin
Referee: Leafe (England)

Brazil (0) **1**, **Wales** (0) **0**
19.6.58 GOTHENBURG
Brazil: Gylmar, De Sordi, Santos N, Zito, Bellini, Orlando, Garrincha, Didi, Mazzola, Pelé (1), Zagalo
Wales: Kelsey, Williams, Hopkins, Sullivan, Charles M, Bowen, Medwin, Hewitt, Webster, Allchurch, Jones
Referee: Seipelt (Austria)

THE SEMI-FINALS

In the Stockholm semi-final, two teams entirely committed to attack faced each other. Brazil led early through Vava, and despite the prolific Fontaine replying for France, the injury sustained by Jonquet reduced them effectively to ten fit men. Didi drove in Brazil's second before the interval and then teenage sensation Pelé demolished them with three second-half goals. France's second goal, through Piantoni, brought the score the respectability their endeavours merited.

In Gothenburg for the first time Sweden, supported by their own frenzied countrymen, promptly fell behind to a volley from Schäfer, but fought back gamely, laying siege to the German goal. Leidholm, playing now as a forward, handed Skoglund an opportunity too good to miss, and the Germans, pressured now by a more mobile and inventive team on the field and a hostile crowd off it, pushed the self-destruct button. Juskowiak kicked out at his fast little tormentor, Hamrin, and was sent off. The Swedes ran the Germans ragged, Gunnar Gren putting them ahead on 80 minutes before Hamrin himself, with a wonderful run and finish, concluded matters and heralded jubilant celebrations.

Semi-Finals

Sweden (1) **3, West Germany** (1) **1**
24.6.58 GOTHENBURG
Sweden: Svensson, Bergmark, Axbom, Borjesson, Gustavsson, Parling, Hamrin (1), Gren (1), Simonsson, Liedholm, Skoglund (1)
West Germany: Herkenrath, Stollenwerk, Juskowiak, Eckel, Erhardt, Szymaniak, Rahn, Walter F, Seeler, Schäfer (1), Cleslarczyk
Referee: Zsolt (Hungary)

Brazil (2) **5, France** (1) **2**
24.6.58 STOCKHOLM
Brazil: Gylmar, De Sordi, Santos N, Zito, Bellini, Orlando, Garrincha, Didi (1), Vava (1), Pelé (3), Zagalo
France: Abbes, Kaelbel, Lerond, Penverne, Jonquet, Marcel, Wisnieski, Fontaine (1), Kopa, Piantoni (1), Vincent
Referee: Griffiths (Wales)

PLAY-OFF FOR THIRD PLACE

In the third and fourth place final, France beat Germany 6–3 in an astonishing match that stood at 0–0 until half-time. The second half was an absolute joy as the two teams attacked remorselessly, Fontaine scoring four, thus increasing his tally for the Tournament to thirteen.

Match for Third Place
France (3) **6, West Germany** (1) **3**
28.6.58 GOTHENBURG
France: Abbes, Kaelbel, Lerond, Penverne, Lafond, Marcel, Wisnieski, Douis (1), Kopa (1 pen), Fontaine (4), Vincent
West Germany: Kwiatkowski, Stollenwerk, Erhardt, Schnellinger, Wewers, Szymaniak, Rahn (1), Sturm, Kelbassa, Schäfer (1), Cleslarczyk (1)
Referee: Brozzi (Argentina)

THE FINAL

In Stockholm's strangely subdued and rain-sodden stadium, Sweden was given an early lead when Leidholm scored brilliantly after a meandering run. Another goal may have been decisive, but Brazil recovered their composure and struck back through Vava. Both sides now sought a second goal; it was

Vava finally who gave it to Brazil, converting with aplomb following a breathtaking run from Garrincha, to go 2–1. The second half saw Brazil dominate, the midfield mastered and significantly Hamrin was denied the time or space to threaten. Pelé juggled and volleyed for another goal, Zagalo made it four, and though Simonsson briefly gave Sweden hope, the phenomenal youngster Pelé managed to lift his header over Svenssen to bring the final score to 5–2. Brazil, after years of frustration, had finally become Champions with a team of extravagant skill.

Final

Brazil (2) **5, Sweden** (1) **2**
29.6.58 STOCKHOLM
Brazil: Gylmar, Santos D, Santos N, Zito, Bellini, Orlando, Garrincha, Didi, Vava (2), Pelé (2), Zagalo (1)
Sweden: Svensson, Bergmark, Axbom, Borjesson, Gustavsson, Parling, Hamrin, Gren, Simonsson (1), Liedholm (1), Skoglund
Referee: Guigue (France)

Brazil were worthy Champions, playing exhilarating football with their multitude of talented team members, Garrincha, Vava, Didi, Zito and the waif-like boy genius Pelé. Their triumph was thoroughly deserved. Sweden for their part had had a fine run in a well-organized Tournament, their winger Hamrin unquestionably one of the major players of the Championship. Germany, the defending World Champions, showed experience in advancing to the semi-finals, though their team were too cautious and consumed by a tidal wave of emotion.

Britain's wonderful achievement through both Wales and Ireland reaching the quarter-finals was somewhat diminished by FIFA absurdly arranging play-offs two days beforehand, which did their chance of further advancement no favours at all.

Finally there was France, who in scoring twenty-three goals, six more than even the Brazilians had managed, epitomized the spirit of a thrilling, captivating competition.

CHAPTER 7

CHILE

1962

Qualifying Tournament
56 Entrants
Brazil qualify as holders, Chile qualify as hosts

Eastern Hemisphere (Africa, Asia, Europe) (39): **Africa** – Egypt, Ethiopia, Ghana, Morocco, Nigeria, Sudan, Tunisia; **Asia** – Indonesia, Japan, South Korea; **Europe** – Belgium, Bulgaria, Cyprus, Czechoslovakia, England, Finland, France, East Germany, West Germany, Greece, Holland, Hungary, Republic of Ireland, Northern Ireland, Israel, Italy, Luxembourg, Norway, Poland, Portugal, Romania, Scotland, Spain, Sweden, Switzerland, Turkey, USSR, Wales, Yugoslavia

Western Hemisphere (North, Central and South America) (17): **North America** – Canada, Mexico, USA; **Central** – Costa Rica, Guatemala, Honduras, Netherlands Antilles, Surinam; **South America** – Argentina, Bolivia, Brazil, Chile, Colombia, Ecuador, Paraguay, Peru, Uruguay

Europe/Africa/Asia

Group 1 (Switzerland, Sweden, Belgium)
Sweden v Belgium 2–0, Belgium v Switzerland 2–4, Switzerland v Belgium 2–1, Sweden v Switzerland 4–0, Belgium v Sweden 0–2, Switzerland v Sweden 3–2

	P	W	D	L	F	A	Pts
Sweden	4	3	0	1	10	3	6
Switzerland	4	3	0	1	9	9	6
Belgium	4	0	0	4	3	10	0

Play-off (in Berlin): Switzerland v Sweden 2–1
Switzerland qualified

Group 2 (Bulgaria, France, Finland)
Finland v France 1–2, France v Bulgaria 3–0, Finland v Bulgaria 0–2, France v Finland 5–1, Bulgaria v Finland 3–1, Bulgaria v France 1–0

	P	W	D	L	F	A	Pts
Bulgaria	4	3	0	1	6	4	6
France	4	3	0	1	10	3	6
Finland	4	3	0	4	3	12	0

Play-off (in Milan): Bulgaria v France 1–0
Bulgaria qualified

Group 3 (West Germany, Northern Ireland, Greece)

Northern Ireland v West Germany 3–4, Greece v West Germany 0–3, Greece v Northern Ireland 2–1, West Germany v Northern Ireland 2–1, Northern Ireland v Greece 2–0, West Germany V Greece 2–1

	P	W	D	L	F	A	Pts
West Germany	4	4	0	0	11	5	8
Northern Ireland	4	1	0	3	7	8	2
Greece	4	1	0	3	3	8	2

West Germany qualified

Group 4 (Hungary, Holland, East Germany)

Hungary v East Germany 2–0, Holland v Hungary 0–3, East Germany v Holland 1–1, East Germany v Hungary 2–3, Hungary v Holland 3–3, Holland v East Germany not played

	P	W	D	L	F	A	Pts
Hungary	4	3	1	0	11	5	7
Holland	3	0	2	1	4	7	2
East Germany	3	0	1	2	3	6	1

Hungary qualified

Group 5 (USSR, Turkey, Norway)

Norway v Turkey 0–1, USSR v Turkey 1–0, USSR v Norway 5–2, Norway v USSR 0–3, Turkey v Norway 2–1, Turkey v USSR 1–2

	P	W	D	L	F	A	Pts
USSR	4	4	0	0	11	3	8
Turkey	4	2	0	2	4	4	4
Norway	4	0	0	4	3	11	0

USSR qualified

Group 6 (England, Portugal, Luxembourg)

Luxembourg v England 0–9, Portugal v Luxembourg 6–0, Portugal v England 1–1, England v Luxembourg 4–1, Luxembourg v Portugal 4–2, England v Portugal 2–0

	P	W	D	L	F	A	Pts
England	4	3	1	0	16	2	7
Portugal	4	1	1	2	9	7	3
Luxembourg	4	1	0	3	5	21	2

England qualified

Group 7
Sub-Group A (Cyprus, Israel, Ethiopia)

First Round
Cyprus v Israel 1–1, 1–6

Second Round
Israel v Ethiopia (in Tel Aviv) 1–0, 3–2

Sub-Group B (Italy, Romania)
Romania withdrew
Israel v Italy 2–4, 0–6
Italy qualified

Group 8 (Czechoslovakia, Scotland, Rep of Ireland)
Scotland v Rep of Ireland 4–1, Rep of Ireland v Scotland 0–3, Czechoslovakia v Scotland 4–0, Scotland v Czechoslovakia 3–2, Rep of Ireland v Czechoslovakia 1–3, Czechoslovakia v Rep of Ireland 7–1

	P	W	D	L	F	A	Pts
Czechoslovakia	4	3	0	1	16	5	6
Scotland	4	3	0	1	10	7	6
Rep of Ireland	4	0	0	4	3	17	0

Play-off (in Brussels): Czechoslovakia v Scotland 4–2
Czechoslovakia qualified

Group 9 (Spain, Wales)
Wales v Spain 1–2, 1–1

Sub-Group 1 (Sudan, Egypt)
Both withdrew

Sub-Group 2 (Morocco, Tunisia)
Morocco v Tunisia 2–1, 1–2
Play-off (in Palermo): Morocco v Tunisia 1–1
(Morocco won on toss-up)

Sub-Group 3 (Ghana, Nigeria)
Ghana v Nigeria 4–1, 2–2

Sub-Group Final
Ghana v Morocco 0–0, 0–1

Group Final
Morocco v Spain 0–1, 2–3
Spain qualified

Group 10 (Yugoslavia, Poland)
Yugoslavia v Poland 2–1, 1–1

Sub-Group 1 (South Korea, Indonesia, Japan)
Indonesia withdrew
South Korea v Japan 2–1, 2–0

Group Final
Yugoslavia v South Korea 5–1, 3–1
Yugoslavia qualified

South America

Group 11 (Argentina, Ecuador)
Ecuador v Argentina 3–6, 0–5
Argentina qualified

Group 12 (Uruguay, Bolivia)
Bolivia v Uruguay 1–1, 1–2
Uruguay qualified

Group 13 (Colombia, Peru)
Colombia v Peru 1–0, 1–1
Colombia qualified

Group 14 (Uruguay)
Play off with North and Central American group winners

North and Central America

Sub-Group 1 (USA, Canada, Mexico)
Canada withdrew
USA v Mexico 3–3, 0–3

Sub-Group 2 (Costa Rica, Guatemala, Honduras)
Costa Rica v Guatemala 3–2, Guatemala v Costa Rica 4–4, Honduras v Costa Rica 2–1, Costa Rica v Honduras 5–1, Honduras v Guatemala 1–1, Guatemala v Honduras 0–2 (abandoned)

	P	W	D	L	F	A	Pts
Costa Rica	4	2	1	1	13	8	5
Honduras	3	1	1	1	3	7	3
Guatemala	3	0	2	1	7	8	2

Play-off (in Guatemala): Honduras v Costa Rica 0–1

Sub-Group 3 (Surinam, Netherlands Antilles)
Surinam v Netherlands Antilles 1–2, 0–0

Group Final
Costa Rica v Mexico 1–0, Costa Rica v Netherlands Antilles 6–0, Mexico v Netherlands 7–0, Mexico v Costa Rica 4 – 1, Netherlands Antilles v Costa Rica 2–0, Netherlands Antilles v Mexico 0–0

	P	W	D	L	F	A	Pts
Mexico	4	2	1	1	11	2	5
Costa Rica	4	2	0	2	8	6	4
Netherlands Antilles	4	1	1	2	2	13	3

Mexico v Paraguay 1–0, 0–0
Mexico qualified

1962 CHILE 30 May–17 June

QUALIFIERS

Argentina	Hungary
Brazil	Italy
Bulgaria	Mexico
Chile	Russia
Colombia	Spain
Czechoslovakia	Switzerland
England	Uruguay
Germany	Yugoslavia

Chile hosted the seventh competition. A country in turmoil, shattered by earthquake, their FIFA representative Charles Dittborn appealed successfully for the sympathy of the game's governing body. 'We have nothing, that is why we must have the World Cup.' Remarkably, by the time the sixteen teams arrived, all of the Chileans' preparations were complete, including two brand new stadia.

Brazil, drawn to play at the coastal town of Viña Del Mar, again were favoured, with nine of their spectacular team of four years earlier still available, but several were at the veteran stage and questions about their collective stamina remained to be answered. Their challengers in Group Three included Spain, a fine team able to call on the talents of their great club side Real Madrid. Goalkeeper Araquistain, Pachin, Gento and Del Sol were joined by their legendary club colleagues Puskas and Di Stefano, neither, of course, of Spanish origin, and Suarez the striker, now playing his football in Turin with Juventus.

The Mexicans in the same group had performed dismally in 1958 and looked to erase the rather painful memories; Reyes and the veteran Cardenas were among their more reliable performers, while the astonishing Carbajal kept goal. The final member of this quartet, Czechoslovakia, had beaten Scotland 4–2 in a play-off. With Popluhar and Masopust in their second Tournament and a new star in midfield in the form of Kvasnak, they were optimistic, though Rudolf Kuecra, their key striker, would be absent through injury.

A thousand miles to the north in the tropical climate of Arica on the Bolivian border, Group One included the Russian team, Champions of Europe and fancied by many experts. Their early opponents would be Colombia, relative minnows embarking on their first World Cup adventure. Yugoslavia, Olympic Champions, replete with their contingent of players from the very fine Partisan of Belgrade Team and the influential Sekularac, their play maker, they would be a dangerous proposition. Uruguay, back after their surprise elimination from the 1958 Tournament, were certainly capable, but not a team of the calibre of ten years earlier.

Much the same could have been said of Hungary, who would play at Rancagua, denied as they were of the services of Puskas, Kocsis and Czibor, all living in exile away from the communist regime. Still, in Florian Albert they possessed a young centre forward of exceptional ability. The Hungarians had prospered in qualification at the expense of Holland. Joining them in Group Four were Bulgaria, surprise conquerors of France in Milan in a qualification play-off and inclined to be horribly negative; Argentina, whose team was enduring a period of transition; and England, with Moore, Charlton and Fulham's Johnny Haynes in their line up, not to mention the predatory Tottenham forward Greaves providing constant menace.

The hosts, Chile, managed astutely by Riera, were based in the national capital Santiago for their Group Two matches. Theirs appeared an unenviable task: Germany, Italy and Switzerland would provide the opposition. Though Chile had in Rojas, Toro and Leonel Sanchez high quality players, they were not expected to progress. Switzerland, once formidable and successful against 1958 finalists Sweden in qualification, were thought to be in decline, though

Antenen, their veteran winger, was undoubtedly world class. The Germans and Italians, former winners and traditionally strong, would be fielding relatively inexperienced teams, but Germany could count on the leadership of Uwe Seeler and the rock-like defensive skills of Karl Heinz Schnellinger, and Italy on the blossoming youngster Rivera and his colleagues in an excellent Milan side, Maldini, David, Mora and the centre forward Altafini.

Group 1

Venue: Arica
Colombia
Russia
Uruguay
Yugoslavia

Group 3

Venue: Viña del Mar
Brazil
Czechoslovakia
Mexico
Spain

Group 2

Venue: Santiago
Chile
Germany
Italy
Switzerland

Group 4

Venue: Rancagna
Argentina
Bulgaria
England
Hungary

THE FIRST SERIES

At the brand new stadium in Santiago on 30 May, Chile kicked off their campaign against the Swiss: level at half-time they eventually won comfortably, Leonel Sanchez scoring twice in their 3–1 win. Meanwhile, in the other Group Two opener Italy and Germany, both anxious not to lose, drew 0–0 in a tense, nervous encounter, the Germans coming closest to scoring when Seeler found space to direct a header against the bar.

Brazil, seeking to emulate Pozzo's great Italian side of the 1930s and defend their title, finally overcame a lively Mexican team in Group Three, though not without difficulty, Zagalo, and then Pelé, striking after a modest first half. Also at the smart little Viña del Mar ground, Czechoslovakia, to general surprise, beat Spain. The largely disappointing Spanish team, shorn of De Stefano through muscle injury, had their solitary goal scored by Stibranyi.

South of Santiago in Group Four at Rancagua, in a stadium owned by the Braden Copper Co., Argentina, through Facundo, finally saw off the horribly sterile Bulgarians intent on their spoiling tactics in a lamentable affair. A day later Hungary repeated a recent friendly victory in Budapest by defeating a rigid, inflexible England eleven. Albert, a striker of infinite talent, snatched a decisive second half winner after England, courtesy of a penalty kick, had equalized Tichy's opener.

So to the North, where Uruguay met Colombia in an all South American encounter. The Uruguayans only just won: the Colombians going down 2–1 acquitted themselves very well indeed. Russia, the tough challengers from the Iron Curtain, completed the first round by beating the dark horses of Yugoslavia 2–0 in a match notable only for the brutality of the tackling: Dubinski, the Russian full back, was hospitalized when his leg was broken.

THE SECOND SERIES

In the second round of matches an appalling exhibition of violence took place as Italy and Chile eclipsed even the carnage witnessed at Berne eight years earlier. Incensed by insensitive remarks made by Italian journalists, the Chileans embarked on a crusade of vengeance. Hostilities commenced early, Sanchez pole-axed and broke the nose of Maschio with a punch and the match degenerated quickly into anarchic chaos as both teams flagrantly disregarded the laws of the game. Ultimately Italy, not the instigators – they claimed the Chileans were spitting at them from the beginning – but certainly not innocents, suffered, two of their players, Ferrini and David, being dismissed. Chile, now playing nine men, took advantage. Their two goals, however, did nothing to eradicate the stain of what had gone before. Later, upon reflection, the Italians sought to lay the blame for the defeat at the feet of Ken Aston, the English referee, though in truth his task of controlling the shambolic spectacle was an impossible one.

Germany, meanwhile, won 2–1 in a dull match in the other Group Two fixture against a poor Swiss side reduced to ten men through injury. It was Seeler who provided what proved to be the winner.

Pelé, a giant of world football, saw his tournament end prematurely at Viña del Mar in Brazil's second game against an obstinate Czechoslovakia, injured while striking the foot of the post in the nearest either side came to a goal. He left the field and thereafter both sides probed cautiously, neither willing to over-commit and thus leave gaps, the match ending 0–0. Also at Viña del Mar, Spain, making five desperate changes, crucially beat Mexico 2–1 and thus retained an interest. It was a last gasp winner that finally sank the enterprising Mexicans, with Piero of Athletico, in at the expense of Martinez, providing the last touch.

England, down south at Rancagua, improved immeasurably in defeating Argentina. Two up early on through another Flowers' penalty kick and a thumping shot by Charlton, Greaves gave them a third before Argentina's

Sanfilippo earned a single consolatory goal for 3–1. Hungary sauntered to victory against their destructive, reluctant Bulgarian opponents. Being 4–0 up by half-time, they relaxed somewhat in the second period, though their 6–1 victory confirmed their status as serious challengers; Albert, a rising star, hit a hat-trick for them.

Real drama was witnessed as first Yugoslavia squeezed by Uruguay 3–1 with Sekularac, their inspiration, and then Russia contrived shockingly to throw away a 4–1 lead in 20 negligent minutes against rank outsiders Colombia. The South Americans, 3–0 behind in quarter of an hour, staged a gallant recovery encouraged by a rare mistake from the normally outstanding Lev Yashin, the Russian goalkeeper. It was Klinger, Colombia's little winger, whose goal brought them a most unlikely draw; indeed, Yashin was twice called upon to deny them a late victory.

THE THIRD SERIES

In Group Two's final round in Santiago, Chilean fervour was dissipated by the ruthless and clinical Germans. Chile attacked with a passion but were repelled by an organized and professional defence, their own weaknesses twice exploited by Szymaniak – a forward employed here as an extra defender – from the penalty spot and then through the ebullient little Hamburg striker, Seeler. Successful though their tactics had been, their miserly approach won Germany few friends amongst neutrals. Italy, the last member of the Group, achieved comfortable victory over poor Switzerland in a lack-lustre affair between two disappointed teams on their way home.

On the coast at Viña del Mar, Spain again shifted their pack and almost succeeded this time against a Brazil now without Pelé. Adelardo snatched the lead after 34 minutes and clung to it; the Brazilians, staring elimination in the face, left it late. Fifteen minutes from time, Amarildo, Pelé's replacement, fired the Champions level and then, showing great promise, poached a second to frustrate and extinguish the hopes of the brave and much improved Spaniards. The final Group Three match ended with a rather surprising win for a jubilant Mexico, though the Czechs' motivation, secure in the knowledge of a quarter-final place, might have been questioned. Either way Mexico deserved their 3–1 triumph, a first for them in their fifth finals appearance.

Back in Arica, Russia, duly warned against complacency by the doughty Colombians, again lived dangerously. In their final game with Uruguay, ahead and playing virtually against ten men following injury to Alvarez, they allowed the South Americans back. Sasia equalized and in the ensuing excitement the ball struck the Russian goal frame three times. Ivanov's 39th minute goal was both fortunate and crucial.

Yugoslavia crushed an exhausted Colombia in the final game, 5–0. The Colombians had had their day of glory and the improving East Europeans, orchestrated again by Sekularc and led at the front by Jerkovic, proved altogether too much for them.

In Group Four a dour finale took place. The Hungarians, a revelation in their first two round matches, rested Albert and suffered accordingly, their goal-free draw at Rancagua a tedious affair with little incident. England, though less impressive, expected better than a 0–0 draw with the depressingly negative Bulgarians. Determined to defend in depth despite already being eliminated, they achieved their objective, as England, needing only a point, lost interest in chasing the game. Few shed tears at their departure.

Final Tournament – Chile

Group 1

Uruguay (0) **2, Colombia** (1) **1**
30.5.62 ARICA
Uruguay: Sosa, Troche, Alvarez E W, Mendez, Goncalvez, Alvarez E, Cubilla (1), Rocha, Langon, Sasia (1), Perez
Colombia: Sanchez C, Gonzalez J, Lopez, Echeverri, Zuluaga (1), Silva, Aceros, Coll, Klinger, Gamboa, Arias
Referee: Dorogi (Hungary)

USSR (0) **2, Yugoslavia** (0) **0**
31.5.62 ARICA
USSR: Yashin, Dubinski, Masionkin, Ostrovsky, Voronin, Netto, Metreveli, Ivanov V (1), Ponedeinik (1), Kanevski, Meschki
Yugoslavia: Soskic, Durkovic, Jusufi, Matus, Markovic, Popovic, Mujic, Sekularac, Jerkovic, Galic, Skoblar
Referee: Dusch (West Germany)

Yugoslavia (2) **3, Uruguay** (1) **1**
2.6.62 ARICA
Yugoslavia: Soskic, Durkovic, Radakovic, Markovic, Jusufi, Popovic, Melic, Sekularac, Jerkovic (1), Galic (1), Skoblar (1)
Uruguay: Sosa, Troche, Alvarez E W, Mendez, Goncalvez, Alvarez E, Rocha, Bergara, Cabrera (1), Sasia, Perez
Referee: Galba (Czechoslovakia)

USSR (3) **4, Colombia** (1) **4**
3.6.62 ARICA
USSR: Yashin, Tschokeli, Voronin, Masionkin, Netto, Chislenko (1), Ivanov V (2), Ponedeinik (1), Kanevski, Meschki
Colombia: Sanchez C, Alzate, Gonzalez J, Echeverri, Lopez, Serrano, Aceros (1), Coll (1), Klinger (1), Rada (1), Gonzalez H
Referee: Filho (Brazil)

USSR (1) **2, Uruguay** (0) **1**
6.6.62 ARICA
USSR: Yashin, Tschokeli, Voronin, Netto, Ostrovsky, Masionkin, Chislenko, Ivanov V (1), Ponedeinik, Mamykin (1), Chusainov
Uruguay: Sosa, Mendez, Alvarez E W, Goncalvez, Alvarez E, Troche, Cubilla, Cortez, Cabrera, Sasia (1), Perez
Referee: Jonni (Italy)

Yugoslavia (2) **5, Colombia** (0) **0**
7.6.62 ARICA
Yugoslavia: Soskic, Durkovic, Jusufi, Radakovic, Markovic, Popovic, Ankovic, Sekularac, Jerkovic (3), Galic (1), Melic (1)
Colombia: Sanchez C, Alzate, Gonzalez J, Echeverri, Lopez, Serrano, Aceros, Coll, Klinger, Rada, Gonzalez H
Referee: Robies (Chile)

	P	W	D	L	F	A	Pts
USSR	3	2	1	0	8	5	5
Yugoslavia	3	2	0	1	8	3	4
Uruguay	3	1	0	2	4	6	2
Colombia	3	0	1	2	5	11	1

Group 2

Chile (1) **3, Switzerland** (1) **1**
30.5.62 SANTIAGO
Chile: Escuti, Eyzaguirre, Sanchez R, Navarro, Contreras, Rojas, Ramirez (1), Toro, Landa, Fouilloux, Sanchez L (2)
Switzerland: Elsener, Groberty, Morf, Weber, Schneiter, Tachella, Antenen, Allemann, Wüthrich (1), Eschmann, Pottier
Referee: Aston (England)

West Germany (0) **0, Italy** (0) **0**
31.5.62 SANTIAGO
West Germany: Fahrian, Nowak, Schnellinger, Schulz, Erhardt, Szyynaniak, Sturm, Haller, Seeler, Brülls, Schäfer
Italy: Buffon, Losi, Robotti, Salvadore, Maldini, Radice, Ferrini, Rivera, Altafini, Sivori, Menichelli
Referee: Davidson (Scotland)

Chile (0) **2, Italy** (0) **0**
2.6.62 SANTIAGO
Chile: Escuti, Eyzaguirre, Sanchez R, Navarro, Contreras, Rojas, Ramirez (1), Toro (1), Landa, Fouilloux, Sanchez L
Italy: Mattrel, David, Robotti, Salvadore, Janich, Tumburus, Mora, Maschio, Altafini, Ferrini, Menichelli
Referee: Aston (England)

West Germany (1) **2, Switzerland** (0) **1**
3.6.62 SANTIAGO
West Germany: Fahrian, Nowak, Schnellinger, Schulz, Erhardt, Szymaniak, Koslowski, Hailer, Seeler (1), Schäfer, Brülls (1)
Switzerland: Elsener, Schneiter (1), Tachella, Groberty, Wüthrich, Weber, Antenen, Vonlanthen, Eschmann, Allemann, Dürr
Referee: Horn (Netherlands)

West Germany (1) **2, Chile** (0) **0**
6.6.62 SANTIAGO
West Germany: Fahrian, Nowak, Schnellinger, Schulz, Erhardt, Giesemann, Kraus, Szymaniak (1 pen), Seeler (1), Schäfer, Brülls
Chile: Escuti, Eyzaguirre, Navarro, Contreras, Sanchez R, Rojas, Moreno, Tobar, Landa, Sanchez L, Ramirez
Referee: Davidson (Scotland)

Italy (1) **3, Switzerland** (0) **0**
7.6.62 SANTIAGO
Italy: Buffon, Losi, Radice, Salvadore, Maldini, Robotti, Mora (1), Bulgarelli (1), Sormani, Sivori, Pascutti (1)
Switzerland: Elsener, Schneiter, Tachella, Groberty, Meier, Weber, Antenen, Vonlanthen, Wüthrich, Allemann, Dürr
Referee: Latyschev (USSR)

	P	W	D	L	F	A	Pts
West Germany	3	2	1	0	4	1	5
Chile	3	2	0	1	5	3	4
Italy	3	1	1	1	3	2	3
Switzerland	3	0	0	3	2	8	0

Group 3

Brazil (0) **2, Mexico** (0) **0**
30.5.62 VIÑA DEL MAR
Brazil: Gylmar, Santos D, Santos N, Zito, Mauro, Zozimo, Garrincha, Didi, Vava, Pelé (1), Zagalo (1)
Mexico: Carbajal, Del Muro, Villegas, Cardenas, Sepulveda, Najera, Del Aguila, Reyes, Hernandez H, Jasso, Diaz
Referee: Dienst (Switzerland)

Czechoslovakia (0) **1, Spain** (0) **0**
31.5.62 VIÑA DEL MAR
Czechoslovakia: Schroif, Lala, Novak, Pluskal, Popluhar, Masopust, Stibranyi (1), Scherer, Kvasnak, Adamec, Jelinek
Spain: Carmelo, Rivilla, Reija, Segarra, Santamaria, Garay, Del Sol, Puskas, Martinez, Suarez, Gento
Referee: Steiner (Austria)

Brazil (0) **0, Czechoslovakia** (0) **0**
2.6.62 VIÑA DEL MAR
Brazil: Gylmar, Santos D, Santos N, Zito, Mauro, Zozimo, Garrincha, Didi, Vava, Pelé, Zagalo
Czechoslovakia: Schroif, Lala, Novak, Pluskal, Popluhar, Masopust, Stibranyi, Scherer, Kvasnak, Adamec, Jelinek
Referee: Schwinte (France)

Spain (0) **1, Mexico** (0) **0**
3.6.62 VIÑA DEL MAR
Spain: Carmelo, Rodriguez, Gracia, Verges, Santamaria, Pachin, Del Sol, Peiro (1), Puskas, Suarez, Gento
Mexico: Carbajal, Del Muro, Jauregui, Cardenas, Sepulveda, Jasso, Najera, Del Aguila, Reyes, Hernandez H, Diaz
Referee: Tesanic (Yugoslavia)

Brazil (0) **2, Spain** (1) **1**
6.6.62 VIÑA DEL MAR
Brazil: Gylmar, Santos D, Santos N, Zito, Mauro, Zozimo, Garrincha, Didi, Vava, Amarildo (2), Zagalo
Spain: Araquistain, Rodreguez, Garcia, Verges, Echeverria, Pachin, Collar, Adelardo (1), Puskas, Peiro, Gento
Referee: Bustamante (Chile)

Mexico (2) **3, Czechoslovakia** (1) **1**
7.6.62 VIÑA DEL MAR
Mexico: Carbajal, Del Muro, Sepulveda, Jauregui, Cardenas, Najera, Del Aguila (1), Hernandez A, Hernandez H (1 pen), Reyes, Diaz
Czechoslovakia: Schroif, Lala, Novak, Pluskal, Popluhar, Masopust, Stibranyi, Scherer, Kvasnak, Adamec, Masek (1)
Referee: Dienst (Switzerland)

	P	W	D	L	F	A	Pts
Brazil	3	2	1	0	4	1	5
Czechoslovakia	3	1	1	1	2	3	3
Mexico	3	1	0	2	3	4	2
Spain	3	1	0	2	2	3	2

Group 4

Argentina (1) **1, Bulgaria** (0) **0**
30.5.62 RANCAGUA
Argentina: Roma, Navarro, Marzolini, Sainz, Sacchi, Paez, Facundo (1), Rossi, Pagani, Sanfilippo, Belen
Bulgaria: Naidenov, Rakarov, Dimitrov, Kitov, Kostov D, Kovatchev, Diev, Velitschkov, Iljev, Yakimov, Kolev
Referee: Gardeazabal (Spain)

Hungary (1) **2, England** (0) **1**
31.5.62 RANCAGUA
Hungary: Grosics, Matrai, Meszöly, Sarosi, Solymosi, Sipos, Sandor, Rakosi, Tichy (1), Albert (1), Fenyvesi
England: Springett, Armfield, Wilson, Moore, Norman, Flowers (1 pen), Douglas, Greaves, Hitchens, Haynes, Charlton R
Referee: Horn (Netherlands)

England (2) **3, Argentina** (0) **1**
2.6.62 RANCAGUA
England: Springett, Armfield, Wilson, Moore, Norman, Flowers (1 pen), Douglas, Greaves (1), Peacock, Haynes, Charlton R
Argentina: Roma, Cap, Marzolini, Sacchi, Navarro, Paez, Oleniak, Rattin, Sosa, Sanfilippo (1), Belen
Referee: Latyschev (USSR)

Hungary (4) **6, Bulgaria** (0) **1**
3.6.62 RANCAGUA
Hungary: Ilku, Matrai, Sarosi, Solymosi (1), Meszöly, Sipos, Sandor, Göröcs, Albert (3), Tichy (2), Fenyvesi
Bulgaria: Naidenov, Rakarov, Kitov, Kostov D, Dimitrov, Kovatchev, Sokolov (1), Velitschkov, Asparoukhov, Kolev, Dermendjiev
Referee: Gardeazabel (Spain)

Hungary (0) **0, Argentina** (0) **0**
6.6.62 RANCAGUA
Hungary: Grosics, Matrai, Sarosi, Solymosi, Meszöly, Sipos, Kuharszky, Göröcs, Monostori, Tichy, Rakosi
Argentina: Dominquez, Sainz, Marzolini, Delgado, Cap, Sacchi, Facundo, Pando, Pagani, Oleniak, Gonzalez
Referee: Yakasaki (Peru)

England (0) **0, Bulgaria** (0) **0**
7.6.62 RANCAGUA
England: Springett, Armfield, Wilson, Moore, Norman, Flowers, Douglas, Greaves, Peacock, Haynes, Charlton R
Bulgaria: Naidenov, Pentshev, Jetchev, Kostov D, Dimitrov, Kovatchev, Kostov A, Velitschkov, Sokolov, Kolev, Dermendjiev
Referee: Blavier (Belgium)

	P	W	D	L	F	A	Pts
Hungary	3	2	1	0	8	2	5
England	3	1	1	1	4	3	3
Argentina	3	1	1	1	2	3	3
Bulgaria	3	0	1	2	1	7	1

THE QUARTER-FINALS

Brazil and England met at the Viña del Mar ground that had staged all of the Brazilians' matches. The English played well and resisted fiercely, equalizing

Garrincha's close range and extremely rare headed goal through Hitchens (in for the injured Alan Peacock) who converted a rebound after Greaves had sent a header crashing on to the bar. With the score 1–1 at half-time, the irresistible little Garrincha turned the game conclusively, first deceiving keeper Springett with a free kick that bounced back into the path of Vava and then whipping a curling 20 yarder directly into the net; the match ended 3–1 but England had not been disgraced.

Chile, to the surprise of everyone but their own hysterical supporters, ousted Russia in Arica. The Soviets, whose form curiously deteriorated during the Tournament, lost two early goals to Sanchez and Rojas and never really recovered, though Ivanov made it close.

The capital, Santiago, saw the typically cautious Germans lose narrowly yet deservedly to their more ambitious Yugoslavian opponents. The late goal from Radakovic rescued the crowd from the prospect of an extra 30 minutes and gave the Yugoslavians ample revenge for previous defeats at German hands.

In the other quarter-final at Rancagua, Hungary outplayed Czechoslovakia – and lost with dreadful misfortune. The Czechs scored early on, exploiting a rare counter-attack and were then given a frightful pounding, surviving only through the excellence of Schroif, their goalkeeper, the thickness of their goal frame – struck three times – and the generosity of officials whose decision to disallow Tichy's 'goal' for Hungary was a contentious one.

Quarter-Finals

Yugoslavia (0) **1, West Germany** (0) **0**
10.6.62 SANTIAGO
Yugoslavia: Soskic, Durkovic, Jusufi, Radakovic (1), Markovic, Popovic, Kovacevic, Sekularac, Jerkovic, Galic, Skoblar
West Germany: Fahrian, Nowak, Schnellinger, Schulz, Erhardt, Giesemann, Brülls, Haller, Seeler, Szymaniak, Schäfer
Referee: Yamasaki (Peru)

Chile (2) **2, USSR** (1) **1**
10.6.62 ARICA
Chile: Escuti, Eyzaguirre, Navarro, Contreras, Sanchez R, Rojas (1), Ramirez, Toro, Landau, Tobar, Sanchez L (1)
USSR: Yashin, Tschokeli, Ostrovsky, Voronin, Maslonkin, Netto, Chislenko (1), Ivanov, Ponedeinik, Mamykin, Meschki
Referee: Horn (Netherlands)

Brazil (1) **3, England** (1) **1**
10.6.62 VIÑA DEL MAR
Brazil: Gylmar, Santos D, Santos N, Zito, Mauro, Zozimo, Garrincha (2), Didi, Vava (1), Amarlido, Zagalo
England: Springett, Armfield, Wilson, Moore, Norman, Flowers, Douglas, Greaves, Hitchens (1), Haynes, Charlton R
Referee: Schwinte (France)

Czechoslovakia (1) **1, Hungary** (0) **0**
10.6.62 RANCAGUA
Czechoslovakia: Schroif, Lala, Novak, Pluskal, Popluhar, Masopust, Pospichal, Scherer (1), Kadraba, Kvasnak, Jelinek
Hungary: Grosics, Matrai, Sarosi, Solymosi, Meszöly, Sipos, Sandor, Rakosi, Tichy, Albert, Fenyvesi
Referee: Latyschev (USSR)

THE SEMI-FINALS

In the semi-final stage at Santiago, Chile suffered the trauma of defeat at the hands of their South American rivals Brazil. Garrincha, an increasingly inspired influence, was their tormentor in chief. Two goals from him, one a glorious shot from distance, gave Brazil the initiative before Toro hammered Chile back into contention before half-time, 2–1. Soon after the interval Vava met Garrincha's centre for Brazil's third. Chile hauled themselves back when Leonel Sanchez converted a penalty, but Vava again, close in, met another cross, this time from Zagalo, to thump a header beyond Escuti to condemn the brave Chileans to a 4–2 defeat. Just before the end Garrincha spoiled a wonderful performance with a petulant kick at Rojas for which he was dismissed. Landa, the Chilean forward, followed him, crudely challenging Zito. The crowd, disappointed, hostile and frenzied, extracted their own retribution on Garrincha. As he headed for the safety of the dressing room, a missile struck him, cutting his head.

Before a tiny and less passionate crowd at Viña del Mar, Czechoslovakia again defied the odds and denied Yugoslavia. Defending cleverly and countering again swiftly and decisively, they broke the Yugoslavian resolve with their third goal, a penalty from Scherer. Goal-free at half-time, Kadraba beat Soskic with a shot that gave the Czechs an unexpected lead. Jerkovic, a menacing presence throughout the competition, equalized, but as Yugoslavia pressed, they were caught by Scherer on the counter for 2–1. Then Markovic with a needless hand-ball gave the same player the opportunity to strike the final blow from the penalty spot for 3–1. Czechoslovakia would play Brazil again, this time in the final.

Semi-Finals

Brazil (2) **4, Chile** (1) **2**
13.6.62 SANTIAGO
Brazil: Gylmar, Santos D, Santos N, Zito, Mauro, Zozimo, Garrincha (2), Didi, Vava (2), Amarlido, Zagalo
Chile: Escuti, Eyzaguirre, Rodriguez, Contreras, Sanchez R, Rojas, Ramirez, Toro (1), Landa, Tobar, Sanchez L (1 pen)
Referee: Yamasaki (Peru)

Czechoslovakia (1) **3, Yugoslavia** (0) **1**
13.6.62 VIÑA DEL MAR
Czechoslovakia: Schroif, Lala, Novak, Pluskal, Popluhar, Masopust, Pospichal, Scherer (2, 1 pen), Kvasnak, Kadraba (1), Jelinek
Yugoslavia: Soskic, Durkovic, Jusufi, Radakovic, Markovic, Popovic, Sijakovic, Sekularac, Jerkovic (1), Galic, Skoblar
Referee: Dienst (Switzerland)

PLAY-OFF FOR THIRD PLACE

On the day prior to the final, the now tiresome custom of third place decider between two physically and emotionally exhausted teams ensued. Chile, with at least the encouragement of a home crowd to lift them, won a dull affair, with the only goal scored by Rojas. However, in truth Yugoslavia, still prompted by Sekularac's vision, were the more accomplished team.

Match for Third Place

Chile (0) **1, Yugoslavia** (0) **0**
16.6.62 SANTIAGO
Chile: Godoy, Eyzaguirre, Rodriguez, Cruz, Sanchez R, Rojas (1), Ramirez, Toro, Campos, Tobar, Sanchez L
Yugoslavia: Soskic, Durkovic, Svinjarevic, Radakovic, Markovic, Popovic, Kovacevic, Sekularac, Jerkovic, Galic, Skoblar
Referee: Gardeazabel (Spain)

THE FINAL

The final took place on 17 June at the purpose-built Santiago stadium. Once more Czechoslovakia challenged conventional wisdom: controlling the early midfield exchanges, they took the lead when Masopust burst through Brazil's defence, collected Scherer's pass and shot past Gylmar. This time, however, their luck ran out, and Schroif, heroic goalkeeper throughout, failed them when it mattered most. Amarildo squeezed an unlikely equalizer almost through him before the interval and then chipped back for Zito to score the simplest of headers early in the second period. Kvasnak and his courageous colleagues laboured against the odds, but Schroif, deceived by the sun, made another dreadful misjudgement, spilling a hopeful pass by Djalma Santos; Vava following in did the rest. Brazil again were Champions.

Final

Brazil (1) 3, Czechoslovakia (1) 1
17.6.62 SANTIAGO
Brazil: Gylmar, Santos D, Santos N, Zito (1), Mauro, Zozimo, Garrincha, Didi, Vava (1), Amarlido (1), Zagalo
Czechoslovakia: Schroif, Tichi, Novak, Pluskal, Popluhar, Masopust (1), Pospichal, Scherer, Kadraba, Kvasnak, Jelinek
Referee: Latyschev (USSR)

Brazil, older and possibly wiser, controlled their destiny admirably. Once recovered from potential defeat against Spain, they improved and adapted, scarcely seeming to notice the absence of Pelé. They were the best team.

Czechoslovakia, underrated and entering the competition without their recognized striker Kucero, played superbly, defending cleverly, conserving energy and striking swiftly. In spite of his final aberration Schroif in goal was a magnificent inspiration.

Hungary were also bright and inventive; they were, of course, desperately unlucky to go out in the quarter-final, and when they did, the Tournament was denied a fascinating and potentially exhilarating final.

For the rest it was largely a disappointing affair, with most concentrating their emphasis on not losing. Then there was the revolting spectacle served up by Italy and Chile. All in all, the conclusion must be that 1962 was of quite modest vintage.

CHAPTER 8

ENGLAND

1966

Qualifying Tournament
71 entries
Brazil qualify as holders, England qualify as hosts

Europe (32): Albania, Austria, Belgium, Bulgaria, Cyprus, Czechoslovakia, Denmark, England, Finland, France, East Germany, West Germany, Greece, Holland, Hungary, Republic of Ireland, Northern Ireland, Israel, Italy, Luxembourg, Norway, Poland, Portugal, Romania, Scotland, Spain, Sweden, Switzerland, Turkey, USSR, Wales, Yugoslavia

South America (10): Argentina, Bolivia, Brazil, Chile, Colombia, Ecuador, Paraguay, Peru, Uruguay, Venezuela

CONCACAF (North, Central America and Caribbean) (9): Costa Rica, Cuba, Honduras, Jamaica, Mexico, Netherlands Antilles, Surinam, Trinidad, USA

Asia, Africa (20): Algeria, Australia, Cameroon, Egypt, Ethiopia, Gabon, Ghana, Guinea, Liberia, Libya, Mali, Morocco, Nigeria, North Korea, Senegal, South Africa, South Korea, Sudan, Syria, Tunisia

Europe

Group 1 (Bulgaria, Belgium, Israel)
Belgium v Israel 1–0, Bulgaria v Israel 4–0, Bulgaria v Belgium 3–0, Belgium v Bulgaria 5–0, Israel v Belgium 0–5, Israel v Bulgaria 1–2

	P	W	D	L	F	A	Pts
Belgium	4	3	0	1	11	3	6
Bulgaria	4	3	0	1	9	6	6
Israel	4	0	0	4	1	12	0

Play-off (in Florence): Bulgaria v Belgium 2–1
Bulgaria qualified

Group 2 (West Germany, Sweden, Cyprus)
West Germany v Sweden 1–1, West Germany v Cyprus 5–0, Sweden v Cyprus 3–0, Sweden v West Germany 1–2, Cyprus v Sweden 0–5, Cyprus v West Germany 0–6

	P	W	D	L	F	A	Pts
West Germany	4	3	1	0	14	2	7
Sweden	4	2	1	1	10	3	5
Cyprus	4	0	0	4	0	19	0

West Germany qualified

Group 3 (France, Norway, Yugoslavia, Luxembourg)

Yugoslavia v Luxembourg 3–1, Luxembourg v France 0–2, Luxembourg v Norway 0–2, France v Norway 1–0, Yugoslavia v France 1–0, Norway v Luxembourg 4–2, Norway v Yugoslavia 3–0, Norway v France 0–1, Luxembourg v Yugoslavia 2–5, France v Yugoslavia 1–0, Francé v Luxembourg 4–1, Yugoslavia v Norway 1–1

	P	W	D	L	F	A	Pts
France	6	5	0	1	9	2	10
Norway	6	3	1	2	10	5	7
Yugoslavia	6	3	1	2	10	8	7
Luxembourg	6	0	0	6	6	20	0

France qualified

Group 4 (Portugal, Czechoslovakia, Romania, Turkey)

Portugal v Turkey 5–1, Turkey v Portugal 0–1, Czechoslovakia v Portugal 0–1, Romania v Turkey 3–0, Romania v Czechoslovakia 1–0, Portugal v Romania 2–1, Czechoslovakia v Romania 3–1, Turkey v Czechoslovakia 0–6, Turkey v Romania 2–1, Portugal v Czechoslovakia 0–0, Czechoslovakia v Turkey 3–1, Romania v Portugal 2–0

	P	W	D	L	F	A	Pts
Portugal	6	4	1	1	9	4	9
Czechoslovakia	6	3	1	2	12	4	7
Romania	6	3	0	3	9	7	6
Turkey	6	1	0	5	4	19	2

Portugal qualified

Group 5 (Switzerland, Northern Ireland, Holland, Albania)

Holland v Albania 2–0, Northern Ireland v Switzerland 1–0, Albania v Holland 0–2, Switzerland v Northern Ireland 2–1, Northern Ireland v Holland 2–1, Holland v Northern Ireland 0–0, Albania v Switzerland 0–2, Switzerland v Albania 1–0, Northern Ireland v Albania 4–1, Holland v Switzerland 0–0, Switzerland v Holland 2–1, Albania v Northern Ireland 1–1

	P	W	D	L	F	A	Pts
Switzerland	6	4	1	1	9	4	9
Northern Ireland	6	3	2	1	9	5	8
Holland	6	2	2	2	6	4	6
Albania	6	0	1	5	2	12	1

Switzerland qualified

Group 6 (Hungary, East Germany, Austria)

Austria v East Germany 1–1, East Germany v Hungary 1–1, Austria v Hungary 0–1, Hungary v Austria 3–0, Hungary v East Germany 3–2, East Germany v Austria 1–0

	P	W	D	L	F	A	Pts
Hungary	4	3	1	0	8	3	7
East Germany	4	1	2	1	5	5	4
Austria	4	0	1	3	1	6	1

Hungary qualified

Group 7 (USSR, Wales, Greece, Denmark)

Denmark v Wales 1–0, Greece v Denmark 4–2, Greece v Wales 2–0, Wales v Greece 4–1, USSR v Greece 3–1, USSR v Wales 2–1, USSR v Denmark 6–0, Greece v USSR 1–4, Denmark v USSR 1–3, Denmark v Greece 1–1, Wales v USSR 2–1, Wales v Denmark 4–2

	P	W	D	L	F	A	Pts
USSR	6	5	0	1	19	6	10
Wales	6	3	0	3	11	9	6
Greece	6	2	1	3	10	14	5
Denmark	6	1	1	4	7	18	3

USSR qualified

Group 8 (Italy, Scotland, Poland, Finland)

Scotland v Finland 3–1, Italy v Finland 6–1, Poland v Italy 0–0, Poland v Scotland 1–1, Finland v Scotland 1–2, Finland v Italy 0–2, Finland v Poland 2–0, Scotland v Poland 1–2, Poland v Finland 7–0, Italy v Poland 6–1, Scotland v Italy 1–0, Italy v Scotland 3–0

	P	W	D	L	F	A	Pts
Italy	6	4	1	1	17	3	9
Scotland	6	3	1	2	8	8	7
Poland	6	2	2	2	11	10	6
Finland	6	1	0	5	5	20	2

Italy qualified

Group 9 (Spain, Rep of Ireland, Syria (withdrew))

Rep of Ireland v Spain 1–0, Spain v Rep of Ireland 4–1
Play-off (in Paris): Spain v Rep of Ireland 1–0
Spain qualified

Group 10 (England)
England qualified as hosts

South America

Group 11 (Uruguay, Peru, Venezuela)
Peru v Venezuela 1–0, Uruguay v Venezuela 5–0, Venezuela v Uruguay 1–3, Venezuela v Peru 3–6, Peru v Uruguay 0–1, Uruguay v Peru 2–1

	P	W	D	L	F	A	Pts
Uruguay	4	4	0	0	11	2	8
Peru	4	2	0	2	8	6	4
Venezuela	4	0	0	4	4	15	0

Uruguay qualified

Group 12 (Chile, Ecuador, Colombia)
Colombia v Ecuador 0–1, Ecuador v Colombia 2–0, Chile v Colombia 7–2, Colombia v Chile 2–0, Ecuador v Chile 2–2, Chile v Ecuador 3–1

	P	W	D	L	F	A	Pts
Chile	4	2	1	1	12	7	5
Ecuador	4	2	1	1	6	5	5
Colombia	4	2	0	3	4	10	2

Play-off (in Lima): Chile v Ecuador 2–1
Chile qualified

Group 13 (Argentina, Paraguay, Bolivia)
Paraguay v Bolivia 2–0, Argentina v Paraguay 3–0, Paraguay v Argentina 0–0, Argentina v Bolivia 4–1, Bolivia v Paraguay 2–1, Bolivia v Argentina 1–2

	P	W	D	L	F	A	Pts
Argentina	4	3	1	0	9	2	7
Paraguay	4	1	1	2	3	5	3
Bolivia	4	1	0	3	4	9	2

Argentina qualified

Group 14 (Brazil)
Brazil qualified as holders

CONCACAF

Group 15
Sub-Group 1 (Jamaica, Netherlands Antilles, Cuba)

Jamaica v Cuba 1–0, Cuba v Netherlands Antilles 1–1, Jamaica v Netherlands Antilles 2–0, Netherlands Antilles v Cuba 1–0, Netherlands Antilles v Jamaica 0–0, Cuba v Jamaica 2–1

	P	W	D	L	F	A	Pts
Jamaica	4	2	1	1	4	2	5
Netherlands Antilles	4	1	2	1	2	3	4
Cuba	4	1	1	2	3	4	3

Sub-Group 2 (Costa Rica, Surinam, Trinidad)

Trinidad v Surinam 4–1, Costa Rica v Surinam 1–0, Costa Rica v Trinidad 4–0, Surinam v Costa Rica 1–3, Trinidad v Costa Rica 0–1, Surinam v Trinidad 6–1

	P	W	D	L	F	A	Pts
Costa Rica	4	4	0	0	9	1	8
Surinam	4	1	0	3	8	9	2
Trinidad	4	1	0	3	5	12	2

Sub-Group 3 (Mexico, USA, Honduras)

Honduras v Mexico 0–1, Mexico v Honduras 3–0, USA v Mexico 2–2, Mexico v USA 2–0, Honduras v USA 0–1, USA v Honduras 1–1

	P	W	D	L	F	A	Pts
Mexico	4	3	1	0	8	2	7
USA	4	1	2	1	4	5	4
Honduras	4	0	1	3	1	6	1

Final round

Costa Rica v Mexico 0–0, Jamaica v Mexico 2–3, Mexico v Jamaica 8–0, Costa Rica v Jamaica 7–0, Mexico v Costa Rica 1–0, Jamaica v Costa Rica 1–1

	P	W	D	L	F	A	Pts
Mexico	4	3	1	0	12	2	7
Costa Rica	4	1	2	1	8	2	4
Jamaica	4	0	1	3	3	19	1

Mexico qualified

Asia/Africa

Group 16 (Australia, North Korea, South Korea)
(In Cambodia)
South Africa were suspended and the other sixteen countries from Africa withdrew
South Korea withdrew
North Korea v Australia 6–1, 3–1
North Korea qualified

1966 ENGLAND 11 July–30 July

QUALIFIERS

Argentina	Mexico
Brazil	North Korea
Bulgaria	Portugal
Chile	Russia
England	Spain
France	Switzerland
Hungary	Uruguay
Italy	West Germany

England, whose form coming into the Tournament had been less then convincing, had the advantage of matches at Wembley Stadium to encourage them and the added good fortune of relatively undistinguished opponents in Group One. Uruguay offered a potential threat, particularly in the guise of Rocha from Penarol, but they were considered hard and sterile, a team less interested in winning than avoiding defeat.

Both Mexico, who had won through the unremarkable Central American qualifier and then failed dismally on a European Tour, and France, conquerors of Yugoslavia in qualification, shorn now of its inspirational 1958 stars, were a modest bunch indeed. England, with Bobby Moore of West Ham United, the consummate defender at their heart, and both Bobby Charlton and Jimmy Greaves prolific goal scorers in international football in attack, were expected to progress without breaking into a sweat. Quite untypically their coach went further. The normally modest, unassuming Ramsay promised 'England *will* win the World Cup.'

At Hillsborough and Villa Park were Group Two, an altogether tougher proposition. Spain, the winners of the European Nations Cup, with Real Madrid players Pirri, Amancio, Gento and Zoco amongst their number, were up against a West German side of consistent performers, with a new and youthful team including Dortmund's Siggi Held and the Munich twenty-one-year-old Franz Beckenbauer. Crafty Seeler, now in his twelfth season as an international striker, retained his place. Argentina, talented but unpredictable, would also provide a formidable obstacle. Their squad included Perfumo, Artime and the River Plate winger Mas. Drawn with these three, Switzerland, back again after twelve years with a modest side, had been unfortunate.

In the north-west Group Three included Brazil. The inimitable Pelé and the nimble little genius Garrincha led a much changed blend of youth and experience playing at Goodison Park. Bulgaria, dour and occasionally brutal, were led by Asparoukhov, and had eliminated Belgium in a qualification play-off in Florence. Hungary, Olympic Champions, aided by Albert, Bene and the splendid Vasas player Janos Farkas, were a thrilling though somewhat fragile team. The fourth Group Three team, Portugal, commanded respect, built as it was on the marvellous Benfica side of the time, four times European Club finalists, with Eusebio, Coluña, Simoes, Augusta and the towering Torres providing their attacking options. The patrons at both Old Trafford and the Everton ground could expect, one way or another, explosive encounters.

Group Four promised to be interesting if nothing else, the USSR numbering Voronin, Yashin, Banischevski and Chislenko amongst their exceptional players. Italy and Chile, to the dismay of all, had also been drawn in Group Four, but the memories of their petulant, despicably violent brawl in Santiago were fresh in the minds of all that had witnessed it. A repetition would be unforgivable. For their part Italy had an immensely skilful line-up, with Milan's Gianni Rivera, Cagliari winger Luigi Riva and the Inter trio of Facchetti, Burgnich and Mazzola regular team members. Chile, a semi-finalist on home soil in 1962, had a point to prove, though theirs was now a new, young and largely inexperienced side. The final member of this quartet, who would compete in the north-eastern strongholds of Middlesbrough and Sunderland, were North Korea. Their presence caused enormous interest: qualifying in Cambodia against Australia, they had disappeared again behind their borders, preserving their mystique, and had, reputedly, spent months in isolation in fastidious preparation.

Group 1

Venues: London, Wembley, White City
England
France
Mexico
Uruguay

Group 3

Venues: Liverpool – Goodison Park, Manchester – Old Trafford
Brazil
Bulgaria
Hungary
Portugal

Group 2

Venues: Birmingham – Villa Park, Sheffield – Hillsborough
Argentina
Spain
Switzerland
West Germany

Group 4

Venues: Sunderland – Roker Park, Middlesbrough – Ayresome Park
Chile
Italy
North Korea
Russia

THE FIRST SERIES

The Tournament began at Wembley Stadium with a predictably cautious and drab affair. Despite England's boundless energy, they lacked the wit and imagination required to overcome an organized Uruguayan team displaying little ambition of their own. England soon floundered, smothered and devoid of invention long before the referee's final merciful whistle. This had been an unsatisfactory beginning, and Ramsay's bold declaration already bore a hollow ring.

So to Goodison Park and the opening Group Three encounter between a nervous Bulgarian side and the Champions, Brazil. Pelé scored spectacularly from an early free kick and Garrincha emulated the feat to make it 2–0. Bulgaria, their attacking options blighted by an injury to their Levski striker Asparoukhov, resorted to robust tackling, particularly targeting Pelé, who received a fierce and savage pounding.

Sheffield witnessed the West Germans in action. Playing Switzerland, the game was a rout. The Swiss, understrength following internal disciplinary problems, collapsed under persistent pressure to lose 5–0, the immaculate Beckenbauer scoring twice and leading a fine team performance.

Wembley Stadium hosted the second match in Group One, a dismal, depressing affair between Mexico and France. The Mexicans through their one outstanding player, Borja, took the lead, and despite Hausser equalizing, they clung on to a 1–1 draw.

Villa Park saw Argentina and Spain contest a sporadically exciting encounter. Artime, the classy Palmeiras centre forward, gave the South Americans the lead until Pirri equalized before Artime scored again, this time decisively.

Portugal in Group Three edged out an uninhibited Hungarian team in a close game at Old Trafford, the thorough Portuguese capitalizing on two goal-keeping calamities to secure the points with a final result of 3–1.

In the north-east Middlesborough's Ayresome Park saw the brave little Koreans bullied and beaten by their physically superior Russian opponents 3–0. They were fast and hard-working but made little impression on the Soviet goal, guarded on this occasion by Kavazashvili, the Moscow Torpedo keeper, instead of regular custodian Yashin.

Chile met Italy at Roker Park. The Italians predictably won without great difficulty; their pre-tournament form was good, but in spite of goals from Barison and Mazzola, Chile, reduced by injury to ten players for more than half an hour, resisted manfully. It finished 2–0, fortunately without the ugly scenes of Santiago.

THE SECOND SERIES

At White City, Uruguay, less threatened by the French, threw off their shackles and played surprisingly brightly. Conceding a penalty kick early on, they took command, the excellent Rocha bringing them level before Cortes scored what proved to be the winner, and all this before half-time.

England, also in Group One, beat Mexico as expected. The timid Mexicans appeared overawed and retreated en masse, intent only on survival. Charlton could not tempt them out, despite beating Calderon with a ferocious shot, and when Hunt swept home from close range they had lost without apparently trying to win. England, though, struggled to break them down and had been largely unimpressive.

In Sheffield, Switzerland in Group Two, smarting from their treatment at the hands of the Germans, made wholesale changes and very nearly reaped the reward. Quentin fired them ahead but in the second half Spain responded, first from Sanchis, their full back, and then Amancio from Real popped up to give the Spanish two valuable points and some hope. Argentina, having gained an advantage by beating Spain, met the West Germans determined not to lose. Not inclined to take the initiative, they waited for an onslaught that never materialized. Germany were evidently perfectly content with a 0–0 draw, showing no greater effort even after Albrecht, the Argentinean defender, was dismissed. Hungary meeting Brazil at Goodison Park replaced the hapless Szentmihalyi with Gelei in goal and prospered, with exhilarating attacking inspired by Florian Albert and Ferenc Bene, overwhelming the Champions

3–1. Brazil had been proven vulnerable. Portugal, courtesy of rare Bulgarian generosity, won 3–0 easily, though again their goals were gifted to them by dreadful defending; Vulzov put the ball through his own net before Eusebio and then Torres completed the scoring.

In Group Four at Middlesbrough the plucky Koreans fought back from a first half drubbing by Chile who led through a penalty kick. They finally earned a point when Pak Seung Zin stabbed a late equalizer past Valentini, the Chilean goalkeeper. Meanwhile at Roker Park, Italy encountered the Russians. Chislenko scored first with a fierce drive and Russia held their advantage to the end. Rugged and capable, but hardly spectacular, they deserved their victory against a disappointingly uninspired Italian team.

THE THIRD SERIES

At Wembley the final Group One encounters took place. Against their clearly inferior Mexican opponents, Uruguay curiously elected to defend. This they did with comfort in a woefully uneventful fixture. England, bringing Ian Callaghan in for Terry Paine, won again. But they were far from convincing, the French cause not helped by the unfortunate injury of their midfield player Herbin, effectively thereafter a passenger. Hunt of Liverpool scored twice either side of half-time, enough to secure a quarter-final place.

From Group Two the Germans at Villa Park eliminated Spain. The short squat figure of Seeler snatched the decisive goal in a game they generally controlled, and the youthful Beckenbauer became an increasingly dominant force in a fine midfield. Argentina joined them in the quarter-finals by beating demoralized Switzerland 2–0, though their performance was once again patchy and unspectacular.

At Goodison Park, Portugal administered the last rites over a depleted Brazilian team, whose coach, Feola, gambled on changes and lost. Replacement keeper Manga, hesitant and uncertain behind a now inexperienced defence, allowed the Portuguese two quick goals, and then saw Pelé, subjected to frightening brutality throughout the Tournament, crippled by a shameful tackle by Morais. Reduced to ten men there was no way back, 3–1 at the end and Portugal deserved winners.

Sensation came next at Ayresome Park as the Italians pressed against the Koreans, creating and squandering goal-scoring opportunities before losing Bulgarelli with an injury on the half-hour. The Koreans, with a numerical advantage, attacked remorselessly, seizing the chance of an enormous upset when Pak Doo Ik hammered the ball beyond Albertosi. Italy, tired and dejected, could not respond. Astonishingly, they would take no further part in the Tournament.

Nor would Chile, beaten 2–1 by a much changed but strangely reluctant Russian team, who at times had seemed perfectly content with a draw. Porkujan scored twice for them. Bulgaria, trying their third goalkeeper in as many games, managed yet another own goal, this time at Old Trafford against Hungary. The Hungarians, trailing 1–0, took full and ruthless advantage, scoring twice more for a comfortable and comprehensive victory, 3–1.

Final Tournament – England
First round

Group 1

England (0) **0, Uruguay** (0) **0**
11.7.66 WEMBLEY
England: Banks, Cohen, Wilson, Stiles, Charlton J, Moore, Ball, Greaves, Hunt, Charlton R, Connelly
Uruguay: Mazurkiewicz, Troche, Manicera, Ubinas, Goncalvez, Caetano, Cortes, Viera, Silva, Rocha, Perez
Referee: Zsolt (Hungary)

France (0) **1, Mexico** (0) **1**
13.7.66 WEMBLEY
France: Aubour, Djorkaeff, Artelesa, Budzinski, De Michele, Bonnel, Bosquier, Combin, Herbin, Gondet, Hausser (1)
Mexico: Calderon, Chaires, Nuñez, Hernandez, Peña, Mercado, Diaz, Reyes, Fragoso, Padilla, Borja (1)
Referee: Ashkenasi (Israel)

Uruguay (2) **2, France** (1) **1**
15.7.66 WHITE CITY
Uruguay: Mazurkiewicz, Troche, Manicera, Ubinas, Goncalvez, Caetano, Cortes (1), Viera, Sasia, Rocha (1), Perez
France: Aubour, Djorkaeff, Artelesa, Budzinski, Bosquier, Bonnel, Simon, Herbet, De Bourgoing (1 pen), Gondet, Hausser
Referee: Galba (Czechoslovakia)

England (1) **2, Mexico** (0) **0**
16.7.66 WEMBLEY
England: Banks, Cohen, Wilson, Stiles, Charlton J, Moore, Paine, Greaves, Hunt (1), Charlton R (1), Peters
Mexico: Calderon, Chaires, Peña, Nuñez, Hernandez, Diaz, Mercado, Reyes, Cisneros, Borja, Padilla
Referee: Lo Bello (Italy)

Uruguay (0) **0, Mexico** (0) **0**
19.7.66 WEMBLEY
Uruguay: Mazurkiewicz, Troche, Manicera, Ubinas, Goncalvez, Caetano, Cortes, Viera, Sasia, Rocha, Perez
Mexico: Calderon, Chaires, Peña, Nuñez, Hernandez, Diaz, Mercado, Reyes, Cisneros, Borja, Padilla
Referee: Lööw (Sweden)

England (1) **2, France** (0) **0**
20.7.66 WEMBLEY
England: Banks, Cohen, Wilson, Stiles, Charlton J, Moore, Callaghan, Greaves, Hunt (2), Charlton R, Peters
France: Aubour, Djorkaeff, Artelesa, Budzinski, Bosquier, Bonnel, Simon, Herbet, Gondet, Herbin, Hausser (1)
Referee: Yamasaki (Peru)

	P	W	D	L	F	A	Pts
England	3	2	1	0	4	0	5
Uruguay	3	1	2	0	2	1	4
Mexico	3	0	2	1	1	3	2
France	3	0	1	2	2	5	1

Group 2

West Germany (3) **5, Switzerland** (0) **0**
12.7.66 HILLSBOROUGH
West Germany: Tilkowski, Höttges, Weber, Schulz, Schnellinger, Beckenbauer (2), Haller (2, 1 pen), Brülls, Seeler, Overath, Held (1)
Switzerland: Elsener, Grobety, Schneiter, Tacchella, Führer, Bäni, Dürr, Odermatt, Künzli, Hosp, Schindelholz
Referee: Phillips (Scotland)

Argentina (0) **2, Spain** (0) **1**
13.7.66 VILLA PARK
Argentina: Roma, Ferreiro, Perfumo, Albrecht, Marzolini, Solari, Rattin, Gonzalez, Artime (2), Onega, Mas
Spain: Iribar, Sanchis, Gallego, Zoco, Eladio, Pirri (1), Suarez, Del Sol, Ufarte, Peiro, Gento
Referee: Rumentschev (Bulgaria)

Spain (0) **2, Switzerland** (1) **1**
15.7.66 HILLSBOROUGH
Spain: Iribar, Sanchis (1), Gallego, Zoco, Reija, Pirri, Del Sol, Amancio (1), Peiro, Suarez, Gento
Switzerland: Elsener, Führer, Brodmann, Leimgruber, Stierli, Bäni, Armbruster, Gottardi, Hosp, Kuhn, Quentin (1)
Referee: Bakhramov (USSR)

West Germany (0) **0, Argentina** (0) **0**
16.7.66 VILLA PARK
West Germany: Tilkowski, Höttges, Weber, Schulz, Schnellinger, Beckenbauer, Haller, Brülls, Seeler, Overath, Held
Argentina: Roma, Ferreiro, Perfumo, Albrecht, Marzolini, Solari, Rattin, Gonzalez, Artime, Onega, Mas
Referee: Zecevic (Yugoslavia)

Argentina (0) **2, Switzerland** (0) **0**
19.7.66 HILLSBOROUGH
Argentina: Roma, Ferreiro, Perfumo, Calics, Marzolini, Solari, Rattin, Gonzalez, Artime (1), Onega (1), Mas
Switzerland: Eichmann, Führer, Bäni, Brodmann, Stierli, Armbruster, Kühn, Gottardi, Künzli, Hosp, Quentin
Referee: Campos (Portugal)

West Germany (1) **2, Spain** (1) **1**
20.7.66 VILLA PARK
West Germany: Tilkowski, Höttges, Weber, Schulz, Schnellinger, Beckenbauer, Overath, Krämer, Seeler (1), Held, Emmerich (1)
Spain: Iribar, Sanchis, Gallego, Zoco, Reija, Glaria, Fusté (1), Amancio, Adelardo, Marcelino, Lapetra
Referee: Marques (Brazil)

	P	W	D	L	F	A	Pts
West Germany	3	2	1	0	7	1	5
Argentina	3	2	1	0	4	1	5
Spain	3	1	0	2	4	5	2
Switzerland	3	0	0	3	1	9	0

Group 3

Brazil (1) **2, Bulgaria** (0) **0**
12.7.66 GOODISON PARK
Brazil: Gylmar, Santos D, Bellini, Altair, Paulo Henrique, Denilson, Lima, Garrincha (1), Alcindo, Pelé (1), Jair
Bulgaria: Naidenov, Chalamanov, Penev, Vutzov, Gaganelov, Kitov, Jetchev, Dermendjiev, Asparoukhov, Yakimov, Kolev
Referee: Tschenscher (West Germany)

Portugal (1) **3, Hungary** (0) **1**
13.7.66 OLD TRAFFORD
Portugal: Carvalho, Morais, Baptista, Vicente, Hilairo, Graca, Coluña, Jose Augusto (2), Eusebio, Torres (1), Simoes
Hungary: Szentmihalyi, Kaposzta, Matrai, Meszöly, Sovari, Nagy I, Sipos, Bene (1), Albert, Farkas, Rakosi
Referee: Callaghan (Wales)

Hungary (1) **3, Brazil** (1) **1**
15.7.66 GOODISON PARK
Hungary: Gelei, Matrai, Kaposzta, Meszöly (1 pen), Sipos, Szepesi, Mathesz, Rakosi, Bene (1), Albert, Farkas (1)
Brazil: Gylmar, Santos D, Bellini, Altair, Paulo Henrique, Gerson, Lima, Garrincha, Alcindo, Tostao (1), Jair
Referee: Dagnall (England)

Portugal (2) **3, Bulgaria** (0) **0**
16.7.66 OLD TRAFFORD
Portugal: Pereira, Morais, Baptista, Vicente, Hilairo, Graca, Coluña, Jose Augusto, Eusebio (1), Torres (1), Simoes
Bulgaria: Naidenov, Chalamanov, Vutzov (o.g.), Gaganelov, Penev, Jetchev, Yakimov, Dermendjiev, Jekov, Asparoukhov, Kolev
Referee: Codesal (Uruguay)

Portugal (2) **3, Brazil** (0) **1**
17.7.66 GOODISON PARK
Portugal: Pereira, Morais, Baptista, Vicente, Hilairo, Graca, Coluña, Jose Augusto, Eusebio (2),Torres, Simoes (1)
Brazil: Manga, Fidelis, Brito, Orlando, Rildo (1), Denilson, Lima, Jair, Silva, Pelé, Parana
Referee: McCabe (England)

Hungary (2) **3, Bulgaria** (1) **1**
20.7.66 OLD TRAFFORD
Hungary: Gelei, Matrai, Kaposzta, Meszöly (1), Sipos, Szepesi, Mathesz, Rakosi, Bene (1), Albert, Farkas
Bulgaria: Simeonov, Penev, Largov, Vutzov, Gaganelov, Jetchev, Davidov (o.g.), Yakimov, Asparoukhov (1), Kolev, Kostov
Referee: Goicoechea (Argentina)

	P	W	D	L	F	A	Pts
Portugal	3	3	0	0	9	2	6
Hungary	3	2	0	1	7	5	4
Brazil	3	1	0	2	4	6	2
Bulgaria	3	0	0	3	1	8	0

Group 4

USSR (2) **3, North Korea** (0) **0**
12.7.66 AYRESOME PARK
USSR: Kavazashvili, Ponomarev, Shesternev, Khurtsilava, Ostrovksky, Sabo, Sichinava, Chislenko, Banischevski (1), Khusainov, Malofeyev (2)
North Korea: Chan Myung, Li Sup, Yung Kyoo, Bong Chil, Zoong Sun, Seung Hwi, Bong Zin, Doo Ik, Ryong Woon, Seung Il, Seung Zin
Referee: Gardeazabal (Spain)

Italy (1) **2, Chile** (0) **0**
13.7.66 ROKER PARK
Italy: Albertosi, Burgnich, Rosato, Salvadore, Facchetti, Bulgarelli, Lodetti, Perani, Mazzola (1), Rivera, Barison (1)
Chile: Olivares, Eyzaguirre, Cruz, Figueroa, Villanueva, Prieto, Marcos (1 pen), Araya, Landa, Fouilloux, Sanchez L
Referee: Dienst (Switzerland)

North Korea (0) **1, Chile** (1) **1**
13.7.66 AYRESOME PARK
North Korea: Chan Myung, Li Sup, Yung Kyoo, Zoong Sun, Yoon Kyung, Seung Zin (1), Seung Hwi, Bong Zin, Doo Ik, Dong Woon, Seung Il
Chile: Olivares, Valentini, Cruz, Figueroa, Villanueva, Prieto, Marcos (1 pen), Araya, Landa, Fouilloux, Sanchez L
Referee: Kandil (Egypt)

USSR (0) **1, Italy** (0) **0**
16.7.66 ROKER PARK
USSR: Yashin, Ponomarev, Shesternev, Khurtsilava, Danilov, Sabo, Voronin, Chislenko (1), Malofeyev, Banischevski, Khusainov
Italy: Albertosi, Burgnich, Rosato, Salvadore, Facchetti, Lodetti, Leoncini, Meroni, Mazzola, Bulgarelli, Pascutti
Referee: Kreitlein (West Germany)

North Korea (1) **1, Italy** (0) **0**
19.7.66 AYRESOME PARK
North Korea: Chan Myung, Zoong Sun, Yung Kyoo, Yung Won, Yoon Kyung, Seung Hwi, Bong Zin, Doo Ik (1), Seung Zin, Bong Hwan, Seung Kook
Italy: Albertosi, Landini, Guarneri, Janich, Facchetti, Bulgarelli, Fogli, Meroni, Mazzola, Rivera, Barison
Referee: Schwinte (France)

USSR (1) **2, Chile** (1) **1**
20.7.66 ROKER PARK
USSR: Kavazashvili, Getmanov, Shesternev, Kornejev, Ostrovsky, Voronin, Afonin, Metreveli, Serebrannikov, Markarov, Porkujan (2)
Chile: Olivares, Valentini, Cruz, Figueroa, Villanueva, Marcos (1), Prieto, Araya, Landa, Yaver, Sanchez L
Referee: Adair (Northern Ireland)

	P	W	D	L	F	A	Pts
USSR	3	3	0	0	6	1	6
North Korea	3	1	1	1	2	4	3
Italy	3	1	0	2	2	2	2
Chile	3	0	1	2	2	5	1

THE QUARTER-FINALS

North Korea, perhaps the unlikeliest quarter-finalist in the competition's thirty-six-year history, took to the field again at Goodison Park. An air of scepticism pervaded the ground and ninety minutes later they had been duly dispatched. In between, however, an extraordinary contest took place as the little men of Asia played with skill and incisiveness to begin with and later with dogged determination and courage, challenging their illustrious opponents to the very end. Scoring within a minute through Pak Seung Jin, they waltzed through Portugal's astonished defence twice more to go 3–0 up in just twenty minutes. But the fabulous Eusebio was to deny them victory. Lifting the Portuguese from their knees with two goals before half-time, he scored twice more after the interval before Augusto added a fifth. Although the game ended 5–3, North Korea's skill and bravery had greatly enhanced the reputation of football on the Asian continent.

At Wembley, England and Argentina played an ill-tempered, occasionally violent, match. The Argentineans finally lost their fragile composure and with it their chance, fouling repeatedly (though England were not entirely blameless) for a succession of first half bookings leading to Rattin's expulsion amid furious and prolonged protest. The second period saw England labour worryingly before Hurst, in at the expense of the injured Greaves, lifted a header over the stranded and despairing goalkeeper Roma thirteen minutes from the end.

Hungary, positive and exciting, went out to Russia at Goodison Park. Finally paying the price for insecure goalkeeping, Gelei had a poor match, Chislenko and Porkujan capitalizing on his weakness for a two-goal lead. While Bene hauled Hungary back to 2–1, it was scant consolation at full time – they had been the better team and lost.

At Hillsborough there were more South American histrionics as Uruguay disgraced themselves against West Germany. Behind to a rather unfortunate deflection, they were denied a penalty kick appeal and resorted to meting out their own savage justice. First Emmerich and then the excellent Haller were left writhing on the ground. The perpetrators, Troche and then the brilliant but temperamental Silva, were dismissed, and the nine remaining Uruguayans were overrun, conceding three more goals for a 4–0 final score.

Quarter-Finals

England (0) **1, Argentina** (0) **0**
23.7.66 WEMBLEY
England: Banks, Cohen, Wilson, Stiles, Charlton J, Moore, Ball, Hunt, Hurst (1), Charlton R, Peters
Argentina: Roma, Ferreiro, Perfumo, Albrecht, Marzolini, Solari, Rattin, Gonzalez, Artime, Onega, Mas
Referee: Kreitlein (West Germany)

West Germany (1) **4, Uruguay** (0) **0**
23.7.66 HILLSBOROUGH
West Germany: Tilkowski, Höttges, Weber, Schulz, Schnellinger, Haller (2), Beckenbauer (1), Overath, Seeler (1), Emmerich, Held
Uruguay: Mazurkiewicz, Troche, Ubinas, Caetano, Manicera, Rocha, Goncalvez, Salva, Cortes, Silva, Perez
Referee: Finney (England)

Portugal (2) **5, North Korea** (3) **3**
23.7.66 GOODISON PARK
Portugal: Pereira, Morais, Baptista, Vicente, Hilario, Graca, Coluña, Jose Augusto (1), Eusebio (4, 2 pens), Torres, Simoes
North Korea: Chan Myung, Zoong Sun, Yung Kyoo, Yung Won, Yoon Kyung, Seung Zin, Seung Hwi, Bong Zin, Doo Ik, Dong Woon (1), Seung Kook (2)
Referee: Ashkenasi (Israel)

USSR (1) **2, Hungary** (0) **1**
23.7.66 ROKER PARK
USSR: Yashin, Ponomarev, Shesternev, Danilov, Voronin, Sabo, Khusainov, Chislenko (1), Banischevski, Malofeyev, Porkujan (1)
Hungary: Gelei, Kaposzta, Matrai, Meszöly, Szepesi, Nagy I, Sipos, Bene (1), Albert, Farkas, Rakosi
Referee: Gardeazabel (Spain)

THE SEMI-FINALS

West Germany, to no one's surprise, overcame Russia at Goodison Park. The industrious physical approach adopted by the Russian team proved no match for the Germans, who attacked from the outset. Sabo, Beckenbauer's marker, injured himself after ten minutes and limped thereafter. Russia were further hampered when, behind to a goal from Haller, they lost the services of

Chislenko, dismissed for a petulant kick at Held, when Beckenbauer smashed a rising shot past Yashin from 20 yards to give Germany a two-goal cushion. A rout threatened, but Russia, to their credit, refused to buckle, and the willing Porkujan gave them an opportunistic header in the dying moments.

At Wembley, England and Portugal met in a memorable contest. The English, defensively sound, finally blossomed as an attacking force and deserved to win a thrilling match. Charlton first, following in Hunt's shot parried by Pereira, gave them the lead, and then from Hurst's cut back ten minutes from time England went two ahead. Though Eusebio, shackled so effectively by Stiles, gave Portugal renewed hope with a second half penalty kick, England held on, Banks denying Coluña at the death.

Semi-Finals

West Germany (1) **2, USSR** (0) **1**
25.7.66 GOODISON PARK
West Germany: Tilkowski, Lutz, Weber, Schulz, Schnellinger, Beckenbauer (1), Overath, Seeler, Haller (1), Held, Emmerich
USSR: Yashin, Ponomarev, Shesternev, Danilov, Voronin, Sabo, Khusainov, Chislenko, Banischevski, Malofeyev, Porkujan (1)
Referee: Lo Bello (Italy)

England (1) **2, Portugal** (0) **1**
26.7.66 WEMBLEY
England: Banks, Cohen, Wilson, Stiles, Charlton J, Moore, Ball, Hunt, Hurst, Charlton R (2), Peters
Portugal: Pereira, Festa, Baptista, Jose Carlos, Hilario, Graca, Coluña, Jose Augusto, Eusebio (1 pen), Torres, Simoes
Referee: Schwinte (France)

PLAY-OFF FOR THIRD PLACE

Before the final, the traditional, wholly unnecessary, third and fourth place match between Portugal and Russia took place. A tired affair, Eusebio put the Portuguese ahead, converting his fourth penalty in three games, and despite Malofeyev gleefully whacking in another Pereira fumble, Torres fired home the winner for Portugal late on, the better of two lamentably uninspired teams.

Match for Third Place

Portugal (1) **2, USSR** (1) **1**
28.7.66 WEMBLEY
Portugal: Pereira, Festa, Baptista, Jose Carlos, Hilario, Graca, Coluña, Jose Augusto, Eusebio (1 pen), Torres (1), Simoes
USSR: Yashin, Ponomarev, Korneev, Khurtsilava, Danilov, Voronin, Sichinava, Serebrannikov, Banischevski, Malofeyev (1), Metreveli
Referee: Dagnall (England)

THE FINAL

On 30 July the final took place at Wembley. England met West Germany on an unforgettable afternoon of heart-stopping drama. The Germans struck first, the blond Haller sweeping home Wilson's hesitant clearance. Hurst, in again at the expense of Greaves, bulleted a header past the Eintracht keeper Tilkowski to equalize 1–1. Peters, then his West Ham colleague, popped up in a crowded goalmouth to rifle the ball in for 2–1. Twelve minutes remained. Seconds from the end Emmerich launched a free kick goalward for the desperate Germans: the ball eluded attackers and defenders alike before Weber, arriving at the far post, drove in an equalizer.

In extra time England demonstrated admirable resolve. Ball, running tirelessly at Schnellinger on the right wing, tore ragged holes in the German defence and finally Hurst, receiving another Ball cross, thundered a shot off the underside of the cross bar – had it crossed the line? The Swiss referee, at first uncertain, consulted with his linesmen at length before giving his verdict. *Goal*. The stadium erupted into wild celebration, and as bravely as the Germans fought thereafter, the momentum had swung away from them. Hurst, powerfully and conclusively, fired a fourth for a hat-trick, the first in a final. England were the Champions.

Final

England (1) **4, West Germany** (1) **2** (aet, 2–2 at 90 mins)
30.7.66 WEMBLEY
England: Banks, Cohen, Wilson, Stiles, Charlton J, Moore, Ball, Hunt, Hurst (3), Charlton R, Peters (1)
West Germany: Tilkowski, Höttges, Weber (1), Schulz, Schnellinger, Haller (1), Beckenbauer, Overath, Seeler, Emmerich, Held
Referee: Dienst (Switzerland)

England, slow starters, were undoubtedly the best team, though both West Germany and Portugal pushed them hard. For the rest, Hungary thrilled, Brazil disappointed and North Korea provided sensation.

Following the trend of the 1962 competition, many of the matches in 1966 were rugged, dreary affairs, played out by teams whose attitude was entirely negative.

Significantly, perhaps, one of those few committed to attacking football prevailed.

CHAPTER 9

MEXICO

1970

Qualifying Tournament
70 entries
England qualify as holders, Mexico qualify as hosts

Europe (30): Austria, Belgium, Bulgaria, Cyprus, Czechoslovakia, Denmark, England, Finland, France, East Germany, West Germany, Greece, Holland, Hungary, Republic of Ireland, Northern Ireland, Italy, Luxembourg, Norway, Poland, Portugal, Romania, Scotland, Spain, Sweden, Switzerland, Turkey, USSR, Wales, Yugoslavia

South America (10): Argentina, Bolivia, Brazil, Chile, Colombia, Ecuador, Paraguay, Peru, Uruguay, Venezuela

CONCACAF (12): Bermuda, Canada, Costa Rica, Guatemala, Haiti, Honduras, Jamaica, Netherlands Antilles, El Salvador, Surinam, Trinidad, USA

Asia/Oceania (7): Australia, Israel, Japan, New Zealand, North Korea, Rhodesia, South Korea

Africa (11): Algeria, Cameroon, Ethiopia, Ghana, Libya, Morocco, Nigeria, Senegal, Sudan, Tunisia, Zambia

Europe

Group 1 (Romania, Greece, Switzerland, Portugal)

Switzerland v Greece 1–0; Portugal v Romania 3–0; Romania v Switzerland 2–0; Greece v Portugal 4–2; Portugal v Switzerland 0–2; Greece v Romania 2–2; Portugal v Greece 2–2; Switzerland v Romania 0–1; Romania v Portugal 1–0; Greece v Switzerland 4–1; Switzerland v Portugal 1–1; Romania v Greece 1–1

	P	W	D	L	F	A	Pts
Romania	6	3	2	1	7	6	8
Greece	6	2	3	1	13	9	7
Switzerland	6	2	1	3	5	8	5
Portugal	6	1	2	3	8	10	4

Romania qualified

Group 2 (Hungary, Czechoslovakia, Denmark, Rep of Ireland)

Denmark v Czechoslovakia 0–3; Czechoslovakia v Denmark 1–0; Rep of Ireland v Czechoslovakia 1–2; Hungary v Czechoslovakia 2–0; Rep of Ireland v Denmark 1–1 (after abandoned game after 51 minutes due to fog); Rep of Ireland v Hungary 1–2; Denmark v Hungary 3–2; Czechoslovakia v Hungary 3–3; Czechoslovakia v Rep of Ireland 3–0; Denmark v Rep of Ireland 2–0; Hungary v Denmark 3–0; Hungary v Rep of Ireland 4–0

	P	W	D	L	F	A	Pts
Hungary	6	4	1	1	16	7	9
Czechoslovakia	6	4	1	1	12	6	9
Denmark	6	2	1	3	6	10	5
Republic of Ireland	6	0	1	5	3	14	1

Play-off (in Marseilles): Czechoslovakia v Hungary 4–1
Czechoslovakia qualified

Group 3 (Italy, East Germany, Wales)

Wales v Italy 0–1; East Germany v Italy 2–2; East Germany v Wales 2–1; Wales v East Germany 1–3; Italy v Wales 4–1; Italy v East Germany 3–0

	P	W	D	L	F	A	Pts
Italy	4	3	1	0	10	3	7
East Germany	4	2	1	1	7	7	5
Wales	4	0	0	4	3	10	0

Italy qualified

Group 4 (USSR, Northern Ireland, Turkey)

Northern Ireland v Turkey 4–1; Turkey v Northern Ireland 0–3; Northern Ireland v USSR 0–0; USSR v Turkey 3–0; USSR v Northern Ireland 2–0; Turkey v USSR 1–3

	P	W	D	L	F	A	Pts
USSR	4	3	1	0	8	1	7
Northern Ireland	4	2	1	1	7	3	5
Turkey	4	0	0	4	2	13	0

USSR qualified

Group 5 (Sweden, France, Norway)

Sweden v Norway 5–0; France v Norway 0–1; Norway v Sweden 2–5; Norway v France 1–3; Sweden v France 2–0; France v Sweden 3–0

	P	W	D	L	F	A	Pts
Sweden	4	3	0	1	12	5	6
France	4	2	0	2	6	4	4
Norway	4	1	0	3	4	13	2

Sweden qualified

Group 6 (Belgium, Yugoslavia, Spain, Finland)

Finland v Belgium 1–2; Yugoslavia v Finland 9–1; Belgium v Finland 6–1; Belgium v Yugoslavia 3–0; Yugoslavia v Spain 0–0; Spain v Belgium 1–1; Belgium v Spain 2–1; Spain v Yugoslavia 2–1; Finland v Yugoslavia 1–5; Finland v Spain 2–0; Spain v Finland 6–0; Yugoslavia v Belgium 4–0

	P	W	D	L	F	A	Pts
Belgium	6	4	1	1	14	8	9
Yugoslavia	6	3	1	2	19	7	7
Spain	6	2	2	2	10	6	6
Finland	6	1	0	5	6	28	2

Belgium qualified

Group 7 (West Germany, Scotland, Austria, Cyprus)

Austria v Cyprus 7–1; Austria v West Germany 0–2; Scotland v Austria 2–1; Cyprus v West Germany 0–1; Cyprus v Scotland 0–5; Scotland v West Germany 1–1; Cyprus v Austria 1–2; West Germany v Austria 1–0; Scotland v Cyprus 8–0; West Germany v Cyprus 12–0; West Germany v Scotland 3–2; Austria v Scotland 2–0

	P	W	D	L	F	A	Pts
West Germany	6	5	1	0	20	3	11
Scotland	6	3	1	2	18	7	7
Austria	6	3	0	3	12	7	6
Cyprus	6	0	0	6	2	35	0

West Germany qualified

Group 8 (Bulgaria, Poland, Holland, Luxembourg)

Luxembourg v Holland 0–2; Bulgaria v Holland 2–0; Holland v Luxembourg 4–0; Poland v Luxembourg 8–1; Bulgaria v Luxembourg 2–1; Holland v Poland 1–0; Bulgaria v Poland 4–1; Poland v Holland 2–1; Luxembourg v Poland 1–5; Holland v Bulgaria 1–1; Poland v Bulgaria 3–0; Luxembourg v Bulgaria 1–3

	P	W	D	L	F	A	Pts
Bulgaria	6	4	1	1	12	7	9
Poland	6	4	0	2	19	8	8
Holland	6	3	1	2	9	5	7
Luxembourg	6	0	0	6	4	24	0

Bulgaria qualified

Group 9 (England)

England qualified as holders

South America

Group 10 (Peru, Bolivia, Argentina)

Bolivia v Argentina 3–1; Peru v Argentina 1–0; Bolivia v Peru 2–1; Peru v Bolivia 3–0; Argentina v Bolivia 1–0; Argentina v Peru 2–2

	P	W	D	L	F	A	Pts
Peru	4	2	1	1	7	4	5
Bolivia	4	2	0	2	5	6	4
Argentina	4	1	1	2	4	6	3

Peru qualified

Group 11 (Brazil, Paraguay, Colombia, Venezuela)

Colombia v Venezuela 3–0; Venezuela v Colombia 1–1; Colombia v Brazil 0–2; Venezuela v Paraguay 0–2; Colombia v Paraguay 0–1; Venezuela v Brazil 0–5; Paraguay v Brazil 0–3; Brazil v Colombia 6–2; Paraguay v Venezuela 1–0; Brazil v Venezuela 6–0; Paraguay v Colombia 2–1; Brazil v Paraguay 1–0

	P	W	D	L	F	A	Pts
Brazil	6	6	0	0	23	2	12
Paraguay	6	4	0	2	6	5	8
Colombia	6	1	1	4	7	12	3
Venezuela	6	0	1	5	1	18	1

Brazil qualified

Group 12 (Uruguay, Chile, Ecuador)

Ecuador v Uruguay 0–2; Chile v Uruguay 0–0; Uruguay v Ecuador 1–0; Chile v Ecuador 4–1; Ecuador v Chile 1–1; Uruguay v Chile 2–0

	P	2	D	L	F	A	Pts
Uruguay	4	3	1	0	5	0	7
Chile	4	1	2	1	5	4	4
Ecuador	4	0	1	3	2	8	1

Uruguay qualified

CONCACAF

Group 13 (Honduras, Costa Rica, Jamaica, Haiti, Guatemala, Trinidad, El Salvador, Surinam, Netherlands Antilles, USA, Canada, Bermuda)

Sub-Group A

Costa Rica v Jamaica 3–0; Jamaica v Costa Rica 1–3; Honduras v Jamaica 3–1; Jamaica v Honduras 0–2; Honduras v Costa Rica 1–0; Costa Rica v Honduras 1–1

	P	W	D	L	F	A	Pts
Honduras	4	3	1	0	7	2	7
Costa Rica	4	2	1	1	7	3	5
Jamaica	4	0	0	4	2	11	0

Sub-Group B

Guatemala v Trinidad 4–0; Trinidad v Guatemala 0–0; Trinidad v Haiti 0–4; Haiti v Trinidad 2–4; Haiti v Guatemala 2–0; Guatemala v Haiti 1–1

	P	W	D	L	F	A	Pts
Haiti	4	2	1	1	9	5	5
Guatemala	4	1	2	1	5	3	4
Trinidad	4	1	1	2	4	10	3

Sub-Group C

Surinam v Netherlands Antilles 6–0; El Salvador v Surinam 6–0; Netherlands Antilles v Surinam 2–0; El Salvador v Netherlands Antilles 1–0; Netherlands Antilles v El Salvador 1–2; Surinam v El Salvador 4–1

	P	W	D	L	F	A	Pts
El Salvador	4	3	0	1	10	5	6
Surinam	4	2	0	2	10	9	4
Netherlands Antilles	4	1	0	3	3	9	2

Sub-Group D

Canada v Bermuda 4–0; Canada v USA 4–2; Bermuda v Canada 0–0; USA v Canada 1–0; USA v Bermuda 6–2; Bermuda v USA 0–2

	P	W	D	L	F	A	Pts
USA	4	3	0	1	11	6	6
Canada	4	2	1	1	8	3	5
Bermuda	4	0	1	3	2	12	1

2nd Round

Haiti v USA 2–0, 1–0; Honduras v El Salvador 1–0, 0–3
Play-off (in Mexico City): El Salvador v Honduras 3–2

3rd Round

Haiti v El Salvador 1–2, 3–0
Play-off (in Kingston): El Salvador v Haiti 1–0
El Salvador qualified

Group 14 (Mexico)

Mexico qualified as hosts

Asia/Oceania

Group 15 (Australia, South Korea, Japan, Rhodesia, Israel, New Zealand)

Sub-Group A (in Seoul)

Australia v Japan 3–1; South Korea v Japan 2–2; Australia v South Korea 2–1; Japan v Australia 1–1; South Korea v Japan 2–0; South Korea v Australia 1–1

	P	W	D	L	F	A	Pts
Australia	4	2	2	0	7	4	6
South Korea	4	1	2	1	6	5	4
Japan	4	0	2	2	4	8	2

Sub-Group B (in Tel Aviv)
North Korea eliminated for refusing to play Israel
Israel v New Zealand 4–0, 2–0

2nd Round (in Lourenco Marques)
Australia v Rhodesia 1–1, 0–0
Play-off: Australia v Rhodesia 3–1

Final Round
Israel v Australia 1–0, 1–1
Israel qualified

Africa

Group 16 (Algeria, Tunisia, Nigeria, Cameroon, Ghana (bye), Morocco, Senegal, Libya, Ethiopia, Zambia, Sudan)
Morocco v Senegal 1–0, 1–2; Play-off (in Las Palmas): Morocco v Senegal 2–0; Algeria v Tunisia 1–2, 0–0; Libya v Ethiopia 2–0, 1–5; Zambia v Sudan 4–2, 2–4 (Sudan winners by scoring more goals in second match); Nigeria v Cameroon 1–1, 3–2

Second Round
Tunisia v Morocco 0–0, 0–0; Play-off: Morocco v Tunisia 2–2 (Morocco won on toss of coin); Ethiopia v Sudan 1–1, 1–3; Nigeria v Ghana 2–1, 1–1

Final Round
Nigeria v Sudan 2–2; Morocco v Nigeria 2–1; Sudan v Nigeria 3–3; Sudan v Morocco 0–0; Morocco v Sudan 3–0; Nigeria v Morocco 2–0

	P	W	D	L	F	A	Pts
Morocco	4	2	1	1	5	3	5
Nigeria	4	1	2	1	8	7	4
Sudan	4	0	3	1	5	8	3

Morocco qualified

1970 MEXICO 31 May–21 June

QUALIFIERS

Belgium	Mexico
Brazil	Morocco
Bulgaria	Peru
Czechoslovakia	Romania
El Salvador	Sweden
England	Uruguay
Israel	USSR
Italy	West Germany

Mexico, only two years earlier hosts to the Olympic Games, now welcomed the participating nations for the ninth World Cup. This time FIFA by allowing the Asian and African continents a qualifying competition ensured a truly global entry. As for the Europeans, they were concerned over the heat and high altitude, which would place them at a disadvantage. Many arrived early in order to acclimatize to the conditions.

Group C at Guadalajara was clearly the strongest of the four, with England the holders and Brazil the favourites drawn along with the robust Romanians, who had surprisingly eliminated Eusebio's Portugal, and Czechoslovakia, so often tough customers in tournament football. England were optimistic; the World Champions still included the commanding influence of Moore, Peters and Hurst, his West Ham United colleagues Banks, the indefatigable Ball, and Bobby Charlton, full of grace and guile. They were, it was generally held, better equipped than in 1966. Brazil possessed in Pelé indisputably the world's finest player. Swearing after his suffering four years earlier never to play in the competition again, he was persuaded to change his mind, undoubtedly aided though by the selection of Zagalo, a former team-mate as coach. Jairzinho, Gerson and Tostao, all of whom had played a small part in England, had grown in stature, and the moustached Rivelino, a thunderous striker of the ball, completed a formidable attacking quintet.

What of Mexico? Drawn in Mexico City with familiar opponents in El Salvador, whose qualification had led to bloodshed, two points appeared certain, though their prospect of advancement relied on another result gained at the expense of the skilful Belgians, conquerors of Spain, and the powerful and organized USSR, with Byshovets, Voronin and the crafty Shesternev highly regarded as potential challengers.

Group B offered tiny Israel a tough debut, qualifying at the expense of Rhodesia, New Zealand and Australia after North Korea had withdrawn.

Uruguay and Italy, masters of denial, were tight in defence whilst seeking to exploit opponents' weakness, and their own encounter promised to be a dull one with potential for explosive violence and histrionics, though Italy, European Champions, had in Riva, Rivera and their captain Fachetti, players of the highest calibre. Sweden completed the line up at a Group to be played in the twin venues of Puebla and Toluca (almost 9000 feet above sea level). Back in the finals for the first time since finishing runners-up in 1958, they had removed both their neighbours Norway and a French side clearly in transition.

Finally to Group D and Leon, north of the capital, where Peru, to the chagrin of Argentina, had made it, on merit, for the first time since 1930. They were a neat attacking team managed by Didi, a Brazilian legend. Germany, with the now mature Franz Beckenbauer, the Bayern Goal Machine Gerd Müller and grizzled little veteran Uwe Seeler, were again a fine team, and it had been Scotland's misfortune to be drawn with them for qualification. Morocco, for Africa, were an unknown quantity, and Bulgaria, who to their credit had accounted for both Holland and Poland, joined them.

Group A

Venue: Mexico
Belgium
El Salvador
Mexico
USSR

Group B

Venues: Puebla, Toluca
Israel
Italy
Sweden
Uruguay

Group C

Venue: Guadalajara
Brazil
Czechoslovakia
England
Romania

Group D

Venue: Leon
West Germany
Peru
Morocco
Bulgaria

THE FIRST SERIES

On 31 May the Tournament kicked off before an enthusiastic media and a wildly excited Mexican public. At the Azteca Stadium in Mexico City the USSR were a tough assignment for the hosts. Predictably as an opening fixture, the game petered out into a tame, cautious draw. There were no goals and precious little entertainment for the 112,000 in attendance.

The Salvadorians' qualification, at the expense of neighbours and rivals

Honduras, sparked a violent and bloody conflict between the two, thus any joy at the tiny nation's participation was tempered by the suffering endured by the country's population. Opening their campaign against European opposition in Belgium, they defended stoutly but were quickly seen to be out of their depth. Belgium snatched an early lead through Van Moer and sauntered to victory, two second-half goals increasing their advantage to 3–0.

In Pueblo, Group B began with Uruguay facing the minnows from Israel. With no need to demonstrate the darker side of their game, the skilful Uruguayans won at a canter. Sweden and Italy played at the giddy height of Toluca, 8,792 feet above sea level. The atmosphere, unfamiliar to both teams, affected the pattern of play. Domenghini scored and the Italians won without looking overly impressive. Fatigue for both teams, however, had taken its toll long before the curtain came down.

England, facing Romania, won with something in hand at Guadalajara, Hurst's second-half strike proving decisive against stubborn, if limited, opponents. Meanwhile Brazil, also in Group C, demolished the Czechs with football of breathtaking extravagance. An early lead given to them by the talented Petras encouraged the Czechs, but thereafter, in spite of determined resistance, Brazil took command. Goals from Rivelino, Pelé and Jairzinho (twice) completed the rout; the favourites quite clearly were in fine form.

Peru, like El Salvador, arrived at the Tournament leaving behind them a nation affected by appalling tragedy. Thousands had died as an earthquake ravaged Lima, the country's capital, and a minute's silence was afforded the victims before their opening match in Leon against Bulgaria. The game itself proved to be exciting, the tough Bulgarians twice finding the net before the interval. Peru, however, fought back; defensively naïve, their inventive attacking play pivoted by the outstanding Cubillas earned them three goals and an unlikely victory to head Group D.

West Germany, the runners-up of 1966, opened their account against Morocco, the first African qualifiers for thirty-six years, and won – just. Taking the lead, the Moroccans displayed considerable skill, until the Germans equalized and then snatched their victory in the closing moments through the predatory Gerd Müller.

THE SECOND SERIES

In Mexico City, now in the second round of matches, the unfortunate men from El Salvador were clinging to parity then suffered from a dreadful piece of refereeing that somehow allowed Mexico to score from a free kick that belonged to their opponents! Incensed, the Salvadorans hoofed the resultant kick off into the crowd, and despite trailing 1–0 at half-time, capitulated to a dismal 4–0 defeat amidst scenes of protracted petulance.

Russia for their part beat Belgium with surprising and consummate ease 4–1, Dynamo Kiev's Anatol Byshovets scoring twice. The meeting of Uruguay and Italy quite typically was a 0–0 draw as the two masters of defensive football played cautiously, neither willing to commit numbers to attack and both apparently content with a point. Sweden and Israel in Toluca desperately needed a win, though neither got it. Sweden took the lead but allowed the plucky Israelis an equalizer that their gallant effort deserved, Spiegler, a persistent centre forward, gaining reward for his endeavours.

In Guadalajara the Group C matches recommenced, and a penalty kick by Dumitrache ensured Romania a 2–1 win over Czechoslovakia, though Petras, the clever Czech forward, scored again and enjoyed his uniquely theatrical celebration.

England and Brazil met in withering heat at the Jalisco stadium, two heavyweights of world football in a titanic struggle. It proved an absorbing give and take contest; Banks denied Pelé with an astonishing save before Pelé astutely picked out Jairzinho's run, the winger driving home decisively. For England there were still opportunities to salvage a point, but Astle, the West Bromwich centre forward, and Alan Ball squandered them wastefully. England had lost, but in temperatures touching 100 °F they had merely been unfortunate. For them all was not yet lost.

Group D in Leon saw Morocco again make nuisances of themselves. Uninhibited by the fierce sunshine, they chased and harried the Peruvians, who relied on a late rally inspired by Cubillas to see them through. However, the score, 3–0, did no justice at all to the brave Africans.

West Germany met Bulgaria, fell behind and then dominated thoroughly, winning at a canter 5–2. With a game still to play, they had secured a quarter-final berth, Müller, the diminutive yet dynamic centre forward, providing three sharp goals.

Poor, hapless El Salvador, twice beaten, faced the formidable USSR in the final round of group matches. To their credit they restricted their opponents to two goals, both by Byshovets. But it was obvious that the Soviets were saving themselves for the sterner challenges ahead – here was a team with ambition.

THE THIRD SERIES

Finally, in Group A, Mexico and Belgium witnessed another dubious decision in favour of the hosts, this one giving them a penalty kick that saw them narrowly through at the intimidating Azteca Stadium. Belgium staged a fierce though unsuccessful revival and went out protesting their harsh treatment. Mexico had qualified but not without difficulty.

Sweden in Group B desperately needed a comprehensive victory against

Uruguay for further progress. Sadly their 1–0 win was not enough. Surprisingly, the South Americans with all the talent at their disposal nervously packed their defence and showed the ugly, sterile tactics for which they were renowned. Still, they were through to a meeting in Mexico City with the dangerous Soviets. Italy, not unexpectedly, joined them, but this result was hardly glorious, as they laboured to another 0–0 draw, this time with the gallant Israelis in a lamentably dreary affair. Group B in six matches had provided the patrons of Puebla and Toluca with just six goals and precious little excitement.

Brazil confirmed their status as favourites in sweeping aside the challenge of Romania: Pelé scored twice and then Jairzinho. In holding them courageously to 3–2, Romania offered hope to the rest. Irresistible going forward, there remained a question mark over their ability to defend. Although England also secured a passage to the last eight, it was an uninspired team that defeated the Czechoslovakians, Allan Clarke, the Leeds United player, converting a penalty kick for a dour 1–0 win over disappointed and dejected opponents.

In Group D both Peru and West Germany, already through, contested top place. The Germans, superbly marshalled by Beckenbauer, won the day, and Müller, the phenomenally prolific striker, remarkably completed a second successive hat-trick. Peru scored but their 3–1 defeat condemned them to the cauldron that was Guadalajara where Zagalo's Brazil awaited them.

Disappointingly for the spectators in Leon, the concluding group match was played between Morocco and Bulgaria. While the Africans finally earned a point, the 1–1 draw was scant reward for their courageous effort. Yet they had represented their continent with great aplomb. The Bulgarians had flattered to deceive and failed again. Consistent qualifiers now, they had yet to win a match in three World Cup finals, and had staged an occasionally exciting, though once again unsuccessful, campaign.

Final Tournament – Mexico

Group A

Mexico (0) **0, USSR** (0) **0**
31.5.70 MEXICO CITY
Mexico: Calderon, Peña, Pérez, Hernández, Lopez, Vantolra, Guzman, Pulido, Velarde (Munguia), Valdivia, Fragoso
USSR: Kavazashvili, Kaplichny, Lovchev, Logofet, Shesternev, Asatiani, Muntian, Serebrannikov (Puzach), Nodia (Khmelnitski), Byshovets, Evryushikhin
Referee: Tchenscher (West Germany)

Belgium (1) **3, El Salvador** (0) **0**
3.6.70 MEXICO CITY
Belgium: Piot, Heylens, Thissen, Dewalque, Dockx, Semmeling (Polleunis), Van Moer (2), Devrindt, Van Himst, Puis, Lambert (1 pen)
El Salvador: Magana, Rivas, Mariona, Osorio, Quintanilla, Rodriguez Lindo (Sermeno), Vasquez, Martinez, Cabezas, Aparicio, Manzano (Mendes C)
Referee: Radulescu (Romania)

USSR (1) **4, Belgium** (0) **1**
6.6.70 MEXICO CITY
USSR: Kavazashvili, Dzodzuashvili (Kiselev), Afonin, Shesternev, Khurtsilava, Kaplichny (Lovchev), Asatiani (1), Muntian, Byshovets (2), Evryushikhin, Khmelnitski (1)
Belgium: Piot, Heylens, Thissen, Dewalque, Jeck, Dockx, Semmeling, Van Moer, Van Himst, Puis, Lambert (1)
Referee: Scheurer (Switzerland)

Mexico (1) **4, El Salvador** (0) **0**
7.6.70 MEXICO CITY
Mexico: Calderon, Vantolra, Peña, Guzman, Pérez, Gonzalez, Munguia, Valdivia (2), Borja (Lopez then Basaguren (1)), Fragoso (1), Padilla
El Salvador: Magana, Rivas, Mariona, Osorio, Mendez C (Monge), Quintanilla, Rodriguez Lindo, Vasquez, Martinez, Cabezas, Aparicio (Mendez S)
Referee: Kandil (Egypt)

USSR (0) **2, El Salvador** (0) **0**
10.6.70 MEXICO CITY
USSR: Kavazashvili, Dzodzuashvili, Khurtsilava, Shesternev, Afonin, Kiselev (Asatiani), Serebrannikov, Muntian, Pusach (Evryushikhin), Byshovets (2), Khmelnitski
El Salvador: Magana, Rivas, Mariona, Castro, Osorio, Vasquez, Portillo, Cabezas (Aparicio), Rodriguez Lindo (Sermeno), Mendez S, Monge
Referee: Hormazabal (Chile)

Mexico (1) **1, Belgium** (0) **0**
11.6.70 MEXICO CITY
Mexico: Calderon, Vantolra, Guzman, Peña (1 pen), Pérez, Pulido, Gonzalez, Munguia, Padilla, Valdivia (Basaguren), Fragoso
Belgium: Piot, Heylens, Thissen, Dewalque, Jeck, Dockx, Semmeling, Van Moer, Van Himst, Puis, Polleunis (Devrindt)
Referee: Coerezza (Argentina)

	P	W	D	L	F	A	Pts
USSR	3	2	1	0	6	1	5
Mexico	3	2	1	0	5	0	5
Belgium	3	1	0	2	4	5	2
El Salvador	3	0	0	3	0	9	0

Group B

Uruguay (1) **2, Israel** (0) **0**
2.6.70 PUEBLA
Uruguay: Mazurkiewicz, Ubinas, Ancheta, Matosas, Mujica (1), Montero Castillo, Rocha (Cortes), Maneiro (1), Cubilla, Esparrago, Losada
Israel: Vissoker, Schwager, Rosen, Rosenthal, Primo, Spiegel, Shum, Spiegler, Talbi (Bar), Faygenbaum, Rom (Vollach)
Referee: Davidson (Scotland)

Italy (1) **1, Sweden** (0) **0**
3.6.70 TOLUCA
Italy: Albertosi, Burgnich, Facchetti, Cera, Niccolai (Rosato), Bertini, Riva, Domenghini (1), Mazzola, Di Sisti, Boninsegna
Sweden: Hellström, Axelsson, Nordqvist, Grip, Svensson, Bo Larsson (Nicklasson), Eriksson (Ejderstedt), Kindvall, Grahn, Cronqvist, Olsson
Referee: Taylor (England)

Uruguay (0) **0, Italy** (0) **0**
6.6.70 PUEBLA
Uruguay: Mazurkiewicz, Ancheta, Matosas, Ubinas, Montero Castillo, Mujica, Cubilla, Esparrago, Maneiro, Bareño (Zubia), Cortes
Italy: Albertosi, Burgnich, Facchetti, Cera, Rosato, Bertini, Riva, Domenghini (Furino), Mazzola, De Sisti, Boninsenga
Referee: Glöckner (East Germany)

Sweden (0) **1, Israel** (0) **1**
7.6.70 TOLUCA
Sweden: Larsson S G, Selander, Axelsson, Olsson, Grip, Svensson, Bo Larsson, Nordahl, Kindvall, Persson (Palsson), Turesson (1)
Israel: Vissoker, Bar, Schwager, Rosen, Rosenthal, Primo, Spiegel, Vollach (Schuruk), Spiegler (1), Faygenbaum, Shum
Referee: Tarekegn (Ethiopia)

Sweden (0) **1, Uruguay** (0) **0**
10.6.70 PUEBLA
Sweden: Larsson S G, Selander, Axelsson, Nordqvist, Grip, Svensson, Bo Larsson, Eriksson, Kindvall (Turesson), Persson, Nicklasson (Grahn (1))
Uruguay: Mazurkiewicz, Ancheta, Matosas, Ubinas, Montero Castillo, Mujica, Esparrago (Fontes), Maneiro, Zubia, Cortes, Losada
Referee: Landauer (USA)

Italy (0) **0, Israel** (0) **0**
11.6.70 TOLUCA
Italy: Albertosi, Burgnich, Facchetti, Cera, Rosato, Bertini, Riva, Domenghini (Rivera), Mazzola, De Sisti, Boninsegna
Israel: Vissoker, Bar, Bello, Primo, Rosen, Rosenthal, Shum, Spiegel, Faygenbaum (Rom), Spiegler, Schwager
Referee: De Moraes (Brazil)

	P	W	D	L	F	A	Pts
Italy	3	1	2	0	1	0	4
Uruguay	3	1	1	1	2	1	3
Sweden	3	1	1	1	2	2	3
Israel	3	0	2	1	1	3	2

Group C

England (0) **1, Romania** (0) **0**
2.6.70 GUADALAJARA
England: Banks, Newton (Wright), Cooper, Mullery, Labone, Moore, Lee (Osgood), Ball, Hurst (1), Charlton R, Peters
Romania: Adamache, Satmareanu, Lupescu, Dinu, Mocanu, Dimitru, Tataru (Neagu), Nunweiler, Dembrovschi, Dumitrache, Lucescu
Referee: Loraux (Belgium)

Brazil (1) **4, Czechoslovakia** (1) **1**
3.6.70 GUADALAJARA
Brazil: Felix, Carlos Alberto, Brito, Piazza, Everaldo, Clodoaldo, Gerson (Paulo Cesar), Rivelino (1), Jairzinho (2), Tostao, Pelé (1)
Czechoslovakia: Viktor, Dobias, Migas, Horvath, Hagara, Kuna, Hrdlicka (Kvasnak), Vesely F (Vesely B), Petras (1), Adamec, Jokl
Referee: Barreto (Uruguay)

Romania (0) **2, Czechoslovakia** (1) **1**
6.6.70 GUADALAJARA
Romania: Adamache, Satmareanu, Dinu, Lupescu, Mocanu, Dumitru (Ghergeli), Nunweiler, Dembrovschi, Neagu (1), Dumitrache (1 pen), Lucescu (Tataru)
Czechoslovakia: Vencel, Dobias, Migas, Horvath, Ziocha, Kuna, Kvasnak, Vesely B, Jurkanin (Adamec), Petras (1), Jokl (Vesely F)
Referee: De Leo (Mexico)

Brazil (1) **1, England** (0) **0**
7.6.70 GUADALAJARA
Brazil: Felix, Carlos Alberto, Brito, Piazza, Everaldo, Clodoaldo, Paulo Cesar, Rivelino, Jairzinho (1), Tostao (Roberto), Pelé
England: Banks, Wright, Cooper, Mullery, Labone, Moore, Lee (Bell), Ball, Charlton R (Astle), Hurst, Peters
Referee: Klein (Israel)

Brazil (2) **3, Romania** (1) **2**
10.6.70 GUADALAJARA
Brazil: Felix, Carlos Alberto, Brito, Fontana, Everaldo (Marco Antonio), Clodoaldo (Edu), Piazza, Paulo Cesar, Jairzinho (1), Tostao, Pelé (2)
Romania: Adamache (Raducanu), Satmareanu, Lupescu, Dinu, Mocanu, Dumitru, Nunweiler, Dembrovschi (1), Lucescu, Neagu, Dumitrache (1) (Tataru)
Referee: Marshall (Austria)

England (0) **1, Czechoslovakia** (0) **0**
11.6.70 GUADALAJARA
England: Banks, Newton, Cooper, Mullery, Carlton J, Moore, Bell, Clarke (1 pen), Astle (Osgood), Charlton R (Ball), Peters
Czechoslovakia: Viktor, Dobias, Hrivnak, Migas, Hagara, Pollak, Kuna, Vesely F, Petras, Adamec, Capkovic (Jokl)
Referee: Machin (France)

	P	W	D	L	F	A	Pts
Brazil	3	3	0	0	8	3	6
England	3	2	0	1	2	1	4
Romania	3	1	0	2	4	5	2
Czechoslovakia	3	0	0	3	2	7	0

Group D

Peru (0) **3, Bulgaria** (1) **2**
2.6.70 LEON
Peru: Rubinos, Campos (Gonzalez J), De la Torre, Chumpitaz (1), Fuentes, Mifflin, Challe, Baylon (Sotil), Leon, Cubillas (1), Gallardo (1)
Bulgaria: Simeonov, Chalamanov, Dimitrov, Davidov, Aladjov, Penev, Bonev (1) (Asparoukhov), Yakimov, Popov (Marachliev), Jekov, Dermendiev (1)
Referee: Sbardella (Italy)

West Germany (0) **2, Morocco** (1) **1**
3.6.70 LEON
West Germany: Maier, Vogts, Schulz, Fichtel, Höttges (Löhr), Haller (Grabowski), Beckenbauer, Overath, Seeler (1), Müller (1), Held
Morocco: Allal, Abdallah, Boujemaa, Khannoussi, Silimani, Maaroufi, Bamous (Faras), El Filali, Said, Ghazouani (Khyati), Houmane (1)
Referee: Van Ravens (Netherlands)

Peru (0) **3, Morocco** (0) **0**
6.6.70 LEON
Peru: Rubinos, Gonzales P, De la Torre, Chumpitaz, Fuentes, Mifflin, Challe (1), Sotil, Leon, Cubillas (2), Gallardo (Ramirez)
Morocco: Allal, Abdallah, Boujemaa (Fadili), Khannoussi, Silimani, Maaroufi, Bamous, El Filali, Said (Alaoui), Ghazouani, Houmane
Referee: Bakhramov (USSR)

West Germany (2) **5, Bulgaria** (1) **2**
7.6.70 LEON
West Germany: Maier, Vogts, Fichtel, Schnellinger, Höttges, Seeler (1), Beckenbauer (Weber), Overath, Libuda (1), Müller (3, 1 pen), Löhr (Grabowski)
Bulgaria: Simeonov, Gaidarski, Jetchev, Nikodimov (1), Gaganelov (Chalamanov), Penev, Bonev, Kolev (1), Marachliev, Asparoukhov, Dermendiev (Mitkov)
Referee: De Mendibil (Spain)

West Germany (3) **3, Peru** (1) **1**
10.6.70 LEON
West Germany: Maier, Vogts, Fichtel, Schnellinger, Höttges (Patzke), Seeler, Beckenbauer, Overath, Libuda (Grabowski), Müller (3), Löhr
Peru: Rubinos, Gonzales P, De la Torre, Chumpitaz, Fuentes, Mifflin, Challe (Cruzado), Sotil, Leon (Ramirez), Cubillas (1), Gallardo
Referee: Aguilar (Mexico)

Bulgaria (1) **1, Morocco** (0) **1**
11.6.70 LEON
Bulgaria: Yordanov, Chalamanov, Penev (Dimitrov), Jetchev (1), Gaidarski, Kolev, Nikodimov, Yakimov (Bonev), Popov, Asparoukhov, Mitkov
Morocco: Hazzaz, Fadili, Silimani, Khannoussi, Boujemaa, Maaroufi, Bamous (Choukri), El Filali, Said, Alaoui (Faras), Ghazouani (1)
Referee: Saldanha (Portugal)

	P	W	D	L	F	A	Pts
West Germany	3	3	0	0	10	4	6
Peru	3	2	0	1	7	5	4
Bulgaria	3	0	1	2	5	9	1
Morocco	3	0	1	2	2	6	1

THE QUARTER-FINALS

At the Azteca, predictably, the USSR attacked and the Uruguayans defended, often en masse, their tough and uncompromising tactics succeeding in stifling the Soviets who could not score. In extra time the Europeans weakened significantly and Uruguay took full advantage, Esparrago rising to head a late and controversial winner, which in spite of furious protest was allowed. So the USSR, surprisingly, were eliminated, beaten as much by exhaustion brought on by heat and high altitude, as by the cautious and volatile Uruguayans.

Up in the clouds at Toluca, Mexico went out; stripped of their huge and passionate Mexico City support, they were no match at all for the Italians, who after falling behind to noisy and rapturous acclaim, dispatched them ruthlessly. Riva (twice), Rivera and Domenghini scored for a team who had previously found goals hard to come by, as ever the rigours of Tournament football increasing their resolve.

At Guadalajara, Brazil and Peru engaged typically in a wonderfully open game. Brazil again were the masters of their South American rivals but the match proved to be a little more difficult than expected, with a final result of 4–2. Jairzinho, who had scored in all three group matches, was amongst the scorers again. Peru throughout had distinguished themselves, playing delightful football, and in Cubillas they had a jewel.

In Leon high and extraordinary drama followed as England contrived to snatch defeat from the jaws of victory! Mullery first and then the dangerous Martin Peters established a two-goal advantage, which they held to the hour. Slowly but bravely the Germans fought back, and England, so thoroughly in command, lost the initiative. Beckenbauer first deceived Bonetti – Gordon Banks' understudy – with a drive from distance, and England succumbed to panic. Grabowski tormented them down the flanks, Seeler equalized, before, amidst the unbearable tension of extra time, Müller escaped his marker to hammer home a point-blank winner. England, who should have won, had thrown away their chance. Ramsey and his team suffered regret and recrimination, while the Germans enjoyed revenge and a second win against their great rivals.

Quarter-Finals

Uruguay (0) **1, USSR** (0) **0** (aet, 0–0 at 90 mins)
14.6.70 MEXICO CITY
Uruguay: Mazurkiewicz, Ancheta, Matosas, Ubinas, Montero Castillo, Mujica, Cubilla, Maneiro, Morales (Gomez), Fontes (Esparrago (1)), Cortes
USSR: Kavazashvili, Dzodzuashvili, Afonin, Shesternev, Khurtsilava (Logofet), Kaplichny, Asatiani (Kiselev), Muntian, Byshovets, Evryushikhin, Khmelnitzki
Referee: Van Ravens (Netherlands)

Italy (1) **4, Mexico** (1) **1**
14.6.70 TOLUCA
Italy: Albertosi, Burgnich, Facchetti, Cera, Rosato, Bertini, Riva (2), Domenghini (1) (Gori), Mazzola (Rivera (1)), De Sisti, Boninsegna
Mexico: Calderon, Vantolra, Guzman, Peña, Pérez, Pulido, Gonzalez (1) (Borja), Munguia (Diaz), Padilla, Valdivia, Fragoso
Referee: Scheurer (Switzerland)

Brazil (2) **4, Peru** (1) **2**
14.6.70 GUADALAJARA
Brazil: Felix, Carlos Alberto, Brito, Piazza, Marco Antonio, Clodoaldo, Gerson (Paulo Cesar), Rivelino (1), Jairzinho (1) (Roberto), Tostao (2), Pelé
Peru: Rubinos, Campos, Fernandez, Chumpitaz, Fuentes, Challe, Mifflin, Baylon (Sotil), Leon (Reyes), Cubillas (1), Gallardo (1)
Referee: Loraux (Belgium)

West Germany (0) **3, England** (2) **2** (aet, 2–2 at 90 mins)
14.6.70 LEON
West Germany: Maier, Vogts, Fichtel, Schnellinger, Höttges (Schulz), Seeler (1), Beckenbauer (1), Overath, Libuda (Grabowski), Müller (1), Löhr
England: Bonetti, Newton, Cooper, Mullery (1), Labone, Moore, Lee, Ball, Hurst, Charlton R (Bell), Peters (1) (Hunter)
Referee: Coerezza (Argentina)

THE SEMI-FINALS

The semi-final pitted together the starkly contrasting football cultures of Brazil and Uruguay. Brazil duly won, but in permitting their opponents an early goal they encouraged them into packed defence and crude, intimidating spoiling. Brazil persisted: Clodoaldo brought them level before the interval. Jairzinho scored another goal before Rivelino saw them through to another final. Uruguay, to the relief of most, had not been rewarded for their cynicism, and had been swept away by an altogether brighter force.

In Mexico City the two surviving European nations battled it out for the dubious privilege of a meeting with Brazil. Italy scored through the sprightly Boninsegna and elected to defend in depth. Germany conjured up another salvage operation, their astonishing resilience seeing them force a last minute draw through the veteran Hamburg striker Seeler. Into extra time an endurance test in the sunshine ensued as Gerd Müller fired the Germans ahead until Burgnich and Riva replied. Italy led 3–2. Germany summoned up another courageous effort, the remarkable Müller dragging them back to 3–3 before the whistle. With the normally elegant Beckenbauer hampered by a shoulder injury, Rivera of Milan struck the winner. German hearts and their resistance had been broken at last. So it was with wild celebration that Italy advanced to the final.

Semi-Finals

Italy (1) **4, West Germany** (0) **3** (aet, 1–1 at 90 mins)
17.6.70 MEXICO CITY
Italy: Albertosi, Burgnich (1), Facchetti, Cera, Rosato (Poletti), Bertini, Riva (1), Domenghini, Mazzola (Rivera (1)), De Sisti, Boninsegna (1)
West Germany: Maier, Vogts, Schnellinger (1), Schulz, Patzke (Held), Beckenbauer, Overath, Grabowski, Seeler, Müller (2), Löhr (Libuda)
Referee: Yamasaki (Peru)

Brazil (1) **3, Uruguay** (1) **1**
17.6.70 GUADALAJARA
Brazil: Felix, Carlos Alberto, Brito, Piazza, Everaldo, Clodoaldo (1), Gerson, Rivelino (1), Jairzinho (1), Tostao, Pelé
Uruguay: Mazurkiewicz, Ubinas, Ancheta, Matosas, Mujica, Montero Castillo, Maneiro (Esparrago), Cortes, Cubilla (1), Fontes, Morales
Referee: De Mendibil (Spain)

PLAY-OFF FOR THIRD PLACE

West Germany still had one final appointment with Uruguay to decide third place, and with changes in the line-up their tired team once more called upon seemingly bottomless reserves of spirit and energy. Remarkably, they won, Overath's single goal enough to ensure victory, though curiously Uruguay, relieved of pressure, played with a style and forcefulness hitherto unseen.

Match for Third Place

West Germany (1) **1, Uruguay** (0) **0**
20.6.70 MEXICO CITY
West Germany: Wolter, Patzke, Weber, Schnellinger (Lorenz), Fichtel, Vogts, Overath (1), Libuda (Löhr), Seeler, Müller, Held
Uruguay: Mazurkiewicz, Ubinas, Ancheta, Matosas, Mujica, Montero Castillo, Maneiro (Sandoval), Cortes, Cubilla, Fontes (Esparrago), Morales
Referee: Sbardella (Italy)

THE FINAL

The final was witnessed by a huge pro-Brazilian crowd at the magnificent Azteca stadium. Italy, the European Champions, expected to pack defence and conserve energy, were denied the opportunity when Pelé accepted an early and simple header after woeful marking for 1–0, and despite the alert Boninsegna latching on to Clodoaldo's careless crossfield back heel to fire home an equalizer, the die was cast. Brazil's irresistible talent and the European's fatigue combined to wear the Italians down. Italy's resolve cracked: first Gerson and then the irrepressible Jairzinho from close in made it 3–1. With just twenty minutes to play, hard though Italy tried, there was no way back. Dramatically, in the closing moments a goal to live in the memory. Italy pressing lost possession and the ball moved rhythmically upfield through seven Brazilians, culminating in Carlos Alberto sweeping a right foot shot past the bemused Dino Albertosi. Brazil were Champions and deservedly so, their victory achieved in such scintillating fashion that it was a triumph of skill over 'the dark ways' that had so dominated world football in the 1960s.

Final

Brazil (1) **4, Italy** (1) **1**
21.6.70 MEXICO CITY
Brazil: Felix, Carlos Alberto (1), Brito, Piazza, Everaldo, Clodoaldo, Gerson (1), Rivelino, Jairzinho (1), Tostao, Pelé (1)
Italy: Albertosi, Burgnich, Facchetti, Cera, Rosato, Bertini (Juliano), Riva, Domenghini, Mazzola, De Sisti, Boninsegna (1) (Rivera)
Referee: Glöckner (East Germany)

Back in England a feeling of what might have been prevailed. Blame was apportioned, largely at the unfortunate reserve goalkeeper Bonetti, and Ramsey was ridiculed for his tactical naiveté in substituting Charlton. The reality was that the Manchester United player, uncomfortable in the heat, was struggling and that England lost because they allowed a team with phenomenal determination a glimmer of hope and were outlasted in the withering conditions. Whatever the reason, however, a good Tournament was perhaps denied its great final.

CHAPTER 10

GERMANY

1974

Qualifying Tournament
99 entries
Brazil qualify as holders, West Germany qualify as hosts

Europe (33): Albania, Austria, Belgium, Bulgaria, Cyprus, Czechoslovakia, Denmark, England, Finland, France, East Germany, West Germany, Greece, Holland, Hungary, Iceland, Republic of Ireland, Northern Ireland, Italy, Luxembourg, Malta, Norway, Poland, Portugal, Romania, Scotland, Spain, Sweden, Switzerland, Turkey, USSR, Wales, Yugoslavia

South America (10): Argentina, Bolivia, Brazil, Chile, Colombia, Ecuador, Paraguay, Peru, Uruguay, Venezuela

CONCACAF (14): Antigua, Canada, Costa Rica, Guatemala, Haiti, Honduras, Jamaica, Mexico, Netherlands Antilles, Puerto Rico, El Salvador, Surinam, Trinidad and Tobago, USA

Asia/Oceania (19): Australia, Hong Kong, India, Indonesia, Iran, Iraq, Israel, Japan, North Korea, South Korea, Kuwait, Malaysia, New Zealand, Philippines, Sri Lanka, Syria, Thailand, United Arab Emirates, South Vietnam

Africa (23): Algeria, Cameroon, Congo, Dahomey, Egypt, Ethiopia, Gabon, Ghana, Guinea, Ivory Coast, Kenya, Lesotho, Madagascar, Mauritius, Morocco, Nigeria, Senegal, Sierra Leone, Sudan, Tanzania, Tunisia, Zaire, Zambia

Seven countries withdrew before the qualifying tournament began: Gabon, India, Jamaica, Madagascar, Philippines, Sri Lanka, Venezuela.

Europe

Group 1 (Austria, Sweden, Hungary, Malta)
Malta v Hungary 0–2, Austria v Malta 4–0, Hungary v Malta 3–0, Sweden v Hungary 0–0, Austria v Sweden 2–0, Sweden v Malta 7–0, Austria v Hungary 2–2, Malta v Austria 0–2, Hungary v Austria 2–2, Sweden v Austria 3–2, Hungary v Sweden 3–3, Malta v Sweden 1–2

	P	W	D	L	F	A	Pts
Sweden	6	3	2	1	15	8	8
Austria	6	3	2	1	14	7	8
Hungary	6	2	4	0	12	7	8
Malta	6	0	0	6	1	20	0

Play-off (in Gelsenkirchen): Austria v Sweden 1–2
Sweden qualified

Group 2 (Italy, Turkey, Switzerland, Luxembourg)
Luxembourg v Italy 0–4, Switzerland v Italy 0–0, Luxembourg v Turkey 2–0, Turkey v Luxembourg 3–0, Italy v Turkey 0–0, Turkey v Italy 0–1, Italy v Luxembourg 5–0, Luxembourg v Switzerland 0–1, Switzerland v Turkey 0–0, Switzerland v Luxembourg 1–0, Italy v Switzerland 2–0, Turkey v Switzerland 2–0

	P	W	D	L	F	A	Pts
Italy	6	4	2	0	12	0	10
Turkey	6	2	2	2	5	3	6
Switzerland	6	2	2	2	2	4	6
Luxembourg	6	1	0	5	2	14	2

Italy qualified

Group 3 (Holland, Belgium, Norway, Iceland)
Belgium v Iceland 4–0, Iceland v Belgium 0–4, Norway v Iceland 4–1, Norway v Belgium 0–2, Holland v Norway 9–0, Belgium v Holland 0–0, Iceland v Norway 0–4, Iceland v Holland 0–5, Holland v Iceland 8–1, Norway v Holland 1–2, Belgium v Norway 2–0, Holland v Belgium 0–0

	P	W	D	L	F	A	Pts
Holland	6	4	2	0	24	2	10
Belgium	6	4	2	0	12	0	10
Norway	6	2	0	4	9	16	4
Iceland	6	0	0	6	2	29	0

Holland qualified

Group 4 (East Germany, Romania, Finland, Albania)
Finland v Albania 1–0, Finland v Romania 1–1, East Germany v Finland 5–0, Romania v Albania 2–0, East Germany v Albania 2–0, Albania v Romania 1–4, Romania v East Germany 1–0, Finland v East Germany 1–5, East Germany v Romania 2–0, Albania v Finland 1–0, Romania v Finland 9–0, Albania v East Germany 1–4

	P	W	D	L	F	A	Pts
East Germany	6	5	0	1	18	3	10
Romania	6	4	1	1	17	4	9
Finland	6	1	1	4	3	21	3
Albania	6	1	0	5	3	13	2

East Germany qualified

Group 5 (Poland, England, Wales)

Wales v England 0–1, England v Wales 1–1, Wales v Poland 2–0, Poland v England 2–0, Poland v Wales 3–0, England v Poland 1–1

	P	W	D	L	F	A	Pts
Poland	4	2	1	1	6	3	5
England	4	1	2	1	3	4	4
Wales	4	1	1	2	3	5	3

Poland qualified

Group 6 (Bulgaria, Portugal, Northern Ireland, Cyprus)

Portugal v Cyprus 4–0, Cyprus v Portugal 0–1, Bulgaria v Northern Ireland 3–0, Cyprus v Bulgaria 0–4, Cyprus v Northern Ireland 1–0, Northern Ireland v Portugal 1–1, Bulgaria v Portugal 2–1, Northern Ireland v Cyprus 3–0 (at Fulham), Northern Ireland v Bulgaria 0–0, Portugal v Bulgaria 2–2, Portugal v Northern Ireland 1–1, Bulgaria v Cyprus 2–0

	P	W	D	L	F	A	Pts
Bulgaria	6	4	2	0	13	3	10
Portugal	6	2	3	1	10	6	7
Northern Ireland	6	1	3	1	5	6	5
Cyprus	6	1	0	5	1	14	2

Bulgaria qualified

Group 7 (Spain, Yugoslavia, Greece)

Spain v Yugoslavia 2–2, Yugoslavia v Greece 1–0, Greece v Spain 2–3, Spain v Greece 3–1, Yugoslavia v Spain 0–0, Greece v Yugoslavia 2–4

	P	W	D	L	F	A	Pts
Spain	4	2	2	0	8	5	6
Yugoslavia	4	2	2	0	7	4	6
Greece	4	0	0	4	5	11	0

Play-off (in Frankfurt): Spain v Yugoslavia 0–1
Yugoslavia qualified

Group 8 (Scotland, Czechoslovakia, Denmark)

Denmark v Scotland 1–4, Scotland v Denmark 2–0, Denmark v Czechoslovakia 1–1, Czechoslovakia v Denmark 6–0, Scotland v Czechoslovakia 2–1, Czechoslovakia v Scotland 1–0

	P	W	D	L	F	A	Pts
Scotland	4	3	0	1	8	3	6
Czechoslovakia	4	2	1	1	9	3	5
Denmark	4	0	1	3	2	13	1

Scotland qualified

Group 9 (USSR, Rep of Ireland, France)

France v USSR 1–0, Rep of Ireland v USSR 1–2, Rep of Ireland v France 2–1, USSR v Rep of Ireland 1–0, France v Rep of Ireland 1–1, USSR v France 2–0

	P	W	D	L	F	A	Pts
USSR	4	3	0	1	5	2	6
Rep of Ireland	4	1	1	2	4	5	3
France	4	1	1	2	3	5	3

Play-off with South American Group 3 winners
USSR v Chile 0–0
USSR disqualified by FIFA for refusing to play return leg in Santiago.
Chile qualified

South America

Group 1 (Uruguay, Colombia, Ecuador)

Colombia v Ecuador 1–1, Colombia v Uruguay 0–0, Ecuador v Colombia 1–1, Ecuador v Uruguay 1–2, Uruguay v Colombia 0–1, Uruguay v Ecuador 4–0

	P	W	D	L	F	A	Pts
Uruguay	4	2	1	1	6	2	5
Colombia	4	1	3	0	3	2	5
Ecuador	4	0	2	2	3	8	2

Uruguay qualified

Group 2 (Argentina, Paraguay, Bolivia)

Bolivia v Paraguay 1–2, Argentina v Bolivia 4–0, Paraguay v Argentina 1–1, Bolivia v Argentina 0–1, Paraguay v Bolivia 4–0, Argentina v Paraguay 3–1

	P	W	D	L	F	A	Pts
Argentina	4	3	1	0	9	2	7
Paraguay	4	2	1	1	8	5	5
Bolivia	4	0	0	4	1	11	0

Argentina qualified

Group 3 (Chile, Peru, Venezuela)
Venezuela withdrew
Peru v Chile 2–0, Chile v Peru 2–0
Play-off (in Montevideo): Chile v Peru 2–1

CONCACAF

Preliminary Round
Group 1
Canada v USA 3–2, Canada v Mexico 0–1, USA v Canada 2–2, Mexico v USA 3–1, Mexico v Canada 2–1, USA v Mexico 1–2

	P	W	D	L	F	A	Pts
Mexico	4	4	0	0	8	3	8
Canada	4	1	1	2	6	7	3
USA	4	0	1	3	6	10	1

Group 2
Guatemala v El Salvador 1–0, 1–0

Group 3
Honduras v Costa Rica 2–1, 3–3

Group 4
Netherlands Antilles v Jamaica (withdrew)

Group 5
Haiti v Puerto Rica 7–0, 5–0

Group 6
Surinam v Trinidad & Tobago 1–2, Trinidad & Tobago v Surinam 1–1, Surinam v Antigua 3–1, Antigua v Surinam 0–6, Trinidad & Tobago v Antigua 11–1, Antigua v Trinidad & Tobago 1–2

	P	W	D	L	F	A	Pts
Trinidad & Tobago	4	3	1	0	16	4	7
Surinam	4	2	1	1	11	4	5
Antigua	4	0	0	4	3	22	0

Final Round (in Haiti)

Honduras v Trinidad & Tobago 2–1, Mexico v Guatemala 0–0, Haiti v Netherlands Antilles 3–0, Mexico v Honduras 1–1, Haiti v Trinidad & Tobago 2–1, Guatemala v Netherlands Antilles 2–2, Haiti v Honduras 1–0, Mexico v Netherlands Antilles 8–0, Trinidad & Tobago v Guatemala 1–0, Netherlands Antilles v Honduras 2–2, Haiti v Guatemala 2–1, Trinidad & Tobago v Mexico 4–0, Honduras v Guatemala 1–1, Trinidad & Tobago v Netherlands Antilles 4–0, Mexico v Haiti 1–0

	P	W	D	L	F	A	Pts
Haiti	5	4	0	1	8	3	8
Trinidad & Tobago	5	3	0	2	11	4	6
Mexico	5	2	2	1	10	5	6
Honduras	5	1	3	1	6	6	5
Guatemala	5	0	3	2	4	6	3
Netherlands Antilles	5	0	2	3	4	19	2

Haiti qualified

Asia/Oceania

Preliminary Round (to determine Group composition)

South Vietnam v Thailand 1–0, Israel v Japan 2–1, Hong Kong v Malaysia 1–0, South Korea bye

Group A (in Seoul)
Sub-Group 1

Hong Kong v South Vietnam 1–0, Hong Kong v Japan 1–0, Japan v South Vietnam 4–0

	P	W	D	L	F	A	Pts
Hong Kong	2	2	0	0	2	0	4
Japan	2	1	0	1	4	1	2
South Vietnam	2	0	0	2	0	5	0

Sub-Group 2

Israel v Malaysia 3–0, Israel v Thailand 6–0, Israel v South Korea 0–0, South Korea v Thailand 4–0, South Korea v Malaysia 0–0, Malaysia v Thailand 2–0

	P	W	D	L	F	A	Pts
Israel	3	2	1	0	9	0	5
South Korea	3	1	2	0	4	0	4
Malaysia	3	1	1	1	2	3	3
Thailand	3	0	0	3	0	12	0

Semi-finals

South Korea v Hong Kong 3–1, Israel v Japan 1–0

Final

South Korea v Israel 1–0

Group B
Sub-Group 1 (in Australia)

New Zealand v Australia 1–1, Indonesia v New Zealand 1–1, Australia v Iraq 3–1, Iraq v New Zealand 2–0, Australia v Indonesia 2–1, Iraq v Indonesia 1–1, Australia v New Zealand 3–3, Indonesia v New Zealand 1–0, Australia v Iraq 0–0, Iraq v Indonesia 3–2, Iraq v New Zealand 4–0, Australia v Indonesia 6–0

	P	W	D	L	F	A	Pts
Australia	6	3	3	0	15	6	9
Iraq	6	3	2	1	11	6	8
Indonesia	6	1	2	3	6	13	4
New Zealand	6	0	3	3	5	12	3

Sub-Group 2 (in Tehran)

North Korea v Iran 0–0, Syria v Kuwait 2–1, Iran v Kuwait 2–1, North Korea v Syria 1–1, Iran v Syria 1–0, Kuwait v North Korea 0–0, North Korea v Iran 1–2, Syria v Kuwait 2–0, Iran v Kuwait 2–0, North Korea v Syria 3–0, Syria v Iran 1–0, Kuwait v North Korea 2–0

	P	W	D	L	F	A	Pts
Iran	6	4	1	1	7	3	9
Syria	6	3	1	2	6	6	7
North Korea	6	1	3	2	5	5	5
Kuwait	6	1	1	4	4	8	3

Final Matches
Australia v Iran 3–0, 0–2, Australia v South Korea 0–0, 2–2
Play-off (in Hong Kong): Australia v South Korea 1–0
Australia qualified

Africa

1st Round
Morocco v Senegal 0–0, 2–1, Algeria v Guinea 1–0, 1–5, Egypt v Tunisia 2–1, 0–2, Sierra Leone v Ivory Coast 0–1, 0–2, Kenya v Sudan 2–0, 0–1, Mauritius v Madagascar (withdrew), Ethiopia v Tanzania 0–0, 1–1, Play-off: Ethiopia v Tanzania 3–0, Lesotho v Zambia 0–0, 1–6, Nigeria v Congo 2–1, 1–1, Dahomey v Ghana 0–5, 1–5, Togo v Zaire 0–0, 0–4, Cameroon v Gabon (withdrew)

2nd Round
Kenya v Mauritius 3–1, 2–2, Guinea v Morocco 1–1, 0–2, Tunisia v Ivory Coast 1–1, 1–2, Ethiopia v Zambia 0–0, 2–4, Nigeria v Ghana 2–3 (abandoned), 0–0, (Nigeria disqualified from competition by FIFA Disciplinary Committee), Cameroon v Zaire 0–1, 1–0
Play-off: Zaire v Cameroon 2–0

3rd Round
Ivory Coast v Morocco 1–1, 1–4, Zambia v Kenya 2–0, 2–2, Ghana v Zaire 1–0, 1–4

Final Round
Zambia v Morocco 4–0, Zambia v Zaire 0–2, Zaire v Zambia 2–1, Morocco v Zambia 2–0, Zaire v Morocco 3–0, Morocco (withdrew) v Zaire (awarded game 2–0)

	P	W	D	L	F	A	Pts
Zaire	4	4	0	0	9	1	8
Zambia	4	1	0	3	5	6	2
Morocco	4	1	0	3	2	9	2

Zaire qualified

1974 GERMANY 13 June–7 July

QUALIFIERS

Argentina	Italy
Australia	Poland
Brazil	Scotland
Bulgaria	Sweden
Chile	Uruguay
East Germany	West Germany
Haiti	Yugoslavia
Holland	Zaire

As with Mexico four years earlier, the World Cup followed the route of the Olympic Games, this time to a German nation anxious to avoid a repetition of the tragic killing of athletes by terrorists in Munich's Olympic Village; security here would be paramount. The Tournament itself had been arranged again into four groups of four, though the knock-out stage had been dispensed with in favour of a further two groups into which eight teams would advance, the winners then contesting the final.

Group One featured the powerful host nation, formidable and deserved European Champions two years earlier, whose team included Beckenbauer, Müller, Overath and Grabowski, veterans all, and they were widely favoured. Opposing them were East Germany, qualified for the first time at the expense of Romania. Joining them were Chile, play-off victors over Peru and hoping to stem a series of depressing results in Europe, and fascinatingly Australia, here like the East Germans, making their debut, genuine football minnows who had accounted in qualification for the collective might of Iraq, Indonesia, New Zealand, Iran and South Korea, finally, after a decisive win in Hong Kong.

For Group Two, Brazil, so elegant in Mexico, were largely a new team with a new coach. Significantly Pelé, their talisman for so long, was absent. Scotland, playing first in Dortmund before moving to Frankfurt, complete with a contingent from the highly successful Leeds United club and the calming influence of Martin Buchan at the heart of their defence, would oppose them, qualifying courtesy of a 2–1 victory over Czechoslovakia after sixteen years in World Cup wilderness. Yugoslavia also had reason to be optimistic: they had triumphed over Spain in a Frankfurt play-off, curiously now the venue for them to open the competition, and in Dragan Dzajic they possessed one of Europe's most outstanding talents. Zaire, the 'Leopards', conquerors with surprising ease of Bali, Zambia and Morocco, represented Africa's interest, although their task in Group Two appeared mountainous.

In Group Three, Holland, fabulous aristocrats whose rise, built on the success of club sides Ajax and Feyenoord, had been meteoric, were a fine and flexible side. With the genius of Cruyff and Neeskens to inspire them, they were favoured by many, yet their qualification, oddly, was a close run thing, only goal difference separating them from neighbour and rivals Belgium. Bulgaria, still without a win in four successive tournaments, Uruguay, they of the fragile temperament, and the Swedes, talented and incisive, would be their challengers.

Group Four featured Italy, so close four years earlier and qualifying without conceding a goal in six matches; Poland, a dark horse, their enterprising new team having eliminated England; and Argentina, free now of their troublesome brood of 1966. The last of the four playing in this Stuttgart- and Munich-based group were remarkably Haiti, whose unlikely presence owed much to the Central American Qualification Tournament being staged on their island. They would need all the native magic they could muster.

Group 1

Venues: West Berlin, Hamburg
Australia
Chile
East Germany
West Germany

Group 3

Venues: Hanover, Düsseldorf, Dortmund
Bulgaria
Holland
Sweden
Uruguay

Group 2

Venues: Frankfurt, Dortmund, Gelsenkirchen
Brazil
Scotland
Yugoslavia
Zaire

Group 4

Venues: Stuttgart, Munich
Argentina
Haiti
Italy
Poland

THE FIRST SERIES

Frankfurt provided the backdrop for the Tournament's first match, Yugoslavia giving Brazil, the holders, a rugged examination of their credentials. Jairzinho and Rivelino, now approaching the veteran stage, were unable to provide a spark and were comfortably contained, resulting in a goal-less and uninspired draw. Scotland in the same Group Two faced tiny Zaire in Dortmund with the opportunity to seize the initiative. They won without difficulty but their two goals through Peter Lorimer and the menacing Joe Jordan, a constant aerial threat, were poor reward. Chances came and went, but 2–0 was all they could manage.

In Group One the Chileans in West Berlin faced the West Germans. An expectant nation urging them on, Chile surprisingly resisted early pressure, though they capitulated ultimately to a wonderful long-range effort from Germany's cavalier full back Paul Breitner. They had won, but the European Champions had failed to impress. Australia playing in Hamburg and taking the world stage for the first time proved strong and organized; here they frustrated their more sophisticated East German opponents until the Europeans finally broke them down. Benefiting from an own goal that calmed them, they had completed an unremarkable victory when Streich scored. Australia had proven themselves brave but limited.

In Group Three, Holland finally provided the Tournament with inspiration. The men in orange poured down on Uruguay, a side still horribly negative yet lacking the confidence or clever tactical guile of previous years. Rep scored twice as Cruyff and Neeskens in particular ran them ragged, the Dutch confirming themselves as an early favourite while the Uruguayans enhanced their reputation as a team prone to violence, Castillo being dismissed after an ugly confrontation with Rensenbrink.

Bulgaria and Sweden, meeting in Düsseldorf, played out a dull 0–0 draw, the Bulgarians, miserably mean, denying the more willing Swedes space; however, their physical endeavours and lack of ambition hinted at an inferiority complex.

Group Four and little Haiti representing Central America in their first World Cup faced the might of Italy in Munich. The Haitians, playing with great self-belief, took the lead, Sanon firing past Zoff and for Italy the spectre of North Korea loomed large. They forged their way back, holding their nerve, finding their form. The bold Haitians were beaten, Rivera instrumental, scoring one of Italy's three goals.

Poland kicked off in Stuttgart against Argentina, back on European soil and with a point to prove. The South Americans played with considerable skill, but Poland confirmed their reputation as a very fine side and edged them out 3–2, little Lato, so incisive, grabbing two goals.

THE SECOND SERIES

In Group Two the second round of matches saw Scotland and Brazil fight out a draw in Frankfurt. The Scots led by the dynamic Bremner chased and harried, creating chances to win the points. Still, they lent further weight to the growing suspicion that Brazil were an ageing and vulnerable team. The 'Leopards' of Zaire were annihilated in embarrassing fashion by a ruthless Yugoslavian team seizing on naive defending and intent on stealing an advantage over their Group rivals. Trailing 6–0 at the interval, the Africans at least saved themselves the indignity of defeat in double figures; 9–0, however, equalled the finals record.

Hamburg now welcomed their heroes as West Germany, though still showing disappointing form, won easily 3–0 against the muscular, hard-working Australians. Often faced with a wall of yellow shirts, it was a comfortable if dull win, and Müller, their predatory striker, opened his account. East Germany and Chile in the same group fought out a 1–1 draw in West Berlin of precious little interest, the East Germans in particular, faced with dogged opponents of limited ambition, failing singularly to take the initiative.

The tight, low-scoring cautious football dominating the Tournament prevailed again in Group Three, hardly surprising in the case of Bulgaria and Uruguay, whose typically brutal 1–1 draw seemed inevitable given the participants' reputations. Holland playing Sweden were deservedly held to 0–0, as the Scandinavians, ably led by the dangerous Edström, competed skilfully in a bright, open contest. Cruyff, Neeskens and their total football created chances but were quite unable to fashion a goal.

Haiti's bubble burst with allegations of drug abuse dominating the days proceeding their Group Four clash with Poland. They played dismally, defeated 7–0, the internal disruption clearly affecting morale against a Polish side prompted by Deyna who took full and clinical advantage of their low morale. Lato with two more and Szarmach, his able accomplice, scoring a hat-trick benefited most from the islanders' generosity.

Italy and Argentina, giants of the modern game, met at Stuttgart in Group Four, and the South Americans, losers to Poland, continued to impress with their commitment to attacking football. Italy, responding in kind, helped provide a satisfying spectacle. Houseman, a fine player, scored for Argentina, but the unfortunate Perfumo gifted Italy an own goal equalizer for 1–1.

THE THIRD SERIES

Group One in Hamburg played amidst high level security. National pride burned fiercely, West meeting East, and all of Germany watched with bated breath. Sadly the players could not respond as the occasion demanded and the game became a drab, tepid affair. The West Germans, stewarded by the majestic Beckenbauer, probed gently, and the East Germans closed ranks and waited, though despite Kreische's attempt, the best opportunity came and went. The pattern continued until, undeservedly, the East stole a late winner through Sparwasser. Schoen, the wily, grizzled West German coach, faced the wrath of the press, his team castigated, but whilst no one dared suggest collusion, defeat undoubtedly gave them an easier passage to the final.

Australia in their final game were allowed to play more enterprisingly, and did their best to lift the spirits of a small West Berlin crowd and in doing so achieved a point against Chile, who had once again proven unable to rise to the challenge of a World Cup. They had fallen far since 1962.

In Group Two, Scotland suffered huge disappointment as they fell behind to the Yugoslavs when Karasi scored. With characteristic grit Scotland hauled themselves back through Jordan, but now cast anxious looks at the Press Box for clues as to the Brazil–Zaire game. Playing in Gelsenkirchen, a shell-shocked Zaire lost to Brazil, thus dashing the slim hopes of the Scots. Brazil, nervous at first, won easily by 3–0 and Scotland were eliminated – strangely without losing. Curiously, as the South Americans applied pressure, there was the extraordinary sight of an African bursting out of their defensive wall to hammer the ball placed for a free kick upfield whilst bemused Brazilians looked on. The culprit received a yellow card and Zaire were dismissed.

In Group Three brain satisfyingly outwitted brawn when the Dutch sauntered into the next stage playing assured and mesmerizing football against an increasingly dejected and disjointed Bulgarian team. Altogether too good, Holland with their fast, mobile football scored four, Neeskens, a wonderful midfield player, responsible for two of them. They were a team to avoid. Sweden, too, swept through as their attacking potential finally bore dividends, their 3–0 victory ejecting a shockingly undisciplined and destructive Uruguayan team who handed out bruises with impunity.

Poland, with two wins and certain of progress from Group Four, beat Italy 2–1 with something in hand, and the 'Azzurri' consequently were eliminated. Their team had been ineffective and unlike the 1970 vintage, unable to rise to the challenges presented to them. Argentina, left to dispatch Haiti for a place in the next round, predictably did so by 4–1; they were an improving team. Haiti, following the debacle after the Italy match, patently were not.

Final Tournament – West Germany
First round

Group 1

West Germany (1) **1, Chile** (0) **0**
14.6.74 WEST BERLIN
West Germany: Maier, Vogts, Schwarzenbeck, Beckenbauer, Breitner (1), Hoeness, Cullmann, Overath (Hölzenbein), Grabowski, Müller, Heynckes
Chile: Vallejos, Garcia, Figueroa, Quintano, Arias, Valdes (Veliz), Rodriguez (Lara), Reinoso, Caszely, Ahumada, Paez
Referee: Babacan (Turkey)

East Germany (0) **2, Australia** (0) **0**
14.6.74 HAMBURG
East Germany: Croy, Kische, Bransch, Weise, Wätzlich, Sparwasser, Irmscher, Pommerenke, Löwe (Hoffmann), Streich (1), Vogel
Australia: Reilly, Utjesenovic, Schafer, Wilson, Curran (o.g.), Richards, Mackay, Rooney, Warren, Alston, Buljevic
Referee: N'Diaye (Senegal)

West Germany (2) **3, Australia** (0) **0**
18.6.74 HAMBURG
West Germany: Maier, Vogts, Schwarzenbeck, Beckenbauer, Breitner, Hoeness, Cullmann (1) (Wimmer), Overath (1), Grabowski, Müller (1), Heynckes (Hölzenbein)
Australia: Reilly, Utjesenovic, Schafer, Wilson, Curran, Richards, Rooney, Mackay, Campbell (Abonyi), Alston, Buljevic (Ollerton)
Referee: Kamel (Egypt)

Chile (0) **1, East Germany** (0) **1**
18.6.74 WEST BERLIN
Chile: Vallejos, Garcia, Figueroa, Quintano, Arias, Valdes (Yavar), Reinoso, Paez, Socias (Farias), Ahumada (1), Veliz
East Germany: Croy, Kische, Bransch, Weise, Wätzlich, Seguin (Kreische), Irmscher, Sparwasser, Hoffmann (1), Streich, Vogel (Ducke)
Referee: Angonese (Italy)

Australia (0) **0, Chile** (0) **0**
22.6.74 WEST BERLIN
Australia: Reilly, Utjesenovic, Wilson, Schafer, Curran (Williams), Richards, Rooney, Mackay, Abonyi, Alston (Ollerton), Buljevic
Chile: Vallejos, Garcia, Quintano, Figueroa, Arias, Paez, Caszely, Reinoso, Valdes (Farias), Ahumada, Veliz (Yavar)
Referee: Namdar (Iran)

East Germany (0) **1, West Germany** (0) **0**
22.6.74 HAMBURG
East Germany: Croy, Kische, Weise, Bransch, Wätzlich, Lauck, Irmscher (Hamann), Kreische, Kurbjuweit, Sparwasser (1), Hoffmann
West Germany: Maier, Vogts, Schwarzenbeck (Höttges), Beckenbauer, Breitner, Hoeness, Cullmann, Overath (Netzer), Grabowski, Müller, Flohe
Referee: Barreto (Uruguay)

	P	W	D	L	F	A	Pts
East Germany	3	2	1	0	4	1	5
West Germany	3	2	0	1	4	1	4
Chile	3	0	2	1	1	2	2
Australia	3	0	1	2	0	5	1

Group 2

Yugoslavia (0) **0, Brazil** (0) **0**
13.6.74 FRANKFURT
Yugoslavia: Maric, Buljan, Katalinski, Bogicevic, Hadziabdic, Muzinic, Oblak, Acimovic, Petkovic, Surjak, Dzajic
Brazil: Leao, Nelinho, Mario Marinho, Pereira, Francesco Marinho, Piazza, Rivelino, Paulo Cesar L, Valdomiro, Jairzinho, Leivinha
Referee: Scheurer (Switzerland)

Scotland (2) **2, Zaire** (0) **0**
14.6.74 DORTMUND
Scotland: Harvey, Jardine, McGrain, Bremner, Holton, Blackley, Dalglish (Hutchison), Hay, Lorimer (1), Jordan (1), Law
Zaire: Kazadi, Mwepu, Mukombo, Buhanga, Lobilo, Kilasu, Myanga (Kembo), Mana, Ndaye, Kidumu (Kibonge), Kakoko
Referee: Schulenberg (West Germany)

Yugoslavia (6) **9, Zaire** (0) **0**
18.6.74 GELSENKIRCHEN
Yugoslavia: Maric, Buljan, Katalinski (1), Bogicevic (1), Hadziabdic, Acimovic, Oblak (1), Surjak (1), Petkovic (1), Bajevic (3), Dzajic (1)
Zaire: Kazadi (Tubilandu), Mwepu, Mukombo, Buhanga, Lobilo, Kilasu, Ndaye, Mana, Kembo, Kidumu, Kakoko (Myanga)
Referee: Delgado (Colombia)

Scotland (0) **0, Brazil** (0) **0**
18.6.74 FRANKFURT
Scotland: Harvey, Jardine, McGrain, Buchan, Holton, Bremner, Dalglish, Hay, Jordan, Lorimer, Morgan
Brazil: Leao, Nelinho, Pereira, Mario Marinho, Francesco Marinho, Piazza, Rivelino, Paulo Cesar L, Jairzinho, Mirandinha, Leivinha (Paulo Cesar C)
Referee: Van Gemert (Netherlands)

Brazil (1) **3, Zaire** (0) **0**
22.6.74 GELSENKIRCHEN
Brazil: Leao, Nelinho, Pereira, Mario Marinho, Francesco Marinho, Piazza (Mirandhina), Rivelino (1), Paulo Cesar C, Jairzinho (1), Leivinha (Valdomiro (1)), Edu
Zaire: Kazadi, Mwepu, Mukombo, Buhanga, Lobilo, Kibonge, Tshinabu (Kembo), Mana, Ntumba, Kidumu (Kilasu), Myanga
Referee: Rainea (Romania)

Yugoslavia (0) **1, Scotland** (0) **1**
22.6.74 FRANKFURT
Yugoslavia: Maric, Buljan, Katalinski, Bogicevic, Hadziabdic, Acimovic, Oblak, Surjak, Petkovic, Bajevic (Karasi (1)), Dzajic
Scotland: Harvey, Jardine, McGrain, Buchan, Holton, Bremner, Dalglish (Hutchison), Hay, Jordan (1), Lorimer, Morgan
Referee: Archundia (Mexico)

	P	W	D	L	F	A	Pts
Yugoslavia	3	1	2	0	10	1	4
Brazil	3	1	2	0	3	0	4
Scotland	3	1	2	0	3	1	4
Zaire	3	0	0	3	0	14	0

Group 3

Holland (1) **2, Uruguay** (0) **0**
15.5.74 HANOVER
Holland: Jongbloed, Suurbier, Rijsbergen, Haan, Krol, Jansen, Neeskens, Van Hanegem, Rep (2), Cruyff, Rensenbrink
Uruguay: Mazurkiewicz, Forlan, Masnik, Juaregui, Pavoni, Esparrago, Montero Castillo, Rocha, Cubilla (Milar), Morena, Mantegazza
Referee: Palotai (Hungary)

Sweden (0) **0, Bulgaria** (0) **0**
15.6.74 DÜSSELDORF
Sweden: Hellström, Olsson, Karlsson, Bo Larsson, Andersson, Grahn, Kindvall (Magnusson), Tapper, Torstensson, Sandberg, Edström
Bulgaria: Goranov, Vassilev Z, Ivkov, Penev, Velitschkov, Kolev, Bonev, Nikodimov, Voinov (Michailov), Panov (Vassilev M), Denev
Referee: Nunez (Peru)

Holland (0) **0, Sweden** (0) **0**
19.6.74 DORTMUND
Holland: Jongbloed, Suurbier, Rijsbergen, Haan, Krol, Jansen, Neeskens, Van Hanegem (De Jong), Rep, Cruyff, Keizer
Sweden: Hellström, Olsson (Grip), Andersson, Karlsson, Nordqvist, Tapper (Persson), Grahn, Bo Larsson, Ejderstadt, Edström, Sandberg
Referee: Winsemann (Canada)

Bulgaria (1) **1, Uruguay** (0) **1**
19.6.74 HANOVER
Bulgaria: Goranov, Vassilev Z, Ivkov, Penev, Velitschkov, Kolev, Bonev (1), Nikodimov (Michailov), Voinov, Panov, Denver
Uruguay: Mazurkiewicz, Forlan, Garrets (Masnik), Jauregui, Pavoni (1), Esparrago, Mantegazza (Cardaccio), Rocha, Milar, Morena, Corbo
Referee: Taylor (England)

Holland (2) **4, Bulgaria** (0) **1**
23.6.74 DORTMUND
Holland: Jongbloed, Suurbier, Rijsbergen, Haan, Krol (o.g.), Jansen, Neeskens (2) (De Jong (1)), Van Hanegem (Israël), Rep (1), Cruyff, Rensenbrink.
Bulgaria: Staikov, Vassilev Z, Ivkov, Penev, Velitschkov, Kolev, Bonev, Stoyanov (Michailov), Voinov, Panov (Borisov), Denev
Referee: Boskovic (Australia)

Sweden (0) **3, Uruguay** (0) **0**
23.6.74 DÜSSELDORF
Sweden: Hellström, Andersson, Nordqvist, Karlsson, Grip, Grahn, Kindvall (Torstensson), Bo Larsson, Magnusson (Ahlström), Edström (2), Sandberg (1)
Uruguay: Mazurkiewicz, Forlan, Garisto (Masnik), Jauregui, Pavoni, Esparrago, Mantegazza, Rocha, Milar, Morena, Corbo (Cubilla)
Referee: Linemayr (Australia)

	P	W	D	L	F	A	Pts
Holland	3	2	1	0	6	1	5
Sweden	3	1	1	0	3	0	4
Bulgaria	3	0	2	1	2	5	2
Uruguay	3	0	1	2	1	6	1

Group 4

Italy (0) **3, Haiti** (0) **1**
15.6.74 MUNICH
Italy: Zoff, Spinosi, Morini, Burgnich, Facchetti, Mazzola, Capello, Rivera (1),
Bennetti (1), Chinaglia (Anastasi (1)), Riva
Haiti: Francillon, Bayonne, Nazaire, Jean-Joseph, Auguste, Francois, Vorbe,
Desir, Antoine, Saint-Vil G (Barthelmy), Sanon (1)
Referee: Llobregat (Venezuela)

Poland (2) **3, Argentina** (0) **2**
15.6.74 STUTTGART
Poland: Tomaszewski, Szymanowski, Zmuda, Gorgón, Musial, Kasperczyk,
Maszczyk, Deyna, Lato (2), Szarmach (1) (Domarski), Gadocha (Cmikiewicz)
Argentina: Carnevali, Wolff, Perfumo, Heredia (1), Sa, Bargas (Telch), Brindisi
(Houseman), Babington (1), Balbuena, Ayala, Kempes
Referee: Thomas (Wales)

Poland (5) **7, Haiti** (0) **0**
19.6.74 MUNICH
Poland: Tomaszewski, Szymanowski, Zmuda, Gorgón (1), Musial (Gut),
Kasperczyk, Maszczyk (Cmikiewicz), Deyna (1), Lato (2), Szarmach (3)
Gadocha
Haiti: Francillon, Bayonne, Nazaire, Vorbe, Auguste, Francois, Desir, Andre
(Barthelmy), Sanon, Antoine, Saint-Vil R (Racine)
Referee: Suppiah (Singapore)

Argentina (1) **1, Italy** (1) **1**
19.6.74 STUTTGART
Argentina: Carnevali, Wolff (Glaria), Perfumo (o.g.), Heredia, Telch, Sa,
Houseman (1), Babington, Ayala, Kempes, Yazalde (Chazarreta)
Italy: Zoff, Spinosi, Morini (Wilson), Burgnich, Facchetti, Mazzola, Capello,
Rivera (Causio), Benetti, Riva, Anastasi
Referee: Kasakov (USSR)

Argentina (2) **4, Haiti** (0) **1**
23.6.74 MUNICH
Argentina: Carnevali, Wolff, Perfumo, Heredia, Sa, Telch, Houseman (1)
(Brindisi), Babington, Ayala (1), Kempes (Balbuena), Yazalde (2)
Haiti: Francillon, Ducoste, Bayonne, Nazaire (Leandre M), Louis, Vorbe, Desir,
Saint-Vil G (Leandre F), Antonine, Racine, Sanon (1)
Referee: Sanchez-Ibañez (Spain)

Poland (2) **2**, **Italy** (0) **1**
23.6.74 STUTTGART
Poland: Tomaszewski, Szymanowski, Zmuda, Gorgón, Musial, Kasperczyk, Maszczyk, Deyna (1), Lato, Szarmach (1) (Cmikiewicz), Gadocha
Italy: Zoff, Spinosi, Morini, Burgnich (Wilson), Facchetti, Mazzola, Benetti, Capello (1), Causio, Chinaglia (Boninsegna), Anastasi
Referee: Weyland (West Germany)

	P	W	D	L	F	A	Pts
Poland	3	3	0	0	12	3	6
Argentina	3	1	1	1	7	5	3
Italy	3	1	1	1	5	4	3
Haiti	3	0	0	3	2	14	0

FINAL POOLS

Group A   **Hanover, Gelsenkirchen, Dortmund**
East Germany   Winner Group 1
Brazil   Runner-up Group 2
Holland   Winner Group 3
Argentina   Runner-up Group 4

Group B   **Frankfurt, Düsseldorf, Stuttgart**
West Germany   Runner-up Group 1
Yugoslavia   Winner Group 2
Sweden   Runner-up Group 3
Poland   Winner Group 4

Arranged into two groups the final eight offered Poland, Yugoslavia, Sweden and West Germany in B. Meanwhile, Holland, Argentina and Brazil were to battle it out in a quite sensational Group A, along with the East Germans who clearly had not prospered from defeating their brothers from the west because it elevated them to the tougher group. The table toppers would advance to the final.

In Hanover, East Germany were given an immediate indication of the magnitude of their task. Pressured constantly, they defended with resolve but were finally undone by the elegant Rivelino, who powered home from a free kick the decisive goal. The victors Brazil, however, had tougher tests ahead, not least from Holland, who served notice of their credentials by crushing Argentina 4–0, Cruyff (with two), Rep and Krol scoring in an outstanding performance. Scoring first to ensure an open game, the Dutch overwhelmed the unfortunate South Americans.

Poland from Group B in Stuttgart, again through the artful Lato, scored and held their lead against the Swedes, but not without difficulty. Though unimpressive this time, the Poles, a strong, tactically adept team, were proving themselves an outstanding contender for the new trophy. Yugoslavia predictably found the task of taking on West Germany in Düsseldorf altogether too much, and were convincingly beaten by a now eager and determined team. So to East Germany: jubilant just a week earlier, they could not turn the trick a second time, and the multi-talented Dutch brushed them aside 2–0. In Group A, Argentina and Brazil, old rivals in unfamiliar settings, battled out a tense affair. Jairzinho, now a veteran, settled matters and ended the Argentinean interest, their final fixture rendered academic.

At Frankfurt, Deyna for Poland, an increasingly influential fixture in their meteoric rise, gave them an advantage against Yugoslavia in the next round of matches in B. However, this penalty kick was quickly equalized by Karasi, who had conceded it. The little figure of Lato saved the Poles once more, snatching a quite crucial winner. Sweden facing West Germany proved again their competitive instincts, taking the lead twice in a roller coaster Group B game in Düsseldorf.

Germany showed their familiar resilience in the face of adversity, clawing their way back and finally breaking the doughty Scandinavians' resistance. Undoubtedly Beckenbauer's side were beginning to achieve their best and most powerful form.

In the final Group A matches East Germany earned a deserved draw with Argentina in a game of little interest and precious little passion. The East Germans gained a sense of restored pride; as newcomers they had done exceedingly well. As for Argentina, they had at least gone some way to erasing the unpleasant memories of 1966, and as hosts four years on, they had the foundation of an enterprising and exciting team. Holland faced Brazil next in Dortmund, an eagerly anticipated clash that would decide the finalist from Group A. Sadly, threatened by a team of infinitely more talent than their own, the Brazilians pitched into Holland with an alarming commitment that startled their opponents. Often outside of the rules, the aggression appeared to work to a degree as the Dutch took stock and retaliated in kind and the game degenerated for a period into a spiteful and unpleasant affair. Slowly Holland composed themselves, however, and moved into their fluid, flexible passing game, bewildering a team who resorted increasingly to petulance and violent challenges. Neeskens and Cruyff broke them finally, each scoring from crisp movements. Pereira, Brazil's rugged central defender, was dismissed for one atrocity too many and Brazil went out ingloriously.

Sweden beat Yugoslavia in a match no longer with significance, 2–1. The Swedes had proven themselves a brave, first class outfit, and it was no coincidence either that they had taken part in some of the competition's better matches.

All eyes now turned to a rain-sodden Frankfurt stadium where in a delayed start on a heavy, waterlogged pitch Poland and West Germany contested the last match of Group B, the Germans in the enviable situation of knowing a draw would suffice. Poland tried hard to deny them, Lato inevitably a constant threat, but the Germans through Gerd Müller found the net first. It proved enough in a tense and unspectacular affair. Germany, however, was truly delighted: its team was through to their third final. Poland's had been a great achievement, as largely unfancied they had proven a revelation in coming so very close to the final itself.

Second Round

Group A

Brazil (0) **1, East Germany** (0) **0**
26.6.74 HANOVER
Brazil: Leao, Pereira, Ze Maria, Mario Marinho, Francesco Marinho, Rivelino (1), Paulo Cesar C, Paulo Cesar L, Valdomiro, Jairzinho, Dirceu
East Germany: Croy, Kische, Bransch, Weise, Wätzlich, Lauck (Löwe), Hamann (Irmscher), Kurbjuweit, Streich, Sparwasser, Hoffmann
Referee: Thomas (Wales)

Holland (2) **4, Argentina** (0) **0**
26.6.74 GELSENKIRCHEN
Holland: Jongbloed, Suurbier (Israël), Rijsbergen, Haan, Krol (1), Jansen, Neeskens, Van Hanegem, Rep (1), Cruyff (2), Rensenbrink
Argentina: Carnevali, Wolff (Glaria), Perfumo, Heredia, Sa, Telch, Balbuena, Squeo, Yazalde, Ayala, Houseman (Kempes)
Referee: Davidson (Scotland)

Holland (1) **2, East Germany** (0) **0**
30.6.74 GELSENKIRCHEN
Holland: Jongbloed, Suurbier, Rijsbergen, Haan, Krol, Jansen, Neeskens (1), Van Hanegem, Rep, Cruyff, Rensenbrink (1)
East Germany: Croy, Kische, Weise, Bransch, Kurbjuweit, Lauck (Kreische), Schnuphase, Sparwasser, Pommerenke, Löwe (Ducke), Hoffmann
Referee: Scheurer (Switzerland)

Brazil (1) **2, Argentina** (1) **1**
30.6.74 HANOVER
Brazil: Leao, Pereira, Ze Maria, Mario Marinho, Francesco Marinho, Rivelino
(1), Paulo Cesar C, Paulo Cesar L, Valdomiro, Jairzinho (1), Dirceu
Argentina: Carnevali, Glaria, Bargas, Heredia, Sa (Carrascosa), Brindisi (1),
Squeo, Babington, Balbuena, Ayala, Kempes (Houseman)
Referee: Loraux (Belgium)

Holland (0) **2, Brazil** (0) **0**
3.7.74 DORTMUND
Holland: Jongbloed, Suurbier, Rijsbergen, Haan, Krol, Jansen, Neeskens (1)
(Israël), Van Hanegem, Rep, Cruyff (1), Rensenbrink (De Jong)
Brazil: Leao, Pereira, Ze Maria, Mario Marinho, Francesco Marinho, Rivelino,
Paulo Cesar C, Paulo Cesar L (Mirandinha), Valdomiro, Jairzinho, Dirceu
Referee: Tschenscher (West Germany)

East Germany (1) **1, Argentina** (1) **1**
3.7.74 GELSENKIRCHEN
East Germany: Croy, Kische, Weise, Bransch, Kurbjuweit, Sparwasser,
Schnuphase, Pommerenke, Löwe (Vogel), Streich (1) (Ducke), Hoffmann
Argentina: Fillol, Wolff, Heredia, Bargas, Carrascosa, Telch, Brindisi,
Babington, Houseman (1), Ayala, Kempes
Referee: Taylor (England)

	P	W	D	L	F	A	Pts
Holland	3	3	0	0	8	0	6
Brazil	3	2	0	1	3	3	4
East Germany	3	0	1	2	1	4	1
Argentina	3	0	1	2	2	7	1

Group B

West Germany (1) **2, Yugoslavia** (0) **0**
26.6.74 DÜSSELDORF
West Germany: Maier, Vogts, Schwarzenbeck, Beckenbauer, Breitner (1),
Wimmer (Hoeness), Overath, Bonhof, Hölzenbein (Flohe), Müller (1), Herzog
Yugoslavia: Maric, Buljan, Katalinski, Muzinic, Hadziabdic, Oblak (Jerkovic),
Acimovic, Surjak, Popivoda, Karasi, Dzajic (Petkovic)
Referee: Marques (Brazil)

Poland (1) **1, Sweden** (0) **0**
26.6.74 STUTTGART
Poland: Tomaszewski, Gut, Gorgón, Szymanowski, Zmuda, Kasperczyk, Deyna, Maszczyk, Lato (1), Szarmach (Kmiecik), Gadocha
Sweden: Hellström, Andersson (Augustsson), Grip, Karlsson, Nordqvist, Bo Larsson, Torstensson, Tapper (Ahlström), Edström, Grahn, Sandberg
Referee: Barreto (Uruguay)

West Germany (0) **4, Sweden** (1) **2**
30.6.74 DÜSSELDORF
West Germany: Maier, Vogts, Schwarzenbeck, Beckenbauer, Breitner, Hoeness (1 pen), Bonhof (1), Overath (1), Hölzenbein (Flohe), Müller, Herzog (Grabowski (1))
Sweden: Hellström, Olsson, Karlsson, Nordqvist, Augustsson, Tapper, Bo Larsson (Ejderstedt), Grahn, Torstensson, Edström (1), Sandberg (1)
Referee: Kasakov (USSR)

Poland (1) **2, Yugoslavia** (1) **1**
30.6.74 FRANKFURT
Poland: Tomaszewski, Szymanowski, Zmuda, Gorgón, Musial, Kasperczyk, Maszczyk, Deyna (1 pen) (Domarski), Lato (1), Szarmach (Cmikiewicz), Gadocha
Yugoslavia: Maric, Buljan, Katalinski, Bogicevic, Hadziabdic, Karasi (1), Oblak (Jerkovic), Acimovic, Petkovic (Petrovic), Bajevic, Surjak
Referee: Glöckner (East Germany)

Sweden (1) **2, Yugoslavia** (1) **1**
3.7.74 DÜSSELDORF
Sweden: Hellström, Olsson, Karlsson, Nordqvist, Augustsson, Tapper, Grahn, Persson, Torstensson (1), Edström (1), Sandberg
Yugoslavia: Maric, Buljan, Katalinski, Hadziabdic, Pavlovic (Peruzovic), Bogicevic, Acimovic, Jerkovic, Petrovic (Karasi), Surjak (1), Dzajic
Referee: Pestarino (Argentina)

West Germany (0) **1, Poland** (0) **0**
3.7.74 FRANKFURT
West Germany: Maier, Vogts, Schwarzenbeck, Beckenbauer, Breitner, Hoeness, Bonhof, Overath, Grabowski, Müller (1), Hölzenbein
Poland: Tomaszewski, Szymanowski, Gorgón, Zmuda, Musial, Kasperczyk (Cmikiewicz), Deyna, Maszczyk (Kmiecik), Lato, Domarski, Gadocha
Referee: Linemayer (Austria)

	P	W	D	L	F	A	Pts
West Germany	3	3	0	0	7	2	6
Poland	3	2	0	1	3	2	4
Sweden	3	1	0	2	4	6	2
Yugoslavia	3	0	0	3	2	6	0

PLAY-OFF FOR THIRD PLACE

Before the final the third and fourth place match between Poland and the disgraced Brazilians ensued. A typically drab affair, it was won at walking pace by Poland's midfield, courtesy of Lato, a remarkable dependable and prolific marksmen for them throughout.

Match for Third Place

Poland (0) **1, Brazil** (0) **0**
6.7.74 MUNICH
Poland: Tomaszewski, Szymanowski, Zmuda, Gorgón, Musial, Kasperczyk (Cmikiewicz), Maszczyk, Deyna, Lato (1), Szarmach (Kapka), Gadocha
Brazil: Leao, Ze Maria, Alfredo, Mario Marinho, Francesco Marinho, Rivelino, Paulo Cesar C, Ademir (Mirandinha), Valdomiro, Jairzinho, Dirceu
Referee: Angonese (Italy)

THE FINAL

In the final Beckenbauer's immovable object came up against Cruyff's irresistible force. The most sensational beginning imaginable ensued as Cruyff, following a period of possession football, darted incisively towards the German goal to be challenged clumsily by Uli Hoeness. With a penalty kick came pandemonium, and Neeskens thumped the ball gratefully beyond Bayern's fine goalkeeper, Maier, for 1–0, and no German had touched the ball. Holland pressed, threatening a second goal, Cruyff fraying the nerves of uncertain defenders, but the Germans clung on to them, refusing to buckle. Their obstinacy was rewarded, wholly against the run of play, when Hölzenbein himself went down under a dubious challenge. The game's second spot kick converted by Paul Breitner levelled the scores and lifted the confidence of the Germans. Encouraged by their calm and assured captain, they began to impose themselves and found the net again, with Müller firing past Jongbloed from ten yards.

Holland, after the break, persisted, and in spite of enforced substitutions and a largely hostile crowd, they and the swaggering genius of Cruyff held sway. But an equalizing goal proved beyond them, as with Beckenbauer sweeping behind, a disciplined and resolute defence repelled them to the whistle. Germany had won the Trophy, Holland the admiration of spectators around the world.

Final

West Germany (2) **2, Holland** (1) **1**
7.7.74 MUNICH
West Germany: Maier, Vogts, Schwarzenbeck, Beckenbauer, Breitner (1 pen), Hoeness, Bonhof, Overath, Grabowski, Müller (1), Hölzenbein
Holland: Jongbloed, Suurbier, Rijsbergen (De Jong), Haan, Krol, Jansen, Neeskens (1 pen), Van Hanegem, Rep, Cruyff, Rensenbrink (Van der Kerhof)
Referee: Taylor (England)

So the Scots returned home frustrated, eliminated without losing, paying the price for an inability to punish the 'Leopards' of Zaire more heavily, thus giving themselves the more difficult task of beating either Brazil or Yugoslavia. They had, however, courage personified in the very being of their captain, Billy Bremner, little in stature, great in heart.

Brazil, in their efforts to combat the vigorous physical examination that had undone them in 1966, attempted to adapt to the European game and perversely were disgraced by a side playing football in the manner of their own victorious campaign in Mexico. Poland, third best nation in the world, had played with patience and style, and in Lato had a goal scorer of the very highest quality.

What of Holland? A team of imagination and mobility, many witnesses considered them unlucky, 'the best team, beaten as were Hungary 20 years earlier, by their inferior German opponents'. This suggestion, though, does not do justice to an excellent West German team, who improved dramatically after the initial Group stage and survived an early Dutch goal and subsequent onslaught to outwit them over 90 fiercely contested minutes. The Germans, dominant in the 1972 European Nations Cup with club sides winning UEFA Trophies, played with tactical awareness. Their apparently shock defeat by the East Germans offered them the greater opportunity of progress, and here is an illuminating parallel with their 1954 counterparts, who without question in the Group match with Hungary lulled the Magyars into a sense of invincibility.

CHAPTER 11

ARGENTINA

1978

Qualifying Tournament
106 entries
West Germany qualify as holders, Argentina qualify as hosts

Europe (32): Austria, Belgium, Bulgaria, Cyprus, Czechoslovakia, Denmark, England, Finland, France, East Germany, West Germany, Greece, Holland, Hungary, Iceland, Republic of Ireland, Northern Ireland, Italy, Luxembourg, Malta, Norway, Poland, Portugal, Romania, Scotland, Spain, Sweden, Switzerland, Turkey, USSR, Wales, Yugoslavia

South America (10): Argentina, Bolivia, Brazil, Chile, Colombia, Ecuador, Paraguay, Peru, Uruguay, Venezuela

CONCACAF (17): Barbados, Canada, Costa Rica, Cuba, Dominican Republic, Guatemala, Guyana, Haiti, Honduras, Jamaica, Mexico, Netherlands Antilles, Panama, El Salvador, Surinam, Trinidad and Tobago, USA

Asia/Oceania (21): Australia, Bahrain, Hong Kong, Indonesia, Iran, Iraq, Israel, Japan, North Korea, South Korea, Kuwait, Malaysia, New Zealand, Qatar, Saudi Arabia, Singapore, Sri Lanka, Syria, Taiwan, Thailand, United Arab Emirates

Africa (26): Algeria, Cameroon, Central Africa, Congo, Egypt, Ethiopia, Ghana, Guinea, Ivory Coast, Kenya, Libya, Malawi, Mauritania, Morocco, Niger, Nigeria, Senegal, Sierra Leone, Sudan, Tanzania, Togo, Tunisia, Uganda, Upper Volta, Zaire, Zambia

Europe

Group 1 (Poland, Portugal, Denmark, Cyprus)
Cyprus v Denmark 1–5, Portugal v Poland 0–2, Denmark v Cyprus 5–0, Poland v Cyprus 5–0, Portugal v Denmark 1–0, Cyprus v Portugal 1–2, Denmark v Poland 1–2, Cyprus v Poland 1–3, Poland v Denmark 4–1, Denmark v Portugal 2–4, Poland v Portugal 1–1, Portugal v Cyprus 4–0

	P	W	D	L	F	A	Pts
Poland	6	5	1	0	17	4	11
Portugal	6	4	1	1	12	6	9
Denmark	6	2	0	4	14	12	4
Cyprus	6	0	0	0	3	24	0

Poland qualified

Group 2 (Italy, England, Finland, Luxembourg)
Finland v England 1–4, Finland v Luxembourg 7–1, England v Finland 2–1, Luxembourg v Italy 1–4, Italy v England 2–0, England v Luxembourg 5–0, Luxembourg v Finland 0–1, Finland v Italy 0–3, Luxembourg v England 0–2, Italy v Finland 6–1, England v Italy 2–0, Italy v Luxembourg 3–0

	P	W	D	L	F	A	Pts
Italy	6	5	0	1	18	4	10
England	6	5	0	1	15	4	10
Finland	6	2	0	4	11	16	4
Luxembourg	6	0	0	6	2	22	0

Italy qualified

Group 3 (East Germany, Austria, Turkey, Malta)
Turkey v Malta 4–0, East Germany v Turkey 1–1, Malta v Austria 0–1, Malta v East Germany 0–1, Austria v Turkey 1–0, Austria v Malta 9–0, Austria v East Germany 1–1, East Germany v Austria 1–1, East Germany v Malta 9–0, Turkey v Austria 0–1, Turkey v East Germany 1–2, Malta v Turkey 0–3

	P	W	D	L	F	A	Pts
Austria	6	4	2	0	14	2	10
East Germany	6	3	3	0	15	4	9
Turkey	6	2	1	3	9	5	5
Malta	6	0	0	6	0	27	0

Austria qualified

Group 4 (Holland, Belgium, Northern Ireland, Iceland)
Iceland v Belgium 0–1, Iceland v Holland 0–1, Holland v Northern Ireland 2–2, Belgium v Northern Ireland 2–0, Belgium v Holland 0–2, Iceland v Northern Ireland 1–0, Holland v Iceland 4–1, Belgium v Iceland 4–0, Northern Ireland v Iceland 2–0, Northern Ireland v Holland 0–1, Holland v Belgium 1–0, Northern Ireland v Belgium 3–0

	P	W	D	L	F	A	Pts
Holland	6	5	1	0	11	3	11
Belgium	6	3	0	3	7	6	6
Northern Ireland	6	2	1	3	7	6	5
Iceland	6	1	0	5	2	12	2

Holland qualified

Group 5 (Bulgaria, France, Rep of Ireland)

Bulgaria v France 2–2, France v Rep of Ireland 2–0, Rep of Ireland v France 1–0, Bulgaria v Rep of Ireland 2–1, Rep of Ireland v Bulgaria 0–0, France v Bulgaria 3–1

	P	W	D	L	F	A	Pts
France	4	2	1	1	7	4	5
Bulgaria	4	1	2	1	5	6	4
Rep of Ireland	4	1	1	3	2	4	3

France qualified

Group 6 (Sweden, Switzerland, Norway)

Sweden v Norway 2–0, Norway v Switzerland 1–0, Switzerland v Sweden 1–2, Sweden v Switzerland 2–1, Norway v Sweden 2–1, Switzerland v Norway 1–0

	P	W	D	L	F	A	Pts
Sweden	4	3	0	1	7	4	6
Norway	4	2	0	2	3	4	4
Switzerland	4	1	0	3	3	5	2

Sweden qualified

Group 7 (Scotland, Czechoslovakia, Wales)

Czechoslovakia v Scotland 2–0, Scotland v Wales 1–0, Wales v Czechoslovakia 3–0, Scotland v Czechoslovakia 3–1, Wales v Scotland 0–2, Czechoslovakia v Wales 1–0

	P	W	D	L	F	A	Pts
Scotland	4	3	0	1	6	3	6
Czechoslovakia	4	2	0	2	4	6	4
Wales	4	1	0	3	3	4	2

Scotland qualified

Group 8 (Yugoslavia, Spain, Romania)

Spain v Yugoslavia 1–0, Romania v Spain 1–0, Yugoslavia v Romania 0–2, Spain v Romania 2–0, Romania v Yugoslavia 4–6, Yugoslavia v Spain 0–1

	P	W	D	L	F	A	Pts
Spain	4	3	0	1	4	1	6
Romania	4	2	0	2	7	8	4
Yugoslavia	4	1	0	3	6	8	2

Spain qualified

Group 9 (USSR, Hungary, Greece)

Greece v Hungary 1–1, USSR v Greece 2–0, Hungary v USSR 2–1, Greece v USSR 1–0, USSR v Hungary 2–0, Hungary v Greece 3–0

	P	W	D	L	F	A	Pts
Hungary	4	2	1	1	6	4	5
USSR	4	2	0	2	5	3	4
Greece	4	1	1	2	2	6	3

Play-off against third-placed team in South American play-off group: Hungary v Bolivia 6–0, 3–2
Hungary qualified

South America

Group 1 (Brazil, Paraguay, Colombia)

Colombia v Brazil 0–0, Colombia v Paraguay 0–1, Paraguay v Colombia 1–1, Brazil v Colombia 6–0, Paraguay v Brazil 0–1, Brazil v Paraguay 1–1

	P	W	D	L	F	A	Pts
Brazil	4	2	2	0	8	1	6
Paraguay	4	1	2	1	3	3	4
Colombia	4	0	2	2	1	8	2

Group 2 (Uruguay, Venezuela, Bolivia)

Venezuela v Uruguay 1–1, Bolivia v Uruguay 1–0, Venezuela v Bolivia 1–3, Bolivia v Venezuela 2–0, Uruguay v Venezuela 2–0, Uruguay v Bolivia 2–2

	P	W	D	L	F	A	Pts
Bolivia	4	3	1	0	8	3	7
Uruguay	4	1	2	1	5	4	4
Venezuela	4	0	1	3	2	8	1

Group 3 (Chile, Peru, Ecuador)

Ecuador v Peru 1–1, Ecuador v Chile 0–1, Chile v Peru 1–1, Peru v Ecuador 4–0, Chile v Ecuador 3–0, Peru v Chile 2–0

	P	W	D	L	F	A	Pts
Peru	4	2	2	0	8	2	6
Chile	4	2	1	1	5	3	5
Ecuador	4	0	1	3	1	9	1

Play-off group (in Colombia)
Brazil v Peru 1–0, Brazil v Bolivia 8–0, Peru v Bolivia 5–0

	P	W	D	L	F	A	Pts
Brazil	2	2	0	0	9	0	4
Peru	2	1	0	1	5	1	2
Bolivia	2	0	0	2	0	13	0

Brazil and Peru qualified

CONCACAF

Group 1 (North) (Canada, USA, Mexico)

Canada v USA 1–1, USA v Mexico 0–0, Canada v Mexico 1–0, Mexico v USA 3–0, USA v Canada 2–0, Mexico v Canada 0–0

	P	W	D	L	F	A	Pts
Mexico	4	1	2	1	3	1	4
USA	4	1	2	1	3	4	4
Canada	4	1	2	1	2	3	4

Play-off for second place (in Haiti): Canada v USA 3–0

Group 2 (Central) (Guatemala, El Salvador, Honduras (withdrew), Costa Rica, Panama)

Panama v Costa Rica 3–2, Panama v El Salvador 1–1, Costa Rica v Panama 3–0, El Salvador v Panama 4–1, Panama v Guatemala 2–4, Guatemala v Panama 7–0, El Salvador v Costa Rica 1–1, Costa Rica v Guatemala 0–0, Guatemala v El Salvador 3–1, Guatemala v Costa Rica 1–1, El Salvador v Guatemala 2–0, Costa Rica v El Salvador 1–1

	P	W	D	L	F	A	Pts
Guatemala	6	3	2	1	15	6	8
El Salvador	6	2	3	1	10	7	7
Costa Rica	6	1	4	1	8	6	6
Panama	6	1	1	4	7	21	3

Group 3 (Caribbean) (Netherlands Antilles, Barbados, Cuba, Guyana, Haiti, Jamaica, Surinam, Trinidad and Tobago, Dominican Republic)

Extra preliminary round
Dominican Republic v Haiti 0–3, 0–3

Preliminary round
Guyana v Surinam 2–0, 0–3, Netherlands Antilles v Haiti 1–2, 0–7, Jamaica v Cuba 1–3, 0–2, Barbados v Trinidad & Tobago 2–1, 0–1,
Play-off: Trinidad & Tobago v Barbados 3–1

Final preliminary round
Surinam v Trinidad & Tobago 1–1, 2–2
Play-off: Surinam v Trinidad & Tobago 3–2
Cuba v Haiti 1–1, 1–1
Play-off: Cuba v Haiti 0–2

Final Round
Guatemala v Surinam 3–2, El Salvador v Canada 2–1, Mexico v Haiti 4–1, Canada v Surinam 2–1, Haiti v Guatemala 2–1, Mexico v El Salvador 3–1, Mexico v Surinam 8–1, Canada v Guatemala 2–1, Haiti v El Salvador 1–0, Mexico v Guatemala 2–1, Canada v Haiti 1–1, El Salvador v Surinam 3–2, Mexico v Canada 3–1, Haiti v Surinam 1–0, Guatemala v El Salvador 2–2

	P	W	D	L	F	A	Pts
Mexico	5	5	0	0	20	5	10
Haiti	5	3	1	1	6	6	7
Canada	5	2	1	2	7	8	5
El Salvador	5	2	1	2	8	9	5
Guatemala	5	1	1	3	8	10	3
Surinam	5	0	0	5	6	17	0

Mexico qualified

Asia/Oceania

Oceania Group (Australia, New Zealand, Taiwan) (in Australia)
Australia v Taiwan 3–0, Taiwan v Australia 1–2, New Zealand v Taiwan 6–0, Taiwan v New Zealand 0–6, Australia v New Zealand 3–1, New Zealand v Australia 1–1

	P	W	D	L	F	A	Pts
Australia	4	3	1	0	9	3	7
New Zealand	4	2	1	1	14	4	5
Taiwan	4	0	0	4	1	17	0

Asia Group 1 (Hong Kong, Indonesia, Malaysia, Thailand, Singapore) (in Singapore)

Singapore v Thailand 2–0, Hong Kong v Indonesia 4–1, Malaysia v Thailand 6–4, Hong Kong v Singapore 2–2, Indonesia v Malaysia 0–0, Thailand v Hong Kong 1–2, Singapore v Malaysia 1–0, Thailand v Indonesia 3–2, Malaysia v Hong Kong 1–1, Indonesia v Singapore 4–0

	P	W	D	L	F	A	Pts
Hong Kong	4	2	2	0	9	5	6
Singapore	4	2	1	1	5	6	5
Malaysia	4	1	2	1	7	6	4
Indonesia	4	1	1	2	7	7	3
Thailand	4	1	0	3	8	12	2

Group Final

Singapore v Hong Kong 0–1

Asia Group 2 (Israel, Japan, South Korea, North Korea)

North Korea withdrew

Israel v South Korea 0–0, Israel v Japan 2–0, Japan v Israel 0–2, South Korea v Israel 3–1, Japan v South Korea 0–0, South Korea v Japan 1–0

	P	W	D	L	F	A	Pts
South Korea	4	2	2	0	4	1	6
Israel	4	2	1	1	5	3	5
Japan	4	0	1	3	0	5	1

Asia Group 3 (Iran, Saudi Arabia, Iraq, Syria)

Iraq withdrew

Saudi Arabia v Syria 2–0, Syria v Saudi Arabia 2–1, Saudi Arabia v Iran 0–3, Syria v Iran 0–1, Iran v Syria (withdrew), match awarded to Iran 2–0, Iran v Saudi Arabia 2–0

	P	W	D	L	F	A	Pts
Iran	4	4	0	0	8	0	8
Saudi Arabia	4	1	0	3	3	7	2
Syria	4	1	0	3	2	6	2

Asia Group 4 (Bahrain, Kuwait, Qatar, UAE) (In Qatar)

UAE withdrew

Bahrain v Kuwait 0–2, Bahrain v Qatar 0–2, Qatar v Kuwait 0–2, Bahrain v Kuwait 1–2, Qatar v Bahrain 0–3, Qatar v Kuwait 1–4

	P	W	D	L	F	A	Pts
Kuwait	4	4	0	0	10	2	8
Qatar	4	1	0	3	3	9	2
Bahrain	4	1	0	3	4	6	2

Final Round

Hong Kong v Iran 0–2, Hong Kong v South Korea 0–1, South Korea v Iran 0–0, Australia v Hong Kong 3–0, Australia v Iran 0–1, Australia v South Korea 2–1, Hong Kong v Kuwait 1–3, South Korea v Kuwait 1–0, Australia v Kuwait 1–2, South Korea v Australia 0–0, Iran v Kuwait 1–0, Hong Kong v Australia 2–5, Kuwait v South Korea 2–2, Iran v South Korea 2–2, Kuwait v Hong Kong 4–0, Iran v Hong Kong 3–0, Kuwait v Australia 1–0, Iran v Australia 1–0, Kuwait v Iran 1–2, South Korea v Hong Kong 5–2

	P	W	D	L	F	A	Pts
Iran	8	6	2	0	12	3	14
South Korea	8	3	4	1	12	8	10
Kuwait	8	4	1	3	13	8	9
Australia	8	3	1	4	11	8	7
Hong Kong	8	0	0	8	5	26	0

Iran qualified

Africa

Extra Preliminary Round

Sierra Leone v Niger 5–1, 1–2, Upper Volta v Mauritania 1–1, 2–0

1st Round

Algeria v Libya 1–0, 0–0, Morocco v Tunisia 1–1, 1–1 (Tunisia won 4–2 on penalties), Togo v Senegal 1–0, 1–1, Ghana v Guinea 2–1, 1–2, Sierra Leone v Nigeria 0–0, 2–6, Congo v Cameroon 2–2, 2–1, Upper Volta v Ivory Coast 1–1, 0–2, Egypt v Ethiopia 3–0, 2–1, Zambia v Malawi 4–0, 1–0
Play-off: Guinea v Ghana 2–0
Zaire v Central Africa (withdrew), Kenya v Sudan (withdrew), Uganda v Tanzania (withdrew)

2nd Round

Zaire withdrew
Tunisia v Algeria 2–0, 1–1, Togo v Guinea 0–2, 1–2, Ivory Coast v Congo 3–2, 3–1, Kenya v Egypt 0–0, 0–1, Uganda v Zambia 1–0, 2–4

3rd Round
Guinea v Tunisia 1–0, 1–3, Ivory Coast v Nigeria 2–2, 0–4, Egypt v Zambia 2–0, 0–0

Final Tournament
Tunisia v Nigeria 0–0, Nigeria v Egypt 4–0, Egypt v Nigeria 3–1, Nigeria v Tunisia 0–1, Egypt v Tunisia 3–2, Tunisia v Egypt 4–1

	P	W	D	L	F	A	Pts
Tunisia	4	2	1	1	7	4	5
Egypt	4	2	0	2	7	11	4
Nigeria	4	1	1	2	5	4	3

Tunisia qualified

1978 ARGENTINA 1 June–26 June

QUALIFIERS

Argentina	Mexico
Austria	Peru
Brazil	Poland
France	Scotland
Holland	Spain
Hungary	Sweden
Iran	Tunisia
Italy	West Germany

There was a pessimistic air pervading as the sixteen finalists disembarked in Argentina for the eleventh competition. The military Junta governing the country was deeply unpopular internationally, constantly attacked by human rights groups such as Amnesty International for its more sinister activities. Football, too, would be under the closest scrutiny with the general consensus being that the world's more formidable nations had not progressed, and had merely marked time since 1974.

The Argentines themselves had been drawn in Group One, the strongest by far. Preparation had for them been moderately successful, Kempes was back from Spain and this potentially volatile team promised to play to an attacking formula. With them in the nation's capital would be Italy, blessed with an abundance of fine players, who had edged out England in qualification. 'I do not expect great achievement,' said their coach Erizo Bearzet defensively – the Italian public, however, would not be sympathetic to failure. France, absent from three successive competitions, brought a younger, altogether more promising team, and their leading club side St Etienne were proving themselves among Europe's very best: the unpredictable Rocheteau was a threat and in Platini they had a midfield player with intoxicating skills. Hungary, the group's fourth member and conquerors of the Soviet Union, Greece and then Bolivia, arrived with the reputation of being a very fine side. Torocsik, their striker, whilst not prolific was a high calibre provider, and Nyilasi nimble and inventive in midfield.

Group Two opening in Buenos Aires would then entertain the twin towns of Rosario and Cordoba. Here Germany would face Poland, Mexico and Tunisia. Despite being shorn of the elegant Beckenbauer and most of his World Cup colleagues, in Karl Heinz Rummenigge Germany had uncovered a gifted new goal scorer, and would give any opposition a stern test with their organized, disciplined approach. Poland, relatively unchanged from four years earlier, had eased into the finals with the loss of just one point, and though many of their players were approaching the veteran stage, Boniek, a new recruit to the cause, was a young midfield player of whom great things were expected. Mexico, boasting a 'new dynamic style', came in reality with a team inexperienced at this level of competition. They and the African representative Tunisia – hammered 4–0 in a friendly with the Dutch – would find further progress difficult.

In Group Three the grumpy Brazilians, complaining bitterly about being based in chilly Mar del Plata, adopted the more physical approach seen in European football. As ever, they were the favourites, and with the young and mercurial Zico joining the old master Rivelino, theirs was a team to contend with. Austria also had reason for optimism: ousting East Germany and firing nine goals past the modest Maltese – where Krankl, their opportunist striker, scored six times – they were a confident squad, unbeaten in fourteen matches. Spain, like France were back in the finals for the first time since 1966, and had mercifully eliminated the dour, destructive Yugoslavians in the qualifying tournament; they would enjoy the majority of the local support and had Cano, their Argentine born winger, Pirri and Migueli to inspire their challenge. Sweden completed the Group, coming with a team largely supplied by their own league clubs and amidst mutterings of discontent. 'The difference between now and 1974,' said their coach Georg Ericson, ' is that I don't have a goal scorer.'

The Dutch in Group Four were hampered, as had become their custom, by internal strife. Cruyff, the opulent and extravagant genius, had refused to play, citing Argentina's appalling human rights record. Nevertheless, they remained a team of outstanding ability, having quality individuals of the calibre of Rep, Krol, Neeskens, the Van der Kerkhof twins and Rensenbrink to call on.

Scotland arrived full of optimism with a team many considered their best to play in a World Cup. They had a powerful midfield supplying Jordan – a human battering ram – and Dalglish, his clever and incisive accomplice. Peru, with perhaps the oldest team in the Tournament, included many of their Mexico squad, the wily Cubillas and Chumpitaz amongst them. Unfortunately their preparation had been disastrous and their results poor. For Iran a glorious adventure awaited, whatever their fate, winning the Asia/Oceania qualifier in style; nine victories in eleven games had brought them this rich reward.

Group 1

Venues: Buenos Aires, Mar del Plata
Argentina
France
Hungary
Italy

Group 2

Venues: Buenos Aires, Cordoba, Rosario
Mexico
Poland
Tunisia
West Germany

Group 3

Venues: Buenos Aires, Mar del Plata
Austria
Brazil
Spain
Sweden

Group 4

Venues: Cordoba, Mendoza
Holland
Iran
Peru
Scotland

THE FIRST SERIES

At the River Plate Stadium, West Germany opened their defence and the Tournament against Poland in Group Two before 80,000 spectators. Here the two fought out the almost inevitable 0–0 draw, the fourth consecutive opening fixture to end in stalemate. Germany, lacking in authority and nervous in defence, showed little urgency, although Bonhof's shot before half-time struck the crossbar. Poland, the better and brighter team, created plentiful chances and should have won except that the normally lethal Lato scorned an opening presented to him after good work by Lubanski and Szarmach.

On the Parana River, at Rosario, Tunisia surprisingly accounted for the young Mexican team. Regardless of having conceded a penalty early on.

Inspired by the solid Dhouieb and the tricky Temine, they ran in three second-half goals and cantered to victory, Africa's first in the competition's history.

The host nation began at the intimidating River Plate against the dangerously unpredictable Hungarians in a stadium near to hysteria. Promptly falling behind to Csapo, they equalized within moments through Luque before both teams indulged in a bruising war of attrition, fouling with impunity. Argentina's Bertoni scored their late and undeserved winner on 76 minutes before the ugliness degenerated into chaos, Torocsik and the brilliant Nyilasi sent off on the Hungarian side whilst Argentina, largely the instigators, scandalously enjoyed the benefit of the Portuguese referee's more lenient and understanding instincts. At the other Group One fixture down at Mar del Plata, France took the lead within forty seconds through Lacombe. But despite their clever play, they could not sustain it. Rossi, Italy's gangly striker, levelled before Zaccarelli, on as a second-half substitute, flashed the winner into the French goal for 2–1; France were beaten, though they had been somewhat unfortunate.

In Group Three a fast and determined Austrian side inspired by Prohaska and Obermayer shocked Spain in Buenos Aires. Level at half-time, Hans Krankl, their bullish centre forward, settled matters. Spain, in spite of the sympathy of the crowd, could not respond.

Brazil, still unhappy at being asked to play at Mar del Plata, the coldest venue – akin to the British winter – kicked off their campaign with an unsatisfactory performance against George Ericson's Swedish charges. The Swedes were fiercely competitive and worthy of a 1–1 draw. Sjöberg and Reinaldo provided the goals. Here, however, an extraordinary climax followed: Brazil, frustrated in extraordinary circumstances, brought unsettling mutterings of conspiracy. In injury time a last gasp corner kick fell invitingly to the blond-headed Zico, who arrived to head beyond Hellström only to discover that Welsh referee Thomas had ended the game whilst the ball was in flight. Furious protests ensued but to no avail as the officious Thomas strode from the pitch, leaving behind an outraged Brazilian team.

Out west Group Four's Peru in Cordoba outwitted a dull and complacent Scotland side, and in so doing poured scorn on the Scots' pretensions. For Scotland it began well, with the forceful Jordan putting them ahead, until Cueto brought the South Americans an equalizer. The Scots, unable to respond to this unexpected challenge, were undone by the veteran genius of the elegant Cubillas, scorer of two quite unstoppable second-half goals to end 3–1. Down near the Chilean border at Mendoza, Holland disposed of Iran with little difficulty, fielding most of their class of '74. Rob Rensenbrink's hat-trick brought them victory; there was undoubtedly more to come from them.

THE SECOND SERIES

France, so unfortunate against Italy, suffered again in the cauldron at Buenos Aires against the hosts. Falling behind to a dubious Passarella penalty, they fought back, Platini driving in gloriously before Luque, the moustachioed Argentine forward, powered in for a second goal and a decisive score. The French were outraged, believing themselves, with some justification, to be the victims of poor refereeing. Here they had the sympathy of others, for if the hostile crowd could not intimidate opponents, it certainly and worryingly appeared to be affecting officials.

Hungary, also in Group One, had cause to rue their encounter with the hosts, for without the impressive Torocsic and their play maker Nyilasi, now suspended, they were no match at all for a relaxed, confident Italy orchestrated by Causio. They lost tamely, 3–1.

Poland, playing up at Rosario, scored through Lato and were forced to hang on, at times grimly, by a lively Tunisian team clearly gaining inspiration in this, their debut in the competition. Poland, 1–0 winners, were jeered derisively and justifiably by the disappointed locals at the final whistle. Mexico at Cordoba fell apart against a rampant German team, stung by criticism of their poor performance against the Poles. Down 2–0 early on, the Mexicans capitulated miserably, eventually losing 6–0, though it might reasonably have been worse. Rummenigge, scorer of two German goals, was a constant thorn in the side of an inadequate and naive defence.

Austria again won at Buenos Aires, 1–0 victors over Sweden, Krankl once more the decisive factor, this time with a penalty kick. Well organized and with the splendid Koncilia in goal, they were worthy and impressive winners over a talented Swedish side that lacked the potency of 1974.

Brazil, at the reviled Mar del Plata, also in Group Three, failed once more, despite changes against cautious Spain in a nervous, timid, goal-less affair that did nothing for either of the participants' reputations.

Holland, in Group Four at Mendoza, again played within themselves, content largely with containing the Peruvians and conserving energy for the later rounds. Disturbingly, they almost paid for their apathy as Peru, skilful and persistent opponents, increased their effort, worrying them constantly in the closing moments.

Scotland, already embarrassed by Peru, suffered humiliation at the hands of an enthusiastic Iranian team lifted by Danaifar's unlikely equalizer. Scotland, though dominant to the whistle, could not manufacture a winner, and looked dejected and demoralized as they trooped off to hoots of derision from their own partisan supporters.

THE THIRD SERIES

Argentina and Italy, both qualified already from Group One, played out their final group match in the frenzied capital. Italy, masters of the counter-attack, defended their opponents' swift movement shrewdly before Bettega ruthlessly punished a lack of concentration by the Argentineans. Italy winning 1–0, try as Argentina might, the huge stadium and their heroes on the pitch could not conjure up a reply. Argentina, therefore, would not play their second stage in the capital, and for that at least the survivors would owe the Italians a debt of gratitude.

France, completing the Group fixtures against Hungary, won 3–1 at Mar del Plata in a now meaningless game between much changed teams. At least the game was entertaining for the spectators, as the freedom afforded by certain elimination allowed both to attack without caution.

Brazil in Group Three faced Austria and the prospect of elimination. Galvanized by the challenge, by introducing Roberto they gave themselves more attacking options, his goal finally separating the teams at the end. Nonetheless, Austria, qualification already confirmed, worried them desperately, Kreuz twice forcing saves before Obermayer blasted a shot tantalizingly wide to leave the beaten Brazilian goalkeeper Leao groping vainly.

Spain and Sweden were condemned to going home, though the Spaniards, relieved of the pressure, now perversely played their best football harrying the dispirited Swedes. Asensi and Cardensoa, forceful providers in midfield, gave them a platform. Uria went close, Cardenosa struck Hellström's goalpost before Asensi decisively shot powerfully and accurately the winner fourteen minutes from time.

In Group Two, West Germany's Jekyll and Hyde competition continued against Tunisia in Cordoba. Forced on the back foot for long periods by eager and inventive opponents enjoying themselves hugely, they were forced to hold on to an unconvincing and rather fortunate 0–0 draw.

Poland swept the inept and outclassed Mexicans aside 3–1 at Cordoba, their midfield master Deyna organizing busily whilst the flame-haired Boniek, having his first World Cup match, took full advantage of generous marking with two fine goals. Mexico did gain consolation through Rangel, but in truth they were once again a poor and ill-prepared team.

Finally to Group Four and Mendoza where the accomplished Dutch faced Scotland, so ragged and uninspired thus far. Astonishingly the Scots, with Souness of Liverpool selected, attacked their opponents constantly, Rioch hitting a post, Dalglish going close, before Rensenbrink, very much against the run of play, made the most of a penalty kick. How Scotland responded! Their pride and spirit gave them the impetus to attack and they were rewarded for their efforts when Dalglish reached a Jordan header to fire past Jongbloed, then taking the lead with a Gemmill penalty. Worse still for the Dutch followed swiftly, once more thanks to Gemmill. This time he collected a ball out wide, drifted into the penalty area, meandered past lazy tackles and unleashed a stunning drive beyond the startled Jongbloed for a third. Holland, now struggling and embarrassed, were forced to respond, and despite Rep crashing a ferocious shot in from twenty-five yards, beating the despairing Rough for 2–3, Scotland, regardless of having already been eliminated, clung on to win magnificently.

Peru secured the last place in the final eight by defeating the Iranians 4–1 with a hat-trick, two penalties and a brilliant piece of individualism from Cubillas putting the lid on it. Rowshan did at least provide Iran with the encouragement of a 40th minute goal, and thereafter sought without success to exploit Peru's apparent vulnerability to high balls.

Final Tournament – Argentina
First Round

Group 1

Argentina (1) **2, Hungary** (1) **1**
2.6.78 BUENOS AIRES
Argentina: Fillol, Olguin, Galvan, Passarella, Tarantini, Ardiles, Gallego, Valencia (Alonso), Houseman (Bertoni (1)), Luque (1), Kempes
Hungary: Gujdar, Török (Martos), Kereki, Kocsis, Toth J, Nyilasi, Pinter, Zombori, Csapo (1), Torocsik, Nagy
Referee: Garrido (Portugal)

Italy (1) **2, France** (1) **1**
2.6.78 MAR DEL PLATA
Italy: Zoff, Scirea, Gentile, Bellugi, Cabrini, Benetti, Causio, Tardelli, Antognoni (Zaccarelli (1)), Rossi (1), Bettega
France: Bertrand-Demanes, Tresor, Janvion, Rio, Bossis, Guillou, Michel, Platini, Dalger, Lacombe (1) (Berdoll), Six (Rouyer)
Referee: Rainea (Romania)

Argentina (1) **2, France** (0) **1**
6.7.78 BUENOS AIRES
Argentina: Fillol, Olguin, Galvan, Passarella (1 pen), Tarantini, Ardiles, Gallego, Valencia (Alonso), Houseman, Luque (1), Kempes
France: Bertrand-Demanes (Baratelli), Tresor, Battiston, Lopez, Bossis, Bathenay, Michel, Platini (1), Rocheteau, Lacombe, Six
Referee: Dubach (Switzerland)

Italy (2) **3, Hungary** (0) **1**
6.6.78 MAR DEL PLATA
Italy: Zoff, Scirea, Gentile, Bellugi, Cabrini (Cuccureddu), Benetti (1), Causio, Tardelli, Antognoni, Rossi (1), Bettega (1) (Graziani)
Hungary: Meszaros, Kereki, Martos, Kocsis, Toth J, Csapo, Pinter, Zombori, Pusztai, Fazekas (Halasz), Nagy (Toth A (1 pen))
Referee: Barretto (Uruguay)

Italy (0) **1, Argentina** (0) **0**
10.6.78 BUENOS AIRES
Italy: Zoff, Scirea, Gentile, Bellugi (Cuccureddu), Cabrini, Benetti, Causio, Tardelli, Antognoni (Zaccarelli), Rossi, Bettega (1)
Argentina: Fillol, Olguin, Galvan, Passarella, Tarantini, Gallego, Ardiles, Valencia, Bertoni, Kempes, Ortiz (Houseman)
Referee: Klein (Israel)

France (3) **3, Hungary** (1) **1**
10.6.78 MAR DEL PLATA
France: Dropsy, Tresor, Janvion, Lopez (1), Bracci, Petit, Bathenay, Papi, Rocheteau (1), Berdoll (1), Rouyer
Hungary: Gujdar, Kereki, Balint, Martos, Toth J, Nyilasi, Pinter, Zombori (1), Pusztai, Torocsik, Nagy (Csapo)
Referee: Coehlo (Brazil)

	P	W	D	L	.	A	Pts
Italy	3	3	0	0	6	2	6
Argentina	3	2	0	1	4	3	4
France	3	1	0	2	5	5	2
Hungary	3	0	0	3	3	8	0

Group 2

West Germany (0) **0, Poland** (0) **0**
1.6.78 BUENOS AIRES
West Germany: Maier, Kaltz, Vogts, Rüssmann, Zimmermann, Bonhof, Beer, Flohe, Müller H, Abramczik, Fischer
Poland: Tomaszewski, Gorgón, Maculewicz, Szymanowski, Zmuda, Masztaler (Kasperczak), Nawalka, Deyna, Lato, Lubanski (Boniek), Szarmach
Referee: Coerezza (Argentina)

Tunisia (0) **3, Mexico** (1) **1**
2.6.78 ROSARIO
Tunisia: Naili, Dhouieb (1), Jendoubi, Jebali, Kaabi (1), Ghommidh (1), Temine (Labidi), Agrebi, Akid, Tarak, Ben Aziza (Karoui)
Mexico: Reyes, Martinez Diaz, Vasquez Ayala (1 pen), Ramos, Teña, De la Torre, Cuellar, Mendizabal (Lugo Gomez), Isiordia, Rangel, Sanchez
Referee: Gordon (Scotland)

Poland (1) **1, Tunisia** (0) **0**
6.6.78 ROSARIO
Poland: Tomaszewski, Gorgón, Szymanowski, Zmuda, Maculewicz, Nawalka, Deyna, Kasperczak, Lato (1), Lubanski (Boniek), Szarmach (Iwan)
Tunisia: Naili, Dhouieb, Jendoubi, Gasmi, Kaabi, Ghommidh, Temine, Agrebi, Akid, Tarak, Jebali
Referee: Martinez (Spain)

West Germany (4) **6, Mexico** (0) **0**
6.6.78 CORDOBA
West Germany: Maier, Kaltz, Vogts, Rüssmann, Dietz, Bonhof, Flohe (2), Müller H (1), Rummenigge (2), Fischer, Müller D (1)
Mexico: Reyes (Soto), Martinez Diaz, Teña, Ramos, Vazquez Ayala, Lopez Zarza (Lugo Gomez), Cuellar, De la Torre, Sanchez, Rangel, Mendizabal
Referee: Bouzo (Syria)

West Germany (0) **0, Tunisia** (0) **0**
10.6.78 CORDOBA
West Germany: Maier, Kaltz, Vogts, Rüssmann, Dietz, Bonhof, Flohe, Rummenigge, Müller H, Fischer, Müller D
Tunisia: Naili, Jebali, Dhouieb, Jendoubi, Kaabi, Ghommidh, Gasmi, Tarak, Agrebi, Temine, Akid (Ben Aziza)
Referee: Orosco (Peru)

Poland (1) **3, Mexico** (0) **1**
10.6.78 ROSARIO
Poland: Tomaszewski, Gorgón, Szymanowski, Zmunda, Kasperczak, Deyna (1), Masztaler, Rudy (Maculewicz), Boniek (2), Lato, Iwan (Lubanski)
Mexico: Soto, Gomez C, Cisneros, De la Torre, Vasquez Ayala, Cuellar, Flores, Cardeñas (Mendizabal), Ortega, Rangel (1), Sanchez
Referee: Namdar (Iran)

	P	W	D	L	F	A	Pts
Poland	3	2	1	0	4	1	5
West Germany	3	1	2	0	6	0	4
Tunisia	3	1	1	1	3	2	3
Mexico	3	0	0	3	2	12	0

Group 3

Austria (1) **2, Spain** (1) **1**
3.6.78 BUENOS AIRES
Austria: Koncilia, Pezzey, Sara, Breitenberger, Obermayer, Prohaska, Kreuz, Hickersberger (Weber), Jara, Schachner (1) (Pirkner), Krankl (1)
Spain: Miguel Angel, Marcelino, Pirri, Migueli, San José, De la Cruz, Asensi, Rexach (Quini), Cardenosa (Leal), Dani (1), Ruben Cano
Referee: Palotai (Hungary)

Sweden (1) **1, Brazil** (1) **1**
3.6.78 MAR DEL PLATA
Sweden: Hellström, Andersson R, Borg, Nordqvist, Erlandsson, Larsson L (Edström), Tapper, Linderoth, Bo Larsson, Sjöberg (1), Wendt
Brazil: Leao, Oscar, Toninho, Amaral, Edinho, Batista, Zico, Cerezo, Gil (Nelinho), Reinaldo (1), Rivelino
Referee: Thomas (Wales)

Austria (1) **1, Sweden** (0) **0**
7.6.78 BUENOS AIRES
Austria: Koncilia, Obermayer, Sara, Pezzey, Breitenberger, Prohaska, Hickersberger, Krieger (Weber), Jara, Krankl (1 pen), Kreuz
Sweden: Hellström, Andersson R, Borg, Nordqvist, Erlandsson, Larsson L, Tapper (Torstensson), Linderoth (Edström), Bo Larsson, Sjöberg, Wendt
Referee: Corver (Netherlands)

Brazil (0) **0, Spain** (0) **0**
7.6.78 MAR DEL PLATA
Brazil: Leao, Amaral, Nelinho (Gil), Oscar, Edinho, Cerezo, Batista, Zico (Mendonca), Dirceu, Toninho, Reinaldo
Spain: Miguel Angel, Olmo, Marcelino, Migueli (Biosca), Uria (Guzman), Leal, Asensi, Cardenosa, San José, Juanito, Santillana
Referee: Gonella (Italy)

Spain (0) **1, Sweden** (0) **0**
11.6.78 BUENOS AIRES
Spain: Miguel Angel, Olmo (Pirri), Marcelino, Biosca, San José, Uria, Leal, Asensi (1), Cardenosa, Juanito, Santillana
Sweden: Hellström, Anderson R, Borg, Nordqvist, Erlandsson, Larsson L, Bo Larsson, Nordin, Nilsson, Sjöberg (Linderoth), Edström (Wendt)
Referee: Biwersi (West Germany)

Brazil (1) **1, Austria** (0) **0**
11.6.78 MAR DEL PLATA
Brazil: Leao, Amaral, Toninho, Oscar, Rodrigues Neto, Batista, Cerezo (Chicao), Dirceu, Gil, Mendonca (Zico), Roberto (1)
Austria: Koncilia, Obermayer, Sara, Pezzey, Breitenberger, Prohaska, Hickersberger (Weber), Krieger (Happich), Jara, Krankl, Kreuz
Referee: Wurtz (France)

	P	W	D	L	F	A	Pts
Austria	3	2	0	1	3	2	4
Brazil	3	1	2	0	2	1	4
Spain	3	1	1	1	2	2	3
Sweden	3	0	1	2	1	3	1

Group 4

Holland (1) **3, Iran** (0) **0**
3.6.78 MENDOZA
Holland: Jongbloed, Suurbier, Rijsbergen, Krol, Haan, Jansen, Neeskens, Van de Kerkhof W, Rep, Rensenbrink (3, 2 pens), Van de Kerkhof R (Nanninga)
Iran: Hejazi, Nazari, Abdullahi, Kazerani, Eskandarian, Parvin, Ghassempour, Sadeghi, Nayeb-Agha, Faraki (Rowshan), Jahani
Referee: Archundia (Mexico)

Peru (1) **3, Scotland** (1) **1**
3.6.78 CORDOBA
Peru: Quiroga, Chumpitaz, Duarte, Manzo, Diaz, Velasquez, Cueto (1) (Rojas), Cubillas (2), Munante, La Rosa (Sotil), Oblitas
Scotland: Rough, Kennedy, Burns, Rioch (Gemmill), Forsyth, Buchan, Dalglish, Hartford, Jordan (1), Masson (Macari), Johnston
Referee: Eriksson (Switzerland)

Scotland (1) **1, Iran** (0) **1**
7.6.78 CORDOBA
Scotland: Rough, Jardine, Donachie, Gemmill, Burns, Buchan (Forsyth), Dalglish (Harper), Hartford, Jordan, Macari, Robertson
Iran: Hejazi, Nazari, Abdullahi, Kazerani, Eskandarian (o.g.), Parvin, Ghassempour, Sadeghi, Danaifar (1) (Nayeb-Agha), Faraki (Rowshan), Jahani
Referee: N'Diaye (Senegal)

Holland (0) **0, Peru** (0) **0**
7.6.78 MENDOZA
Holland: Jongbloed, Suurbier, Rijsbergen, Krol, Poortvliet, Neeskens (Nanninga), Van de Kerkhof W, Jansen, Haan, Van de Kerkhof R (Rep), Rensenbrink
Peru: Quiroga, Chumpitaz, Duarte, Manzo, Diaz, Velasquez, Cueto, Cubillas, Munante, La Rosa (Sotil), Oblitas
Referee: Prokop (East Germany)

Peru (3) **4, Iran** (1) **1**
11.6.78 CORDOBA
Peru: Quiroga, Chumpitaz, Duarte, Manzo (Leguia), Diaz, Velasquez (1), Cueto, Cubillas (3, 2 pens), Munante, La Rosa (Sotil), Oblitas
Iran: Hejazi, Nazari, Abdullahi, Kazerani, Allahvardi, Parvin, Ghassempour, Sadeghi, Danaifar, Faraki (Jahani), Rowshan (1) (Fariba)
Referee: Jarguz (Poland)

Scotland (1) **3, Holland** (1) **2**
11.6.78 MENDOZA
Scotland: Rough, Kennedy, Donachie, Rioch, Forsyth, Buchan, Dalglish (1), Hartford, Jordan, Gemmill (2, 1 pen), Souness
Holland: Jongbloed, Suurbier, Rijsbergen (Wildschut), Krol, Poortvliet, Neeskens (Boskamp), Jansen, Van de Kerkhof W, Rep (1), Van de Kerkhof R, Rensenbrink (1 pen)
Referee: Linemayer (Austria)

	P	W	D	L	F	A	Pts
Peru	3	2	1	0	7	2	5
Holland	3	1	1	1	5	3	3
Scotland	3	1	1	1	5	6	3
Iran	3	0	1	2	2	8	1

Second Round

Group A	Group B
Venues: Buenos Aires,	**Venues: Rosario,**
Cordoba	**Mendoza**
West Germany	Brazil
Holland	Argentina
Italy	Poland
Austria	Peru

THE SECOND ROUND

The second stage opened with Italy, now cautiously installed as the new favourites, struggling hard to contain the vigorous challenge presented to them by West Germany. Both teams were left to rue squandered opportunities and ultimately they emerged with a draw. Dietz and Vogts expertly shackled Rossi, and Causio and Fischer, particularly aided by the sleek Rummenigge, menaced the Italian rearguard constantly. Despite a goal-less draw, Bettega's shot scrambled off the goal line and Cabrini thumping a shot off the upright provided gripping entertainment.

Peru, hampered by enforced substitutions, went down to their old nemesis Brazil at Mendoza 3–0. Dirceu scored with an outrageous swerving free kick and then almost immediately benefited from Quiroga's eccentric goalkeeping for 2–0. Peru, though they fought gallantly, could find no way back, and were condemned to defeat by Zico's successful penalty kick after Duarte's foolish lunge at Roberto.

Also in Group B, Argentina won 2–0 against a disappointing Polish team. Kempes headed in from close range and the Poles' task, in front of a large provincial crowd, proved too much. It was Kempes again who drove a second decisive goal beyond Tomaszewski.

Holland playing Austria before a meagre crowd in Cordoba also grabbed the early initiative, as Brandts, one of four changes, found himself with time to place a lofted free kick past Koncilia. Austria responded undeterred, both Jara and then Sara forcing saves, and Krankl, a collosus, worrying the Dutch. As Austria sought their reward, they were exposed in an instant, Rensenbrink first scoring from a penalty, before, one minute later, supplying a teasing cross for Rep to apply the final touch. Down 3–0 and beaten, the Austrians continued to create chances after the interval, but Holland again provided the more ruthless finishing, Rep taking charge with a fourth goal. Obermayer finally hit the Dutch net ten minutes from the end but it was too late to matter, and Van der Kerkhof with another for Holland added to the Austrian misery. As an attacking force, Holland had been impressive.

Argentina, provoked by rough and distasteful tackles, responded with relish in a foul-filled, unpleasant match at Rosario. Their opponents and bitter rivals Brazil, better organized and the more inventive, enjoyed the upper hand. However, it was Ortiz, seizing Bertoni's low cross, who missed the game's most significant chance for Argentina. The Peruvians at Mendoza against Poland stumbled to a second successive defeat, beaten comprehensively though by only 1–0. Deyna in dominant form, with the increasingly assured and youthful Boniek, controlled affairs, and Lato finally forced an error from Navarro to cross for Szarmach's tumbling header.

At the River Plate, Italy ruthlessly triumphed over Austria, looking at times a hugely talented outfit. Taking a 13th minute lead, they suffocated their unfortunate opponents, breaking swiftly from compact defence. Graziani, a substitute, was guilty of missing a gilt-edged chance for them for 2–0 and a more comfortable win than their control deserved.

There was drama at Cordoba as the Germans, beginning again forcefully, stole the early advantage when Abramczik – making his first appearance – dived to head them a goal for a lead after two minutes. Holland toiled but Germany repelled them with their fine defensive unit until Ari Haan struck a quite staggering shot beyond Maier from fully forty yards to level. The two Europeans sparred: Rummenigge, now partnered by Müller, probed, while Rensenbrink, the imaginative Dutchman, prompted his team-mates, but as Holland appeared to have control, Müller complemented the German resilience with a second goal, another point blank header on 70 minutes. Facing defeat, the Dutch found salvation six minutes from time, Rene Van der Kerkhof swaying away from markers before striking the net with a spectacular curling effort that defeated the excellent Maier for 2–2. Nanninga, a substitute, still found time to get himself sent off just eight minutes after arriving on the field. 'For "laughing at me",' said Referee Ramon Barreto! Holland were left playing out to the whistle with ten men.

Brazil, in Mendoza, overcame the early loss of their playmaker Zico and a storming attack by Poland, boldly carrying the fight, and ultimately won 3–1. Nelinho gave them an ideal start with another perfectly executed free kick, but thereafter they were pinned back by their determined, strong opponents. Lato levelled after Boniek's powerful defence-splitting run. It was Roberto who sealed the Poles' fate, twice gathering rebounds to force home from the closest of range. Poland responded, though let down at times by woeful finishing, and bowed out as impressive at least as in Germany. This time, however, unlike four years earlier, their cutting edge had deserted them crucially. Brazil's eyes turned now to Rosario, where Argentina needed a miracle against Peru to deny them.

Germany, too, failed dismally. Desperate to win heavily, their desire was fully exploited by the wily Austrians in Cordoba. Leading early on through

Rummenigge, an outstanding striker, they allowed Austria an unlikely equalizer, Vogts deflecting into his own net before Krankl unleashed a spectacular volley past Maier to give Austria the lead. Hans Müller brought Germany level but it was too little too late, and Krankl provided the Austrians with their first victory over the Germans for forty-seven years, brushing aside Rüssmann and Vogts before sweeping the ball past the stranded Maier.

So to Buenos Aires and the glorious triumph of Holland who defeated Italy to confirm themselves finalists. Outplayed thoroughly and behind to Brandts' own goal, they gathered themselves and raised their game. Brandts, making amends, smashed home a marvellous equalizer before Haan, remarkably, thundered another enormous drive from an unlikely distance beyond the groping Zoff for 2–1. At the end there was Dutch jubilation, for the Italians despair. Bearzots' 'Azzurri', who often had looked quite the best team in the Tournament, were out of the reckoning.

Finally to Rosario, where Argentina fashioned an improbable result against a shockingly inept Peruvian team. Needing to win by four, they annihilated a depressingly obliging opponents 6–0 with an exhilarating and breathless display of fast moving, attacking football. Post and bar were struck as Kempes and Luque scored twice, Tarantini and Houseman completing the rout. Argentina were through, Brazil without losing were eliminated, and Peru had been castigated.

Second Round

Group A

West Germany (0) **0, Italy** (0) **0**
14.6.78 BUENOS AIRES
West Germany: Maier, Kaltz, Vogts, Rüssmann, Dietz, Bonhof, Flohe (Beer), Zimmermann (Konopa), Holzenbein, Rummenigge, Fischer
Italy: Zoff, Scirea, Gentile, Bellugi, Cabrini, Tardelli, Benetti, Antognoni (Zaccarelli), Causio, Rossi, Bettega
Referee: Maksimovic (Yugoslavia)

Holland (3) **5, Austria** (0) **1**
14.6.78 CORDOBA
Holland: Schrijvers, Wildschut, Brandts (1) (Van Kraay), Krol, Poortvliet, Jansen, Haan, Van de Kerkhof W (1), Rep (2), Van de Kerkhof R (Schoenaker), Rensenbrink (1)
Austria: Koncilia, Obermayer (1), Sara, Pezzey, Breitenberger, Hickersberger, Prohaska, Jara, Krieger, Kreuz, Krankl
Referee: Gordon (Scotland)

Italy (1) **1, Austria** (0) **0**
18.6.78 BUENOS AIRES
Italy: Zoff, Scirea, Bellugi (Cuccureddu), Gentile, Cabrini, Benetti, Zaccarelli, Tardelli, Causio, Rossi (1), Bettega (Graziani)
Austria: Koncilia, Obermayer, Sara, Pezzey, Strasser, Hickersberger, Prohaska, Kreuz, Krieger, Schachner (Pirkner), Krankl
Referee: Rion (Belgium)

West Germany (1) **2, Holland** (1) **2**
18.6.78 CORDOBA
West Germany: Maier, Kaltz, Vogts, Rüssmann, Dietz, Bonhof, Holzenbein, Beer, Abramczik (1), Müller D (1), Rummenigge
Holland: Schrijvers, Wildschut (Nanninga), Brandts, Krol, Poortvliet, Jansen, Haan (1), Van de Kerkhof W, Rep, Van de Kerkhof R (1), Rensenbrink
Referee: Barreto (Uruguay)

Holland (0) **2, Italy** (1) **1**
21.6.78 BUENOS AIRES
Holland: Schrijvers (Jongbloed), Brandts (o.g., 1), Krol, Poortvliet, Jansen, Haan (1), Neeskens, Van de Kerkhof W, Rep (Van Kraay), Van de Kerkhof R, Rensenbrink
Italy: Zoff, Scirea, Gentile, Cuccureddu, Cabrini, Tardelli, Zaccarelli, Benetti (Graziani), Causio (Sala C), Rossi, Bettega
Referee: Martinez (Spain)

Austria (0) **3, West Germany** (1) **2**
21.6.78 CORDOBA
Austria: Koncilia, Obermayer, Sara, Pezzey, Strasser, Hickersberger, Prohaska, Kreuz, Krieger, Schachner (Oberacher), Krankl (2)
West Germany: Maier, Kaltz, Vogts (o.g.), Rüssmann, Dietz, Bonhof, Holzenbein (1), Beer (Müller H), Abramczik, Müller D (Fisher), Rummenigge (1)
Referee: Klein (Israel)

	P	W	D	L	F	A	Pts
Holland	3	2	1	0	9	4	5
Italy	3	1	1	1	2	2	3
West Germany	3	0	2	1	4	5	2
Austria	3	1	0	2	4	8	2

Group B

Argentina (1) **2, Poland** (0) **0**
14.6.78 ROSARIO
Argentina: Fillol, Olguin, Galvan, Passarella, Tarantini, Ardiles, Gallego, Valencia (Villa), Houseman (Ortiz), Bertoni, Kempes (2)
Poland: Tomaszewski, Kasperczak, Szymanowski, Zmunda, Maculewicz, Masztaler (Mazur), Deyna, Nawalka, Boniek, Lato, Szarmach
Referee: Eriksson (Sweden)

Brazil (2) **3, Peru** (0) **0**
14.6.78 MENDOZA
Brazil: Leao, Amaral, Toninho, Oscar, Rodrigues Neto, Batista, Cerezo (Chicao), Dirceu (2), Gil (Zico (1 pen)), Mendonca, Roberto
Peru: Quiroga, Chumpitaz, Diaz (Navarro), Manzo, Duarte, Velasquez, Cueto, Cubillas, La Rosa, Munante, Oblitas (Rojas P)
Referee: Rainea (Romania)

Argentina (0) **0, Brazil** (0) **0**
18.6.78 ROSARIO
Argentina: Fillol, Olguin, Galvan, Passarella, Tarantini, Ardiles (Villa), Gallego, Ortiz (Alonso), Kempes, Bertoni, Luque
Brazil: Leao, Amaral, Toninho, Oscar, Rodrigues Neto (Edinho), Chicao, Batista, Dirceu, Mendonca (Zico), Gil, Roberto
Referee: Palotai (Hungary)

Poland (0) **1, Peru** (0) **0**
18.6.78 MENDOZA
Poland: Kukla, Gorgón, Szymanowski, Zmunda, Maculewicz, Masztaler (Kasperczak), Nawalka, Deyna, Lato, Boniek (Lubanski), Szarmach (1)
Peru: Quiroga, Chumpitaz, Duarte, Manzo, Navarro, Cueto, Quezada, Cubillas, La Rosa (Sotil), Munante (Rojas P), Oblitas
Referee: Partridge (England)

Brazil (1) **3, Poland** (1) **1**
21.6.78 MENDOZA
Brazil: Leao, Amaral, Toninho, Oscar, Nelinho (1), Cerezo (Rivelino), Batista, Dirceu, Zico (Mendonca), Gil, Roberto (2)
Poland: Kukla, Gorgón, Szymanowski, Zmunda, Maculewicz, Kasperczak (Lubanski), Nawalka, Deyna, Boniek, Lato (1), Szarmach
Referee: Silvagno (Chile)

Argentina (2) **6, Peru** (0) **0**
21.6.78 ROSARIO
Argentina: Fillol, Olguin, Galvan, Passarella, Tarantini (1), Larrosa, Gallego (Oviedo), Kempes (2), Bertoni (Houseman (1)), Luque (2), Ortiz
Peru: Quiroga, Chumpitaz, Duarte, Manzo, Rojas R, Cueto, Velasquez (Gorriti), Cubillas, Quezada, Munante, Oblitas
Referee: Wurtz (France)

	P	W	D	L	F	A	Pts
Argentina	3	2	1	0	8	0	5
Brazil	3	2	1	0	6	1	5
Poland	3	1	0	2	2	5	2
Peru	3	0	0	3	0	10	0

PLAY-OFF FOR THIRD PLACE

Before the final a surprisingly interesting and keen contest for third and fourth place ensued. Italy, opening brightly, dominated, full again of their clever football. Causio gave them a deserved lead, Nelinho on the hour brought Brazil parity with a swerving dipping shot from an impossible angle close to the touchline, and Dirceu put them ahead from a distance 2–1. Although Bettega hit the bar as the Italians pressed, the South Americans held on to gain some small consolation.

Match for Third Place

Brazil (0) **2, Italy** (1) **1**
24.6.78 BUENOS AIRES
Brazil: Leao, Amaral, Nelinho (1), Oscar, Rodrigues Neto, Batista, Cerezo (Rivelino), Dirceu (1), Gil (Reinaldo), Roberto, Mendonca
Italy: Zoff, Scirea, Gentile, Cuccureddu, Maldera, Cabrini, Antognoni (Sala C), Sala P, Causio (1), Rossi, Bettega
Referee: Klein (Israel)

THE FINAL

There was immediate controversy as Holland took the field and waited fully five minutes for their Argentine opponents to emerge beneath a huge ticker tape shower, Further delay occurred as the gamesmanship continued when

Rene Van der Kerkhof's bandaged hand was objected to. Ten minutes late, the game began with the Dutch tackling furiously, determined to disrupt Argentina's rhythm. Passarella forced Jongbloed into an early save and then missed again. Rep for Holland with a still better opportunity allowed Fillol to parry away safely. Holland, happy to concede midfield, were punished after 37 minutes, Kempes finding space to drive the ball home. Rensenbrink might have scored for the Dutch right on the half-time whistle, allowing the ball to be cleared off his toe a yard out.

In the second half Haan of the hammer shot twice, latched on to indecisive clearances to test Fillol, as the Dutch, increasingly urgent, raked their hosts. Yet Argentina clung comfortably to their lead. Nanninga, a substitute, finally produced a goal: tall, gangling and troublesome to the Argentine defence, he turned Van der Kerkhof's high centre over the goal line with nine minutes left for 1–1. Extra time beckoned and for the Dutch one final opportunity came and went – Rensenbrink struck the foot of the post in the 89th minute.

It was Kempes who rescued the home nation from its seemingly inevitable fate in the fourteenth minutes of extra time tension, squeezing the ball expertly in through a posse of flailing legs. Holland now lost their composure, kicking out indiscriminately as time deserted them, and their fate was finally sealed on 116 minutes when Bertoni, put through by the wonderful Kempes, stabbed a third and killer goal for 3–1. The celebration could begin in earnest.

Final

Argentina (1) **3, Holland** (0) **1** (aet, 1–1 at 90 mins)
25.6.78 BUENOS AIRES
Argentina: Fillol, Olguin, Galvan, Passarella, Tarantini, Ardiles (Larrosa), Gallego, Kempes (2), Bertoni (1), Luque, Ortiz (Houseman)
Holland: Jongbloed, Poortvliet, Krol, Brandts, Jansen (Suurbier), Neeskens, Haan, Van de Kerkhof W, Van de Kerkhof R, Rep (Nanninga (1)), Rensenbrink
Referee: Gonella (Italy)

Argentina gained the Crown Jewel, World Champions, a title their people and the Military Junta had craved. They had played fiercely and largely deserved their victory, though later, much later, sinister undertones would emerge to discredit their achievements: Peru stood accused of throwing away their decisive encounter in order to gain political and financial favour. Holland, immensely talented, denied again by a host nation, had proven themselves the best of the rest, their bold challenge undermined by the absence of Johann Cruyff.

Brazil were rightly aggrieved. Without exception the best team in their seven matches, they were eliminated without loss in contentious circumstances. Italy, too, assured and skilful, illuminated the Tournament and enjoyed their finest day when cleverly condemning Argentina to defeat in front of the disbelieving hordes at the River Plate Stadium. As for the rest, Germany, less talented now shorn of Beckenbauer and Müller, defended cleverly, though lacked attacking inspiration, and Poland once more played with power and flair despite Lato and his colleagues lacking their clinical edge of 1974.

Scotland, who promised much, were ruined by overconfidence and imploded miserably, an unrealistic assessment of their own capabilities leading them to complacency and failure. But who knows how far this excellent team, so resolute against the Dutch, may have travelled under more constrained and conservative leadership.

CHAPTER 12

SPAIN

1982

Qualifying Tournament
108 entries
Argentina qualify as holders, Spain qualify as hosts

Europe (33): Albania, Austria, Belgium, Bulgaria, Cyprus, Czechoslovakia, Denmark, England, Finland, France, East Germany, West Germany, Greece, Holland, Hungary, Iceland, Republic of Ireland, Italy, Luxembourg, Malta, Northern Ireland, Norway, Poland, Portugal, Romania, Scotland, Spain, Sweden, Switzerland, Turkey, USSR, Wales, Yugoslavia

South America (10): Argentina, Bolivia, Brazil, Chile, Colombia, Ecuador, Paraguay, Peru, Uruguay, Venezuela

CONCACAF (15): Canada, Costa Rica, Cuba, Grenada, Guatemala, Guyana, Haiti, Honduras, Mexico, Netherlands Antilles, Panama, El Salvador, Surinam, Trinidad and Tobago, USA

Asia/Oceania (22): Australia, Bahrain, China, Fiji, Hong Kong, Indonesia, Iran, Iraq, Israel, Japan, North Korea, South Korea, Kuwait, Macao, Malaysia, New Zealand, Qatar, Saudi Arabia, Singapore, Syria, Taiwan, Thailand

Africa (28): Algeria, Cameroon, Central Africa, Egypt, Ethiopia, Gambia, Ghana, Guinea, Kenya, Lesotho, Liberia, Libya, Madagascar, Malawi, Morocco, Mozambique, Niger, Nigeria, Senegal, Sierra Leone, Somalia, Sudan, Tanzania, Togo, Tunisia, Uganda, Zaire, Zambia

Europe

Group 1 (West Germany, Austria, Bulgaria, Finland, Albania)
Finland v Bulgaria 0–2, Albania v Finland 2–0, Finland v Austria 0–2, Bulgaria v Albania 2–1, Austria v Albania 5–0, Bulgaria v West Germany 1–3, Albania v Austria 0–1, Albania v West Germany 0–2, West Germany v Austria 2–0, Bulgaria v Finland 4–0, Finland v West Germany 0–4, Austria v Bulgaria 2–0, Austria v Finland 5–1, Finland v Albania 2–1, West Germany v Finland 7–1, Austria v West Germany 1–3, Albania v Bulgaria 0–2, Bulgaria v Austria 0–0, West Germany v Albania 8–0, West Germany v Bulgaria 4–0

	P	W	D	L	F	A	Pts
West Germany	8	8	0	0	33	3	16
Austria	8	5	1	2	16	6	11
Bulgaria	8	4	1	3	11	10	9
Albania	8	1	0	7	4	22	2
Finland	8	1	0	7	4	27	2

West Germany and Austria qualified

Group 2 (Holland, France, Belgium, Rep of Ireland, Cyprus)

Cyprus v Rep of Ireland 2–3, Rep of Ireland v Holland 2–1, Cyprus v France 0–7, Rep of Ireland v Belgium 1–1, France v Rep of Ireland 2–0, Belgium v Holland 1–0, Rep of Ireland v Cyprus 6–0, Cyprus v Belgium 0–2, Belgium v Cyprus 3–2, Holland v Cyprus 3–0, Holland v France 1–0, Belgium v Rep of Ireland 1–0, France v Belgium 3–2, Cyprus v Holland 0–1, Holland v Rep of Ireland 2–2, Belgium v France 2–0, Holland v Belgium 3–0, Rep of Ireland v France 3–2, France v Holland 2–0, France v Cyprus 4–0

	P	W	D	L	F	A	Pts
Belgium	8	5	1	2	12	9	11
France	8	5	0	3	20	8	10
Rep of Ireland	8	4	2	2	17	11	10
Holland	8	4	1	3	11	7	9
Cyprus	8	0	0	8	4	29	0

Belgium and France qualified

Group 3 (Czechoslovakia, USSR, Wales, Turkey, Iceland)

Iceland v Wales 0–4, Iceland v USSR 1–2, Turkey v Iceland 1–3, Wales v Turkey 4–0, USSR v Iceland 5–0, Wales v Czechoslovakia 1–0, Czechoslovakia v Turkey 2–0, Turkey v Wales 0–1, Turkey v Czechoslovakia 0–3, Czechoslovakia v Iceland 6–1, Wales v USSR 0–0, Iceland v Turkey 2–0, Czechoslovakia v Wales 2–0, Iceland v Czechoslovakia 1–1, USSR v Turkey 4–0, Turkey v USSR 0–3, Wales v Iceland 2–2, USSR v Czechoslovakia 2–0, USSR v Wales 3–0, Czechoslovakia v USSR 1–1

	P	W	D	L	F	A	Pts
USSR	8	6	2	0	20	2	14
Czechoslovakia	8	4	2	2	15	6	10
Wales	8	4	2	2	12	7	10
Iceland	8	2	2	4	10	21	6
Turkey	8	0	0	8	1	22	0

USSR and Czechoslovakia qualified

Group 4 (England, Norway, Romania, Switzerland, Hungary)
England v Norway 4–0, Norway v Romania 1–1, Romania v England 2–1, Switzerland v Norway 1–2, England v Switzerland 2–1, Switzerland v Hungary 2–2, England v Romania 0–0, Hungary v Romania 1–0, Norway v Hungary 1–2, Switzerland v England 2–1, Romania v Norway 1–0, Hungary v England 1–3, Norway v Switzerland 1–1, Norway v England 2–1, Romania v Hungary 0–0, Romania v Switzerland 1–2, Hungary v Switzerland 3–0, Hungary v Norway 4–1, Switzerland v Romania 0–0, England v Hungary 1–0

	P	W	D	L	F	A	Pts
Hungary	8	4	2	2	13	8	10
England	8	4	1	3	13	8	9
Romania	8	2	4	2	5	5	8
Switzerland	8	2	3	3	9	12	7
Norway	8	2	2	4	8	15	6

Hungary and England qualified

Group 5 (Italy, Yugoslavia, Greece, Denmark, Luxembourg)
Luxembourg v Yugoslavia 0–5, Yugoslavia v Denmark 2–1, Luxembourg v Italy 0–2, Denmark v Greece 0–1, Italy v Denmark 2–0, Italy v Yugoslavia 2–0, Denmark v Luxembourg 4–0, Greece v Italy 0–2, Greece v Luxembourg 2–0, Luxembourg v Greece 0–2, Yugoslavia v Greece 5–1, Luxembourg v Denmark 1–2, Denmark v Italy 3–1, Denmark v Yugoslavia 1–2, Greece v Denmark 2–3, Yugoslavia v Italy 1–1, Italy v Greece 1–1, Yugoslavia v Luxembourg 5–0, Greece v Yugoslavia 1–2, Italy v Luxembourg 1–0

	P	W	D	L	F	A	Pts
Yugoslavia	8	6	1	1	22	7	13
Italy	8	5	2	1	12	5	12
Denmark	8	4	0	4	14	11	8
Greece	8	3	1	4	10	13	7
Luxembourg	8	0	0	8	1	23	0

Yugoslavia and Italy qualified

Group 6 (Scotland, Sweden, Portugal, Northern Ireland, Israel)
Israel v Northern Ireland 0–0, Sweden v Israel 1–1, Sweden v Scotland 0–1, Northern Ireland v Sweden 3–0, Scotland v Portugal 0–0, Israel v Sweden 0–0, Portugal v Northern Ireland 1–0, Portugal v Israel 3–0, Israel v Scotland 0–1, Scotland v Northern Ireland 1–1, Scotland v Israel 3–1, Northern Ireland v Portugal 1–0, Sweden v Northern Ireland 1–0, Sweden v Portugal 3–0, Scotland v Sweden 2–0, Portugal v Sweden 1–2, Northern Ireland v Scotland 0–0, Israel v Portugal 4–1, Northern Ireland v Israel 1–0, Portugal v Scotland 2–1

	P	W	D	L	F	A	Pts
Scotland	8	4	3	1	9	4	11
Northern Ireland	8	3	3	2	6	3	9
Sweden	8	3	2	3	7	8	8
Portugal	8	3	1	4	8	11	7
Israel	8	1	3	4	6	10	5

Scotland and Northern Ireland qualified

Group 7 (Poland, East Germany, Malta)

Malta v Poland 0–2, Malta v East Germany 1–2, Poland v East Germany 1–0, East Germany v Poland 2–3, East Germany v Malta 5–1, Poland v Malta 6–0

	P	W	D	L	F	A	Pts
Poland	4	4	0	0	12	2	8
East Germany	4	2	0	2	9	6	4
Malta	4	0	0	4	2	15	0

Poland qualified

South America

Group 1 (Bolivia, Brazil, Venezuela)

Venezuela v Brazil 0–1, Bolivia v Venezuela 3–0, Bolivia v Brazil 1–2, Venezuela v Bolivia 1–0, Brazil v Bolivia 3–1, Brazil v Venezuela 5–0

	P	W	D	L	F	A	Pts
Brazil	4	4	0	0	11	2	8
Bolivia	4	1	0	3	5	6	2
Venezuela	4	1	0	3	1	9	2

Brazil qualified

Group 2 (Colombia, Peru, Uruguay)

Colombia v Peru 1–1, Uruguay v Colombia 3–2, Peru v Colombia 2–0, Uruguay v Peru 1–2, Peru v Uruguay 0–0, Colombia v Uruguay 1–1

	P	W	D	L	F	A	Pts
Peru	4	2	2	0	5	2	6
Uruguay	4	1	2	1	5	5	4
Colombia	4	0	2	2	4	7	2

Peru qualified

Group 3 (Chile, Ecuador, Paraguay)
Ecuador v Paraguay 1–0, Ecuador v Chile 0–0, Paraguay v Ecuador 3–1, Paraguay v Chile 0–1, Chile v Ecuador 2–0, Chile v Paraguay 3–0

	P	W	D	L	F	A	Pts
Chile	4	3	1	0	6	0	7
Ecuador	4	1	1	2	2	5	3
Paraguay	4	1	0	3	3	6	2

Chile qualified

CONCACAF

Group 1 (Caribbean)
Preliminary Round
Guyana v Grenada 5–2, 3–2

Sub-Group 1A (Cuba, Surinam, Guyana)
Cuba v Surinam 3–0, Surinam v Cuba 0–0, Guyana v Surinam 0–1, Surinam v Guyana 4–0, Cuba v Guyana 1–0, Guyana v Cuba 0–3

	P	W	D	L	F	A	Pts
Cuba	4	3	1	0	7	0	7
Surinam	4	2	1	1	5	3	5
Guyana	4	0	0	4	0	9	0

Sub-Group 1B (Haiti, Trinidad and Tobago, Netherlands Antilles)
Haiti v Trinidad & Tobago 2–0, Trinidad & Tobago v Haiti 1–0, Haiti v Netherlands Antilles 1–0, Trinidad & Tobago v Netherlands Antilles 0–0, Netherlands Antilles v Trinidad & Tobago 0–0, Netherlands Antilles v Haiti 1–1

	P	W	D	L	F	A	Pts
Haiti	4	2	1	1	4	2	5
Trinidad & Tobago	4	1	2	1	1	2	4
Netherlands Antilles	4	0	3	1	1	2	3

Group 2 (North) (Mexico, Canada, USA)
Canada v Mexico 1–1, USA v Canada 0–0, Canada v USA 2–1, Mexico v USA 5–1, Mexico v Canada 1–1, USA v Mexico 2–1

	P	W	D	L	F	A	Pts
Canada	4	1	3	0	4	3	5
Mexico	4	1	2	1	8	5	4
USA	4	1	1	2	4	8	3

Group 3 (Central) (Costa Rica, El Salvador, Guatemala, Honduras, Panama)

Panama v Guatemala 0–2, Panama v Honduras 0–2, Panama v Costa Rica 1–1, Panama v El Salvador 1–3, Costa Rica v Honduras 2–3, El Salvador v Panama 4–1, Guatemala v Costa Rica 0–0, Honduras v Guatemala 0–0, El Salvador v Costa Rica (awarded 2–0 to El Salvador when Costa Rica refused to play there for security reasons), Costa Rica v Panama 2–0, Guatemala v El Salvador 0–0, Guatemala v Panama 5–0, Honduras v Costa Rica 1–1, El Salvador v Honduras 2–1, Costa Rica v Guatemala 0–3, Honduras v El Salvador 2–0, Guatemala v Honduras 0–1, Costa Rica v El Salvador 0–0, Honduras v Panama 5–0, El Salvador v Guatemala 1–0

	P	W	D	L	F	A	Pts
Honduras	8	5	2	1	15	5	12
El Salvador	8	5	2	1	12	5	12
Guatemala	8	3	3	2	10	2	9
Costa Rica	8	1	4	3	6	10	6
Panama	8	0	1	7	3	24	1

Final Round

(In Honduras)

Mexico v Cuba 4–0, Canada v El Salvador 1–0, Honduras v Haiti 4–0, Haiti v Canada 1–1, Mexico v El Salvador 0–1, Honduras v Cuba 2–0, El Salvador v Cuba 0–0, Mexico v Haiti 1–1, Honduras v Canada 2–1, Haiti v Cuba 0–2, Mexico v Canada 1–1, Honduras v El Salvador 0–0, Haiti v El Salvador 0–1, Cuba v Canada 2–2, Honduras v Mexico 0–0

	P	W	D	L	F	A	Pts
Honduras	5	3	2	0	8	1	8
El Salvador	5	2	2	1	2	1	6
Mexico	5	1	3	1	6	3	5
Canada	5	1	3	1	6	6	5
Cuba	5	1	2	2	4	8	4
Haiti	5	0	2	3	2	9	2

Honduras and El Salvador Qualified

Asia/Oceania

Group 1 (Australia, Fiji, Indonesia, New Zealand, Taiwan)

New Zealand v Australia 3–3, Fiji v New Zealand 0–4, Taiwan v New Zealand 0–0, Indonesia v New Zealand 0–2, Australia v New Zealand 0–2, Australia v Indonesia 2–0, New Zealand v Indonesia 5–0, New Zealand v Taiwan 2–0, Fiji v Indonesia 0–0, Fiji v Taiwan 2–1, Australia v Taiwan 3–2, Indonesia v Taiwan 1–0, Taiwan v Indonesia 2–0, Fiji v Australia 1–4, Taiwan v Fiji 0–0, Indonesia v Fiji 3–3, Australia v Fiji 10–0, New Zealand v Fiji 13–0, Indonesia v Australia 1–0, Taiwan v Australia 0–0

	P	W	D	L	F	A	Pts
New Zealand	8	6	2	0	31	3	14
Australia	8	4	2	2	22	9	10
Indonesia	8	2	2	4	5	14	6
Taiwan	8	1	3	4	5	8	5
Fiji	8	1	3	4	6	35	5

Group 2 (Saudi Arabia, Bahrain, Iraq, Qatar, Syria) (in Saudi Arabia)

Qatar v Iraq 0–1, Syria v Bahrain 0–1, Iraq v Saudi Arabia 0–1, Qatar v Bahrain 3–0, Syria v Saudi Arabia 0–2, Iraq v Bahrain 2–0, Qatar v Syria 2–1, Bahrain v Saudi Arabia 0–1, Iraq v Syria 2–1, Qatar v Saudi Arabia 0–1

	P	W	D	L	F	A	Pts
Saudi Arabia	4	4	0	0	5	0	8
Iraq	4	3	0	1	5	2	6
Qatar	4	2	0	2	5	3	4
Bahrain	4	1	0	3	1	6	2
Syria	4	0	0	4	2	7	0

Group 3 (South Korea, Iran (withdrew), Kuwait, Malaysia, Thailand)

(In Kuwait)

Malaysia v South Korea 1–2, Kuwait v Thailand 6–0, South Korea v Thailand 5–1, Kuwait v Malaysia 4–0, Malaysia v Thailand 2–2, Kuwait v South Korea 2–0

	P	W	D	L	F	A	Pts
Kuwait	3	3	0	0	12	0	6
South Korea	3	2	0	1	7	4	4
Malaysia	3	0	1	2	3	8	1
Thailand	3	0	1	2	3	13	1

Group 4 (China, North Korea, Hong Kong, Japan, Macao, Singapore)
(In Hong Kong)

Preliminary Round
Hong Kong v China 0–1, North Korea v Macao 3–0, Singapore v Japan 0–1

Sub-Group 4A
China v Macao 3–0, China v Japan 1–0, Japan v Macao 3–0

Sub-Group 4B
Hong Kong v Singapore 1–1, Singapore v North Korea 0–1, Hong Kong v North Korea 2–2

Semi-finals
North Korea v Japan 1–0, China v Hong Kong 0–0 (China won 5–4 on penalties)

Final
China v North Korea 4–2

Final Round
China v New Zealand 0–0, New Zealand v China 1–0, New Zealand v Kuwait 1–2, China v Kuwait 3–0, Saudi Arabia v Kuwait 0–1, Saudi Arabia v China 2–4, China v Saudi Arabia 2–0, New Zealand v Saudi Arabia 2–2, Kuwait v China 1–0, Kuwait v Saudi Arabia 2–0, Kuwait v New Zealand 2–2, Saudi Arabia v New Zealand 0–5

	P	W	D	L	F	A	Pts
Kuwait	6	4	1	1	8	6	9
New Zealand	6	2	3	1	11	6	7
China	6	3	1	2	9	4	7
Saudi Arabia	6	0	1	5	4	16	1

Play-off (in Singapore): New Zealand v China 2–1
Kuwait and New Zealand qualified

Africa

1st Round (Zimbabwe, Sudan, Liberia, Togo byes)
Libya v Gambia 2–1, 0–0, Ethiopia v Zambia 0–0, 0–4, Sierra Leone v Algeria 2–2, 1–3, Senegal v Morocco 0–1, 0–0, Guinea v Lesotho 3–1, 1–1, Tunisia v Nigeria 2–0, 0–2 (Nigeria won 4–3 on penalties), Cameroon v Malawi 3–0, 1–1, Kenya v Tanzania 3–1, 0–5, Zaire v Mozambique 5–2, 2–1, Niger v Somalia 0–0, 1–1, Egypt v Ghana (withdrew), Madagascar v Uganda (withdrew)

2nd Round

Cameroon v Zimbabwe 2–0, 0–1, Sudan v Algeria 1–1, 0–2, Madagascar v Zaire 1–1, 2–3, Morocco v Zambia 2–0, 0–2 (Morocco won 5–4 on penalties), Nigeria v Tanzania 1–1, 2–0, Liberia v Guinea 0–0, 0–1, Niger v Togo 0–1, 2–1, Egypt v Libya (withdrew)

3rd Round

Guinea v Nigeria 1–1, 0–1, Zaire v Cameroon 1–0, 1–6, Morocco v Egypt 1–0, 0–0, Algeria v Niger 4–0, 0–1

4th Round

Nigeria v Algeria 0–2, 1–2, Morocco v Cameroon 0–2, 1–2
Algeria and Cameroon qualified

1982 SPAIN 13 June–11 July

QUALIFIERS

Algeria	El Salvador	Northern Ireland
Argentina	England	Peru
Austria	France	Poland
Belgium	Honduras	Scotland
Brazil	Hungary	Spain
Cameroon	Italy	USSR
Chile	Kuwait	West Germany
Czechoslovakia	New Zealand	Yugoslavia

Spain, a football-worshipping nation but strangely unsuccessful in the Tournament, were host to the twelfth World Cup. Unfortunately, with many of those participating in political crisis or conflict, the mood was a sombre one. Britain, with three representatives, had been at war with Argentina. Poland and El Salvador were in turmoil, and Spain, themselves threatened perennially by the terrorism of Basque separatists, feared withdrawals from this, the biggest spectacle ever organized. Twenty-four teams would now challenge rather than the traditional sixteen, creating six groups of four, from which in the second round the twelve best teams would advance into four groups of three to determine semi-finalists.

Group One, on the northern coast at La Coruña and at Vigo near the Portuguese border, featured Italy, so close in 1978. Their gifted team included

Rossi, the striker, returning after a two-year suspension for alleged match rigging, Antognoni, their play maker, and Zoff, their veteran goalkeeper and captain. Qualification for them had been a comfortable affair despite Denmark in Copenhagen embarrassing them temporarily. Cameroon, one of two African nations catered for, had squeezed out previous representatives Zaire (1974) and Morocco (1970), and whilst still an outsider, had players participating regularly in European leagues. Peru, so good and then so appallingly bad in Argentina, promised much by way of entertainment. Conquerors of Uruguay and benefiting still from the experience and flair of Oblitas and the veteran skills of Cubillas, they were considered amongst the best of the dark horses. Their goalkeeper Quiroga, who delighted in his nickname 'El Loco', caused both amusement and concern. Poland completed the Group. Their team, shown to be aged in 1978, had a new look, though Zmuda remained to organize, Lato for the third time to provide goals, and Boniek for imagination; they were much respected in spite of the trouble in their homeland.

From Group Two in the northern towns of Gijon and Oviedo were the West Germans, awesome in qualification where they won every game, scoring thirty-three times and conceding just three goals. Justifiably they were co-favourites for the competition, their team tough in defence and incisive in attack, boasting the talents of Rummenigge and the nimble running of Littbarski. Chile, last seen in 1974, had benefited from being drawn in the weakest South American group and given the relatively simple task of beating Ecuador and Paraguay. Furthermore, because they were renowned for their travel sickness, they were lightly regarded.

Austria, a fine side built on the remnants of their Argentina squad, had strangely been drawn again with their German rivals with whom they qualified. Koncilia, Obermayer, Prohaska and Krankl would all be there, and Hintermaier, a newcomer to their midfield, offered an extra dimension. The last of the group, Algeria, making the short trip across the Mediterranean, were Africa's other entry. The Algerians, known to be tricky, energetic customers, with Madjer, Dhaleb and the very accomplished Belloumi in the ranks, arrived hoping to build on the achievement of neighbouring Tunisia four years earlier.

In Group Three the champions Argentina, for whom Passarella, Ardiles, Bertoni and Kempes played, would be joined by the mercurial twenty-one-year-old Maradona. Preparing thoroughly for four months, they again had high expectations. Belgium, often deplorably defensive, were still effective, with the notable scalp of Holland during a rugged qualification campaign, their star performer being Ceulemans. Hungary, Group winners from the most competitive of the European pools despite two defeats by England, had Nyilasi, a still more influential figure for them. Unfortunately, their form away from Budapest was largely unimpressive. Finally came El Salvador, whose surprise presence was the result of a shock victory over Mexico. Little was known of them, but as in 1970, their qualification had been achieved at a time when their country was undergoing crisis.

In Group Four, England, so shaky early on, had finally booked their passage courtesy of a spectacular success over Hungary. With the muscular Robson, elegant Wilkins commanding and instigating their attacks, and Keegan harrying defenders, they came with hope. Czechoslovakia, European Champions to general astonishment in 1976, had also been drawn in Valladolid and Bilbao, the heart of Basque country, edging out the brave Welsh. However, in spite of the excellent Nehoda and recent draws with Argentina and Brazil, they were thought to be in decline. The same could not be said of France, with Tigana, Platini and Giresse in a cavalier midfield, the powerful Tresor in defence, and a fast, mobile attack. At their best they constituted a threat to even the finest, and had beaten both Italy and Holland (but curiously lost to Wales and Peru in warm-ups). Kuwait, the fourth member from the Asia/Oceania qualifiers, boasted credible results against Czechoslovakia with whom they had drawn, and Spain who had beaten them narrowly. Still, here in this company they would begin very much an outsider.

In Group Five the hosts Spain were guaranteed a large and vocal support in the cities of Zaragoza and Valencia, with a hard, uncompromising defence giving them stability. Having a very favourable draw, optimism abounded despite the youth of their team, with Real Madrid's rising star Juanito carrying much of the nation's hope on his shoulders. Honduras, making their debut, had finally won through winning the weak CONCACAF final tournament that they themselves had hosted. Though unbeaten there, this would be a searching test for their inexperienced players. The same could have been said of Northern Ireland who had qualified ahead of both Sweden and Portugal. Organized and hard working, theirs had already been a magnificent achievement. Yugoslavia, the fourth of this quartet, had scored freely in finishing ahead of the Italians to confirm their participation and their status as one of the competition's dark horses.

Finally, Group Six's matches were set in the sunny climes of the south at Malaga and Seville. Brazil, the favourites, had a thoroughly changed team both in playing staff and philosophy. Zico, now a mature and dominating force, had been joined by Falcao, the elegant Socrates and Junior in a team with talent the envy of most. Qualification for them against Venezuela and Bolivia had been merely academic. New Zealand had earned the dubious honour of competing against them after finishing behind Kuwait in the Asia/Oceania competition. Their final win, a crushing 5–0 victory over Saudi Arabia, had earned then an unlikely play-off in Singapore with China, and they seized their chance. Robust and compact, they relied heavily on Rufer to provide their attacking options. The Soviets, as ever, were viewed with caution despite constantly underachieving. Their team, easy and unbeaten qualifiers, would represent a threat with a mean defence and fine players, Blokhin, Shengelia and Baltacha amongst their squad. The last of the group would be Scotland, resurgent and eager to erase the bitter memories of Argentina. Their team, fiercely competitive, would be led by the powerful Souness, the diminutive ball player Strachan, and Liverpool's fine defender, Hansen.

Group 1

Venues: Vigo, La Coruña
Cameroon
Italy
Peru
Poland

Group 2

Venues: Gijon, Oviedo
Algeria
Austria
Chile
West Germany

Group 3

Venues: Elche, Alicante
Argentina
Belgium
El Salvador
Hungary

Group 4

Venues: Bilbao, Valladolid
Czechoslovakia
England
France
Kuwait

Group 5

Venues: Valencia, Zaragoza
Honduras
Northern Ireland
Spain
Yugoslavia

Group 6

Venues: Seville, Malaga
Brazil
New Zealand
Scotland
USSR

THE FIRST SERIES

In a foul-infested opener played out in front of 95,000 at the Nou camp, Argentina floundered on the rock that was Belgium. Stifled and unable to find inspiration, they were undone by Van den Bergh's second-half goal, Coeck positioned in front of the Belgian back four effective in shackling Maradona. Also in Group Three, carnage ensued as Hungary savaged the unfortunate Salvadorans. Behind in minutes and 3–0 down by half-time, they collapsed pitifully as the Hungarians achieved the remarkable feat of scoring ten goals.

Zapata in scoring for the tiny American nation provided little consolation, nor did it conceal their embarrassment as their defending bordered on the farcical long before the end.

Group One's first game up at Vigo saw Italy and Poland manufacture a tense and nervous 0–0 draw. Italy, beginning brighter, saw Tardelli strike the cross bar, but Poland, resolute, fought back determinedly in the second half before both accepted a point. The next day at La Coruña saw Cameroon give Peru a fright, enjoying the better of another surprisingly uneventful draw before a frustrated audience.

In Group Two, Algeria remarkably registered a shock to equal that of North Korea when they deservedly and dramatically accounted for West Germany. Quick and incisive, encouraged by a large and noisy band of compatriots, the North Africans launched themselves at increasingly unsettled opponents, though as half-time approached, the Germans had appeared to have restored a semblance of order to proceedings. In the second half, as Germany pressed, they were caught out; Magath managed to block Belloumi on a darting run and shot, but the lurking Madjer rammed home the rebound. The fiercely competitive European champions responded with a series of rugged challenges, gaining the upper hand to ultimately equalize through Rummenigge, only to relax and allow an immediate response from the clever Belloumi, who was engulfed by his jubilant colleagues. At 2–1 they held on for a famous victory. Austria, facing a Chilean side lacking in conviction, won without difficulty with Schachner's shot. Prohaska excelled and the Chileans seldom threatened Koncilia in the Austrian goal.

In Bilbao, England scored sensationally in 27 seconds through Robson's close-range left footer, and despite an equalizer from Larios, they built on the foundation to record a fine win over a dispirited and despairing French side, Robson rising to thump a header beyond Ettori before Mariner hammered a third to complete an impressive win. At Valladolid the unconvincing Czechs were held to a draw by Kuwait, taking the lead through a contentious penalty kick taken by Panenka. They allowed their lively opponents to seize the initiative and were punished when Al Dakheel snatched a second half reply.

The party in Valencia fizzled out rapidly as the hosts, arriving amidst pomp and ceremony, were rudely upstaged by the bold minnows of Honduras. Pressing forward tentatively in the opening five minutes, Spain were frustrated. Betancourt strode forward purposefully, slipped the ball to Zelaya who, to the amazement of the home crowd, directed his shot beyond the reach of Arconada in the Spanish goal. Riding their luck and enduring the histrionics of increasingly desperate opponents, the gallant Hondurans hung on grimly for a further 66 minutes until Villegas fouled Saura clumsily and Ufarte dispatched the resultant penalty. Still, at the end Honduras had their unlikely and glorious draw. On the following day Northern Ireland and Yugoslavia facing each other in Zaragoza settled for a dreary 0–0 draw, the two sides sparring cautiously in an often physical encounter.

On the Costa del Sol the imaginative Brazilians and their more mechanical though dangerous Soviet opponents fought out an absorbing contest. Brazil won, just, but both served notice on the rest. The Soviets took the lead, silencing the rhythmic samba, Bal smashing the ball past Waldir Peres from thirty-five yards. Shengelia and Blokhin stretched Brazil's defence ceaselessly, whilst the South Americans, regaining their composure, probed with intelligence against uncompromising and resourceful defending. Finally an equalizer came when Socrates, turning away from markers, shot high into the net from a distance, and though the Soviets had cause for protest when a justifiable penalty appeal was refused, Eder shot another magical, dipping drive beyond the transfixed Dasayev for last minute triumph. Scotland also enjoyed victory over the hard working but limited New Zealand team. Up 3–0 at half-time and appearing in total command, they allowed their brave opponents moments of second-half success but still won easily 5–2.

THE SECOND SERIES

In the second series Group One began at Vigo. Italy, handed the advantage through Bruno Conti, stumbled again to an undistinguished draw, Diaz up from the back for Peru giving the South Americans a late equalizer and a deserved but slightly surprising draw. The following day Poland also made heavy weather of their game with Cameroon. Harried and harassed throughout they escaped rather fortunately with a 0–0 draw against willing, troublesome opponents.

In Group Two, Germany, embarrassed by Algeria, crushed the unfortunate Chileans. Outclassed by the rampaging Germans, they fell quickly behind and were dispatched ruthlessly 4–1, Rummenigge and Littbarski tormenting them endlessly. At Oviedo the gallant Algerians went down 2–0 to Austria. Belloumi, their tireless inspiration, gave them momentum, and Zidane, a thorn in the Austrian's side, was twice foiled by Koncilia. The Africans looked the likelier before Schachner punished their generous marking after Degeorgi's shot was parried. Krankl, almost inevitably, drove a second goal spectacularly past Cerbah.

Argentina from Group Three found their form, exposing the free scoring Hungarians, defensive limitations. Maradona at his bewitching best scored twice as the Argentines raced to 4–0. Pölöskei, fifteen minutes from the end, earned a degree of respectability for Hungary, though they had been thoroughly outplayed by infinitely superior opponents. In the tiny town of Elche,

Belgium, forced by negative Salvadorian opponents to take the unfamiliar role of aggressors, won 1–0 courtesy of a goal from Coeck. They were, however, hugely disappointing, and El Salvador, determined and brave, at least restored their shattered pride.

At Bilbao, England won 2–0 against Czechoslovakia. England were less impressive than in their opener, but Francis and the towering Mariner provided the goals against a much changed Czech side who lacked confidence in attack. Meanwhile, France in Valladolid overwhelmed Kuwait amidst bizarre scenes. Ahead 3–1 and dominating, France added a fourth through Giresse, which precipitated a remarkable walk off by the Arabs, claiming that a whistle blown from the crowd had distracted them. They behaved with the dignity of unruly children before finally being persuaded by their President to continue. Stranger still, the referee upon restarting chose to disallow the goal, much to the chagrin of the bemused French, and awarded a drop ball. France eventually gained reward for retaining composure in farcical circumstances, the stalwart Bossis adding a legitimate fourth. Unfortunately, the ugliness and resentment continued. Hidalgo, the French coach, blasted the heavy-handed approach applied by both police and organizers: 'They are treating us all like domestic animals, not responsible people,' he said. Kuwait were fined £6,500 for their antics – small change for a nation so wealthy.

In the cauldron at Valencia, Spain, fraught with anxiety, fell behind quickly to Gudelj's strike before recovering to beat a cautious Yugoslavian team. Benefiting from a ludicrous penalty and weak refereeing, Saura sent the fervent crowd home in raptures with his late, scarcely deserved winner. Northern Ireland, meantime, finding themselves cast unusually in the role of favourites, pressed hard against the relaxed and seemingly carefree Hondurans, gaining the lead when Armstrong headed conclusively past Arzu after two consecutive efforts from McIlroy and Nicholl had rattled the bar. The Hondurans rallied as Ireland tired: Betancourt fired powerfully against the goal frame before Laing, a substitute on for just two minutes, arrived to deflect a near post corner into the Irish net to earn themselves another draw.

At Seville, Group Six's Scotland played with panache and composure, scoring a magnificent goal through David Narey, hammered home gloriously from thirty yards, before succumbing to the exhilarating attacking flair of Brazil. Zico fired the South Americans level; Oscar, Eder with an astonishing shot and Falcoa won it 4–1, but Scotland had played their part in Malaga. So unlucky against Brazil, the USSR again demonstrated fine technique and hard, forceful football. As Shengelia teased tortuously once more, Baltacha, Blokhin and Gavrilov finished mercilessly. New Zealand, quite unable to resist, were swept aside.

THE THIRD SERIES

In Group One, Poland, without a goal in their opening two fixtures, ran riot. Three goals in six second-half minutes destroyed Peru, who wilted visibly in the sunshine. Buncol exchanging sharp passes with the quick-thinking Boniek made it four. Ciolek stabbed a fifth before La Rosa, a lonely isolated figure, snatched late consolation for Peru; they had been a disappointment. Italy, at Vigo, struggled nervously against a vibrant Cameroon, but confirmed their further qualification with a 1–1 draw. Graziani powered a header home on the hour, and though M'Bida gave the Africans hope, they were eliminated without losing a match, having greatly enhanced their reputation.

In Group Two the other African nation, Algeria, built on their miraculous win over Germany, astonishing demoralized Chile with their fast attacking movement to score three first-half goals. Chile responded as the Algerians again failed to sustain their effort, dragging themselves back to 3–2. They were out, but the Algerians turned their attention to Gijon, where Austria were playing their West German neighbours. Scandalously, on the following day the two Europeans conspired unforgivably to ensure the Africans' departure. Germany needing to win did so 1–0. Austria, assured of qualification unless defeated heavily, achieved their goal, and the game resembled a practice session punctuated with pass backs and slow laborious keep ball. Algeria and their fresh invigorating approach had been denied by age-old cynicism.

At Elche, Group Three's Hungary, playing boldly with four strikers against Belgium, scored first through Varga their left back but were frustrated by the wily Ceulemans. Weaving past two defenders, he drilled his cross into the path of Czerniatynski, who from ten yards out made no mistake. Argentina, needing merely to beat El Salvador to secure a place in the second stage, completed the task easily, Bertoni and Passarella booking their passage. Mercifully for the Salvadorans, they contented themselves with 2–0.

France in Group Four failed in a poor game at Valladolid to beat the Czechs, their 1–1 draw leaving them to rely on England beating Kuwait. For Czechoslovakia, a nation with a great football tradition, elimination and ignominy was suffered. Theirs had been a lamentable campaign. England duly beat Kuwait 1–0 competently, though without great inspiration, in a dull match. The French at least were grateful.

Joe Jordan, Scotland's old war horse, earned a recall against the USSR for their final Group Six match at Malaga. It was he, running on to Narey's long ball, who fired past Dasayev to give the Scots a lead they needed to hold. Sadly, their effort was again in vain. Their defence self-destructed as Chivadze, running on to a half clearance, curled a fierce shot past Rough and equalized before Shengelia, seizing on a collision between Miller and Hansen, moved in to give the Soviets a lead in the withering Malaga heat. Undeterred, the Scots retaliated bravely through Souness, who levelled at 2–2 three minutes from time. But their draw condemned them to an early exit. Brazil in Seville predictably proved altogether too much for New Zealand. Playing at half pace, they won with great ease 4–0, Zico providing the highlight, stretching up into the night sky to fashion a bicycle kick that flew into the startled Van Hattum's net.

Honduras were finally beaten at Zaragoza, offering the conquering Yugoslavians the possibility of qualification. Surprisingly resilient throughout the competition, the underdogs clung on desperately against their stronger, yet unimaginative, opponents, until Petrovic converted a penalty kick. The little American nation had, however, won the deserved affection of the Spanish crowds.

In Group Five and the final game, the stout hearts of Northern Ireland shocked their hosts with an unlikely and courageous triumph. Under enormous pressure and threatening occasionally on swift sorties into Spanish territory, they were rewarded to the disbelief of the Valencian throng when Armstrong of Tottenham thumped the ball gleefully into the horrified Arconada's net. Spain redoubled their effort but Ireland resisted to the finish, 1–0. For the Irish there was glory and a place in the second stage; Yugoslavia were eliminated.

Final Tournament – Spain
First round

Group 1

Italy (0) **0, Poland** (0) **0**
14.6.82 VIGO
Italy: Zoff, Gentile, Scirea, Collovati, Cabrini, Marini, Antognoni, Tardelli, Conti, Rossi, Graziani
Poland: Mlynarczyk, Jalocha, Majewski, Zmuda, Janas, Buncol, Lato, Boniek, Matysik, Iwan (Kusto), Smolarek
Referee: Vautrot (France)

Peru (0) **0, Cameroon** (0) **0**
15.6.82 LA CORUÑA
Peru: Quiroga, Duarte, Salguero, Diaz, Olaechea, Uribe, Cueto, Velasquez, Leguia (La Rosa), Cubillas (Barbadillo), Oblitas
Cameroon: N'Kono, M'Bom, Aoudou, Onana, Kaham, Abega, M'Bida, Kunde, Milla (Tokoto), N'Djeya, N'Guea (Bakohen)
Referee: Wohrer (Austria)

Italy (1) **1, Peru** (0) **1**
18.6.82 VIGO
Italy: Zoff, Cabrini, Collovati, Gentile, Scirea, Antognoni, Marini, Tardelli, Conti (1), Graziani, Rossi (Causio)
Peru: Quiroga, Duarte, Diaz (1), Salguero, Olaechea, Cueto, Velasquez (La Rosa), Cubillas, Uribe, Oblitas, Barbadillo (Leguia)
Referee: Eschweiler (West Germany)

Poland (0) **0, Cameroon** (0) **0**
19.6.82 LA CORUÑA
Poland: Mlynarczyk, Majewski, Janas, Zmuda, Jalocha, Lato, Buncol, Boniek, Iwan (Szarmach), Palasz (Kusto), Smolarek
Cameroon: N'Kono, Kaham, Onana, N'Djeya, M'Bom, Aoudou, Abega, Kunde, M'Bida, Milla, N'Guea (Tokoto)
Referee: Ponnet (Belgium)

Poland (0) **5, Peru** (0) **1**
22.6.82 LA CORUÑA
Poland: Mlynarczyk, Majewski, Janas, Zmuda, Jalocha (Dziuba), Buncol (1), Matysik, Kupcewiez, Lato (1), Boniek (1), Smolarek (1) (Ciolek (1))
Peru: Quiroga, Duarte, Diaz, Salguero, Olaechea, Cubillas (Uribe), Velasquez, Cueto, Leguia, La Rosa (1), Oblitas (Barbadillo)
Referee: Rubio (Mexico)

Italy (0) **1, Cameroon** (0) **1**
23.6.82 VIGO
Italy: Zoff, Gentile, Collovati, Scirea, Cabrini, Oriali, Tardelli, Antognoni, Conti, Rossi, Graziani (1)
Cameroon: N'Kono, Kaham, N'Djeya, Onana, M'Bom, Aoudou, Kunde, M'Bida (1), Abega, Milla, Tokoto
Referee: Dotschev (Bulgaria)

	P	W	D	L	F	A	Pts
Poland	3	1	2	0	5	1	4
Italy	3	0	3	0	2	2	3
Cameroon	3	0	3	0	1	1	3
Peru	3	0	2	1	2	6	2

Group 2

Algeria (0) **2, West Germany** (0) **1**
16.6.82 GIJON
Algeria: Cerbah, Guendouz, Kourichi, Merzekane, Mansouri, Belloumi (1), Dhaleb, Fergani, Madjer (1) (Larbes), Zidane (Bensaoula), Assad
West Germany: Schumacher, Kaltz, Stielike, Förster K H, Briegel, Breitner, Magath (Fischer), Dremmler, Rummenigge (1), Hrubesch, Littbarski
Referee: Labo (Peru)

Austria (1) **1, Chile** (0) **0**
17.6.82 OVIEDO
Austria: Koncilia, Krauss, Obermayer, Pezzey, Degeorgi (Baumeister), Hattenberger, Hintermaier, Weber (Jurtin), Prohaska, Krankl, Schachner (1)
Chile: Osben, Garrido, Figueroa, Valenzuela, Bigorra, Bonvallet, Dubo, Neira (Manuel Rojas), Moscoso (Gamboa), Yañez, Caszely
Referee: Cardellino (Uruguay)

West Germany (1) **4, Chile** (0) **1**
20.6.82 GIJON
West Germany: Schumacher, Kaltz, Stielike, Förster K H, Briegel, Dremmler, Breitner (Matthäus), Magath, Littbarski (Reinders (1)), Hrubesch, Rummenigge (3)
Chile: Osben, Garrido, Figueroa, Valenzuela, Bigorra, Dubo, Bonvallet, Soto (Letelier), Moscoso (1), Yañez, Gamboa (Neira)
Referee: Galler (Switzerland)

Algeria (0) **0, Austria** (0) **2**
21.6.82 OVIEDO
Algeria: Cerbah, Guendouz, Kourichi, Merzekane, Mansouri, Belloumi (Bensaoula), Dhaleb (Tiemcani), Fergani, Madjer, Zidane, Assad
Austria: Koncilia, Krauss, Obermayer, Degeorgi, Pezzey, Hattenberger, Hintermaier, Baumeister (Welzl), Prohaska (Weber), Krankl (1), Schachner (1)
Referee: Boscovic (Austria)

Algeria (3) **3, Chile** (0) **2**
24.6.82 OVIEDO
Algeria: Cerbah, Kourichi, Merzekane, Guendouz, Larbes, Mansouri (Dhaleb), Fergani, Assad (2), Bensaoula (1), Bourebbou (Yahi), Madjer
Chile: Osben, Galindo, Valenzuela, Figueroa, Bigorra, Bonvallet (Soto), Dubo, Neira (1 pen), Yañez, Caszely (Letelier (1)), Moscoso
Referee: Mendez (Guatemala)

West Germany (1) **1, Austria** (0) **0**
25.6.82 GIJON
West Germany: Schumacher, Kaltz, Stielike, Förster K H, Briegel, Dremmler, Breitner, Magath, Littbarski, Hrubesch (1) (Fischer), Rummenigge (Matthäus)
Austria: Koncilia, Krauss, Pezzey, Obermayer, Degeorgi, Hattenberger, Prohaska, Hintermaier, Weber, Schachner, Krankl
Referee: Valentine (Scotland)

	P	W	D	L	F	A	Pts
West Germany	3	2	0	1	6	3	4
Austria	3	2	0	1	3	1	4
Algeria	3	2	0	1	5	5	4
Chile	3	0	0	3	3	8	0

Group 3

Argentina (0) **0, Belgium** (0) **1**
13.6.82 BARCELONA
Argentina: Fillol, Olguin, Galvan, Passarella, Tarantini, Ardiles, Gallego, Maradona, Bertoni, Diaz (Valdano), Kempes
Belgium: Pfaff, Gerets, Millecamps L, De Schrijver, Baecke, Coeck, Vercauteren, Vandersmissen, Czerniatynski, Van den Bergh (1), Ceulemans
Referee: Christov (Czechoslovakia)

Hungary (3) **10, El Salvador** (0) **1**
15.6.82 ELCHE
Hungary: Meszaros, Martos, Balint, Toth (1), Garaba, Müller (Szentes (1)), Nyilasi (2), Sallai, Fazekas (2), Torocsik (Kiss (3)), Pölöskei (1)
El Salvador: Mora, Castillo, Jovel, Rodriguez, Recinos, Rugamas (Zapata (1)), Ventura, Huezo, Hernandez F, Gonzalez, Rivas
Referee: Al-Doy (Bahrain)

Argentina (2) **4, Hungary** (0) **1**
18.6.82 ALICANTE
Argentina: Fillol, Olguin, Galvan, Passarella, Tarantini (Barbas), Ardiles (1), Gallego, Maradona (2), Bertoni (1), Valdano (Calderon), Kempes
Hungary: Meszaros, Martos (Fazekas), Balint, Toth, Varga, Garaba, Nyilasi, Sallai, Rab, Kiss (Szentes), Pölöskei (1)
Referee: Lacarne (Algeria)

Belgium (1) **1, El Salvador** (0) **0**
19.6.82 ELCHE
Belgium: Pfaff, Gerets, Meeuws, Baecke, Millecamps L, Vandersmissen (Van der Elst), Coeck (1), Vercauteren, Ceulemans (Van Moer), Van den Bergh, Czerniatynski
El Salvador: Mora, Osorto (Diaz), Jovel, Rodriguez, Recinos, Fagoaga, Ventura, Huezo, Zapata, Gonzalez, Rivas
Referee: Moffat (Northern Ireland)

Belgium (0) **1, Hungary** (1) **1**
22.6.82 ELCHE
Belgium: Pfaff, Gerets (Plessers), Millecamps L, Meeuws, Baecke, Coeck, Vercauteren, Vandersmissen (Van Moer), Czerniatynski (1), Van den Bergh, Ceulemans
Hungary: Meszaros, Martos, Kerekes (Sallai), Garaba, Varga (1), Nyilasi, Müller, Fazekas, Torocsik, Kiss (Csongradi), Pölöskei
Referee: White (England)

Argentina (1) **2, El Salvador** (0) **0**
23.6.82 ALICANTE
Argentina: Fillol, Olguin, Galvan, Passarella (1 pen), Tarantini, Ardiles, Gallego, Kempes, Bertoni (1) (Diaz), Maradona, Calderon (Santamaria)
El Salvador: Mora, Osorto (Arevalo), Jovel, Rodriguez, Rugamas, Fagoaga, Ventura (Alfaro), Huezo, Zapata, Gonzalez, Rivas
Referee: Barrancos (Bolivia)

	P	W	D	L	F	A	Pts
Belgium	3	2	1	0	3	1	5
Argentina	3	2	0	1	6	2	4
Hungary	3	1	1	1	12	6	3
El Salvador	3	0	0	3	1	13	0

Group 4
England (1) **3, France** (1) **1**
16.6.82 BILBAO
England: Shilton, Mills, Sansom (Neal), Thompson, Butcher, Robson (2), Coppell, Wilkins, Mariner (1), Francis, Rix
France: Ettori, Battiston, Bossis, Tresor, Lopez, Larios (Tigana), Girard, Giresse, Rocheteau (Six), Platini, Soler (1)
Referee: Garrido (Portugal)

Czechoslovakia (1) **1, Kuwait** (0) **1**
17.6.82 VALLADOLID
Czechoslovakia: Hruska, Barmos, Jurkemik, Fiala, Kukucka, Panenka (1 pen),
Berger, Kriz (Bicovsky), Janecka (Petrzela), Nehoda, Vizek
Kuwait: Al Tarabulsi, Naeem Saed, Mayoof, Mahboub, Waleed Jasem, Al Buloushi,
Saeed Al Houti, Karam (Fathi Kameel), Al Dakheel (1), Jasem Yacoub, Al Anbari
Referee: Dwomoha (Ghana)

England (0) **2, Czechoslovakia** (0) **0**
20.6.82 BILBAO
England: Shilton, Mills, Thompson, Butcher, Sansom, Coppell, Robson
(Hoddle), Wilkins, Francis (1), Mariner (1), Rix
Czechoslovakia: Seman (Stromsik), Barmos, Fiala, Radimec, Vojacek,
Jurkemik, Chaloupka, Vizek, Berger, Janecka (Masny), Nehoda
Referee: Corver (Holland)

France (2) **4, Kuwait** (0) **1**
21.6.82 VALLADOLID
France: Ettori, Amoros, Tresor, Janvion, Bossis (1), Giresse, Platini (1) (Girard),
Genghini (1), Soler, Lacombe, Six (1)
Kuwait: Al Tarabulsi, Naeem Saed, Mayoof, Mahboub, Waleed Jasem (Al
Shemmari), Al Buloushi (1), Saed Al Houti, Karam (Fathi Kameel), Al Dakheel,
Jasem Yacoub, Al Ambari
Referee: Stupar (USSR)

France (0) **1, Czechoslovakia** (0) **1**
24.6.82 VALLADOLID
France: Ettori, Amoros, Tresor, Janvion, Bossis, Giresse, Platini, Genghini, Soler
(Girard), Lacombe (Couriol), Six (1)
Czechoslovakia: Stromsik, Barmos, Fiala, Stambacher, Vojacek, Jurkemik, Kriz
(Masny), Bicovsky, Vizek, Janecka (Panenka (1 pen)), Nehoda
Referee: Casarin (Italy)

England (1) **1, Kuwait** (0) **0**
25.6.82 BILBAO
England: Shilton, Neal, Thompson, Foster, Mills, Coppell, Hoddle, Wilkins,
Rix, Mariner, Francis (1)
Kuwait: Al Tarabulsi, Naeem Saed, Mahboub, Mayoof, Waleed Jasem (Al
Shemmari), Saed Al Houti, Al Buloushi, Al Suwayed, Fathi Kameel, Al
Dakheel, Al Anbari
Referee: Aristizabal (Colombia)

	P	W	D	L	F	A	Pts
England	3	3	0	0	6	1	6
France	3	1	1	1	6	5	3
Czechoslovakia	3	0	1	2	2	6	1
Kuwait	3	0	1	2	2	6	1

Group 5

Spain (0) **1, Honduras** (1) **1**
16.6.82 VALENCIA
Spain: Arconada, Gordillo, Camacho, Alonso, Alesanco, Tendillo, Juanito (Saura), Joaquin (Sanchez), Satrustegui, Zamora, Lopez Ufarte (1 pen)
Honduras: Arzu, Gutierrez, Costly, Villegas, Bulnes, Zelaya (1), Gilberto, Maradiaga, Norales (Caballero), Betancourt, Figueroa
Referee: Ithurralde (Argentina)

Northern Ireland (0) **0, Yugoslavia** (0) **0**
17.6.82 ZARAGOZA
Northern Ireland: Jennings, Nicholl J, Nicholl C, McClelland, Donaghy, McIlroy, O'Neill M, McCreery, Armstrong, Hamilton, Whiteside
Yugoslavia: Pantelic, Gudelj, Zajec, Stojkovic, Petrovic, Slijivo, Zlatko Vujovic, Susic, Juvanovic, Hrstic, Surjak
Referee: Fredriksson (Sweden)

Spain (1) **2, Yugoslavia** (1) **1**
20.6.82 VALENCIA
Spain: Arconada, Camacho, Tendillo, Alesanco, Gordillo, Alonso, Sanchez (Saura (1)), Zamora, Juanito (1 pen), Satrustegui (Quini), Lopez Ufarte
Yugoslavia: Pantelic, Krmpotic, Zajec, Stojkovic, Jovanovic (Halilhodzic), Gudelj (1), Petrovic, Sljivo, Zlatko Vujovic (Sestic), Surjak, Susic
Referee: Lund-Sorensen (Denmark)

Honduras (0) **1, Northern Ireland** (1) **1**
21.6.82 ZARAGOZA
Honduras: Arzu, Gutierrez, Villegas, Cruz J L, Costly, Maradiaga, Gilberto, Zelaya, Norales (Laing (1)), Betancourt, Figueroa
Northern Ireland: Jennings, Nicholl J, Nicholl C, McClelland, Donaghy, O'Neill M (Healy), McCreery, McIlroy, Whiteside (Brotherston), Armstrong (1), Hamilton
Referee: Chan Tam Sun (Hong Kong)

Honduras (0) **0, Yugoslavia** (0) **1**
24.6.82 ZARAGOZA
Honduras: Arzu, Droumond, Villegas, Costly, Bulnes, Zelaya, Gilberto, Maradiaga, Cruz J (Laing), Betancourt, Figueroa
Yugoslavia: Pantelic, Krmpotic, Stojkovic, Zajec, Juvanovic (Halilhodzic), Slijivo, Gudelj, Surjak, Zlatko Vujovic (Sestic), Susic, Petrovic (1 pen)
Referee: Castro (Chile)

Northern Ireland (0) **1, Spain** (0) **0**
25.6.82 VALENCIA
Northern Ireland: Jennings, Nicholl J, Nicholl C, McClelland, Donaghy, O'Neill M, McCreery, McIlroy (Cassidy), Armstrong (1), Hamilton, Whiteside (Nelson)
Spain: Arconada, Camacho, Tendillo, Alesanco, Gordillo, Sanchez, Alonso, Saura, Juanito, Satrustegui (Quini), Lopez Ufarte (Gallego)
Referee: Ortiz (Paraguay)

	P	W	D	L	F	A	Pts
Northern Ireland	3	1	2	0	2	1	4
Spain	3	1	1	1	3	3	3
Yugoslavia	3	1	1	1	2	2	3
Honduras	3	0	2	1	2	3	2

Group 6

Brazil (0) **2, USSR** (1) **1**
14.6.82 SEVILLE
Brazil: Valdir Peres, Leandro, Oscar, Luizinho, Junior, Socrates (1), Serginho, Zico, Eder (1), Falcao, Dirceu (Paulo Isidoro)
USSR: Dasayev, Sulakvelidze, Chivadze, Baltacha, Demyanenko, Shengelia (Andreyev), Bessonov, Gavrilov (Susloparov), Blokhin, Bal (1), Daraselia
Referee: Lamo Castillo (Spain)

Scotland (3) **5, New Zealand** (0) **2**
15.6.82 MALAGA
Scotland: Rough, McGrain, Gray F, Hansen, Evans, Souness, Strachan (Narey), Dalglish (1), Wark (2), Brazil (Archibald (1)), Robertson (1)
New Zealand: Van Hattum, Elrick, Hill, Malcolmson (Cole), Almond (Herbert), Sumner (1), Mackay, Cresswell, Boath, Rufer W, Wooddin (1)
Referee: El Ghoul (Libya)

Brazil (1) **4, Scotland** (1) **1**
18.6.82 SEVILLE
Brazil: Valdir Peres, Leandro, Oscar (1), Luizinho, Junior, Cerezo, Falcao (1), Socrates, Serginho (Paulo Isidoro), Zico (1), Eder (1)
Scotland: Rough, Narey (1), Gray F, Souness, Hansen, Miller, Strachan (Dalglish), Hartford (McLeish), Archibald, Wark, Robertson
Referee: Siles (Costa Rica)

USSR (1) **3, New Zealand** (0) **0**
19.6.82 MALAGA
USSR: Dasayev, Sulakvelidze, Chivadze, Baltacha (1), Demyanenko, Shengelia, Bessonov, Bal, Daraselia (Oganesian), Gavrilov (1) (Rodionov), Blokhin (1)
New Zealand: Van Hattum, Dods, Herbert, Elrick, Boath, Cole, Sumner, Mackay, Cresswell, Rufer W, Wooddin
Referee: El Ghoul (Libya)

Scotland (1) **2, USSR** (0) **2**
22.6.82 MALAGA
Scotland: Rough, Narey, Gray F, Souness (1), Hansen, Miller, Strachan (McGrain), Archibald, Jordan (1) (Brazil), Wark, Robertson
USSR: Dasayev, Sulakvelidze, Chivadze (1), Baltacha, Demyanenko, Borovsky, Shengelia (1) (Andreyev), Bessonov, Gavrilov, Bal, Blokhin
Referee: Rainea (Romania)

Brazil (2) **4, New Zealand** (0) **0**
23.6.82 SEVILLE
Brazil: Valdir Peres, Leandro, Oscar (Edinho), Luizinho, Junior, Cerezo, Socrates, Zico (2), Falcao (1), Serginho (1) (Paulo Isidoro), Eder
New Zealand: Van Hattum, Dods, Herbert, Elrick, Boath, Sumner, Mackay, Cresswell (Turner B), Almond, Rufer W (Cole), Wooddin
Referee: Matovinovic (Yugoslavia)

	P	W	D	L	F	A	Pts
Brazil	3	3	0	0	10	2	6
USSR	3	1	1	1	6	4	3
Scotland	3	1	1	1	8	8	3
New Zealand	3	0	0	3	2	12	0

Second Round

Group A

Venue: Barcelona
Poland
Belgium
USSR

Group B

Venue: Madrid
West Germany
England
Spain

Group C

Venue: Barcelona
Argentina
Brazil
Italy

Group D

Venue: Madrid
Austria
France
Northern Ireland

THE SECOND ROUND

Poland, continuing where they left off against Peru, shattered the Belgians' prospects in the Group A opener at the Santiago Bernabeu. The flame-haired Boniek – despite criticism by his coach, Plechniczek – was the architect, with a superb hat-trick, and denying their destructive, negative opponents the opportunity to frustrate and suffocate, Poland strolled delightfully to a 3–0 win.

In Group B, West Germany faced England in Madrid. Neither gained the upper hand, but England was by far the more positive, earning the plaudits, though Rummenigge for the Germans came closest of all, almost snapping Shilton's cross bar four minutes from time. A draw then, 0–0, fascinating if a little ponderous, and a tangible sense of nervous relief was felt at the end. Defeat for these great rivals had been avoided and hope for both remained.

In Group C at Barcelona's neat little Sarna stadium, the Italians handled little Maradona roughly and surprisingly found the form to win in an oppressive atmosphere with constant interruption. Argentina, their little general Ardiles the most effective player, gained the upper hand, but it was Italy, finding at last venomous finishing to match their neat passing, who took the lead. Tardelli comfortably beat Fillol from an Antognoni pass, Maradona struck a post, Passarella was fouled by Zoff before Italy again punished vulnerable defending. After Conti's darting run, Rossi's shot was parried, Cabrini applying the decisive touch 2–0. Argentina's goal when it came proved too little and too late.

In Group D, France edged out Austria. Genghini, their inspiration in the absence of Platini, beat the excellent Koncilia with a first-half strike, and though their neat passing proved dominant, that was that. Austria, through the powerful running of Krankl, remaining a constant worry and France, 1–0 victors, caused themselves unnecessary anxiety through an inability to accept a hat full of chances.

Back in Barcelona the Soviet Union began their Group A campaign against dull Belgium, a team now evidently both tired and tiresome. Oganesian squeezed a second-half effort into Munaron's goal and the USSR had their win. Belgium, in truth, hardly tried to recover. It was a disappointing end to a disappointing team.

In Group B, West Germany denied a huge Bernabeau crowd the result they so craved, beating Spain 2–1. Far too accomplished to be intimidated and more positive than against England, the Germans controlled the pace of the game throughout. With Littbarski darting and dangerous and the frightening, imposing figure of Förster commanding an untroubled defence, they held a comfortable two-goal lead. Spain replied late against relaxed opponents, the result and the winners never in doubt.

Argentina, desperate to win, lost their heads, the game and the championship, as Brazil, wonderful again in their movement and bewildering in invention, outplayed them. Zico, Junior and Serginho condemned the Argentineans, all too much for the young Maradona, dismissed for impetuously retaliating. Brazil, their bitterest rival, had been far too good.

In Group D, Ireland again produced an unlikely and courageous result, leading Austria twice before settling ultimately for an honourable and deserved 2–2 draw in Madrid, Billy Hamilton supplying their goals.

Poland from Group A played the final match, cagily forcing a draw with USSR and securing for themselves a semi-final place. The Soviets pressed and then tired as the Poles, staging a series of counter-attacks, threatened their flanks, 0–0. In Madrid, England, much the better team, failed to score against stubborn, goal shy Spain. Rix creative on the left and Wilkins patiently prompting in the centre brought opportunities. Notably falling to Sansom, Robson and Francis, all were thwarted, and as England rolled their final dice, both Keegan and Brooking failed tantalizingly to apply finishing touches. At the final whistle they sank to their knees in despair. England, without ever being threatened with defeat in the competition, were eliminated, they had, however, confirmed themselves as a very fine team indeed.

In Barcelona's Sarna stadium Italy shocked Brazil in an epic encounter. Rossi, wasteful moments earlier, given time and space headed Cabrini's teasing cross beyond Peres. Brazil responded immediately, forcing the game as Italy retreated into their own half. Socrates accelerating on to Zico's astute through ball brought them reward. Italy, exhibiting hitherto unseen pace and character, composed themselves, weathered the storm with grim determination and remarkably took the lead again: Rossi, seizing on to an extraordinary and careless pass played by Cerezo to the luckless Junior, advanced on goal and ripped his shot into the net from fifteen yards. The South Americans allowed their annoyance and frustration to show, their incomparable skills breaking down on Italy's rock-like defence, until finally, having seen Rossi miss a simple chance for a hat-trick, Falcoa ran on to Junior's inviting pass to thunder the ball with enormous velocity past Dino Zoff for 2–2. Twenty minutes to go, Brazil seemed set to qualify. Italy in this topsy-turvy and scintillating contest had other ideas, and it was inevitably Rossi who re-wrote the script. After Bergomi's effort had been deflected into his path off Socrates, he swivelled back to goal, rifling home the winner. At 3–2 Italy hung on in the face of considered and unrelenting pressure to confirm themselves deserved semi-finalists.

It was the end of the road for the brave Irish from Group D in Madrid, tired in body and spirit and broken cruelly, just as they were in their 1958 adventure, by a remorseless French team, full of flair and supreme confidence. Platini back again from injury, supported ably by Tigana and Giresse, ran them ragged, though the obdurate Armstrong scored near the end, defiantly salvaging their enormous pride for 4–1.

Second Round

Group A

Poland (2) **3, Belgium** (0) **0**
28.6.82 BARCELONA
Poland: Mlynarczyk, Dziuba, Zmuda, Janas, Majewski, Kupcewicz (Ciolek), Buncol, Matysik, Lato, Boniek (3), Smolarek
Belgium: Custers, Renquin, Millecamps L, Meeuws, Plessers (Baecke), Van Moer, (Van der Elst), Coeck, Vercauteren, Czerniatynski, Van den Bergh, Ceulemans
Referee: Siles (Costa Rica)

Belgium (0) **0, USSR** (0) **1**
1.7.82 BARCELONA
Belgium: Munaron, Renquin, Millecamps L, Meeuws, De Schrijver (Millecamps M), Verheyen, Coeck, Vercauteren, Vandersmissen (Czerniatynski), Van den Bergh, Ceulemans
USSR: Dasayev, Borovsky, Chivadze, Baltacha, Demyanenko, Bal (Daraselia), Oganesian (1), Bessonov, Shengelia (Rodionov), Gavrilov, Blokhin
Referee: Vautrot (France)

Poland (0) **0, USSR** (0) **0**
4.7.82 BARCELONA
Poland: Mlynarczyk, Dziuba, Zmuda, Janas, Majewski, Kupcewicz (Ciolek), Buncol, Matysik, Lato, Boniek, Smolarek
USSR: Dasayev, Sulakvelidze, Chivadze, Baltacha, Demyanenko, Borovsky, Oganesian, Bessonov, Shengelia (Andreyev), Gavrilov (Daraselia), Blokhin
Referee: Valentine (Scotland)

	P	W	D	L	F	A	Pts
Poland	2	1	1	0	3	0	3
USSR	2	1	1	0	1	0	3
Belgium	2	0	0	2	0	4	0

Group B

West Germany (0) **0, England** (0) **0**
29.6.82 MADRID
West Germany: Schumacher, Kaltz, Förster K H, Stielike, Förster B, Müller (Fischer), Breitner, Dremmler, Briegel, Rummenigge, Reinders (Littbarski)
England: Shilton, Mills, Thompson, Butcher, Sansom, Coppell, Wilkins, Robson, Rix, Francis (Woodcock), Mariner
Referee: Coelho (Brazil)

Spain (0) **1, West Germany** (0) **2**
2.7.82 MADRID
Spain: Arconada, Camacho, Gordillo, Alonso, Tendillo, Alesanco, Juanito (Lopez Ufarte), Zamora (1), Urquiaga, Santillana, Quini (Sanchez)
West Germany: Schumacher, Kaltz, Förster K H, Stielike, Förster B, Breitner, Briegel, Dremmler, Littbarski (1), Fischer (1), Rummenigge (Reinders)
Referee: Casarin (Italy)

England (0) **0, Spain** (0) **0**
5.7.82 MADRID
England: Shilton, Mills, Thompson, Butcher, Sansom, Wilkins, Robson, Rix (Brooking), Francis, Mariner, Woodcock (Keegan)
Spain: Arconada, Camacho, Gordillo, Alonso, Tendillo (Macedo), Alesanco, Satrustegui, Zamora, Urquiaga, Saura (Uralde), Santillana
Referee: Ponnet (Belgium)

	P	W	D	L	F	A	Pts
West Germany	2	1	1	0	1	1	3
England	2	0	2	0	0	0	2
Spain	2	0	1	1	1	2	1

Group C

Italy (0) **2, Argentina** (0) **1**
29.6.82 BARCELONA
Italy: Zoff, Gentile, Collovati, Scirea, Cabrini (1), Oriali (Marini), Tardelli (1), Antognoni, Conti, Rossi (Altobelli), Graziani
Argentina: Fillol, Olguin, Passarella (1), Galvan, Tarantini, Ardiles, Gallego, Maradona, Bertoni, Diaz (Calderon), Kempes (Valencia)
Referee: Rainea (Romania)

Brazil (1) **3, Argentina** (0) **1**
2.7.82 BARCELONA
Brazil: Valdir Peres, Leandro (Edevaldo), Oscar, Luizinho, Junior (1), Cerezo, Falcao, Socrates, Serginho (1), Zico (1) (Batista), Eder
Argentina: Fillol, Olguin, Barbas, Passarella, Tarantini, Ardiles, Galvan, Maradona, Bertoni (Santamaria), Calderon, Kempes (Diaz (1))
Referee: Rubio (Mexico)

Italy (2) **3, Brazil** (1) **2**
5.7.82 BARCELONA
Italy: Zoff, Collovati (Bergomi), Gentile, Scirea, Cabrini, Oriali, Antognoni, Tardelli (Marini), Conti, Graziani, Rossi (3)
Brazil: Valdir Peres, Leandro, Oscar, Luizinho, Junior, Cerezo, Falcao (1), Socrates (1), Zico, Serginho (Paulo Isidoro), Eder
Referee: Klein (Israel)

	P	W	D	L	F	A	Pts
Italy	2	2	0	0	5	3	4
Brazil	2	1	0	1	5	4	2
Argentina	2	0	0	2	2	5	0

Group D

France (1) **1, Austria** (0) **0**
28.6.82 MADRID
France: Ettori, Battiston, Janvion, Tresor, Bossis, Giresse, Genghini (1) (Girard), Tigana, Soler, Lacombe (Rocheteau), Six
Austria: Koncilia, Krauss, Obermayer, Pezzey, Degeorgi (Baumeister), Hattenberger, Hintermaier, Jara (Welzl), Schachner, Prohaska, Krankl
Referee: Palotai (Hungary)

Northern Ireland (1) **2, Austria** (0) **2**
1.7.82 MADRID
Northern Ireland: Platt, Nicholl J, Nicholl C, McClelland, Nelson, McCreery, O'Neill M, McIlroy, Armstrong, Hamilton (2), Whiteside (Brotherston)
Austria: Koncilia, Krauss, Obermayer, Pezzey (1), Schachner, Prohaska, Pichler, Hagmayr (Welzl), Balimeister, Pregesbauer (Hintermaier (1)), Jurtin
Referee: Prokop (East Germany)

Northern Ireland (0) **1, France** (1) **4**
4.7.82 MADRID
Northern Ireland: Jennings, Nicholl J, Nicholl C, McClelland, Donaghy, McIlroy, McCreery (O'Neill J), O'Neill M, Armstrong (1), Hamilton, Whiteside
France: Ettori, Amoros, Janvion, Tresor, Bossis, Giresse (2), Genghini, Tigana, Platini, Soler (Six), Rocheteau (2) (Couriol)
Referee: Jarguz (Poland)

	P	W	D	L	F	A	Pts
France	2	2	0	0	5	1	4
Austria	2	0	1	1	2	3	1
Northern Ireland	2	0	1	1	3	6	1

THE SEMI-FINALS

The semi-final in Barcelona was highlighted only by Rossi scoring two more goals to make it five for the week, as Poland, without the suspended Boniek, were unable to galvanize any real attacking momentum and were beaten. They did, however, manage the not inconsiderable feat of being rougher than the Italians. Majewski in particular benefited from the Uruguayan referee's leniency when he scythed down the troublesome Rossi with a quite disgraceful lunge. Antognoni, having an excellent Tournament, dictated much of Italy's more imaginative work as an unpressured Italian defence repelled Poland's outnumbered and feeble attack and it was he who provided the cross from which Rossi, aided by Tardelli's diversionary run, fired home. Poland, irritated, responded with still greater emphasis on the hard and brutal side of their nature, and Italy, always willing, matched them with relish. Still, Conti at the end found time to avoid yet another crude hack to plant a cross on the head of the irrepressible Rossi, the match ending 2–0.

For France in Seville there was heartbreak. As much the better and more creative side, they went out in the most dramatic and traumatizing circumstances to a robust and remarkably resourceful German team. Platini, in spite of Dremmler's close attention, and Giresse, who eluded poor Breitner throughout, gave the German defence a hard time, engineering ever widening cracks through which Six and the enigmatic Rocheteau flowed. Yet it was West Germany, composed in the face of the storm, who stole the lead. Fischer, running on to a pass from the overworked Brietner, fired against the knees of Ettori; Littbarski lurking did the rest. France now showed their own fortitude, Platini placing a penalty kick into Schumacher's net after Förster fouled Rocheteau clumsily. In the second half amid growing tension Battiston, the substitute, was put through on goal by an exquisite pass from Giresse, and seemingly certain to score was almost decapitated by Schumacher's hideous flying kick. The French remonstrated angrily with the Dutch official while the distressed Battiston was administered oxygen and removed from the field. Appallingly, the goalkeeper's barbarism went unpunished.

Extra time arrived and the French finally appeared to have the reward their skilful effort warranted. Tresor volleyed Giresse's free kick, 2–1, and then Giresse himself scored beautifully to end a move he himself initiated, 3–1. Germany, on the verge of being swept away, hung on, not succumbing to panic. Rummenigge gave them hope by gently rolling the ball in for 3–2, and then unbelievably Fischer equalized with three minutes left, an overhead kick reminiscent of Müller's twelve years earlier in Leon. So it was 3–3 and for the very first time a penalty shoot out and injustice. Stielike missed, but Six, losing his nerve, failed to capitalize. Then the unfortunate Bossis gave the Germans their chance when he shot tamely. Hrubesch duly accepted it and Germany advanced; France was shaken by disappointment, disbelief and sorrow.

Semi-Finals

Poland (0) **0, Italy** (1) **2**
8.7.82 BARCELONA
Poland: Mlynarczyk, Dziuba, Zmuda, Janas, Majewski, Kupcewicz, Buncol, Matysik, Lato, Ciolek (Palasz), Smolarek (Kusto)

Italy: Zoff, Bergomi, Collovati, Scirea, Cabrini, Oriali, Antognoni (Marini), Tardelli, Conti, Rossi (2), Graziani (Altobelli)
Referee: Cardellino (Uruguay)

West Germany (1) **3**, **France** (1) **3** (aet, 1–1 at 90 mins, West Germany won 5–4 on penalties)
8.7.82 SEVILLE
West Germany: Schumacher, Kaltz, Förster K H, Stielike, Förster B, Briegel (Rummenigge (1)), Dremmler, Breitner, Littbarski (1), Fischer (1), Magath (Hrubesch)
France: Ettori, Amoros, Janvion, Tresor (1), Bossis, Genghini (Battiston) (Lopez), Platini (1 pen), Giresse (1), Rocheteau, Six, Tigana
Referee: Corver (Holland)

PLAY-OFF FOR THIRD PLACE

Preceding the Final, the traditional match for third place was played, as ever, by two weary and dejected teams. Poland won a more than passable match, strengthened as they were by the return of Boniek. France, shattered by their German defeat, rested Rocheteau, Platini, Ghengini, Tigana, Giresse and poor Bossis, and predictably lost. Poland, trailing, snatched three goals before and just after half-time; it proved to be enough, though Couriol, enjoying a rare outing at the Tournament, chipped Mlynarczyk in Poland's goal delightfully to reduce French arrears to 2–3 late on.

Match for Third Place

France (1) **2**, **Poland** (2) **3**
10.7.82 ALICANTE
France: Castaneda, Amoros, Mahut, Tresor, Janvion (Lopez), Tigana (Six), Girard (1), Larios, Couriol (1), Soler, Bellone
Poland: Mlynarczyk, Dziuba, Janas, Zmuda, Majewski (1), Matysik (Wojcicki), Kupcewicz (1), Buncol, Lato, Szarmach (1), Boniek
Referee: Garrido (Portugal)

THE FINAL

Sunday, 11 June, and for Italy the final began catastrophically. Antognoni, so effective throughout, lost through injury before the start, was joined after eight minutes by the bullish Graziani who sustained a dislocated shoulder in a collision. Quickly they settled into their usual rhythm of blatant fouling and dangerous and sporadic raids. From one such sortie Conti collapsed in a heap under Stielike's clumsy challenge for a penalty; Cabrini given the gilt-edged opportunity squandered it pitifully, his shot weak and wide. Still the Germans could not raise themselves. Their team, without conviction or distinction, were finalists largely through good fortune, and here in Madrid it began to run out. Rossi, the inevitable Italian hero, deflected Gentile's deep cross in, 1–0, and this time the West German's fate was quickly sealed. Ruthlessly Tardelli exploited time and space as Germany took chances, his fierce drive making it 2–0 before substitute Altobelli grabbed a third, latching on to Conti's pass for 3–0, when twelve minutes earlier it had been goal-less. There were no more miraculous revivals for Germany, though the veteran Breitner managed a consolation effort near the end. Their luck, it proved, had been used up against the French.

Italy, with a peculiar mixture of brilliance and cynicism, had triumphed, and claimed the honour of being the twelfth World Champions.

Final

West Germany (0) **1, Italy** (0) **3**
11.7.82 MADRID
West Germany: Schumacher, Kaltz, Förster K H, Stielike, Förster B, Breitner (1), Dremmler (Hrubesch), Littbarski, Briegel, Fischer, Rummenigge (Müller)
Italy: Zoff, Bergomi, Cabrini, Collovati, Scirea, Gentile, Oriali, Tardelli (1), Conti, Graziani (Altobelli (1)) (Causio), Rossi (1)
Referee: Arnaldo Coelho (Brazil)

Italy, who began with an atrocious draw with Poland and appeared miserably uncertain against Peru and Cameroon, improved suddenly and dramatically, beating both Argentina and Brazil with stunning displays, and in truth crushed a German team bereft of ideas and tired from their monumental exertions in the semi-final. Simply unable when all else failed them to draw again on exhausted reserves of fighting spirit, Poland suffered from the absence of Boniek against the wily Italians, though their team exceeded the expectations of most given the turmoil surrounding their preparation. France and Brazil delighted all, but the Final that should have been, could have been, was lost because neither from position of strength that their superior football brought them could sustain it or resist persistent and indomitable opponents when it mattered most.

CHAPTER 13

MEXICO

1986

Qualifying Tournament
Record 120 entries
Italy qualify as holders, Mexico qualify as hosts

Europe (33): Albania, Austria, Belgium, Bulgaria, Cyprus, Czechoslovakia, Denmark, England, Finland, France, East Germany, West Germany, Greece, Holland, Hungary, Iceland, Northern Ireland, Republic of Ireland, Italy, Luxembourg, Malta, Norway, Poland, Portugal, Romania, Scotland, Spain, Sweden, Switzerland, Turkey, USSR, Wales, Yugoslavia

South America (10): Argentina, Bolivia, Brazil, Chile, Colombia, Ecuador, Paraguay, Peru, Uruguay, Venezuela

CONCACAF (18): Antigua, Barbados, Canada, Costa Rica, Grenada, Guatemala, Guyana, Haiti, Honduras, Jamaica, Mexico, Netherlands Antilles, Panama, Puerto Rico, El Salvador, Surinam, Trinidad and Tobago, USA

Asia (26): Bahrain, Bangladesh, Brunei, China, Hong Kong, India, Indonesia, Iran, Iraq, Japan, Jordan, North Korea, South Korea, Kuwait, Macao, Malaysia, Nepal, Oman, Qatar, Saudi Arabia, Singapore, Syria, Thailand, UAE, North Yemen, South Yemen

Africa (29): Algeria, Angola, Benin, Cameroon, Egypt, Ethiopia, Gambia, Ghana, Guinea, Ivory Coast, Kenya, Lesotho, Liberia, Libya, Madagascar, Malawi, Mauritius, Morocco, Niger, Nigeria, Senegal, Sierra Leone, Sudan, Tanzania, Togo, Tunisia, Uganda, Zambia, Zimbabwe

Oceania (4): Australia, Israel, New Zealand, Taipei

Europe

Group 1 (Poland, Belgium, Greece, Albania)
Belgium v Albania 3–1, Poland v Greece 3–1, Poland v Albania 2–2, Greece v Belgium 0–0, Albania v Belgium 2–0, Greece v Albania 2–0, Belgium v Greece 2–0, Belgium v Poland 2–0, Greece v Poland 1–4, Albania v Poland 0–1, Poland v Belgium 0–0, Albania v Greece 1–1

	P	W	D	L	F	A	Pts
Poland	6	3	2	1	10	6	8
Belgium	6	3	2	1	7	3	8
Greece	6	1	2	3	5	10	4
Albania	6	1	2	3	6	9	4

Poland qualified
Belgium to play-off with runner-up of Group 5

Group 2 (West Germany, Czechoslovakia, Sweden, Portugal, Malta)

Sweden v Malta 4–0, Sweden v Portugal 0–1, Portugal v Czechoslovakia 2–1, West Germany v Sweden 2–0, Czechoslovakia v Malta 4–0, Portugal v Sweden 1–3, Malta v West Germany 2–3, Malta v Portugal 1–3, Portugal v West Germany 1–2, West Germany v Malta 6–0, Malta v Czechoslovakia 0–0, Czechoslovakia v West Germany 1–5, Sweden v Czechoslovakia 2–0, Sweden v West Germany 2–2, Czechoslovakia v Portugal 1–0, Portugal v Malta 3–2, Czechoslovakia v Sweden 2–1, West Germany v Portugal 0–1, West Germany v Czechoslovakia 2–2, Malta v Sweden 1–2

	P	W	D	L	F	A	Pts
West Germany	8	5	2	1	22	9	12
Portugal	8	5	0	3	12	10	10
Sweden	8	4	1	3	14	9	9
Czechoslovakia	8	3	2	3	11	12	8
Malta	8	0	1	7	6	25	1

West Germany and Portugal qualified

Group 3 (England, Northern Ireland, Romania, Turkey, Finland)

Finland v Northern Ireland 1–0, Northern Ireland v Romania 3–2, England v Finland 5–0, Turkey v Finland 1–2, Northern Ireland v Finland 2–1, Turkey v England 0–8, Northern Ireland v England 0–1, Romania v Turkey 3–0, Northern Ireland v Turkey 2–0, Romania v England 0–0, Finland v England 1–1, Finland v Romania 1–1, Romania v Finland 2–0, Turkey v Northern Ireland 0–0, England v Romania 1–1, Finland v Turkey 1–0, Romania v Northern Ireland 0–1, England v Turkey 5–0, England v Northern Ireland 0–0, Turkey v Romania 1–3

	P	W	D	L	F	A	Pts
England	8	4	4	0	21	2	12
Northern Ireland	8	4	2	2	8	5	10
Romania	8	3	3	2	12	7	9
Finland	8	3	2	3	7	12	8
Turkey	8	0	1	7	2	24	1

England and Northern Ireland qualified

Group 4 (France, Yugoslavia, East Germany, Bulgaria, Luxembourg)

Yugoslavia v Bulgaria 0–0, Luxembourg v France 0–4, East Germany v Yugoslavia 2–3, Luxembourg v East Germany 0–5, France v Bulgaria 1–0, Bulgaria v Luxembourg 4–0, France v East Germany 2–0, Yugoslavia v Luxembourg 1–0, Yugoslavia v France 0–0, Bulgaria v East Germany 1–0, Luxembourg v Yugoslavia 0–1, Bulgaria v France 2–0, East Germany v Luxembourg 3–1, Bulgaria v Yugoslavia 2–1, East Germany v France 2–0, Luxembourg v Bulgaria 1–3, Yugoslavia v East Germany 1–2, France v Luxembourg 6–0, France v Yugoslavia 2–0, East Germany v Bulgaria 2–1

	P	W	D	L	F	A	Pts
France	8	5	1	2	15	4	11
Bulgaria	8	5	1	2	13	5	11
East Germany	8	5	0	3	16	9	10
Yugoslavia	8	3	2	3	7	8	8
Luxembourg	8	0	0	8	2	27	0

France and Bulgaria qualified

Group 5 (Austria, Hungary, Holland, Cyprus)

Cyprus v Austria 1–2, Hungary v Austria 3–1, Holland v Hungary 1–2, Austria v Holland 1–0, Cyprus v Hungary 1–2, Cyprus v Holland 0–1, Holland v Cyprus 7–1, Hungary v Cyprus 2–0, Austria v Hungary 0–3, Holland v Austria 1–1, Austria v Cyprus 4–0, Hungary v Holland 0–1

	P	W	D	L	F	A	Pts
Hungary	6	5	0	1	12	4	10
Holland	6	3	1	2	11	5	7
Austria	6	3	1	2	9	8	7
Cyprus	6	0	0	6	3	18	0

Hungary qualified
Holland to play-off with runner-up of Group 1

European Play-off
Belgium v Holland 1–0, 1–2
Belgium qualified on away goals

Group 6 (USSR, Denmark, Rep of Ireland, Switzerland, Norway)
Rep of Ireland v USSR 1–0, Norway v Switzerland 0–1, Denmark v Norway
1–0, Norway v USSR 1–1, Switzerland v Denmark 1–0, Norway v Rep of
Ireland 1–0, Denmark v Rep of Ireland 3–0, Switzerland v USSR 2–2, Rep of
Ireland v Norway 0–0, USSR v Switzerland 4–0, Rep of Ireland v Switzerland
3–0, Denmark v USSR 4–2, Switzerland v Rep of Ireland 0–0, USSR v Denmark
1–0, Denmark v Switzerland 0–0, Norway v Denmark 1–5, USSR v Rep of
Ireland 2–0, USSR v Norway 1–0, Switzerland v Norway 1–1, Rep of Ireland v
Denmark 1–4

	P	W	D	L	F	A	Pts
Denmark	8	5	1	2	17	6	11
USSR	8	4	2	2	13	8	10
Switzerland	8	2	4	2	5	10	8
Rep of Ireland	8	2	2	4	5	10	6
Norway	8	1	3	4	4	10	5

Denmark and USSR qualified

Group 7 (Spain, Scotland, Wales, Iceland)
Iceland v Wales 1–0, Spain v Wales 3–0, Scotland v Iceland 3–0, Scotland v
Spain 3–1, Wales v Iceland 2–1, Spain v Scotland 1–0, Scotland v Wales 0–1,
Wales v Spain 3–0, Iceland v Scotland 0–1, Iceland v Spain 1–2, Wales v
Scotland 1–1, Spain v Iceland 2–1

	P	W	D	L	F	A	Pts
Spain	6	4	0	2	9	8	8
Scotland	6	3	1	2	8	4	7
Wales	6	3	1	2	7	6	7
Iceland	6	1	0	5	4	10	2

Spain qualified
Scotland to play-off with winner of Oceania Group

South America

Group 1 (Argentina, Peru, Colombia, Venezuela)

Colombia v Peru 1–0, Venezuela v Argentina 2–3, Colombia v Argentina 1–3, Venezuela v Peru 0–1, Peru v Colombia 0–0, Argentina v Venezuela 3–0, Peru v Venezuela 4–1, Argentina v Colombia 1–0, Venezuela v Colombia 2–2, Peru v Argentina 1–0, Colombia v Venezuela 2–0, Argentina v Peru 2–2

	P	W	D	L	F	A	Pts
Argentina	6	4	1	1	12	6	9
Peru	6	3	2	1	8	4	8
Colombia	6	2	2	2	6	6	6
Venezuela	6	0	1	5	5	15	1

Argentina qualified
Peru and Colombia to play-offs

Group 2 (Chile, Ecuador, Uruguay)

Ecuador v Chile 1–1, Uruguay v Ecuador 2–1, Chile v Ecuador 6–2, Chile v Uruguay 2–0, Ecuador v Uruguay 0–2, Uruguay v Chile 2–1

	P	W	D	L	F	A	Pts
Uruguay	4	3	0	1	6	4	6
Chile	4	2	1	1	10	5	5
Ecuador	4	0	1	3	4	11	1

Uruguay qualified
Chile to play-offs

Group 3 (Brazil, Paraguay, Bolivia)

Bolivia v Paraguay 1–1, Bolivia v Brazil 0–2, Paraguay v Bolivia 3–0, Paraguay v Brazil 0–2, Brazil v Paraguay 1–1, Brazil v Bolivia 1–1

	P	W	D	L	F	A	Pts
Brazil	4	2	2	0	6	2	6
Paraguay	4	1	2	1	5	4	4
Bolivia	4	0	2	2	2	7	2

Brazil qualified
Paraguay to play-offs

Semi-Finals
Play-off between the runners-up of Groups 1 and 2
Chile v Peru 4–2, 1–0
Play-off between the runners-up of Groups 3 and third-placed team in Group 1
Paraguay v Colombia 3–0, 1–2

Final Play-off
Paraguay v Chile 3–0, 2–2
Paraguay qualified

CONCACAF

1st Round
Group 1 (El Salvador, Puerto Rico, Canada, Jamaica (expelled), Netherlands Antilles, USA)
El Salvador v Puerto Rico 5–0, 3–0, Netherlands Antilles v USA 0–0, 0–4, Canada (walked over)

Group 2 (Barbados (withdrew), Costa Rica (walked over), Panama, Honduras, Guatemala (walked over))
Panama v Honduras 0–3, 0–1

Group 3 (Trinidad and Tobago, Grenada (withdrew), Antigua, Haiti, Surinam, Guyana)
Antigua v Haiti 0–4, 2–1, Surinam v Guyana 1–0, 1–1, Trinidad and Tobago (walked over)

2nd Round
Group 1 (El Salvador, Honduras, Surinam)
Surinam v El Salvador 0–3, El Salvador v Surinam 3–0, Surinam v Honduras 1–1, Honduras v Surinam 2–1, El Salvador v Honduras 1–2, Honduras v El Salvador 0–0

	P	W	D	L	F	A	Pts
Honduras	4	2	2	0	5	3	6
El Salvador	4	2	1	1	7	2	5
Surinam	4	0	1	3	2	9	1

Group 2 (Canada, Haiti, Guatemala)
Canada v Haiti 2–0, Canada v Guatemala 2–1, Haiti v Guatemala 0–1, Guatemala v Canada 1–1, Haiti v Canada 0–2, Guatemala v Haiti 4–0

	P	W	D	L	F	A	Pts
Canada	4	3	1	0	7	2	7
Guatemala	4	2	1	1	7	3	5
Haiti	4	0	0	4	0	9	0

Group 3 (USA, Costa Rica, Trinidad and Tobago)
Trinidad and Tobago v Costa Rica 0–3, Costa Rica v Trinidad and Tobago 1–1, Trinidad and Tobago v USA 1–2, USA v Trinidad and Tobago 1–0, Costa Rica v USA 1–1, USA v Costa Rica 0–1

	P	W	D	L	F	A	Pts
Costa Rica	4	2	2	0	6	2	6
USA	4	2	1	1	4	3	5
Trinidad and Tobago	4	0	1	3	2	7	1

3rd Round
Costa Rica v Honduras 2–1, Canada v Costa Rica 1–1, Honduras v Canada 0–1, Costa Rica v Canada 0–0, Honduras v Costa Rica 3–1, Canada v Honduras 2–1

	P	W	D	L	F	A	Pts
Canada	4	2	2	0	4	2	6
Honduras	4	1	1	2	7	6	3
Costa Rica	4	0	3	1	4	5	3

Canada qualified

Asia

1st Round
Group 1
Sub-Group 1A (Saudi Arabia, UAE, Oman (withdrew))
Saudi Arabia v UAE 0–0, 0–1

Sub-Group 1B (Iraq, Lebanon, Qatar, Jordan)
Jordan v Qatar 1–0, Iraq v Lebanon 6–0, Lebanon v Iraq 0–6, Qatar v Lebanon 7–0 (Lebanon withdrew, record expunged), Jordan v Iraq 2–3, Qatar v Iraq 3–0, Qatar v Jordan 2–0, Iraq v Jordan 2–0, Iraq v Qatar 2–1

	P	W	D	L	F	A	Pts
Iraq	4	3	0	1	7	6	6
Qatar	4	2	0	2	6	3	4
Jordan	4	1	0	3	3	7	2

Group 2
Sub-Group 2A (Kuwait, North Yemen, Syria)
Syria v Kuwait 1–0, North Yemen v Syria 0–1, Kuwait v North Yemen 5–0, Kuwait v Syria 0–0, Syria v North Yemen 3–0, North Yemen v Kuwait 1–3

	P	W	D	L	F	A	Pts
Syria	4	3	1	0	5	0	7
Kuwait	4	2	1	1	8	2	5
North Yemen	4	0	0	4	1	12	0

Sub-Group 2B (Bahrain, South Yemen, Iran excluded)
South Yemen v Bahrain 1–4, Bahrain v South Yemen 3–3

Group 3
Sub-Group 3A (Malaysia, Nepal, South Korea)
Nepal v South Korea 0–2, Malaysia v South Korea 1–0, Nepal v Malaysia 0–0, Malaysia v Nepal 5–0, South Korea v Nepal 4–0, South Korea v Malaysia 2–0

	P	W	D	L	F	A	Pts
South Korea	4	3	0	1	8	1	6
Malaysia	4	2	1	1	6	2	5
Nepal	4	0	1	3	0	11	1

Sub-Group 3B (Thailand, India, Bangladesh, Indonesia)
Indonesia v Thailand 1–0, Indonesia v Bangladesh 2–0, Indonesia v India 2–1, Thailand v Bangladesh 3–0, Thailand v India 0–0, Thailand v Indonesia 0–1, Bangladesh v India 1–2, Bangladesh v Indonesia 2–1, Bangladesh v Thailand 1–0, India v Indonesia 1–1, India v Thailand 1–1, India v Bangladesh 2–1

	P	W	D	L	F	A	Pts
Indonesia	6	4	1	1	8	4	9
India	6	2	3	1	7	6	7
Thailand	6	1	2	3	4	4	4
Bangladesh	6	2	0	4	5	10	4

Group 4
Sub-Group 4A (China, Hong Kong, Macao, Brunei)
Macao v Brunei 2–0, Hong Kong v China 0–0, Macao v China 0–4, Hong Kong v Brunei 8–0, China v Brunei 8–0, Brunei v China 0–4, Brunei v Hong Kong 1–5, Brunei v Macao 1–2, Macao v Hong Kong 0–2, Hong Kong v Macao 2–0, China v Macao 6–0, China v Hong Kong 1–2

	P	W	D	L	F	A	Pts
Hong Kong	6	5	1	0	19	2	11
China	6	4	1	1	23	2	9
Macao	6	2	0	4	4	15	4
Brunei	6	0	0	6	2	29	0

Sub-Group 4B (Japan, North Korea, Singapore)
Singapore v North Korea 1–1, Singapore v Japan 1–3, Japan v North Korea 1–0, North Korea v Japan 0–0, Japan v Singapore 5–0, North Korea v Singapore 2–0

	P	W	D	L	F	A	Pts
Japan	4	3	1	0	9	1	7
North Korea	4	1	2	1	3	2	4
Singapore	4	0	1	3	2	11	1

2nd Round
UAE v Iraq 2–3, 2–1, Bahrain v Syria 1–1, 0–1, South Korea v Indonesia 2–0, 4–1, Japan v Hong Kong 3–0, 2–1

3rd Round
Syria v Iraq 0–0, Iraq v Syria 3–1
Japan v South Korea 1–2, South Korea v Japan 1–0
Iraq and South Korea qualified

Africa

1st Round
Egypt v Zimbabwe 1–0, 1–1, Kenya v Ethiopia 2–1, 3–3, Mauritius v Malawi 0–1, 0–4, Zambia v Uganda 3–0, 0–1, Madagascar v Lesotho (withdrew), Tanzania v Sudan 1–1, 0–0, Sierra Leone v Morocco 0–1, 0–4, Libya v Niger (withdrew), Benin v Tunisia 0–2, 0–4, Ivory Coast v Gambia 4–0, 2–3, Nigeria v Liberia 3–0, 1–0, Angola v Senegal 1–0, 0–1 (Angola won 4–3 on penalties), Guinea v Togo (withdrew)

2nd Round
Zambia v Cameroon 4–1, 1–1, Morocco v Malawi 2–0, 0–0, Angola v Algeria 0–0, 2–3, Kenya v Nigeria 0–3, 1–3, Egypt v Madagascar 1–0, 0–1 (Egypt won 4–2 on penalties), Guinea v Tunisia 1–0, 0–2, Sudan v Libya 0–0, 0–4, Ivory Coast v Ghana 0–0, 0–2

3rd Round

Algeria v Zambia 2–0, 1–0, Ghana v Libya 0–0, 0–2, Nigeria v Tunisia 1–0, 0–2, Egypt v Morocco 0–0, 0–2

4th Round

Tunisia v Algeria 1–4, 0–3, Morocco v Libya 3–0, 0–1
Algeria and Morocco qualified

Oceania
1st Round

Israel v Taipei 6–0, Taipei v Israel 0–5, New Zealand v Australia 0–0, New Zealand v Taipei 5–1, Israel v Australia 1–2, Taipei v New Zealand 0–5, Australia v Israel 1–1, Australia v Taipei 7–0, New Zealand v Israel 3–1, Taipei v Australia 0–8, Australia v New Zealand 2–0, Israel v New Zealand 3–0

	P	W	D	L	F	A	Pts
Australia	6	4	2	0	20	2	10
Israel	6	3	1	2	17	6	7
New Zealand	6	3	1	2	13	7	7
Taipei	6	0	0	6	1	36	0

Australia qualified for play-off (see above)

Final Play-off

Scotland v Australia 2–0, 0–0
Scotland qualified

1986 MEXICO 31 May–29 June

QUALIFIERS

Algeria	France	Poland
Argentina	Hungary	Portugal
Belgium	Iraq	Scotland
Bulgaria	Italy	South Korea
Brazil	Mexico	Spain
Canada	Morocco	Uruguay
Denmark	Northern Ireland	USSR
England	Paraguay	West Germany

The thirteenth Tournament would be hosted by Mexico once more, after Colombia, a small impoverished nation with little or no football heritage, withdrew, the burden of the event on their frail economy too great to bear. Though Europeans had learned greatly from 1970 and preparation techniques had advanced with enormous strides, clearly they would be disadvantaged. Heat would be a problem to many, altitude and its debilitating effects on the body a problem to most.

Twenty-four teams would compete again, initially in six groups of four. Here the similarity with 1982 mercifully ended. FIFA elected to dispense with the unsatisfactory 'second group system' and, for the first time since 1966, reverted back to a knock-out competition for those survivors from the group stages. In achieving this there was an added complication, however: four 'third' place teams would need to qualify to balance the draw. Absurdly, therefore, after two weeks competition and thirty-six matches, only eight teams would be eliminated.

In Group A, Italy, the Champions, Argentina their predecessors, Bulgaria and gritty South Korea were to compete. The Italians, again with Enzo Bearzot at the helm, were a team thought to be in decline. Gentile, scourge of attacking players, was gone as was the tough marker Tardelli, Dino Zoff and, most significantly perhaps, Paulo Rossi, striker 'extraordinaire'. Altobelli remained, forceful as ever, as did little Conti and the shrewd Bergomi; their challenge had a platform, but was it creaking? Argentina by consent were a team to be feared, replete as they were with fine performers and the stocky, breathtakingly audacious genius of Maradona, twenty-five years old and already hailed the world's greatest player. Curiously, however, in qualification they had proven unconvincing, losing almost fatally in Lima to Peru. For South Korea, winners along with Iraq from the Asian section, a long awaited opportunity presented itself – for a nation of adoring football lovers – to compete in a World Cup, the country's first since an abortive and embarrassing entry in 1954. This time fast, fit, tenacious and rugged as the occasion demanded, they would not be a pushover. Finally Bulgaria, who owed their presence to a dour yet courageous defensive action in East Germany. Perennial contenders, their record in past finals had been poor, the demands imposed on them by Group A perhaps beyond them.

From Group B the hosts were based, as they were sixteen years earlier, in the capital Mexico City. Unlike, though, the Tournament of 1970, there were reasons for genuine optimism from their wildly enthusiastic support. Thomas Boy, tall, visionary midfielder, and the inimitable Hugo Sanchez, predatory goal scorer and Mexican icon, would add considerable substance to their challenge. Belgium also represented a threat; at their best defensively mean with Gerets organizing capably, they had the grizzled veteran Ceulemans again in the ranks, playing alongside the raw and exciting talent of Scifo, their elegant young playmaker born in Sicily. Iraq's qualification campaign had started disastrously with humiliating defeat in Qatar and then ended in jubilation after victory over Syria. Now they had arrived at the summit of their ambitions, their mettle and a lack of experience at the highest level would surely and painfully be put to the test. Paraquay were considered the nation's finest for many a year, and boasting Romero and his strike partner Cabañas, they had qualified via a difficult and testing route, removing in turn Colombia and Chile.

Leon coupled with Irapuato would stage Group C's matches. Canada, managed by former England goalkeeper Tony Walters and representing CONCACAF, faced three mighty European rivals. The USSR, beaten recently by England and unimpressive generally, had a new coach, Valeri Labanovski, and he had revived their fortunes, galvanizing the team with a large Dynamo Kiev contingent. Hungary, well fancied, with a settled team and an emphatic qualification record, had accounted for both Austria and Holland. Then there was France, hugely talented European Champions, with Platini, Giresse and Tigana in their midfield, and Amoros, a marvellous attacking full back prepared to support his forwards.

In Group D, Brazil fortuitously playing at Guadalajara counted again on Mexican empathy so generously offered to the class of 1970. They were the favourites, a team of extravagant talents returned to a land where they enjoyed support bettered only by that of the Mexican hosts. Doughty Northern Ireland, tiny in size and population, huge in courage and determination, would be one of their opponents. Jennings was an inspiration in goal, but many of the key performers had reached the veteran stage together, and some wondered how they would fare in the heat and humidity. Spain, still bearing the scars of Valencia, would approach Ireland with trepidation. More worryingly, both Scotland and Wales had inflicted defeats on them during qualification. Nevertheless, they were here with a strong team, Viktor, Camacho and Goicoechea were strong performers, and Butragueño 'the Vulture' a dynamic goal scorer. Algeria, so desperately unfortunate in Spain where Austria and West Germany had conspired disgracefully to eliminate them, were back with greater experience. Madjer and the industrious Belloumi, so influential then, were back once more to threaten the footballing establishment.

At Queretaro and Neza a highly competitive group battled it out, instantly dubbed 'The Group of Death'. Scotland were here, as were Denmark, Uruguay and the West Germans. Scotland, who had narrowly and rather luckily qualified ahead of Wales, had fine midfield players in Souness and Strachan, though Dalglish, the mercurial striker, was absent through injury, and to general surprise his club colleague at Liverpool, Alan Hansen, a composed, elegant centre half, had been excluded. Jock Stein, the coach, had died suddenly before the Tournament, and Alex Ferguson, so successful at Aberdeen, had taken over. Denmark in recent years had been a revelation, with their own brand of total football, practised as it was by such luminaries as Michael Laudrup, the outrageously gifted Juventus forward, Preben Elkjaer, left footed, pacey centre forward, and the rock-like Morten Olsen in defence. They were justifiably among the favourites. So, too, were Germany, this in spite of coach Beckenbauer's insistence that his team was too young, too inexperienced, and here just to learn. Few listened. Schumacher, their villainous goalkeeper from 1982, remained, as did Berthold, Briegel, Förster, Augenthaler and the old warrior Rummenigge; Matthäus and Brehme represented the younger generation. Qualification from an apparently difficult group had been achieved with embarrassing ease. Uruguay, the last of the four, were an enigma. Immensely talented and with their brilliant forward Francescoli potentially a star of the Tournament, they still had a tendency to be unduly negative and destructive, violence surfacing its ugly head all too frequently.

Over in Monterrey were Group F's England, with Hoddle their playmaker, Lineker of Everton an eager elusive goal scorer, and Brian Robson a brave and forceful captain, although a succession of injuries left question marks over his fitness. They looked a well-balanced team. Portugal, qualifiers with Germany for this, their first Tournament since the glorious effort of 1966, were in rancour. Undeniably talented, dissent over pay, bonus, lack of preparation and general distrust between players and officials did not bode well for a successful competition. Poland by contrast were happy and carefree, and had enjoyed relatively good form. Yet inexplicably they had managed only a draw with weak Albania. Boniek, Majewski and Kubicki would again be present but theirs appeared an ageing team. Morocco, the final member of the quartet, came to further enhance the growing reputation enjoyed by African football. Inspired by Timoumi and Bouderbala, they had eased by Sierra Leone, Malawi, Egypt and Libya to confirm their return to the world stage in the country where they had begun it… Mexico.

Group A
Venues: Mexico City, Puebla
Argentina
Bulgaria
Italy
South Korea

Group D
Venues: Guadalajara, Monterrey
Algeria
Brazil
Northern Ireland
Spain

Group B

Venues: Mexico City, Toluca
Belgium
Iraq
Mexico
Paraguay

Group E

Venues: Queretaro, Neza
Denmark
Scotland
Uruguay
West Germany

Group C

Venues: Irapuato, Leon
Canada
France
Hungary
USSR

Group F

Venues: Monterrey, Guadalajara
England
Morocco
Poland
Portugal

THE FIRST SERIES

Italy and Bulgaria began the Tournament at the Azteca and at once the derision afforded Mexico's president – roundly jeered before the match – was turned on the two contestants. Bulgaria at least were willing, their attacks floundering on the Italians' well-drilled defence. Italy, the classic counter puncher, waited, seeking to break swiftly against the Bulgarians' increasingly vulnerable rearguard. Inevitably the goal came, Di Gennaro on the stroke of half-time finding the lurking Altobelli unmarked on the far post, his volley driven home. Now with the game firmly in their grasp, their football plainly superior, the 'Azzurri' relaxed, content to hold their lead, Scirea and Bergomi particularly ruthless with crude scything tackles when threatened. Cabrini arriving to meet Altobelli's deft flick might have sealed it fifteen minutes from time, his header flying over. Remarkably, it was soon after that Bulgaria earned their draw, Kostadinov whipping in a cross, Sirakov eluding Scirea and Vierchowod to squeeze the ball acutely between the underemployed Galli and his right hand post. At 1–1 Italy left the field disappointed and with the contemptuous whistling of a frustrated audience ringing in their ears.

At the Olympiaco stadium South Korea, predictably outclassed in every department by a vibrant Argentine side, resorted to violence, the mercurial Maradona singled out for particularly spiteful and malevolent treatment. Mercifully without injury, the South Americans swept their puny challengers away. Ten minutes had passed when Maradona's free kick struck the red-shirted defensive wall and ran to Valdano who shot clinically for 1–0. Straight after, Burruchaga almost made it two, his shot rapping the upright before Ruggeri did. Another free kick was awarded for a ludicrous foul on Burruchaga ten yards from the ball, and Maradona's curling delivery met with precision for 2–0. Fifteen minutes played and the game drifted. Valdano made it three early in the second half, reaching Maradona's low cross before the Koreans replied, Chang-Sun from twenty-five yards shooting gloriously home. Ending 3–1, the Argentineans sensibly reluctant to involve themselves had won at a canter. The Koreans benefiting from lenient refereeing had shown a competitive instinct bordering on the maniacal, though their naiveté had been punished in spite of their physical endeavours.

In Group D in the Jalisco stadium at Guadalajara, Brazil, unimpressively and not without the aid of a huge slice of luck, squeezed to victory over a Spanish team weakened considerably by stomach illness. Cautious and dull in the 95 ºF heat, the game burst into life with its moment of controversy, Miguel Gonzalez hammering a ferocious drive against the Brazilian crossbar and down on to the line. Had it crossed? Referee Bambridge of Australia thought not, his American linesman concurred, and despite furious Spanish protest, Brazil had escaped. Awoken from their slumber, stewarded as ever by the elegant Socrates, Brazil galvanized themselves, Edhino bundled the ball over Spain's line with a hand and was promptly penalized. The wily Butragueño, masterful throughout, missed an opportunity for Spain, before Brazil finally scrambled a winner as untidy as the match itself. Casagrande's pass found Careca, his shot thumped on to the bar and Socrates following up bundled the ball into the Spanish net. Defeated, for depleted Spain worse still was to come. Television replays had confirmed what at once they had suspected, that Gonzalez's shot had indeed been a 'goal' – the bitterest blow of all.

In the 3rd de Marzo stadium Northern Ireland took an early lead and then fell away, toiling strenuously in the midday sun. Algeria, perhaps more comfortable in the searing heat, came back to earn themselves a deserved point. Whiteside's fifth minute effort appeared to set the Irish on their way, but they could not sustain their effort, and by conserving their energy and electing to defend, they allowed the Africans, increasingly confident, the initiative. Zidane on the hour dispatched a powerful free kick beyond Jennings for an equalizer, and thereafter the game fizzled out, its pattern and rhythm disrupted by fatigue.

France in Group C at Leon made surprisingly heavy weather of beating tough, industrious Canada, undistinguished in midfield despite the presence of Platini. Eleven minutes from the end Papin finally gave them their win, seizing on an error by the unfortunate Canadian goalkeeper, Paul Dolan. 'I was really afraid we were not going to win,' said French coach Henri Michel in the aftermath. 'I take my hat off to the Canadians, but we have taken two points and that is what counts. I also know that several players are not at their peak and will improve.'

In Irapuato there was sensation when Russia demolished Hungary 6–0. Unsettled by two goals within five minutes, the Hungarians fell apart catastrophically as the Russian attack, orchestrated brilliantly by Igor Belanov, launched a series of devastating raids on a deflated Magyar defence. The Russians, a team so lacking in confidence in the spring, had brought in a new coach, Valeri Lobanovski, and he in turn brought new players from Ukraine's Dynamo Kiev. They had transformed themselves into genuine and surprise contenders.

At Neza, denied their striker Dalglish through injury, Scotland played with purpose but lacked the cutting edge to unhinge the Danes and were beaten ultimately by a strike on 58 minutes by Preben Elkjaer. Deft of touch and quick of feet, receiving a pass from Arnesen he eluded the luckless Miller to swivel and shoot past Leighton for 1–0. Largely outplayed by a team of verve and bewildering movement – reminiscent perhaps of the Dutch of 1974 – Scotland dug in, closed down and held on, Berggreen's outrageous and cynical challenge on Nicholas six minutes from time giving them a last opportunity. Souness pumped the ball goalwards, McAvennie launched himself acrobatically, his touch diverting the kick agonizingly beyond Rasmussen's upright. Denmark had won the day impressively, though Scotland in defeat had distinguished themselves. Also in the 'Group of Death', Germany and Uruguay played a typically ill-tempered encounter, peppered with fouls. Alzamendi gave the Americans the lead after four minutes, seizing on Thomas Berthold's casual backpass. Allofs finally beat the quite outstanding Alvez in Uruguay's goal on 85 minutes to salvage a point. What filled the time in between only marginally resembled a game of football. As Germany became increasingly frenzied in their search for an equalizer – Berthold twice going close, Augenthaler striking post and bar – Uruguay resorted to the cynical brutality that has sadly become their trademark. Germany, physically capable, responded in kind as the game became littered with sly trips and blatant obstructions. Franz Beckenbauer, Germany's elegant coach, appeared not to have noticed what had gone before in his after match comments. 'We were much superior for 70 minutes and should have won. The goal was a relief. I take my hat off to the team. The players went to the limit of their ability and endurance.' Almost unbelievably, Omar Barras, the Uruguayan counterpart, chose to question the referee's integrity. 'The referee clearly favoured West Germany. He waved play on when they attacked my players. I am genuinely worried by the referees' performances.'

In England's Group F, Morocco and Poland played out a dull, tentative match in Monterrey. The Africans, seeking above all not to lose, achieved their objective without difficulty as Poland, struggling plainly with the unfamiliar conditions, lacked energy and inspiration. Nevertheless, Urban, their substitute, almost rescued them, his shot beating Zaki in Morocco's goal, but not his goalpost – 0–0. Picchniczek, Poland's coach, as is the modern way, chose not to be too downhearted. 'It is always hard to start off by playing the little team. It was obvious my players felt the pressures; we lack cohesion and didn't play as well as we can.'

Mexico at the Azteca accounted for Belgium amidst a heavy downpour causing treacherous conditions. Thomas Boy gave the Belgians a scare on seven minutes, his free kick skidding into the grateful body of Pfaff. Due warning served, five minutes later Mexico had their lead, Quirarte rising highest to thump his header beyond the startled goalkeeper. On thirty eight minutes 1–0 became 2–0, Hugo Sanchez, darling of all Mexico, connecting with a Flores flick to tumultuous ovation. On the interval Vandenbergh reduced the arrears from Gerets' long throw in. Come the second half, hitherto disappointing Belgium steeled themselves and fought back hard, gaining control of midfield and causing 80,000 partisans great anxiety to the whistle.

Also in Group B at Toluca, Paraguay, rather fortunately, overcame Iraq courtesy of Romero's delightful lob on 35 minutes. Iraq, far more willing and adventurous through the first half, forced home an equalizer when Radii leapt high to score, only to discover the referee's whistle to end the half had beaten the ball to the net. Deflated by the incident, Iraq's second-half effort suffered. Twice Paraguay struck the woodwork, though at the end referee Picon of Mauritius received a damning verdict on the night's work, leaving the pitch in undignified fashion as the incensed crowd pelted him with paper cups.

England, in the long grass at Monterrey, huffed and puffed against a Portuguese team disgruntled and enraged by the treatment meted out to them by their own authorities. Defeat considered unthinkable beforehand was confirmed through Carlos Manuel's far post shot after Diamantino had stolen in behind Sansom to provide the telling cross. England, unbeaten in eleven matches coming to the event, played without confidence but still managed to squander a succession of chances to guarantee victory. After the match, coach Bobby Robson was particularly scathing of Portugal's often nine-man defence, at the same time dismissing England's defeat as largely meaningless. 'I thought the Portuguese were frightened of us. I know how disappointed everyone at home will be but I also know my team. You have to lose sometime and the consolation is that it was here and not in the knock-out stages.'

THE SECOND SERIES

For the fourth successive Tournament, Argentina and Italy came together. As ever, the encounter in Puebla proved a contest between two technical masters, both prone to bouts of indiscipline and fraying temper. Six minutes in and Italy had the lead, Altobelli dispatching a penalty kick awarded rather generously by Referee Keizer of Holland for a handball against the unfortunate Garre. Argentina toiled for their equalizer, the darting Maradona skipping around defenders, his audacity often terminated with brutality. After 33 minutes they were level, Valdano's angled pass finding Maradona, his shot from a difficult angle unerringly accurate. For the rest it was just gentle sparring, both evidently content with a draw, though Italy's Cabrini came closest to helping Italy steal the points. The other Group A match at Mexico City saw South Korea frustrate Bulgaria's quest for a first ever 'finals' win. Getov gave the East Europeans a perfect start, cleverly lobbing the goalkeeper on eleven minutes. They could not hold on. Supremely fit and willing, back came Korea, their 70th minute equalizer a virtuoso effort by substitute Jong-Boo and just reward for their immense effort.

At Guadalajara's Jalisco stadium Brazil were once more unconvincing and stumbled to the narrowest of triumphs over gallant Algeria. The Africans from the start showed little respect for their revered opponents and with Belloumi their pivotal player having a significant influence on proceedings, they threatened an upset. Twice he was denied by desperate defending until Edinho was forced to scramble off the goal line after Belloumi and Assad had linked cleverly. Brazil, as against Spain, improved. Julio Cesar thumped a swerving free kick on to the bar, Leau Branco a shot against the post and then finally they had their goal. Careca, taking advantage of Abdallah's indecision, reached the rampaging Müller's cross to pick his spot. At 1–0 Brazil had had to endure the noisy criticism of their own usually devoted supporters. Also in Group D, Northern Ireland fell behind after a minute and then, when 2–0 down to Spain, exhibited enormous resources of pride and resilience to fight their way back into the contest, and almost saved themselves. It was Butragueño who struck immediately, sending them on their way to defeat. The little 'vulture', alert as ever, moved swiftly on to Michels' pass, and before defenders could react, drilled his shot sweetly into Jennings' net. Outplayed in the midfield area in spite of the industry of McCreery, the Irish seemed beaten after the quarter-hour. Butragueño turned Worthington and the ball, moved quickly across the area and found Viktor, whose deliberate pass was hammered on the volley into the Irish net by Julio Salinas. Rolling their sleeves up, the courageous Irish found their combative best. Clark instinctively earned them a consolatory goal, though for all of their earnest endeavour the equalizer they sought remained to the end beyond them.

In Group C a match of infinite promise was delivered as France and the Soviets demonstrated their respective qualities: French flair and an irresistible touch challenged by Russian thrust and power. Physically the stronger, the Soviets closed down their opponents as well as they could. Aleinikov struck the bar and Demyanenko went close as France were forced on to the back foot. Platini, though, held largely in check, rattled the Soviet upright with a fiercely driven free kick in the second half. Rats drove thunderously into the French net from twenty yards before inevitably the slick one-touch movement of the French brought its reward, Fernandez stealing on to Giresse's exquisite chip to beat Dasayev immaculately. Finishing 1–1, it was an indication that the Europeans in the field could sustain a credible challenge.

At Irapuato, Hungary, seeking to salvage pride following their savaging at the hands of the Soviets, did so at the expense of the limited Canadians, thus clinging to slender qualification hopes. Esterhazy, capitalizing within two minutes on slack marking, steered Kiprich's cross in for an early and reassuring lead. Detari confirmed victory as Canada, increasingly vulnerable to counterattack as they searched in vain for an equalizer, were punished by Kiprich's run, which Lettieri could only parry. For Canada there was an unwanted statistic, Mike Sweeney's 86th minute dismissal for a second bookable offence the first of the Tournament.

Remarkable goings on took place at Queretaro where Group E's Denmark, playing with a freedom and verve the envy of all, dismantled and demoralized the defensive masters from Uruguay. The loss of Bossio, sent off after 19 minutes, could hardly have helped the South Americans cause, but in truth, twelve or even thirteen may have been needed to contain these rampant Danes. Elkjaer, a massive presence, ran through them at will, helping himself to a hat-trick. Laudrup mesmerized them, completing a fine match with a bewildering run and shot a goal of stunning virtuosity for 6–1 before the merciful end. Morten Olsen, the thirty-six-year-old sweeper, was left to sum up his team's attitude and philosophy: 'We play the way we like to. Laudrup and Elkjaer consider Italian League football as work. This is their hobby!'

Poor Scotland, playing with conviction at Queretaro, threatened to unhinge the Germans when Strachan ran on to Aitken's pass to score from an acute angle. But resourceful as ever, Beckenbauer's team recovered their composure, gained control of midfield for significant periods, and scored the two goals needed for victory. Allofs chipped Leighton to send Völler in on an empty goal, and then as the second half began Völler returned the compliment, evading Narey's clumsy challenge to feed Allofs, who made no mistake. At 2–1 Scotland fought to the end, McAvennie and then Gough almost rescuing them and earning the point their courage perhaps warranted.

In Toluca for Group B, before a tiny crowd Belgium accelerated quickly to a two-goal advantage over Iraq before allowing the undisciplined Asians to score through Radi and worry then unnecessarily to the end. Scifo, a jewel for the Belgians, and Claesen with a penalty kick set the largely unimpressive 'Les Rouges Diables' on their way, Iraq's resistance all the more admirable after Gorgis's dismissal reduced them to ten men.

At the Azteca, Mexico playing before an enormous and passionate audience of 114,000 took the lead through Flores but failed to contain a dangerous though unpredictable Paraguay in what ultimately proved a sorry spectacle. It was Romero, revered in Brazil where he played his club football, who snatched an equalizer, but the game by then as an entertainment was over, littered disgracefully with seventy-seven fouls and suffering constant and pitiful interruption as both teams harangued the referee, constantly feigned injury, wasted time and sought through gamesmanship to gain unfair advantage. Strangely, afterwards Paraguay's coach Cayetano Re sought to justify his side's part in the anarchic exhibition: 'Football's a man's game,' he announced to a somewhat baffled press.

England in Group F survived the dismissal of Ray Wilkins for an uncharacteristic display of petulance and earned themselves a draw at Monterrey in an otherwise uneventful game. Morocco, curiously handed a numerical advantage, made little attempt to win the game, seemingly content with a 0–0 draw. For England mumblings of discontent and insurrection drifted out of the dressing room and upwards to the offices of the ever attentive pressmen.

The following day, however, England found themselves thrown a lifeline as their conquerors, Portugal, capitulated pitifully to Smolarek's second strike in a miserable match. If the English could now defeat Poland, they would redeem themselves.

THE THIRD SERIES

France at Leon, improving fast, duly dispatched a wary Hungary, short on confidence and by the end thoroughly outclassed. The Hungarians, however, started with positive aspirations, threatening intermittently, though France on the half-hour shook themselves from their lethargy after an injury to Papin offered the opportunity for an impromptu team meeting in the centre circle. Moments after the restart, Stopyra's accurate header gave them the lead and deflated the Hungarians. Giresse and then Platini almost extended their lead. Hungary's Dajka struck the crossbar before the extravagant talents of Rocheteau, a second-half substitute, settled matters. First he escaped his marker to provide Tigana with a goal at the near post, then he put the lid on it by shooting past Diszti to make it 3–0. The strolling French, quite untroubled by their opponents, had played with the calm normally afforded a practice match.

Also in Group C, the powerful Soviets, fielding almost a reserve eleven against Canada, dominated at Irapuato but struggled to finish off the spirited, physical North Americans. Blokhin on the hour finally relieved the anxiety, stealing on to Belanov's pass to force the ball in and Zavarov, on as a substitute, wrapped it up. Canada went home, competitive throughout through their pugnacity but their football had won them few admirers.

In Group A at Puebla, Italy confirmed their qualification to the knock-out stages with an uncomfortably close 3–2 win over gallant South Korea. Altobelli gave the 'Azzurri' the lead on 18 minutes, arriving on cue to rifle home Di Gennaro's cross before half-time. Altobelli spurned the chance of a second when his penalty kick, after a foul on Galderisi by Huh Jung-Moo, thumped against the post. In the second half the Koreans redoubled their efforts making up for their physical disadvantages with an astonishing work rate and ferocious, often reckless, tackling. Choi Soon-Ho fired them gloriously level from twenty-five yards. Italian nerves frittered, Altobelli rescued them, bundling in Conti's chipped free kick; then as Korea reeled, he drove De Napoli's cross in off the unfortunate Cho Kwang-Rae. With eight minutes to go the score was 3–1 and Korea was beaten, yet they mustered the fight to score again, Hung Jung-Moo steering home a consolation they richly deserved. At Mexico City, Argentina, secure in qualification, and a Bulgarian team intent on damage limitation played out a deplorably negative encounter dictated by nine-man defences. In spite of this, Valdano, allowed space, picked his spot for a fifth-minute header, though the goal changed little. Bulgaria heading for defeat were strangely reluctant and Argentina perfectly content. Burruchaga on 80 minutes hammered home Maradona's cross to make it 2–0 and at least temporarily lifted the gloom that had descended over those unfortunate enough to witness the spectacle.

Northern Ireland, electing to defend in depth at Guadalajara against the Brazilians, paid a heavy price, because with Clarke of Bournemouth engaged as a lone striker and the midfield conceded, the South Americans advanced on the massed ranks of the anxious Irish defence. Careca demolished Ireland's battle plan, sweeping in Müller's low cross; Josimar, the marvellously fluent right back, condemned them to defeat before the interval. His shot fired in at an extraordinary angle and from thirty-five yards had pace, movement and accuracy. Jennings, a goalkeeper of genuine world class, never got near it. At 2–0 the second half drew to a close, a third goal merely an embellishment, Zico's pass met powerfully by Careca. Ireland's defeat and dismissal from the Tournament had been disappointingly tame. Spain also confirmed themselves qualifiers from D, goals from Calderé, Salinas and Eloy comfortably dispatching an increasingly violent Algerian team intent on fearful provocation that tested both the temper and composure of the Spaniards to the full. Spain resisted with aplomb, Salinas the architect of their triumph whilst Algeria's tough tactics ultimately backfired on them.

At Toluca, Paraguay had much the better of it against Belgium, but were left to rue missed chances as the Belgians escaped with a draw. Dominant throughout the opening period, the South Americans contrived to fall behind to an inspired finish by Vercauteren, whose lob utterly defeated Fernandez. After the interval Paraguay promptly drew level, Cabañas, capitalizing on slack marking, shooting home fiercely. Tempers now began to fray, though Belgium kept their composure better. Veyt gave them a scarcely deserved lead on the hour. For Paraguay elimination loomed large. Cabañas's goal twelve minutes from time saved them, rifling past Pfaff after neatly controlling Cañete's pass. At 2–2 that was that, but Paraguay's coach Re still found time to be ordered from the touchline by the Bulgarian referee. Mexico, again before a passionate and intimidating crowd, booked their passage to the last sixteen. However, their 1–0 victory did not reflect the superiority of their play nor the measure of their control over a modest Iraqi team. Forced to defend in depth, Iraq clung on, riding their luck as a succession of chances came and went. The desperate siege continued unabated before, amidst scenes of delirium, the decisive moment came. Fifty-five minutes had passed when Quirarte set off in pursuit of Negrete's apparently innocuous free kick. Reaching it first, he shot from the narrowest of angles, his audacity rewarded as Nusseif, surprised, was beaten. Mexico deservedly had their win.

In Group F, England, forced into changes by the absence of their captain Brian Robson, finally and belatedly found their best form and contemptuously brushed aside Poland 3–0. Trevor Steven and Steve Hodge giving the side width provided the ammunition, Gary Lineker the instinctive execution as he helped himself to a first half hat-trick. The whole team benefited enormously from the invention and unselfishness of Peter Beardsley, whose first appearance significantly coincided with the improvement. Remarkably, in the Guadalajara tie Morocco overwhelmed Portugal 3–1 and thus qualified as group winners. Timoumi proved the inspiration, aided by Khairi, Bouderbala and Krimau, as the Africans' policy of contain and counter-attack devastated the increasingly despondent Portuguese defenders.

In Neza against Uruguay, Scotland needing to win were frustrated and eliminated in a bad-tempered, ugly match almost synonymous with the appearance of the Uruguayans. Pantomime villains of world football, once again the South Americans demonstrated both sides of their nature. Reduced to ten men after Batista's astonishingly violent first-minute challenge on Strachan, exquisite touch and movement far too good for the Scots mingled uncomfortably with cynicism and gamesmanship. Time wasting, ludicrous feigning of injury, spiteful challenges and spitting, were all weapons in their despicable armoury but they still celebrated at the end, capitalizing on their opponents' naiveté, Nicol spurned Scotland's only opportunity, shooting feebly after running on to Aitken's glorious cross. For their part, Uruguay when they chose to play their football embarrassed Scotland's eleven men regularly, Cabrera with a header going closest, denied only by an instinctive save from Leighton. After the match, FIFA imposed a fine of £8,000 on Uruguayan coach Omar Barras for 'ungentlemanly conduct'. 'Uruguay,' said Alex Ferguson, his opposite number, 'are a disgrace.'

At Queretaro, meanwhile, Group E qualifiers already, West Germany and Denmark rested players ready for the knock-out stages and served up a memorable encounter won by the Danes in their own inimitable fashion. Attacking with verve from the beginning, Denmark startled the Germans with quick and elusive movement, threatening to overrun their besieged defences and creating confusion and uncertainty. Resourceful as ever, the Germans took stock and responded purposefully, Allofs testing substitute goalkeeper Hogh. Brehme pounded the Danish crossbar with a mighty drive, and Matthäus, too, was denied by Hogh. Typically, dangerous and unpredictable as ever, Denmark took the lead when it appeared they had lost control, Morten Olsen powering into the penalty area halted crudely by Rolff, Jesper Olsen sliding the resultant spot kick past Schumacher with ease. Given the confidence of a goal Denmark flowed forward, gaining further reward just past the hour: Arnesen escaping on the right crossed, Eriksen the substitute appeared on cue to tap the ball in – simple. A perfect day? Almost, but Arnesen dismissed in the last minute for lashing out at Lother Matthäus tarnished it. He would be absent when his team lined up against Spain.

The Round of Sixteen

Argentina v Uruguay
Belgium v USSR
Brazil v Poland
Bulgaria v Mexico
Denmark v Spain
England v Paraguay
France v Italy
Morocco v West Germany

Final Tournament – Mexico
First round

Group A

Bulgaria (0) **1, Italy** (1) **1**
31.5.86 MEXICO CITY
Bulgaria: Mikhailov, Arabov, Zdravkov, Dimitrov, Markov A, Sirakov (1), Iskrenov (Kostadinov), Sadkov, Mladenov, Gospodinov (Jeliaskov), Getov
Italy: Galli, Bergomi, Cabrini, De Napoli, Vierchowod, Scirea, Conti (Vialli), Di Gennaro, Galderisi, Bagni, Altobelli (1)
Referee: Fredriksson (Sweden)

Argentina (2) **3, South Korea** (0) **1**
2.6.86 MEXICO CITY
Argentina: Pumpido, Clausen, Brown, Ruggeri (1), Garre, Giusti, Batista (Olarticoechea), Burruchaga, Pasculli (Tapia), Maradona, Valdano (2)
South Korea: Oh Yun-Kyo, Park Kyung-Hoon, Jung Yong-Hwan, Cho Min-Kook, Kim Yong-See (Byun Byung-Joo), Huh Jung-Moo, Kim Pyung-Suk (Cho Kwang-Rae), Park Chang-Sun (1), Choi Soon-Ho, Kim Joo-Sung, Cha Bum-Kun
Referee: Sanchez Arminio (Spain)

Italy (1) **1, Argentina** (1) **1**
5.6.86 PUEBLA
Italy: Galli, Bergomi, Cabrini, De Napoli (Baresi), Vierchowod, Scirea, Conti (Vialli), Di Gennaro, Galderisi, Bagni, Altobelli (1 pen)
Argentina: Pumpido, Cuciuffo, Brown, Ruggeri, Garre, Giusti, Batista (Olarticoechea), Burruchaga, Borghi (Enrique), Maradona (1), Valdano
Referee: Keizer (Holland)

South Korea (0) **1, Bulgaria** (1) **1**
2.6.86 MEXICO CITY
South Korea: Oh Yun-Kyo, Park Kyung-Hoon, Jung Yong-Hwan, Cho Young-Jeung, Cho Kwang-Rae (Choe Min-Kook), Huh Jung-Moo, Park Chang-Sun, No Soo-Jin (Kim Jong-Boo (1)), Byun Byung-Joo, Kim Joo-Sung, Cha Bum-Kun
Bulgaria: Mikhailov, Arabov, Zdravkov, Dimitrov, Petrov, Sirakov, Iskrenov, Sadkov, Mladenov, Gospodinov (Jeliaskov), Getov (1) (Kostadinov)
Referee: Aj-Shanar (Saudi Arabia)

Argentina (1) **2, Bulgaria** (0) **0**
10.6.86 MEXICO CITY
Argentina: Pumpido, Cuciuffo, Brown, Ruggeri, Garre, Giusti, Batista (Enrique), Burruchaga (1), Borghi (Olarticoechea), Maradona, Valdano (1)
Bulgaria: Mikhailov, Sirakov, Markov A, Dimitrov, Jordanov, Markov P, Petrov, Jeliaskov, Mladenov (Velitchkov), Sadkov, Getov
Referee: Ulloa (Costa Rica)

South Korea (0) **2, Italy** (1) **3**
10.6.86 PUEBLA
South Korea: On Yun-Kyo, Park Kyung-Hoon, Jung Yong-Hwan, Cho Young-Jeung, Cho Kwang-Rae (o.g.), Huh Jung Moo (1), Park Chang-Sun, Byun Byung-Joo (Kim Jong-Boo), Choi Soon-Ho (1), Kim Joo-Sung (Chung Jong-Soo), Cha Bum-Kun
Italy: Galli, Collovati, Cabrini, De Napoli, Vierchowod, Scirea, Conti, Di Gennaro, Galderisi (Vialli), Bagni (Baresi), Altobelli (2)
Referee: Socha (USA)

	P	W	D	L	F	A	Pts
Argentina	3	2	1	0	6	2	5
Italy	3	1	2	0	5	4	4
Bulgaria	3	0	2	1	2	4	2
South Korea	3	0	1	2	4	7	1

Group B

Belgium (1) **1, Mexico** (2) **2**
3.6.86 MEXICO CITY
Belgium: Pfaff, Gerets, Van der Elst F, Broos, De Wolf, Scifo, Vandereycken, Vercauteren, Desmet (Claesen), Vandenbergh (1) (Demol), Ceulemans
Mexico: Larios, Trejo, Quirarte (1), Felix Cruz, Servin, Muños, Aguirre, Negrete, Boy (España), Sanchez (1), Flores (Javier Cruz)
Referee: Esposito (Argentina)

Paraguay (1) **1, Iraq** (0) **0**
4.6.86 TOLUCA
Paraguay: Fernandez, Torales, Zabala, Schettina, Delgado, Nuñez, Ferreira, Romero (1), Cabañas, Cañete, Mendoza (Guasch)
Iraq: Hammoudi, Allawi, Shaker N, Shaker B, Hussein, Mohammed (Hameed), Radi, Saeed, Gorgis (Quassen), Hashem, Uraibi
Referee: Picon (Mauritius)

Mexico (1) **1, Paraguay** (0) **1**
7.6.86 MEXICO CITY
Mexico: Larios, Trejo, Quirarte, Felix Cruz, Servin, Muños, Aguirre, Negrete, Boy (España), Sanchez, Flores (1) (Javier Cruz)
Paraguay: Fernandez, Torales (Hicks), Zabala, Schettina, Delgado, Nuñez, Ferreira, Romero (1), Cabañas, Cañete, Mendoza (Guasch)
Referee: Courtney (England)

Iraq (0) **1, Belgium** (2) **2**
8.6.86 TOLUCA
Iraq: Hammoudi, Allawi, Shaker N, Shaker B, Hussein, Mohammed, Radi (1), Saddam (Hameed), Gorgis, Hashem, Uraibi
Belgium: Pfaff, Gerets, Van der Elst F, Demol (Grun), De Wolf, Scifo (1) (Clysters), Vandereycken, Vercauteren, Desmet, Claesen (1 pen), Ceulemans
Referee: Diaz (Colombia)

Paraguay (0) **2, Belgium** (1) **2**
11.6.86 TOLUCA
Paraguay: Fernandez, Torales, Zabala, Delgado, Guasch, Nuñez, Ferreira, Romero, Cabañas (2), Cañete, Mendoza (Hicks)
Belgium: Pfaff, Grun (Van der Elst L), Broos, Renquin, Vervoort, Scifo, Demol, (Ceulemans), Vercauteren (1), Veyt (1), Claesen
Referee: Dochev (Bulgaria)

Iraq (0) **0, Mexico** (0) **1**
11.6.86 MEXICO CITY
Iraq: Jasim, Majeed, Allawi, Nadhum, Hussein, Ghanem, Hashem, Radi, Abid (Shaker N), Minshed, Kassim (Hameed)
Mexico: Larios, Amador (Dominguez), Quirarte (1), Felix Cruz, Servin, De los Cobos (Javier Cruz), Aguirre, Negrete, Boy, España, Flores
Referee: Petrovic (Yugoslavia)

	P	W	D	L	F	A	Pts
Mexico	3	2	1	0	4	2	5
Paraguay	3	1	2	0	4	3	4
Belgium	3	1	1	1	5	5	3
Iraq	3	0	0	3	1	4	0

Group C

Canada (0) **0, France** (0) **1**
1.6.86 LEON
Canada: Dolan, Lenarduzzi, Wilson, Bridge, Samuel, Ragan, Valentine, Norman, James (Segota), Sweeney (Lowery), Vrablic
France: Bats, Amoros, Tusseau, Battiston, Bossis, Fernandez, Giresse, Tigana, Papin (1), Platini, Rocheteau (Stopyra)
Referee: Silva Arce (Chile)

USSR (3) **6, Hungary** (0) **0**
2.6.86 IRAPUATO
USSR: Dasayev, Larionov, Bessonov, Kuznetsov, Demyanenko, Yaremchuk (2), Yakovenko (1) (Yevtushenko), Rats, Belanov (1 pen) (Rodionov (1)), Zavarov, Aleinikov (1)
Hungary: Disztl P, Sallai, Roth (Burcsa), Garaba, Kardos, Kiprich, Nagy, Detari, Peter (Dajka), Esterhazy, Bognar
Referee: Agnolin (Italy)

France (0) **1, USSR** (0) **1**
5.6.86 LEON
France: Bats, Amoros, Ayache, Battiston, Bossis, Fernandez (1), Giresse (Vercruysse), Tigana, Papin (Bellone), Platini, Stopyra
USSR: Dasayev, Larionov, Bessonov, Kuznetsov, Demyanenko, Yaremchuk, Yakovenko, Rats (1), Belanov, Zavarov (Blokhin), Aleinikov
Referee: Arrpi Filho (Brazil)

Hungary (1) **2, Canada** (0) **0**
6.6.86 IRAPUATO
Hungary: Szendrei, Sallai, Varga, Garaba, Kardos, Kiprich, Nagy (Dajka), Detari (1), Burcsa (Roth), Esterhazy (1), Bognar
Canada: Lettieri, Lenarduzzi, Wilson (Sweeney), Bridge, Samuel, Ragan, Valentine, Norman, James (Segota), Gray, Vrablic
Referee: Al-Sharis (Syria)

Hungary (0) **0, France** (1) **3**
9.6.86 LEON
Hungary: Disztl P, Sallai, Roth, Varga, Kardos, Garaba, Hannich (Nagy), Detari, Dajka, Esterhazy, Kovacs (Bognar)
France: Bats, Ayache, Amoros, Battiston, Bossis, Fernandez, Giresse, Tigana (1), Papin (Rocheteau (1)), Platini, Stopyra (1) (Ferreri)
Referee: Silva (Portugal)

USSR (0) **2, Canada** (0) **0**
9.6.86 IRAPUATO
USSR: Chanov, Morozov, Bubnov, Kuznetsov, Bal, Litovchenko, Yevtushenko, Aleinikov, Rodionov, Protasov (Belanov), Blokhin (1) (Zavarov (1))
Canada: Lettieri, Lenarduzzi, Wilson, Bridge, Samuel, Ragan, Valentine, Norman, James (Segota), Gray (Pakos), Mitchell
Referee: Traore (Mali)

	P	W	D	L	F	A	Pts
USSR	3	2	1	0	9	1	5
France	3	2	1	0	5	1	5
Hungary	3	1	0	2	2	9	2
Canada	3	0	0	3	0	5	0

Group D

Spain (0) **0, Brazil** (0) **1**
1.6.86 GUADALAJARA
Spain: Zubizarreta, Tomas, Camacho, Maceda, Giocoechea, Julio Alberto, Michel, Victor, Butragueño, Francisco (Señor), Julio Salinas
Brazil: Carlos, Branco, Edson, Edhino, Julio Cesar, Junior (Falcao), Alemao, Casagrande (Müller), Careca, Socrates (1), Elzo
Referee: Bambridge (Australia)

Algeria (0) **1, Northern Ireland** (1) **1**
3.6.86 GUADALAJARA
Algeria: Larbi, Medjadi, Mansouri, Kourichi, Guendouz, Kaci Saïd, Assad, Benmabrouk, Zidane (1) (Belloumi), Maroc, Madjer (Harkouk)
Northern Ireland: Jennings, Nicholl, Donaghy, O'Neill, McDonald, Worthington, Penney (Stewart), McIlroy, McCreery, Hamilton, Whiteside (1) (Clarke)
Referee: Butenko (USSR)

Northern Ireland (0) **1, Spain** (2) **2**
7.6.86 GUADALAJARA
Northern Ireland: Jennings, Nicholl, Donaghy, O'Neill, McDonald, Worthington (Hamilton), Penney (Stewart), McIlroy, McCreery, Clarke (1), Whiteside
Spain: Zubizarreta, Tomas, Camacho, Gallego, Giocoechea, Gordillo (Calderé), Michel, Victor, Butragueño (1), Francisco, Julio Salinas (1) (Señor)
Referee: Brummener (Austria)

Brazil (0) **1, Algeria** (0) **0**
6.6.86 GUADALAJARA
Brazil: Carlos, Edson (Falcao), Branco, Edinho, Julio Cesar, Junior, Alemao, Casagrande (Müller), Careca (1), Socrates, Elzo
Algeria: Drid, Medjadi, Mansouri, Megharia, Guendouz, Kaci Saïd, Assad (Bensaoula), Benmabrouk, Menad, Belloumi (Zidane), Madjer
Referee: Molina (Guatemala)

Algeria (0) **0, Spain** (1) **3**
12.6.86 MONTERREY
Algeria: Drid (Larbi), Megharia, Mansouri, Kourichi, Guendouz, Kaci Saïd, Madjer, Maroc, Harkouk, Belloumi, Zidane (Menad)
Spain: Zubizarreta, Tomas, Camacho, Gallego, Goicoechea, Calderé (2), Michel (Señor), Victor, Butragueño (Eloy (1)), Francisco, Julio Salinas
Referee: Takada (Japan)

Northern Ireland (0) **0, Brazil** (2) **3**
12.6.86 GUADALAJARA
Northern Ireland: Jennings, Nicholl, Donaghy, O'Neill, McDonald, McCreery, McIlroy, Stewart, Clarke, Whiteside (Hamilton), Campbell (Armstrong)
Brazil: Carlos, Josimar (1), Julio Cesar, Edinho, Branco, Elzo, Alemao, Junior, Socrates (Zico), Müller (Casagrande), Careca (2)
Referee: Kirschen (East Germany)

	P	W	D	L	F	A	Pts
Brazil	3	3	0	0	5	0	6
Spain	3	2	0	1	5	2	4
Northern Ireland	3	0	1	2	2	6	1
Algeria	3	0	1	2	1	5	1

Group E

Uruguay (1) **1, West Germany** (0) **1**
4.6.86 QUERETARO
Uruguay: Alvez, Gutierrez, Acevedo, Diogo, Bossio, Batista, Alzamendi (1) (Ramos), Barrios (Saralegui), Da Silva, Francescoli, Santin
West Germany: Schumacher, Briegel, Berthold, Förster, Augenthaler, Eder, Matthäus (Rummenigge), Magath, Brehme (Littbarski), Völler, Allofs (1)
Referee: Christov (Czechoslovakia)

Scotland (0) **0, Denmark** (0) **1**
4.6.86 NEZA
Scotland: Leighton, Gough, Malpas, Souness, McLeish, Miller, Strachan (Bannon), Aitken, Nicol, Nicholas, Sturrock (McAvennie)
Denmark: Rasmussen, Busk, Olsen M, Nielsen, Lerby, Olsen J (Mølby), Berggreen, Elkjaer (1), Laudrup, Bertelsen, Arnesen (Sivebaek)
Referee: Nemeth (Hungary)

Denmark (2) **6, Uruguay** (1) **1**
8.6.86 NEZA
Denmark: Rasmussen, Busk, Olsen M, Nielsen, Lerby (1), Andersen, Berggreen, Elkjaer (3), Laudrup (1) (Olsen J (1)), Bertelsen (Mølby), Arnesen
Uruguay: Alvez, Gutierrez, Acevedo, Diogo, Bossio, Batista, Alzamendi (Ramos), Saralegui, Da Silva, Francescoli (1), Santin (Salazar)
Referee: Marquez (Mexico)

West Germany (1) **2, Scotland** (1) **1**
8.6.86 QUERETARO
West Germany: Schumacher, Briegel (Jakobs), Berthold, Förster, Augenthaler, Eder, Matthäus, Magath, Littbarski (Rummenigge), Völler (1), Allofs (1)
Scotland: Leighton, Gough, Malpas, Souness, Narey, Miller, Strachan (1), Aitken, Nicol (McAvennie), Archibald, Bannon (Cooper)
Referee: Igna (Romania)

Scotland (0) **0, Uruguay** (0) **0**
13.6.86 NEZA
Scotland: Leighton, Gough, Albiston, Aitken, Narey, Miller, Strachan, McStay, Sharp, Nicol (Cooper), Sturrock (Nicholas)
Uruguay: Alvez, Diogo, Acevedo, Gutierrez, Pereyra, Batista, Ramos (Saralegui), Barrios, Cabrera, Francescoli (Alzamendi), Santin
Referee: Quiniou (France)

Denmark (1) **2, West Germany** (0) **0**
13.6.86 QUERETARO
Denmark: Hogh, Sivebaek, Busk, Olsen M, Andersen, Arnesen, Lerby, Mølby, Laudrup, Olsen J (1 pen) (Simonsen), Elkjaer (Eriksen (1))
West Germany: Schumacher, Berthold, Jakobs, Förster (Rummenigge), Herget, Eder, Brehme, Matthäus, Völler, Rolff (Littbarski), Allofs
Referee: Ponnet (Belgium)

	P	W	D	L	F	A	Pts
Denmark	3	3	0	0	9	1	6
West Germany	3	1	1	1	3	4	3
Uruguay	3	0	2	1	2	7	2
Scotland	3	0	1	2	1	3	1

Group F

Morocco (0) **0, Poland** (0) **0**
2.6.86 MONTERREY
Morocco: Zaki, Labd, Lemriss, El-Biyaz, Bouyahiaoui, Mustapha El-Haddaoui (Souleimani), Dolmy, Bouderbala, Krimau, Timoumi (Khairi), Merry
Poland: Mlynarczyk, Ostrowski, Wojcicki, Majewski, Matysik, Kubicki, Komornicki (Przybys), Buncol, Smolarek, Dziekanowski (Urban), Boniek
Referee: Martinez Bazan (Uruguay)

Portugal (0) **1, England** (0) **0**
3.6.86 MONTERREY
Portugal: Beneto, Alvaro, Frederico, Oliveira, Inacio, Diamantino (José Antonio), André, Carlos Manuel (1), Pacheco, Sousa, Gomes (Futre)
England: Shilton, Stevens, Sansom, Hoddle, Fenwick, Butcher, Robson (Hodge), Wilkins, Hateley, Lineker, Waddle (Beardsley)
Referee: Roth (West Germany)

England (0) **0, Morocco** (0) **0**
6.6.86 MONTERREY
England: Shilton, Stevens, Sansom, Hoddle, Fenwick, Butcher, Robson (Hodge), Wilkins, Hateley (Stevens G A), Lineker, Waddle
Morocco: Zaki, Labd, Lemriss (Heina), El-Biyaz, Bouyahiaoui, Khairi, Dolmy, Bouderbala, Krimau, Timoumi, Merry (Souleimani)
Referee: Gonzalez (Paraguay)

Poland (0) **1, Portugal** (0) **0**
7.6.86 MONTERREY
Poland: Mlynarczyk, Ostrowski, Wojcicki, Majewski, Matysik, Urban, Komornicki (Karas), Pawlak, Smolarek (1) (Zgutczynski), Dziekanowski, Boniek
Portugal: Damas, Alvaro, Frederico, Oliveira, Inacio, Diamantino, André (Magalhães), Carlos Manuel, Pacheco, Sousa, Gomes (Futre)
Referee: Ali ben Nasser (Tunisia)

England (3) **3, Poland** (0) **0**
11.6.86 MONTERREY
England: Shilton, Stevens, Sansom, Hoddle, Fenwick, Butcher, Steven, Reid, Lineker (3) (Dixon), Beardsley (Waddle), Hodge
Poland: Mlynarczyk, Ostrowski, Wojcicki, Matysik (Buncol), Urban, Majewski, Smolarek, Komonicki (Karas), Pawlak, Dziekanowski, Boniek
Referee: Daina (Switzerland)

Portugal (0) **1, Morocco** (2) **3**
11.6.86 GUADALAJARA
Portugal: Damas, Alvaro (Aguas), Frederico, Oliveira, Inacio, Magalhães, Carlos Manuel, Pacheco, Sousa (Diamantino (1)), Gomes, Futre
Morocco: Zaki, Labd, Lemriss, El-Biyaz, Bouyahiaoui, Dolmy, Mustapha El-Haddaoui (Souleimani), Bouderbala, Krimau (1), Timoumi, Khairi (2)
Referee: Snoddy (Northern Ireland)

	P	W	D	L	F	A	Pts
Morocco	3	1	2	0	3	1	4
England	3	1	1	1	3	1	3
Poland	3	1	1	1	1	3	3
Portugal	3	1	0	2	2	4	2

THE ROUND OF SIXTEEN

At an Azteca Stadium throbbing with noise and emotion, Mexico, the host, faced up to Bulgaria. As if inspired by the crescendo of sound, the Mexicans began splendidly, moving the ball rhythmically and applying steady pressure whilst their opponents contented themselves with a policy of containment and counter. Getov and Kostadinov working in tandem on the right flank threatened sporadically, though Bulgaria's early rather casual approach seemed peculiar. Sanchez for Mexico missed a golden opportunity on the half hour from six yards, firing wastefully straight at the body of Mikhailov, and as the Europeans' composure ebbed away, Negrete punished them, spectacularly twisting in mid-air to strike a shoulder-height left-footed volley into the net for 1–0. After the interval, the Bulgarians belatedly began to assert themselves without causing a resolute Mexican rearguard a problem. It was Servin who finished them with a second for Mexico, leaping to bundle Negrete's corner over the line from five yards. So Bulgaria were out and in doing so maintained their appalling record in the World Cup competition – no wins at all in sixteen matches. Mindful of this, perhaps their confidence had been undermined. Whatever the case, their departure had been a timid one. *World Soccer Magazine* dismissed their efforts later, rather unkindly: 'Bulgaria were a disgrace to football,' it claimed.

In a remarkable contest played at Leon there was a remarkable result as Belgium, hitherto a disappointment and plagued by injury, plunged inexperienced players into their team against the Soviets, hitherto a revelation, and won a glorious match after 120 minutes of pulsating football.

Belanov opened the scoring for the Soviets on 27 minutes, cracking a ferocious shot beyond Pfaff. Crucially then, as half-time approached, his header struck a post. Two goals down surely would have proven too much for the Belgians. After the half-time break, the elegant Scifo fired Belgium level before on 70 minutes Belanov found himself again in the right place. At 2–1 surely now the Soviets, thus far the better team, would prevail? Not a bit of it, lady luck conspiring with the veteran Jan Ceulemans to deny them. Seven minutes from time, receiving Vervoort's long pass he ran goalwards. The Soviets hesitated fatally, anticipating an offside flag that did not come, and Ceulemans, outstanding throughout, scored the goal that took the tie into gruelling extra time. Deflated and dismayed by the apparent injustice suffered, the Soviets' concentration wavered, and worse followed for them. Demol, a novice, climbed to head Belgium ahead for the first time and Claesen accepted a fourth. The score was 4–2 but still the endless drama continued. When Belanov converted a penalty kick for 4–3, the Soviets recovered their collective nerve and went in search of an equalizer. It was not to be, Pfaff denying them acrobatically at the death. 'I have never doubted our ability throughout,' said Belgian coach Guy Thys afterwards. 'That was one of the most passionate matches we have seen at these finals.' His opposite number agreed entirely. 'It was a superb spectacle,' but he added unhappily, 'the Belgians' second goal was offside'.

The following day Brazil faced a determined Polish team appearing none the worse for their debacle against England and intent on further progress. Josimar turned Tarasiewicz's cross intended for Smolarek past his own goalkeeper Carlos. But fortune favoured him as the ball struck the upright and fell into Carlos's relieved hands. Ten minutes later Karas lashed his shot goalwards after a mistake by Branco, only to see it strike the underside of the bar and fly to safety. After their early onslaught, Poland's effort, despite the influence of Dziekanowski, began to fade, and Brazil, shocked by their opponents early dominance, seized control, never again to relinquish it. Tarasiewicz launched himself foolishly at Careca in the 28th minute and Socrates arrogantly converted the penalty kick. Poland resisted bravely as Brazil found their most irresistible form. Josimar with an outrageous dribble and vicious swerving shot extinguished their challenge on 52 minutes. Down 2–0 and their cause an almost impossible one, Poland's disappointment manifested itself as a tired team, attacked mercilessly, withered and fell apart. Edinho scored a third goal courtesy of Careca's cheeky back header before, eight minutes from the end, Careca scored a penalty after Zico's surging run was roughly and abruptly terminated. The match ended 4–0.

At Puebla a potentially savage match between bitter rivals Uruguay and Argentina proved comparatively calm, thanks perhaps to referee Luis Agnolin, whose performance allowed skill and not violence to flourish. Undeniably talented in their own right, the Uruguayans were thus unable to control the mesmerizing little magician Maradona, and he dominated them thoroughly, darting constantly towards and then through fearful defenders. Pasculli settled it, his goal a simple affair after farcical defending had allowed Valdano's pass to present him with an empty net. That was it, but for Uruguay it might have been an embarrassment. Maradona struck a thirty-yard free kick on to their bar before his bewitching skills provided Valdano and Pasculli with opportunities they squandered. At the whistle Argentina celebrated It had taken sixty-eight years to avenge the defeat of 1930, their reward a place in the quarter-finals. As they trudged away dejected, their mood scarcely helped by a deluge of driving rain, the Uruguayans may very well have contemplated defeat and wondered why the national team had abandoned the wondrous, flowing football that had been their tradition in favour of the mean sterility that was their modern game.

The following day in Mexico City, France, the Tournament's artists, played Italy, the defending Champions. France began brightly, patient and cunning, denying the Italian midfield possession and gaining a vice-like grip on the match. Soon control brought its reward: Fernandez, allowed space all after-noon, fed Rocheteau, who resisted a challenge before laying the ball into the path of Platini. The French playmaker did the rest for 1–0. Nevertheless, France dominated, their movement bemusing the cautious Italians. Fernandez, a human dynamo, struck a fierce shot against the bar from thirty-five yards. Ayache and the hugely talented Amoros, providing width from full back, saun-tered forward, creating further problems. At half-time Bearzot removed Platini's marker Giusseppe Baresi and introduced the more gifted Di Gennaro, but by then it was too late. French swagger had turned into a tide threatening to engulf them. Stopyra scored a second in the 56th minute, rifling home Rocheteau's pass after Tigana had set him free. And so France had a rare win over old rivals and in achieving it had managed to inflict upon Italy a still rarer thing: a lesson in possession football. 'For a long time,' said French coach Henri Michel, 'we had complexes about the Italians. Today we didn't. That was per-haps the key to the match.'

In Monterrey, Morocco, showing an acute lack of ambition against the Germans, smothered and stifled, in a desperately drab affair under a baking sun. Germany did their best, Rummenigge denied by Zaki missing the only opportunity of arguably the dullest first half of the Tournament. 'Morocco played more backwards than forwards and made it very difficult for us,' said Franz Beckenbauer later. Perhaps, but the Germans, despite applying enormous pressure, lacked imagination, and as extra time beckoned, their frustration became evident, players uncharacteristically squabbling amongst themselves. It was Matthäus who saved them, his last minute free kick, low and powerful, tore through a hole in the defensive wall and beat the unsighted Zaki. 'It takes two teams to make an attractive match,' responded Beckenbauer to criticism of such poor fare.

In the Azteca stadium England, with fortunes revived, faced the Paraguayans, subtle and fluid in attack though nervous and uncertain in defence. Raiding quickly before the English had settled, Paraguay threatened, Mendoza almost stole through, Canets' shot fiercely forcing Shilton to save, Mendoza again weaved goalward only to shoot tamely. Then, perversely, England had the lead. Hodge picked out Hoddle, whose cross eluded defenders and attackers alike. Fernandez pursued the loose ball vainly but lost the race to Hodge whose pass to Lineker left the Everton man with the simplest of chances from two yards. Deflated Paraguay never recovered. Lineker almost made it two with a sweetly struck volley, before Beardsley took that role, in the 55th minute seizing on another error by Fernandez – fumbling a Terry Butcher header – to drive the ball into the unguarded net. Hoddle, given time and space, dominated proceedings and the Paraguayans – resorting increasingly to spiteful challenges – were carved open at will, their discipline and resolve shattered. Lineker finished them, racing in on 73 minutes to touch home the cross of Gary Stevens. At 3–0 England, in spite of a distinctly uncomfortable beginning, had cause to be optimistic about their prospects.

In Queretaro another extraordinary game took place between steady Spain, a talented resolute bunch, and Denmark, the competition sensation. It began, perhaps, in routine fashion when Olsen from the penalty spot put the Danes ahead. Thereafter the form book was simply ripped up by the ruthless Spaniards. Olsen himself inadvertently handed Spain the initiative, casually and inexplicably rolling the ball across his own penalty area into the path of 'the vulture' Emilio Butragueño. The lethal little striker shot gratefully past Hogh. At 1–1 and just two minutes before half-time, Denmark's horrible afternoon had begun in earnest. Just before the hour Butragueño scored again, taking advantage of slack marking to head his second. Dispirited and menaced constantly by Butragueño, the Danes fell apart, fouling the twisting, turning figure twice as he raced into their penalty area. Giocoechea converted the first, Butragueño himself two minutes from time the second. Sandwiched between another, for the little predator, Eloy with pace and accuracy provided the cross, the finish clinical. It was 5–1 for Spain and for Butragueño four goals, a remarkable achievement.

Second Round

Mexico (1) **2, Bulgaria** (0) **0**
15.6.86 MEXICO CITY
Mexico: Larios, Amador, Quirarte, Felix, Cruz, Servin (1), España, Aguirre, Muños, Boy (De los Cobos), Sanchez, Negrete (1)
Bulgaria: Mikhailov, Arabov, Zdravkov, Dimitrov, Petrov, Jordanov, Sadkov, Kostadinov, Getov (Sirakov), Gospodinov, Paschev (Iskrenov)
Referee: Arppi Filho (Brazil)

USSR (1) **3, Belgium** (0) **4** (aet, 2–2 at 90 mins)
15.6.86 LEON
USSR: Dasayev, Bessonov, Bal, Kuznetsov, Demyanenko, Yaremchuk, Yakovenko (Yevtushenko), Aleinikov, Rats, Belanov (3, 1 pen), Zavarov (Rodionov)
Belgium: Pfaff, Gerets, Grun (Clijsters), Vervoort, Demol (1), Renquin, Scifo (1), Vercauteren, Claesen (1), Veyt, Ceulemans (1)
Referee: Frederiksson (Sweden)

Brazil (1) **4, Poland** (0) **0**
16.6.86 GUADALAJARA
Brazil: Carlos, Josimar (1), Branco, Edinho (1), Julio Cesar, Alemao, Müller (Silas), Socrates (1 pen) (Zico), Careca (1 pen), Junior, Elzo
Poland: Mlynarczyk, Ostrowski, Majewski, Wojcicki, Przybs (Furtok), Urban (Zmuda), Karas, Tarasiewicz, Dziekanowski, Boniek, Smolarek
Referee: Roth (West Germany)

Argentina (1) **1, Uruguay** (0) **0**
16.6.86 PUEBLA
Argentina: Pumpido, Cuciuffo, Brown, Garre, Giusti, Ruggeri, Batista (Olarticoechea), Burruchaga, Pasculli (1), Maradona, Valdano
Uruguay: Alvez, Rivero, Bossio, Gutierrez, Acevedo (Paz), Pereyra, Ramos, Cabrera (Da Silva), Francescoli, Barrios, Santin
Referee: Agnolin (Italy)

France (1) **2, Italy** (0) **0**
17.6.86 MEXICO CITY
France: Bats, Ayache, Amoros, Battiston, Bossis, Fernandez (Tusseau), Giresse, Tigana, Rocheteau, Platini (1) (Ferreri), Stopyra (1)
Italy: Galli, Bergomi, Cabrini, De Napoli, Vierchowod, Scirea, Conti, Bagni, Galderisi (Vialli), Baresi (Di Gennaro), Altobelli
Referee: Esposito (Argentina)

Morocco (0) **0, West Germany** (0) **1**
17.6.86 MONTERREY
Morocco: Zaki, Labd, Lemriss, Bouyahiaoui, Dolmy, Mustapha El-Haddaoui, Bouderbala, Krimau, Timoumi, Hcina, Khairi
West Germany: Schumacher, Berthold, Briegel, Jakobs, Förster, Eder, Matthäus (1), Rummenigge, Völler (Littbarski), Magath, Allofs
Referee: Petrovic (Yugoslavia)

England (1) **3, Paraguay** (0) **0**
18.6.86 MEXICO CITY
England: Shilton, Stevens, Sansom, Hoddle, Martin, Butcher, Steven, Reid (Stevens G A), Lineker (2), Beardsley (1) (Hateley), Hodge
Paraguay: Fernandez, Torales (Guasch), Zabala, Schettina, Delgado, Nuñez, Ferreira, Romero, Cabañas, Canets, Mendoza
Referee: Al-Sharif (Syria)

Denmark (1) **1, Spain** (1) **5**
18.6.86 QUERETARO
Denmark: Hogh, Andersen (Eriksen), Olsen M, Busk, Nielsen, Lerby, Olsen J (1 pen) (Mølby), Bertelsen, Laudrup, Berggreen, Elkjaer
Spain: Zubizarreta, Tomas, Camacho, Gallego, Giocoechea (1 pen), Julio Alberto, Victor, Michel (Francisco), Butragueño (4, 1 pen), Calderé, Julio Salinas (Eloy)
Referee: Keizer (Holland)

Quarter-Finals

Brazil v France
West Germany v Mexico
Argentina v England
Spain v Belgium

THE QUARTER-FINALS

What always promised to be a magnificent contest proved to be just that. Brazil and France meeting in Guadalajara provided the Tournament with a match of epic proportions. Brazil at the outset appeared stronger, their midfield largely in control, Socrates probing and prompting, Careca darting this way and that picked out on fifteen minutes. Bats rescued France, saving desperately then smothering the ball as Careca pounded into the penalty area. Three minutes later Careca earned his reward, guiding Junior's pass into the net. At 1–0 France, thoroughly outplayed, might have been out of it. Müller slammed a shot on to the post as they reeled under their opponent's rhythmic onslaught. Threatened with elimination, France pocketed an undeserved equalizer. Rocheteau fired in a low cross, the ball aided by deflection skidding across the goalmouth, and in at the far post came Platini – anonymous for forty minutes – to shoot gleefully home. France belatedly found their form now and the match moved at a breathtaking pace from one end to the other as chances came and went in the 120 °F heat. Zico, on as a substitute, could have, should have, won it, his pass putting Branco through on goal. Bats was quickly out to the danger, spread himself, missed the ball and took the man. Penalty. In the fateful 73rd minute Zico, who had only just come on, elected unwisely to take the kick himself. Bats diving to his left saved.

In extra time both sides found enough reserves of courage and stamina to continue. Sixteen goal attempts for Brazil, fifteen for France and then at the bitter end the French dramatically might have snatched it. Platini steering a precise, incisive pass invited Bellone to run. Run he did, surging goalward until, one on one with Carlos, he was halted crudely by the goalkeeper on the edge of the penalty area. No foul. At least not in the eyes of referee Igna. That was that. Destiny, it appeared, had determined that this most memorable of games would be decided by a penalty shoot out. For Brazil, Socrates missed, but then amidst mounting tension Platini blotted his copybook, thumping his kick high over the bar. Josimar stepped up next, intent on giving Brazil the lead and failed, leaving Luis Fernandez, solid, reliable and underrated, the chance for glory. He took it. France had triumphed, a team of immense talent rescued by their one artisan.

There was another penalty shoot-out at Monterrey but far less excitement as Germany with a precious knack of winning awful matches disposed of Mexico. The Mexicans had their chance when Berthold was dismissed just past the hour, reducing the Germans for the remainder to ten men. For all their numerical advantage and familiarity with the strength-sapping heat and altitude, the best Mexico could muster was an effort by Aguirre, saved comfortably enough by Schumacher. Aguirre himself saw red during extra time, his dismissal leaving the two teams of ten resigned to their fate. Mexico's nerve failed them, Schumacher saving the kicks of Servin and Quirarte, while for Germany, Allofs, Brehme, Matthäus and Littbarski with nerveless efficiency all did their duty. 'It was a physical match,' said Beckenbauer, 'we were forced to play cautiously because Mexico only played with one forward.' And the French? 'France are a very fine team and have been one of the best for the last three or four years, but we believe we will have a chance against them in our semifinal.'

On Sunday in Mexico City before a passionate and partisan crowd, England faced Argentina. Enemies at war four years earlier, they were now happily reunited in sport.

England were surprisingly negative in the early stages but Beardsley might still have given them an early lead. Chasing an apparently lost cause when Hoddle misdirected a through ball, he benefited from Pumpido's stumble to win the ball, but the acute angle proved too much, the shot curling harmlessly into the side netting. Until the interval, there was little indication of the drama to follow, though the short, stocky Maradona, instigator of much of it, had begun ominously to exert influence. Twisting and turning he threatened wary defenders. Five minutes into the second half and the sterile ultra-cautious approach adopted by Bobby Robson was rendered useless. A goal for Argentina was taken in a manner that brought prolonged and furious protest, Maradona as ever the centre of the controversy. Jorge Valdano receiving a quick wall pass from Maradona looped a deflected return, high, over the heads of the English defence, and though Maradona pursued it into the path of the advancing Shilton, it seemed inconceivable that the tiny Argentinean could outjump England's goalkeeper. It was inconceivable yet he achieved it, lifting the ball over him and sending it bouncing into the yawning net. England at once were stunned, and then as realization dawned that the goal was given, surrounded the referee angrily. Maradona had used his forearm and all but Ali Ben Nasser, the Tunisian official, had seen it. Around the world astonished audiences watched as slow motion replays confirmed the fact, but beneath the baking sun at the Azteca, England needed to regain their composure and switch to Plan B. They were given no time, and badly shaken they were undone again, this time legitimately. Receiving the ball in his own half, Maradona changed direction majestically and accelerated, swerving past Reid, Stevens, Sansom, Butcher and Fenwick before slipping around Shilton to score. Genius. England were shaken to their foundations. Maradona captivated the crowd. From this shambolic and apparently hopeless situation England sought to save themselves. Gathering their senses they made changes and fought back. First Chris Waddle and then the enigmatic John Barnes were introduced, and Argentina attacked on both flanks by wingers began to struggle. With ten minutes left Barnes scorched past the unfortunate Giusti and crossed, Lineker heading securely for 2–1. Six minutes later, four from the end, Barnes again produced a tantalizing cross. Lineker, a yard out this time, failed by the width of a coat of paint to apply the finishing touch and thus take the tie to extra time. So England went out, deeply distressed, inconsolable at the unjust manner of their defeat. Maradona later claimed mischievously that 'the hand of God' had done for them; not so, but undeniably, brave though they were at the end, England had been beaten by a better team and a player of quite wonderful ability.

So to Puebla where most had expected to see the Soviets play Denmark.

Instead it was Spain and Belgium. Shackling Butragueño to great effect, the Belgians took the lead in 34 minutes. Vercauteren delivered the cross and Ceulemans the tumbling header for 1–0. Belgium after the interval should have finished it but Veyt with the opportunity fired wide wastefully. Spain pressed, their best efforts floundering on the rock like Belgian defence, and then as defeat appeared inevitable, Señor, a substitute, hammered his shot into Pfaff's net from thirty yards. Extra time came and went, leading to penalty kicks, the cruellest of tie-breakers, to settle it. Eloy, the winger for Spain, missed, foiled by Pfaff diving to his right, and that was that. Van der Elst, the fifth consecutive Belgian to score, sealed a place for them in the semi-final and a meeting with Maradona.

Quarter-Finals

Brazil (1) **1, France** (1) **1** (aet, 1–1 at 90 mins, France won 2–1 on penalties)
21.6.86 GUADALAJARA
Brazil: Carlos, Josimar, Branco, Edinho, Julio Cesar, Müller (Zico), Alemao, Careca (1), Socrates, Junior (Silas), Elzo
France: Bats, Amoros, Tusseau, Battiston, Bossis, Fernandez, Giresse (Ferreri), Tigana, Rocheteau (Bellone), Platini (1), Stopyra
Referee: Igna (Romania)

West Germany (0) **0, Mexico** (0) **0** (aet, 0–0 at 90 mins, West Germany won 4–1 on penalties)
21.6.86 MONTERREY
West Germany: Schumacher, Berthold, Briegel, Jakobs, Förster, Eder (Littbarski), Matthäus, Brehme, Rummenigge (Hoeness), Magath, Allofs
Mexico: Larios, Amador (Javier Cruz), Felix Cruz, Quirarte, Servin, Muños, Aguirre, España, Boy (De los Cobos), Negrete, Sanchez
Referee: Diaz (Colombia)

Argentina (0) **2, England** (0) **1**
22.6.86 MEXICO CITY
Argentina: Pumpido, Ruggeri, Cuciuffo, Olarticoechea, Brown, Giusti, Batista, Burruchaga (Tapia), Enrique, Maradona (2), Valdano
England: Shildon, Stevens, Sansom, Hoddle, Butcher, Fenwick, Steven (Barnes), Reid (Waddle), Lineker (1), Beardsley, Hodge
Referee: Ali B'en Nasser (Tunisia)

Spain (0) **1**, **Belgium** (1) **1** (aet, 1–1 at 90 mins, Belgium won 5–4 on penalties)
22.6.86 PUEBLA
Spain: Zubizarreta, Chendo, Camacho, Gallego, Tomas (Señor (1)), Michel, Victor, Calderé, Butragueño, Julio Alberto, Julio Salinas (Eloy)
Belgium: Pfaff, Gerets, Renquin, Demol, Vervoort, Grun, Scifo, Veyt (Broos), Claesen, Ceulemans (1), Vercauteren (Van der Elst L)
Referee: Kirschen (East Germany)

THE SEMI-FINALS

At the Azteca, predictably, Argentina (and particularly Maradona) proved far too good for gallant Belgium, the Tournament's overachievers. Defending in depth, conceding territorial advantage and reliant on swift counters, the Belgians clung on grittily, Ceulemans and Scifo striving to provide inspiration against a far better side than their own. Content to dominate the first half, Argentina seized the lead in the second with Burruchaga's cross and Maradona's instinctive left-foot volley. Unable to shackle the little man in spite of employing two markers, Belgian resistance crumbled, victim of the Argentines' towering talent. Picking the ball up just past the hour, he darted goalwards, attacking bewildered defenders. In a matter of yards he weaved himself past four before slamming the ball joyously past Pfaff. Belgium for all their resolve were a beaten team, and though they tried to the end, Argentina always seemed the likelier to score and thus increase their lead. The crowd, as well as anxious Belgian defenders, trembled in awe and anticipation every time the ball ran into Maradona's path. 'We marked him well in the first half,' said Guy Thuys, 'we were organized until the second half when he escaped more often and he punished us twice. He is incredible. Although the final should be fairly even, I think Argentina will win because of him.' Carlos Bilardo, coach to Argentina, conceded that his captain was 'playing well', achieving in doing so an understatement of quite staggering proportions.

At Guadalajara, France and West Germany reunited after their epic contest in Seville four years earlier. Germany, fresher and physically stronger, dominated the early stages and took a deserved 10th-minute lead. Rummenigge, halted unfairly by Bossis, gave them a free kick, Magath rolled it to Brehme and he thundered his shot mightily around the wall. Bats, probably unsighted, was deceived by its flight, and cruelly it wriggled beneath his body and into the French goal. France responded, lifted briefly by their vaunted midfield trio, Giresse, Platini and Tigana, all of whom might have scored, before Germany gained complete control, tackling ferociously. Rummenigge could twice have scored: Bats produced two miraculous saves with flailing legs, and despite the sympathies of the Mexican crowd, the wilting French – though they tried vainly – were so obviously fatigued by victories over Italy and Brazil. They could find no more with which to offer a sustained threat. When France needed him most, Platini faded, hounded out of the game by the willing Rolff. Then at the end as the Germans repelled another feeble French attack, Allofs broke, whipped the ball into substitute Völler, whose clever chip stranded the advancing Bats and left him with the simplest of tasks. With the score at 2–0, Germany were in another final, while France, who had played quite the best football of the Tournament, had been frustrated again by German organization, combined this time with their own exhaustion.

Semi-Finals

Argentina (0) **2, Belgium** (0) **0**
25.6.86 MEXICO CITY
Argentina: Pumpido, Cuciuffo, Ruggeri, Brown, Olarticoechea, Giusti, Batista, Burruchaga (Bochini), Enrique, Maradona (2), Valdano
Belgium: Pfaff, Gerets, Renquin (Desmet), Demol, Vervoort, Veyt, Grun, Scifo, Claesen, Ceulemans, Vercauteren
Referee: Marquez (Mexico)

France (0) **0, West Germany** (1) **2**
25.6.86 GUADALAJARA
France: Bats, Amoros, Ayache, Battiston, Bossis, Fernandez, Giresse (Vercruysse), Tigana, Bellone (Xuereb), Platini, Stopyra
West Germany: Schumacher, Brehme (1), Briegel, Jakobs, Förster, Eder, Matthäus, Rolff, Rummenigge (Völler (1)), Magath, Allofs
Referee: Agnolin (Italy)

PLAY-OFF FOR THIRD PLACE

An uninspired Belgium team entered the play-off for third place at Puebla. 'Its not important. The Tournament is over for us and I am not very concerned about it,' said Thuys rather honestly beforehand. France, their opponents, reflected their team's weariness by making seven changes, including thirty-four-year-old Giresse and their playmaker Platini.

Starting as ever in combative mood, Belgium took the lead in eleven minutes through the dependable Ceulemans. Thereafter the French asserted themselves, the enthusiasm of squad players given their opportunity proving too much for the Belgians. Ferreri and Papin fired France ahead before the interval, and though Claesen took one of a number of their second-half chances, Belgium had simply nothing left in extra time. Genghini scored a third and Amoros converting a late penalty for 4–2 sealed it. Belgium in finishing fourth went home to be hailed heroes, but for the French only disappointment and recrimination awaited.

Match for Third Place

Belgium (1) **2**, **France** (2) **4**
28.6.86 PUEBLA
Belgium: Pfaff, Gerets, Vervoort, Demol, Renquin (Van der Elst F), Grun, Scifo (Van der Elst L), Mommens, Claesen (1), Ceulemans (1), Veyt
France: Rust, Bibard, Amoros (1 pen), Le Roux (Bossis), Battiston, Vercruysse, Genghini (1), Tigana (Tusseau), Papin (1), Ferreri (1), Bellone
Referee: Courtney (England)

THE FINAL

Argentina, with the extravagant skills of Maradona, were cautiously favoured. Against opponents courageous and resilient as ever and capable evidently of stifling and then defeating teams infinitely more talented than themselves, for the Germans organization would be the key. That and the performance of Lothar Matthäus assigned the unenviable task of silencing Maradona.

Twenty largely uneventful minutes passed as the teams sparred, Germany in particular content to pursue a 'wait and see' policy. Maradona – policed doggedly by his vigilant marker – showed frustration, talking himself into a caution when disputing a free kick awarded against Brown. Matthäus inevitably followed, bemused by Maradona's clever back heel and scything him down. Within a minute Argentina had a precious lead. Burruchaga's resultant free kick tempted and deceived Schumacher in its flight and Brown thumped his header into the unguarded net for 1–0. Now Germany attacked, forced to chase a game they instead had hoped to steal, but in the 55th minute their new-found ambition was punished. Their plight, already appearing desperate, became worse. Maradona for once found space, and in turn Enrique, who moved the ball swiftly to Valdano. Surging forward, the striker beat Schumacher's dive with his calm finish. Behind 2–0 and struggling to make any impact on powerful Argentinean defenders, Germany sought inspiration and found it in substitutes Hoeness and Völler.

Brehme in the 73rd minute delivered his corner towards the near post, Völler helped it on and Rummenigge, reacting first, stabbed it home. Fearsome competitors always, the Germans now encouraged sensed and sought an unlikely equalizer, while Argentina for the first time betrayed their anxiety, seeking only to preserve their lead. Eight minutes later another Brehme corner and another German goal. This time Berthold provided the flick and the fair-headed Völler the vital finish – 2–2. The game now headed for extra time and the result for the first time since the 22nd minute was in doubt – would German resilience wear down plainly superior opponents again? The question was answered critically within a minute. There would be no extra time and Argentina would prevail. Burruchaga, quite the best player on the pitch, raced on to Maradona's pass as German concentration wavered fatally. Schumacher again advanced and again was beaten comprehensively – 3–2. Argentina, led by their diminutive captain, received the Trophy, a triumph their collective talents richly deserved.

Final

Argentina (1) **3, West Germany** (0) **2**
29.6.86 MEXICO CITY
Argentina: Pumpido, Cuciuffo, Olarticoechea, Ruggeri, Brown (1), Giusti, Burruchaga (1) (Trobbiani), Batista, Valdano (1), Maradona, Enrique
West Germany: Schumacher, Berthold, Briegel, Jakobs, Förster, Eder, Brehme, Matthäus, Allofs (Völler (1)), Magath (Hoeness), Rummenigge (1)
Referee: Arppi Filho (Brazil)

CHAPTER 14

ITALY

1990

Qualifying Tournament
112 entries
Argentina qualify as holders, Italy qualify as hosts

Europe (33): Albania, Austria, Belgium, Bulgaria, Cyprus, Czechoslovakia, Denmark, England, Finland, France, East Germany, West Germany, Greece, Holland, Hungary, Iceland, Northern Ireland, Republic of Ireland, Italy, Luxembourg, Malta, Norway, Poland, Portugal, Romania, Scotland, Spain, Sweden, Switzerland, Turkey, USSR, Wales, Yugoslavia

South America (10): Argentina, Bolivia, Brazil, Chile, Colombia, Ecuador, Paraguay, Peru, Uruguay, Venezuela

CONCACAF (15): Antigua, Canada, Costa Rica, Cuba, Guatemala, Guyana, Honduras, Jamaica, Mexico, Netherlands Antilles, Panama, Puerto Rico, El Salvador, Trinidad and Tobago, USA

Asia (25): Bahrain, Bangladesh, China, Hong Kong, India, Indonesia, Iran, Iraq, Japan, Jordan, North Korea, South Korea, Kuwait, Malaysia, Nepal, Oman, Pakistan, Qatar, Saudi Arabia, Singapore, Syria, Thailand, UAE, North Yemen, South Yemen

Africa (24): Algeria, Angola, Burkina Faso, Cameroon, Egypt, Gabon, Ghana, Guinea, Ivory Coast, Kenya, Lesotho, Liberia, Libya, Malawi, Morocco, Nigeria, Rwanda, Sudan, Togo, Tunisia, Uganda, Zaire, Zambia, Zimbabwe

Oceania (4 + 1): Australia, Fiji, New Zealand, Taipei + Israel

Europe

Group 1 (Denmark, Bulgaria, Romania, Greece)
Greece v Denmark 1–1, Bulgaria v Romania 1–3, Romania v Greece 3–0, Denmark v Bulgaria 1–1, Greece v Romania 0–0, Bulgaria v Denmark 0–2, Romania v Bulgaria 1–0, Denmark v Greece 7–1, Bulgaria v Greece 4–0, Denmark v Romania 3–0, Greece v Bulgaria 1–0, Romania v Denmark 3–1

	P	W	D	L	F	A	Pts
Romania	6	4	1	1	10	5	9
Denmark	6	3	2	1	15	6	8
Greece	6	1	2	3	3	15	4
Bulgaria	6	1	1	4	6	8	3

Romania qualified

Group 2 (England, Poland, Sweden, Albania)

England v Sweden 0–0, Poland v Albania 1–0, Albania v Sweden 1–2, Albania v England 0–2, England v Albania 5–0, Sweden v Poland 2–1, England v Poland 3–0, Sweden v England 0–0, Sweden v Albania 3–1, Poland v England 0–0, Poland v Sweden 0–2, Albania v Poland 1–2

	P	W	D	L	F	A	Pts
Sweden	6	4	2	0	9	3	10
England	6	3	3	0	10	0	9
Poland	6	2	1	3	4	8	5
Albania	6	0	0	6	3	15	0

Sweden and England qualified

Group 3 (USSR, East Germany, Austria, Iceland, Turkey)

Iceland v USSR 1–1, Turkey v Iceland 1–1, USSR v Austria 2–0, East Germany v Iceland 2–0, Austria v Turkey 3–2, Turkey v East Germany 3–1, East Germany v Turkey 0–2, USSR v East Germany 3–0, Turkey v USSR 0–1, East Germany v Austria 1–1, USSR v Iceland 1–1, Iceland v Austria 0–0, Austria v Iceland 2–1, Austria v USSR 0–0, Iceland v East Germany 0–3, Iceland v Turkey 2–1, East Germany v USSR 2–1, Turkey v Austria 3–0, USSR v Turkey 2–0, Austria v East Germany 3–0

	P	W	D	L	F	A	Pts
USSR	8	4	3	1	11	4	11
Austria	8	3	3	2	9	9	9
Turkey	8	3	1	4	12	10	7
East Germany	8	3	1	4	9	13	7
Iceland	8	1	4	3	6	11	6

USSR and Austria qualified

Group 4 (West Germany, Holland, Wales, Finland)

Finland v West Germany 0–4, Holland v Wales 1–0, Wales v Finland 2–2, West Germany v Holland 0–0, Holland v West Germany 1–1, Wales v West Germany 0–0, Finland v Holland 0–1, Finland v Wales 1–0, West Germany v Finland 6–1, Wales v Holland 1–2, West Germany v Wales 2–1, Holland v Finland 3–0

	P	W	D	L	F	A	Pts
Holland	6	4	2	0	8	2	10
West Germany	6	3	3	0	13	3	9
Finland	6	1	1	4	4	16	3
Wales	6	0	2	4	4	8	2

Holland and West Germany qualified

Group 5 (France, Scotland, Yugoslavia, Norway, Cyprus)

Norway v Scotland 1–2, France v Norway 1–0, Scotland v Yugoslavia 1–1, Cyprus v France 1–1, Cyprus v Norway 0–3, Yugoslavia v France 3–2, Yugoslavia v Cyprus 4–0, Cyprus v Scotland 2–3, Scotland v France 2–0, Scotland v Cyprus 2–1, France v Yugoslavia 0–0, Norway v Cyprus 3–1, Norway v Yugoslavia 1–2, Norway v France 1–1, Yugoslavia v Scotland 3–1, Yugoslavia v Norway 1–0, France v Scotland 3–0, Cyprus v Yugoslavia 1–2, Scotland v Norway 1–1, France v Cyprus 2–0

	P	W	D	L	F	A	Pts
Yugoslavia	8	6	2	0	16	6	14
Scotland	8	4	2	2	12	12	10
France	8	3	3	2	10	7	9
Norway	8	2	2	4	10	9	6
Cyprus	8	0	1	7	6	20	1

Yugoslavia and Scotland qualified

Group 6 (Spain, Hungary, Northern Ireland, Rep of Ireland, Malta)

Northern Ireland v Malta 3–0, Northern Ireland v Rep of Ireland 0–0, Hungary v Northern Ireland 1–0, Spain v Rep of Ireland 2–0, Malta v Hungary 2–2, Spain v Northern Ireland 4–0, Malta v Spain 0–2, Northern Ireland v Spain 0–2, Hungary v Rep of Ireland 0–0, Spain v Malta 4–0, Hungary v Malta 1–1, Malta v Northern Ireland 0–2, Rep of Ireland v Spain 1–0, Rep of Ireland v Malta 2–0, Rep of Ireland v Hungary 2–0, Northern Ireland v Hungary 1–2, Hungary v Spain 2–2, Rep of Ireland v Northern Ireland 3–0, Spain v Hungary 4–0, Malta v Rep of Ireland 0–2

	P	W	D	L	F	A	Pts
Spain	8	6	1	1	20	3	13
Rep of Ireland	8	5	2	1	10	2	12
Hungary	8	2	4	2	8	12	8
Northern Ireland	8	2	1	5	6	12	5
Malta	8	0	2	6	3	18	2

Spain and Rep of Ireland qualified

Group 7 (Belgium, Portugal, Czechoslovakia, Switzerland, Luxembourg)

Luxembourg v Switzerland 1–4, Luxembourg v Czechoslovakia 0–2, Belgium v Switzerland 1–0, Czechoslovakia v Belgium 0–0, Portugal v Luxembourg 1–0, Portugal v Belgium 1–1, Portugal v Switzerland 3–1, Belgium v Czechoslovakia 2–1, Czechoslovakia v Luxembourg 4–0, Luxembourg v Belgium 0–5, Switzerland v Czechoslovakia 0–1, Belgium v Portugal 3–0, Switzerland v Portugal 1–2, Czechoslovakia v Portugal 2–1, Luxembourg v Portugal 0–3, Switzerland v Belgium 2–2, Czechoslovakia v Switzerland 3–0, Belgium v Luxembourg 1–1, Portugal v Czechoslovakia 0–0, Switzerland v Luxembourg 2–1

	P	W	D	L	F	A	Pts
Belgium	8	4	4	0	15	5	12
Czechoslovakia	8	5	2	1	13	3	12
Portugal	8	4	2	2	11	8	10
Switzerland	8	2	1	5	10	14	5
Luxembourg	8	0	1	7	3	22	1

Belgium and Czechoslovakia qualified

South America

Group 1 (Uruguay, Peru, Bolivia)

Bolivia v Peru 2–1, Peru v Uruguay 0–2, Bolivia v Uruguay 2–1, Peru v Bolivia 1–2, Uruguay v Bolivia 2–0, Uruguay v Peru 2–0

	P	W	D	L	F	A	Pts
Uruguay	4	3	0	1	7	2	6
Bolivia	4	3	0	1	6	5	6·
Peru	4	0	0	4	2	8	0

Uruguay qualified

Group 2 (Paraguay, Colombia, Ecuador)

Colombia v Ecuador 2–0, Paraguay v Colombia 2–1, Ecuador v Colombia 0–0, Paraguay v Ecuador 2–1, Colombia v Paraguay 2–1, Ecuador v Paraguay 3–1

	P	W	D	L	F	A	Pts
Colombia	4	2	1	1	5	3	5
Paraguay	4	2	0	2	6	7	4
Ecuador	4	1	1	2	4	5	3

Colombia qualified for play-off with Oceania winner

Group 3 (Brazil, Chile, Venezuela)

Venezuela v Brazil 0–4, Venezuela v Chile 1–3, Chile v Brazil 1–1, Brazil v Venezuela 6–0, Chile v Venezuela 5–0, Brazil v Chile 1–0 (abandoned 59th minutes, match awarded 2–0 to Brazil)

	P	W	D	L	F	A	Pts
Brazil	4	3	1	0	13	1	7
Chile	4	2	1	1	9	4	5
Venezuela	4	0	0	4	1	18	0

Brazil qualified

CONCACAF

1st Round

Guyana v Trinidad and Tobago 0–4, 0–1, Cuba v Guatemala 0–1, 1–1, Jamaica v Puerto Rico 1–0, 2–1, Antigua v Netherlands Antilles 0–1, 1–0 (Netherlands Antilles won 3–1 on penalties), Costa Rica v Panama 1–1, 2–0

2nd Round

Netherlands Antilles v El Salvador 0–1, 0–5, Jamaica v USA 0–0, 1–5, Trinidad and Tobago v Honduras 0–0, 1–1, Costa Rica v Mexico (disqualified), Guatemala v Canada 1–0, 2–3

3rd Round

Guatemala v Costa Rica 1–0, Costa Rica v Guatemala 2–1, Costa Rica v USA 1–0, USA v Costa Rica 1–0, USA v Trinidad and Tobago 1–1, Trinidad and Tobago v Costa Rica 1–1, Costa Rica v Trinidad and Tobago 1–0, USA v Guatemala 2–1, El Salvador v Costa Rica 2–4 (match abandoned after 84 mins, score allowed to stand), Costa Rica v El Salvador 1–0, Trinidad and Tobago v El Salvador 2–0, El Salvador v Trinidad and Tobago 0–0, Guatemala v Trinidad and Tobago 0–1, Trinidad and Tobago v Guatemala 2–1, El Salvador v USA (in Honduras) 0–1, Guatemala v USA 0–0, USA v El Salvador 0–0, Trinidad and

Tobago v USA 0–1, Guatemala v El Salvador and El Salvador v Guatemala not played due to deterioration of the political situation in El Salvador, FIFA annulled the fixtures

	P	W	D	L	F	A	Pts
Costa Rica	8	5	1	2	10	6	11
USA	8	4	3	1	6	3	11
Trinidad and Tobago	8	3	3	2	7	5	9
Guatemala	6	1	1	4	4	7	3
El Salvador	6	0	2	4	2	8	2

Costa Rica and USA qualified

Asia

1st Round
Group 1 (Iraq, Qatar, Jordan, Oman)
Qatar v Jordan 1–0, Oman v Iraq 1–1, Oman v Qatar 0–0, Jordan v Iraq 0–1, Jordan v Oman 2–0, Qatar v Iraq 1–0, Jordan v Qatar 1–1, Iraq v Oman 3–1, Qatar v Oman 3–0, Iraq v Jordan 4–0, Oman v Jordan 0–2, Iraq v Qatar 2–2

	P	W	D	L	F	A	Pts
Qatar	6	3	3	0	8	3	9
Iraq	6	3	2	1	11	5	8
Jordan	6	2	1	3	5	7	5
Oman	6	0	2	4	2	11	2

Group 2 (Saudi Arabia, Syria, North Yemen, Bahrain (withdrew))
North Yemen v Syria 0–1, Saudi Arabia v Syria 5–4, North Yemen v Saudi Arabia 0–1, Syria v North Yemen 2–0, Syria v Saudi Arabia 0 0, Saudi Arabia v North Yemen 1–0

	P	W	D	L	F	A	Pts
Saudi Arabia	4	3	1	0	7	4	7
Syria	4	2	1	1	7	5	5
North Yemen	4	0	0	4	0	5	0

Group 3 (Kuwait, UAE, Pakistan, South Yemen (withdrew))
Pakistan v Kuwait 0–1, Kuwait v UAE 3–2, UAE v Pakistan 5–0, Kuwait v Pakistan 2–0, UAE v Kuwait 1–0, Pakistan v UAE 1–4

	P	W	D	L	F	A	Pts
UAE	4	3	0	1	12	4	6
Kuwait	4	3	0	1	6	3	6
Pakistan	4	0	0	4	1	12	0

Group 4 (South Korea, Singapore, Malaysia, Nepal, India (withdrew))
All matches played in South Korea
Malaysia v Nepal 2–0, Singapore v South Korea 0–3, Malaysia v Singapore 1–0, Nepal v South Korea 0–9, Singapore v Nepal 3–0, South Korea v Malaysia 3–0
All matches played in Singapore
Singapore v Malaysia 2–2, South Korea v Nepal 4–0, Malaysia v South Korea 0–3, Nepal v Singapore 0–7, Singapore v South Korea 0–3, Malaysia v Nepal 3–0

	P	W	D	L	F	A	Pts
South Korea	6	6	0	0	25	0	12
Malaysia	6	3	1	2	8	8	7
Singapore	6	2	1	3	12	9	5
Nepal	6	0	0	6	0	28	0

Group 5 (China, Iran, Thailand, Bangladesh)
Thailand v Bangladesh 1–0, China v Bangladesh 2–0, Thailand v Iran 0–3, Bangladesh v Iran 1–2, Thailand v China 0–3, Bangladesh v China 0–2, Bangladesh v Thailand 3–1, Iran v Bangladesh 1–0, Iran v Thailand 3–0, China v Iran 2–0, Iran v China 3–2, China v Thailand 2–0

	P	W	D	L	F	A	Pts
China	6	5	0	1	13	3	10
Iran	6	5	0	1	12	5	10
Bangladesh	6	1	0	5	4	9	2
Thailand	6	1	0	5	2	14	2

Group 6 (North Korea, Japan, Indonesia, Hong Kong)
Indonesia v North Korea 0–0, Hong Kong v Japan 0–0, Hong Kong v North Korea 1–2, Indonesia v Japan 0–0, Hong Kong v Indonesia 1–1, Japan v North Korea 2–1, Japan v Indonesia 5–0, Japan v Hong Kong 0–0, Indonesia v Hong Kong 3–2, North Korea v Japan 2–0, North Korea v Hong Kong 4–1, North Korea v Indonesia 2–1

	P	W	D	L	F	A	Pts
North Korea	6	4	1	1	11	5	9
Japan	6	2	3	1	7	3	7
Indonesia	6	1	3	2	5	10	5
Hong Kong	6	0	3	3	5	10	3

2nd Round (in Singapore)
UAE v North Korea 0–0, China v Saudi Arabia 2–1, South Korea v Qatar 0–0, Qatar v Saudi Arabia 1–1, South Korea v North Korea 1–0, China v UAE 1–2, China v South Korea 0–1, North Korea v Qatar 2–0, Saudi Arabia v UAE 0–0, UAE v Qatar 1–1, North Korea v China 0–1, Saudi Arabia v South Korea 0–2, UAE v South Korea 1–1, Saudi Arabia v North Korea 2–0, Qatar v China 2–1

	P	W	D	L	F	A	Pts
South Korea	5	3	2	0	5	1	8
UAE	5	1	4	0	4	3	6
Qatar	5	1	3	1	4	5	5
China	5	2	0	3	5	6	4
Saudi Arabia	5	1	2	2	4	5	4
North Korea	5	1	1	3	2	4	3

South Korea and UAE qualified

Africa

1st Round
Group 1
Angola v Sudan 0–0, 2–1, Zimbabwe v Lesotho (withdrew), Zambia v Rwanda (withdrew), Uganda v Malawi 1–0, 1–3

Group 2
Libya v Burkina Faso 3–0, 0–2, Ghana v Liberia 0–0, 0–2, Tunisia v Guinea 5–0, 0–3, Gabon v Togo (withdrew)

2nd Round
Group A (Algeria, Ivory Coast, Zimbabwe, Libya)
Algeria v Zimbabwe 3–0, Ivory Coast v Libya 1–0, Libya v Algeria (Libya refused to play, claiming state of war against the USA, match awarded 2–0 to Algeria), Zimbabwe v Ivory Coast 0–0, (Libya withdrew at this point and their record was expunged), Ivory Coast v Algeria 0–0, Zimbabwe v Algeria 1–2, Ivory Coast v Zimbabwe 5–0, Algeria v Ivory Coast 1–0

	P	W	D	L	F	A	Pts
Algeria	4	3	1	0	6	1	7
Ivory Coast	4	1	2	1	5	1	4
Zimbabwe	4	0	1	3	1	10	1

Group B (Egypt, Kenya, Malawi, Liberia)

Egypt v Liberia 2–0, Kenya v Malawi 1–1, Malawi v Egypt 1–1, Liberia v Kenya 0–0, Kenya v Egypt 0–0, Liberia v Malawi 1–0, Malawi v Kenya 1–0, Liberia v Egypt 1–0, Egypt v Malawi 1–0, Kenya v Liberia 1–0, Egypt v Kenya 2–0, Malawi v Liberia 0–0

	P	W	D	L	F	A	Pts
Egypt	6	3	2	1	6	2	8
Liberia	6	2	2	2	2	3	6
Malawi	6	1	3	2	3	4	5
Kenya	6	1	3	2	2	4	5

Group C (Cameroon, Nigeria, Gabon, Angola)

Nigeria v Gabon 1–0, Cameroon v Angola 1–1, Gabon v Cameroon 1–3, Angola v Nigeria 2–2, Nigeria v Cameroon 2 -0, Angola v Gabon 2–0, Angola v Cameroon 1–2, Gabon v Nigeria 2–1, Nigeria v Angola 1–0, Cameroon v Gabon 2–1, Cameroon v Nigeria 1–0, Gabon v Angola 1–0

	P	W	D	L	F	A	Pts
Cameroon	6	4	1	1	9	6	9
Nigeria	6	3	1	2	7	5	7
Angola	6	1	2	3	6	7	4
Gabon	6	2	0	4	5	9	4

Group D (Morocco, Zaire, Tunisia, Zambia)

Morocco v Zambia 1–0, Zaire v Tunisia 3–1, Tunisia v Morocco 2–1, Zambia v Zaire 4–2, Zaire v Morocco 0–0, Zambia v Tunisia 1–0, Zambia v Morocco 2–1, Tunisia v Zaire 1–0, Morocco v Tunisia 0–0, Zaire v Zambia 1–0, Tunisia v Zambia 1–0, Morocco v Zaire 1–1

	P	W	D	L	F	A	Pts
Tunisia	6	3	1	2	5	5	7
Zambia	6	3	0	3	7	6	6
Zaire	6	2	2	2	7	7	6
Morocco	6	1	3	2	4	5	5

3rd Round
Algeria v Egypt 0–0, 0–1, Cameroon v Tunisia 2–0, 1–0
Egypt and Cameroon qualified

Oceania

1st Round
Group 1
Taipei v New Zealand 0–4, 1–4

Group 2
Fiji v Australia 1–0, 1–5

2nd Round
Israel v New Zealand 1–0, Australia v New Zealand 4–1, Israel v Australia 1–1,
New Zealand v Australia 2–0, New Zealand v Israel 2–2, Australia v Israel 1–1

	P	W	D	L	F	A	Pts
Israel	4	1	3	0	5	4	5
Australia	4	1	2	1	6	5	4
New Zealand	4	1	1	2	5	7	3

Play-off: Colombia v Israel 1–0, 0–0
Colombia qualified

1990 ITALY 8 June–8 July

QUALIFIERS

Argentina	Egypt	Spain
Austria	England	Sweden
Belgium	Holland	UAE
Brazil	Italy	United States
Cameroon	Republic of Ireland	Uruguay
Colombia	Romania	USSR
Costa Rica	Scotland	West Germany
Czechoslovakia	South Korea	Yugoslavia

Group A

Venues: Rome, Florence
Austria
Czechoslovakia
Italy
USA

Group B

Venues: Milan, Bari, Naples
Argentina
Cameroon
Romania
USSR

Group C

Venues: Genoa, Turin
Brazil
Costa Rica
Scotland
Sweden

Group D

Venues: Bologna, Milan
Colombia
UAE
West Germany
Yugoslavia

Group E

Venues: Verona, Udine
Belgium
South Korea
Spain
Uruguay

Group F

Venues: Cagliari, Palermo
Egypt
England
Holland
Republic of Ireland

THE FIRST SERIES

Opening the Tournament in Milan before retreating south to their Naples head-quarters, Argentina the Champions suffered a shocking and embarrassing 1–0 defeat at the hands of Africa's self-ordained indomitable 'Lions', the men from Cameroon. Tough and tenacious, fouling Maradona – to the delight of the crowd – with impunity, the 'Lions' battered Argentina out of their imperious style. Regardless of being reduced to nine men at the end, with Massing and Kana-Biyik sent off for assaulting Caniggia, their win was undeniably deserved, Pumpido decisively and disastrously fumbling Omam-Biyik's header over his own goal-line. For the Soviet side in the same Group, a surprise defeat also, at the hands of the clever Romanians despite the absence of little Hagi. Beaten in the end by the darting Lacatus, often the target of their patient, elaborate and often ultimately incisive movement, his two goals settled a strangely subdued affair, with the disappointing Soviets appearing thoroughly lacking in self belief.

In Group A, Italy proved demonstrably superior to a robust Austrian side of limited ambition. However, confirmation of victory was late in coming. Italy, inspired by 'libero' Baresi, produced at times breathtaking football, orchestrated more often than not by Donadoni. Yet they were frustrated by negative opponents who held their nerve, shape and discipline. Carnevale, the victim of a maniacal lunge by Artner, ultimately was withdrawn injured and perversely this was to prove the Austrians' undoing, as his replacement, Schillaci, seized the chance on 77 minutes to fire Italy ahead, 1–0. The USA celebrated their return to world football in horrible fashion, losing dismally to the sharper Czechoslovakians in Florence by 5–1. Skuhravy, a tall, gangly striker, was a constant worry that ultimately destroyed them, first steering Moravcik's inviting cross in for 1–0 and then helping the Czechs to 3–0, after America had briefly threatened a revival when Caligiuri rounded Stejskal for 3–1. It was Skuhravy on 81 minutes who rose to head the goal to dispel doubts; shortly afterwards, Bilek squandered a penalty before Luhovy stabbed home a fifth.

Brazil, in Group C at Turin, faced the Swedes. Sweden, willing and organized, pushed them hard before going down 2–1. Brazil, unusually employing a sweeper, pressed with a will, and Careca on the stroke of half-time raced on to an inviting Branco pass, repulsed the attentions of Ravanelli and side-footed home. From Limpar's cross Brolin then went close for the Scandinavians, before Careca completed a glorious move, instigated by Jorginho quickly on to the eager Müller who pounded down the wing before crossing. Careca, escaping Larsson his marker, swept home for 2–0. Sweden dug in bravely and earned their reward: the impish Brolin evading Mozer on the edge of the area fired home beautifully. Brazil were winners to the joy of the vast majority in attendance and their form was undeniably impressive. Sadly for Scotland in Genoa, their inexplicable failures suffered at the hands of 'minnows' continued, Costa Rica capitalizing on the Scots' hesitancy and lack of conviction to heap further scorn on a troubled team already humbled in preparation by the Egyptians. Cayasso applied the coup de grace, rifling in Jara's clever back-heel on 50 minutes. Scotland for all of their pressure were smothered efficiently. Conejo, troubled rarely, denied Johnston and McStay at the death as Scotland launched a late, desperate assault. Unfortunately, they lacked the imagination or variety to wreak havoc on so massed a defence as the Costa Ricans.

Down in Cagliari, England and Ireland, banished to Sicily, served up a dreary, ugly affair, full of vigorous endeavour but woefully short on sophistication. The English, with the more creative players, were suffocated by more industrious opponents eager for the battle. Nevertheless, Lineker gave them a lead on eight minutes, breasting the ball past Bonner from Waddle's cross, staggering as defenders bore down on him before recovering to slide his shot into the empty goal, 1–0. Ireland, however, clawed their way back with tenacity and finally earned a point, McMahon, on as a substitute to shore up England's defence, giving the ball injudiciously to Sheedy, the Everton man firing his left-footer past Shilton. Holland at Palermo outplayed their Egyptian opponents through-out the first half, Van Basten volleying splendidly but wide after Gullit headed into his path. The North Africans applied themselves resolutely, and even after Kieft finally put the Dutch ahead on the hour, they refused to be discouraged, pushing the European Champions back on the defensive. Nine minutes from the end, Hassan, tugged outside the penalty area by Koeman, managed to throw himself inside. Abedelghani converted the penalty kick for 1–1. There was still time for the Dutch to redeem themselves, though neither Rijkaard nor a tired Gullit were able to hit the target given presentable openings.

In Group E up in Verona, Belgium, forced to abandon their patient counter-attacking style, still proved too strong for the South Koreans and won 2–0. Scifo was at the hub of their best movements with his willingness to run at defend-ers, and he finally unlocked a packed defence on 52 minutes, his cross from the left creating confusion, and Degryse sweeping home. De Wolf ten minutes later exploded a twenty-five yard kick high into the roof of the Korean net for 2–0, completing the scoring, though the Asians were unfortunate when Soon-Ho beat Preud'homme with a header, only to see the goal-bound ball deflect freakishly off the heel of Gerets to safety. Also in Group E at Udine were Uruguay and Spain in a predictably goal-less draw. Unusually, the South Americans demonstrated surprising enterprise in a match spoiled rather typi-cally by sly fouling, feigned injury and the inevitable thespian tendencies. Uruguay, territorially dominant, threw away victory when Sosa, quite out-standing otherwise, squandered a penalty kick given for a handball against Villaroya, his shot flying high and handsomely wide.

In Group D at Bologna, Colombia, the competition eccentrics, laboured in their own rather casual way before easing by the UAE 2–0. Valderrama, he of the 'big hair', scored and largely controlled proceedings in his own peculiarly languid, if effective, manner. Redin, the forceful little striker, provided the other goal, and condemned by superior opponents to chasing aimlessly about the pitch, the Arabs were sunk without trace. The next day in Milan, Germany against the highly regarded Yugoslavians displayed at once their credentials, winning at a canter with an awe-inspiring combination of pace and power. The Slavs, showing ambition, attacked at the outset, but Matthäus, the German captain, scored first on the half-hour, taking a dropping ball, rounding Jozic and firing home in one smooth movement. Then crucially a second came before the Slavs could regain their composure, Völler distracting defenders allowing Klinsmann time and space to meet Brehme's cross for 2–0. Jozic on 54 minutes gave the East Europeans hope with a header, but as they pressed hard for an equalizer, they were exposed again by Germany's 'contain and counter' policy, the hugely impressive Matthäus surging through a gap and driving home superbly from twenty yards for 3–1. Völler, seizing on an Ivkovic han-dling error, put the lid on it, 4–1.

THE SECOND SERIES

In Rome, Italy expecting a landslide stuttered to unimpressive victory over a determined young American team who retained their organization and discipline in the face of the expected and ferocious onslaught. Giannini scored in eleven minutes, skipping by two American challenges before shooting past Meola. But the promised avalanche did not materialize for all of Italy's possession: Vialli struck the post from a penalty kick after Berti was hauled down, and as the Italian crowd whistled their derision, there was anxiety for the 'Azzurri', Vermes on a rare raid shooting past Zenga, Ferri racing back, clearing as the ball rolled towards the empty goal. Italy, the 1–0 victors at the end, had failed even to spark optimism amongst their own passionate Roman compatriots.

Bilek in the same Group A settled the other match in Czechoslovakia's favour, his penalty struck into the corner of the goal after Lindenberger, trying to rescue Pfeffer's woeful back pass, bundled over Chovanek. This was enough to beat an unduly cautious Austrian team. Hasek, Kubik and the swashbuckling Bilek lent considerable guile to an adventurous performance, Skuhravy one of several to miss chances to underline their total domination in the closing stages.

Now at Naples, adopted home of Maradona, the 'Hand of God' surfaced once more. Argentina faced off against the Soviets, both already staring at the bleak prospect of an undignified and improbable elimination. The Russians replaced goalkeeper Dasayev with Uvarov and trod with great caution, keen to counter from a platform of strong defence. Maradona threatened early, showing glimpses of the outrageous gifts so compelling in Mexico, before Zygmantovich shackled him. Argentina, numerically superior in midfield, dominated before Pumpido, their goalkeeper, clattered into his own defenders and broke his leg. Sensing an opportunity with the uneasy Goycoechea replacing him, the Soviets pressed and Kuznetzov, with a near post header, seemed to have scored only to see a flailing hand – Maradona's – divert the ball off the goal-line to safety. The Soviets protested loud and furiously, but referee Fredriksson would have none of it. What was this strange and mesmerising spell the little man cast over normally competent officials? Deflated temporarily, the Soviets lost concentration and fell behind on 27 minutes to a powerful header from Troglio, and Bessonov's sending off for pulling down the quick-silver Caniggia condemned them. Bravely though the ten men tried, they could find no way back; Burruchaga, hero of '86, scored Argentina's second.

In Bari, to the great surprise of most, the extraordinary 'indomitable Lions' of Cameroon triumphed again, this time over the more talented if less motivated Romanians. Again the Africans, fearsome and occasionally brutal in the tackle, showed no respect at all for their opponents, their remarkable substitute, the thirty-eight-year-old Roger Milla, securing victory with two individual efforts in the 76th and 86th minutes. Two minutes later Balint allowed Romania brief hope, but at the whistle it was another unlikely African celebration.

Up at Bologna in a dull game, Yugoslavia finally found the winning habit. The team of whom Scotland coach Andy Roxburgh's pre-Tournament appraisal had been 'the most highly gifted set of players I have ever seen' had failed to win in eight months, though Colombia, who meandered with no thrust about the pitch in their customary fashion, obligingly and inexplicably failed to galvanize themselves after Jozic had edged Yugoslavia in front. Germany, the first round's most impressive performers, underlined their potential in a crushing and ruthless victory over the hapless UAE by 5–1. Chasing shadows, the game but outclassed Arabs remained in contention for almost an hour. Völler and Klinsmann within a minute eased the Germans to a comfortable 2–0 lead at half-time, before Mubarak, after the restart, fired fiercely and jubilantly past Illgner 2–1. Now the teutonic giant, disturbed from its slumber by the audacious newcomer, shook itself back into shape, the marvellous pace and power game returned at once, forcing the UAE into submission. Matthäus replied within a minute for three, Bein rammed a fourth past the despairing Faraj and Völler a fifth. Germany clearly would be ready, whatever the challenge.

In Group C at Genoa the enigma that was Scotland continued. Beaten by little Costa Rica, they now rose up and battered Sweden to comprehensive defeat. McCall started them off in good style, shooting home after ten minutes. The Scandinavians, lacking pace in defence, were rattled, never allowed fully to regain their composure, Brolin only once threatening in the second half. Victory was confirmed for the delirious 'Tartan Army' packed in the stadium by Maurice Johnston's calm spot kick after Aitken's burgeoning run was halted abruptly and unfairly. At 2–0 and with nine minutes left, Sweden's goal through Strömberg was too little and far too late.

Also in Group C at Turin, Brazil tore into Costa Rica for 90 one-sided minutes but managed just one goal on the half-hour. Müller's shot from a Mozer flick deflecting past the wonderfully acrobatic Conejo for 1–0. Costa Rica, who rarely broke into Brazilian territory and could not muster a shot, did at least demonstrate great resilience as their penalty area resembled the Alamo. With twenty-two shots, three off the goal frame, the score ended just 1–0; Conejo and his defiant colleagues had lost the match but achieved respectability and no little admiration.

England and Holland in Cagliara met looking to stamp their authority on Group F. Neither succeeded, though England, surprisingly the better and more dominant team, undeniably benefited more from their 0–0 draw. Gullit was largely anonymous as a result of Parker's attentions, and Van Basten found himself isolated and reduced to the role of spectator, producing little of the threat posed to rivals in the European Championship of 1988, while the darting Lineker and the tigerish Gascoigne caused great discomfort to the 'Men in Orange', Lineker forcing home a 'goal' to be rightly penalized for hand ball, on 74 minutes. In the final seconds there was another 'goal', as Pearce from the right struck a free kick with enormous velocity through a crowded area into Van Breukelen's net, but again it was disallowed, awarded as indirect – it had made no contact on its path. England could count themselves as most unfortunate. Ireland in Palermo, lacking imaginative creativity, found the stubborn Egyptians a tough nut to crack, and endured the frustration of a goal-less draw against opponents largely unwilling to come out from behind the imaginary sandbags placed in their half. The 20,000 travelling Irishmen roaring encouragement went home disappointed. Coach Jack Charlton, pointedly blamed the sterile Africans for the poor spectacle, barely able to control his anger post-match. 'What match?' he blustered, 'I don't think we played a match today. I have been in football many years. I have watched the game all my life. I've seen 10–0 results, but I've never seen a team that didn't create one chance in ninety minutes. I didn't like the game. I didn't like the way the Egyptians played, I didn't like their time wasting tactics. We must take a little bit of the blame ourselves because we didn't score, but at least we tried.'

In the north at Udine, South Korea, another of the minnows, proved themselves considerably more enterprising, but were beaten comprehensively 3–1 by the powerful though unconvincing Spaniards. Michel, Spain's saviour, gave them an early lead before completing a hat-trick; the Koreans earned late reward for their tenacious approach, Hwang Kwan-Bo supplying a goal.

Belgium surprised the highly regarded Uruguayans in Verona, starting brightly, Clijsters soaring to head an opener with great power and then the immensely talented Schifo hammered in a quite wonderful swerving shot, beating the startled Alvarez from thirty yards. Poor Uruguay were outplayed and largely outthought. Their afternoon, which looked to have improved significantly with the dismissal of the veteran Gerets for a hack at Sosa on 41 minutes, collapsed beyond redemption when the ten remaining 'Rouge Diables' conjured a third decisive goal on 46 minutes, Ceulemans surging through to beat Alvez for 3–0. Try though the South Americans might, their elaborate passing movements could not break down the organized Belgian resistance, and Bengoechea's headed goal when it did arrive was far too late to offer realistic hope.

THE THIRD SERIES

In Group B, Argentina played Romania in Naples where the South Americans started at their fluent best, Caniggia snatching at a presentable opportunity in the second minute. Romania slowly, however, began to gain a foothold, Maradona inevitably the recipient of heavy, often illegal, challenges. First the Europeans matched their opponents, and then with the roaming Hagi out-playing Batista in the pivotal midfield area began to dominate. As half-time approached the wily Carpathian almost broke the deadlock twice, firing high over Goycoechea's crossbar. It was Argentina though who took the lead, after Balint at the other end had been crowded out; from a Maradona corner Monzon rose highest at the near post to direct his header past Lung. For Romania all was not lost: Lacatus with 20 minutes left swung over a cross, the ball travelled across goal where it was headed back and Balint rocketed a close range header high into the roof of the net for 1–1. The spoils shared, now both would wait for the calculations that would decide their destiny.

The Cameroons, certain already of progress, faced the Soviet Union in Bari. Weary, listless and dishevelled from their endeavours, the Africans fell apart against determined opponents desperate for a convincing win to bolster flimsy hopes. Protasov and Zygmantovich provided the Russians with a two-goal lead, and Zavarov and Drobrovolski doubled the advantage in the second half. At the whistle, news from Naples filtered through; the Soviets despaired, their last gasp effort now to no avail.

In Rome against Czechoslovakia the prodigal son, Baggio, scored a 77th-minute goal of breathtaking quality to bring the house down and confirm Italy winners of Group A. Collecting from Giannini, the Italian demigod set off on a mesmerizing run from the left wing, weaving by Hasek and dummying Kadlec before stroking the ball past Stejskal. Earlier the Czechs had defended cautiously, intent on damage limitation in the cauldron-like atmosphere. Behind early to Schillaci's stooping header after Giannini's misdirected shot skidded across the goalmouth, they showed limited ambition. Berti found the net with his hand in the second half but grinned sheepishly as he was booked for his deception. Griga, in spite of Czech reluctance, did find the net for them, momentarily creating anxiety on the terrace, but he was judged off-side. Then came Baggio. Italy were through and significantly would stay in Rome.

The Austrians overcame the USA in a poor quality, often ill-tempered game in Florence. Austria, desperate for goals, looked to Pecl and his forceful runs down the right flank to provide ammunition, but were frustrated by the young American team playing for pride and experience. Ultimately they succeeded, Ogris running on to a through ball for the first goal, Rodax ten minutes later adding a simple second. By the end the Austrians had their victory, though Andrew Murray had reduced their lead to 2–1 and Peter Aigner's sending off left them with ten men; their chance of further progress rested now in the hands of others.

In Group D at Bologna, encouraged by the win over Colombia, Yugoslavia predictably demolished the UAE. Pancev, in for Katanec, gave a fine performance, inspiring his colleagues. Susic fired the first after just four minutes and Pancev scoring shortly afterwards when Mubarak's error suggested a rout. Despite playing with great aplomb, the Yugoslavs mercifully slackened their grip, allowing the Arabs a lifeline. Ali Juma'a headed past Ivkovic for 2–1 before Yugoslavia went away, Pancev making it three before K G Mubarak received a red card. Now the ten could not resist, and eleven minutes from time Prosinecki brought down a high cross and chipped impudently over startled defenders for a fourth. Germany and Colombia staged a late, late show in Milan. The Germans showing greater urgency had the better of the early going, Völler missing, Klinsmann foiled by the eccentric Higuita, and Matthäus lifting a shot on to the bar. The Colombians responded with their trademark patient, neat passing orchestrated by the mop-haired Valderrama, and the game appeared destined for an uneventful draw. Littbarski, on as a substitute, changed it all in the 88th minute, receiving Völler's pass in his stride to dispatch his shot coolly into the net. Down 1–0 and facing the prospect of elimination, Colombia finally showed their mettle. Valderrama in the third minute of injury time slipped an exquisite through ball into the path of Rincon, who shot through Illgner's legs for 1–1, the drama of the final five minutes doing much to extinguish the memory of what had gone before.

Scotland, playing with great courage and conviction in Turin, went down to Brazil in tragic circumstances, Alemao's eightieth minute shot spilled by Leighton into the path of Careca whose attempt to scramble the ball in, though foiled by Gillespie's desperate clearance, fell to Müller who forced it into the empty goal. Poor Scotland, roared on by a vociferous crowd, had emerged unscathed from a period of intense pressure by the rhythmic Americans to threaten themselves, Aitken on 78 minutes seeing his header cleared off the Brazilian goal line, and in injury time they found one last gasp chance, Johnston reacting swiftly to thunder the ball goalwards, Taffarel flinging himself athletically to deny them parity. How bitterly the Scots would regret defeat by the moderate Costa Ricans.

Sweden, after two defeats, sought improbable qualification through spectacular victory over Costa Rica and failed dismally. Ekström did score, side footing home after Schwarz's free kick was parried by Conejo, but they lacked self belief and were tired. Costa Rica, awoken by the appearance of Medford, their substitute, punished a defence short of pace. Flores headed an equalizer fifteen minutes from time and the dispirited Swedes reeled. Medford, the spark in the revival, cracked home the shock winner four minutes from time. Costa

Rica to general astonishment were through. Sweden disastrously and shambolically went home.

In Group F at Cagliari, England finally breached the stubborn defences of the dour Egyptians. Gascoigne carried the ball with urgency at their massed forces, Lineker worked tirelessly but without great effect, the Africans were lamentably negative and suffocated successfully and the game threatened to wander aimlessly. Enter Mark Wright, centre half, arriving to meet Waddle's 58th-minute free kick with a firm header for 1–0. England had won but it had not been pretty. Holland at Palermo launched themselves at the doughty Irish in a bid to overwhelm them. Gullit, after just ten minutes, received Koeman's pass, played a swift one-two with Kieft and slid the ball deftly across Packy Bonner from the angle of the six yard area and into the net. Ireland typically fought back admirably in a thrilling give and take. McGrath shot early in the second half but his thirty-yard effort was tipped over by Van Breukelen. Aldridge also went close, stretching in vain to reach Staunton's searching cross. Quinn, distracted, reached the loose ball but he shot feebly. Gullit at the other end found himself twice smothered as he set to shoot, before Quinn on 71 minutes scored a crucial and deserved Irish equalizer. Freakishly, Van Aerle's deflection of Cascarino's header skidded off of Van Breukelen's chest into the path of the rangy Irishman, who drove the ball in gleefully. For Ireland the draw was reward for their efforts, Houghton and Sheedy becoming increasingly influential. Holland now faced a daunting task in the second stage in Milan against the Germans and worries, too, over the form of Van Basten, their star, so ineffective again.

In Group E, Spain at Verona surprised the previously impressive Belgians in a dull match, largely brought about by their security in the group standing. Spain, courtesy of goals from Michel and Gorriz, would face Yugoslavia in the same stadium. Belgium, whose defeat was illuminated by Vervoort's strike, would face the English at Bologna. South Korea, up at Udine, lost again in heartbreaking fashion in an uneventful game with the wily Uruguayans. Tackling again ferociously, they chased an upset, suffered the loss of Deuk-Yeo (sent off for time wasting) and continued boldly. They were cruelly disappointed in the 89th minute when Uruguay floated a free kick goalwards and negligent marking allowed Fonseca a simple, unchallenged head past Choi In-Young. Uruguay, barely deserving, had scrambled through, but now the stakes were raised: the Italians awaited them in Rome.

Final Tournament – Italy
First round

Group A

Italy (0) **1, Austria** (0) **0**
9.6.90 ROME
Italy: Zenga, Maldini, Ferri, Baresi, Bergomi, De Napoli, Ancelotti (De Agostini), Donadoni, Giannini, Carnevale (Schillaci (1)), Vialli
Austria: Lindenberger, Russ, Streiter, Pecl, Aigner, Artner (Zsak), Herzog, Schöttel, Linzmaier (Hörtnagl), Ogris, Polster
Referee: Wright (Brazil)

Czechoslovakia (2) **5, USA** (0) **1**
10.6.90 FLORENCE
Czechoslovakia: Stejskal, Hasek (1), Kocian, Kadlec, Straka, Moravcik (Weiss), Chovanec, Kubik, Bilek (1 pen), Knoflicek (Luhovy (1)), Skuhravy (2)
USA: Meola, Armstrong, Stollmeyer (Balboa), Windischmann, Trittschuh, Caligiuri (1), Ramos, Harkes, Wynalda, Vermes, Murray (Sullivan)
Referee: Röthlisberger (Switzerland)

Italy (1) **1, USA** (0) **0**
14.6.90 ROME
Italy: Zenga, Bergomi, Ferri, Baresi, Maldini, De Napoli, Berti, Giannini (1), Donadoni, Carnevale (Schillaci), Vialli
USA: Meola, Armstrong, Windischmann, Doyle, Banks (Stollmeyer), Ramos, Balboa, Caligiuri, Harkes, Vermes, Murray (Sullivan)
Referee: Codesal (Mexico)

Austria (0) **0, Czechoslovakia** (0) **1**
15.6.90 FLORENCE
Austria: Lindenberger, Russ (Ogris), Aigner, Pecl, Pfeffer, Hörtnagl, Zsak, Schöttel (Streiter), Herzog, Rodax, Polster
Czechoslovakia: Stejskal, Hasek, Kadlec, Kocian, Nemecek, Moravcik, Chovanec (Bielik), Kubik, Bilek (1 pen), Skuhravy, Knoflicek (Weiss)
Referee: Smith (Scotland)

Italy (1) **2, Czechoslovakia** (0) **1**
19.6.90 ROME
Italy: Zenga, Bergomi, Ferri, Baresi, Maldini, Donadoni (De Agostini), De Napoli (Vierchowod), Giannini, Berti, Baggio (1), Schillaci (1)
Czechoslovakia: Stejskal, Hasek, Kadlec, Kinier, Nemecek (Bielik), Moravcik, Chovanec, Weiss (Griga), Bilek, Skuhravy, Knoflicek
Referee: Quiniou (France)

Austria (0) **2, USA** (0) **1**
19.6.90 FLORENCE
Austria: Lindenberger, Streiter, Aigner, Pecl, Pfeffer, Artner, Zsak, Herzog, Rodax (1) (Glatzmeyer), Polster (Reisinger), Ogris (1)
USA: Meola, Doyle, Windischmann, Banks (Wynalda), Armstrong, Caligiuri (Bliss), Harkes, Ramos, Balboa, Murray (1), Vermes
Referee: Sharif Jamal (Egypt)

	P	W	D	L	F	A	Pts
Italy	3	3	0	0	4	0	6
Czechoslovakia	3	2	0	1	6	3	4
Austria	3	1	0	2	2	3	2
United States	3	0	0	3	2	8	0

Group B

Argentina (0) **0, Cameroon** (0) **1**
8.6.90 MILAN
Argentina: Pumpido, Ruggeri (Caniggia), Fabbri, Simon, Lorenzo, Batista, Sensini (Calderon), Balbo, Basualdo, Burruchaga, Maradona
Cameroon: Nkono, Tataw, Ebwelle, Massing, Ndip, Kunde, Mbouh, Kana-Biyik, Mfede (Libih), Makanaky (Milla), Omam-Biyik (1)
Referee: Vautrot (France)

USSR (0) **0, Romania** (1) **2**
9.6.90 BARI
USSR: Dasayev, Kuznetsov, Khidiatulin, Gorlukovich, Rats, Aleinikov, Bessonov, Litovchenko (Yaremchuk), Zavarov, Protasov, Dobrovolski (Borodyuk)
Romania: Lung, Rednic, Andone, Popescu, Klein, Rotariu, Timofte, Sabau, Lupescu, Lacatus (2, 1 pen) (Dumitrescu), Raducioiu (Balint)
Referee: Cardelino (Uruguay)

Argentina (1) **2, USSR** (0) **0**
13.6.90 NAPLES
Argentina: Pumpido (Goycoechea), Monzon (Lorenzo), Serrizuela, Simon, Olarticoechea, Batista, Basualdo, Burruchaga (1), Troglio (1), Maradona, Caniggia
USSR: Uvarov, Bessonov, Kuznetsov, Khidiatulin, Gorlukovich, Zygmantovich, Aleinikov, Shalimov, Zavarov (Liuti), Dobrovolski, Protasov (Litovchenko)
Referee: Fredriksson (Sweden)

Cameroon (0) **2, Romania** (0) **1**
14.6.90 BARI
Cameroon: Nkono, Tataw, Onana, Ndip, Ebwelle, Kunde (Pagal), Mbouh, Mfede, Maboang (Milla (2)), Makanaky, Omam-Biyik
Romania: Lung, Rednic, Andone, Popescu, Klein, Rotariu, Sabau, Timofte, Hagi (Dumitrescu), Raducioiu (Balint (1)), Lacatus
Referee: Valente (Portugal)

Argentina (0) **1, Romania** (0) **1**
18.6.90 NAPLES
Argentina: Goycoechea, Simon, Serrizuela, Monzon (1), Troglio (Giusti), Batista, Burruchaga (Dezotti), Basualdo, Olarticoechea, Maradona, Caniggia
Romania: Lung, Rednic, Andone, Popescu, Klein, Rotariu, Sabau (Mateut), Lupescu, Hagi, Lacatus, Balint (1) (Lupu)
Referee: Valente (Portugal)

USSR (2) **4, Cameroon** (0) **0**
18.6.90 BARI
USSR: Uvarov, Khidiatulin, Kuznetsov, Demianenko, Gorlukovich, Aleinikov, Litovchenko (Yaremchuk), Zygmantovich (1), Shalimov (Zavarov (1)), Protasov (1), Dobrovolski (1)
Cameroon: Nkono, Onana, Ebwelle, Kunde (Milla), Tataw, Ndip, Kana-Biyik, Mbouh, Mfede, Makanaky (Pagal), Omam-Biyik
Referee: Wright (Brazil)

	P	W	D	L	F	A	Pts
Cameroon	3	2	0	1	3	5	4
Romania	3	1	1	1	4	3	3
Argentina	3	1	1	1	3	2	3
USSR	3	1	0	2	4	4	2

Group C

Brazil (1) **2, Sweden** (0) **1**
10.6.90 TURIN
Brazil: Taffarel, Mauro Galvao, Mozer, Ricardo Gomes, Jorginho, Branco, Dunga, Alemao, Valdo (Silas), Müller, Careca (2)
Sweden: Ravelli, Nilsson R, Larsson P, Ljung (Strömberg), Limpar, Thern, Schwarz, Ingesson, Nilsson J, Brolin (1), Magnusson (Pettersson)
Referee: Lanese (Italy)

Costa Rica (0) **1, Scotland** (0) **0**
11.6.90 GENOA
Costa Rica: Conejo, Chavarria, Flores, Marchena, Montero, Chavez, Gonzalez, Gomez, Ramirez, Jara (Medford), Cayasso (1)
Scotland: Leighton, Gough (McKimmie), McPherson, McLeish, Malpas, McStay, Aitken, McCall, Bett (McCoist), Johnston, McInally
Referee: Loustau (Argentina)

Brazil (1) **1, Costa Rica** (0) **0**
16.6.90 TURIN
Brazil: Taffarel, Mauro Galvao, Jorginho, Mozer, Ricardo Gomes, Branco, Dunga, Alemao, Valdo (Silas), Careca (Bebeto), Müller (1)
Costa Rica: Conejo, Flores, Chavarria, Marchena, Gonzalez, Montero, Chavez, Gomez, Ramirez, Jara (Myers), Cayasso (Guimaraes)
Referee: Jouini (Tunisia)

Scotland (1) **2, Sweden** (0) **1**
16.6.90 GENOA
Scotland: Leighton, McPherson, Levein, McLeish, Malpas, Aitken, MacLeod, McCall (1), Fleck (McCoist), Durie (McStay), Johnston (1 pen)
Sweden: Ravelli, Nilsson R, Larsson P (Strömberg (1)), Hysén, Schwarz, Ingesson, Thern, Limpar, Nilsson J, Brolin, Pettersson (Ekström)
Referee: Maciel (Paraguay)

Brazil (0) **1, Scotland** (0) **0**
20.6.90 TURIN
Brazil: Taffarel, Jorginho, Mauro Galvao, Ricardo Rocha, Ricardo Gomes, Branco, Alemao, Dunga, Valdo, Careca, Romario (Müller (1))
Scotland: Leighton, McKimmie, McPherson, Aitken, McLeish, Malpas, McCall, McStay, MacLeod (Gillespie), Johnston, McCoist (Fleck)
Referee: Kohl (Austria)

Costa Rica (0) **2, Sweden** (1) **1**
20.6.90 GENOA
Costa Rica: Conejo, Marchena, Flores (1), Gonzalez, Montero, Chavarria, Gomez (Medford (1)), Chaves, Cayasso, Ramirez, Jara
Sweden: Ravelli, Nilsson R, Larsson P, Hysén, Schwarz, Pettersson, Strömberg (Engqvist), Ingesson, Nilsson J, Ekström (1), Brolin (Gren)
Referee: Petrovic (Yugoslavia)

	P	W	D	L	F	A	Pts
Brazil	3	3	0	0	4	1	6
Costa Rica	3	2	0	1	3	2	4
Scotland	3	1	0	2	2	3	2
Sweden	3	0	0	3	3	6	0

Group D

Colombia (0) **2, UAE** (0) **0**
9.6.90 BOLOGNA
Colombia: Higuita, Escobar, Gildardo Gomez, Herrera, Perea, Gabriel Gomez, Valderrama (1), Redin (1), Alvarez, Rincon, Iguaran (Estrada)
UAE: Faraj, Mubarak K G, Abdulrahman I, Abdulrahman E (Sultan), Mohamed Y, Juma'a, Abdullah Moh, Abbas, Mubarak N, Mubarak K (Bilal), Talyani
Referee: Courtney (England)

Yugoslavia (0) **1, West Germany** (2) **4**
10.6.90 MILAN
Yugoslavia: Ivkovic, Vulic, Hadzibegic, Jozic (1), Spasic, Katanec, Baljic, Susic (Brnovic), Savicevic (Prosinecki), Stojkovic, Vujovic
West Germany: Illgner, Reuter, Berthold, Augenthaler, Brehme, Buchwald, Matthäus (2), Bein (Möller), Hässler (Littbarski), Klinsmann (1), Völler (1)
Referee: Mikkelsen (Denmark)

Yugoslavia (0) **1, Colombia** (0) **0**
14.6.90 BOLOGNA
Yugoslavia: Ivkovic, Stanojkovic, Spasic, Hadzibegic, Jozic (1), Brnovic, Susic, Katanec (Jarni), Stojkovic, Sabanadzovic, Vujovic (Pancev)
Colombia: Higuita, Herrera, Perea, Gildardo Gomez, Escobar, Gabriel Gomez, Alvarez, Valderrama, Redin (Estrada), Rincon (Hernandez), Iguaran
Referee: Agnolin (Italy)

West Germany (2) **5, UAE** (0) **1**
15.6.90 MILAN
West Germany: Illgner, Reuter, Buchwald, Augenthaler, Brehme, Berthold (Littbarski), Matthäus (1), Hässler, Bein (1), Klinsmann (1) (Riedle), Völler (2)
UAE: Faraj, Abdulrahman E, Mubarak K G, Mohamed Y, Abdulrahman I (Al Haddad), Abdullah Moh, Juma'a, Mubarak N, Mubarak K (1) (Hussain), Abbas, Talyani
Referee: Spirin (USSR)

West Germany (0) **1, Colombia** (0) **1**
19.6.90 MILAN
West Germany: Illgner, Reuter, Buchwald, Augenthaler, Pflugler, Berthold, Matthäus, Hässler (Thon), Bein (Littbarski (1)), Klinsmann, Völler
Colombia: Higuita, Herrera, Escobar, Perea, Gildardo Gomez, Gabriel Gomez, Alvarez, Estrada, Fajardo, Valderrama, Rincon (1)
Referee: Snoddy (Northern Ireland)

Yugoslavia (2) **4, UAE** (1) **1**
19.6.90 BOLOGNA
Yugoslavia: Ivkovic, Stanojkovic, Spasic, Hadzibegic, Jozic, Brnovic, Susic (1), Stojkovic, Sabanadzovic (Prosinecki (1)), Pancev (2), Vujovic (Vulic)
UAE: Faraj, Mubarak K G, Abdulrahman I, Abdulrahman E, Al Haddad, Juma'a (1) (Mubarak F K), Abdullah Moh, Abbas, Mubarak N (Sultan), Mubarak I, Talyani
Referee: Takada (Japan)

	P	W	D	L	F	A	Pts
West Germany	3	2	1	0	10	3	5
Yugoslavia	3	2	0	1	6	5	4
Colombia	3	1	1	1	3	2	3
UAE	3	0	0	3	2	11	0

Group E

Belgium (0) **2, South Korea** (0) **0**
12.6.90 VERONA
Belgium: Preud'homme, Gerets, Clijsters, Demol, De Wolf (1), Emmers, Van der Elst, Scifo, Versavel, Degryse (1), Van der Linden (Ceulemans)
South Korea: Choi In-Young, Choi Kang-Hee, Chung Yong-Hwan, Hong Myung-Bo, Park Kyung-Joon, Gu Sang-Bum, Lee Young-Jin (Cho Min-Kook), Noh Soo-Jin (Lee Tae-Hoo), Choi Soon-Ho, Hwang Seon-Hong, Kim Joo-Sung
Referee: Mauro (USA)

Spain (0) **0, Uruguay** (0) **0**
13.6.90 UDINE
Spain: Zubizarreta, Chendo, Sanchis, Andrinua, Jimenez, Martin Vazquez, Roberto, Villaroya (Gorriz), Michel, Manolo (Paz), Butragueño
Uruguay: Alvez, Herrera, Gutierrez, De Leon, Dominguez, Ruben Pereira (Correa), Perdomo, Paz, Alzamendi (Aguilera), Francescoli, Sosa
Referee: Kohl (Austria)

Spain (1) **3, South Korea** (1) **1**
17.6.90 UDINE
Spain: Zubizarreta, Chendo, Andrinua, Sanchis, Gorriz, Michel (3), Villaroya, Roberto (Bakero), Martin Vazquez, Butragueño (Fernando), Julio Salinas
South Korea: Choi In-Young, Park Kyung-Joon (Chung Jong-Soo), Choi Kang-Hee, Hong Myung-Bo, Yoon Deuk-Yeo, Hwang Kwan-Bo (1), Chung Hae-Won (Noh Soo-Jin), Kim Joo-Sung, Gu Sang-Bum, Byun Byung-Joo, Choi Soon-Ho
Referee: Guerrero (Ecuador)

Belgium (2) **3, Uruguay** (0) **1**
17.6.90 VERONA
Belgium: Preud'homme, Gerets, Grun, Clijsters (1) (Emmers), Demol, De Wolf, Versavel (Vervoort), Van der Elst, Scifo (1), Degryse, Ceulemans (1)
Uruguay: Alvez, Herrera, Gutierrez, De Leon, Dominguez, Ostalaza (Bengoechea (1)), Perdomo, Paz, Alzamendi (Aguilera), Francescoli, Sosa
Referee: Kirschen (East Germany)

Spain (2) **2, Belgium** (1) **1**
21.6.90 VERONA
Spain: Zubizarreta, Chendo, Sanchis, Andrinua, Villaroya, Gorriz (1), Michel (1 pen), Roberto, Martin Vazquez, Butragueño (Alcorta), Julio Salinas (Pardeza)
Belgium: Preud'homme, Staelens (Van der Linden), Albert, Demol, De Wolf, Van der Elst, Emmers (Plovie), Vervoort (1), Scifo, Degryse, Ceulemans
Referee: Loustau (Argentine)

Uruguay (0) **1, South Korea** (0) **0**
21.6.90 UDINE
Uruguay: Alvez, Gutierrez, De Leon, Herrera, Dominguez, Perdomo, Ostolaza (Aguilera), Francescoli, Paz, Martinez, Sosa (Fonseca (1))
South Korea: Choi In-Young, Park Kyung-Joon, Choi Kang-Hee, Chung Jong-Soo, Hong Myung-Bo, Yoon Deuk-Yeo, Hwang Kwan-Bo (Chung Hae-Won), Lee Heung-Sil, Kim Joon-Sung (Hwang Seon-Hong), Byun Byung-Joo, Choi Soon-Ho
Referee: Lanese (Italy)

	P	W	D	L	F	A	Pts
Spain	3	2	1	0	5	2	5
Belgium	3	2	0	1	6	3	4
Uruguay	3	1	1	1	2	3	3
South Korea	3	0	0	3	1	6	0

Group F

England (1) 1, Rep of Ireland (0) 1
11.6.90 CAGLIARI
England: Shilton, Stevens, Walker, Butcher, Pearce, Robson, Beardsley (McMahon), Gascoigne, Waddle, Barnes, Lineker (1) (Bull)
Rep of Ireland: Bonner, Morris, McCarthy, Moran, Staunton, McGrath, Houghton, Sheedy (1), Aldridge (McLoughlin), Townsend, Cascarino
Referee: Schmidhuber (West Germany)

Egypt (0) 1, Holland (0) 1
12.6.90 PALERMO
Egypt: Shoubeir, Hassan I, Yaken, Ramzi H, Yassine, Youssef, Ramzi A (Abdel Rahmane), Hassan H, Abdelhamid (Tolba), Abdelghani (1 pen), Abdou
Holland: Van Breukelen, Van Aerle, Rutjes, Koeman R, Van Tiggelen, Vanenburg (Kieft (1)), Wouters, Rijkaard, Koeman E (Witschge), Van Basten, Gullit
Referee: Aladren (Spain)

England (0) 0, Holland (0) 0
16. 9.90 CAGLIARI
England: Shilton, Parker, Walker, Wright, Butcher, Pearce, Robson (Platt), Waddle (Bull), Gascoigne, Barnes, Lineker
Holland: Van Breukelen, Van Aerle, Rijkaard, Koeman R, Van Tiggelen, Wouters, Gullit, Witschge, Van't Schip (Kieft), Gillhaus, Van Basten
Referee: Petrovic (Yugoslavia)

Egypt (0) 0, Rep of Ireland (0) 0
17.6.90 PALERMO
Egypt: Shoubeir, Hassan I, Yaken, Ramzi H, Yassine, Abdelghani, Orabi, Tolba (Abou Seid), Youssef, Abdou (Abdelhamid), Hassan H
Rep of Ireland: Bonner, Morris, McCarthy, Moran, Staunton, McGrath, Houghton, Townsend, Sheedy, Aldridge (McLoughlin), Cascarino (Quinn)
Referee: Van Langehove (Belgium)

England (0) **1, Egypt** (0) **0**
21.6.90 CAGLIARI
England: Shilton, Parker, Wright (1), Walker, Pearce, Waddle (Platt), McMahon, Gascoigne, Barnes, Lineker, Bull (Beardsley)
Egypt: Shoubeir, Hassan I, Yaken, Ramzi H, Yassine, Youssef, Abdelghani, Abdou (Soliman), Ramzi A, Abdelhamid (Abdel Rahmane), Hassan H
Referee: Röthlisberger (Switzerland)

Rep of Ireland (0) **1, Holland** (1) **1**
21.6.90 PALERMO
Rep of Ireland: Bonner, Morris, McCarthy, Moran, Staunton, McGrath, Houghton, Townsend, Sheedy (Whale), Aldridge (Cascarino), Quinn (1)
Holland: Van Breukelen, Van Aerle, Rijkaard, Koeman R, Van Tiggelen, Wouters, Witschge (Fraser), Van Basten, Gullit (1), Gillhaus, Kieft (Van Loen)
Referee: Vautrot (France)

	P	W	D	L	F	A	Pts
England	3	1	2	0	2	1	4
Rep of Ireland	3	0	3	0	2	2	3
Holland	3	0	3	0	2	2	3
Egypt	3	0	2	1	1	1	2

The Last Sixteen

Cameroon v Colombia
Czechoslovakia v Costa Rica
Argentina v Brazil
West Germany v Holland
Republic of Ireland v Romania
Italy v Uruguay
Spain v Yugoslavia
England v Belgium

THE ROUND OF SIXTEEN

In Naples, Cameroon and the Colombians indulged in a crazy match. The Africans, committing themselves in their forthright, direct way, gave a thoroughly undisciplined performance, collecting a series of yellow cards for brutal unnecessary challenges whilst the Colombians strolled around, weaving intricate passing movements of little purpose or thrust. The game meandered into extra time. Now the South Americans, infinitely the more talented, allowed their eccentricity to dictate matters. Milla, the veteran, again a substitute, cleaved his way through the Colombian defence, smashing a left-footer home to give Cameroon the lead. Higuito, strolling out of goal, offered himself for a square ball from Perea, Milla gratefully intercepted, shrugged off the reckless goalkeeper's attempts to foul him and fired home the simplest of goals. Though Redin brought Colombia back to 2–1, by the end they were out, perishing at the hands of their own peculiar brand of complacency. 'We just have a goalkeeper who has certain characteristics,' said coach Francisco Mantowana, showing remarkable restraint in the aftermath.

At Bari the rampaging Czechs threatened to overrun Costa Rica, scoring in just ten minutes when Skuhravy rose to meet Moravcik's testing cross. Thereafter they bore down on the Americans' goal until half-time. At least the Costa Ricans demonstrated their ability to defend in depth and ride their luck. After the interval, as the Czechs relaxed, they were punished. Gonzalez, at nineteen the Tournament's youngest player, rose to head home Ramirez's free kick past Stejskal. Shocked out of their lethargy, Czechoslovakia found themselves and responded mightily and decisively, Skuhravy again arriving to meet a Moravcik cross with a brave header on the hour. In mere moments 2–1 became 3–1, Kubik sending in a rasping free kick. The Czechs in Skuhravy held the battering ram to beat down the Costa Rican ramparts, his presence creating panic as he exploited their weakness with high balls. On 82 minutes, Skuhravy scored another goal for a hat-trick, firmly heading past Barrantes from Chovanec's corner, 4–1 at the end. Nonetheless, the Costa Ricans' achievement had been immense, though Scots watching would reflect ruefully on their defeat in Genoa two weeks earlier.

Two South American giants collided in Turin as Brazil encountered Argentina. The Brazilians, dominant throughout, put Careca in within a minute but his shot flew wide of goal. Dunga then headed on to the post as Alemao commanded midfield whilst Maradona for the Argentineans was subjected to a succession of assaults, body checks, sly trips and shirt pulling designed to nullify his effectiveness. Argentina resisted with admirable efficiency in spite of Brazil's abundance of possession, rarely themselves constructing attacking movements. In the second half Brazil persisted, Careca grazing the bar, Valdo whipping in crosses, Alemao forcing Goycoechea to a desperate save, though as the crowd grew apathetic, bored almost with the steady procession towards Goycoechea's goal, Maradona drew on the genius of 1986, accelerating without impediment past three defenders. Drawing three more towards him, he slipped a pass with precision into the feet of the darting Caniggia. The new darling of the Pampas swerved around Taffarel and coolly slid the ball home. At 1–0, for the remaining 10 minutes Argentina exhibited the professionalism of the previous 80. Brazil, bewildered and inconsolable at the end, had maintained control throughout and been beaten.

In Milan a taut, tense contest was played out by familiar rivals Germany and Holland, affected in no small measure by two sending offs. After 20 minutes, Rijkaard, penalized for a crude challenge on Völler, found himself cautioned and in the aftermath was dismissed, foolishly, for spitting at the same player after Völler was ordered off for violently remonstrating with the referee. With Rijkaard's petulance perhaps went Dutch aspirations as the Germans reorganized better to the demands of the ten-man game. Buchwald early in the second half pushed up to support Klinsmann, shrugged off Winter on the left and provided his striker with a chance he duly dispatched. Holland's tired Gullit floundered, Van Basten completed a miserable Tournament of great personal expectation, a sorrowful, largely anonymous figure, and though Kieft struck the German goal-frame, Brehme, after Littbarski had been denied, curled an 85th minute shot decisively past Van Breukelen, the Dutch defence shredded. Holland, for the sake of pride, staged a mini revival, Koeman converting a last minute penalty after Kohler bundled over Van Basten. But they were out; for the neutrals theirs had been a desperately disappointing campaign.

On a humid evening in Rome the hosts faced Uruguay and tore into them eagerly. Schillaci almost gave them an immediate lead, stabbing the ball wide from Baggio's incisive cross. Uruguay, however, enhanced their reputation, gathering their composure in the hostile environment, defending astutely and playing neat though laborious football, hoping to turn the Italian flanks. Italy, untroubled but frustrated, lost their way and the game petered out into a series of niggling fouls and histrionics. Serena, a second-half substitute, provided the much-needed impetus, galvanizing an Italian attack increasingly bereft of ideas. De Agostini saw his free kick saved by Alvez before Schillaci, the idol of a nation, received Serena's pass to blast a thunderous shot into the Uruguayan net for 1–0. Uruguay were beaten, deflated by the disappointment as Italy rose like giants in response to the crescendo of noise urging them forward. Giannini's cross put the lid on it seven minutes from the end, met emphatically by the inspirational Serena. The Italian coach, Vicini, summarized briefly, 'Schillaci stupendi,' he opined. The man himself remained modesty itself: 'I am going through a magical moment. I just hope I can keep my feet on the ground.'

In Genoa there was more remarkable drama as Romania and the Republic of Ireland slugged it out like two heavyweight boxers, the former applying science and finesse, the latter courage and willpower. McGrath for the Irish worked tirelessly, the elegant Hagi often foiled by the energetic McCarthy. Romania started the brighter, Sabau firing wide after linking with Hagi. In the second half Bonner denied the clever Raducioiu, and Hagi, allowed rare space, blasted over. For Ireland, Townsend, Quinn and Sheedy missed in succession and an intense period of extra time followed. Houghton for Ireland came closest, his header flying wide. Penalty kicks, then, would settle the issue, and with each in the unbearably tense atmosphere converting four, Timofte stepped up for Romania, his shot brilliantly saved by Bonner flinging himself to his right. Enter David O'Leary, a veteran of less successful times in Ireland's football history. His kick flew past Lung and amidst joyous and triumphant celebrations Ireland looked forward to a date in Rome with the Italian 'Azzurri'.

In Verona, Yugoslavia, seeking to conserve their energy in the 90 ºF heat, started slowly and almost paid the price against Spain. Butragueño on eight minutes, seizing on an error by Ivkovic, fired across the gaping goal as Spain showed greater urgency, inspired by the magnificent Martin Vazquez, while Yugoslavia resisted and with great patience waited for opportunities to turn defence to attack. The Spanish, who might have led when Butragueño headed wastefully on to an upright from eight yards, saw Ivkovic fumbled a header from Gorriz on to the same post and then, suddenly, found themselves behind and with time running out. Stojkovic, the mercurial menace, carrying the ball deep into the Spanish area dragged it back, wrong-footing defenders, and unleashed a ferocious shot beyond Zubizarreta with 12 minutes left. Curiously, Spain now found their scoring touch, Salinas sweeping the persistent Vazquez's cross ball past the previously charmed Ivkovic on 84 minutes. In extra time Stojkovic settled it with one majestic free kick after Savicevic had been pulled down by Roberto. Twenty-five yards out, he roared in and powered the ball delightfully around the wall and curling back into Zubizarreta's net for 2–1. Spain fought to the end; stronger in the heat, they dominated though Savicevic on another rapier-like counter almost embarrassed them a third time. At the end the day belonged to Stojkovic and his compatriots.

An absorbing contest between England and Belgium took place in Bologna. Ceulemans for the Belgians, playing behind the strikers, struck a post in an eventful first half, while Barnes of England rose to head a seemingly perfect goal past Preud'homme. To his chagrin, however, Mr Middelsen ruled him offside. In the second half Lineker was denied by the goalkeeper's legs as Waddle began to gain ascendancy over De Wolf, and England took control. The marvellously elusive Scifo almost won the game for his 'Diables Rouge' with a breathtaking effort from more than thirty yards, which thumped against the inside of Shilton's goal-post. In extra time, and to the consternation of the English supporters, Belgium appeared the fresher. Van der Elst exploiting space vacated by McMahon's substitution probed, and England clung on. And then as the faint-hearted braced themselves for the inevitable penalty shoot out, England found a winner. Gascoigne, an inspiration to his team, found yet more energy, carrying the ball sixty yards to the heart of Belgium's defence before being upended by Gerets. Rising to his feet he fired the free kick quickly toward the left hand side of the Belgian penalty area and Platt, a substitute with the happy knack of scoring goals, watched the ball fall out of the night sky and with perfect timing crashed an unstoppable volley past the despairing Preud'homme from ten yards. It was a wonderful match decided by a wonderful goal; at the whistle Gascoigne and coach Robson embraced – England would go to Naples.

Second Round

Cameroon (0) **2, Colombia** (0) **1** (aet, 0–0 at 90 mins)
23.6.90 NAPLES
Cameroon: Nkono, Tataw, Ndip, Onana, Ebwelle, Kana-Biyik, Mbouh, Maboang, Mfede (Milla (2)), Omam-Biyik, Makanaky (Djonkep)
Colombia: Higuita, Herrera, Perea, Escobar, Gildardo Gomez, Alvarez, Gabriel Gomez (Redin (1)), Rincon, Fajardo (Iguaran), Valderrama, Estrada
Referee: Lanese (Italy)

Czechoslovakia (1) **4, Costa Rica** (0) **1**
23.6.90 BARI
Czechoslovakia: Stejskal, Hasek, Kadlec, Kocian, Straka, Moravcik, Chovanec, Kubik (1), Bilek, Skuhravy (3), Knoflicek
Costa Rica: Barrantes, Chavarria (Guimaraes), Marchena, Flores, Montero, Chavez, Ramirez, Gonzalez (1), Obando (Medford), Cayasso, Jara
Referee: Kirschen (East Germany)

Argentina (0) **1, Brazil** (0) **0**
24.6.90 TURIN
Argentina: Goycoechea, Basualdo, Monzon, Simon, Ruggeri, Olarticoechea, Giusti, Burruchaga, Maradona, Troglio (Calderon), Caniggia (1)
Brazil: Taffarel, Jorginho, Ricardo Rocha, Ricardo Gomes, Mauro Galvao (Renato), Branco, Alemao (Silas), Dunga, Valdo, Careca, Müller
Referee: Quiniou (France)

West Germany (0) **2, Holland** (0) **1**
24.6.90 MILAN
West Germany: Illgner, Reuter, Kohler, Augenthaler, Brehme (1), Buchwald, Berthold, Matthäus, Littbarski, Völler, Klinsmann (1) (Riedle)
Holland: Van Breukelen, Van Aerie (Kieft), Koeman R (1 pen), Van Tiggelen, Wouters, Rijkaard, Witschge (Gillhaus), Winter, Gullit, Van Basten, Van't Schip
Referee: Loustau (Argentina)

Rep of Ireland (0) **0, Romania** (0) **0** (aet, Rep of Ireland won 5–4 on penalties)
25.6.90 GENOA
Rep of Ireland: Bonner, Morris, McCarthy, Moran, Staunton (O'Leary), McGrath, Townsend, Houghton, Sheedy, Aldridge (Cascarino), Quinn
Romania: Lung, Rednic, Andone, Popescu, Klein, Rotariu, Lupescu, Sabau (Timofte), Hagi, Raducioiu (Lupu), Blaint
Referee: Wright (Brazil)

Italy (0) **2, Uruguay** (0) **0**
25.6.90 ROME
Italy: Zanga, Bergomi, Ferri, Baresi, Maldini, De Agostini, De Napoli, Berti (Serena (1)), Giannini, Schillaci (1), Baggio (Vierchowod)
Uruguay: Alvez, Saldana, Gutierrez, De Leon, Dominguez, Ostolaza (Alzamendi), Perdomo, Francescoli, Ruben Pereira, Aguilera (Sosa), Fonseca
Referee: Courtney (England)

Spain (0) **1, Yugoslavia** (0) **2** (aet, 1–1 at 90 mins)
26.6.90 VERONA
Spain: Zubizarreta, Chendo, Gorriz, Andrinua (Jimenez), Sanchis, Villaroya, Martin Vazquez, Roberto, Michel, Butragueño (Rafa Paz), Julio Salinas (1)
Yugoslavia: Ivkovic, Sabanadzovic, Spasic, Brnovic, Katanec (Vulic), Hadzibegic, Jozic, Susic, Stojkovic (2), Pancev (Savicevic), Vujovic
Referee: Schmidhuber (West Germany)

England (0) **1, Belgium** (0) **0** (aet, 0–0 at 90 mins)
26.6.90 BOLOGNA
England: Shilton, Parker, Butcher, Wright, Walker, Pearce, Waddle, Gascoigne, McMahon (Platt (1)), Barnes (Bull), Lineker
Belgium: Preud'homme, Gerets, Grun, Demol, Clijsters, De Wolf, Van der Elst, Scifo, Versavel (Vervoort), Ceulemans, Degryse (Claesen)
Referee: Middelsen (Denmark)

THE QUARTER-FINALS

At Florence, Argentina overcame an infinitely more talented Yugoslavian team after a 0–0 draw and the trauma of a penalty competition. Perversely with Maradona effectively, though fairly, shackled by Sabanadzovic and Stojkovic, roughly dealt with by Olarticoechea, Sabanadzovic was somewhat ironically dismissed for a mistimed challenge on 31 minutes whilst Olarticoechea stayed to the end to perpetrate his full and comprehensive repertoire – including an elbow in the face and a kick on the knee – on the unfortunate Stojkovic. The ten

Europeans persisted, more menacing in attack whilst defending stoutly until tiring in extra time. Argentina might at the very end have clinched it, Burruchaga bundling the ball into goal. 'Handball,' said referee Röthlisberger, though replays later indicated otherwise. Were the gods finally deserting the Argentineans? No. As the penalty shoot-out progressed, it fell to the quite outstanding centre back Hagzibegic to keep the Slavs in it, but to his and their despair he failed.

Ireland in Rome against Italy failed to turn back the tide as the 'Azzurri', roared on by fervent support, advanced to the semi-final. The Irish, however, battled mightily to the end, with their busy, pressing game forcing Italy into error. They enjoyed moments of supremacy, Niall Quinn towering up above the Italian defence forcing Zenga to a fine save. Schillaci responded in kind, his header going wide, before, as half-time approached, came the game's decisive moment. Donadoni's shot was parried by the unsighted Bonner into the path of Schillaci, who steered the ball calmly into the net. Freed now from their inhibitions, Italy sought to press home their advantage, the inspirational Schillaci giving them a cutting edge that the Irish, hard as they fought, lacked. First he struck the bar thunderously and then when bearing down on goal in the final moments he was adjudged offside. Ending 1–0, the Irish achievement with the Tournament's oldest squad had been a magnificent one. Jack Charlton, their occasionally abrasive coach, reflected philosophically afterwards: 'Maybe this type of game we play shows a little bit of merit; maybe it's shown the way that others can go.'

In Milan the Germans predictably disposed of Czechoslovakia in a disappointing and largely one-sided fixture. The Czechs, seemingly lacking the conviction and confidence their own previous form might have brought, proved reluctant, their lack of self-belief allowing Germany to attack them remorselessly. Stejskal, beaten by a Matthäus penalty after Klinsmann was clumsily felled by Chovanek midway through the first half, produced a string of fine saves to hold the Germans to 1–0. Curiously for the Czechs in the embers of the game and after Moravcik's dismissal had reduced them to ten men, there was a chance for salvation. Kocian fed Nemecek, whose shot beat Ilgner but, sadly for the Czechs, the post as well. Sinking to the ground, head in hands, Nemecek knew now what the referee's whistle would confirm – Germany would go to the Turin semi-final.

In Naples there was real drama as England threatened to snatch defeat from the jaws of victory against Cameroon, before emerging from a heart-stopping extra period the narrowest of winners. It all began routinely, Gascoigne, with his penetrating runs unsettling a nervous African defence, and Pearce galloping up the left-hand side a constant source of danger. Platt finally arrived to meet a Pearce cross heading fiercely past Nkono on 25 minutes for 1–0. England continued to press, Lineker in particular being subjected to crude and distasteful fouling. As half-time approached, Makanaky and Biyik began to turn defenders, Libih was presented with an easy chance which he spurned, England wobbled, and the tide turned. Milla, the extraordinary veteran substitute, arrived to weave his crafty spells, Pagal and Libih found attackers with unexpected angles and Cameroon seized the initiative. First Milla bursting through on the hour was hauled down for a penalty that Kunde converted, and then four minutes later Milla, again the orchestrater, put through Ekeke for 2–1. To their credit England recovered their composure and went in search of an equalizer. Lineker with just eight minutes to go answered their prayers, converting a penalty he himself had earned when an incisive run was ended by Kunde's flailing feet. At 2–2 there was still time for Biyik at the very end to force a fine save from Shilton. In extra time Biyik again wasted an opportunity, shooting hopelessly wide, before Gascoigne controlled and passed instantly and exquisitely into the path of Lineker's darting sortie. This time Nkono brought him down; again he got up and smashed his penalty kick home, decisively 3–2, and the wilting but courageous Africans could find no more. 'At one time,' said England coach Bobby Robson afterwards, 'I thought we were on the plane home; we never underestimated Cameroon but they still surprised us through their speed, strength and running off the ball. We pulled it out of the fire, I don't really know how. I thought we showed a lot of spirit and a willingness to fight to the end. They were the better team when they went ahead, but it was a see-saw saga of a match and now we are in the world's top four and I'm proud of our footballers for having achieved that.'

Quarter-Finals

Argentina (0) **0, Yugoslavia** (0) **0** (aet, Argentina won 3–2 on penalties)
30.6.90 FLORENCE
Argentina: Goycochea, Simon, Ruggeri, Serrizuela, Basualdo, Olarticoechea (Troglio), Giusti, Burruechaga, Calderon (Dezotti), Caniggia, Maradona
Yugoslavia: Ivkovic, Hadzibegic, Spasic, Brnovic, Vulic, Sabanadzovic, Jozic, Susic (Savicevic), Prosinecki, Stojkovic, Vujovic
Referee: Röthlisberger (West Germany)

Rep of Ireland (0) **0, Italy** (1) **1**
30.6.90 ROME
Rep of Ireland: Bonner, Morris, McCarthy, Moran, Staunton, McGrath, Houghton, Townsend, Sheedy, Quinn (Cascarino), Aldridge (Sheridan)
Italy: Zenga, Bergomi, Ferri, Baresi, Maldini, De Agostini, Donadoni, De Napoli, Giannini (Ancelotti), Baggio (Serena), Schillaci (1)
Referee: Valente (Portugal)

Czechoslovakia (0) **0, West Germany** (1) **1**
1.7.90 MILAN
Czechoslovakia: Stejskal, Hasek, Straka, Kocian, Kadlec, Moravcik, Chovanec, Bilek (Nemecek), Kubik (Griga), Skuhravy, Knoflicek
West Germany: Illgner, Berthold, Kohler, Augenthaler, Brehme, Buchwald, Matthäus (1 pen), Bein (Möller), Littbarski, Riedle, Klinsmann
Referee: Kohl (Austria)

Cameroon (0) **2, England** (1) **3** (aet, 2–2 at 90 mins)
1.7.90 NAPLES
Cameroon: Nkono, Tataw, Massing, Kunde (1 pen), Ebwelle, Maboang (Milla), Libih, Pagal, Makanaky, Mfede (Ekeke (1)), Omam-Biyik
England: Shilton, Parker, Butcher (Steven), Wright, Walker, Pearce, Waddle, Platt (1), Gascoigne, Barnes (Beardsley), Lineker (2 pens)
Referee: Codesal (Mexico)

THE SEMI-FINALS

The semi-finals provided quite breathtaking drama. First in Naples, Italy before a wildly enthusiastic crowd faced Argentina with Diego Maradona, formerly of Napoli, back on his old stomping ground. In the days preceding the match he attempted to divide the sympathy and loyalties of a public that once adored him. It worked not one jot: the loathing filtering down from the terraces was almost tangible. From the start Italy took command, forcing the Argentineans back. Eager to impose themselves, their reward came quickly, the dynamic Giannini cleverly lobbing Simon and heading into the path of Vialli, whose shot fiercely struck was blocked by Goycoechea, only for Schillaci to react quickest, the rebound firmly fired home. At 1–0 Italy in control relaxed, fatally allowing Argentina to patiently find their way back, the blond-haired Caniggia, one of the Tournament's danger men, arriving at the near post to deftly lift Maradona's cross over both defenders and goalkeeper for 1–1. Italy now raised themselves from their lethargy, huffing and puffing mightily but with little success, a deep sense of foreboding hanging over proceedings. Much later Schillaci would say, 'When they equalized I knew we would lose,' and so it proved. Extra time served the same fare, Italy pressing purposefully but with little penetration, Argentina defending and stifling in organized fashion unhindered, in spite of Giusti's dismissal for an off the ball incident with Baggio. At the last the offended Baggio did at least force an acrobatic save from Goycoechea, but that was that. Penalty kicks would decide the first finalist. Predictably Argentina prevailed, just as they had in similar circumstances against Yugoslavia. As the Italian nerve weighed down by the expectation of their own vociferous crowd cracked, Donadoni, so influential in their progress and Serena were the two to endure the surreal experience of sudden and total failure. The Italians trudged off, tears shed in anguish, whilst Maradona cast in the role of arch villain celebrated with his colleagues a fortuitous and unlikely triumph. 'Argentina,' said one acerbic scribe in the immediate aftermath, 'are a fortunate and reviled team.'

The following evening in Turin the best match of the Tournament took place between Germany, from the outset the team everyone had to beat, and England, who had grown in confidence and stature, beyond recognition now from those nervous Sicilian beginnings. The French media, enthusiastic in their coverage despite their own team's absence, described the contest as 'a match between the irresistible Germans and the indestructible English'. 'West Germany have similar qualities,' offered the English coach Bobby Robson. 'They are a very durable team, I think it will be a battle of wills,' and so it proved.

England in the early stages held sway, their forceful, thoughtful promptings keeping the Germans on the back foot. Then against the run of play, on 59 minutes a foul by Pearce on Hässler gave the Germans a free kick from Andreas Brehme, which thumped into the white-shirted defensive wall, looped freakishly up into the air and then down beyond and behind Peter Shilton into the net – 1–0. England did not dwell on their misfortune; instead, they redoubled their efforts, desperate for an equalizer. Gascoigne, commanding the midfield, unsettled the Germans, and with Walker, Butcher and Wright solid and secure against Völler and Klinsmann, the platform for recovery was in place. Butcher ultimately was sacrificed for Steven, on as a last gamble. Ten minutes from time a goal almost inevitably came from the boot of Lineker. Parker's innocuous cross misjudged by both Kohler and Augenthaler fell to the Englishman who spun and shot with precision for 1–1. Extra time delivered more thrills as the commitment of the combatants continued unwaveringly. Shilton denied the athletic Klinsmann, Waddle struck the inside of the post, before Buchwald fired against England's goal frame. A draw and again the dreaded agony of a penalty competition. For Pearce and Waddle there was utter despair – they missed, the Germans did not, and England's campaign in devastating circumstances was over. They had played well, very well indeed, always the equals and often the betters of an indisputably fine German team. Theirs from humble beginnings had been a great campaign.

Semi-Finals

Argentina (0) **1, Italy** (1) **1** (aet, 1–1 at 90 mins, Argentina won 4–3 on penalties)
3.7.90 NAPLES
Argentina: Goycoechea, Simon, Ruggeri, Serrizuela, Giusti, Calderon (Troglio), Burruchaga, Basualdo (Batista), Olarticoechea, Caniggia (1), Maradona
Italy: Zenga, Bergomi, Baresi, Ferri, De Napoli, De Agostini, Donadoni, Maldini, Giannini (Baggio), Schillaci (1), Vialli (Serena)
Referee: Vautrot (France)

West Germany (0) **1, England** (0) **1** (aet, 1–1 at 90 mins, West Germany won 4–3 on penalties)
4.7.90 TURIN
West Germany: Illgner, Berthold, Augenthaler, Buchwald, Kohler, Hässler (Reuter), Matthäus, Thon, Brehme (1), Klinsmann, Völler (Riedle)
England: Shilton, Parker, Butcher (Steven), Wright, Walker, Pearce, Platt, Gascoigne, Waddle, Beardsley, Lineker (1)
Referee: Wright (Brazil)

PLAY-OFF FOR THIRD PLACE

To their credit England and Italy, tired and disappointed teams, galvanized themselves, both shorn of hugely influential midfielders, Donadoni for the 'Azzurri' and Gascoigne for the English. They played out an enterprising and entertaining match at Bari. Baggio scored first, Platt equalized with a searing header, before Schillaci settled affairs from the penalty spot. Italy winning 2–1 at the end, the suspicion remained that the third place play-off would prove a far more attractive encounter than the final itself.

Match for Third Place

Italy (0) **2, England** (0) **1**
7.7.90 BARI
Italy: Zenga, Bergomi, Baresi, Ferrara, Maldini, Vierchowod, De Agostini (Berti), Ancelotti, Giannini (Ferri), Baggio (1), Schillaci (1 pen)
England: Shilton, Stevens, Wright (Waddle), Parker, Walker, Dorigo, Steven, Platt (1), McMahon (Webb), Beardsley, Lineker
Referee: Quiniou (France)

THE FINAL

So to the final in Rome where Germany, overwhelming favourites now, took the game to the South Americans. The Argentineans without Caniggia laboured hard to contain and stifle their more imaginative opponents driven by Hässler. Germany, while they sought at least to play a game approximating football, found the hard, sterile tactics of Argentina frustrating them endlessly. Maradona, marshalled expertly by Buchwald, found himself unable to exert influence, and the match, after the thrills of Turin and the drama of Italy's elimination in Naples, floundered dismally. Germany, running out of ideas, were encouraged by the expulsion of Monzon, sent off on 64 minutes – the first sending off in a final – for a dreadful hack at the unfortunate Klinsmann. Augenthaler, put through by Matthäus, was smothered, but still the ten stubborn Argentineans resisted, though now even less ambitious than at the beginning. There was finally a goal six minutes from time, a shambles befitting the game itself, as Sensini racing with Völler for a through ball lunged in desperation, conceding a dubious penalty kick. Pandemonium ensued as the volatile South Americans protested fruitlessly; Brehme, when all was calm, hammered home the kick. At 1–0 there was no way back. The coveted championship slipping from the Argentineans' grasp, their disappointment manifested itself into petulance and disgrace. Dezotti, two minutes from the end, also received his marching orders amid anarchic scenes after wrestling Kohler to the ground. Germany were crowned, while Maradona wept. But few wept with him, his team's contribution to the Tournament almost entirely negative, their conduct in a final watched around the globe quite deplorable.

Final

West Germany (0) **1, Argentina** (0) **0**
8.7.90 ROME
West Germany: Illgner, Berthold (Reuter), Kohler, Augenthaler, Buchwald, Brehme (1 pen), Littbarski, Hässler, Matthäus, Völler, Klinsmann
Argentina: Goycochea, Lorenzo, Serrizuela, Sensini, Ruggeri (Monzon), Simon, Basualdo, Burruchaga (Calderon), Maradona, Troglio, Dezotti
Referee: Codesal (Mexico)

CHAPTER 15

USA

1994

Qualifying Tournament
143 entries
Argentina qualify as holders, USA qualify as hosts

Europe (37): Albania, Austria, Belgium, Bulgaria, Cyprus, Czechoslovakia, Denmark, England, Republic of Ireland, Estonia, Faroe Isles, Finland, France, Germany, Greece, Holland, Hungary, Iceland, Israel, Italy, Latvia, Lithuania, Luxembourg, Malta, Northern Ireland, Norway, Poland, Portugal, Romania, Russia, San Marino, Scotland, Spain, Sweden, Switzerland, Turkey, Wales

South America (9): Argentina, Bolivia, Brazil, Colombia, Ecuador, Paraguay, Peru, Uruguay, Venezuela

CONCACAF (23): Antigua, Barbados, Bermuda, Canada, Costa Rica, Cuba, Dominican Republic, El Salvador, Guatemala, Guyana, Haiti, Honduras, Jamaica, Mexico, Netherlands Antilles, Nicaragua, Panama, Puerto Rico, St Lucia, St Vincent, Surinam, Trinidad and Tobago, USA

Asia (28): Bahrain, Bangladesh, China, Hong Kong, India, Indonesia, Iran, Iraq, Japan, Jordan, Lebanon, North Korea, Kuwait, Macao, Malaysia, Oman, Pakistan, Qatar, Saudi Arabia, Singapore, South Korea, Sri Lanka, Syria, Taiwan, Thailand, UAE, Vietnam, Yemen

Africa (40): Algeria, Angola, Benin, Botswana, Burkina Faso, Burundi, Cameroon, Congo, Egypt, Ethiopia, Gabon, Gambia, Ghana, Guinea, Ivory Coast, Kenya, Liberia, Libya, Madagascar, Malawi, Mali, Mauritania, Morocco, Mozambique, Namibia, Niger, Nigeria, Sao Tome e Principe, Senegal, Sierra Leone, South Africa, Sudan, Swaziland, Tanzania, Togo, Tunisia, Uganda, Zaire, Zambia, Zimbabwe

Oceania (6): Australia, Fiji, New Zealand, Solomon Islands, Tahiti, Vanuatu

Europe
Group 1 (Estonia, Italy, Malta, Portugal, Scotland, Switzerland)
Estonia v Switzerland 0–6, Switzerland v Scotland 3–1, Italy v Switzerland 2–2, Scotland v Portugal 0–0, Malta v Estonia 0–0, Scotland v Italy 0–0, Switzerland v Malta 3–0, Malta v Italy 1–2, Malta v Portugal 0–1, Scotland v Malta 3–0, Portugal v Italy 1–3, Italy v Malta 6–1, Switzerland v Portugal 1–1, Italy v Estonia 2–0, Malta v Switzerland 0–2, Portugal v Scotland 5–0, Switzerland v Italy 1–0, Estonia v Malta 0–1, Estonia v Scotland 0–3, Scotland v Estonia 3–1, Portugal v Malta 4–0,

Estonia v Portugal 0–2, Scotland v Switzerland 1–1, Estonia v Italy 0–3, Portugal v Switzerland 1–0, Italy v Scotland 3–1, Portugal v Estonia 3–0, Italy v Portugal 1–0, Malta v Scotland 0–2, Switzerland v Estonia 4–0

	P	W	D	L	F	A	Pts
Italy	10	7	2	1	22	7	16
Switzerland	10	6	3	1	23	6	15
Portugal	10	6	2	2	18	5	14
Scotland	10	4	3	3	14	13	11
Malta	10	1	1	8	3	23	3
Estonia	10	0	1	9	1	27	1

Italy and Switzerland qualified

Group 2 (England, Holland, Norway, Poland, San Marino, Turkey)

Norway v San Marino 10–0, Norway v Holland 2–1, Poland v Turkey 1–0, San Marino v Norway 0–2, England v Norway 1–1, Holland v Poland 2–2, Turkey v San Marino 4–1, England v Turkey 4–0, Turkey v Holland 1–3, England v San Marino 6–0, Holland v Turkey 3–1, San Marino v Turkey 0–0, Holland v San Marino 6–0, Turkey v England 0–2, England v Holland 2–2, Norway v Turkey 3–1, Poland v San Marino 1–0, San Marino v Poland 0–3, Poland v England 1–1, Norway v England 2–0, Holland v Norway 0–0, England v Poland 3–0, Norway v Poland 1–0, San Marino v Holland 0–7, Holland v England 2–0, Poland v Norway 0–3, Turkey v Poland 2–1, Turkey v Norway 2–1, San Marino v England 1–7, Poland v Holland 1–3

	P	W	D	L	F	A	Pts
Norway	10	7	2	1	25	5	16
Holland	10	6	3	1	29	9	15
England	10	5	3	2	26	9	13
Poland	10	3	2	5	10	15	8
Turkey	10	3	1	6	11	19	7
San Marino	10	0	1	9	2	46	1

Norway and Holland qualified

Group 3 (Albania, Denmark, Republic of Ireland, Latvia, Lithuania, Northern Ireland, Spain)

Spain v Albania 3–0, Northern Ireland v Lithuania 2–2, Rep of Ireland v Albania 2–0, Albania v Lithuania 1–0, Latvia v Lithuania 1–2, Latvia v Denmark 0–0, Rep of Ireland v Latvia 4–0, Northern Ireland v Albania 3–0, Latvia v Spain 0–0, Lithuania v Denmark 0–0, Denmark v Rep of Ireland 0–0, Northern Ireland v Spain 0–0, Lithuania v Latvia 1–1, Albania v Latvia 1–1, Northern Ireland v Denmark 0–1, Spain v Rep of Ireland 0–0, Spain v Latvia 5–0, Albania v Northern

Ireland 1–2, Spain v Lithuania 5–0, Denmark v Spain 1–0, Rep of Ireland v Northern Ireland 3–0, Denmark v Latvia 2–0, Lithuania v Albania 3–1, Rep of Ireland v Denmark 1–1, Spain v Northern Ireland 3–1, Latvia v Albania 0–0, Lithuania v Northern Ireland 0–1, Albania v Rep of Ireland 1–2, Denmark v Albania 4–0, Latvia v Northern Ireland 1–2, Lithuania v Spain 0–2, Latvia v Rep of Ireland 0–2, Lithuania v Rep of Ireland 0–1, Denmark v Lithuania 4–0, Albania v Denmark 0–1, Rep of Ireland v Lithuania 2–0, Northern Ireland v Latvia 2–0, Albania v Spain 1–5, Denmark v Northern Ireland 1–0, Rep of Ireland v Spain 1–3, Northern Ireland v Rep of Ireland 1–1, Spain v Denmark 1–0

	P	W	D	L	F	A	Pts
Spain	12	8	3	1	27	4	19
Rep of Ireland	12	7	4	1	19	6	18
Denmark	12	7	4	1	15	2	18
Northern Ireland	12	5	3	4	14	13	13
Lithuania	12	2	3	7	8	21	7
Latvia	12	0	5	7	4	21	5
Albania	12	1	2	9	6	26	4

Spain and Republic of Ireland qualified

Group 4 (Belgium, Cyprus, Czechoslovakia, Faroe Islands, Romania, Wales)

Belgium v Cyprus 1–0, Romania v Faroe Islands 7–0, Romania v Wales 5–1, Faroe Islands v Belgium 0–3, Faroe Islands v Cyprus 0–2, Czechoslovakia v Belgium 1–2, Wales v Faroe Islands 6–0, Czechoslovakia v Faroe Islands 4–0, Belgium v Romania 1–0, Cyprus v Wales 0–1, Romania v Czechoslovakia 1–1, Belgium v Wales 2–0, Cyprus v Romania 1–4, Cyprus v Belgium 0–3, Cyprus v Czechoslovakia 1–1, Wales v Belgium 2–0, Romania v Cyprus 2–1, Cyprus v Faroe Islands 3–1, Czechoslovakia v Wales 1–1, Belgium v Faroe Islands 3–0, Czechoslovakia v Romania 5–2, Faroe Islands v Wales 0–3, Faroe Islands v Czechoslovakia 0–3, Wales v Czechoslovakia 2–2, Faroe Islands v Romania 0–4, Romania v Belgium 2–1, Wales v Cyprus 2–0, Czechoslovakia v Cyprus 3–0, Wales v Romania 1–2, Belgium v Czechoslovakia 0–0

	P	W	D	L	F	A	Pts
Romania	10	7	1	2	29	12	15
Belgium	10	7	1	2	16	5	15
Czechoslovakia	10	4	5	1	21	9	13
Wales	10	5	2	3	19	12	12
Cyprus	10	2	1	7	8	18	5
Faroe Islands	10	0	0	10	1	38	0

Romania and Belgium qualified

Group 5 (Greece, Hungary, Iceland, Luxembourg, Russia)

Greece v Iceland 1–0, Hungary v Iceland 1–2, Luxembourg v Hungary 0–3, Iceland v Greece 0–1, Russia v Iceland 1–0, Russia v Luxembourg 2–0, Greece v Hungary 0–0, Greece v Luxembourg 2–0, Hungary v Greece 0–1, Luxembourg v Russia 0–4, Russia v Hungary 3–0, Luxembourg v Iceland 1–1, Russia v Greece 1–1, Iceland v Russia 1–1, Iceland v Hungary 2–0, Hungary v Russia 1–3, Iceland v Luxembourg 1–0, Luxembourg v Greece 1–3, Hungary v Luxembourg 1–0, Greece v Russia 1–0

	P	W	D	L	F	A	Pts
Greece	8	6	2	0	10	2	14
Russia	8	5	2	1	15	4	12
Iceland	8	3	2	3	7	6	8
Hungary	8	2	1	5	6	11	5
Luxembourg	8	0	1	7	2	17	1

Russia and Greece qualified

Group 6 (Austria, Bulgaria, Finland, France, Israel, Sweden)

Finland v Bulgaria 0–3, Bulgaria v France 2–0, Finland v Sweden 0–1, Sweden v Bulgaria 2–0, France v Austria 2–0, Austria v Israel 5–2, Israel v Sweden 1–3, France v Finland 2–1, Israel v Bulgaria 0–2, Israel v France 0–4, Austria v France 0–1, Austria v Bulgaria 3–1, France v Sweden 2–1, Bulgaria v Finland 2–0, Bulgaria v Israel 2–2, Finland v Austria 3–1, Sweden v Austria 1–0, Sweden v Israel 5–0, Finland v Israel 0–0, Sweden v France 1–1, Austria v Finland 3–0, Finland v France 0–2, Bulgaria v Sweden 1–1, France v Israel 2–3, Bulgaria v Austria 4–1, Sweden v Finland 3–2, Israel v Austria 1–1, Austria v Sweden 1–1, Israel v Finland 1–3, France v Bulgaria 1–2

	P	W	D	L	F	A	Pts
Sweden	10	6	3	1	19	8	15
Bulgaria	10	6	2	2	19	10	14
France	10	6	1	3	17	10	13
Austria	10	3	2	5	15	16	8
Finland	10	2	1	7	9	18	5
Israel	10	1	3	6	10	27	5

Sweden and Bulgaria qualified

South America

Group A (Argentina, Colombia, Paraguay, Peru)

Colombia v Paraguay 0–0, Peru v Argentina 0–1, Paraguay v Argentina 1–3, Peru v Colombia 0–1, Colombia v Argentina 2–1, Paraguay v Peru 2–1,

Argentina v Peru 2–1, Paraguay v Colombia 1–1, Argentina v Paraguay 0–0, Colombia v Peru 4–0, Argentina v Colombia 0–5, Peru v Paraguay 2–2

	P	W	D	L	F	A	Pts
Colombia	6	4	2	0	13	2	10
Argentina	6	3	1	2	7	9	7
Paraguay	6	1	4	1	6	7	6
Peru	6	0	1	5	4	12	1

Colombia qualified
Argentina qualified for play-off with Australia or Canada

Group B (Brazil, Bolivia, Ecuador, Uruguay, Venezuela)

Ecuador v Brazil 0–0, Venezuela v Bolivia 1–7, Bolivia v Brazil 2–0, Venezuela v Uruguay 0–1, Uruguay v Ecuador 0–0, Venezuela v Brazil 1–5, Bolivia v Uruguay 3–1, Ecuador v Venezuela 5–0, Bolivia v Ecuador 1–0, Uruguay v Brazil 1–1, Bolivia v Venezuela 7–0, Brazil v Ecuador 2–0, Brazil v Bolivia 6–0, Uruguay v Venezuela 4–0, Brazil v Venezuela 4–0, Ecuador v Uruguay 0–1, Uruguay v Bolivia 2–1, Venezuela v Ecuador 2–1, Brazil v Uruguay 2–0, Ecuador v Bolivia 1–1

	P	W	D	L	F	A	Pts
Brazil	8	5	2	1	20	4	12
Bolivia	8	5	1	2	22	11	11
Uruguay	8	4	2	2	10	7	10
Ecuador	8	1	3	4	7	7	5
Venezuela	8	1	0	7	4	34	2

Brazil and Bolivia qualified

CONCACAF
Pre-preliminary round
Caribbean Region (North) (Dominican Republic, Puerto Rico, St Lucia, St Vincent)

Dominican Republic v Puerto Rico, 1–2, Puerto Rico v Dominican Republic 1–1, St Lucia v St Vincent 1–0, St Vincent v St Lucia 3–1
Puerto Rico and St Vincent qualified for Preliminary round

Preliminary Round
Caribbean Region (North) (Bermuda, Cuba, Haiti, Jamaica, Puerto Rico, St Vincent)
Cuba withdrew
Bermuda v Haiti 1–0, Haiti v Bermuda 2–1, Jamaica v Puerto Rico 2–1, Puerto Rico v Jamaica 0–1
Bermuda, Jamaica and St Vincent qualified for Round 1

Caribbean Region (South) (Antigua, Barbados, Guyana, Netherlands Antilles, Surinam, Trinidad & Tobago)
Netherlands Antilles v Antigua 1–1, Antigua v Netherlands Antilles 3–0, Guyana v Surinam 1–2, Surinam v Guyana 1–1, Barbados v Trinidad & Tobago 1–2, Trinidad & Tobago v Barbados 3–0
Antigua, Surinam and Trinidad & Tobago qualified for Round 1

Round 1
Central Region (Costa Rica, El Salvador, Guatemala, Honduras, Nicaragua, Panama)
Guatemala v Honduras 0–0, Honduras v Guatemala 2–0, Nicaragua v El Salvador 0–5, El Salvador v Nicaragua 5–1, Panama v Costa Rica 1–0, Costa Rica v Panama 5–1
Honduras, El Salvador, Costa Rica qualified for Round 2

Caribbean Region (Antigua, Bermuda, Jamaica, Surinam, St Vincent, Trinidad & Tobago)
Antigua v Bermuda 0–3, Bermuda v Antigua 2–1, Trinidad & Tobago v Jamaica 1–2, Jamaica v Trinidad & Tobago 1–1, Surinam v St Vincent 0–0, St Vincent v Surinam 2–1
Bermuda, Jamaica and St Vincent qualified for Round 2

Round 2
Group A (Costa Rica, Honduras, Mexico, St Vincent)
Costa Rica v Honduras 2–3, St Vincent v Mexico 0–4, Mexico v Honduras 2–0, St Vincent v Costa Rica 0–1, Mexico v Costa Rica 4–0, St Vincent v Honduras 0–4, Honduras v St Vincent 4–0, Costa Rica v Mexico 2–0, Honduras v Costa Rica 2–1, Mexico v St Vincent 11–0, Costa Rica v St Vincent 5–0, Honduras v Mexico 1–1

	P	W	D	L	F	A	Pts
Mexico	6	4	1	1	22	3	9
Honduras	6	4	1	1	14	6	9
Costa Rica	6	3	0	3	11	9	6
St Vincent	6	0	0	6	0	29	0

Mexico and Honduras qualified for Final Round

Group B (Bermuda, Canada, El Salvador, Jamaica)

Jamaica v Canada 1–1, Bermuda v El Salvador 1–0, El Salvador v Canada 1–1, Bermuda v Jamaica 1–1, Canada v Jamaica 1–0, El Salvador v Bermuda 4–1, Canada v El Salvador 2–3, Jamaica v Bermuda 3–2, Canada v Bermuda 4–2, Jamaica v El Salvador 0–2, Bermuda v Canada 0–0, El Salvador v Jamaica 2–1

	P	W	D	L	F	A	Pts
El Salvador	6	4	1	1	12	6	9
Canada	6	2	3	1	9	7	7
Jamaica	6	1	2	3	6	9	4
Bermuda	6	1	2	3	7	12	4

El Salvador and Canada qualified for Final Round

Final Round (Canada, El Salvador, Honduras, Mexico)

El Salvador v Mexico 2–1, Honduras v Canada 2–2, Mexico v Honduras 3–0, Canada v El Salvador 2–0, Canada v Honduras 3–1, Mexico v El Salvador 3–1, Mexico v Canada 4–0, Honduras v El Salvador 2–0, Honduras v Mexico 1–4, El Salvador v Canada 1–2, Canada v Mexico 1–2, El Salvador v Honduras 2–1

	P	W	D	L	F	A	Pts
Mexico	6	5	0	1	17	5	10
Canada	6	3	1	2	10	10	7
El Salvador	6	2	0	4	6	11	4
Honduras	6	1	1	4	7	14	3

Mexico qualified

Canada qualified for play-off with Australia

Asia

Round 1
Group A (China, Iraq, Jordan, Pakistan, Yemen)
Matches played in Amman, Jordan
Jordan v Yemen 1–1, Pakistan v China 0–5, Jordan v Iraq 1–1, Yemen v Pakistan 5–1, Jordan v China 0–3, Yemen v Iraq 1–6, Pakistan v Iraq 0–8, Yemen v China 1–0, Jordan v Pakistan 3–1, Iraq v China 1–0
Matches played in Beijing, China
Yemen v Jordan 1–1, China v Pakistan 3–0, Iraq v Jordan, 4–0, Pakistan v Yemen 0–3, China v Jordan 4–1, Iraq v Yemen 3–0, Iraq v Pakistan 4–0, China v Yemen 1–0, Pakistan v Jordan 0–5, China v Iraq 2–1

	P	W	D	L	F	A	Pts
Iraq	8	6	1	1	28	4	13
China	8	6	0	2	18	4	12
Yemen	8	3	2	3	12	13	8
Jordan	8	2	3	3	12	15	7
Pakistan	8	0	0	8	2	36	0

Iraq qualified for Round 2

Group B (Iran, Myanmar (formerly Burma), Oman, Syria, Taiwan)
Myanmar withdrew
Matches played in Tehran, Iran
Iran v Oman 0–0, Taiwan v Syria 0–2, Oman v Syria 0–0, Iran v Taiwan 6–0, Oman v Taiwan 2–1, Iran v Syria 1–1
Matches played in Damascus, Syria
Oman v Iran 0–1, Syria v Taiwan 8–1, Syria v Oman 2–1, Taiwan v Iran 0–6, Taiwan v Oman 1–7, Syria v Iran 1–1

	P	W	D	L	F	A	Pts
Iran	6	3	3	0	15	2	9
Syria	6	3	3	0	14	4	9
Oman	6	2	2	2	10	5	6
Taiwan	6	0	0	6	3	31	0

Iran qualified for Round 2

Group C (Indonesia, North Korea, Qatar, Singapore, Vietnam)
Matches played in Doha, Qatar
Qatar v Indonesia 3–1, North Korea v Vietnam 3–0, North Korea v Singapore 2–1, Qatar v Vietnam 4–0, North Korea v Indonesia 4–0, Vietnam v Singapore 2–3, Qatar v Singapore 4–1, Vietnam v Indonesia 1–0, Indonesia v Singapore 0–2, Qatar v North Korea 1–2
Matches played in Singapore
Indonesia v Qatar 1–4, Vietnam v North Korea 0–1, Singapore v North Korea 1–3, Vietnam v Qatar 0–4, Indonesia v North Korea 1–2, Singapore v Vietnam 1–0, Singapore v Qatar 1–0, Indonesia v Vietnam 2–1, Singapore v Indonesia 2–1, North Korea v Qatar 2–2

	P	W	D	L	F	A	Pts
North Korea	8	7	1	0	19	6	15
Qatar	8	5	1	2	22	8	11
Singapore	8	5	0	3	12	12	10
Indonesia	8	1	0	7	6	19	2
Vietnam	8	1	0	7	4	18	2

North Korea qualified for Round 2

Group D (Bahrain, Hong Kong, India, Lebanon, South Korea)
Matches played in Beirut, Lebanon
Lebanon v India 2–2, Hong Kong v Bahrain 2–1, Bahrain v South Korea 0–0, Lebanon v Hong Kong 2–2, India v Hong Kong 1–2, Lebanon v South Korea 0–1, Lebanon v Bahrain 0–0, India v South Korea 0–3, Hong Kong v South Korea 0–3, Bahrain v India 2–1
Matches played in Seoul, South Korea
South Korea v Hong Kong 3–0, Bahrain v Lebanon 0–0, India v Bahrain 0–3, South Korea v Lebanon 2–0, Hong Kong v Lebanon 1–2, South Korea v India 7–0, India v Lebanon 1–2, Bahrain v Hong Kong 3–0, South Korea v Bahrain 3–0, Hong Kong v India 1–3

	P	W	D	L	F	A	Pts
South Korea	8	7	1	0	22	0	15
Bahrain	8	3	3	2	9	6	9
Lebanon	8	2	4	2	8	9	8
Hong Kong	8	2	1	5	8	18	5
India	8	1	1	6	8	22	3

South Korea qualified for Round 2

Group E (Kuwait, Macao, Malaysia, Saudi Arabia)

Matches played in Kuala Lumpur, Malaysia
Saudi Arabia v Macao 6–0, Malaysia v Kuwait 1–1, Kuwait v Macao 10–1, Malaysia v Saudi Arabia 1–1, Saudi Arabia v Kuwait 0–0, Malaysia v Macao 9–0
Matches played in Riyadh, Saudi Arabia
Malaysia v Kuwait 0–2, Saudi Arabia v Macao 8–0, Macao v Kuwait 0–8, Saudi Arabia v Malaysia 3–0, Malaysia v Macao 5–0, Saudi Arabia v Kuwait 2–0

	P	W	D	L	F	A	Pts
Saudi Arabia	6	4	2	0	20	1	10
Kuwait	6	3	2	1	21	4	8
Malaysia	6	2	2	2	16	7	6
Macao	6	0	0	6	1	46	0

Saudi Arabia qualified for Round 2

Group F (Bangladesh, Japan, Sri Lanka, Thailand, UAE)

Matches played in Tokyo, Japan
Japan v Thailand 1–0, Sri Lanka v UAE 0–4, Japan v Bangladesh 8–0, Thailand v Sri Lanka 1–0, Sri Lanka v Bangladesh 0–1, UAE v Thailand 1–0, Japan v Sri Lanka 5–0, UAE v Bangladesh 1–0, Japan v UAE 2–0, Thailand v Bangladesh 4–1
Matches played in Dubai, UAE
Thailand v Japan 0–1, UAE v Sri Lanka 3–0, Bangladesh v Japan 1–4, Thailand v UAE 1–2, Bangladesh v UAE 0–7, Sri Lanka v Thailand 0–3, Bangladesh v Thailand 1–4, Sri Lanka v Japan 0–6 Bangladesh v Sri Lanka 3–0, UAE v Japan 1–1

	P	W	D	L	F	A	Pts
Japan	8	7	1	0	28	2	15
UAE	8	6	1	1	19	4	13
Thailand	8	4	0	4	13	7	8
Bangladesh	8	2	0	6	7	28	4
Sri Lanka	8	0	0	8	0	26	0

Japan qualified for Round 2

Round 2 (Iran, Iraq, Japan, North Korea, Saudi Arabia, South Korea)

Matches played in Doha, Qatar
North Korea v Iraq 3–2, Saudi Arabia v Japan 0–0, Iran v South Korea 0–3, North Korea v Saudi Arabia 1–2, Japan v Iran 1–2, Iraq v South Korea 2–2, North Korea v Japan 0–3, Iran v Iraq 1–2, South Korea v Saudi Arabia 1–1, Iraq v Saudi Arabia 1–1, Japan v South Korea 1–0, Iran v North Korea 2–1, South Korea v North Korea 3–0, Saudi Arabia v Iran 4–3, Iraq v Japan 2–2

	P	W	D	L	F	A	Pts
Saudi Arabia	5	2	3	0	8	6	7
South Korea	5	2	2	1	9	4	6
Japan	5	2	2	1	7	4	6
Iraq	5	1	3	1	9	9	5
Iran	5	2	0	3	8	11	4
North Korea	5	1	0	4	5	12	2

Saudi Arabia and South Korea qualified

Africa

Round 1
Group A (Algeria, Burundi, Ghana, Uganda)
Uganda withdrew

Algeria v Burundi 3–1, Burundi v Ghana 1–0, Ghana v Algeria 2–0, Burundi v Algeria 0–0, Ghana v Burundi 1–0, Algeria v Ghana 2–1

	P	W	D	L	F	A	Pts
Algeria	4	2	1	1	5	4	5
Ghana	4	2	0	2	4	3	4
Burundi	4	1	1	2	2	4	3

Algeria qualified for Round 2

Group B (Cameroon, Liberia, Swaziland, Zaire)
Liberia withdrew

Cameroon v Swaziland 5–0, Swaziland v Zaire 1–0, Zaire v Cameroon 1–2, Swaziland v Cameroon 0–0, Cameroon v Zaire 0–0, Zaire v Swaziland was not played

	P	W	D	L	F	A	Pts
Cameroon	4	2	2	0	7	1	6
Swaziland	3	1	1	1	1	5	3
Zaire	3	0	1	2	1	3	1

Cameroon qualified for Round 2

Group C (Angola, Egypt, Sierra Leone (Togo), Zimbabwe)

Sierra Leone withdrew and were replaced by Togo

Egypt v Angola 1–0, Zimbabwe v Togo 1–0, Togo v Egypt 1–4, Zimbabwe v Egypt 2–1, Angola v Zimbabwe 1–1, Togo v Zimbabwe 1–2, Angola v Egypt 0–0, Egypt v Togo 3–0, Zimbabwe v Angola 2–1, Egypt v Zimbabwe 2–1 (Result declared void after a protest)

Replay (in Lyons): Egypt v Zimbabwe 0–0, Togo v Angola 0–1, Angola v Togo was not played

	P	W	D	L	F	A	Pts
Zimbabwe	6	4	2	0	8	4	10
Egypt	6	3	2	1	9	3	8
Angola	5	1	2	2	3	4	4
Togo	5	0	0	5	2	11	0

Zimbabwe qualified for Round 2

Group D (Congo, Libya, Nigeria, Sao Tome e Principe, South Africa)

Sao Tome e Principe and Libya withdrew

Nigeria v South Africa 4–0, South Africa v Congo 1–0, Congo v Nigeria 0–1, South Africa v Nigeria 0–0, Congo v South Africa 0–1, Nigeria v Congo 2–0

	P	W	D	L	F	A	Pts
Nigeria	4	3	1	0	7	0	7
South Africa	4	2	1	1	2	4	5
Congo	4	0	0	4	0	5	0

Nigeria qualified for Round 2

Group E (Botswana, Ivory Coast, Niger, Sudan)

Sudan withdrew

Ivory Coast v Botswana 6–0, Niger v Ivory Coast 0–0, Botswana v Niger 0–1, Botswana v Ivory Coast 0–0, Ivory Coast v Niger 1–0, Niger v Botswana 2–1

	P	W	D	L	F	A	Pts
Ivory Coast	4	2	2	0	7	0	6
Niger	4	2	1	1	3	2	5
Botswana	4	0	1	3	1	9	1

Ivory Coast qualified for Round 2

Group F (Ethiopia, Malawi (Benin), Morocco, Tunisia)
Malawi withdrew and were replaced by Benin
Morocco v Ethiopia 5–0, Tunisia v Benin 5–1, Ethiopia v Tunisia 0–0, Benin v
Morocco 0–1, Tunisia v Morocco 1–1, Ethiopia v Benin 3–1, Ethiopia v Morocco
0–1, Benin v Tunisia 0–5, Tunisia v Ethiopia 3–0, Morocco v Benin 5–0, Benin v
Ethiopia 1–0, Morocco v Tunisia 0–0

	P	W	D	L	F	A	Pts
Morocco	6	4	2	0	13	1	10
Tunisia	6	3	3	0	14	2	9
Ethiopia	6	1	1	4	3	11	3
Benin	6	1	0	5	3	19	2

Morocco qualified for Round 2

Group G (Gabon, Mauritania, Mozambique, Senegal)
Mauritania withdrew
Gabon v Mozambique 3–1, Mozambique v Senegal 0–1, Gabon v Senegal 3–2,
Mozambique v Gabon 1–1, Senegal v Mozambique 6–1, Senegal v Gabon 1–0

	P	W	D	L	F	A	Pts
Senegal	4	3	0	1	10	4	6
Gabon	4	2	1	1	7	5	5
Mozambique	4	0	1	3	3	11	1

Senegal qualified for Round 2

Group H (Burkina Faso (Namibia), Madagascar, Tanzania, Zambia)
Tanzania withdrew. Burkina Faso withdrew and were replaced by Namibia
Madagascar v Namibia 3–0, Namibia v Zambia 0–4, Madagascar v Zambia
2–0, Namibia v Madagascar 0–1, Zambia v Namibia 4–0, Zambia v Madagascar
3–1

	P	W	D	L	F	A	Pts
Zambia	4	3	0	1	11	3	6
Madagascar	4	3	0	1	7	3	6
Namibia	4	0	0	4	0	12	0

Zambia qualified for Round 2

Group I (Kenya, Gambia, Guinea, Mali)
Gambia and Mali withdrew
Guinea v Kenya 4–0, Kenya v Guinea 2–0

	P	W	D	L	F	A	Pts
Guinea	2	1	0	1	4	2	2
Kenya	2	1	0	1	2	4	2

Guinea qualified for Round 2

Round 2
Group A (Algeria, Ivory Coast, Nigeria)

Algeria v Ivory Coast 1–1, Ivory Coast v Nigeria 2–1, Nigeria v Algeria 4–1, Ivory Coast v Algeria 1–0, Nigeria v Ivory Coast 4–1, Algeria v Nigeria 1–1

	P	W	D	L	F	A	Pts
Nigeria	4	2	1	1	10	5	5
Ivory Coast	4	2	1	1	5	6	5
Algeria	4	0	2	2	3	7	2

Nigeria qualified

Group B (Morocco, Senegal, Zambia)

Morocco v Senegal 1–0, Zambia v Morocco 2–1, Senegal v Morocco 1–3, Senegal v Zambia 0–0, Zambia v Senegal 4–0, Morocco v Zambia 1–0

	P	W	D	L	F	A	Pts
Morocco	4	3	0	1	6	3	6
Zambia	4	2	1	1	6	2	5
Senegal	4	0	1	3	1	8	1

Morocco qualified

Group C (Cameroon, Guinea, Zimbabwe)

Cameroon v Guinea 3–1, Guinea v Zimbabwe 3–0, Zimbabwe v Cameroon 1–0, Guinea v Cameroon 0–1, Zimbabwe v Guinea 1–0, Cameroon v Zimbabwe 3–1

	P	W	D	L	F	A	Pts
Cameroon	4	3	0	1	7	3	6
Zimbabwe	4	2	0	2	3	6	4
Guinea	4	1	0	3	4	5	2

Cameroon qualified

Oceania

Group 1 (Australia, Solomon Islands, Tahiti)
Solomon Islands v Tahiti 1–1, Solomon Islands v Australia 1–2, Tahiti v Australia 0–3, Australia v Tahiti 2–0, Australia v Solomon Islands 6–1, Tahiti v Solomon Islands 4–2

	P	W	D	L	F	A	Pts
Australia	4	4	0	0	13	2	8
Tahiti	4	1	1	2	5	8	3
Solomon Islands	4	0	1	3	5	13	1

Australia qualified for Final play-off

Group 2 (Fiji, New Zealand, Vanuatu)
New Zealand v Fiji 3–0, Vanuatu v New Zealand 1–4, New Zealand v Vanuatu 8–0, Fiji v Vanuatu 3–0, Fiji v New Zealand 0–0, Vanuatu v Fiji 0–3

	P	W	D	L	F	A	Pts
New Zealand	4	3	1	0	15	1	7
Fiji	4	2	1	1	6	3	5
Vanuatu	4	0	0	4	1	18	0

New Zealand qualified for Final play-off

Final Play-off (Australia, New Zealand)
New Zealand v Australia 0–1, Australia v New Zealand 3–0
Australia won 4–0 on aggregate and met Canada in a play-off

1st Play-off (Australia, Canada)
Canada v Australia 2–1, Australia v Canada 2–1
Australia won 4–1 on penalties and qualified for play-off with Argentina

2nd Play-off (Argentina, Australia)
Australia v Argentina 1–1, Argentina v Australia 1–0
Argentina won 2–1 on aggregate and qualified

1994 UNITED STATES 17 June–17 July

QUALIFIERS

Argentina	Greece	Romania
Belgium	Holland	Russia
Bolivia	Italy	Saudi Arabia
Brazil	Mexico	South Korea
Bulgaria	Morocco	Spain
Cameroon	Nigeria	Sweden
Colombia	Norway	Switzerland
Germany	Republic of Ireland	United States

For the very first time the Tournament moved away from its traditional host continents South America and Europe on to a new North American stage. The United States by and large welcomed the competition with enthusiasm, though the development of football (or soccer as they call it) was still in its infancy. Again there would be twenty-four teams in six groups, sixteen survivors to the knock-out rounds and the drama of penalty shoot-outs awaiting those unable to decide matters in regulation or extra time. As for the organization itself, it was as excellent and thorough as it was expected to be. In so vast a country disruption caused by lengthy travel, no matter how sophisticated, was a concern. Not since the Brazilian event of 1950 would so many miles be clocked up on the road to glory. The United States, the hosts, deemed by comparison with their formidable group opponents a weakling, were in A, confronted at once by a revitalized Switzerland, with quite their best team for a generation; Romania, the European enigma; and Colombia, their South American counterparts considered by many on the strength of an annihilation of Argentina, fragile but worthy favourites. The USA, whilst achieving an occasionally pleasing result, had modest ambitions for their squad, and to succeed even with these, the key players (including Meola, a highly capable goalkeeper, Lalas, an eccentric though rugged centre half and the industrious John Harkes) would need to inspire their colleagues. Switzerland, coached by Londoner Ray Hodgson, were back in the finals for the first time since 1966, and had qualified impressively, with Sforza their pivotal player and Dortmund's Chapuisat further forward offering a considerable threat. Romania, good or bad? Here was a team often brutal in defence and of questionable temperament but undeniably at their breathtaking, audacious best serious challengers to all. Fast and fluid and with the wonderfully cavalier Hagi at their helm, theirs promised, whether short or long in duration, to be an eventful and exciting campaign. Colombia, astonishingly incisive in

Buenos Aires, were controlled masterfully by Valderrama. This was a patient and elegant passing team whose recent record suggested that potency, in the diminutive form of Asprilla, had been discovered to enhance their always attractive football. Indeed, none other than Pelé himself had selected them as the probable winners.

In Group B were another favourite, Brazil, a much weakened Russian team, Cameroon (a revelation four years earlier) and Sweden, eager to atone for their debacle in Italy. The Brazilian coach, Carlos Alberto Parreira, had been scathingly criticized by the nation's media; his team, it was said, reflected his bias toward European-based players and indeed had adopted a more steely and cautious approach. Yet theirs was a team capable of rare and inspirational brilliance, Dunga epitomizing the new European style, while the peerless Romario assisted by Bebeto represented South American artistry at its maverick best. Russia would rely greatly on a newly found team spirit following the withdrawal of the disenchanted mercenaries plying their trade in the West. However, shorn of many established internationals now returned to their new independent countries (Georgia and Ukraine, for example) the loss of Shalimov, Konchelskis et al would be hard to bear. For Cameroon, at last a known quantity, came the opportunity to enhance their reputation as an emerging footballing power. Fearsomely competitive, Libilh, Oman and Kana-Byik would again provide thrust; remarkably Roger Milla also would be present, aged forty-two. One notable absentee was Pagal, ever present at 1990, so incensed by his exclusion that at Orly Airport he met the departing heroes and provoked a fight, in which Henri Michel, the coach and principal object of his vitriol, was struck in the face! Sweden included again the talented Brolin and he, twinned with Martin Dahlin, were looked to, for the goals that would launch their campaign. Behind them came the dreadlocked Larsson. Thern and Schwarz, powerful midfielders remained, with a dependable if sluggish defence.

The Champions, Germany, returned with lofty aspirations and the foundations of their 1990 triumph still in place. Opposing them were Bolivia, back after an absence of forty-four years, South Korea, Asia's finest, and a familiar adversary, Spain, perennial underachievers in Tournament football. Matthäus, inspirational captain and now a sweeper, held Germany's key, supported ably as ever by Buchwald and Kohler, commanding defender, the industrious Hässler in midfield and the predatory Klinsmann, reunited with Völler his partner in attack in 1990. Bolivia, relying largely on the goal-scoring instincts of Ramallo, were an unknown quantity, though in Sanchez and Etcheverry they possessed high-class midfield players. Their qualification at the expense of Uruguay had surprised many and proven them a durable and diligent squad. What of South Korea? They qualified for the third successive time from an increasingly competitive Asian Federation with a team of players no longer confined to their own borders. Joo Sung and Sun-Hong earned their living in Germany's Bundesliga, Hong-Gi was a talented defender, and their goalkeeper In-Young enjoyed a reputation as one of Asia's outstanding players. Spain, with a new team which had qualified comfortably and achieved the not inconsiderable feat of victory in fortress Dublin, had Zubizarreta, the veteran goalkeeper, to provide stability, Guerrero and Caminero industry, and Salinas and Luis Enrique goals in Spain's one area of concern since the departure of the mighty Butragueño.

In Group D Argentina faced the interesting prospect of Nigeria's 'Super Eagles' and Balkan neighbours Bulgaria and Greece. Maradona was back for Argentina, a veteran now, yet still a talisman for a talented but often destructive force; Caniggia, banned for a year for drug abuse, would be back to aid him, as was Balbo and the gifted Batistuta, both playing their football in Italy's Serie A. Nigeria came to the Tournament fresh from success in the African Nations Cup, supremely confident of launching a lengthy campaign; Oliseh and Okocha (considered by Pelé the potential star of the competition) would give direction and purpose, Amokachi and Ikpeka, the thrust. The darkest of horses, some pundits believed Africa could perhaps be celebrating an unlikely victory in Los Angeles on 7 July. Greece would enjoy their first competition in the country's long and colourful football history, though how much was open to question. Deserved qualifiers, their subsequent form had been poor, confidence undermined by a savaging from England at Wembley; still, they were a neat, competent team, with Tassos Mitropoulos at thirty-six looked to for inspiration. Bulgaria, so regularly qualifiers and so often disappointing, came this time with reason for optimism; Hristo Stoichkov, moody but magnificent, was their spearhead, supported by Kostadinov and Sirakov in attack, and prompted by Balakov and Lechkov from the midfield area. Theirs had the look of a well balanced if not exceptional team.

Group E offered a mouth-watering proposition with Italy, the aristocrats, facing the powerful twin assault of Ireland and Norway, both strong willed, capable and immensely difficult to beat. Adding Mexico to the equation, elegant, confident and a far more formidable prospect than in previous years, and the possibilities in this toughest of all groups appeared endless. The Italians, whose club side Milan were proving so dominant in European competition, boasted Baresi, Costacurta, Tassoti and Maldini, fine defenders from that triumphant team, and in Roberto Baggio they possessed arguably the most gifted individual in world football. Ireland arrived with their reputation enhanced by wins in both Germany and Holland, remarkable achievements both. Feet firmly on the ground yet with expectation high, they approached the Tournament as a team growing in conviction and confidence. Norway, considered hard sterile and direct, conceded little and had proven, as England had found to their cost, steadfastly resolute. Venturing forward themselves, Fjørtoft and Flo would be relied on to provide the goals that in a tight group would make the difference. Mexico, so poor in preparation when suffering heavy defeats to both Switzerland and Russia, remained a threat; neat and patient, their defensive frailties could be negated by an inventive and incisive forward line led by the veteran Hugo Sanchez and his young protégé Luis Garcia, and in the flamboyant Campos they had an inspired though somewhat eccentric goalkeeper.

In Group F, Holland were without Gullit, who had stayed at home, it was said, to sulk, and Van Basten, perennially injured and in decline. Theirs was still a fine young team that had accounted somewhat controversially for England in qualification. Rijkaard, Koeman, the de Boer twins and Bergkamp would provide industry and influence, but concern remained over Bergkamp's poor form in Serie A for Internazionale. Belgium again would oppose them, as experienced a squad in World Cup terms as any of the entrants. Scifo, Van der Elst, Grün, Preud'homme and Degryse offered much needed nous and in Weber, with six goals in two friendlies, it was hoped they had discovered a cutting edge to their resolute and disciplined approach. Morocco, another of Africa's representatives, had amassed a wealth of experience from their two previous campaigns on the American continent where they had performed ably against the world's elite. Moreover, their schedule offering fixtures against both of their European rivals in the heat of Orlando would be much to their liking. They would not be overawed. Finally, Saudi Arabia, another making their debut in the Tournament, unsung and considered by many pampered by fixtures largely played at home, were both vibrant and proficient, Al Muwallid a gifted playmaker and Majed Mohammed 'the Desert Pelé' ready and able to take advantage of complacency.

Venues: New York, Orlando, Washington, Chicago, Boston, Dallas, Los Angeles, San Francisco, Detroit

Group A

Colombia
Romania
Switzerland
United States

Group D

Argentina
Bulgaria
Greece
Nigeria

Group B

Brazil
Cameroon
Russia
Sweden

Group C

Bolivia
Germany
Spain
South Korea

Group E

Italy
Mexico
Norway
Republic of Ireland

Group F

Belgium
Holland
Morocco
Saudi Arabia

THE FIRST SERIES

It fell to Germany, the holders, to open the Tournament in Chicago after the familiar extravagant ceremonies, their opponents Bolivia. On a hot afternoon the Germans finally prevailed over the self-assured and competent South Americans, though not without difficulty. Forced to defend in depth, the Bolivians sat back, patiently allowing Germany to dictate and breaking imaginatively but without real purpose. On the hour the decisive moment came: Hässler advanced, beating the off-side trap on the left, drew Trucco from Bolivia's goal and rolled the ball to the unmarked Klinsmann. A simple goal; thereafter the Germans threatened sporadically, and Bolivia, galvanized momentarily by the appearance of Etcheverry as substitute, responded without success, their fate sealed when Etcheverry completed his remarkable cameo with a sulky kick at Matthäus and received a red card.

In Dallas, also in Group C, Spain sauntered into a two-goal lead provided to them by Goicoechea and Salinas, then relaxed their effort fatally. Cue the revival as the Koreans inspired by Choi Yung Il lifted themselves, astonishingly saving the game with two goals from Seo Jung-Won and Hong Myung Bo as the horrified Spaniards looked on disbelievingly, unable to raise their game again.

The United States opened in the Pontiac Silverdrome before 73,000 enthusiastic patrons, undeterred by 100 ºF heat and a Swiss team of considerable reputation. They deservedly earned their point, defending stoutly and sensibly, and countering to great effect. Unfortunately, they had to recover from Bregy's fierce free kick that defeated Meola, giving Switzerland an early lead, Wynalda though equalized, scoring exquisitely after Sforza had hauled down Harkes twenty-five yards out. 'If we had held our lead to half-time I think we would have won,' moaned Swiss coach Ray Hodgson afterwards. 'We're still alive,' commented Boris Milutinovich, his American counterpart somewhat gloomily, though in truth his team, had Harkes not spurned a free close-range header, may have stolen unexpected victory.

Colombia, skilful and operating, as ever, their intricate passing movements, did so to no great effect in Los Angeles. They allowed Hagi the freedom to rampage around the field creating havoc, and were beaten comprehensively to the surprise of most experts. Under pressure and starved of the ball for fifteen minutes, Romania promptly stole both it and the lead, demonstrating the one talent their opponents lacked. Hagi's incisive pass sent in Raducioiu, who swerved past two defenders to fire home. With the pattern set, so it continued, Colombia probing patiently, Romania counterattacking with cunning. Hagi's genius created a second goal for them, an extraordinary chip from an impossible angle, bewildering Cordoba in the South American goal. To their credit the disconsolate Colombians refused to give up the ghost, laying siege to Stelea's goal. Valencia met Perez's corner for a header of stunning simplicity, but thereafter their efforts were frustrated by disciplined defending and inspired goalkeeping. One minute from time Hagi and Raducioiu combined again, the quicksilver forward guiding his shot for a third conclusive goal.

In Group E at New York's Giants Stadium another large crowd turned up to witness the clash between Ireland and Italy, two nations with huge communities within the United States. The Irish, roared on lustily by a horde estimated at 50,000 and swathed in green, won the day, triumphing once more against the odds. McGrath was dominant in defence, nullifying the subtle promptings of Signori and constantly arriving at precisely the right time to frustrate Baggio. Harrying and hastening the Italians, Ireland pressed home the advantage their energetic efforts brought them, Staunton shooting wide in ten seconds and then Houghton on twelve minutes spectacularly striking the goal. Costacurta, harassed by Coyne, headed in the direction of Baresi, whose lazy clearance was seized by the Liverpool man, controlled quickly with a chest trap and struck sweetly goalward. Pagliuca, off his line, watched, hopelessly beaten as the volley looped up over his head and into the net. Delirium. Ireland, in control on and off the field, persisted. Houghton was foiled by Pagliuca on a second occasion and Sheridan fired a shot against the crossbar as the disenchanted Italians struggled to stem the flow, Signori going closest for them, denied acrobatically. At the end, two-thirds of the crowd left in rapture and the blue third filed away in dejected silence. 'My wife and children were in the stadium and I looked for them but I couldn't see them,' said the goalscorer Houghton, 'I thought it was a dream.' Back home in Italy, the Italian media wished it had been. 'Betrayal,' screamed *Corriere Dellosport*, 'A legendary fiasco,' claimed *La Stampa*. Italy clearly would have to improve.

In Washington at the R.F.K. Stadium, Mexico provided craft and invention but lacked the pace to unsettle Norway, and lost out to stronger, physically superior opponents at the death. Generally dominant, the Scandinavians proved wasteful; Fjørtoft 'scored' to be ruled off-side, then found himself through again, only to be denied by the athletic Campos. Worse followed as Bratseth, free and with Campos stranded, contrived to head woefully wide. Zague for Mexico almost punished them with a header as their controlled passing bore dividends before Norway returned to attack, Fjørtoft missing again before finally Rekdal stole through to beat Mexico's colourful goalkeeper from close range on 84 minutes. At 1–0, that was almost it, though Zague again made a nuisance of himself, another header striking the post in injury time, before in the ensuing scramble Berg blocked a second effort. Norway had won, just, but contributed greatly to their own anxieties.

Brazil opened their account in the Stanford Stadium, San Francisco, despatching an impoverished Russia 2–0 without ever producing the antici-pated fireworks. Romario and Bebeto, guilty of overelaboration, missed when they might have scored, before Tsymbalar woke them from their lethargy, his fiercely struck effort smothered by the grateful Taffarel. Thereafter the passive Russians retreated, surrendering time and space in pursuit of damage limita-tion. Romario broke through first, skipping impishly away from his marker to direct Bebeto's inswinger corner in at the far post on 30 minutes. Greatly encouraged, the South Americans showed considerable urgency. Bebeto shot over the bar before Romario again contributed decisively; the little man, spin-ning away from one defender and flicking the ball past Ternavski, was sent sprawling. Rai duly placed the penalty kick past Kharine. The sea of yellow and green in the stadium celebrated jubilantly and Brazil finally found their fluent rhythmic passing game, threatening a rout. That they did not owed more to Russia's policy of sly and often crude fouling; however, at the end Romario did seize on an opportunity created by Bebeto to be thwarted by the excellent Kharine.

The second Group B match at Los Angeles saw Cameroon and Sweden clash unremarkably in the Rose Bowl and witnessed relief for both as defeat was avoided. Cameroon started nervously and Ljung, with a far post header, punished their hesitancy. As ever, the Africans responded positively. Embe forced home on the half-hour after Sweden's defence failed to clear, and then Omam-Byik, back on the world stage, gave them the lead, stealing between Ravelli and Andersson to crash the ball into the net. But Sweden saved them-selves and deservedly so: Bell reacted acrobatically and turned Larsson's shot on to the bar but was helpless to prevent Dahlin sweeping home the rebound.

Holland in Group F prevailed at the R.F.K against Saudi Arabia, though theirs was an unconvincing effort and a fortunate win. Warned within a minute by the leap of Majed Mohammed whose header flew wide, the Dutch were constantly exposed by the swift, uninhibited counters of an Arab team delighting in its role of underdog. Overmars and Roy raided the flanks, giving Holland width, and Rikjaard, arriving for one teasing cross, headed the first of a series of wasted chances tamely at Al Deayea, the Saudi keeper. Then suddenly, the earlier warnings unheeded, Holland fell behind with another high cross, more indecision and sloppy marking, and Amin's header crashed into an unguarded net. Responding with alacrity, Koeman providing impetus, the Dutch surged forward but their shooting remained awry, whilst the Saudis, with pace and deliberation, caused great discomfort to their overextended defenders. Jonk finally powered home an equalizer that had looked increasingly unlikely, before, in a last gasp finale, Taument the substitute answered Dutch prayers with a free and easy header on 87 minutes. Desperately disappointed, the Saudis had lost with great honour. In Orlando at the Citrus Bowl high humidity and a determined Moroccan team could and should have defeated Belgium, who, given a lead after eleven minutes by a beautifully timed header from Marc Degryse, wilted visibly in the fierce Floridian sunshine, Mohammed Chaouch twice hitting the crossbar for the desperately unlucky Africans. 'We can thank the heavens,' said Belgian coach Van Himst afterwards, acknowledging his team's good fortune. 'They were a much stronger team than we expected. The humidity here is a real problem, it's a killer.'

In Group D, Argentina roared into Boston firing on all cylinders and demolished the modest Greeks as they wished. Inspired by the sprightly little veteran Maradona, the South Americans scored in a minute, the fleet-footed Batistuta shooting through the legs of Minou whose frustration was evident. Poor Minou; the die was now cast, and nobly though he tried to stem the procession bearing down on his goal, he was beaten again before the interval, Batistuta again reacting quickest after Chamot had broken through the bewildered Greek defence. Maradona made it 3–0, curling his shot deliciously into the net after a series of short sharp passes on the hour before Batistuta completed his hat trick and the Europeans' misery from a penalty kick given rather harshly against Apostolakis for hand ball near the end. At 4–0, for Maradona, substituted seven minutes from time, there was the rapturous acclaim of an appreciative audience. Faced by a stubborn, strong-looking Bulgarian team in Dallas, Nigeria's 'Super Eagles' made an astonishing Tournament debut, beating their ultimately demoralized opponents utterly in the Cotton Bowl. Perhaps Hristo Stoichkov's free kick 'equalizer' disallowed – it had been awarded as indirect – may have revived failing Bulgarian spirits. But thereafter, behind already to Yekini's 21st minute effort, they capitulated; Amokachi, stumbling, recovered to prod a second past Mikhailov before the interval, Amunike adding a third in the second half, racing through a startled defence to place a firm, diving header into the Bulgarian net for 3–0. Nigeria had undoubtedly arrived.

THE SECOND SERIES

In Chicago, Germany, cautious and largely outplayed by a more inventive and enterprising Spanish team, fought back from conceding an early goal and held on for a draw they scarcely deserved. Spain, beginning brightly and with Caminero the game's single greatest influence, created bewildering passing patterns and exploited a lack of pace in the German ranks which saw Sergi first denied by Illgner before Goicoechea fluked an outrageous goal on the quarter-hour. His harmless looking cross deceived the German goalkeeper in flight, dropping in off the inside of the far post for 1–0. Early in the second half and against the flow, Klinsmann stole an equalizer heading down into the turf from Hässler's promising cross, the ball bounced hard, leaping sharply upward and surprising Zubizarreta. Drawing 1–1 when having come so close to winning, Spain contrived almost to lose it at the last. Klinsmann, with two minutes left, raced on to Effenberg's inviting pass but fired wide. Defeat would have been too cruel to contemplate for a team who, try as they did through the valiant Hierro, could not conjure a second goal. Bolivia playing Korea in the Foxboro Stadium, Boston, and managed for the second time to finish with ten men, Cristaldo sent off nine minutes from the end for an undisciplined lunge, though here at least they clung on desperately for a 0–0 draw. The Asians, much the better team in a dreary game, spurned a hatful of chances, Hwang blazing over in the tenth minute, the worst and most prolific offender, his failure to shoot accurately with Trucco out of his goal at the half-hour condemning the Koreans to their second successive draw.

Group A and Romania in Detroit showed the other side of their character against the obdurate and pacey Swiss, and fell apart, a shambles quite unrecognizable from the team that had destroyed the Colombians in the Pasadena Rose Bowl. Adrian Knup, absent against the United States, returned to wreak havoc. Sutter, though denied by an off-side flag on twelve minutes, brought Switzerland their opener just three minutes later, rifling in Chapuisat's subtle lay off, and while the imperious Hagi struck home a fine equalizer, the Swiss, ignoring the heat, carried the game to Romania, seeking to press home their obvious advantage. Chapuisat made it 2–1 after a dreadful hash had been made of Ohrel's cross, and then Knup took over, first rolling Sforza's cross over the line and then in the 73rd minute ducking low at the near post to glance Bregy's free kick into the Romanian net. Down 4–1 there was still time for the disconsolate Romanians to heap further ignominy on themselves, Viadiou being dismissed for a quite disgraceful hack at Ohrel. The scale of Romania's defeat by the end was comprehensive and truly shocking. In Pasadena once again the Colombians played lamentably and were punished emphatically by an American team full of passion and purpose. Rocked by an own goal when Escobar tragically intercepted a Harkes cross and directed it past his own goalkeeper, Colombia fell further behind only minutes into the second half when Stewart won a race with Perea and Cardoba to steer the ball home 2–0. There was no urgency from the lethargic South Americans, their goal from Valencia in the last minute no more than consolation; 2–1 and the USA were unlikely winners in this topsy-turvy group. From the camp of the troubled Colombians, there were sinister rumours of a squad undermined by death threats from home.

In New York, faced with adversity, Italy triumphed courageously over a Norwegian team lacking ambition. Their goal fashioned by Signori's cross was completed by Dino Baggio's thumping header from close in on 68 minutes; for Norway it was a massive disappointment. Playing ten men after Italian goalkeeper Pagliuca was sent off for a reckless challenge on Leonhardsen, they forced one effort over the line. Disallowed for a foul. Few were sympathetic; theirs had been a deplorably negative effort.

Ireland, in withering heat measured at 120 °F, lost miserably in Florida to the fast and skilful Mexico revelling in familiar conditions. In a furiously competitive first half, Staunton fired wide for the Irish, and Sheridan with a stooping header was denied by Campos, resplendent in his psychedelic kit. Mexico, too, threatened intermittently before Luis Garcia broke the deadlock, cutting across the penalty area to beat Bonner with a hard, low drive a minute from the interval. Worse for Ireland followed: three times Campos denied them before Garcia again collected Aspe's cross to fire a second, startling goal. Bonner quick off his line denied the alert Mexican his hat-trick before Aldridge reached McAteer's precise cross with a glorious header to bring the Irish hope and set up a frenzied assault on the Mexican goal for the final seven minutes. Jack Charlton, Ireland's coach, while recognizing the difficult conditions afterwards, paid tribute to Mexico. 'I'm not blaming the heat; we had to work harder than we ever had to work and were beaten by a very good team.

Brazil, beginning in unanimously languid style, found their form as Cameroon finally sought to venture out from behind their sandbags, and dispatched the Africans with ease. Troubled first on the half-hour in quick succession by both MFede and Embe, finally the Brazilians discovered the creativity they craved. Romario, again the rapier, burst between two Africans to slip the ball beyond the advancing Bell. Down 1–0 at the interval, a steep hill to climb became insurmountable on the hour as Songo'o hacked at Bebeto on the right wing and received a red card. The game swiftly went away from them, Santos guiding Jorginho's cross in for 2–0 and the rampaging Brazilians pressed hard, their fluidity fully restored, Bebeto shooting a third goal, a hard, low drive 16 minutes from time. Brazil continued to improve whilst suspicion abounded that Cameroon, so effective in 1990, were in decline. In Detroit, Sweden, a goal behind in four minutes to Russia, recovered in style to destroy a team forced to play almost all of the second half with ten players, Dahlin the orchestrator. Salenko's penalty after Ljung's indiscreet foul gave the Russians hope, but Brolin equalized in similar fashion after Dahlin had been manhandled, and when Gorlukovich was dismissed, Dahlin again had a hand, he being the victim of a wild tackle from behind. Not content with his role, Dahlin headed the Swedes ahead on the hour and then powered in a third to settle matters. Russia's misery, compounded by Radchenko's late 'goal' being disallowed, was complete.

Argentina met Nigeria and outlasted them in an exciting, often rugged, encounter in Boston. The Nigerians, open and instinctive, began where they had left off against Bulgaria, playing in vibrant rhythmic fashion and took the lead deservedly, Yekini feeding Siasia who beat Ruggeri with a body swerve and clipped the ball cheekily over the head of Islas and into the Argentine net for 1–0. Argentina responded, keeping possession for long periods whilst the Africans pursued them fruitlessly, Caniggia twice scoring as the South Americans restored the proper order before half-time. At the end, whilst neither had committed fully, the Nigerians were beaten, though not without demonstrating considerable potential. For Argentina, Redondo, a busy midfielder, was emerging from the shadow of Maradona, whilst the little man himself, shorn of the pace and audacity of 1986, remained a player of razor sharp awareness and surprising stamina. 'I am beaten up all over,' he said alluding in the aftermath to the Nigerians' rough treatment of him.

Poor Greece, so overwhelmed by Argentina they now plunged into further disaster against Balkan neighbours Bulgaria. Stoichkov sparked the rout, twice converting penalties before Lechkov, after a one-two with Ivanov, added a third. The Greeks, thoroughly demoralized, could not compete with the slick passing and movement of a much improved Bulgarian team, and Borimirov added to their misery in the last minute. At the end the Bulgarians were delirious and with good reason; remarkably this was their first win in eighteen finals matches spanning thirty-two years!

In Group F, Saudi Arabia became the second beneficiaries of Morocco's wayward finishing, beating them courtesy of Al-Jaber's early penalty and Filad Amin's colossal thirty-yard effort on the stroke of half-time. In between times the Africans largely ran the game, though Chaouch scoring in 28 minutes was their scant reward. Frustratingly for the Moroccans, the second half proved similarly unprofitable, their nimble football ruined by hurried and wasteful shooting, and Arabia's inspired rearguard action. 'Thank Allah for our goalkeeper,' said captain Abdul Jawad at the end. Morocco, a good team without a cutting edge, would not.

In a leisurely contest played out in the Florida sunshine, Belgium and Holland served up an action-packed encounter for the patrons at the Citrus Bowl. The Dutch, with their strolling passing movements playing in their own inimitable way, created the greater chances, but for all of Rijkaard's panache and subtlety and the menace of Bergkamp, all were squandered. The Belgians carved out a succession of their own, with a similar lack of success, until Weber's jump confused the Dutch defence, allowing Albert to guide the winner beneath Wouters. No greater urgency displayed, Holland went down, and though the suspicion remained that both teams had coasted, Belgium, patient and stubborn defensively, aided by Scifo's ability to launch swift counters, appeared better suited to the unfamiliar tropical climate.

THE THIRD SERIES

In Pasadena the final act of Group A took place, as Romania, threatened with elimination, revived their fortunes and defeated the United States with little difficulty. The Americans, urged on by a huge crowd, huffed and puffed without penetration, their efforts falling on the central defensive rock of Prodan and Belodedici. For Romania, both patient and potent, Petrescu put through by Raducioiu's clever pass, finished emphatically. Conserving energy in temperatures souring to 115 ºF, they strolled to victory, their invention still proving the more likely source of a further goal. Colombia finally displayed the undoubted talent that had warranted their inclusion as favourites, beating Switzerland, evidently already content with their efforts in qualifying. Marco Pascolo denied the elegant South Americans a rout, but Gaviria with a close range header and Lozano, a substitute, confirmed victory with a last minute second. For Switzerland there was a place in Washington in the second series, whilst Colombia served only to underline their potential when their fate was sealed. Elimination ensued for Valderrama and company, a team wholly undermined by chaotic political wranglings at home, amid allegations of match fixing and the influence of drug barons.

In Dallas, Germany stumbled through, if without authority, against South Korea. Hampered by horribly naive defending and inept goalkeeping by their captain Choi, the Asians staged another monumental recovery, almost re-enacting their fierce fightback against Spain. Almost, but not quite. Germany, beginning the brighter, took the lead. Klinsmann received Hässler's pass and, allowed time, spun to shoot home. For Korea more calamity followed: Choi misjudged Buchwald's weak effort and watched in horror as the ball ricocheted off the post to the grateful Riedle. Cho and Kim forced Illgner to athletic saves as Korea belatedly mounted their challenge, though Choi, in allowing Klinsmann's shot to slip through him for 3–0, had seemingly undone them. Remarkably, in the second half they surged forward, perhaps given heart by the replacement of Choi by substitute custodian Lee. Hwang brought them

hope, chipping Park's through pass over Illgner for 3–1, and Hong with astonishing velocity drove in from thirty-five yards for 3–2. Playing now with the
authority and conviction normally associated with their illustrious opponents,
the Koreans ploughed forward in pursuit of an equalizer; it did not come.
Floundering, exhausted at the end, the Germans kept them out, and Korea,
with considerable honour, were eliminated. Spain, increasingly assured, swept
past Bolivia in Chicago, though in doing so lost Caminero, a major influence,
as he was awarded a second yellow card for their next match. The Bolivians
began forcefully, Ramallo a constant thorn in the Spaniards' side, striking the
post after two minutes. Thereafter, Spain quietly assumed control. After ten
minutes, a flowing movement terminated by a combined assault on Felipe by
Borja and Pena resulted in a penalty slotted in by Guardiola. In the second half
Caminero applied the killer blows: first hitting a post, he redeemed himself
moments later, slipping Sergi's astute pass underneath Trucco for 2–0. Bolivia
gamely fought on, inspired by Sanchez and Ramallo, Sanchez firing a speculative shot that deflected off the bewildered Voro to deceive Zubizarretta to
reduce the deficit, before Caminero completed his day's work, chesting down
Ferrer's cross and hammering the ball past a bemused Trucco. Ending 3–1,
Spain progressed full of hope, whilst Bolivia left the competition with hard lessons to learn.

In Group E in New York and Washington four anxious teams peered over
the precipice of failure. In an inglorious first half at the R.F.K., Italy and
Mexico, nerves betraying them, played cautiously, spellbound by the fear of
error and the prospect of elimination. Massaro dramatically changed matters
moments after arriving as a second-half substitute. Positive, where before all
had been negative, the Milan striker seized on Albertini's pass, bearing down
on goal and shooting firmly beneath the despairing Campos. Italy belatedly
came to life, Massaro again leaping, this time to head threateningly. Italy's
ambition, however, expired quickly as Mexico found a lifeline, Signori making
a hash of Hermosillo's innocuous pass, Bernal accepting the gift with aplomb.

At 1–1, there it stayed, though Mexico, encouraged, played to the end with
great freedom and thrust, rampaging down on a tired and harassed 'Azzurri'
rearguard. The Italians had been fortunate but coach Sacchi waiting now for
results that would decide their fate thought otherwise. 'We deserve to advance,
we played three strong opponents and held our own.'

In the first half in New York was more pitifully sterile football, with Norway
packing defence in search of a draw, while Ireland, invited to take the initiative,
did so only sporadically. The Irish came closest, Townsend and Sheridan both
missing acceptable chances. For Norway, more positive in the second half,
Rekdal provided menace with spectacular shooting. But by the end, as the
arithmetic was done, they learned that their stalemate had not been enough.
An unimaginative and poor campaign was at an end.

Cameroon, needing a convincing victory over the fast fading Russians, fell swiftly behind in debilitating fashion and collapsed to embarrassing defeat; neither would progress. Salenko, the Valencia striker, exploiting space and uncharacteristically generous African defending, ran amok, seizing five goals and a place in World Cup history books. Behind 3–0 to a Salenko hat-trick at half-time, the remarkable Milla, now forty-three years old, offered Cameroon a glimpse of salvation two minutes after the interval, though Salenko with rapier-like incisiveness, closed the door firmly on their prospects, his fourth and fifth goals in a three-minute spell in the final quarter. Beaten comprehensively and thoroughly disenchanted, Cameroon stumbled from the pitch disbelievingly, but not before Dimitry Radchenko had added a sixth to Russia's total and deepened their gloom.

In Detroit, Brazil faced a patient, organized Swedish side prepared to defend with calm for long periods. Unable to instigate their fluid creative passing with any success, the South Americans were further frustrated by Brolin. Lively throughout, he picked out the gangling Andersson with a searching crossfield ball. Suddenly in disarray, Mauro Silva lunged in too late as the tall Swede directed his shot beyond Taffarel. Threatened, the Brazilians replied predictably, Dunga and Romario firing in long shots that Ravelli repelled. Finally Romario struck, gliding past Schwarz and Larsson to shoot in at a narrow angle. Finishing 1–1, Sweden's effort was commendable and achieved without Dahlin. Brazil was left to contemplate still more formidable challenges ahead.

In Washington, fatigued by the heat, Belgium went behind to a sensational goal in just five minutes and were beaten by the Saudis. For the Belgians the disappointment of defeat was accentuated by the task it condemned them to – Orlando, hotter and more draining still, and the prospect of a demanding though as yet undecided opponent. It might have been different. Chances came and went, squandered chiefly by Weber and Wilmots, against obdurate opponents quick to counter-attack in strength-sapping conditions far more to their liking. The goal that proved decisive was an astonishing piece of individualism scored by Owairan and from the Maradona School of Audacity. Collecting the ball deep in his own half, he ploughed forward, accelerating past Medved, swerving around De Wolf, racing towards goal, beating Schmidts before steering the ball past Albert's lunge and beyond the groping Preud'homme. Stunning. At the end coach Solari reminded all of his pre-Tournament prophecy, 'I told you we would get to second place. Here today we did what we promised you!' Belgium's Van Himst could not conceal his gloom. 'It was a catastrophic second half for us, the way the heat affected our players. It's going to be very tough for us to play Germany or Argentina.' Soon he would discover it would be the Germans.

Holland squeezed by the willing Moroccans, but, as ever, the Africans acquitted themselves with distinction. Bergkamp gave the Dutch the lead, taking over from Van Vossen to cleverly chip Alaoui in the Moroccan goal. After the interval, Nader stunned them with an equalizer, and at home in the conditions they pressed for further glory, De Goey brilliantly denying a Daoudi free kick. Struggling with persistent opponents and tiring visibly, the Dutch, not for the first time, found a lifeline in a crisis, Bergkamp feeding Bryan Roy, who drove in from eight yards. At 2–1 the Europeans had looked distinctly ill at ease.

The sensation of the Tournament sadly did not come as a moment of breathtaking skill or a courageous resolute stand by the small against the mighty. Instead Maradona, already a figure of controversy and loathed by so many, disgraced himself further, and in doing so cast a shadow that threatened even to undermine and engulf his own formidable genius.

As Argentina prepared in Dallas for their final group match, shocking developments began to undermine their campaign as news filtered through that a player at the Nigerian game in Chicago had tested positive for a banned stimulant. Quickly, as the Press descended, the Argentinean Football Association moved to protect themselves. Maradona, with a history of drug abuse and the media's chief 'suspect', was withdrawn from their team and effectively 'thrown to the wolves'. Dr Pablo Abbatangelo explained the decision had been taken ahead of the results of the second, corroborating urine sample, 'to avoid more serious sanctions from FIFA'. Maradona, it was reported, had taken ephedrine, a drug that quickens the heartbeat and increases the flow of blood to the muscles, though later a medical report from the Sports Administrating Body revealed 'a cocktail of drugs', all stimulants. For all of his denials, the little man, the greatest footballing talent for thirty years, cut a forlorn and tragic figure, shorn of his crown, his dignity and the adulation, shamed publicly and certain to be banished from a game synonymous with his name.

Maradona often courting controversy had always been forgiven, his genius on the pitch always his salvation. Now at the very end his obvious vulnerabilities had betrayed him and he left this great stage to derision, portrayed as corrupt and a cheat. Sadly, while few in the history of football have been so admired, still fewer have proven so deeply unpopular.

In the aftermath of the Maradona fiasco Argentina predictably suffered a loss of form. Perhaps more surprising still, the buoyant Bulgarians proved good enough to take full advantage, winning 2–0 and qualifying ahead of the South Americans in the process. Initially treating the Argentines' lethargy with extreme suspicion, the Bulgarians slowly gained control and once encouraged they never relinquished it, Stoichkov almost providing Sirakov with a goal from a clever chip before Kostadinov, surging through, was smothered by the alert Islas. In the second half the threat constantly posed by Stoichkov finally bore dividends as the temperamental striker tore through to score on the hour.

At 1–0 Argentina, not without some provocation, reverted to their dark side. Bulgaria joined the battle with relish, resulting ultimately in the dismissal of Tzvetanov. It hardly mattered, as Argentina, clearly demoralized, could find no inspiration, and Sirakov scoring in the last minute rubbed salt in their considerable wounds. Nigeria, recovering from their defeat by Argentina, beat Greece 2–0 with ease in a dull match often played at half pace. For all of Nigeria's evident superiority, the Greeks might have saved themselves, their concentration crucially betraying them in the last minute of each half, Finidi and the bullish Amokachi giving Africa a representative in the Second Stage and a Group winner at that. The Greeks' debut had proven a most miserable experience.

Final Tournament – USA
First round

Group A

USA (1) **1, Switzerland** (1) **1**
18.6.94 DETROIT
USA: Meola, Kooiman, Balboa, Lalas, Caligiuri, Ramos, Dooley, Sorber, Wynalda (1) (Wegerle), Harkes, Stewart (Jones)
Switzerland: Pascolo, Hottiger, Herr, Geiger, Quentin, Ohrel, Bregy (1), Sforza (Wyss), Sutter, Bickel (Subiat), Chapuisat
Referee: Lamolina (Argentina)

Colombia (1) **1, Romania** (2) **3**
18.6.94 LOS ANGELES
Colombia: Cordoba, Herrera, Perea, Escobar, Perez, Alvarez, Valderrama, Rincon, Gomez, Asprilla, Valencia (1)
Romania: Stelea, Belodedici, Prodan, Mihali, Petrescu, Lupescu, Popescu, Hagi (1), Munteanu, Dumitrescu (Selymes), Raducioiu (2) (Papura)
Referee: Al Sharif (Syria)

Romania (1) **1, Switzerland** (1) **4**
22.6.94 DETROIT
Romania: Stelea, Belodedici, Prodan, Mihali, Petrescu, Lupescu (Panduru), Popescu, Munteanu, Hagi (1), Dumitrescu (Vladiou), Raducioiu
Switzerland: Pascolo, Hottiger, Herr, Geiger, Quentin, Ohrel (Sylvestre), Bregy, Sforza, Sutter (1) (Bickel), Knup (2), Chapuisat (1)
Referee: Jouini (Tunisia)

USA (1) **2, Colombia** (0) **1**
24.6.94 LOS ANGELES
USA: Meola, Balboa, Clavijo, Lalas, Caligiuri, Ramos, Harkes, Dooley, Sorber, Stewart (1) (Jones), Wynalda (Wegerle)
Colombia: Cordoba, Perez, Perea, Escobar (o.g.), Herrera, Alvarez, Valderrama, Rincon, Gaviria, Asprilla (Valencia (1)), De Avila (Valenciano)
Referee: Baldas (Italy)

USA (0) **0, Romania** (1) **1**
26.6.94 LOS ANGELES
USA: Meola, Clavijo, Balboa, Lalas, Caligiuri, Harkes, Dooley, Ramos (Jones), Sorber (Wegerle), Stewart, Wynalda
Romania: Prunea, Belodedici (Mihali), Petrescu (1), Selymes, Lupescu, Prodan, Hagi, Popescu, Munteanu, Dumitrescu, Raducioiu (Galca)
Referee: Van der Ende (Holland)

Switzerland (0) **0, Colombia** (1) **2**
28.6.94 SAN FRANCISCO
Switzerland: Pascolo, Hottiger, Herr, Geiger, Quentin, Ohrel, Bregy, Sforza, Sutter (Subiat), Knup (Grassi), Chapuisat
Colombia: Cordoba, Herrera, Mendoza, Escobar, Perez, Gaviria (1) (Lozano (1)), Alvarez, Valderrama, Rincon, Valencia (De Avila), Asprilla
Referee: Mikkelsen (Denmark)

	P	W	D	L	F	A	Pts
Romania	3	2	0	1	5	5	5
Switzerland	3	1	1	1	5	4	4
USA	3	1	1	1	3	3	4
Colombia	3	1	0	2	4	5	3

Group B
Cameroon (1) **2, Sweden** (1) **2**
20.6.94 LOS ANGELES
Cameroon: Bell, Song-Bahanag, MBouh, Kalla-Nkongo, Tataw, Libiih, MFede (Maboang-Kessack), Foe, Agbo, Omam-Byik (1), Embe (1) (Mouyeme)
Sweden: Ravelli, Nilsson, Andersson P, Björklund, Ljung (1), Ingesson (Andersson K), Thern, Schwarz, Blomqvist (Larsson), Brolin, Dahlin (1)
Referee: Tejada (Peru)

Brazil (1) **2, Russia** (0) **0**
20.6.94 SAN FRANCISCO
Brazil: Taffarel, Jorginho, Ricardo Rocha (Aldair), Marcio Santos, Leonardo, Dunga (Mazinho), Rai (1 pen), Mauro Silva, Zinho, Bebeto, Romario (1)
Russia: Kharine, Nikiforov, Khlestov, Ternavski, Gorlukovich, Karpin, Kuznetsov, Piatnitski, Radchenko (Borodyuk), Tsymbalar, Yuran (Salenko)
Referee: Lim Kee Chong (Mauritius)

Brazil (1) **3, Cameroon** (0) **0**
24.6.94 SAN FRANCISCO
Brazil: Taffarel, Jorginho, Aldair, Marcio Santos (1), Leonardo, Rai (Muller), Mauro Silva, Dunga, Zinho (Paulo Sergio), Bebeto (1), Romario (1)
Cameroon: Bell, Song-Bahanag, Kalla-Nkono, MBouh, Tataw, Libiih, MFede (Maboang-Kessack), Foe, Agbo, Embe (Milla), Omam-Byik
Referee: Brizio Carter (Mexico)

Sweden (1) **3, Russia** (1) **1**
25.6.94 DETROIT
Sweden: Ravelli, Nilsson, Andersson P, Björklund (Erlingmark), Ljung, Brolin (1 pen), Schwarz, Thern, Ingesson, Dahlin (2), Andersson K (Larsson)
Russia: Kharine, Nikiforov, Gorlukovich, Kuznetsov, Mostovoi, Khlestov, Onopko, Borodyuk (Galjamin), Popov (Karpin), Radchenko, Salenko (1 pen)
Referee: Quiniou (France)

Brazil (0) **1, Sweden** (1) **1**
28.6.94 DETROIT
Brazil: Taffarel, Jorginho, Aldair, Marcio Santos, Leonardo, Dunga, Mauro Silva (Mazinho), Rai (Paulo Sergio), Zinho, Romario (1), Bebeto
Sweden: Ravelli, Nilsson, Andersson P, Kåmark, Ljung, Larsson (Blomqvist), Schwarz (Mild), Thern, Ingesson, Andersson K (1), Brolin
Referee: Puhl (Hungary)

Russia (3) **6, Cameroon** (0) **1**
28.6.94 SAN FRANCISCO
Russia: Cherchesov, Nikiforov, Ternavski, Khlestov, Tetradze, Onopko, Korneyev (Radchenko (1)), Karpin, Lediakhov (Beschastnykh), Tsymbalar, Salenko (5–1 pen)
Cameroon: Songoo, Tataw, Kalla-Nkongo, Ndip-Akem, Agbo, Libiih, Kana-Byik, MFede (Milla (1)), Foe, Omam-Byik, Embe (Tchami)
Referee: Al Sharif (Syria)

	P	W	D	L	F	A	Pts
Brazil	3	2	1	0	6	1	7
Sweden	3	1	2	0	6	4	5
Russia	3	1	0	2	7	6	3
Cameroon	3	0	1	2	3	11	1

Group C

Germany (1) **1, Bolivia** (0) **0**
17.6.94 CHICAGO
Germany: Illgner, Matthäus, Kohler, Berthold, Effenberg, Hässler (Strunz), Sammer, Möller, Brehme, Riedle (Basler), Klinsmann (1)
Bolivia: Trucco, Quinteros, Rimba, Sandy, Borja, Soria, Erwin Sanchez, Melgar, Cristaldo, Ramallo (Etcheverry), Baldivieso (Moreno)
Referee: Brizio Carter (Mexico)

Spain (0) **2, South Korea** (0) **2**
18.6.94 DALLAS
Spain: Canizares, Nadal, Ferrer, Sergi, Fernandez, Alkorta, Goicoechea (1), Hierro, Guerrero (Caminero), Luis Enrique, Salinas (1) (Felipe)
South Korea: Choi In-Young, Hong-Gi, Kim Pan-Keun, Park Jung-Bae, Lee Young-Jin, Noh Jung-Yoon (Ha Seok-Ju), Kim Joo-Sung (Seo Jung-Won (1)), Ko Jeong-Woon, Choi Young-Il, Hong Myong-Bo (1), Hwang Sun-Hong
Referee: Mikkelsen (Denmark)

Germany (0) **1, Spain** (1) **1**
21.6.94 CHICAGO
Germany: Illgner, Matthäus, Kohler, Berthold, Strunz, Hässler, Effenberg, Sammer, Brehme, Möller (Völler), Klinsmann (1)
Spain: Zubizarreta, Ferrer, Aberlardo, Alkorta, Sergi, Goicoechea (1) (Bakero), Hierro, Caminero, Guardiola (Camarasa), Luis Enrique, Salinas
Referee: Filippi Cavani (Uruguay)

South Korea (0) **0, Bolivia** (0) **0**
24.6.94 BOSTON
South Korea: Choi In-Young, Hong Myung-Bo, Kim Pan-Keun, Shin Hong-Gi, Noh Jung-Yoon (Choi Young-Il), Park Jung-Bae, Ko Jeong-Woon, Lee Young-Jin, Kim Joo-Sung, Hwang Sun-Hong, Seo Jung-Won (Ha Seok-Ju)
Bolivia: Trucco, Rimba, Quinteros, Sandy, Cristaldo, Borja, Melgar, Soria, Erwin Sanchez, Baldivieso, Ramallo (Pena)
Referee: Mottram (Scotland)

Bolivia (0) **1, Spain** (1) **3**
27.6.94 CHICAGO
Bolivia: Trucco, Rimba, Pena, Sandy, Soruco, Borja, Erwin Sanchez (1), Soria (Castillo), Melgar, Ramallo, Ramos (Moreno)
Spain: Zubizarreta, Ferrer, Voro, Abelardo, Sergi, Goicoechea, Guardiola (1 pen), Guerrero, Caminero (2), Felipe (Hierro), Salinas
Referee: Badilla (Costa Rica)

Germany (3) **3, South Korea** (0) **2**
27.6.94 DALLAS
Germany: Illgner, Matthäus (Möller), Kohler, Berthold, Effenberg (Helmer), Hässler, Buchwald, Sammer, Brehme, Riedle (1), Klinsmann (2)
South Korea: Choi In-Young (Lee Won-Jae), Hong Myung-Bo (1), Kim Pan-Keun, Choi Young-Il, Park Jung-Bae, Cho Jin-Ho (Seo Jung-Won), Lee Young-Jin (Chung Jong-Son), Kim Joo-Sung, Shin Hong-Gi, Ko Jeong-Woon, Hwang Sun-Hong (1)
Referee: Quiniou (France)

	P	W	D	L	F	A	Pts
Germany	3	2	1	0	5	3	7
Spain	3	1	2	0	6	4	5
South Korea	3	0	2	1	4	5	2
Bolivia	3	0	1	2	1	4	1

Group D

Argentina (2) **4, Greece** (0) **0**
21.6.94 BOSTON
Argentina: Islas, Ruggeri, Sensini, Caceres, Chamot, Simeone, Redondo, Maradona (1) (Ortega), Balbo (Mancuso), Caniggia, Batistuta (3, 1 pen)
Greece: Minou, Manolas, Apostolakis, Kolitsidakis, Kalitzakis, Tsiantakis (Marangos), Tsalouchidis, Nioplias, Koifidis, Saravakos, Machlas (Mistropoulos)
Referee: Angeles (USA)

Bulgaria (0) **0, Nigeria** (2) **3**
22.6.94 DALLAS
Bulgaria: Mikhailov, Hubchev, Kremenliev, Ivanov, Tzvetanov, Borimirov (Yordanov), Lechkov (Sirakov), Balakov, Yankov, Kostadinov, Stoichkov
Nigeria: Rufai, Nwanu, Eguavoen, Uche, Iroha, Siasia (Adepoju), Finidi (Ezeugo), Oliseh, Amunike (1), Amokachi (1), Yekini (1)
Referee: Badilla (Costa Rica)

Argentina (2) **2, Nigeria** (1) **1**
25.6.94 BOSTON
Argentina: Islas, Sinisl (Diaz), Caceres, Ruggeri, Chamot, Balbo (Mancuso), Simeone, Maradona, Redondo, Batistuta, Caniggia (2)
Nigeria: Rufai, Nwanu, Eguavoen, Okechukwu, Finidi, Siasia (1) (Adepoju), Emenalo, Oliseh (Okocha), Amokachi, Yekini, Amunike
Referee: Karlsson (Sweden)

Bulgaria (1) **4, Greece** (0) **0**
26.6.94 CHICAGO
Bulgaria: Mikhailov, Hubchev, Kremenliev, Ivanov, Tzvetanov (Kiriakov), Yankov, Lechkov (1), Balakov, Kostadinov (Borimirov (1)), Sirakov, Stoichkov (2 pens)
Greece: Atmatzidis, Apostolakis, Karataidis, Karagiannis, Kalitzakis, Marangos, Nioplias, Hantzidis (Mistropoulos), Kofidis, Machlas, Alexoudis (Dimitriadis)
Referee: Bujsaim (UAE)

Greece (0) **0, Nigeria** (1) **2**
1.7.94 BOSTON
Greece: Karkamanis, Alexiou, Hantzidis, Karagiannis, Kofidis (Dimitriadis), Nioplias, Kalitzakis, Tsalouchidis, Alexandris, Machlas, Mitropoulos (Tsiantakis)
Nigeria: Rufai, Keshi, Okechukwu, Nwanu, Siasia, Amokachi (1), Oliseh, Finidi (1) (Adepoju), Emenalo, Yekini (Okocha), Amunike
Referee: Mottram (Scotland)

Argentina (0) **0, Bulgaria** (0) **2**
1.7.94 DALLAS
Argentina: Islas, Caceres, Ruggeri, Chamot, Diaz, Rodriguez (Medina), Simeone, Redondo, Balbo, Batistuta, Caniggia (Ortega)
Bulgaria: Mikhailov, Hubchev, Kremenliev, Ivanov, Kostadinov (Kiriakov), Lechkov (Borimirov), Yankov, Balakov, Tzvetanov, Sirakov (1), Stoichkov (1)
Referee: Jouini (Tunisia)

	P	W	D	L	F	A	Pts
Nigeria	3	2	0	1	6	2	6
Bulgaria	3	2	0	1	6	3	6
Argentina	3	2	0	1	6	3	6
Greece	3	0	0	3	0	10	0

Group E

Italy (0) **0, Rep of Ireland** (1) **1**
18.6.94 NEW YORK
Italy: Pagliuca, Tassoti, Baresi, Costacurta, Maldini, Donadoni, Baggio D, Albertini, Evani (Massaro), Baggio R, Signori (Berti)
Republic of Ireland: Bonner, Irwin, McGrath, Babb, Phelan, Houghton (1) (McAteer), Keane, Sheridan, Townsend, Staunton, Coyne (Aldridge)
Referee: Van der Ende (Holland)

Norway (0) **1, Mexico** (0) **0**
19.6.94 WASHINGTON
Norway: Thorstvedt, Håland, Bratseth, Berg, Bjørnebye, Flo, Bohinen, Mykland (Rekdal (1)), Leonhardsen, Jakobsen (Halle), Fjørtoft
Mexico: Campos, Gutierrez (Bernal), Suarez, Juan de Dios Ramirez, Jesus Ramirez, Ambriz, Del Olmo, Valdez (Galdino), Luis Garcia, Zague, Sanchez
Referee: Puhl (Hungary)

Italy (0) **1, Norway** (0) **0**
23.6.94 NEW YORK
Italy: Pagliuca, Benarrivo, Costacurta, Baresi (Apolloni), Maldini, Berti, Albertini, Baggio D (1), Signori, Casiraghi (Massaro), Baggio R (Marchegiani)
Norway: Thorstvedt, Håland, Berg, Bratseth, Bjørnebye, Rushfeldt (Jakobsen), Leonhardsen, Mykland (Rekdal), Bohinen, Flo, Fjørtoft
Referee: Krug (Germany)

Mexico (1) **2, Rep of Ireland** (0) **1**
24.6.94 FLORIDA
Mexico: Campos, Del Olmo, Suarez, Juan de Dios Ramirez, Rodriguez (Salvador), Bernal, Ambriz, Luis Garcia (2), Garcia Aspe, Hermosillo (Gutierrez), Zague
Republic of Ireland: Bonner, Irwin, McGrath, Babb, Phelan, Houghton, Keane, Sheridan, Townsend, Staunton (Aldridge (1)), Coyne (McAteer)
Referee: Röthlisberger (Switzerland)

Rep of Ireland (0) **0, Norway** (0) **0**
28.6.94 NEW YORK
Republic of Ireland: Bonner, Kelley G, McGrath, Babb, Staunton, Keane, McAteer, Sheridan, Townsend (Whelan), Houghton, Aldridge (Kelley D)
Norway: Thorstvedt, Berg, Bratseth, Johnsen, Halle (Jakobsen), Flo, Mykland, Leonhardsen (Bohinen), Rekdal, Bjørnebye, Sørloth
Referee: Torres Cadena (Colombia)

Italy (0) **1, Mexico** (0) **1**
28.6.94 WASHINGTON
Italy: Marchegiani, Benarrivo, Apolloni, Costacurta, Maldini, Berti, Albertini, Baggio D (Donadoni), Signori, Baggio R, Casiraghi (Massaro (1))
Mexico: Campos, Rodriguez, Suarez, Juan de Dios Ramirez, Del Olmo, Bernal (1), Ambriz, Luis Garcia (Chabaz), Garcia Aspe, Hermosillo, Zague
Referee: Lamolina (Argentina)

	P	W	D	L	F	A	Pts
Mexico	3	1	1	1	3	3	4
Republic of Ireland	3	1	1	1	2	2	4
Italy	3	1	1	1	2	2	4
Norway	3	1	1	1	1	1	4

Group F

Belgium (1) **1, Morocco** (0) **0**
19.6.94 FLORIDA
Belgium: Preud'homme, De Wolf, Grün, Smidts, Staelens, Van der Elst, Scifo, Boffin (Borkelmans), Degryse (1), Weber, Nilis (Emmers)
Morocco: Azmi (Alaoul El Achraf), Naybet, Abdella, Triki, El Hadrioui, Hababi, Azzouzi, El Haddaoui (Bahja), Daoudi, Hadji, Chaouch (Samadi)
Referee: Torres Cadena (Colombia)

Holland (0) **2, Saudi Arabia** (1) **1**
21.6.94 WASHINGTON
Holland: De Goey, Koeman, Van Gobbel, De Boer F, Rijkaard, Jonk (1), Wouters, Bergkamp, Overmars (Taument (1)), De Boer R, Roy (Van Vossen)
Saudi Arabia: Al Deayea, Al Dosari, Al Khlawi, Madani, Al Jawad, Al Bishi, Owairan (Saleh), Amin (1), Jebreen, Al Muwallid, Mohammed (Falatah)
Referee: Vega Diaz (Spain)

Belgium (0) **1, Holland** (0) **0**
25.6.94 FLORIDA
Belgium: Preud'homme, De Wolf, Grün, Albert (1), Emmers (Medved), Scifo, Van der Elst, Staelens, Borkelmans (Smidts), Weber, Degryse
Holland: De Goey, Koeman, Valckx, De Boer F, Taument (Overmars), Rijkaard, Bergkamp, Jonk, Wouters, Roy, De Boer R (Witschge)
Referee: Marsiglia (Brazil)

Saudi Arabia (1) **2, Morocco** (1) **1**
25.6.94 NEW YORK
Saudi Arabia: Al Deayea, Al Jawad, Al Anazi (Zebermawi), Madani, Al Khiaiwi, Al Bishi, Amin (1), Jebreen, Al Muwallid, Al-Jaber (1) (Al Ghesheyan), Owairan
Morocco: Azmi, Naybet, Abdellah (El Ghrissi), Triki, El Hadrioui, Hababi (Hadji), Azzouzi, El Khalej, Daoudi, Bahja, Chaouch (1)
Referee: Don (England)

Morocco (0) **1, Holland** (1) **2**
29.6.94 ORLANDO
Morocco: Alaoui, El Khalej, Negrouz, Triki, El Hadrioui, Samadi, Azzouzi (Daoudi), Hababi, Nader (1), Bahja, Bouyboud (Hadji)
Holland: De Goey, Koeman, De Boer F, Valckx, Winter, Jonk, Wouters, Witschge, Overmars (Taument), Bergkamp (1), Van Vossen (Roy (1))
Referee: Tejada (Peru)

Belgium (0) **0, Saudi Arabia** (1) **1**
29.6.94 WASHINGTON
Belgium: Preud'homme, De Wolf, Smidts, Albert, Medved, Staelens, Van der Elst, Scifo, Boffin, Degryse (Nilis), Wilmots (Weber)
Saudi Arabia: Al Deayea, Zebermawi, Madani, Al Khaiwi, Al Jawad, Al Bishi, Saleh, Owairan (1) (Al Dosari), Jebreen, Mohammed (Al Muwallid), Falatah
Referee: Krug (Germany)

	P	W	D	L	F	A	Pts
Holland	3	2	0	1	4	3	6
Saudi Arabia	3	2	0	1	4	3	6
Belgium	3	2	0	1	2	1	6
Morocco	3	0	0	3	2	5	0

THE SECOND STAGE

Germany and Belgium, old rivals, faced off in Chicago on a day when the heat relented and a climate far more familiar to both prevailed. The Germans immediately stamped their authority on matters, Matthäus slipping the ball to the evasive Völler, who flashed his shot past Preud'homme. Five minutes gone and 1–0, two minutes later Grün capitalized on a misdirected header to fire the Belgians level. Klinsmann concluded a remarkable opening in the tenth minute with a goal to restore the German lead from Völler's inviting pass. At 2–1 the Germans threatened a rout against steadfast but unimaginative opponents.

Klinsmann's clever running unnerved them and when Völler scored a third before the interval the Belgians appeared thoroughly beaten. Remarkably, chances came and went, most falling to Klinsmann, playing irresistibly, before Belgium launched a revival and sparked a controversy. Twenty minutes from the end Thomas Helmer lunged at Josip Weber, causing the Belgian to tumble, a clear penalty to all but referee Röthlisberger. When Albert shot smartly home for 3–2 Belgium had good reason to complain that they might have drawn, though it would have hardly reflected the balance of play. Later German coach Berti Vogts put things in perspective, claiming quite reasonably that his team might have scored five or six times. 'Yes, we started the Tournament slowly but maybe we can now do as we have done before,' he said, sounding ominously self-assured.

In Washington an infinitely improved Spain met a rugged and confident Switzerland. Hierro pushed forward to replace the suspended Caminero, opened the scoring running between the startled Geiger and Herr, before advancing unchallenged to shoot past the unprotected Pascolo. Switzerland produced – when they needed their characteristic resilience – their least convincing performance, and were further handicapped by the last minute withdrawal of Sutter, victim of a broken toe. They had no answer. Thoroughly outplayed, Switzerland futilely chased the swift moving Spanish shadows. In the second half Goicoechea struck the Swiss goal frame after a brisk and inventive movement started by Hierro and carried on in turn by Luis Enrique and Ferrer. Then on 74 minutes another and decisive goal was scored by Luis Enrique and created by the rampaging Sergi. Berguiristain at the end added a third from the penalty spot after Pascolo had launched himself at Ferrer before the referee mercifully ended the Swiss torment. Their Tournament, which had begun with such promise, had been terminated in disappointing fashion. Spain for their part advanced; arriving largely unheralded, their compact defending and fluent attacking suggested a team capable at the very least of challenging those with still greater aspirations.

In Pasadena, Argentina and Romania played out a high quality contest full of spellbinding excitement. Argentina controlled the early stages, probing Romania's defences searching for weakness, Balbo missing a fine early chance put through by Simeone's dribble and pass, but Prunea smothered swiftly as he fatally delayed his shot. Dumitrescu punished Argentina instantly, curling a wicked free kick over a three-man wall and in from thirty-five yards. Undeterred, Argentina persisted and won their reward when Batistuta was pushed down by Prodan in the penalty area; the offended player himself fired home the kick. Now Romania belatedly showed their true creative genius, inspired again by the mesmerizing skills of little Hagi. Playing a one-two to gain time, he spotted Dumitrescu's penetrating near-post run and with a surgeon's precision stroked the ball into his path. Dumitrescu calmly, almost

nonchalantly, rolled his gift into the startled Islas's net. Redondo began to galvanize Argentina, Batistuta's fierce drive thwarted by Prunea. Then a further
penalty appeal was denied as they pressed purposefully for parity. Like a
cobra Hagi struck again. Dumitrescu ran swiftly at the South Americans'
retreating defence and ignored Selymes on the left wing, picking Hagi out
instead in huge space on the right, his blistering drive quite unstoppable for
3–1. Argentina did recover to score a late consolation but at the end they were
beaten; undone by genius, their own equally gifted playmaker, Maradona, sat
in disgrace, watching from the stands doubtless pondering what might have
been.

In the strength-sapping heat of the Cotton Bowl in Dallas, Sweden, so
impressive against Brazil, met Saudi Arabia, the competition's major surprise.
In the opening moments as Sweden sought to settle, Al-Jaber fired wastefully
wide from Falatah's pull back. Almost behind, the Scandinavians responded
immediately, Kennet Andersson's hopeful long cross evading the Saudi
defence but not the elegant Dahlin, who thumped his header into the net.
Sweden now commanded, restricting the Arabs to pacey counter-attacking
which brought them scant reward. The sweltering conditions favoured the
Saudi Arabians heavily, and as half-time approached Sweden visibly tired. In
the second half, benefiting from the interval, the Swedes went for broke, determined to finish the game before fatigue set in again. Dahlin and Ingesson
missed clumsily before Andersson seized on a slip by Al Khlawi to shoot them
2–0 ahead. The Saudis fought back furiously, Ravelli brilliantly saving from Al
Muwallid, and Ingesson clearing Falatah's header off the line. Sweden
laboured, desperate for the end, and with four minutes remaining concern
turned to anxiety as the Saudis finally produced the goal their efforts merited,
Al Ghesheyan turning inside Ljung to smash a rising shot into the roof of the
net. With the score at 2–1, for the exhausted Europeans the appalling prospect
of extra time loomed large. Andersson dispelled their fears, winning for them
at the death a game they had always seemed likely to prosper from, though not
without great discomfort.

In Orlando, Ireland, buoyant from their qualification, met the gifted Dutch
head on and might have scored within a minute, Staunton's drive deflected out
of harm's way by Overmars. Thereafter Holland dominated, Van Vossen and
the turbocharged Overmars whistling up the flanks pinning back the Irish
full backs, Kelly and Phelan. A goal threatened and duly arrived: the
harassed Phelan mistiming a headed back-pass and saw Overmars seize on
the error and whip a cross into the path of Bergkamp, who shot with great
certainty past Bonner for 1–0. Ireland's response proved robust and positive,
Coyne and Sheridon narrowly failing to reach Kelly's inviting cross, but
Holland, increasingly assured, continued to hold sway. Koeman, Rijkaard
and Overmars all went desperately close but it was Jonk who fired their

second goal in a seemingly harmless effort that the waiting Bonner misjudged horribly, the ball looping up off his gloves to nestle in the Irish net, 2–0 at half-time. Ireland fought to the end, their courage in the heat admirable. Yet at the end their disappointment was etched into the faces of tired and demoralized players. 'There's nobody else to blame but me,' said the refreshingly honest Bonner. Jack Charlton, their inspiring coach, was philosophical, 'If we had to go out, I'm glad it was to the Dutch,' he said. Dick Advocaat, Holland's mentor, paid tribute to the Irish spirit: 'They really went for it in the second half. You have to wait for the final whistle to be sure you have really won against the Irish.'

On 4 July, American Independence Day, the USA faced up in Paolo Alto to a formidable barrier to their progress: Brazil. A huge crowd willed them to improbable triumph. The Brazilians began cautiously and were troubled by America's purposeful beginning, Ramos in the 12th minute slipping casually beyond his marker to rifle the ball towards Dooley, whose sharp effort defeated Taffarel's groping dive to flash wide of the far post. As Brazil began to work their fluent passing game, the USA retreated, defenders and midfielders alike snapping eagerly into their illustrious opponents; and unhappy at his own personal attentions, Leonardo's frustrations culminated in violence in the 43rd minute. Jostled by Tab Ramos near the touchline, he lashed out petulantly with his elbow in full view of the officials and was dismissed. With no goals and reduced to ten men in a hostile environment, the imperious South Americans were threatened by their upstart hosts. Remarkably, Brazil now found their invention. Romario struck Meola's goal frame and tortured the beleaguered American defence, Dooley headed his chip off the goal line and Meola watched gratefully as the little Brazilian skipped around him to shoot wastefully wide of the gaping goal. But it was Romario who had the final say as extra time approached, carving through on another bewildering run to present Bebeto with a simple and decisive goal.

An initially tepid encounter between Bulgaria and Mexico in the Giants Stadium produced the Tournament's most dramatic moments to date. Bulgaria, without three key players through suspension, were deprived also of the services of Kremenliev before the hour. However, they played with tremendous character throughout, snuffing out Mexican forays with little difficulty, dominating for long spells and launching menacing attacks, with Stoichkov their instrument of torment. It was Stoichkov on seven minutes who seized on to Yordanov's pass, surged through despairing defenders and drove powerfully past Campos. Now Kremenliev began his difficult day: penalized and booked already for little more than standing his ground, Syrian referee Al Sharif, dreadful throughout, awarded a penalty kick and dismissed him. Aspe gratefully slotted Mexico level. Bulgaria, forced with ten men to conserve energy, played cautiously now as the game drifted aimlessly, though Kostadinov did rattle Campos's upright with a whistling free kick late on. Luis Zague joined Kremenliev, equally unfortunate to be sent off, and two teams concluded 120 sterile minutes playing ten a side and arriving inevitably at a penalty shoot-out. Unbelievably, here Mexico, the beneficiaries of all the luck thus far, contrived to miss their first three kicks, and it fell to the talented Iodan Lechkov to fire Bulgaria into the quarter-finals. 'God,' said Stoichkov, 'is a Bulgarian.'

In Boston the 'Azzurri' of Italy and Nigeria's 'Super Eagles' faced off in a fiercely contested encounter the Africans relished, their pace and power causing Italy difficulties despite Maldini's switch to centre back. Roberto Baggio, looking lethargic and lacking inspiration, provided little outlet for an often besieged defence and Amunike's goal, hooked in after Finidi's free kick deflected off Maldini, appeared inevitable. Quite unable to find their smooth passing game, Italy instead displayed their considerable and formidable fighting spirit. Baggio, showing belated interest, arriving to meet Benarrivo's cross appeared to be pushed off balance by Nwanu. The referee thought otherwise. Enter Dino Baggio for the second half to further strengthen the Italians' competitive edge. His first kick struck a post but Nigeria continued to resist resolutely. Fifteen minutes from time there was an Italian tragedy when Zola, the substitute, frustrated by Nwanu's rough treatment, lost his head and was dismissed. Down 1–0 with ten men left, it was bad enough but might have been worse. Yekini, clean though crudely fouled by Maldini, was this time given a yellow card and then, perhaps almost providentially, came the unlikeliest of equalizers. Two minutes from time the pony-tailed Roberto Baggio, finding time and space in Nigeria's penalty area, where none had been before, drove Mussi's long, low pass beyond Rufai. In extra time Nigeria, for so long the likely winners, began to buckle under bombardment from depleted Italy's astonishing and brave revival. In 12 minutes Benarrivo helped complete a heroic turnabout by the ten men. Receiving Roberto Baggio's clever chip, he advanced from the left into the African area, but Eguavoen's horrible lunge, ill-timed and unnecessary, stopped him in his tracks. Roberto Baggio duly dispatched the resultant kick and an exhausted Italy, regardless of Yekini's late effort, were through, their team resembling a small child stumbling unstoppably and relentlessly forward without ever appearing to recover its balance.

Second Round

Germany (3) **3, Belgium** (1) **2**
2.7.94 CHICAGO
Germany: Illgner, Matthäus (Brehme), Helmer, Kohler, Berthold, Hässler, Buchwald, Sammer, Wagner, Völler (2), Klinsmann (1) (Kuntz)
Belgium: Preud'homme, De Wolf, Grün (1), Albert (1), Emmers, Van der Elst, Scifo, Staelens, Smidts (Bovin), Weber, Nilis (Czerniatynski)
Referee: Röthlisberger (Switzerland)

Spain (1) **3, Switzerland** (0) **0**
2.7.94 WASHINGTON
Spain: Zubizarreta, Alkorta, Nadal, Abelardo, Ferrer, Hierro (1) (Otero), Camarasa, Goicoechea (Berguiristain (1 pen)), Bakero, Sergi, Luis Enrique (1)
Switzerland: Pascolo, Hottiger, Herr, Geiger, Quentin (Studer), Ohrel (Subiat), Bregy, Sforza, Bickel, Knup, Chapuisat
Referee: Van der Ende (Holland)

Saudi Arabia (0) **1, Sweden** (1) **3**
3.7.94 DALLAS
Saudi Arabia: Al Deayea, Madani, Zebermawi, Al Khlawi, Al Jawed (Al Ghesheyan (1)), Al Bishi (Al Muwallid), Amin, Owairan, Saleh, Al-Jaber, Falatah
Sweden: Ravelli, Nilsson, Andersson P, Björklund (Kåmark), Ljung, Brolin, Schwarz, Thern (Mild), Ingesson, Andersson K (2), Dahlin (1)
Referee: Marsiglia (Brazil)

Romania (2) **3, Argentina** (1) **2**
3.7.94 LOS ANGELES
Romania: Prunea, Belodedici, Petrescu, Prodan, Munteanu, Mihali, Hagi (1) (Galca), Lupescu, Popescu, Selymes, Dumitrescu (2) (Papura)
Argentina: Islas, Sensini (Medina Bello), Caceres, Ruggeri, Chamot, Simeone, Basualdo, Redondo, Ortega, Balbo (1), Batistuta (1 pen)
Referee: Parietto (Italy)

Holland (2) **2, Republic of Ireland** (0) **0**
4.7.94 ORLANDO
Holland: De Goey, Koeman, Valckx, De Boer F, Rijkaard, Winter, Jonk (1), Witschge (Numan), Overmars, Bergkamp (1), Van Vossen (Roy)
Republic of Ireland: Bonner, Kelly G, McGrath, Babb, Phelan, Houghton, Keane, Sheridan, Townsend, Staunton (McAteer), Coyne (Cascarino)
Referee: Mikkelsen (Denmark)

Brazil (0) **1, USA** (0) **0**
4.7.94 SAN FRANCISCO
Brazil: Taffarel, Jorginho, Aldair, Marcio Santos, Leonardo, Mazinho, Dunga, Mauro Silva, Zinho (Cafu), Romario, Bebeto (1)
USA: Meola, Clavijo, Balboa, Lalas, Caligiuri, Ramos (Wynalda), Sorber, Dooley, Perez (Wegerle), Jones, Stewart
Referee: Quiniou (France)

Nigeria (1) **1, Italy** (0) **2**
5.7.94 BOSTON
Nigeria: Rufai, Nwanu, Eguavoen, Okechukwu, Emenalo, Finidi, Okocha, Oliseh, Amunike (1) (Oliha), Amokachi (Adepoju), Yekini
Italy: Marchigiani, Mussi, Costacurta, Maldini, Benarrivo, Berti (Baggio D), Albertini, Donadoni, Signori (Zola), Baggio R (2, 1 pen), Massaro
Referee: Arturo Brizio Carter (Mexico)

Mexico (1) **1, Bulgaria** (1) **1**
5.7.94 NEW YORK
Mexico: Campos, Rodriguez, Juan de Dios Ramirez, Suarez, Jesus Ramirez, Bernal, Ambriz, Luis Garcia, Garcia Aspe (1 pen), Zague, Galindo
Bulgaria: Mikhailov, Hubchev, Yordanov, Kremenliev, Kiriakov, Sirakov (Guentchev), Borimirov, Lechkov, Balakov, Stoichkov (1), Kostadinov (Mitarski)
Referee: Al Sharif (Syria)

THE QUARTER-FINALS

In the Giants Stadium at New York, Germany faced a Bulgarian team exuding confidence after their unprecedented success. It was not long before they troubled their celebrated opponents, Sirakov shooting across goal to be foiled by Illgner before Stoichkov evaded Wagner to pass back to Balakov, his shot thumped against the foot of the post with 12 minutes gone. The fluid imaginative movement of the men from the Balkans, inspired by Lechkov, Balakov and Kostadinov, held sway over the contrasting pace and power of Germany. Hässler busied himself working diligently to beak up the Bulgarian rhythm, and finding time to provide Klinsmann with a cross, the blond striker stretched full length to head goalwards, Mikhailov saving instinctively. The flow continued after the interval, Wagner's 48th minute cross creating confusion, and Lechkov in the ensuing mêlée caught Klinsmann; Matthäus struck the penalty home for 1–0. Bulgaria did not collapse as the Germans piled forward, Helmer drove wide of Mikhailov's goal, Möller struck a post. Bulgaria persisted though, neat and thoughtful, and finally after 75 minutes it reaped its rich reward – Stoichkov, always a danger, pulled down by Muller twenty yards out, picked himself up and floated the free kick over a six-man wall into the helpless Illgner's net. Three minutes later, as the Germans reeled from the shock, Lechkov finished it, rising to loop a spectacular header home for 2–1. Germany in their customary fashion fought desperately to the whistle. Bulgaria, however, hung on to clinch a marvellous and deserved win.

In San Francisco, Romania and Sweden, bidding for a place in the semi-final, engaged in another nerve-jangling encounter. Early on Ingesson broke free on the right, his hard driven cross causing consternation among Romanian defenders, Dahlin stooping to head agonizingly against the post. Soon the Romanians began to find their flowing, destructive football, Ravelli denying both Lupescu and early in the second half Petrescu, while Hagi typically endured the close attentions of Ingesson and, when he escaped him, rough handling from the combative Swedish midfield. Without the influence of the swashbuckling Hagi, Romania persisted, commanding proceedings with leisurely, patient probing that brought no reward, before the pace of the game altered dramatically, courtesy of a wonderfully engineered goal by the hitherto cautious Swedes from a free kick. Schwarz shaped to shoot but instead Mild flicked the ball into the path of Brolin's astute run, the little striker spun and thrashed the ball into the roof of the net. Down 1–0 with ten minutes left, Romania responded fiercely and in the final minute were thrown a lifeline. A hopeful cross eluded Sweden's defence and from close range Raducioiu forced the equalizer. In extra time if Raducioiu appeared to have settled it for Romania, driving past Ravelli from eighteen yards, Sweden's plight appeared desperate when Schwarz made matters worse by being dismissed shortly afterwards. To their credit, however, the ten men fought back. Outplayed and outthought, they manufactured an unlikely equalizer in the 115th minute, Andersson unforgivably outjumping the hesitant Prunea to set up another dramatic penalty shoot-out. Two tired teams stepped up to begin a battle of nerves. Mild lost his first, giving Romania the advantage, but Petrescu shot indecisively and was thwarted by Ravelli's dive. Sudden death, and it fell to the hugely impressive Belodedici to draw Romania level. Sadly he was not up to the task. Trudging forward without enthusiasm, he shot feebly, Ravelli beat it out joyously and Scandinavian celebrations began in earnest. 'There had to be a winner,' said Anghel Iordanescu, Romania's coach, afterwards, 'but it is a game that shows no mercy.' For little Hagi, perhaps the competition's outstanding performer, the adventure was over.

Brazil and Holland in the Cotton Bowl at Dallas always threatened to be an epic encounter. In the event it did not disappoint. The South Americans took control and scarcely relinquished their iron grip. In the first half whilst the Dutch relied on sporadic raids, the fluid movement of the Brazilians tormented them. Aldair failed though where both Romario or Bebeto would have been expected to succeed, and had the best chance before the interval. Encouraged by their dominance, in the second period Brazil accelerated their play, sharper, more incisive. On 47 minutes Romario, pursued as ever by his marker, Valckx, should have scored, but it served merely as a rehearsal. Five minutes later Rijkaard was dispossessed, Dunga's pass sent Bebeto away down the flank, and his cross was met crisply on the half volley by the predatory Romario. Shaken, soon all of Holland was outraged as Romario, plainly offside and assuredly interfering, allowed the ball to pass him by and into the path of Bebeto, who shot unerringly beyond Ravelli's reach. At 2–0 that should have been that; for 62 minutes the Dutch had played out the role of dutiful, respectable sparring partners, resisting stoutly but seldom pushing back. Now to their eternal credit they took the game to their apparent masters. Bergkamp, gloriously talented though thus far anonymous, stole a yard on Marcio Santos two minutes later to plunder a goal, and as Brazilian concentration wavered, Winter rose ahead of the hesitant Taffarel to thump his header home for an astonishing and spirited equalizer just 14 minutes from time. Brazil steeled themselves, regained composure, and in spite of Holland's policy of organized harassment in midfield, gained the initiative once more. With just nine minutes left and extra time beckoning, Branco stepped up to a free kick and drove it hard and low, the ball hit the defensive wall and its change of direction, albeit slight, deceived De Goey fatally. Ending 3–2, though the Dutch protested long and loud, in truth they had left their best efforts far too late and had succumbed to a more accomplished team than their own.

In Boston an Italian team with the priceless knack of rescuing lost causes faced Spain marching purposefully forward with ever-increasing confidence. Cautious at first, the game erupted into life on 26 minutes with Dino Baggio pounding the ball into Zubizarreta's net from thirty yards. Spain's response was immediate, Caminero's downward header forcing Pagliuca to a groping save at his near post. Spain continued to press after the interval, pushing the Italians back, forcing an assortment of niggling fouls and one deplorable assault on Luis Enrique by Tassoti, which left the Spaniard with a split nose. Unaccountably, the incident went unpunished. Caminero, lively throughout, finally rewarded their industry, his raking shot thumping into Benarrivo looped high in the air and beyond the unfortunate Pagliuca. With an equalizer to fortify them Spain persisted, and the Italians, their enormous resilience pressured to the point of collapse, visibly wilted under the onslaught. Eight minutes from the end Salinas strode forward, advancing on goal. Pagliuca tore out too late and realizing his error appeared to compound it by retreating. Salinas surged into the area, certain to score, hesitated and the desperate Pagliuca flung himself feet first to deny the Barcelona player a winner his team indisputably deserved. As injury time began, Spain, the stronger and more incisive, seemed the likely winners in extra time. It was not to be; as they tore upfield they were punished. Committing seven players to attack, they conceded possession. Signori quick as a flash directed an exquisite chipped pass into Roberto Baggio's run and their patron saint of lost causes evaded Zubizarreta's dive to guide the ball in from the narrowest of angles. Spanish hearts were broken while the Italians again had defied logic, 'God is an Italian', screamed Spanish newspaper *El Periodico*, but how would the Italians deal with the majestic Stoichkov in their semi-final with Bulgaria? 'I don't know, maybe with a pistol,' offered Sacci, wryly.

Quarter-Finals

Italy (1) **2, Spain** (0) **1**
9.7.94 BOSTON
Italy: Pagliuca, Tassotti, Costacurta, Maldini, Benarrivo, Conte (Berti), Baggio D (1), Albertini (Signori), Donadoni, Baggio R (1), Massaro
Spain: Zubizarreta, Nadal, Ferrer, Abelardo, Alkorta, Otero, Goicoechea, Bakero (Hierro), Caminero (1), Sergi (Salina), Luis Enrique
Referee: Puhl (Hungary)

Holland (0) **2, Brazil** (0) **3**
9.7.94 DALLAS
Holland: De Goey, Koeman, Valckx, Wouters, Winter (1), Rijkaard (De Boer R), Jonk, Witschge, Overmars, Bergkamp (1), Van Vossen (Roy)
Brazil: Taffarel, Jorginho, Aldair, Marcio Santos, Branco (1) (Cafu), Mazinho (Rai), Dunga, Mauro Silva, Zinho, Bebeto (1), Romario (1)
Referee: Badilla (Costa Rica)

Bulgaria (0) **2, Germany** (0) **1**
10.7.94 NEW YORK
Bulgaria: Mikhailov, Hubchev, Ivanov, Yankov, Kiriakov, Lechkov (1), Sirakov, Balakov, Tzvetanov, Kostadinov (Guentchev), Stoichkov (1) (Yordanov)
Germany: Illgner, Matthäus (1 pen), Kohler, Helmer, Berthold, Hässler (Brehme), Buchwald, Möller, Wagner (Strunz), Völler, Klinsmann
Referee: Torres Cadena (Colombia)

Sweden (0) **2, Romania** (0) **2** (aet, 1–1 after 90 mins, Sweden won 5–4 on penalties)
10.7.94 SAN FRANCISCO
Sweden: Ravelli, Nilsson, Andersson P, Björklund (Kåmark), Ljung, Brolin (1), Schwarz, Mild, Ingesson, Andersson K (1), Dahlin (Larsson)
Romania: Prunea, Belodedici, Prodan, Popescu, Lupescu, Petrescu, Selymes, Hagi, Munteanu (Panduru), Dumitrescu, Raducioiu (2)
Referee: Don (England)

THE SEMI-FINALS

In Los Angeles, Brazil, now the favourites, faced an obdurate and almost entirely negative Sweden. Allowed command of midfield from the beginning by the Swedes' tiresome insistence on retreating behind the ball, the Brazilians bore down in a steady procession on Sweden's goal, Romario's shot in the third minute forcing Ravelli to punch clear. In eight minutes Branco called the eccentric keeper into action again with a flying save from a fiercely struck free kick. Sweden's cautious approach consisting of sporadic ineffective raids offered little hope, and Mild, on a rare foray, was denied comfortably by the under-employed Taffarel. At least Sweden were level, their overworked defence surviving diligently and on occasions miraculously. Zinho missed when put through by Bebeto. Romario, quicksilver, darted by Ljung and Björklund, beat Ravelli and pounded the ground in frustration as first Patrik Andersson forced the ball off the line and then the wasteful Mazinho following up, fired horribly and inexplicably wide of the gaping goal. Romario himself was next to be consumed with guilt. Bebeto and Jorginho carved the Swedes open and Brazil's talisman delayed his shot and allowed himself to be smothered. As the pattern persisted, the Swedes became yet more withdrawn, Brolin their sole midfielder, Dahlin and Kennett Anderson spectators further forward. Ravelli for his part continued his heroics, again defying Romario and then flinging himself acrobatically to his left to deny Zinho's goalbound shot. When Thern was dismissed for a spiteful lunge at Dunga, even the Swedes' inspired resistance seemed certain to break, though doggedly they clung on, their determination, if not their stunted ambition, deserving grudging respect. It was Romario who finally confirmed Brazil's safe passage to the final, their first in twenty-four years, his far-post header from Jorginho's cross nine minutes from time finally beating the courageous Ravelli. Brazil had won, though the final would surely provide a sterner test. Sweden, while defending stoutly, had offered little but the thought that by eliminating the imaginative Romanians they had denied the Tournament a far more fitting and entertaining spectacle.

Up at New York, Italy and Bulgaria met to contest a semi-final that would ensure a European representative in the Rose Bowl in Pasadena. Beginning like a chess match with probing and counter probing, the game exploded into life in the 21st minute, the instinctive genius of Roberto Baggio wandering past Yankov and then sweeper Hubchev before driving venomously into Mikhailov's net. At 1–0 Italy, the sleeping giant so fortunate to have arrived at the semi-final stage, finally shook itself mightily to inflict irreparable damage on Bulgarian aspirations. Immediately Albertini crashed a shot against the goalpost and then forced Mikhailov to an athletic save. The Italians were irresistible, running Bulgaria ragged. Albertini, again an incisive and destructive weapon, floated an exquisite chip into the path of the majestic Roberto Baggio. This time he placed his shot with precision inside the goalkeeper's left-hand post for 2–0. Twenty-five minutes had passed and in four minutes of glorious football Italy had bewildered Bulgaria hopelessly and surely destined them to an ignonimous exit. Italy's purple patch, however, could not last; it did not, and slowly, their nerve holding splendidly, the men from the Balkans found themselves. Stoichkov, often prompting from the left, sought weakness and finally on 43 minutes he offered his team a lifeline: Sirakov's run into the penalty area curtailed by Pagliuca's trip allowed Stoichkov to slam the penalty home with conviction. Italy, now threatened, showed their old anxieties. Costacurta, booked for a lunge at Stoichkov, would miss the final, and though they clung on without too much difficulty, their Jekyll and Hyde character offered hope to Brazil, their opponents in the final. For Italy there was always Baggio, creative genius and scorer of crucial goals at crucial times. Could he, would he, manage it one last time? Bulgaria bowed out. Theirs had been a magnificent achievement. 'We played with a lot of dignity and determination,' said coach Penev of his vanquished team. 'We really can't be upset with our defence for allowing Roberto Baggio those two wonderful goals.'

Semi-Finals

Italy (2) **2, Bulgaria** (1) **1**
13.7.94 NEW YORK
Italy: Pagliuca, Mussi, Costacurta, Maldini, Benarrivo, Berti, Albertini, Baggio D (Conte), Donadoni, Casiraghi, Baggio R (2) (Signori)
Bulgaria: Mikhailov, Kiriakov, Ivanov, Hubchev, Tzvetanov, Yankov, Lechkov, Balakov, Sirakov, Kostadinov (Yordanov), Stoichkov (1 pen) (Guentchev)
Referee: Quiniou (France)

Brazil (0) **1, Sweden** (0) **0**
13.7.94 LOS ANGELES
Brazil: Taffarel, Jorginho, Aldair, Marcio Santos, Branco, Dunga, Mauro Silva, Mazinho (Rai), Zinho, Bebeto, Romario (1)
Sweden: Ravelli, Nilsson, Andersson P, Björklund, Ljung, Mild, Brolin, Thern, Ingesson, Dahlin (Rehn), Andersson K
Referee: Torres Cadena (Colombia)

Bulgaria, tired and demoralized by their defeat in the semi-finals, faced in Sweden a team eager to erase the memory of a much-criticized performance devoid of ambition against Brazil. Brolin, a lonely and forlorn figure three days earlier, proved the catalyst for the highly motivated Scandinavians after eight minutes when he fired them ahead, and with Bulgaria failing to find the spark with which to retaliate, his constant threat opened them up at will. On 30 minutes Mild duly scored a second, running on to Brolin's inviting pass. Now the floodgates opened: Henrik Larsson hammered a third and the rangy Kennett Andersson loped in to head Sweden 4–0 up by half-time. Bulgaria, with no way back in the second half, managed at least to avoid further embarrassment, as Sweden contented themselves with a margin of victory of unlikely proportions. 'You have to remember,' said Brolin afterwards, 'that Brazil are a stronger team than Bulgaria; we could not play the same way. It is not a case of being disappointed to lose to Brazil and not make the final. We got third place and this medal is a huge thing for the Swedish team.' Coach Svensson endorsed the little striker's sentiments, 'It was fantastic to go this far.' For Bulgaria's Dimitar Penev the irrelevance of this final match could not be overstated. 'We were tired from our previous games; this one should not have taken place.'

Match for Third Place

Sweden (4) **4, Bulgaria** (0) **0**
16.7.94 LOS ANGELES
Sweden: Raveilli, Nilsson, Andersson P, Björklund, Kåmark, Brolin (1), Schwarz, Mild (1), Ingesson, Andersson K (1), Larsson (1) (Limpar)
Bulgaria: Mikhailov (Nikolov), Kiriakov, Ivanov (Kremenliev), Hubchev, Tzvetanov, Yankov, Lechkov, Sirakov (Yordanov), Balakov, Stoichkov, Kostadinov
Referee: Bujsaim (UAE)

The final, better certainly than the miserable affair of 1990 but still an encounter gripped with fear and tension, was contested by two teams possessing enormous talent. Eyeing one another with caution for 120 minutes of stalemate, Italy's midfield, Abertini, Dino, Baggio and Donadoni, were slightly the better, though Brazil, with Bebeto and Romario, were the livelier in attack. It was

Romario whose invention offered the first threat. Running hard at the 'Azzurri' defence, he released Bebeto with a precise pass, Bebeto shaped and shot from a narrow angle, but the immaculate Maldini, reading the danger, stepped across to block the ball to safety. Italy came alive, Aldair's slip allowing Massaro space to surge forward and shoot. Taffarel spread himself to save. Never dreary but always tentative, the game ran its course. Roberto Baggio, half fit and ineffective, still found himself with opportunities to score, but his shooting failed him. Then 15 minutes from time good fortune again smiled on the Italians, Marcio Santos's thirty-yard effort deceiving Pagliuca in flight, slipping through his gloves to bounce gently against the goal post and back into his grateful arms. The relieved goalkeeper stepped back to plant an affectionate kiss on the woodwork. In extra time Italian luck held out: three minutes in, Bebeto, left a simple chance after Cafu's cross defeated Pagliuca, missed in embarrassing fashion. For the first time penalty kicks would settle the World Cup final.

Italy began the nerve jangling ritual. The recalled Baresi, excellent in their cause for 120 minutes, shot high over the bar. Distraught, he retreated to the blue-shirted scrum to watch. Marcia Santos, denied earlier by Pagliuca, stepped up to suffer the same fate again. Now steely souls made their mark, Albertini and Evani for the Italians, Romario and Branco for Brazil, 2–2. Massaro came forward, his shot clawed away by Taffarel, who then watched the rugged Dunga fire his team ahead. Enter Roberto Baggio to try and save his team, not for the first time. Sadly for him, his team, his country, the well of miracles from which he had drawn prodigiously had finally run dry, his weary effort rising harmlessly up and over the crossbar.

Brazil, to joyous celebration, had won their fourth Championship. Italy, in the cruellest manner, had lost; their luck, monumental throughout the competition, had betrayed them at the last and tallest hurdle.

Final

Brazil (0) **0, Italy** 0 (aet, 0–0 after 90 mins, Brazil won 3–2 on penalties)
17.7.94 LOS ANGELES
Brazil: Taffarel, Jorginho (Cafu), Marcio Santos, Aldair, Branco, Mazinho, Mauro Silva, Dunga, Zinho (Viola), Bebeto, Romario
Italy: Pagliuca, Mussi (Apolloni), Maldini, Baresi, Benarrivo, Donadoni, Albertini, Baggio D (Evani), Berti, Baggio R, Massaro
Referee: Puhl (Hungary)

CHAPTER 16

FRANCE

1998

Qualifying Tournament
174 entries
Brazil qualify as holders, France qualify as hosts

Europe (49): Albania, Armenia, Austria, Azerbaijan, Belarus, Belgium, Bosnia-Herzegovina, Bulgaria, Croatia, Cyprus, Czech Republic, Denmark, England, Estonia, Faroe Isles, Finland, Georgia, Germany, Greece, Holland, Hungary, Iceland, Ireland, Israel, Italy, Latvia, Liechtenstein, Lithuania, Luxembourg, Macedonia, Malta, Moldova, Northern Ireland, Norway, Poland, Portugal, Romania, Russia, San Marino, Scotland, Spain, Slovakia, Slovenia, Sweden, Switzerland, Turkey, Ukraine, Wales, Yugoslavia

South America (10): Argentina, Bolivia, Brazil, Chile, Colombia, Ecuador, Paraguay, Peru, Uruguay, Venezuela

CONCACAF (30): Antigua, Aruba, Barbados, Bahamas (withdrew), Belize, Bermuda (withdrew), Canada, Cayman Islands, Costa Rica, Cuba, Dominican Republic, El Salvador, Grenada, Guatemala, Guyana, Haiti, Honduras, Jamaica, Mexico, Netherlands Antilles, Nicaragua, Panama, Puerto Rico, St Kitts & Nevis, St Lucia, St Vincent & the Grenadines, Surinam, Trinidad and Tobago, USA

Asia (36): Bahrain, Bangladesh, Cambodia, China, Hong Kong, India, Indonesia, Iran, Iraq, Japan, Jordan, Lebanon, Khazakhstan, Korean Republic, Kyrgyzstan, Kuwait, Macao, Malaysia, Maldives, Nepal, Oman, Pakistan, Philippines, Qatar, Saudi Arabia, Singapore, Sri Lanka, Syria, Taiwan, Tajikistan, Thailand, Turkmenistan, UAE, Uzbekistan, Vietnam, Yemen

Africa (38) (2 withdrew): Algeria, Angola, Burkina Faso, Burundi, Cameroon, Congo, Egypt, Gabon, Gambia, Ghana, Guinea, Guinea-Bissau, Ivory Coast, Kenya, Liberia, Madagascar, Malawi, Mauritania, Mauritius, Morocco, Mozambique, Namibia, Nigeria, Rwanda, Senegal, Sierra Leone, South Africa, Sudan, Swaziland, Tanzania, Togo, Tunisia, Uganda, Zaire, Zambia, Zimbabwe

Oceania (10): Australia, Cook Islands, Fiji, New Zealand, Papua New Guinea, Solomon Islands, Tahiti, Tonga, Vanuatu, Western Samoa

Europe

Group 1 (Boznia-Herzegovina, Croatia, Denmark, Greece, Slovenia)

Greece v Slovenia 2–0, Greece v Bosnia-Herzegovina 3–0, Slovenia v Denmark 0–2, Croatia v Bosnia-Herzegovina 4–1, Denmark v Greece 2–1, Slovenia v Bosnia-Herzegovina 1–2, Croatia v Greece 1–1, Croatia v Denmark 1–1, Croatia v Slovenia 3–3, Bosnia-Herzegovina v Greece 0–1, Denmark v Slovenia 4–0, Greece v Croatia 0–1, Denmark v Bosnia-Herzegovina 2–0, Bosnia-Herzegovina v Denmark 3–0, Croatia v Bosnia-Herzegovina 3–2, Slovenia v Greece 0–3, Denmark v Croatia 3–1, Bosnia-Herzegovina v Slovenia 1–0, Greece v Denmark 0–0, Slovenia v Croatia 1–3

	P	W	D	L	F	A	Pts
Denmark	8	5	2	1	14	6	17
Croatia	8	4	3	1	17	12	15
Greece	8	4	2	2	11	4	14
Bosnia	8	3	0	5	9	14	9
Slovenia	8	0	1	7	5	20	1

Denmark qualify
Croatia play-off

Group 2 (England, Georgia, Italy, Moldovia, Poland)

Moldova v England 0–3, Moldova v Italy 1–3, England v Poland 2–1, Italy v Georgia 1–0, Georgia v England 0–2, Poland v Moldova 2–1, England v Italy 0–1, Italy v Moldova 3–0, Poland v Italy 0–0, England v Georgia 2–0, Italy v Poland 3–0, Poland v England 0–2, Georgia v Moldova 2–0, Poland v Georgia 4–1, England v Moldova 4–0, Georgia v Italy 0–0, Moldova v Georgia 0–1, Moldova v Poland 0–3, Italy v England 0–0, Georgia v Poland 3–0

	P	W	D	L	F	A	Pts
England	8	6	1	1	15	2	19
Italy	8	5	3	0	11	1	18
Poland	8	3	1	4	10	12	10
Georgia	8	3	1	4	7	9	10
Moldova	8	0	0	8	2	21	0

England qualify
Italy play-off

Group 3 (Azerbaijan, Finland, Hungary, Norway, Switzerland)

Norway v Azerbaijan 5–0, Azerbaijan v Switzerland 1–0, Hungary v Finland 1–0, Finland v Switzerland 2–3, Norway v Hungary 3–0, Switzerland v Norway 0–1, Azerbaijan v Hungary 0–3, Azerbaijan v Finland 1–2, Norway v Finland 1–1, Switzerland v Hungary 1–0, Finland v Azerbaijan 3–0, Hungary v Norway 1–1, Hungary v Switzerland 1–1, Finland v Norway 0–4, Switzerland v Finland 1–2, Azerbaijan v Norway 0–1, Hungary v Azerbaijan 3–1, Norway v Switzerland 5–0, Finland v Hungary 1–1, Switzerland v Azerbaijan 5–0

	P	W	D	L	F	A	Pts
Norway	8	6	2	0	21	2	20
Hungary	8	3	3	2	10	8	12
Finland	8	3	2	3	11	12	11
Switzerland	8	3	1	4	11	12	10
Azerbaijan	8	1	0	7	3	22	3

Norway qualify
Hungary play-off

Group 4 (Austria, Belarus, Estonia, Latvia, Scotland, Sweden)

Sweden v Belarus 5–1, Austria v Scotland 0–0, Belarus v Estonia 1–0, Latvia v Sweden 1–2, Estonia v Belarus 1–0, Latvia v Scotland 0–2, Sweden v Austria 0–1, Belarus v Latvia 1–1, Austria v Latvia 2–1, Scotland v Sweden 1–0, Estonia v Scotland 0–0, Scotland v Estonia 2–0, Scotland v Austria 2–0, Austria v Estonia 2–0, Sweden v Scotland 2–1, Latvia v Belarus 2–0, Estonia v Latvia 1–3, Estonia v Sweden 2–3, Latvia v Austria 1–3, Belarus v Scotland 0–1, Estonia v Austria 0–3, Belarus v Sweden 1–2, Austria v Sweden 1–0, Scotland v Belarus 4–1, Latvia v Estonia 1–0, Sweden v Latvia 1–0, Belarus v Austria 0–1, Austria v Belarus 4–0, Scotland v Latvia 2–0, Sweden v Estonia 1–0

	P	W	D	L	F	A	Pts
Austria	10	8	1	1	17	4	25
Scotland	10	7	2	1	15	3	23
Sweden	10	7	0	3	16	9	21
Latvia	10	3	1	6	10	14	10
Estonia	10	1	1	8	4	16	4
Belarus	10	1	1	8	5	21	4

Austria qualify
Scotland as Europe's best finished runner-up and qualify

Group 5 (Bulgaria, Cyprus, Israel, Luxembourg, Russia)

Israel v Bulgaria 2–1, Russia v Cyprus 4–0, Luxembourg v Bulgaria 1–2, Israel v Russia 1–1, Cyprus v Israel 2–0, Luxembourg v Russia 0–4, Cyprus v Bulgaria 1–3, Israel v Luxembourg 1–0, Cyprus v Russia 1–1, Luxembourg v Israel 0–3, Bulgaria v Cyprus 4–1, Israel v Cyprus 2–0, Russia v Luxembourg 3–0, Bulgaria v Luxembourg 4–0, Russia v Israel 2–0, Bulgaria v Israel 1–0, Luxembourg v Cyprus 1–3, Bulgaria v Russia 1–0, Cyprus v Luxembourg 3–0, Russia v Bulgaria 4–2

	P	W	D	L	F	A	Pts
Bulgaria	8	6	0	2	18	9	18
Russia	8	5	2	1	19	5	17
Israel	8	4	1	3	9	7	13
Cyprus	8	3	1	4	10	15	10
Luxembourg	8	0	0	8	2	22	0

Bulgaria qualify
Russia to play-off

Group 6 (Czech Republic, Faroe Isles, Malta, Slovakia, Spain, Yugoslavia)

Yugoslavia v Faroe Islands 3–1, Yugoslavia v Malta 6–0, Faroe Isles v Slovakia 1–2, Faroe Isles v Spain 2–6, Czech Republic v Malta 6–0, Slovakia v Malta 6–0, Faroe Isles v Yugoslavia 1–8, Czech Republic v Spain 0–0, Slovakia v Faroe Isles 3–0, Yugoslavia v Czech Republic 1–0, Spain v Slovakia 4–1, Spain v Yugoslavia 2–0, Malta v Spain 0–3, Spain v Malta 4–0, Malta v Slovakia 0–2, Czech Republic v Yugoslavia 1–2, Malta v Faroe Isles 1–2, Yugoslavia v Spain 1–1, Yugoslavia v Slovakia 2–0, Faroe Isles v Malta 2–1, Spain v Czech Republic 1–0, Czech Republic v Faroe Isles 2–0, Slovakia v Czech Republic 2–1, Faroe Isles v Czech Republic 0–2, Slovakia v Yugoslavia 1–1, Malta v Czech Republic 0–1, Slovakia v Spain 1–2, Malta v Yugoslavia 0–5, Spain v Faroe Isles 3–1, Czech Republic v Slovakia 3–0

	P	W	D	L	F	A	Pts
Spain	10	8	2	0	26	6	26
Yugoslavia	10	7	2	1	29	7	23
Czech Republic	10	5	1	4	16	6	16
Slovakia	10	5	1	4	18	14	16
Faroe Isles	10	2	0	8	10	31	6
Malta	10	0	0	10	2	37	0

Spain qualify
Yugoslavia play-off

Group 7 (Belgium, Holland, San Marino, Turkey, Wales)

San Marino v Wales 0–5, Belgium v Turkey 2–1, Wales v San Marino 6–0, Wales v Holland 1–3, San Marino v Belgium 0–3, Holland v Wales 7–1, Turkey v San Marino 7–0, Wales v Turkey 0–0, Belgium v Holland 0–3, Holland v San Marino 4–0, Wales v Belgium 1–2, Turkey v Holland 1–0, Turkey v Belgium 1–3, San Marino v Holland 0–6, Belgium v San Marino 6–0, Turkey v Wales 6–4, Holland v Belgium 3–1, San Marino v Turkey 0–5, Belgium v Wales 3–2, Holland v Turkey 0–0

	P	W	D	L	F	A	Pts
Holland	8	6	1	1	26	4	19
Belgium	8	6	0	2	20	11	18
Turkey	8	4	2	2	21	9	14
Wales	8	2	1	5	20	21	7
San Marino	8	0	0	8	0	42	0

Holland qualify
Belgium play-off

Group 8 (Iceland, Ireland, Liechtenstein, Lithuania, Macedonia, Romania)

Macedonia v Liechtenstein 3–0, Iceland v Macedonia 1–1, Liechtenstein v Ireland 0–5, Romania v Lithuania 3–0, Lithuania v Iceland 2–0, Iceland v Romania 0–4, Ireland v Macedonia 3–0, Lithuania v Liechtenstein 2–1, Liechtenstein v Macedonia 1–11, Ireland v Iceland 0–0, Macedonia v Romania 0–3, Romania v Liechtenstein 8–0, Lithuania v Romania 0–1, Macedonia v Ireland 3–2, Liechtenstein v Lithuania 0–2, Romania v Ireland 1–0, Ireland v Liechtenstein 5–0, Macedonia v Iceland 1–0, Iceland v Lithuania 0–0, Liechtenstein v Iceland 0–4, Ireland v Lithuania 0–0, Romania v Macedonia 4–2, Iceland v Ireland 2–4, Liechtenstein v Romania 1–8, Lithuania v Macedonia 2–0, Romania v Iceland 4–0, Lithuania v Ireland 1–2, Iceland v Liechtenstein 4–0, Ireland v Romania 1–1, Macedonia v Lithuania 1–2

	P	W	D	L	F	A	Pts
Romania	10	9	1	0	37	4	28
Ireland	10	5	3	2	22	8	18
Lithuania	10	5	2	3	11	8	17
Macedonia	10	4	1	5	22	18	13
Iceland	10	2	3	5	11	16	9
Liechtenstein	10	0	0	10	3	52	0

Romania qualify
Ireland play-off

Group 9 (Albania, Armenia, Germany, Northern Ireland, Portugal, Ukraine)

Northern Ireland v Ukraine 0–1, Armenia v Portugal 0–0, Northern Ireland v Armenia 1–1, Ukraine v Portugal 2–1, Albania v Portugal 0–3, Armenia v Germany 1–5, Albania v Armenia 1–1, Germany v Northern Ireland 1–1, Portugal v Ukraine 1–0, Portugal v Germany 0–0, Northern Ireland v Albania 2–0, Albania v Ukraine 0–1, Northern Ireland v Portugal 0–0, Albania v Germany 2–3, Ukraine v Northern Ireland 2–1, Germany v Ukraine 2–0, Armenia v Northern Ireland 0–0, Ukraine v Armenia 1–1, Ukraine v Germany 0–0, Portugal v Albania 2–0, Northern Ireland v Germany 1–3, Portugal v Armenia 3–1, Ukraine v Albania 1–0, Germany v Portugal 1–1, Armenia v Albania 3–0, Albania v Northern Ireland 1–0, Germany v Armenia 4–0, Germany v Albania 4–3, Portugal v Northern Ireland 1–0, Armenia v Ukraine 0–2

	P	W	D	L	F	A	Pts
Germany	10	6	4	0	23	9	22
Ukraine	10	6	2	2	10	6	20
Portugal	10	5	4	1	12	4	9
Armenia	10	1	5	4	8	17	8
Northern Ireland	10	1	4	5	6	10	7
Albania	10	1	1	8	7	20	4

Germany qualify
Ukraine play-off

Play-offs
First Legs
Croatia v Ukraine 2–0, Russia v Italy 1–1, Ireland v Belgium 1–1, Hungary v Yugoslavia 1–7

Second Legs
Belgium v Ireland 2–1, Italy v Russia 1–0, Ukraine v Croatia 1–1, Yugoslavia v Hungary 5–0
Belgium, Italy, Croatia and Yugoslavia qualify

South America

Argentina v Bolivia 3–1, Colombia v Paraguay 1–0, Ecuador v Peru 4–1, Venezuela v Uruguay 0–2, Ecuador v Argentina 2–0, Peru v Colombia 1–1, Uruguay v Paraguay 0–2, Venezuela v Chile 1–1, Bolivia v Venezuela 6–1, Chile v Ecuador 4–1, Colombia v Uruguay 3–1, Peru v Argentina 0–0, Argentina v Paraguay 1–1, Bolivia v Peru 0–0, Colombia v Chile 4–1, Ecuador v Venezuela 1–0, Uruguay v Bolivia 1–0, Ecuador v Colombia 2–1, Paraguay v Chile 2–1, Venezuela v Argentina 2–5, Peru v Venezuela 4–1, Bolivia v Colombia 2–2, Paraguay v Ecuador 1–0, Chile v Uruguay 1–0, Venezuela v Colombia 0–2, Bolivia v Paraguay 0–0, Argentina v Chile 1–1, Uruguay v Peru 2–0, Peru v Chile 2–1, Bolivia v Ecuador 2–0, Venezuela v Paraguay 0–2, Uruguay v Argentina 0–0, Bolivia v Chile 1–1, Colombia v Argentine 0–1, Ecuador v Uruguay 4–0, Paraguay v Peru 2–1, Bolivia v Argentina 2–1, Paraguay v Colombia 2–1, Peru v Ecuador 1–1, Uruguay v Venezuela 3–1, Chile v Venezuela 6–0, Colombia v Peru 0–1, Paraguay v Uruguay 3–1, Argentina v Ecuador 2–1, Argentina v Peru 2–0, Ecuador v Chile 1–1, Uruguay v Colombia 1–1, Venezuela v Bolivia 1–1, Chile v Colombia 4–1, Paraguay v Argentina 1–2, Peru v Bolivia 2–1, Venezuela v Ecuador 1–1, Argentina v Venezuela 2–0, Bolivia v Uruguay 1–0, Chile v Paraguay 2–1, Colombia v Ecuador 1–0, Colombia v Bolivia 3–0, Ecuador v Paraguay 2–1, Uruguay v Chile 1–0, Venezuela v Peru 0–3, Chile v Argentina 1–2, Colombia v Venezuela 1–0, Paraguay v Bolivia 2–1, Peru v Uruguay 2–1, Argentina v Uruguay 0–0, Chile v Peru 4–0, Ecuador v Bolivia 1–0, Paraguay v Venezuela 1–0, Argentina v Colombia 1–1, Chile v Bolivia 3–0, Peru v Paraguay 1–0, Uruguay v Ecuador 5–3

	P	W	D	L	F	A	Pts
Argentina	16	8	6	2	23	13	30
Paraguay	16	9	2	5	21	14	29
Colombia	16	8	4	4	23	15	28
Chile	16	7	4	5	32	18	25
Peru	16	7	4	5	19	20	25
Ecuador	16	6	3	7	22	21	21
Uruguay	16	6	3	7	18	21	21
Bolivia	16	4	5	7	18	21	17
Venezuela	16	0	3	13	8	41	3

CONCACAF

First round (Caribbean zone)
Dominican Republic v Aruba 3–2, Aruba v Dominican Republic 1–3, Bahamas withdrew v St Kitts & Nevis w.o., Guyana v Grenada 1–2, Grenada v Guyana 6–0, Dominican Republic v Antigua 3–3, Antigua v Dominican Republic 1–3

Second round (Caribbean zone)
Bermuda withdrew v Trinidad and Tobago w.o., Puerto Rico v St Vincent & the Grenadines 1–2, St Vincent & the Grenadines v Puerto Rico 7–0, Cuba v Cayman Islands 5–0, Cayman Islands v Cuba 0–1, St Kitts & Nevis v St Lucia 5–1, St Lucia v St Kitts & Nevis 0–1, Haiti v Grenada 6–1, Grenada v Haiti 0–1, Surinam v Jamaica 0–1, Jamaica v Surinam 1–0, Dominican Republic v Barbados 0–1, Barbados v Dominican Republic 1–0, Dominican Republic v Netherlands Antilles 2–1, Netherlands Antilles v Dominican Republic 0–0

Third round (Caribbean zone)
Cuba v Haiti 6–1, Haiti v Cuba 1–1, Dominican Republic v Trinidad and Tobago 1–4, Trinidad and Tobago v Dominican Republic 8–0, Barbados v Jamaica 0–1, Jamaica v Barbados 2–0, St Kitts & Nevis v St Vincent 2–2, St Vincent v St Kitts & Nevis 0–0

First round (Central American zone)
Nicaragua v Guatemala 0–1, Guatemala v Nicaragua 2–1, Belize v Panama 1–2, Panama v Belize 4–1

Semi-Final Round
Group 1
Trinidad & Tobago v Costa Rica 0–1, Trinidad & Tobago v Guatemala 1–1, USA v Guatemala 2–0, USA v Trinidad & Tobago 2–0, Costa Rica v Guatemala 3–0, Guatemala v Costa Rica 1–0, Trinidad & Tobago v USA 0–1, Costa Rica v USA 2–1, Guatemala v Trinidad & Tobago 2–1, USA v Costa Rica 2–1, Costa Rica v Trinidad & Tobago 2–1, Guatemala v USA 2–2
USA and Costa Rica progress

Group 2
Canada v Panama 3–1, Cuba v El Salvador 0–5, Cuba v Panama 3–1, Panama v El Salvador 1–1, Canada v Cuba 2–0, Cuba v Canada 0–2, Panama v Canada 0–0, Canada v El Salvador 1–0, El Salvador v Panama 3–2, El Salvador v Cuba 3–0, Panama v Cuba 3–1, El Salvador v Canada 0–2
El Salvador and Canada progress

Group 3

Jamaica v Honduras 3–0, St Vincent & the Grenadines v Mexico 0–3, Honduras v Mexico 2–1, St Vincent & the Grenadines v Jamaica 1–2, St Vincent & the Grenadines v Honduras 1–4, Mexico v Jamaica 2–1, Honduras v Jamaica 0–0, Mexico v St Vincent & the Grenadines 5–1, Mexico v Honduras 3–1, Jamaica v St Vincent & the Grenadines 5–0, Honduras v St Vincent & the Grenadines 11–3, Jamaica v Mexico 1–0

Jamaica and Mexico progress

Finals

Mexico v Canada 4–0, Jamaica v USA 0–0, USA v Canada 3–0, Costa Rica v Mexico 0–0, Costa Rica v USA 3–2, Canada v El Salvador 0–0, Mexico v Jamaica 6–0, USA v Mexico 2–2, Canada v Jamaica 0–0, El Salvador v Costa Rica 2–1, Costa Rica v Jamaica 3–1, Jamaica v El Salvador 1–0, Canada v Costa Rica 1–0, El Salvador v Mexico 0–1, El Salvador v USA 1–1, Costa Rica v El Salvador 0–0, USA v Costa Rica 1–0, Jamaica v Canada 1–0, Jamaica v Costa Rica 1–0, El Salvador v Canada 4–1, USA v Jamaica 1–1, Mexico v El Salvador 5–0, Canada v Mexico 2–2, Mexico v USA 0–0, Canada v USA 0–3, El Salvador v Jamaica 2–2, Mexico v Costa Rica 3–3, Jamaica v Mexico 0–0, Costa Rica v Canada 3–1, USA v El Salvador 4–2

	P	W	D	L	F	A	Pts
Mexico	10	4	6	0	23	7	18
USA	10	4	5	1	17	9	17
Jamaica	10	3	5	2	7	12	14
Costa Rica	10	3	3	4	13	12	12
El Salvador	10	2	4	4	11	16	10
Canada	10	1	3	6	5	20	6

Mexico, USA and Jamaica qualify

Asia

First Round
Group 1

Taiwan v Saudi Arabia 0–2, Malaysia v Bangladesh 2–0, Bangladesh v Taiwan 1–3, Malaysia v Saudi Arabia 0–0, Bangladesh v Saudi Arabia 1–4, Malaysia v Taiwan 2–0, Taiwan v Malaysia 0–0, Saudi Arabia v Bangladesh 3–0, Taiwan v Bangladesh 1–2, Saudi Arabia v Malaysia 3–0, Bangladesh v Malaysia 0–1, Saudi Arabia v Taiwan 6–0

Group 2

Maldives v Iran 0–17, Syria v Maldives 12–0, Kyrgzstan v Iran 0–7, Syria v Iran 0–1, Kyrgyzstan v Maldives 3–0, Iran v Kyrgyzstan 3–1, Maldives v Syria 0–12, Iran v Maldives 9–0, Kyrgyzstan v Syria 2–1, Iran v Syria 2–2, Maldives v Kyrgyzstan 0–6

Group 3

Jordan v UAE 0–0, Bahrain v UAE 1–2, Bahrain v Jordan 1–0, Jordan v Bahrain 4–1, UAE v Bahrain 3–0, UAE v Jordan 2–0

Group 4

Nepal v Macao 1–1, Oman v Japan 0–1, Macao v Japan 0–10, Oman v Nepal 1–0, Nepal v Japan 0–6, Oman v Macao 4–0, Japan v Macao 10–0, Nepal v Oman 0–6, Japan v Nepal 3–0, Macao v Oman 0–2, Japan v Oman 1–1, Macao v Nepal 2–1

Group 5

Indonesia v Cambodia 8–0, Indonesia v Yemen 0–0, Cambodia v Yemen 0–1, Cambodia v Indonesia 1–1, Yemen v Uzbekistan 0–1, Yemen v Cambodia 7–0, Uzbekistan v Cambodia 6–0, Indonesia v Uzbekistan 1–1, Yemen v Indonesia 1–1, Uzbekistan v Indonesia 3–0, Cambodia v Uzbekistan 1–4, Uzbekistan v Yemen 5–1

Group 6

Hong Kong v South Korea 0–2, Thailand v South Korea 1–3, Thailand v Hong Kong 2–0, Hong Kong v Thailand 3–2, South Korea v Hong Kong 4–0, South Korea v Thailand 0–0

Group 7

Lebanon v Singapore 1–1, Singapore v Kuwait 0–1, Kuwait v Lebanon 2–0, Singapore v Lebanon 1–2, Kuwait v Singapore 4–0, Lebanon v Kuwait 1–3

Group 8

Tajikistan v Vietnam 4–0, Turkmenistan v China 1–4, Tajikistan v China 0–1, Turkmenistan v Vietnam 2–1, Vietnam v China 1–3, Turkmenistan v Tajikistan 1–2, Vietnam v Tajikstan 0–4, China v Turkmenistan 1–0, Vietnam v Turkmenistan 0–4, China v Vietnam 4–0, Tajikistan v Turkmenistan 5–0

Group 9

Kazakhstan v Pakistan 3–0, Pakistan v Iraq 2–6, Iraq v Kazakhstan 1–2, Pakistan v Kazakhstan 0–7, Iraq v Pakistan 6–1, Kazakhstan v Iraq 3–1

Group 10
Qatar v Sri Lanka 3–0, India v Philippines 2–0, Qatar v Philippines 5–0, Sri Lanka v India 1–1, Philippines v Sri Lanka 0–3, Qatar v India 6–0

Second Round
Group A
China v Iran 2–4, Saudi Arabia v Kuwait 2–1, Iran v Saudi Arabia 1–1, Qatar v Kuwait 0–2, Kuwait v Iran 1–1, Qatar v China 1–1, Iran v Qatar 3–0, China v Saudi Arabia 1–0, Kuwait v China 1–2, Saudi Arabia v Qatar 1–0, Iran v China 4–1, Kuwait v Saudi Arabia 2–1, Saudi Arabia v Iran 1–0, Kuwait v Qatar 0–1, China v Qatar 2–3, Iran v Kuwait 0–0, Saudi Arabia v China 1–1, Qatar v Iran 2–0, China v Kuwait 1–0, Qatar v Saudi Arabia 0–1

	P	W	D	L	F	A	Pts
Saudi Arabia	8	4	2	2	8	6	14
Iran	8	3	3	2	13	8	12
China	8	3	2	3	11	14	11
Qatar	8	3	1	4	7	10	10
Kuwait	8	2	2	4	7	8	8

Group B
South Korea v Kazakhstan 3–0, Japan v Uzbekistan 6–3, South Korea v Uzbekistan 2–1, UAE v Kazakhstan 4–0, UAE v Japan 0–0, Kazakhstan v Uzbekistan 1–1, Uzbekistan v UAE 2–3, Japan v South Korea 1–2, Kazakhstan v Japan 1–1, South Korea v UAE 3–0, Kazakhstan v South Korea 1–1, Uzbekistan v Japan 1–1, Uzbekistan v South Korea 1–5, Kazakhstan v UAE 3–0, Uzbekistan v Kazakhstan 4–0, Japan v UAE 1–1, South Korea v Japan 0–2, UAE v Uzbekistan 0–0, Japan v Kazakhstan 5–1, UAE v South Korea 1–3

	P	W	D	L	F	A	Pts
South Korea	8	6	1	1	19	7	19
Japan	8	3	4	1	17	9	13
UAE	8	2	3	3	9	12	9
Uzbekistan	8	1	3	4	13	18	6
Kazakhstan	8	1	3	4	7	19	6

South Korea and Saudi Arabia qualify

Play-off (Malaysia)
Iran v Japan 2–3
Japan qualify

Africa

First round

Sudan v Zambia 2–0, Namibia v Mozambique 2–0, Tanzania v Ghana 0–0, Swaziland v Gabon 0–1, Uganda v Angola 0–2, Mauritius v Zaire 1–5, Malawi v South Africa 0–1, Madagascar v Zimbabwe 1–2, Guinea-Bissau v Guinea 3–2, Rwanda v Tunisia 1–3, Congo v Ivory Coast 2–0, Kenya v Algeria 3–1, Burundi v Sierra Leone 1–0, Mauritania v Burkina Faso 0–0, Togo v Senegal 2–1, Gambia v Liberia 2–1, Algeria v Kenya 1–0, Senegal v Togo 1–1, South Africa v Malawi 3–0, Sierra Leone v Burundi 0–1, Angola v Uganda 3–1, Gabon v Swaziland 2–0, Guinea v Guinea-Bissau 3–1, Ivory Coast v Congo 1–1, Mozambique v Namibia 1–1, Tunisia v Rwanda 2–0, Burkina Faso v Mauritania 2–0, Zaire v Mauritius 2–0, Zambia v Sudan 3–0, Zimbabwe v Madagascar 2–2, Ghana v Tanzania 2–1, Liberia v Gambia 4–0

Second Round
Group 1

Nigeria v Burkina Faso 2–0, Guinea v Kenya 3–1, Kenya v Nigeria 1–1, Burkina Faso v Guinea 0–2, Nigeria v Guinea 2–1, Kenya v Burkina Faso 4–3, Kenya v Guinea 1–0, Burkina Faso v Nigeria 1–2, Nigeria v Kenya 3–0, Guinea v Burkina Faso 3–1, Guinea v Nigeria 1–0, Burkina Faso v Kenya 2–4

	P	W	D	L	F	A	Pts
Nigeria	6	4	1	1	10	4	13
Guinea	6	4	0	2	10	5	12
Kenya	6	3	1	2	11	12	10
Burkina Faso	6	0	0	6	7	17	0

Nigeria qualify

Group 2

Egypt v Namibia 7–1, Liberia v Tunisia 0–1, Namibia v Liberia 0–0, Tunisia v Egypt 1–0, Liberia v Egypt 1–0, Namibia v Tunisia 1–2, Namibia v Egypt 2–3, Tunisia v Liberia 2–0, Egypt v Tunisia 0–0, Liberia v Namibia 1–2, Egypt v Liberia 5–0, Tunisia v Namibia 4–0

	P	W	D	L	F	A	Pts
Tunisia	6	5	1	0	10	1	16
Egypt	6	3	1	2	15	5	10
Liberia	6	1	1	4	2	10	4
Namibia	6	1	1	4	6	17	4

Tunisia qualify

Group 3

South Africa v Zaire 1–0, Congo v Zambia 1–0, Zambia v South Africa 0–0, Zaire v Congo 1–1, Congo v South Africa 2–0, Zaire v Zambia 2–2, Zaire v South Africa 1–2, Zambia v Congo 3–0, Congo v Zaire 1–0, South Africa v Zambia 3–0, South Africa v Congo 1–0, Zambia v Zaire 2–0

	P	W	D	L	F	A	Pts
South Africa	6	4	1	1	7	3	13
Congo	6	3	1	2	5	5	10
Zambia	6	2	2	2	7	6	8
Zaire	6	0	2	4	4	9	2

South Africa qualify

Group 4

Angola v Zimbabwe 2–1, Togo v Cameroon 2–4, Cameroon v Angola 0–0, Zimbabwe v Togo 3–0, Angola v Togo 3–1, Cameroon v Zimbabwe 1–0, Cameroon v Togo 2–0, Zimbabwe v Angola 0–0, Angola v Cameroon 1–1, Togo v Zimbabwe 2–1, Zimbabwe v Cameroon 1–2, Togo v Angola 1–1

	P	W	D	L	F	A	Pts
Cameroon	6	4	2	0	10	4	14
Angola	6	2	4	0	7	4	10
Zimbabwe	6	1	1	4	6	7	4
Togo	6	1	1	4	6	14	4

Group 5

Morocco v Sierra Leone 4–0, Gabon v Ghana 1–1, Sierra Leone v Gabon 1–0, Ghana v Morocco 2–2, Sierra v Leone v Ghana 1–1, Gabon v Morocco 0–4, Sierra Leone v Morocco 0–1, Ghana v Gabon 3–0, Morocco v Ghana 1–0, Morocco v Gabon 2–0, Ghana v Sierra Leone 0–2

	P	W	D	L	F	A	Pts
Morocco	6	5	1	0	14	2	16
Sierra Leone	5	2	1	2	4	6	7
Ghana	6	1	3	2	7	7	6
Gabon	5	0	1	4	1	11	1

Gabon and Sierra Leone not played
Morocco qualify

Oceania

First Round
Melanesian Group
Papua New Guinea v Solomon Islands 1–1, Solomon Islands v Vanuatu 1–1, Papua New Guinea v Vanuatu 2–1

Polynesian Group
Tonga v Cook Islands 2–0, Western Samoa v Cook Islands 2–1, Tongav Western Samoa 1–0

Play-off
Tonga v Solomon Islands 0–4, Solomon Islands v Tonga 9–0

Second Round
Group 1
Australia v Solomon Islands 13–0, Australia v Tahiti 5–0, Solomon Islands v Tahiti 4–1, Solomon Islands v Australia 2–6, Tahiti v Australia 0–2, Tahiti v Soloman Islands 1–1

Group 2
Papua New Guinea v New Zealand 1–0, Fiji v New Zealand 0–1, New Zealand v Papua New Guinea 7–0, Fiji v Papua New Guinea 3–1, New Zealand v Fiji 5–0, Papua New Guinea v Fiji 0–1

Third Round
Winner of Group 1 v Winner of Group 2; Third Round Winner plays team finishing fourth in Asia
New Zealand v Australia 0–3, Australia v New Zealand 2–0

Oceania/Asian Play off
Iran v Australia 1–1, Australia v Iran 2–2 (Iran win on away goals) Iran qualify

1998 FRANCE 10 June–12 July

QUALIFIERS

Argentina	Jamaica
Austria	Japan
Belgium	Mexico
Brazil	Morocco
Bulgaria	Nigeria
Cameroon	Norway
Chile	Paraguay
Colombia	Romania
Croatia	Saudi Arabia
Denmark	Scotland
England	South Africa
France	South Korea
Germany	Spain
Holland	Tunisia
Iran	United States
Italy	Yugoslavia

In 1998 France hosted the World Cup for the second time, a huge media circus greater by far than any of its predecessors. Thirty-two teams would compete for the prize in what generally was held to be the most open event in a very long time. Eight groups of four would allow sixteen winners and runners-up to advance to the knockout stages and begin the road all hoped would lead to the Stade de France in Paris on 12 July. Astonishingly, Africa, without a representative until 1966, now had five. One new rule introduced to encourage positive play in extra time was 'The Golden Goal': the first team to score during the period would instantly win the match, less cruel perhaps than elimination by penalty kicks, but only just.

Group A would feature Champions and favourites Brazil, the highly regarded Morocco, and two Europeans, Scotland and Norway, both enjoying a period of renaissance. Brazil in preparation had not been entirely successful, suffering defeats by Norway and the USA and embarrassing draws with Jamaica and Guatemala. However, they had the shaven-headed Ronaldo, arguably the world's greatest player, the dazzling Denilson and the little genius of Romario to call upon, and would hope to emulate their team of 1958 and carry the Trophy away from the host continent for only the second time. Morocco, coached by Frenchman Henri Michel, would come with an interesting blend of youth and experience, and genuine hopes of progress. Naybet of

Deportivo provided strength in defence, Hadji and Bassir guile and punch further forward. Scotland were a fast-improving team, a team without stars but packed with disciplined commitment and defensively sound. Kevin Gallacher would be expected to provide goals while his Blackburn Rovers colleague, Colin Hendry, a towering, commanding centre half, would lead by example. What of Norway? Eager to make amends for 1994, theirs was a hard, uncompromising team of mercenaries largely plying their trade in England. Easy qualifiers from a poor group, their robust, direct style would not be relished by the opposition, least of all Brazil, beaten in Oslo a year earlier 4–2.

Italy had been seeded in Group B under the questionable system adopted by FIFA. Undeniably talented, their team included both Baggios, the forceful Di Matteo of Chelsea, golden boy Del Piero of Juventus and the coach Maldini's own son Paulo on the left flank. England, though, had eclipsed them in qualification, and their self-belief was damaged. The Group also comprised Austria, Chile and Cameroon, nations of vastly different cultures and traditions. Austria, a team with a reputation as a dour and efficient side, whose victory over Sweden both home and away had seen them top their qualification group, had Herzog as their neat playmaker and Toni Polster, a top-class marksman, both of whom earned a living in the highly competitive German Bundesliga. Chile came with a greatly enhanced reputation. Thought to be defensively frail, they had distinguished themselves mightily with a friendly victory at Wembley over England, and with Zamorano of Italy's Internazionale and Salas, a striker of phenomenal quality, had players capable of unsettling the very best in the Tournament. Cameroon, too, had played in London, though on a cold November evening and had looked bereft of ideas, appearing content merely on damage limitation. Still, Mboma would provide a goal threat and sixteen-year-old Soloman Olembe, the competition's youngest player, offered great hope for the future.

Could France perhaps deliver the Trophy to an expectant nation? Host and seeded in Group C, theirs was a fine side sprinkled liberally with marvellously gifted performers, Zidane, Djorkaeff, Desailly, Lizarazu and Didier Deschamps. Goalscoring for them had been a problem, and the inclusion of Trezeguet, a dashing young striker from Monaco, hoped to redress this. Memories of Euro '96 lingered, where they had appeared paralyzed with fear, too afraid of the prospect of losing to win. South Africa, debutantes, stout and resourceful, replete with players competing throughout Europe, had Mark Fish, a centre half, Phil Masinga and Lucas Radebe. Whatever the results, 'Bafana Bafana' ('the Boys, the Boys') would enjoy their adventure. Denmark, surprisingly, made only their second appearance. Not a team of the quality of 1986 nor indeed the European Championship side of 1992, they still boasted the wonderfully talented Laudrup brothers and perhaps the world's finest goalkeeper in Schmeichel. Impressive early in qualification, their form had meandered somewhat, finally secured in a nervy and fortunate draw with Greece in Athens. Finally for Group C came Saudi Arabia, whose qualification from the Asian Group A had been achieved with comfort. Theirs was a young team, with Al-Jaber a useful striker and Al-Deayea a veteran goalkeeper who performed notably in the USA competition four years earlier. They looked to build on their previous success where victories over Morocco and then Belgium had commanded respect.

In Group D four tough customers had been drawn together, Spain very much the form team, Bulgaria fourth in 1994, Olympic Champions Nigeria, and Paraguay with a team they believed to be the best in their history. The scribes rejoiced: here again was a 'Group of Death'. Spain were the fancy of many, durable and skilful with a record over four seasons, and since Javier Clemente took the reins, of just one defeat – to France in Marseilles. At Euro '96 they had proven themselves formidable. Much the better team, they had been unfortunate to be eliminated in a penalty shoot-out against England, their hosts. It was hoped that twenty-year-old Raul would provide their inspiration, and in the toughest qualification group of all, featuring Yugoslavia, the Czech Republic and Slovakia, they had won at a canter. Bulgaria opposed Spain again, just as they had in Euro '96. Their poor performance then had fuelled suspicion that theirs was an ageing team in decline. Yet they had rebounded gloriously, dramatically winning a decisive group qualification match in Sofia against Russia. The surly though lethal Stoichkov would again feature for them, as would Kostadinov, Balakov and the wonderfully composed Letchkov, so effective in the United States. Nigeria, capable of almost anything, wondered whether they could fulfil Walter Winterbottom's prophecy forty years earlier that an African team could win the Championship by the turn of the century? Certainly in Sunday Oliseh and Jay Jay Okocha they had players of sublime talent, and had beaten strong Argentinean and Brazilian teams to claim Olympic Gold. They would be further reinforced by their captain and pivot Nwanko Kanu, returned after career-threatening heart surgery. However, Nigeria's preparation had been horrible. Ejected from the African Nations Cup and condemned universally for their poor record on Human Rights, the Military Junta unnecessarily delayed the installation of a new coach and appeared determined to hamper in every conceivable manner the team's progress. Paraguay, coached by Brazilian Paulo Cesar Carpeggiani, were a strong, well-organized team. Difficult to break down and with credible victories over Chile, Colombia, Peru and Uruguay, they enjoyed the respect of South American football. Playing for them were Roberto Acuña, a fine organizer in midfield, and Jose Luis Chilavert, goalkeeper extraordinare, occasionally brilliant, always inspirational, though inclined to maniacal outbursts or provocation designed to, and often prompting, wild and unseemly brawls; would he and Paraguay self-destruct?

In Group E, Holland had been seeded and drawn with their neighbours Belgium, plus South Korea and Mexico. A team of outstanding individual talent, with Bergkamp hailed as one of the world's finest, Overmars, Kluivert, Seedorf and David, theirs was a squad the envy of most, although the whole often seemed less than its parts and the Dutch habitually seemed a disunited group. Curiously, Belgium had opposed Holland in qualification and had finally won through in a play-off against the Irish. Despite Luc Nilis, a dangerous striker playing for PSV Eidhoven, and the experienced and often inspired Scifo, they appeared an unimpressive team for traditionally so effective a footballing nation. South Korea for the third successive time had forced their way to the finals, better prepared now, and with fine players in Yong-Soo, a prolific goalscorer, and Myung-Bo, an accomplished defender, optimism abounded. Mexico completing the quartet also had expectations of progress; a settled team including their flamboyant goalkeeper Campos, they had qualified with ease from the CONCACAF group, and on their travels at last appeared a more resolute proposition.

Germany headed Group F, European Champions and a formidable team by any standards, joining the Yugoslavians, Iran and the United States. The Germans had qualified unconvincingly, their team struggling desperately to overcome Albania. But with Klinsmann, their blond-haired marksman, Kohler, the consummate defender, and Bierhoff, prolific at Euro '96 and a huge success for Udinese in Italy's Serie A, they were a fearsome proposition. Iran had already proven themselves the great survivors. Beaten into second place in qualification by the Koreans in Asia's Group A and again by Japan in a play-off, they succeeded finally against the unfortunate Australians and from the distinctly unpromising position of 2–0 behind. However, in Azizi they possessed Asia's player of the year and Bagheri had scored a remarkable seventeen goals for them in qualification. The United States had enjoyed their moment of triumph in Mexico City, holding the Mexicans for the first time to an away draw in front of 114,000 supporters eager to witness their destruction. Given this platform they had qualified with ease and subsequently had defeated a below par Brazil in a startling upset. Kasey Keller, their goalkeeper, an assured figure, the experienced Dooley and injury-prone playmaker Tab Ramos would be key figures. The Yugoslavians were an enigma; Stojkovic and Savicevic were present, as was Predrag Mijatovic, the Real Madrid striker, who had been instrumental in the annihilation of poor Hungary by a staggering aggregate of 12–1 in the play-off. Theirs was an attack to trouble the best, though defeat in Madrid by Spain suggested old frailties lingered.

Romania headed Group G with the thirty-two-year-old Hagi, Petrescu of Chelsea (a talented full back) and Munteanu, their midfield organizer. Easy qualifiers and seeded for the Tournament, they were nevertheless disappointed with the draw. 'We had hoped to avoid England,' said coach Iordanescu

glumly. So what of England? Winners of a group featuring Italy and conquerors of both France and the Italians in 'Le Tournoi', they were considered by
many one of a handful of serious contenders. With Seaman an excellent goalkeeper, Adams in defence a rock, Ince an abrasive, combative midfield player,
theirs was an immensely powerful team. Despite the precocious talents of
Beckham, Campbell, Rio Ferdinand and Owen, worryingly Shearer, powerful
and inspirational centre forward, had suffered a lengthy lay off through injury,
and as the Tournament approached, doubts continued over the form of
Gascoigne, supremely gifted and a key galvanizing force during their campaign. In the event, coach Glen Hoddle resisted the temptation to use
Gascoigne, sensationally axing him. Colombia, as they had been in the United
States, were an unfathomable commodity. Skilful and at times quite irresistible,
this was a team commanding respect; but they could be vulnerable. Asprilla
would provide a constant threat, Valderrama again would weave his intricate
patterns in midfield, and the world waited to see which Colombian team, good
or bad, would be in competition. Tunisia playing in their second Tournament
expected huge support. Well organized and defensively sound, they had
excelled in African football, and coached by Henri Kasperczak, the former
Polish international, and prompted by Adel Sellimi, they would be ready and
able to capitalize on any complacency.

Argentina were seeded in Group H and found themselves in a fascinating
contest indicative of the Tournament's embracement of all corners of the
globe. Here were Japan from Asia, Jamaica from the Central and North
American Federation, and Croatia, a new nation in Europe of considerable
talent. Argentina had progressed during qualification; initially threatened,
they had blossomed under the stewardship of Daniel Passarella. Crespo and
Batistuta offered striking options the envy of most, and Ortega was a talented
and explosive playmaker. Japan for the first time had made it to the finals, a
reconnaissance for 2002 when, with the Koreans, they would host the
Championship. For Japan, winners over Iran in a play-off, Nakata, a youthful playmaker, would be an influence, as would Wagner Lopes,
Brazilian-born but a hero now in his adopted country. Croatia, sound in
defence and with threatening attack, had nudged aside Ukraine in a play-off.
A team of experience and ability, they had Stimac and Bilic, masterful in
defence, Suker and Boksic, creative further forward, and Boban, wonderfully composed between. Lastly, Jamaica, the 'Reggae Boyz', would make
their debut. Improved dramatically by an influx from the English professional game, their results suggested increasing confidence. Draws with Brazil
and Nigeria had carried them into a Tournament where their inexperience
would be tested. Deone Burton, hitherto an unsung journeyman striker
for Portsmouth Football Club, had become a celebrity of almost folk hero
proportions.

Venues: Paris, Lens, Bordeaux, Nantes, Toulouse, Montpellier, St Etienne, Marseilles, Lyons

Group A

Brazil
Norway
Scotland
Morocco

Group B

Italy
Austria
Chile
Cameroon

Group C

France
South Africa
Saudi Arabia
Denmark

Group D

Spain
Nigeria
Paraguay
Bulgaria

Group E

Holland
South Korea
Belgium
Mexico

Group F

Germany
USA
Yugoslavia
Iran

Group G

Romania
Colombia
England
Tunisia

Group H

Argentina
Jamaica
Croatia
Japan

THE FIRST SERIES

The honour of opening the Tournament fell to Scotland, at the Stade de France, against the defending Champions Brazil. Before a large colourful and enthusiastic audience they set about their unenviable task with grim determination before losing out narrowly and unfortunately. Brazil set out in dominating fashion, Sampaio, arriving at the near post in three minutes to meet Bebeto's corner, took advantage of generous marking, his header beating Leighton with ease. The Scots, terrorized by Ronaldo, almost self-destructed: Hendry under pressure beat his own goalkeeper with a desperate header, which missed the yawning goal by inches before Ronaldo emphasized his menace. Receiving the ball by the touchline, turning away from Hendry he twisted past Boyd and inside Jackson, his shot bravely parried by the forty-year-old Leighton. Scotland hung on, found their form and retaliated, their more direct approach unsettling the Champions, Jackson's penetrating pass to Durie cut out at the death by Junior Baiano. On 36 minutes the Scots earned reward for their efforts. Christian Dailly's seemingly innocuous header pursued by the eager Gallacher caused consternation, and Sampaio bundled the little Blackburn striker to the floor. Penalty, and John Collins, quite outstanding in the first half, slotted home coolly. In the second period Brazil again exerted considerable pressure, Rivaldo twice close while Scotland, largely outplayed, threatened occasionally. Gallacher crossing fiercely created panic as the Brazilians scrambled the ball from under their crossbar, away for a corner. Then, as is Scotland's way in the competition, misfortune struck. Playing patiently, Brazil sought an opening, and Dunga's chip invited Cafu to advance on goal. Leighton was out quickly to block the shot but the rebound struck Boyd and dribbled over the line. At 2–1 to Brazil, hard though Scotland fought, the die was cast. Gallacher almost saved them four minutes from time scooping the ball over the bar from ten yards, but it was not to be. Their defeat had been honourable and offered encouragement, but more significantly, their brave stand had perhaps shown Brazil to have defensive vulnerabilities.

In Montpellier, Morocco, tidy and compact, almost surprised the powerful Norwegians, leading twice before settling for a 2–2 draw in an absorbing contest of very different footballing philosophies. Norway began the brighter, showing clever touches for a side dubbed direct and physical. Solskjaer spurned an early opportunity, arriving at the far post to blast over from six yards, and Tore Andre Flo provided a menacing presence with his marauding runs. Morocco, however, gained a measure of composure and slowly but surely their lengthier spells of possession began to dictate affairs. Hadji, pony-tailed midfielder of Deportivo, constantly threatened the tough Scandinavians' defence, twice testing Grodås with powerful shooting before finally defeating him utterly with a movement and shot of the highest quality. Receiving the ball in the 37th minute, the lithe Moroccan swept in from the left, stepped over the ball to deceive a defender, cut inside and fired spectacularly into the net. Down 1–0 and all at sea, Norway were saved by a fortuitous goal scored at a crucial moment. On the stroke of half-time Benzekri, pressured by Berg, fumbled a harmless free kick that Chippo inadvertently headed into his own goal. At the interval the score was 1–1, though in the second half the green-shirted Moroccans held sway, Bassir almost embarrassing Grodås before Hadda pounced, sprinting on to a through ball to drive home fiercely from six yards. Again Norway's response came quickly and again owed much to the unfortunate Benzekri, Bjørnebye's free kick forcing more uncertainty from the floundering goalkeeper, his weak parry falling to Eggen who headed back past him gratefully. At the end, as the Africans visibly tired, Norway's strength almost won it, Leonhardsen twice, Harvard Flo and Solbakken all going close to forcing a winner they scarcely deserved. In truth Morocco, given competent goalkeeping, would have taken all the points, and Egil Olsen's pre-match statement, 'We don't give the ball away in midfield because we play over it,' had a ring of self delusion about it.

Italy playing at Bordeaux in Group B, the favourites of many, struggled to 2–2 against a resolute Chilean team blessed with formidable attacking talents. They were saved in the end by a highly dubious penalty award converted by Roberto Baggio four minutes from time. All for the white-shirted 'Azzurri' began well, Paulo Maldini's long ball searching out Roberto Baggio whose instinctive pass found Vieri quite unmarked and thus was able to slide his shot home with ease. Ten minutes had elapsed and the Italians, playing with authority, assumed control, worried only by sporadic raids by Zamorano and his diminutive partner Salas. Baggio on 15 minutes weaved majestically into the Chilean penalty area; the last ditch tackle that denied him ran to Di Matteo whose shot cleared the bar. Ten minutes later Vieri shot again but his goalbound effort struck Rojas. In between Salas served due warning on the Italians, speeding elusively forward, wriggling free of despairing defenders, his avenue closed down only when in sight of goal. A minute later Zamorano's looping header fell to him a yard out but the angle proved too acute. Italy's grip was such that a Chilean goal appeared a remote prospect. It was astonishing then when it came and also its manner, as the 'Azzurri' defence, by tradition so mean, lost its concentration in first-half injury time. A corner swung in towards Zamorano was won cleanly, the knock down falling into the path of Salas who found time and space to swivel and crash the ball unstoppably past Pagliuca from six yards. For Italy worse was to follow as the second half began, little Salas with remarkable timing outjumping his much taller marker Cannavaro, deftly diverting a long diagonal cross inside the despairing Pagliuca's far post. Chile now controlled the game, showing patience and invention, though Italy in their desperation produced a string of half chances. De Livio, Vieri and Inzaghi all failed before, and on the verge of defeat, lady luck arrived on cue to save them. Baggio, searching for options, chipped powerfully towards goal, the ball struck Fuentes on the right hand before he could react and referee Bouchardeau pointed rather harshly to the spot. Chile, so deserving victory, might at the end have suffered cruel defeat. Baggio's last minute free kick punched clear by Tapia fell to Inzaghi, who drove narrowly wide. 'We did make some mistakes in defence,' said Italian coach Cesare Maldini afterwards, 'but I believe it was a fair result.' Perhaps, but the Chileans would beg to differ.

In Toulouse also in Group B rugged Cameroon and stubborn Austria played out a predictable draw achieved in a thoroughly unpredictable fashion. Often hard and physical, both sides began in dour cautious mood, the greater experience of the Austrians pitted against the youthful exuberance of their African opponents. Herzog provided the first of what little entertainment was on offer in the opening period, his shot flying past Songo'o's upright. Angibeau next tested Konsel with a wicked cross that threatened to dip under the veteran keeper's bar as Cameroon raised the tempo, and then again the African, perhaps the most influential player on the field, arrived to head off target. As Austria clung on, Konsel came to their rescue once more, shovelling away Wome's fierce free kick. As referee Chavez signalled half-time, the paying spectators whistled their displeasure at both teams' lack of ambition. In the second half Cameroon at least showed greater urgency, whilst Toni Polster, Austria's prolific goal scorer, cut a forlorn figure isolated by team-mates unwilling to offer support. Dominating, Njanka on 72 minutes finally gave the Africans reward for their positive play, a goal of stunning individuality. Breaking forward from inside his own half and dancing through tackles, he thundered into Austria's penalty area, cut inside Schöttel and despatched a glorious drive beyond Konsel's reach. Faced with defeat, coach Prohaska gambled and won, replacing three midfield players with substitutes. Austria finally rolled forward, and as victory moved ever closer to them, Cameroon became increasingly apprehensive. In injury time their nerve finally betrayed them. Feiersinger's corner headed on by Pfeffer found the underemployed Polster lurking alone and with time to drive a half volley in off the underside of the bar for 1–1. While Austria celebrated, Cameroon could only question their marking, which was not so much generous as non-existent. For both with Chile and Italy awaiting, only considerable improvement would do.

In Lens from Group C there was a dreary opening encounter between Denmark and Saudi Arabia, spoiled by a surprising lack of enterprise from the Asian qualifiers flattered by their 1–0 defeat. Denmark, overrunning the Saudis in midfield, created enough chances, but poor finishing threatened to undermine their clever football. In the end a defender, Marc Rieper of Glasgow Celtic, saved them on 68 minutes, arriving unmarked and onside to meet Brian Laudrup's cross and power his header beyond Al Deayea. Only now on the verge of defeat did the Saudis show urgency, though their efforts to the whistle failed to trouble Schmeichel, a reassuring figure in the Danish goal. 'The result,' declared the *Politiken* newspaper in Copenhagen, 'was better than the game.'

In Marseilles, the hosts France facing South Africa overcame courageous opponents and high winds to ultimately run out comfortable 3–0 winners. Poor South Africa, try though they did, could find no way through a remarkably strong and increasingly dominant French defence led with authority by Desailly. France, given the platform and 60,000 enthusiastic supporters, exerted pressure, Deschamps and Petit, solid performers both, policing midfield, and

Zinedine Zidane released to probe the South African rearguard. Resisting with little difficulty for half an hour, the 'Bafana Bafana' were undone by a goal owing a little to good fortune and a lot to slack defending. Zidane's inswinging corner, met by the lunging head of substitute Christian Dugarry, flew past the advancing goalkeeper Hans Vonk and in off the inside of the upright. The South Africans fought back. Issa – whose evening was soon to be ruined – missed a presentable opportunity, reaching Nyathi's free kick but heading wide. Unlikely to score but resolute in the face of heavy pressure, the Africans continued to frustrate their superior opponents until the final 15 minutes, then their world, and particularly that of the unfortunate Issa's, fell apart. First the defender stretched to divert Djorkaeff's weak shot past Vonk, and then in the final minute he helped Henry's shot into his own net for a second own goal. France's sports paper *L'Equipe* enthused. 'France were at Force Three as their journey to destiny begins.' South Africa's *Star* reacted less cheerfully, 'Bafana,' it moaned, 'gone with the wind.'

Paraguay and Bulgaria played in Group D at Montpellier in a goal-less, often dull match, yet sprinkled with enough incident to hold the interest until the end. Referee Al-Zeid also made his mark, brandishing the Tournament's first red card, the unfortunate recipient Nankov two minutes from time. In truth the Bulgarian contributed to his own fate: already on a yellow card, his scything tackle on Yegros condemned him, though coach Bonev, angered by the decision, argued otherwise. 'People come to the World Cup to see football played in a man's way; this will stop it. I think my player was unfairly done by. I have seen much harsher things than this let go.'

Bulgaria in the first half attacked nervous opponents; Stoichkov struck an upright and created problems with darting runs, and Ivanov firing in a free kick found himself frustrated by Chilavert, 'the Bull Dog', as eccentric a goalkeeper as the Tournament has ever seen. As penalty kick and free kick taker, he would have his moment, but not before Penev, receiving Stoichkov's inviting pass, fired way over from eight yards. The glare afforded him by Stoichkov, not noted for his cheerful disposition, summed up the moment. In the 72nd minute there was a free kick and the extraordinary sight of Chilavert striding upfield to place the ball twenty-five yards out. The attempt – a curling, dipping effort, struck with great velocity – produced from Zdravkov a breathtaking save as he flung himself upwards to tip the ball over. 'I thought it had gone in,' said Chilavert afterwards, 'what a moment that would have been.' Despite not adding to his tally of forty-one goals, he had produced the enduring memory from an otherwise strangely lack lustre affair.

At Nantes also in Group D an exhilarating match ensued between powerful, unpredictable Nigeria and tough and inventive Spain, the Africans not so much winning, as the Spanish throwing it away and losing. In the early stages Spain threatened a rout, Raul first forcing Rufai to a fine save, then clipping the crossbar. Nigeria, with poor preparation and rumoured internal strife, appeared disjointed, and though the rampaging Ikpeba worried the Spanish defences sporadically, they appeared bound for defeat in the 35th minute when Hierro's well struck free kick cannoned off Okechukwu's chest, leaving Rufai helpless. Instead, the Africans responded within minutes, Adepoju rising to force a header in off Sergi. Encouraged, Nigeria produced their most forceful football, edging the remainder of the first half, only to be undone by the rapier-like Raul within seconds of the restart. The young Real Madrid striker produced a stunning volley as he arrived to meet Hierro's deep diagonal pass. That should perhaps have been that, as Spain assumed command and Nigeria floundered. Then on 73 minutes an astonishing error by the veteran goalkeeper and Spanish captain threw them a lifeline. Lawal, off balance, stumbled after Yekini's pass down the left touchline, retrieved the ball and fired in a low hopeful cross. Whether or not Zubizarreta was deceived by its angle is debatable, but the goalkeeper's attempt at stopping the ball saw him inadvertently turn it into his own goal. At 2–2, and whilst the horrified Spaniards fought to regain their composure, Nigeria capitalized on their good fortune. Twelve minutes from time Sunday Oliseh, a beautifully balanced midfield player, unleashed a ferocious twenty-five-yard half volley, which Zubizarreta could only tip on to the inside of the upright and into his net. Spain might have saved themselves in injury time when Sergi's curling, deliberate shot beat Rufai but flew inches too high. So Spain had lost, Nigeria had won, and few were left in any doubt that both would play their part in the drama yet to unfold.

There was controversy in Lyon as the willing Koreans took a fortuitous lead, saw the goal scorer dismissed after half an hour and capitulated to a persistent and inventive Mexican attack. After a drab opening during which the Koreans afforded Mexico far too much respect, they took the lead. Ha Seok-Ju, swinging in a free kick, saw it strike the Mexican defensive wall and deflect away from the stranded goalkeeper, Campos, into the net. At 1–0 Korea's euphoria proved to be short lived. Two minutes later a wild scything tackle by Seok-Ju on Jesus Ramirez earned him a red card and the Asians the unenviable task of defending their lead with ten men for an hour. A stiff test for the best, it was far too demanding a challenge for the gallant but limited Koreans. Campos denied Jong Soo shortly before half-time, but thereafter Mexico took command. Palaez drilled an equalizer in after 50 minutes and then Hernandez, Mexico's golden boy, took over, 15 minutes from the end shooting his country into the lead and then on 83 minutes putting the lid on it. Allowed time to turn by tiring opponents, he struck the ball beyond the despairing Ji Kim for 3–1.

Holland, facing fierce rivals Belgium in Saint Denis, might have won but spurned chances to secure a comfortable victory and saw Patrick Kluivert dismissed near the end and settled for what for them was a disappointing 0–0 draw. Holland, exuding confidence, took the game to their ageing neighbours, but in spite of fielding six players over thirty, the Belgians resisted. Marc Overmars, Arsenal's winger, created the most discomfort, his speed and trickery causing Belgium to withdraw his marker, Crasson, after just 20 minutes. Deflandre contained him rather more effectively, though a series of brutal lunges earned him a yellow card within ten minutes of being introduced. Belgium, unable to sustain any attacking momentum, contented themselves with a craven policy of frustration, nine men behind the ball and intimidating tackling. It succeeded, but they rode their luck. Wilde denied Frank De Boer and the rebound falling to Hasselbaink was driven back across the face of goal. Wilde twice foiled the dangerous Hasselbaink in the second half and then when he erred with a wayward punch, Deflandre saved him, heading to safety from under his own bar. Kluivert, a perennial menace, finally condemned his own side to a miserable failure. Always temperamental, the elegant striker responded to the taunts of Lorenzo Staelens' with a foolish shove and the Belgian collapsed disgracefully as though shot. 'Staelens shouted out something to do with my private life in the past. Take it from me, it was below the belt,' Kluivert later explained. Nonetheless he was off, dismissed by a referee who from Staelens writhing theatrics perhaps wrongly assumed a fist or elbow had been used. Even at the end the ten remaining Dutch almost contrived a late winner, Deflandre again rescuing his team on the line from Philip Cocu's whipped inswinging corner. At 0–0 Belgium were the more pleased, while the Dutch, infinitely more talented, would look ahead with the greater confidence.

Germany in Paris overcame a brave but limited United States team 2–0. The Americans, organized and stout defenders with an aptitude for working hard and denying space, were shocked in eight minutes, Möller rising to head home after Klinsmann had touched on a corner. Behind and thus required to show more willingness to attack, the USA's game plan was immediately undermined. Obdurate but not inventive, the task always appeared beyond them. Thon, Germany's sweeper, moved forward at will and initiated attacks, and the Europeans' mobile formation, while lazily going through the motions, at least gave an early indication of their capabilities. Hejduk, an American substitute who clearly had not read the script, flashed a header goalwards, forcing Köpke to an undignified tumble that momentarily inspired the Germans to a more positive and creative effort. Klinsmann typically concluded matters, scoring a classical goal on 65 minutes, Bierhoff's high cross taken cleverly on his chest and placed delicately between Kasey Keller and his far post.

Coach Berti Vogls was critical of his charges afterwards and praised the American effort. 'Hopefully after an early goal you go on and control the game, but we did not do that. The Americans picked up a bit of steam and I was glad to see Jurgen Klinsmann's goal. They played well – there are no poor cousins in international football any more.' Perhaps, but the Germans, far from impressive, would need to improve dramatically.

Patrons at St Etienne might have been forgiven for their optimism when attending the Yugoslavia and Iran Group F opener. With ninety-eight goals the combined total of the teams in qualification, the game promised much and Yugoslavia arrived at the Tournament with praise ringing in their ears. Dark horses certainly, but in this subdued encounter they more closely resembled cart horses, winning only courtesy of a fortuitous Mihajlovic free kick. Iran for their part, perhaps lacking self-belief, failed to see what appeared plainly obvious from the start: the undermotivated Yugoslavians were vulnerable. Iran's direct strong running game led by Ali Deai and Khodadad Azizi embarrassed their opponents frequently, yet the Asians refused to abandon their cautious approach. The goal when it came, after 72 mediocre minutes, was in itself a typically messy affair, Mihajlovic firing in from twenty yards after Nima Nakisa had first disorganized the defensive wall and then compounded his error by positioning himself out of reach of a shot that flew in unforgivably, almost in the middle of his goal.

In Group G in the afternoon heat of Marseilles, England began their campaign, their entry preceded by predictable and tiresome scenes of street violence and the surfacing of ugly nationalism as supporters clashed. At least the team rose above this sickening anarchy, dispatching Tunisia with consummate ease. Surprisingly, the Africans began sharply, their first attack in three minutes being the best they would manage. Souayah played in cleverly but delayed his shot, allowing Campbell the opportunity to block. With the English defence looking increasingly secure, they began to dominate; Le Saux's cross met – albeit not cleanly – by the head of Scholes was desperately hooked to safety by the flailing legs of El Ouaer in Tunisia's goal. Unable to relieve the pressure for any length of time, the Africans could only endure, Sheringham's speculative effort from long range forcing El Ouaer to remarkable acrobatics. Scholes, once more arriving undetected, fastened quickly on to Sheringham's cross though without great power, but El Ouaer again clawed the ball away gratefully. Then on the verge of half-time the threatened goal duly arrived. Shearer, fouled on the right of the penalty area, left the kick to Le Saux and Anderton. Le Saux's delivery swung in towards him and the England striker leapt highest, his header this time beating the gallant goalkeeper emphatically. Ahead and with complete control afforded them by the wonderfully combative Batty and Ince, England played within themselves, Adams in particular stifling the threat offered by the darting Sellimi. In the final moments Scholes put the lid on it. Taking the ball from Ince he looked up twenty yards from goal and curled his shot with deadly accuracy into Tunisia's net. Winning 2–0, afterwards England coach Glen Hoddle expressed his satisfaction on a job well done. 'This was a tricky game for us. The worst time to play Tunisia was here and in this heat. This was their World Cup Final.'

Also in Group G, Romania, showing greater urgency throughout the first half, seized the lead through Ilie in injury time and clung to it in spite of Colombia's determined and despairing efforts. How the South Americans must have rued another of their peculiarly languid openings. Romania, invited to attack from the beginning, did, but their momentum brought little excitement to the Lyons crowd. Moldovan came closest to scoring, facing an empty goal, inches from reaching a cross that eluded all and left him to pound the ground in frustration. Physical and organized, the Romanians persisted, Mondragon producing the game's highlight, a wondrous double save to deny Ilie and Munteanu before the unfortunate Moldovan under pressure ballooned the ball over the Colombian cross bar. Then as half-time approached the disappointing Colombians were made to pay for their mediocrity. Hagi's clever back heel fell to Ilie, who surged past Lozano and Bermudez before beating the advancing Mondragon with the deftest of touches.

Colombia to no one's surprise improved considerably after the interval, Rincon and Valencia going closest as they showed far greater urgency. Victory, however, was celebrated at the end by the more deserving team. 'The team went on to the pitch very timidly,' agreed Colombian coach Hernan Gomez, 'there was no spontaneity. Now we have to find our cohesion and make sure we win next time.' Anghel Iordanescu, his Romanian counterpart, was pleased with his side and particularly with their first-half performance. 'The second half was a bit more difficult,' he added honestly.

Argentina, emerging as a strong Tournament favourite, won in Toulouse, though their narrow 1–0 victory over debutants Japan was a trifle fortunate against willing and wonderfully composed opponents. Neat passing and swift movement, often instigated by the team's twenty-one-year-old pivot Nakata, gave the South Americans a torrid opening. But Batistuta rescued them, the predatory Florentina striker seizing on a defensive error to settle matters. Japanese newspaper *Asahi* had predicted, 'An Argentine victory is not a foregone conclusion,' and Japan began full of confidence, closing down their aristocratic opponents with a vigour. Ortega's reputation as the 'New Maradona' was not enhanced, and for all of Veron's fierce drive the Argentineans floundered until Batistuta's intervention on 28 minutes. Nanami misread Ortega's pass and played the ball inadvertently into the striker's path. Reacting with speed and deftness of touch, Batistuta scored with aplomb, lifting the ball gently and with great accuracy over the enrushing Kawaguchi and into the net. So Japan went down to narrow defeat. 'I was pleased we played so positively and aggressively,' said Japanese coach Takeshi Okada. Daniel Passarella, distinctly less pleased, conceded he was happy to win, but as to the performance? 'Half pleased and half sad,' said the Argentina coach.

In Lens from Group H, Jamaica, roared on by their own very vocal and colourful support, went down gloriously to skilful Croatia in a delightful match. New to the Tournament themselves, the highly regarded Croats sought to take early advantage of Caribbean nerves and defensive naiveté, Suker and Bilic being denied by Warren Barrett before, almost inevitably, their goal came. Asanovic got behind Jamaica's right flank and pulled the ball back to Stimac, whose shot struck the underside of the crossbar and fell to Stanic to force over the line. Jamaica's difficult task now began to look impossible. Soldo hit their woodwork and Suker again saw Barrett foul him when he might have scored. Nevertheless, their constant pressing in midfield and tenacity in defence brought unexpected and spectacular reward. Ricardo Gardener, the left back, fired a cross in, whereupon Robbie Earle arriving at speed outjumped Stimac to plant a thumping header into Drazen Ladic's net from fifteen yards. At 1–1 bedlam ensued.

After the interval, Croatia took nine minutes to quell the celebrations. A cruel goal was scored by the game's outstanding individual, Robert Prosinecki; his hopeful centre delivered right-footed from the left wing swung over goalkeeper Barrett and past sweeper Onandy Lowe, left to despair on the goal line. At 2–1 and destined for defeat, Jamaica's fate was sealed 20 minutes from time. Davor Suker, cleverly losing markers, collected Stanic's cross and fired in at goal. Whether Barrett may have saved it or not, he was left to watch helplessly as the flailing leg of Goodison diverted the ball over him. Guaranteed victory, Croatia went through the full repertoire of their passing movements, whilst Jamaica, denied the ball for long periods, chased in vain. Yet at the end the 'Reggae Boyz' emerged with their pride and dignity intact, their introduction into world football had seen them and their Brazilian coach, Rene Simoes, emerge with great credit.

THE SECOND SERIES

Scotland and Norway at Bordeaux fought out a predictably rugged and tense match, both ultimately settling for the point a 1–1 draw brought them. Scotland, the more thoughtful and composed team, began the brighter, ample possession allowing Collins and Lambert to dictate from midfield. Only Durie came close, however, leaping to send Gallacher's cross just beyond the far post. Largely outplayed, the forthright Norwegians carved out opportunities on sporadic raids. Strand, frustrated by Leighton's alertness as he bore down on goal, turned provider seven minutes from half-time, his inviting cut back blasted horribly high by Solbakken. But within a minute of the second half Norway had the advantage: Riseth furrowing forward outpaced Calderwood and aimed a cross beyond the far post, Harvard Flo pulling away from Dailly made room for himself and left Leighton groping despairingly with a precise header. Scotland trailing and facing the awful prospect of defeat and with it elimination saved themselves with the kind of directness Norway would have been proud of. David Weir, thumping the ball forward, found Craig Burley charging goalwards. The Celtic man's touch was assured, his crisp lofted shot leaving the astonished Grodås stranded. For the remaining 24 minutes the Scots held sway as Norway struggled to contain them, and at the end, while the Norwegians pondered the awesome prospect of achieving a result against Brazil in order to progress, Scotland could be quietly confident that a draw in St Etienne against Morocco might just be enough.

Brazil in Group A continued their imperious march to the knockout stages with the 3–0 dismantling of disappointing Morocco. Full of swagger and adventure six days earlier, here the Africans, plainly intimidated by their opponents, capitulated miserably, offering little resistance. Brazil in any event took the lead before Morocco's nerve had settled. Ronaldo of all people was allowed to drift away from markers, received Rivaldo's astute early pass and thundered his shot into Benzekri's net. Shortly afterwards, recognizing the threat belatedly perhaps, Chiba with raised studs ruthlessly clattered into the Brazilian striker, sending him writhing to the floor and temporarily out of the game. Remarkably lenient, Levnikov, the Russian referee, chose not to issue the culprit with even a caution. Morocco, temporarily finding their rhythm and led ably by the talented Maustopha El Hadji, Tahar and Chippo, might have scored, but at the other end their open football invited trouble. Rivaldo brought it. The play switched sumptuously through Bebeto, Leonardo, Bebeto again, on to Cafu and then finally to the lithe midfielder who side-footed accurately and arrogantly for 2–0. Shortly after the interval a third goal killed all African hopes. Ronaldo, full of power, pace and purpose, seized on an error by Saber, shredded the Moroccan rearguard and delivered the ball to Bebeto a yard out. Brazil mercifully relaxed, sated. The remaining half an hour ressembled an exhibition of South American skills as their opponents wilted, demoralized and beaten.

For Chile in Group B there was cruel disappointment as another horribly negative Austrian performance brought undeserved reward. Indeed, one was moved to wonder why this dreary muscular team of limited ambition had bothered to come at all. This was the second successive match in which they sought to spoil the game, break up any creative flow and counter-attack – though without conviction. Chile sadly, bright and inventive against the Italians, struggled to be effective against such negativity, yet all that resembled football came from them, their twin strikers Zamorano and Salas offering a constant and very mobile threat. Finally on 70 minutes there was a goal. Sierra, a revelation as second-half substitute, chipped his free kick towards Zamorano, and the forward's header pushed out by Konsel fell to Salas, who forced the ball over the line. The 1–0 score might have been 2–0, Zamorano's searching drive finger-tipped away by Konsel, Austria's only outstanding player. And then, scarcely credibly and three minutes into injury time, Austria scored.

Capitalizing on Chilean anxiety, Vastic, a substitute, collecting a pass from Mählich, drifted away from inexcusably slack marking and rifled his shot into Tapia's net. At 1–1 the points would be shared. Austria, so wilfully destructive in achieving two draws, would somehow now need to secure a victory in their third fixture. Italy in St Denis awaited them.

At Montpellier, Italy played with great self-belief to defeat a young Cameroon team whose aggression occasionally degenerated into violence. Ten of their players finished the game where a less lenient referee might easily have seen them with only seven or eight. Di Biagio gave Italy the start they craved, his header in a crowded goalmouth diverting Roberto Baggio's cross past Songo'o for 1–0. Worse for Cameroon was to follow, as after a period of spirited resistance, Nkongo launched himself into a two-footed tackle on Di Biagio and was dismissed. As the second half progressed, Italy smoothly moved through the gears. The Africans, losing their discipline, resorted to a series of crude and spiteful fouls. Vieri 15 minutes from the end scored a second goal and then in the 89th minute the lanky Athletico Madrid striker grabbed another, seizing on an error by Wome to shoot home his team's third.

In Group C it was a black day indeed at Toulouse, where an open, often exciting encounter between two enterprising teams was ultimately ruined by overofficious refereeing and the quite unnecessary dismissal of three players. Denmark scored first, South Africa earned their point in the 51st minute, but these statistics were overshadowed by Mr Toro Rendon and his ruthless interpretation of the rule book. Allan Nielsen's goal, sandwiched between two Danish attempts that struck the woodwork, was reward for their early superiority, his volley off Brian Laudrup's lofted cross beating Hans Vonk at his far post in 12 minutes. Largely outplayed in an attractive first half, South Africa dug deep and found a response, Shaun Bartlett's back heel finding Benny McCarthy, who wriggled free of both Høgh and Colding to slide the ball under Schmeichel. Now the game as a spectacle was ended. First Molnar, a Danish substitute on for 13 minutes, challenged Radebe clumsily and received his marching orders. Two minutes later a South African substitute, Phiri, followed for flailing an arm at Thomas Helveg. Ten a side and five minutes from time there was further controversy as yet another substitute, Denmark's Wieghorst, fouled McCarthy and became the third victim of Toro Rendon's unforgiving red card.

Astonishingly, at the end FIFA statistics vividly demonstrated Denmark's cause for complaint. They had committed six fouls in the match and received two yellow and two red cards for their sins. Mark Fish, stalwart South African central defender, also derided the match official in the aftermath. 'I think the referee was not up to standard. He should have taken the game in context. I don't think the first dismissal should have been a red card and I think he thought he'd done something wrong by levelling it. The third red card was ridiculous.'

In Paris 75,000 came to acclaim the hosts as France duly thrashed poor Saudi Arabia 4–0. Revellers' celebrations, however, were tempered by the dismissal for stamping of the French talisman Zinedine Zidane and the knowledge that his suspension could have the gravest consequences for his team's prospects. The Asians with their hands full before the contest began saw their task grow to monumental proportions on 19 minutes when Al Khilaiwi's mistimed tackle on the elusive Lizarazu earned him a red card. Now the French tide simply swept over their limited opponents as chances came and went at an astonishing rate. Throughout the first half, gallant blocks, misses and brave defiant goalkeeping by Al Deayea all contributed to frustrate Gaelic flair for 36 minutes, before the inevitable. Lizarazu again pounded down the flanks, crossing for Henry to cut inside and shoot home. The 1–0 score at half-time became 2–0 in 68 minutes as the Saudi hero Al Deayea turned villain. His fumbling of an innocuous Lillian Thuram cross presented Trezeguet with the simplest of tasks from five yards. After the departure of Zidane – the game's outstanding player – Henry and Lizarazu completed the scoring as France strutted in front of their own adoring public. Impressive as they had been, the Saudis, physically fit but thoroughly outclassed, had proven no more than an exercise in fine tuning for the sterner challengers ahead.

In Paris for Group D the adventures of perhaps Africa's only serious challengers continued as Nigeria, at first outplayed, consequently outlasted Bulgaria in the sunshine to register their second win, this time by 1–0. Technically brilliant if unconventional, the Africans dominated the early stages, Oliseh and Amokachi close to scoring before Ikpeba duly obliged, completing a sublime movement after 27 minutes. Amokachi found Finidi George, whose return pass he deftly flicked into the path of Ikpeba's darting run. With work to do, the African Player of the Year shimmied past Ivanov and rolled the ball into Zdravkov's net. Until half-time the pattern continued, Okocha and Oliseh taking charge, Babayaro, a teenage wing back, giving width. The chances came and went, though Bulgaria at least served notice in the half's last minute of their attacking threat. Balakov, avoiding Taribo West, lifted the ball over Rufai and by fractions over the helpless goalkeeper's crossbar. Slowly, as the second half unravelled, the Nigerians relinquished control to a Bulgarian team recognizing its perilous position and showing greater urgency. Stoichkov, persistent and petulant moaner but a marvellously instinctive striker nonetheless, almost saved them, redirecting Kostadinov's powerful drive beyond the stranded Rufai but agonizingly inches wide of goal. Nigeria, with some difficulty, held on in an increasingly open and wildly fluctuating game. At the end the Africans celebrated the remarkable achievement of qualification from the 'Group of Death' in just two matches, whilst Bulgaria were left to ponder Lens and Spain, where anything other than victory would condemn them to elimination.

At St Etienne, after making five changes, Spain huffed and puffed to no great effect against a resilient, organized Paraguayan team. Ending 0–0, and leaving the Spaniards on the precipice of disaster, it was a failure that would not be tolerated nor could have been contemplated by an expectant nation at home. Sitting back as they had against the Bulgarians, Paraguay took stock. Ayala, a commanding figure at the heart of their defence, aided by goalkeeper Chilavert, held Spain at bay. They combined to prevent Raul's shot crossing the line after Chilavert had earlier denied Pizzi's 21st minute header, turning it athletically to safety. Growing in confidence, the South Americans began to threaten, Rojas on the stroke of half-time, denied only by Aguilera's desperate tackle while Miguel Benitez terrorized the Spanish rearguard with well-timed incisive runs, twice forcing Zubizarreta to save. At the end, while the distraught Spaniards hung their heads, Paraguay celebrated joyously, their task of reaching the second phase still in their own capable hands.

In Group E a dramatic match took place at Nantes where Mexico, reduced to ten men after 29 minutes, recovered from 2–0 down to earn a draw against an ageing and fatigued Belgian team suffering visibly in the fierce afternoon heat. Always the more imaginative of the two sides and having already struck the bar through Sanchez, Mexico's cause was seriously undermined by Pardo's dismissal for, in truth, a reckless lunge on Borkelmans, with an hour to go. Outnumbered and being bullied by a physically stronger team, their crisis deepened rapidly. Wilmots ran in a goal on the stroke of half-time and then the robust striker did it again within minutes of the restart, crashing through Mexican tackles with the subtlety of a bulldozer, before hammering his shot past the startled Campos. Down and almost out, what saved gallant Mexico was the swiftness of their response and the circumstances that brought it. Only eight minutes after Wilmots' second goal, Jesus Ramirez strode boldly into the Belgian penalty area and was scythed down by Verheyen. The penalty duly converted by Garcia Aspe made it 2–1, and the expelled Belgian midfielder joined Pardo as an unhappy spectator. Greatly encouraged and no longer playing a man short, the more youthful Mexicans tore into weary opponents before Blanco finally brought them their deserved equalizer, meeting Ramirez's cross field pass with a spectacular close range volley. Remarkably, at 2–2 with temperature on the pitch at more than 100 ºF, the frenzied frenetic pace continued unabated to the whistle, with Mexico looking the likelier to score, though failing to take a chance to considerably ease their passage to the last sixteen. 'To say I am unhappy would be an understatement,' said Belgian coach Georges Leekens, 'at 2–0 with eleven man against ten, the victory was ours.' Almost.

Holland in Marseilles crushed South Korea 5–0, sending a message to all with aspirations of winning the Tournament. Digging in bravely, Asia's most consistent qualifiers challenged hard, often embarrassing their illustrious opponents with surging attacks before inevitably succumbing, Cocu's flashing drive on 39 minutes leaving goalkeeper Byung-Ji wrong footed and hopelessly beaten. As the Koreans sought to regroup, they were punished. Overmars finding room cut inside from the left and rifled his shot into the net for 2–0. Given breathing space, the Dutch attacked irresistibly, driven by Davids, their swift interchanging of position sending them flowing through the overworked, undermanned Korean defence and overwhelming them. Bergkamp, the offensive pivot, set them on the journey from victory to rout in the 72nd minute, nimbly working the ball around his marker and scoring with a prod off the outside of his boot from eighteen yards – a touch of such skill and delicacy, achieved so effortlessly. Korea's courage and defiance had finally been broken; in boxing parlance, they had stopped punching back. Hooijdonk headed a fourth, and then seven minutes from the end the cruellest blow of all: Ronald de Boer hammering the fifth goal. Within hours Cha Bum-Kun, Korean coach, had been relieved of his duties, the country's football authorities apparently quite unable to recognize the enormity of their team's task.

In Group F there was another remarkable comeback from those Patron Saints of Lost Causes, as Germany, rarely the equals of their talented Yugoslavian opponents, snatched a 2–2 draw from seemingly certain defeat. Outplayed handsomely by technically superior opponents, the Germans fell behind to a goal by the Real Madrid forward Mijatovic after 13 minutes and were left to lumber about the field in vain as the Yugoslavians passed with assurance, embarrassing them, an almost arrogant swagger to their play. Worse was to come for the Germans in the second half, as after Matthäus, Tarnat and Kirsten had replaced Hamann, Ziege and Möller to no great effect, the Yugoslavian veteran playmaker Dragon Stojkovic, a masterful performer, seized on a horrible fumble by Köpke off Stankovic's driven cross to make it 2–0. Woeful and reeling, Germany appeared destined for a defeat of crushing proportions with 20 minutes remaining. Crucially now the Slavs, apparently content with their afternoon's work, relaxed their effort and not for the first time lady luck smiled down benignly on the German team. After Mihajlovic's ill-judged intervention, Tarnat's fiercely struck if apparently harmless free kick deflected wildly into the helpless Kralj's net and revived flagging German spirits. Scenting blood, the Germans pressed, and the Yugoslavians, unable to reproduce their earlier form, began for the first time to look second best, bullied by Teutonic urgency. It was Bierhoff who finally equalized, rising to meet Thon's corner and sending his header from six yards ripping into Kralj's net. Ending 2–2 Germany could have won it, as Yugoslavia defended nervously; justice saw to it that they did not. Yugoslavia, by far the better side, could not have suffered to lose to a team that scarcely deserved a draw. Afterwards Berti Vogts, German coach, paid glowing tribute to his opponents while criticizing his own team's lackadaisical approach. 'A big compliment to Yugoslavia who played brilliant football, but I was angry with my team who didn't seem to realize they were playing in the World Cup. I was very angry with the way we played in the first 60 minutes. We invited them to play good football and didn't close them down.'

Iran and the USA played in Lyon, a match almost overshadowed by political undertones and begun only after protracted and heartening gestures of goodwill. The Americans roared immediately on to the offensive, seizing the initiative; Reyna's free kick in the third minute met by McBride's thumping header crashed against the Iranian crossbar. A moment later the dreadlocked Cobi Jones wriggled free and cut the ball across the face of the gaping goal. No American read his intention and the ball ran free. Iran slowly settled and hit back. Azizi, a constant threat, raced through, and Keller's challenge on him brought furious Iranian protests but no foul. With both teams adopting positive attitudes, the game flowed, full of pace. Bagheri fired narrowly over Keller's goal. Reyna for the USA struck another free kick, beating Abedzadeh but not his goalpost. A goal as half-time approached seemed imminent, and it was Iran to deafening acclaim who scored it. Forty minutes had passed when Javad Zarincheh sent in his cross, whereupon Hamid Estili rose quite unmarked to head the ball beyond the reach of Keller. At 1–0 to Iran, America left to consider their own rather generous defending.

In the second half Iran, now inspired, held the upper hand. The role of counter-attacker switched to the Americans. They had their chances too, notably through the influential Reyna and the veteran Dooley, but defensively they were stretched. Mahdavikia, demonstrating astonishing stamina as he tore forward at every opportunity from full back, proved a constant worry. It was he who settled matters six minutes from time, racing over the halfway line, drawing Keller and ramming his shot joyously into the net. There was still time for the USA to score and three minutes later they did though McBride's effort proved little more than consolation. Ending 2–1 to Iran, it was an exhilarating, dramatic affair making nonsense of predictions of an ugly confrontation between enemy states.

In unfortunate circumstances at Toulouse, England paid the ultimate price for defensive lapses against a patient, clever Romanian team intent on heading Group G. In a nervous opening the Romanians began the stronger, as England, unable to press effectively or retain possession for significant periods, surrendered the initiative. Hagi, diminutive veteran, troubled them constantly, strolling about the pitch and appearing unexpectedly in dangerous positions. Twice in the first half he drifted away from markers to shoot high and wide. Ilie, too, menaced, darting back and forth, seeking always to exploit a loss of concentration. Sheringham might have scored, hooking an Anderton corner across Stelea's goalmouth, before almost immediately after the interval Moldovan for Romania finally did. Hagi, catching Le Saux on the wrong side from a throw in, lobbed the ball into the England penalty area where Adams, surprised, allowed the ball to fall into the striker's path. Gratefully accepting the invitation, Moldovan swiftly chested and volleyed the ball in one movement, beating Seaman's dive from eight yards. Belatedly England found a sense of urgency and drive. Beckham, a substitute, and Anderton began to run at retreating defenders, creating consternation. Sheringham might have scored, but unable to connect with Anderton's ferocious drive as it flashed across the goal line, his chance had gone, withdrawn for England's boy wonder Michael Owen, a slight eighteen-year-old blessed with astonishing pace. The game appeared to have drifted back in England's favour, and Owen in adding to his burgeoning reputation confirmed the suspicion, ramming in Shearer's low cross for an 80th minute equalizer. Romania did not capitulate; England now were undeniably the stronger. Pressing for an injury time winner, they were caught by Munteanu's long crossfield pass. Le Saux won the race with Petrescu, a club colleague at Chelsea, but as he attempted to hold off the Romanian, the ball was prodded from around his legs under Seaman's body for 2–1. Owen almost saved England within a minute. Advancing purposefully, his low thirty-yard drive beat Stelea comprehensively but thumped against the upright and flew to safety. At the end for England there was disappointment, though little doubt now that Owen and not the pedantic Sheringham would partner Shearer when England faced Colombia in need of a result. For Romania, Petrescu the hero summed up the joy felt: 'I am in heaven. I didn't sleep last night. England were unlucky on the night but they are lucky they can still go through with a draw against Colombia.'

In a spectacularly open game in Montpellier, Colombia met Tunisia, both losers in Group G's opening fixtures. For Colombia the remarkable Carlos Valderrama – playing his third Tournament – prompted their most inventive moments, and there were many: De Avila denied by El Ouaer, Lozano flashing a header wide, Aristizabel also frustrated by the excellence of Tunisia's athletic goalkeeper. In the meantime the Africans also threatened regularly, Mehdi Ben Slimane twice testing Mondragon before providing Zoubeir Baya with a glorious chance. Sadly for the Tunisians he could not accept, the shot flashing inches too high. There was a goal, finally, in the 89th minute, scored by Leider Preciado, a young man with good reason to reflect on his fortune. 'When I was two,' he said later, 'a tidal wave in my village killed hundreds of people. I was lucky.' No luck was needed with the goal. Running hard and directly, Preciado resisted the challenges of Clayton and Trabelsi before beating El Ouaer with ease. The Tunisians deserved sympathy; they had played their full part in an uninhibited and flowing match. Testimony to that came with the statistics, forty-three shots, twenty-one on goal. Colombia for their part had qualification back on their agenda and England looming on the horizon. 'Yes, we have a chance to qualify but it will be tough – very tough,' said coach Hernan Gomez cautiously.

Japan, whose magnificent effort against Argentina brought no reward, lost again and were consequently eliminated by the Croatians after another spirited and disciplined performance that brought their football still more admirers. Japan through their industrious midfielders Nanami and the gifted playmaker Nakata dominated the 'Brazil of Europe' for surprisingly long periods, forcing them to resort to counter-attacks usually directed by the bearded Prosinecki and led by Davor Suker, a constant threat to Japan's defence. Nakata, however, remained the game's most creative influence throughout the first half, as Japan, to the delight of their huge throng of support, attacked at every opportunity. It was he who picked out the willing Nakayama whose shot was saved by Ladic after 34 minutes. Soma and Jo might also have scored for them, whilst the wily Suker shot over and later escaped his marker only to be denied by Nakanishi's last ditch, but well judged, tackle. Inevitably it was Suker who settled it for Croatia: after earlier beating Kawaguchi with the cleverest of lobs, only to see the ball strike the cross bar, he finally earned reward for his endeavours. In the 77th minute Asanovic's cross eluded all but Suker, his touch and finish emphatically beating Kawaguchi. At 1–0, in spite of Japan's best efforts they were left to reflect on what might have been, and, what indeed they could hope to achieve in 2002 as hosts should they unearth a striker of the Croatian's ability.

Jamaica, Group H's other minnows, faced Argentina in Paris and fell behind to a goal by the diminutive genius Ariel Ortega. They saw Darryl Powell sent off for a second bookable offence and were overwhelmed by their ruthless opponents. Initially, the 'Reggae Boyz' resisted bravely, competitive in midfield and composed in defence, and with goalkeeper Winston Barrett assuming an air of confidence, all seemed well. Even after Ortega's goal brilliantly flicked in as he met Veron's incisive pass, Jamaica played with a degree of composure. Powell's dismissal, however, coming after a succession of fouls on Ortega, condemned them to a second-half drubbing. Ortega started the goal rush with his second. Taking a return pass from Claudio Lopez, he burst into the Jamaican penalty area and with exquisite touch lifted the ball over the onrushing Barrett for 2–0. The predatory Batistuta, unforgivably given time and space, struck a volley of enormous power past Barrett for three goals, and then five minutes later struck again, his finish from Simeone's pass equally unstoppable. Jamaica without ever throwing in the towel were now being outclassed. Little Ortega tormented them, and as he wriggled forward, this time Dawes managed a crude challenge to give Argentina a penalty. Batistuta strode forward to convert the kick, complete a hat-trick and conclude the scoring at 5–0.

THE THIRD SERIES

At Marseilles in Group A, Brazil, the Kings widely expected to be reinvested, faced sturdy resolute Norway, an examination at least of the Champions' credentials. In the event it became a frustration and ultimately an embarrassment as Norway staged a late and remarkable recovery to steal the points. It might all have been different had Ronaldo not misdirected a third-minute volley into the side netting, but thereafter the tall, muscular Norwegians smothered all invention, their red-shirted wall strung across the pitch challenging Brazil to break them down. For an hour and more they could not, and while Tore Andre Flo rampaged alone and fruitlessly in search of a Norwegian goal, the Scandinavians were at least level, reducing the Brazilians to long and speculative efforts, one of which from Roberto Carlos stung the hands of Grodås as he beat it away to safety. And then from Denilson came Brazilian inspiration. Climbing from his knees, he tricked his way forward and delivered a cross on to the head of Bebeto six yards out. Goal. Norway, now faced with certain elimination, launched themselves forward in desperation, and within five minutes found an unlikely equalizer. The powerful Flo loped forward hopefully, turned Junior Baiano and unleashed a rifling shot beyond the reach of Taffarel. At 1–1 that appeared to be that. However, Norway persisted, galvanized by substitute Harvard Flo whose physical approach had an unsettling effect on the wary Brazilian defenders. Astonishingly and in contentious fashion, the Norwegians won the day just two minutes from time. Bjørnebye collided with Junior Baiano and referee Baharmast saw what few had: a foul, and most crucially a penalty kick. Kjetil Rekdal, as industrious as any in the midfield battle, stepped up and drove the ball home.

Scotland, having succeeded in difficult circumstances in staying in contention, now faced Morocco, dangerous certainly but surely less so than their earlier opponents. Sadly, any expectation was crushed ruthlessly by a clever, fast-moving African team far too good on this day at St Etienne. It took Morocco just 18 minutes to capitalize on their greater penetration. El Khalej, driving the ball forward, found Bassir streaking away on the left who slipped the ball between Leighton and his near post. Burley for the Scots provided their only notable effort, his shot from Collins' pass parried by Benzekri five minutes before the interval. Harassed by pacey counter-attacks, Scotland's world fell apart two minutes after the restart. Hadji, an inspiration, collected the ball after a succession of short passes and opened them up with a raking long pass to Hadda, whose attempt to lift the ball over Leighton was palmed up by the goalkeeper and towards goal. Tragically, though Leighton set off to rescue the situation, the ball won the race, looping agonizingly into the Scotland net. Facing near certain defeat, worse soon followed. Burley crashed into the back of Bassir in the 53rd minute and received for his enthusiasm a red card. Ten

Scots could not succeed where eleven had failed; bravely as they resisted, Morocco would not be denied a third, Bassir's 85th minute shot deflecting in off Hendry. Thus ended Scotland's campaign. Morocco celebrated at the whistle but their joy proved short lived as news of Norway's unexpected triumph in Marseilles drifted in…

Group B, where the football had been the least entertaining, continued in the same disappointing vein in St Etienne, where an Italian team lacking cohesion had great difficulty in overcoming dour Austria. The first half was among the most uneventful yet seen, illuminated only by Alessandro Del Piero whose weaving runs threatened Austria sporadically. Ironically, it was the ultra cautious Austrians who might have stolen the lead, Bergomi, hero of 1982, reacting swiftly to block Vastic's shot a minute before the interval. On 49 minutes mercifully there was a goal. Del Piero's cross allowed Vieri to bull himself through a ruck of players and power his header into Konsel's net for 1–0 Italy. Predictably, now Austria showed greater ambition, and something more closely resembling football took shape. Wetl with an overhead kick troubled Pagliuca, yet still Italy appeared the more likely. Inzaghi and Baggio, pace and guile, were introduced as substitutes and created doubt. Moriero seizing onto an Inzaghi pass shot woefully wide with the goal at his mercy. In the end it fell to Baggio to seal it. Exchanging swift passes with Inzaghi, he drilled Italy emphatically into the knockout stages. At 2–0 with one minute left, Austria were doomed. Herzog replied almost instantly from the penalty spot after Costacurta's clumsy challenge on Reinmayr, but they were out, their contribution to the Tournament depressingly negative.

Chile also booked their passage through, though the enterprise shown against the Italians gave way to skittish nervousness in the face of a brutal onslaught by a Cameroon team reduced to nine men by full time. It all began serenely for the South Americans. Song, a talented but wildly undisciplined defender, sporting one red and one yellow boot, thumped into the unfortunate Zamorano. Sierra punished the indiscretion, putting the resultant free kick past Songo'o in the Cameroon goal. Six minutes after half-time Song compounded his error and was sent off for an elbow aimed at the face of Salas. Backs to the wall, Cameroon responded with marvellous fortitude as Chile retreated before the ten men. Mboma brought them level, lifting his header beyond Tapia. Then disgracefully referee Vagner denied them a remarkable triumph and qualification. Another Mboma header found its way to the veteran Oman-Biyik and his shot swept in sweetly, but astonishingly Vagner had seen a 'phantom' foul. Cameroon went out protesting furiously and claiming conspiracy, though not before Etame, too, had seen Mr Vagner's red card. So unconvincing, Chile would face Brazil with little reason for confidence, while the referee presumably would review any future plans for an African holiday!

France in Group C, this time at Lyons, won once more. Denmark at least managed to provide them with something of a challenge. Making numerous changes and without the suspended Zidane, Aime Jacquet demonstrated great confidence in the strength of his squad. His faith appeared vindicated a early as the 13th minute: Candela, replacing Lizarazu, burst from defence, strode purposefully forward into Danish territory and picked out Trezeguet lurking in the penalty area. Høgh, alert to the danger, moved in swiftly and in doing so brought down the French striker unfairly. Djorkaeff stepped up and though goalkeeper Schmeichel got a hand to his shot, he was beaten by power and placement. Still eager to impress, France continued their onslaught with flowing, sumptuous football, Trezeguet and Vieira foiled by Schmeichel, Vieira again and Diomede blazing high. Denmark resisted – just. There was little more they could do and the dam appeared ready to burst. Then, as it seems is often the case, Danish spirits were lifted. Jørgensen receiving a quickly taken free kick moved forward, whereupon Candela blocking his route to goal was rather harshly judged to have fouled him. Another penalty, another goal. Remarkably Denmark against all probabilities were level. But France would not be denied. Denmark, organized and swift on the counter, simply could not hold them. Just before the hour Petit confirmed them winners. Vieira, his Arsenal team-mate, shot, the ball charged down, and fell to the pony-tailed midfield player, whose shot zipped into the net off the flailing boot of Schmeichel. At 2–1 France persisted to the whistle searching for a third, while Denmark resigned themselves to defeat. A succession of half chances came and went but goals did not. France had won, and more pleasingly for the many thousands supporting them, they had won with the flamboyant Gaelic swagger expected, almost demanded, by their public.

In Bordeaux, also in Group C, South Africa, some way short of the impression they had been expected to leave, bowed out. Saudi Arabia in earning their first point at least left the competition on a happier note. For the Africans Shaun Bartlett scored an 18th minute goal to give them hope. Denmark, by now losing in Lyon to France, held only the smallest goal difference advantage. It was not to be, Pierre Issa, scorer of two unwanted own goals against France, now excelled himself, two injudicious challenges, two penalty kicks, two goals, the first by Al-Jaber on the stroke of half-time, the second by Al-Thynyan for 2–1. Bartlett's equalizer, curiously another penalty converted in injury time, proving no more than academic to disappointed South African coach Phillipe Troussier. The Sheffield Wednesday-bound Frenchman, displaying an iron fist, had already banished two of his squad for breaking curfew and night clubbing until 6 a.m. Afterwards, his parting remarks, aimed at South Africa's finest criticized their apparent lack of motivation: 'Talent is fine, but without that will and commitment to go on and get that result, you cannot go very far. I never felt there was that collective commitment that makes you go for the ball and fight together.'

In Group D a joyful Paraguay with discipline and no little verve overcame a much changed Nigerian team in Toulouse and thus ensured their qualification. Without Okechukeu, Adepoju, Okocha, Ikpeba and Finidi, the Africans suffered a further blow before kick off with Amokachi pulling up injured in the warm up. Sensing weakness in this depleted line up, Paraguay took the initiative and were rewarded within a minute, Arce flighting his free kick over, Ayala meeting the ball with a precise header. Stung, Nigeria to their credit responded furiously: Babangida freed by the extravagantly skilled Sunday Oliseh slid the ball into Oruma who stabbed his shot past Chilavert. As the pressure intensified, Paraguay might easily have succumbed. That they did not owed much to their combative spirit, as tackle after shuddering tackle thudded into the elusive Africans. Through it all Chilavert provided inspiration, a colossus in their goal, defying in turn Oliseh, West and Yekini twice with breathtaking agility. After the interval Paraguay again raised themselves as Nigeria's effort slackened. Benitez on the hour scored decisively, his venomously struck shot from long range curling high into Nigeria's net. Beaten now in midfield and showing alarming lapses in defence, Nigeria's misery and Paraguayan ecstasy was completed four minutes from the end, Cardoso beating Rufai's despairing dive with a fiercely struck cross shot. At 3–1 Paraguay would have the unenviable task of facing France in Lens.

Poor Spain could only blame themselves for their failure to defeat Nigeria. The subsequently tame draw with Paraguay had left them vulnerable, and here in Lens a glorious demonstration of their potential came to nothing as the thrashing of a feeble Bulgarian side was rendered meaningless by news filtering through from Lens of Nigeria's capitulation at the hands of the Paraguayans. Needing to win, Hierro set Spain on their way, cracking home a penalty kick after Jordanov recklessly lunged at Luis Enrique. With Morientes and Etxeberria troubling them with their ability to attack crosses, Bulgaria's defences began to unravel. Luis Enrique, full of pace and invention, catalyst of so many attacks, scored a second in the 18th minute, cutting inside from the wing to drive the ball comprehensively beyond Zdravkov. Though Bulgaria sought to gain momentum, their rearguard was being overwhelmed by the elusive Spaniards. Penev with a rare opportunity might have done better than force Zubizarreta to an athletic save. Then the floodgates truly opened and Spain poured through. Aguilera struck the bar, Luis Enrique saw his effort smothered by Zdravkov, then the third and conclusive goal: Morientes, put through by another incisive pass from Luis Enrique, slipped his shot easily past the despairing goalkeeper. The score was 3–0. Kostadinov brought Bulgaria spectacular consolation just before the hour, pounding a ferocious shot past the startled Zubizarreta, but that was the end of their resistance. Shuffling his pack, believing goals scored to be vital, Javier Clemente introduced more forwards. One of them, Raul, created a fourth, guiding the ball into the path of

Morientes before another, Kiko, wrapped it up, his two simple goals in the final three minutes making it 6–1. What a pity that the brooding majesty that is Hristo Stoichkov should have had this for a final World Cup appearance. Withdrawn early in the second half, his role was reduced to that of a scowling, anonymous spectator. For Bonev the coach, the dispirited disintegration proved the final straw, 'I am a man of principles, and after what I saw I cannot go on.' For Clemente it was the bitterest of pills. His team often accused of under-achieving had quite typically produced glorious football only when it was too late. 'I think that the Nigeria result really bothered our confidence. You have to congratulate Paraguay. I feel sad, but life goes on.'

On the following day Holland confirmed their qualification for the knockout stages, in so doing demonstrating their strengths and weaknesses. An irresistible revelation, playing football the equal of any, they faded eventually satisfied, thus allowing resilient Mexico the chance to regroup and strike back. Outplayed and overwhelmed early on, Mexico's plight appeared hopeless within 20 minutes. Bergkamp, after just four minutes, sent Cocu in on goal. The Eindhoven striker left Suarez trailing in his wake and beat the exposed Campos easily for 1–0. Fourteen minutes later it became 2–0. Ronald De Boer surged into the Mexican penalty area and bounced off three challenges, his momentum carrying him on, and slipped the ball beneath Campos. As Mexican humiliation threatened, they clung on, waited and prayed for the Dutch, full of style and swagger, to lose some interest. Their patience and resolve brought reward. Holland slowly but surely relaxed. Fifteen minutes from time Pelaez for the gallant Central Americans punished Dutch complacency, and given hope Mexico summoned up their remaining reserves of stamina. In the fourth minute of injury time courage and determination brought them level, Hernandez stole in, swept the ball home and sent Mexicans everywhere into delirium. They, too, would go through.

Belgium went out, their first exit at the group stage since 1970. A disappointing team lacking ambition against Holland, and stamina against Mexico, they failed to keep an inferior South Korean side, full of pride and fight, at arms length and paid the price with elimination. Scifo after five minutes might already have given the Belgians the lead, before one minute later Nilis, a tall gangly centre forward, did. Vidovic leapt to meet Oliveira's corner kick. His header was scrambled away by the Koreans but only into the path of Nilis who smashed the ball past Kim Byung-Ji. For the rest of the first half the Belgians controlled matters; physically stronger they dominated but without the nous to threaten a second. Slowly but surely Korea fought back. They were as committed a team as any in the Tournament, and Min-sung provided their inspiration, beating Staelens. His shot parried by Van de Walle appeared goalbound. Staelens, however, recovered to hack the ball to safety. Now the game flowed back and forth. Nilis crashed a shot against the Korean bar and then found himself frustrated by Byung-Ji who smothered a close range effort. With 17 minutes left the Asians grabbed their equalizer, Ha Seok-Ju's innocuous cross evading all but the jubilant Yoo Sang Chui who arrived at the far post with exquisite timing to thump a rising shot past Van de Walle. At 1–1 in spite of growing pressure from the Belgians desperate to avoid elimination, Korea held on for their draw.

Yugoslavia booked their passage in Nantes, beating an enterprising American team with a goal scored within four minutes. Their performance, however, had been far from convincing. For the United States it might have proven a very different story had Cobi Jones's intended cross within thirty seconds not hit an upright. Barely three minutes later Yugoslavia had the lead. Mihajlovic hammered in a shot, Friedel replacing Kasey Keller couldn't hold it and Komljenovic pounced, heading in from an acute angle. The Liverpool-based goalkeeper redeemed himself, denying in turn Stankovic and Milosevic. The game was open but the clever, elegant Yugoslavians, so much more incisive, held all the aces. Throughout the second half the American exuberance continued. Abandoning all caution they posed the Slavs problems, hounding them with increasing confidence, McBride, tall and youthful, offering an enthusiastic target. Twice his presence caused consternation, twice Kralj thwarted him. Yugoslavia had noticeably relaxed their effort and won. The United States had suffered three defeats but had shown themselves to be competitive.

Germany, as expected, won, poor courageous Iran simply not good enough, their collective experience proving ultimately too much for gallant opponents in Montpellier. Tough and at times overtly physical, the Germans were unsettled in the opening stages, worried by pacey opponents and in particular Mahdavikia, a young and tireless presence on the Iranians' flank. Twice he might have created a sensation, first thumping a rasping free kick into the gloves of Köpke, and then a moment later bearing down on goal to be frustrated by alert goalkeeping. Endurance and resilience, traits of German teams almost by inheritance, turned things around. Never pretty, always thorough and effective, they smothered and nullified eager Iranians desperate for victory to ensure unlikely qualification. Hässler's cross on 50 minutes found Bierhoff, and his header, unerringly accurate, was in Iran's net. If Iran could compete technically, they could not cope with German tenacity. Slowly and irreversibly the tide turned against them. Heinrich's header from veteran Matthäus' right wing cross found Bierhoff, and this time the Italian-based striker struck the post but the lurking Klinsmann did the rest. The score at 2–0, Bierhoff might have made it three, missing with a fierce drive. For the spirited Asians playing with great pride it would have been a cruel and undeserved blow. Germany had won, but in the rarefied atmosphere of the later stages, clearly they would need to improve. Many good judges doubted their ageing team could.

England in Lens introduced their young starlets, midfield playmaker David Beckham and speedy teenage striker Michael Owen, and at once rediscovered themselves. Physically dominant, fast and fluent, their football proved altogether too much for Colombia, dispirited and broken long before the end and flattered by a 2–0 defeat. Scholes almost set the English on their way, his third-minute shot beaten away by Mondragon with the greatest difficulty. Owen shortly afterwards demonstrated his alertness, spinning to volley over the crossbar and Le Saux arriving at the far post steered the ball wastefully wide of goal from Beckham's deep right wing cross. Colombia, under siege, reeled under the onslaught, unable to gain a foothold in a game played at an uncomfortably fast tempo. Beckham's short and long passing was unerringly accurate, Anderton and Le Saux providing width, Ince indomitable in midfield. Colombia wilted. On 20 minutes came a goal long overdue: Owen delivered the cross, Scholes jumping with Moreno the distraction, Anderton waiting at the far post, a magnificently struck shot. The ball driven from the acutest of angles beat Mondragon comprehensively and roared upwards into the roof of the net. If the South Americans prayed for a respite, their prayers went unanswered. Ten minutes later, moments after Owen again had struck a shot narrowly over, the contest was all but decided. Ince again burst forward and was halted unfairly. Beckham, twenty-five yards out, ran in and curled his shot up over the wall and then dipping and turning in at angle of crossbar and goalpost. England were elated, Colombia shattered. Rampant now and until the end, it might have been six by the finish. Instead, Mondragon, performing heroics behind an increasingly disorganized and shambolic defence, denied them. Scholes, Shearer, Scholes again, Beckham and Owen all went close. Campbell, a giant in England's masterful rearguard, sauntered forward from deep in his own half, the leggy Tottenham player breaking or hurdling tackle after tackle as he bore down on goal until a late desperate challenge knocked the ball away as he prepared to shoot. Owen, exhilarating throughout, might have had the last word, his blistering pace carrying him within range. Unfortunately, Bermudez with a meticulously timed block frustrated him. At the whistle England had perhaps done more than win. They had exorcised the ghosts of Romania in Toulouse and in so doing served notice on the rest. It would be a supremely confident English team that would meet Argentina in St Etienne.

In St Denis a complacent performance from a Romanian team already assured of qualification saw them come close to being punished by lively, positive Tunisians. In the event a draw was enough to head the group and send them to Bordeaux to meet the Croatians. If Tunisia, taking the lead after just nine minutes, caused a surprise, it was not the first of the contest. Romania emerged from the tunnel sporting bleached yellow heads, legacy of a bet with their coach Anghel Iordanescu. Tunisia's goal came from their greatest source of inspiration, Adel Sellimi. Tricking his way into the penalty area, his run unsettled Christian Dulca. The defender's clumsy challenge brought Sellimi down and Souayah stepped up to rifle home the penalty for 1–0. Already troubled by Slimane after two minutes, Stelea and his over-worked defence resisted the sprightly Africans. Popescu, on as a substitute after half an hour for poor Dulca, stabilized matters, and after the interval Viovel Moldovan and Adrian Ilie, forced on to the field, galvanized their team. Ilie might have scored in the 53rd minute: put through by Hagi, he squandered his chance. Thirteen minutes later he made amends. Cleverly chipping the advancing El Ouaer, Chouchane's desperate defensive header cleared the ball from immediate danger but only into the path of the predatory Moldovan, who scored with ease. Romania had avoided embarrassment but it had been a close-run thing.

In Bordeaux from Group H came a match between the two hitherto undefeated teams, Argentina and the Tournament's most accomplished newcomers Croatia. Argentina, dominant and relatively untroubled, won at a canter. Given confidence by a well drilled defence marshalled by Ayala, the Argentineans probed gently from the beginning. Veron of Sampdoria was the orchestrator of much of their best work. Ortega, small mobile and clever, aided by Gallardo, provided Batistuta with menacing support. Croatia resisted well, though often beyond the rules until the 36th minute when they contributed negligently to their own downfall. Bilic of Everton, a tower of strength at the heart of their defence, was caught, his pocket picked as he advanced. The eager Ortega, guiding the ball into the space he had vacated, found Pineda, whose volley was dispatched sweetly into the net guarded by Ladic. Always outplayed, in a 'chess match' often at strolling pace, Croatia might have dragged themselves back, Vlaovic crashing an effort against the bar just past the hour. But thereafter the South Americans ground out their win with a degree of comfort. Afterwards Argentine coach Passarella summed up his feeling at qualifying: 'Croatia are a very strong team, so we are delighted that we have come out of this achieving our aim. We have won the group and that means that we can stay at our base near St Etienne and prepare for the next round there on Tuesday night. We always had the edge and we created more chances. The team is still improving, but we have come through all three games strongly and are in good shape now for the rest of the Tournament.' For all of Croatia's evident disappointment, however, their draw for the knockout stages appeared kinder than the task demanded of their imperious conquerors.

Was there ever an unlikelier pairing in the World Cup Finals than Jamaica and Japan? Jamaica won their contest in Lyon, largely through the efforts of Theodore Whitmore, while Japan, full of neat, tidy passing movement, were left again to rue their lack of a cutting edge. Japan, driven as ever by their thoughtful playmaker Nakata, might have taken the lead. Jo, shooting narrowly wide after receiving Nakata's curling cross, came closest, but then after 39 minutes any illusion of supremacy was shattered. Hall received Gayle's headed clearance, and though his control was clumsy, Whitmore proved the beneficiary, picking the ball up and seizing the chance to beat Kawaguchi. After the interval the Japanese continued to press. Nakata direct from a corner worried

Lawrence, the Jamaican goalkeeper, and Yamaguchi agonizingly struck his fierce shot the wrong side of the upright. Jamaica under pressure broke away to steal a second. Whitmore again wide on the right cut inside, leaving Soma stranded, and buried his left-footed shot in Kawaguchi's net.

Still Japan attacked. Narahashi crashed his shot against a post, Jo should have scored but failed dismally, and then Nakayama deservedly drove home. The score remained at 2–1 despite frantic efforts. Lopes might have saved Japan in injury time but his simplest of opportunities was wasted horribly. Both teams could go home and reflect on their adventure. For Jamaica there were lessons to be learned before they sought to qualify again. Japan, as co-hosts, would be there; they would hope in the meantime to improve on their finishing.

Final Tournament – France
First Round

Group A

Brazil (1) **2, Scotland** (1) **1**
10.6.98 PARIS
Brazil: Taffarel, Cafu, Junior Baiano, Aldair, Roberto Carlos, Cesar Sampaio (1), Giovanni (Leonardo), Dunga, Rivaldo, Ronaldo, Bebeto (Denilson)
Scotland: Leighton, Calderwood, Hendry, Dailly (McKinlay T), Lambert, Burley, Collins (1 pen), Boyd (o.g.), Gallacher, Durie, Jackson (McKinlay W)
Referee: Garcia-Aranda (Spain)

Morocco (1) **2, Norway** (1) **2**
10.6.98 MONTPELLIER
Morocco: Benzekri, Saber, Rossi, Naybet, Chiba, El Khalej (Azzouzi), Chippo (o.g.) (Amzine), Hadji (1), Bassir, Hadda (1) (El Khattabi)
Norway: Grodås, Berg, Eggen (1), Johnsen, Bjørnebye, Flo H (Solbakken), Leonhardsen, Rekdal, Mykland, Solskjaer (Riseth), Flo T A
Referee: Un-Prasert (Thailand)

Scotland (0) **1, Norway** (0) **1**
16.6.98 BORDEAUX
Scotland: Leighton, Calderwood (Weir), Hendry, Boyd, Burley (1), Lambert, Collins, Dailly, Jackson (McNamara),Gallacher, Durie
Norway: Grodås Bjørnebye, Eggen, Johnsen, Berg (Halle), Strand, Rekdal, Solbakken, Flo H (1) (Jakobsen), Riseth (Østenstad), Flo T A
Referee: Vagner (Hungary)

Brazil (2) **3, Morocco** (0) **0**
16.6.98 NANTES
Brazil: Taffarel, Cafu, Junior Baiano, Aldair, Roberto Carlos, Cesar Sampaio (Doriva), Dunga, Leonardo, Rivaldo (1) (Denilson), Bebeto (1) (Edmundo), Ronaldo (1)
Morocco: Benzekri, Saber (Abrami), Rossi, Naybet, El Hadrioui, Chiba (Amzine), Tahar, Chippo, Hadji, Bassir, Hadda (El Khattabi)
Referee: Levnikov (Russia)

Brazil (0) **1, Norway** (0) **2**
23.6.98 MARSEILLES
Brazil: Taffarel, Cafu, Junior Baiano, Goncalves M, Roberto Carlos, Dunga, Leonardo, Rivaldo, Denilson, Bebeto (1), Ronaldo
Norway: Grodås, Berg, Eggen, Johnsen, Bjørnebye, Flo H (Solskjaer o.g.), Leonhardsen, Rekdal (1 pen), Strand (Mykland), Riseth, Flo T A (1)
Referee: Baharmast (USA)

Scotland (0) **0, Morocco** (1) **3**
23.6.98 ST ETIENNE
Scotland: Leighton, Weir, Hendry, Boyd, McNamara (McKinlay T), Burley, Lambert, Collins, Dailly, Gallacher, Durie (Booth)
Morocco: Benzekri, Saber, Rossi, Naybet, Triki, Abrami, Amzine (Azzouzi), El Khalej, Chippo (Sellami), Hadji, Bassir (2), Hadda (1)
Referee: Bujsaim (UAE)

	P	W	D	L	F	A	Pts
Brazil	3	2	0	1	6	3	6
Norway	3	1	2	0	5	4	5
Morocco	3	1	1	1	5	5	4
Scotland	3	0	1	2	2	6	1

Group B

Italy (1) **2, Chile** (1) **2**
11.6.98 BORDEUX
Italy: Pagliuca, Nesta, Costacurta, Cannavaro, Di Livio (Chiesa), Baggio D, Albertini, Di Matteo (Di Biagio) Maldini, Vieri (1) (Inzaghi), Baggio R (1 pen)
Chile: Tapia, Fuentes, Margas (Ramirez P), Reyes, Estay (Sierra), Villarroel, Acuña (Cornejo), Parraguez, Rojas, Salas (2), Zamorano
Referee: Bouchardeau (Niger)

Austria (0) **1, Cameroon** (0) **1**
11.6.98 TOULOUSE
Austria: Konsel, Schöttel, Feiersinger, Pfeffer, Cerny (Haas), Mählich, Kühbauer, Pfeifenberger (Stöger), Wetl, Herzog (Vastic), Polster (1)
Cameroon: Songo'o, Njanka (1), Kalla Nkongo, Song, Ndo, (Olembe), Mboma, Angibeau, Wome, Oman-Biyik (Tchami), Ipoua (Job)
Referee: Chavez (Paraguay)

Chile (0) **1, Austria** (0) **1**
17.6.98 PARIS
Chile: Tapia, Margas, Fuentes, Reyes, Rojas, Parraguez, Acuña, Villarroel (Castaneda), Estay (Sierra), Salas (1), Zamorano
Austria: Konsel, Pfeffer, Schöttel, Feiersinger, Cerny (Schoppe), Kühbauer (Herzog), Mählich, Pfeifenberger, Wetl, Haas (Vastic (1)), Polster
Referee: Ghandour (Egypt)

Italy (1) **3, Cameroon** (0) **0**
17.6.98 MONTPELLIER
Italy: Pagliuca, Cannavaro, Costacurta, Nesta, Maldini, Baggio D, Albertini (Di Matteo), Di Biagio (1), Moriero (Di Livio), Vieri (2), Baggio R (Del Piero)
Cameroon: Songo'o, Njanka, Kalla Nkongo, Song, Wome, Ndo, Angibeau, Mboma (Eto'o), Olembe, Ipoua (Job), Oman-Biyik (Tchami)
Referee: Lennie (Australia)

Italy (2) **2, Austria** (0) **1**
23.6.98 ST DENIS
Italy: Pagliuca, Costacurta, Cannavaro, Nesta (Bergomi), Moriero, Passotto, Baggio D, Di Biagio, Maldini, Del Piero (Baggio R (1)), Vieri (1) (Inzaghi)
Austria: Konsel, Feiersinger, Schöttel, Pfeffer, Mählich, Kühbauer (Stöger), Pfeifenberger (Herzog (1 pen)), Reinmayr, Wetl, Vastic, Polster (Haas)
Referee: Durkin (England)

Chile (1) **1, Cameroon** (0) **1**
23.6.98 NANTES
Chile: Tapia, Reyes, Fuentes, Margas, Villarroel (Cornejo), Acuña, Parraguez, Rojas (Ramirez P), Sierra (1) (Estay), Salas, Zamorano
Cameroon: Songo'o, Pensee, Njanka, Song, Mahouve, Ndo (Etame), Olembe (Angibeau), Wome, Mboma (1), Oman-Biyick, Job
Referee: Vagner (Hungary)

	P	W	D	L	F	A	Pts
Italy	3	2	1	0	7	3	7
Chile	3	0	3	0	4	4	3
Austria	3	0	2	1	3	4	2
Cameroon	3	0	2	1	2	5	2

Group C

Saudi Arabia (0) **0, Denmark** (0) **1**
12.6.98 LENS
Saudi Arabia: Al Deayea, Al Jahani, Al Khiaiwi, Zubromawi, Sulimani, Amin (Saleh), Al Owairan S (Al Dosari), Al Muwalid, Al Owairan, Al Shahrani, Al Jaber (Al Thynyan)
Denmark: Schmeichel, Rieper (1), Høgh, Colding, Schjønberg, Helveg, Wieghorst (Nielsen), Jørgensen (Frandsen), Laudrup M, Laudrup B (Heintze), Sand
Referee: Castrilli (Argentina)

France (1) **3, South Africa** (0) **0**
12.6.98 MARSEILLE
France: Barthez, Desailly, Blanc, Lizarazu, Thuram, Deschamps, Petit (Boghossian), Henry, Zidane, Djorkaeff (Trezeguet), Guivarc'h (Dugarry (1))
South Africa: Vonk, Issa (2 o.g.), Fish, Radebe, Nyathi, Jackson, Moshoeu, Fortune, Augustine (Mkhalele), McCarthy (Bartlett), Masinga
Referee: de Freitas (Brazil)

South Africa (0) **1, Denmark** (1) **1**
18.6.98 TOULOUSE
South Africa: Vonk, Fish, Issa, Radebe, Mkhalele, Augustine (Phiri), Moshoeu, Fortune, Nyathi (Buckley), Bartlett (Masinga), McCarthy (1)
Denmark: Schmeichel, Colding, Rieper, Høgh, Schjønberg (Wieghorst), Jørgensen, Helveg, Nielsen (1), Laudrup M (Heintze), Sand (Molnar), Laudrup B
Referee: Rendon (Colombia)

France (1) **4, Saudi Arabia** (0) **0**
18.6.98 PARIS
France: Barthez, Desailly, Blanc, Lizarazu (1), Thuram, Deschamps, Boghossian, Henry (2), Zidane, Diomede, Dugarry (Trezeguet (1))
Saudi Arabia: Al Deayea, Al Jahani, Zubromawi, Al Khilaiwi, Sulimani, Amin, Al Owairan K, Saleh, Al Shahrani, Al Owairan S, Al Jaber
Referee: Carter (Mexico)

South Africa (1) **2, Saudi Arabia** (1) **2**
24.6.98 BORDEAUX
South Africa: Fish, Issa, Jackson, Buckley, Nyathi, Mkhalele, Radebe, Fortune (Khumalo), Moshoeu, McCarthy (Sikhosana), Bartlett (2, pen)
Saudi Arabia: Al Deayea, Al Jahani, Amin, Zubromawi, Sulimani, Al Temyat, Al Owairan, Al Thynyan (1 pen) (Al Harbi), Saleh, Al Jaber (1 pen), Al Mehalel (Al Shahrani)
Referee: Yanten (Chile)

France (1) **2, Denmark** (1) **1**
24.6.98 LYONS
France: Barthez, Karembeu, Leboeuf, Desailly, Candela, Vieira, Petit (1) (Boghossian), Diomede, Pires (Henry), Trezeguet (Guivarc'h), Djorkaeff (1 pen)
Denmark: Schmeichel, Laursen (Colding), Rieper, Høgh, Heintze, Jørgensen (Sand), Helveg, Nielsen, Laudrup M (1), Schjønberg, Laudrup B (Tøfting)
Referee: Collina (Italy)

	P	W	D	L	F	A	Pts
France	3	3	0	0	9	1	9
Denmark	3	1	1	1	3	3	4
South Africa	3	0	2	1	3	6	2
Saudi Arabia	3	0	1	2	2	7	1

Group D

Paraguay (0) **0, Bulgaria** (0) **0**
12.6.98 MONTPELLIER
Paraguay: Chilavert, Gamarra, Ayala, Sarabia, Benitez, Morales (Caniza), Acuña, Paredes, Campos, Cardozo (Ramirez), Campos (Yegros)
Bulgaria: Zdravkov, Nankov, Yordanov, Ivanov, Petkov, Iliev (Borimirov), Balakov, Kichichev, Yankov, Penev (Kostadinov), Stoichkov
Referee: Al-Zeid (Saudi Arabia)

Spain (1) **2, Nigeria** (1) **3**
13.6.98 NANTES
Spain: Zubizarreta, Ferrer (Amor), Alkorta, Campo, Nadal, Sergi, Hierro (1), Luis Enrique, Raul (1), Alfonso (Exteberria), Kiko
Nigeria: Rufai, Oparaku (Yekini), West, Okechukwu, Babayaro, Oliseh (1), Lawal (1) (Okpara), Okocha, Finidi, Adepoju (1), Ikpeba (Babangida)
Referee: Baharmast (USA)

Nigeria (1) **1, Bulgaria** (0) **0**
19.6.98 PARIS
Nigeria: Rufai, Adepoju, Uche, West, Finidi (Babangida), Oliseh, Okocha, Lawal, Babayaro, Amokachi (Kanu), Ikpeba (1) (Yekini)
Bulgaria: Zdravkov, Kichichev, Ivanov, Guentchev, Iliev (Penev), Yankov (Batchev), Balakov, Hristov (Borimirov), Petkov, Kostadinov, Stoichkov
Referee: Yanten (Chile)

Spain (0) **0, Paraguay** (0) **0**
19.6.98 ST ETIENNE
Spain: Zubizarreta, Aguilera, Alkorta, Abelardo (Celades), Sergi, Hierro, Amor, Etxeberria, Luis Enrique, Raul (Kiko), Pizzi (Morientes)
Paraguay: Chilavert, Sarabia, Gamarra, Ayala, Caniza, Benitez, Arce, Enciso, Acuña (Yegros), Campos (Paredes), Rojas (Ramirez)
Referee: McLeod (South Africa)

Spain (2) **6, Bulgaria** (0) **1**
24.6.98 LENS
Spain: Zubizarreta, Aguilera, Nadal, Alkorta, Sergi, Amor, Hierro (1 pen), Luis Enrique (1) (Guerrero), Alfonso (Kiko (2)), Etxeberria (Raul), Morientes (2)
Bulgaria: Zdravkov, Ivanov, Kichichev, Jordanov, Guentchev, Nankov (Penev), Borimirov, Batchev, Balakov (Hristov), Kostadinov (1), Stoichkov (Iliev)
Referee: Van der Ende (Holland)

Nigeria (1) **1, Paraguay** (1) **3**
24.6.98 TOULOUSE
Nigeria: Rufai, Eguavoen, Okafor, West, Iroha, Oliseh (Okpara), Babangida, Oruma (1) (Finidi), Lawal, Yekini, Kanu
Paraguay: Chilavert, Sarabia, Ayala (1), Gamarra, Arce, Enciso, Paredes, Caniza (Yegros), Benitez (1) (Acuña), Cardozo (1), Brizuela (Rojas)
Referee: Un-Prasert (Thailand)

	P	W	D	L	F	A	Pts
Nigeria	3	2	0	1	5	5	6
Paraguay	3	1	2	0	3	1	5
Spain	3	1	1	1	8	4	4
Bulgaria	3	0	1	2	1	7	1

Group E

Belgium (0) **0, Holland** (0) **0**
13.6.98 ST DENIS
Belgium: De Wilde, Borkelmans, Clement, Crasson (Deflandre), Staelens, Verstraeten, Boffin, Van der Elst, Nilis, Oliveira, Mpenza E, Wilmots
Holland: Van der Sar, De Boer F, Numan, Stam, De Boer R (Jonk), Cocu, Seedorf (Zenden), Winter, Kluivert, Overmars, Hasselbaink (Bergkamp)
Referee: Collina (Italy)

South Korea (1) **1, Mexico** (0) **3**
13.6.98 LYONS
South Korea: Kim Byun-Ji, Kim Tae-Young, Hong Myung-Bo, Lee Min-Sung, Ko Jong-Soo (Seo Jung-Won), Lee Sang-Yoon, Ha Seok-Ju (1), Yoo Sang-Chul, Kim Doh-Keun (Choi Sung-Yong), Yun Noh-Jung (Jang Hyung-Seok), Kim Do-Hoon
Mexico: Campos, Suarez, Davino, Pardo, Ramirez, Garcia Aspe (Bernal), Ordiales (Palaez (1)), Lara, Luna (Arellano), Hernandez (2), Blanco
Referee: Benkö (Austria)

Holland (2) **5, South Korea** (0) **0**
20.6.98 MARSEILLES
Holland: Van der Sar, Winter, Stam, De Boer F, De Boer R (1) (Zenden), Jonk, Davids, Numan (Bogarde), Overmars (1), Cocu (1), Bergkamp (1) (Van Hooijdonk (1))
South Korea: Kim Byung-Ji, Choi Young-Il, Hong Myung-Bo, Lee Min-Sung, Choi Sung-Young (Kim Tae-Young), Le Sang-Yoon, Kim Doh-Keun, Yoo Sang-Chul, Seo Jung-Won (Lee Dong-gook), Kim Do-Hoon (Do Jong-Soo), Choi Yong-Soo
Referee: Wojcik (Poland)

Belgium (1) **2, Mexico** (0) **2**
20.6.98 BORDEAUX
Belgium: De Wilde, Deflandre, Vidovic, Staelens, Borkelmans, Wilmots (2), Van der Elst (De Boeck), Boffin (Verheyen), Scifo, Nilis (M'Penza), Oliveira
Mexico: Campos, Pardo, Sanchez, Suarez, Davino, Ramirez, Garcia Aspe (1 pen) (Lara), Palencia (Arellano), Ordiales (Villa), Hernandez, Blanco (1)
Referee: Dallas (Scotland)

Holland (1) **2, Mexico** (0) **2**
25.6.98 ST ETIENNE
Holland: Van der Sar, Reiziger, Stam, De Boer F, Numan (Bogarde), De Boer R (1), Jonk (Winter), Davids, Overmars, Bergkamp (Hasselbaink), Cocu (1)
Mexico: Campos, Sanchez (Pelaez (1)), Suarez, Davino, Carmona, Villa, Ramirez, Luna (Arellano), Blanco, Hernandez (1)
Referee: Al Zeid (Saudi Arabia)

Belgium (1) **1, South Korea** (0) **1**
25.6.98 PARIS
Belgium: Van de Walle, Staelens, Borkelmans, Vidovic, Deflandre, Wilmots, Van Kerckhoven, Clement (Mpenza L), Scifo (Van der Elst), Oliveira (Mpenza M), Nilis (1)
South Korea: Kim Byung-Ji, Hong Myung-Bo, Lee Sang-Hun (Jang Hyung-Seok), Kim Tae-Young, Choi Sung-Yong (Lee Lim-Saeng), Kim Doh-Keun (Ko Jong-Soo), Ha Seok-Ju, Lee Min-Sung, Yoo Sang-Chul (1), Choi Yong-Soo, Seo Jung-Won
Referee: Freitas (Brazil)

	P	W	D	L	F	A	Pts
Holland	3	1	2	0	7	2	5
Mexico	3	1	2	0	7	5	5
Belgium	3	0	3	0	3	3	3
South Korea	3	0	1	2	2	9	1

Group F

Iran (0) **0, Yugoslavia** (0) **1**
14.6.98 ST ETIENNE
Iran: Nakisa, Zarincheh, Khakpour, Mohammadkhani, Pashazadeh, Mahdavikia, Bagheri, Estili (Mansourian), Minavand Chal, Azizi, Daei
Yugoslavia: Kralj, Mirkovic, Djorovic, Mihajlovic (1), Petrovic, Jokanovic, Stojkovic (Kovacevic), Brnovic (Stankovic), Jugovic, Milosevic (Ognjenovic), Mijatovic
Referee: Noriega (Peru)

Germany (1) **2, United States** (0) **0**
15.6.98 PARIS
Germany: Köpke, Wörns, Thon, Kohler, Reuter (Ziege), Jeremies, Möller (1) (Babbel), Hässler (Hamann), Heinrich, Klinsmann (1), Bierhoff
United States: Keller, Pope, Dooley, Regis, Burns (Hejduk), Deering (Ramos), Maisonneuve, Reyna, Jones, Wynalda (Wegerle), Stewart
Referee: Belqola (Morocco)

Iran (1) **2, United States** (0) **1**
21.6.98 LYONS
Iran: Abedzadeh, Zarincheh (Saadavi), Khakpour, Mohammadkhani (Peyravani), Pashazadeh, Mahdavikia (1), Minavand Chal, Bagheri, Estili (1), Azizi (Mansourian), Daei
United States: Keller, Pope, Dooley (Maisonneuve), Regis, Moore, Hejduk, Ramos (Stewart), Reyna, Jones (Preki), McBride (1), Wegerle (Radosavljevic)
Referee: Meier (Switzerland)

Germany (0) **2, Yugoslavia** (1) **2**
21.6.98 LENS
Germany: Köpke, Thon, Kohler, Wörns, Heinrich, Möller (Kirsten), Jeremies, Hamann (Matthäus), Ziege (Tarnat), Klinsmann, Bierhoff (1)
Yugoslavia: Kralj, Djorovic, Mihajlovic (o.g.), Komljenovic, Petrovic (Stevic), Jokanovic, Stojkovic (1), Stankovic (Govedarica), Jugovic, Mijatovic (1), Kovacevic (Ognjenovic)
Referee: Nielsen (Denmark)

Germany (0) **2, Iran** (0) **0**
25.6.98 MONTPELLIER
Germany: Kohler, Thon (Hamann), Wörns, Heinrich, Matthäus, Helmer, Tarnat (Ziege), Hässler (Kirsten), Bierhoff (1), Klinsmann (1)
Iran: Abedzadeh, Khakpour, Mohammadkhani, Pashazadeh, Zarincheh, Mohammadi, Mahdavikia, Estili, Minavand Chal, Bagheri, Azizi, Daei
Referee: Chavez (Paraguay)

United States (0) **0, Yugoslavia** (1) **1**
25.6.98 NANTES
United States: Friedel, Burns, Dooley, Regis, Hejduk, Reyna, Maisonneuve, Stewart, Moore, Jones, McBride
Yugoslavia: Kralj, Djorovic, Mihajlovic, Petrovic, Komljenovic (1), Stankovic, Stojkovic, Jugovic, Jokanovic, Milosevic, Mijatovic (Ognjenovic)
Referee: Ghandour (Egypt)

	P	W	D	L	F	A	Pts
Germany	3	2	1	0	6	2	7
Yugoslavia	3	2	1	0	4	2	7
Iran	3	1	0	2	2	4	3
USA	3	0	0	3	1	5	0

Group G

England (1) **2, Tunisia** (0) **0**
15.6.98 MARSEILLES
England: Seaman, Southgate, Adams, Campbell, Anderton, Batty, Scholes (1), Ince, Le Saux, Sheringham (Owen), Shearer (1)
Tunisia: El Ouaer, Boukadida, Badra, Trabelsi S, Trabelsi H (Thabet), Ghodbane, Souayah (Baya), Chihi, Clayton, Sellimi, Ben Slimane (Ben Younes)
Referee: Okada (Japan)

Romania (1) **1, Colombia** (0) **0**
15.6.98 LYONS
Romania: Stelea, Petrescu, Cibotariu, Gica Popescu, Filipescu, Gabriel Popescu (Stanga), Galca, Hagi (Marinescu), Munteanu, Moldovan (Niculescu), Ilie (1)
Colombia: Mondragon, Cabrera, Bermudez, Palacios, Santa, Aristizabal (Valencia), Lozano, Serna, Rincon, Valderrama, Asprilla (Preciado)
Referee: Chong (Mauritius)

Romania (0) **2, England** (0) **1**
22.6.98 TOULOUSE
Romania: Stelea, Petrescu (1), Ciobotariu, Gheorghe Popescu, Filipescu, Munteanu, Hagi (Stanga, Marinescu), Galca, Gabriel Popescu, Moldovan (1) (Lacatus). Ilie
England: Seaman, Neville, Adams, Campbell, Anderton, Ince (Beckham), Scholes, Batty, Le Saux, Sheringham (Owen (1)), Shearer
Referee: Batta (France)

Colombia (0) **1, Tunisia** (0) **0**
22.6.98 MONTPELLIER
Colombia: Mondragon, Cabrera, Bermudez, Palacios, Santa, Rincon (Aristizabal), Serna (Bolano), Lozano, Valderrama, Valencia (Preciado (1)), De Avila
Tunisia: El Ouaer, Thabet (Godhbane), Trabelsi S, Chouchane, Chihi, Clayton, Baya (Ben Ahmed), Ben Slimane, Bouazizi, Souayah, Sellimi (Ben Younes)
Referee: Heynemann (Germany)

England (2) **2, Colombia** (0)
26.6.98 LENS
England: Seaman, Neville, Adams, Campbell, Anderton (1) (Lee), Ince (Batty), Beckham (1), Scholes (McManaman), Le Saux, Owen, Shearer
Colombia: Mondragon, Palacios, Bermudez, Moreno, Cabrera, Serna (Aristizabal), Lozano, Valderrama, Rincon, De Avila (Ricard), Preciado (Valencia)
Referee: Carter (Mexico)

Romania (0) **1, Tunisia** (1) **1**
26.6.98 ST DENIS
Romania: Stelea, Dobos, Dulca (Gheorge Popescu), Ciobotariu, Petrescu, Galca, Marinescu, Munteanu, Hagi, Dumitrescu (Moldovan (1)), Lacatus (Ilie)
Tunisia: El Ouaer, Bouazizi, Chouchane, Trabelsi S, Boukadida, Chihi, Ghodbane (Thabet), Souayah (1) (Ben Younes), Baya, Ben Slimane (Jelassi), Sellimi
Referee: Lennie (Australia)

	P	W	D	L	F	A	Pts
Romania	3	2	1	0	4	2	7
England	3	2	0	1	5	2	6
Colombia	3	1	0	2	1	3	3
Tunisia	3	0	1	2	1	4	1

Group H

Argentina (1) **1, Japan** (0) **0**
14.6.98 TOULOUSE
Argentina: Roa, Zanetti, Vivas, Ayala, Sensini (Chamot), Ortega, Almeyda, Veron, Simeone, Batistuta (1), Lopez (Balbo)
Japan: Kawaguchi, Narahashi, Nakanishi, Akita, Ihara, Soma (Hirano), Yamaguchi, Nanami, Nakayama (Lopes), Nakata, Jo
Referee: Van der Ende (Holland)

Jamaica (1) **1, Croatia** (1) **3**
14.6.98 LENS
Jamaica: Barrett, Sinclair, Goodison, Lowe, Gardener, Earle (Williams), Whitmore, Cargill (Powell), Simpson, Burton, Hall (Boyd)
Croatia: Ladic, Stimac, Soldo, Bilic, Simic, Boban, Asanovic, Prosinecki (1), Jarni, Stanic (1) (Vlaovic), Suker (1)
Referee: Pereira (Portugal)

Japan (0) **0, Croatia** (0) **1**
20.6.98 NANTES
Japan: Kawaguchi, Akita, Ihara, Nakanishi, Narahashi (Morishima), Yamaguchi, Nanami (Lopes), Soma, Nakata, Nakayama (Okano), Jo
Croatia: Ladic, Bilic, Soldo, Stimac (Vlaovic), Jurcic, Simic, Prosinecki (Maric), Asanovic, Jarni, Stanic (Tudor), Suker (1)
Referee: Ramdhan (Trinidad and Tobago)

Argentina (1) **5, Jamaica** (0) **0**
21.6.98 PARIS
Argentina: Roa, Sensini (Vivas), Ayala, Chamot, Simeone (Pineda), Lopez (Gallardo), Almeyda, Veron, Zanetti, Ortega (2), Batistuta (3, 1 pen)
Jamaica: Barrett, Malcolm (Boyd), Goodison, Dawes, Sinclair, Gardener, Simpson, Powell, Whitmore (Earle), Burton (Cargill), Hall
Referee: Pedersen (Norway)

Japan (0) **1, Jamaica** (1) **2**
26.6.98 LYONS
Japan: Kawaguchi, Akita, Ihara, Omura (Hirano), Narahashi, Nanami (Ono), Yamaguchi, Soma, Nakata, Nakayama (1), Jo (Lopes)
Jamaica: Lawrence, Sinclair, Lowe, Goodison, Malcolm, Dawes, Simpson (Earle), Whitmore (2), Gardener, Hall (Boyd), Gayle, Burton
Referee: Benkö (Austria)

Argentina (1) **1, Croatia** (0) **0**
26.6.98 BORDEAUX
Argentina: Roa, Vivas, Ayala, Paz, Zanetti (Simeone), Almeyda, Veron, Pineda (1), Gallardo (Berti), Ortega (Lopez), Batistuta
Croatia: Ladic, Soldo, Bilic, Simic, Maric (Vlaovic), Prosinecki (Stimac), Boban, Jarni, Asanovic, Suker, Stanic
Referee: Belqola (Morocco)

	P	W	D	L	F	A	Pts
Argentina	3	3	0	0	7	0	9
Croatia	3	2	0	1	4	2	6
Jamaica	3	1	0	2	9	3	3
Japan	3	0	0	3	1	4	0

Round of Sixteen

Italy v Norway
Brazil v Chile
France v Paraguay
Nigeria v Denmark
Germany v Mexico
Holland v Yugoslavia
Romania v Croatia
Argentina v England

THE ROUND OF SIXTEEN

The knockout stages began in Marseilles with Italy, thus far uninspired, playing Norway, here courtesy of their ferocious fightback against the Brazilians. The Italians began in serious mood, out to nullify and thus reduce the threat posed by Norway's long ball game and physical approach. They succeeded where others had failed, their finesse as ever matched by steely determination. Norway, unable to create offensive movement, were left to toil fruitlessly and resist Italy's more subtle probings instead. Alessandro Del Piero, mobile and clever, threatened fearful defenders, twice isolating and beating markers, twice seeing his shots saved by Grodås. It was Vieri who gave Italy the lead: tall and powerful, his bustling run on 18 minutes was picked out by Di Biagio's – quite the game's most outstanding performer – sublime pass, and the big striker hit his shot beneath Grodås's despairing dive. For the rest Norway, whose last gasp assault caused such panic in the Brazilian ranks, could do little but endure as Italian efficiency smothered them. Long before the end the conclusion was inevitable. Finishing 1–0, Egil Olsen, Norway's coach, painfully honest as ever, admitted his team had not performed as he had expected. He did not, he went on, think very much of the Italians either. Cesare Maldini in his post-match summary offered an insight into Italian philosophy as he expressed satisfaction in the result: 'We didn't make any mistakes.'

In Paris in the evening, as if to make up for the afternoon's sterility, Brazil and Chile were hugely entertaining in an open contest full of invention and craft. Chile, fired up, began brightly, their twin threat Zamorano and Salas seeking to steal in behind Brazil's suspect defence. Cruelly, after this period of superiority the Chileans fell behind to the first genuine attack they faced, a free kick angled in, met with precision by Cesar Sampaio, who celebrated in extravagant fashion. Chile for all their positive play were vulnerable to Brazilian rhythm and thrust. Driven by Dunga – a powerful, all-purpose midfield player in the European mould – Brazil had a second within half an hour. Another free kick, another Cesar Sampaio goal, unforgivably allowed time and space to rifle his shot home. To their credit Chile never yielded, though now up against a rampant Brazilian team producing short passing movements at bewildering pace, they were merely resisting. Before half-time it was over; Ronaldo advancing menacingly into the penalty area was felled by Nelson Tapia's desperate dive. Penalty kick – Ronaldo himself stepped up and duly dispatched the ball into Chile's net for 3–0. After the interval Chile reduced arrears briefly. Zamorano, a star of this Tournament if not the match, leapt and hung in the night sky. His header was beaten away by Taffarel but ran to Salas, who flashed his shot into the net. Brazil's response was immediate. Within a minute Ronaldo pursuing substitute Denilson's pass was bearing down again on the unfortunate Tapia. This time the goalkeeper was given no chance to foul, the shot hard, low and accurate made it 4–1. Until the end it was a sumptuous demonstration from Brazil, Roberto Carlos flying up the flanks, Rivaldo, Ronaldo and the eye-catching Denilson mesmerizing defenders with his speed and trickery. At last it was over; Zamorano and Ronaldo, team-mates at Internazionale of Milan, embraced. Chile were out, their approach both refreshing and perhaps naive. For Brazil it was a performance full of verve and flair. However, bigger and more demanding challengers lay on the horizon.

France strode on to the field at Lens to face a Paraguayan team determined to continue its World Cup adventure. Missing the inspiration of their playmaker Zinedine Zidane – suspended for his indiscretion against the Saudis – France laboured while Paraguay, delighting in their role of underdogs, dug in admirably, Chilavert their captain and goalkeeper defiant to the point of absolute heroism. Initially Paraguay resembled perhaps a parody of all the ugliness associated with South American football, negativity and extreme cynicism. Time wasting, feigned injury and petulance part of their armoury, in the face of such odds and evident superiority their gallantry by the end was remarkable. French frustration against staunch and disciplined defending was clearly evident. Deschamps huffed and puffed without purpose, and Djorkaeff was clever but lacking on the day the penetration required to storm this stockade. After a listless first half, France at least threatened with more menace during the second. Henry, pacey and positive, bounded through, Chilavert came to him quickly, the shot cannoning off the goalkeeper's post. Was Paraguay's only hope to hold on and advance on a penalty shoot-out? It certainly appeared so. When Robert Pires, a substitute replacing Thierry Henry, came on, French hopes appeared bleak, with Sarabia quite magnificent in his marshalling of the red-and-white-clad rearguard. Penalties loomed large. But it was Pires who burst through late in extra time, Chilavert, a giant in goal, spreading himself to save. With seven minutes to play in this utterly one-sided match, the veteran Laurent Blanc stepped forward to rescue his toothless team-mates. A cross from Pires found the disappointing Trezeguet; his leap and touch fell into the path of the big defender who thundered the ball finally past the courageous Chilavert. A 'Golden Goal' and Paraguay's Tournament was over with honour. For France there was sheer relief, and the quarter-final would see Zidane amongst them again. Aime Jacquet, French coach, summed up succinctly afterwards: 'We would have preferred to win earlier. We dominated and created plenty of opportunities but we lacked lucidity and confidence.' And so to Paris and the Italians.

Nigeria, Africa's only realistic hope of success, faced Denmark, talented certainly but yet to stamp their mark on the competition. In the event the match in Paris's Stade de France proved an enthralling if surprisingly one-sided contest in which subtlety subdued power. Denmark started at a breathtaking pace, Möller firing them ahead after just three minutes. Nielsen began the move, picking out Michael Laudrup on the right hand side of the penalty area. The veteran swung over his cross and Möller, lurking unmarked, did the rest, his left-foot shot ripping past the helpless Peter Rufai. Already stunned, Nigeria looked increasingly uncertain. Ten minutes later, from a free kick, Michael Laudrup set up Möller for a fierce drive. Rufai managed to parry, but only to Brian Laudrup who thumped the ball back past him for 2–0. Resting on their laurels and seeking to counter, Denmark now sat back. Kanu almost punished them, Schmeichel leaping to smother at his feet, and then Okocha twice found space, though both times his shooting was untypically wasteful. The patient Danes almost stole a third before half-time, Rieper denied by Rufai's alertness before Brian Laudrup, endlessly torturing Nigeria's uncertain defence, fed Möller, free again. Rufai again rescued his team. The second half continued in the same vein, Danish wit and imagination giving Nigeria a torrid time. Laudrup hit the bar, Rufai – without whom Nigeria's plight would have been quite desperate – beating out another Möller effort. On the hour Bo Johannsen sent on Sand, and within thirty seconds with his first touch the substitute sealed it for Denmark. Michael Laudrup provided the pass, Sand surprisingly alertly flicked the ball away from Okocha and, running on, beat Rufai with aplomb. Game over. Yet there was still time for another for the rampant Danes, Helveg gratefully accepting Jørgensen's cross, Nigeria's defence non-existent. Two minutes later Babangida at least gave the Africans consolation with a fiercely struck shot across the body of Schmeichel, but they had been well beaten, pitifully poor against a Danish attack that had proven itself simply devastating.

Mexico, a team who had three times come from behind to save themselves, faced Germany and the odds in Montpellier. From the beginning Germany held sway forcing the game, their physical might too much for a Mexican team content to contain and counter. Typically it was Germany who created chances and Jorge Campos – Mexico's colourful goalkeeper – who foiled them. On 20 minutes he smothered the ball as Klinsmann looked to prod a Bierhoff cross home. Seven minutes from the interval witnessed another gloriously athletic save, diving to deny Tarnat's rasping strike. Another two minutes and the towering Oliver Bierhoff – quite outstanding in the air – leapt to meet Hässler's near perfect cross. This time the crossbar came to Mexico's aid.

Despite Germany's apparent superiority, Mexico had offered enough in reply to give them hope, Palencia almost through on the stroke of half-time only to be frustrated by Köpke's alertness. After 47 minutes Hernandez, their outstanding striker, shocked the Germans. Collecting Blanco's pass he advanced, leaving Tarnat and Wörns in his wake before steering the ball past Köpke for 1–0. Germany vigorously pursued the game, with Mexico evidently conserving energy and ever more willing to launch dangerous raids into German territory. From one on the hour Arellano could have settled matters, seizing on to a misdirected pass to cleave his way through the German defence. Köpke did just enough, his flailing hand stretching to touch the ball to safety via the goalpost. And then as Hernandez sought to capitalize on the German's disarray, the big goalkeeper scrambled up to knock the ball away once more.

When all else fails, German will and resilience remains a formidable weapon. Here again it surfaced, though only an error allowed them back. Fifteen minutes from time, with Mexico harbouring genuine hope of a famous victory, they were undone, Lara guiding his clearing header only into the path of Jurgen Klinsmann. The fair-haired veteran needed no second invitation and drove the ball back, beating Campos for 1–1. Given encouragement the remarkable German machine, ageing though it was, became stronger, slowly but surely beating their courageous opponents into submission. Bierhoff inevitably with a header four minutes from time won it, again leaping highest to dispatch Kirsten's right wing cross and leave Campos beating the ground in despair. For Mexico there was no way back.

A genuinely mouth-watering prospect awaited those heading to Toulouse for the potentially exhilarating encounter between Yugoslavia and Holland: a chance to view two of the Tournament's most technically adept teams in a direct 'winner take all' confrontation.

In the event it was a slightly disappointing evening, with Yugoslavia, perhaps believing themselves to be inferior and consequently vulnerable in an open, free flowing match, electing to defend cautiously and breaking whenever possible. The pattern was set almost from the kick off. The Dutch strolled forward retaining possession comfortably, their attack less an onslaught and more a reconnaissance of Yugoslavia's fortress. Ultimately, Holland, allowed to dictate affairs by retreating, craven opposition, had to score. On 37 minutes they finally did. Bergkamp, escaping his marker, pursued Frank De Boer's long pass and ran on to the left-hand side of the penalty area. Bouncing off a challenge, the Arsenal man looked up and coolly picked his spot, beating Kralj comprehensively at his near post. Belatedly after the interval the Yugoslavians switched to Plan B. More aggressive and positive they immediately reaped the reward and in so doing exposed serious deficiencies in Holland's defending. On 49 minutes the mercurial veteran Stojkovic – now thirty-three – fired in a pinpoint free kick from his favoured left side. Komljenovic jumped quite unmarked and crashed a stunning header into Van Der Saar's net. At 1–1, if after almost an hour of domination the situation was cause of Dutch concern, their plight appeared close to desperate just two minutes later. Jugovic, racing towards goal with Stam, was impeded – in the opinion of referee Garcia-Aranda – unfairly, and a penalty kick awarded. Mijatovic stepped up, beat the goalkeeper and watched, mortified as the ball thumped on to the crossbar and rebounded away to safety. Until the end the Dutch remained the more ambitious, and Cocu from Frank De Boer's surging run and cross might have done better with a diving header. In the last minute with the spectre of extra time looming large, Holland finally and deservedly claimed a quarter-final berth. The dreadlocked Edgar Davids, so long a controversial figure at odds with coach Gus Hiddink, receiving the ball twenty yards out sent his shot whistling into the Yugoslavian net. The score 2–1, the Dutch with an intoxicating mixture of maverick enterprise were through. Curiously though, at the end as celebrations began in earnest, defender Bogarde and goalkeeper Van Der Saar exchanged blows, leaving others to speculate on whether once again off the field relationships were less than cordial.

At Bordeaux on a hot, muggy afternoon, Romania, winners of Group G, faced their East European rivals Croatia, with Germany awaiting the survivor. The Croatians, sensing an opportunity, began strongly by driving Romania back and laying siege to their goal. Only six minutes had passed when the elusive Davor Suker forced Bogdan Stelea to a fine double save. Throughout the first half the grip of the rampaging midfield, Stanic, Jurcic and Boban, was vicelike, while Suker continued to outwit and threaten Romania's troubled defence. On ten minutes Stelea again came to his team's rescue, leaping to thwart Vlaovic, whose powerful shot appeared goalbound. Asanovic, too, saw an effort beaten away, and while Romania offered little by way of retaliation, they seemed destined to start the second half undeservedly level. Senor Castrilli, the Argentinean referee, dashed their hopes. Asanovic, tearing goalwards after a speculative long ball, reached the penalty area and there collided with Popescu. Despite anguished protest, Sr. Castrilli awarded a penalty kick. Suker converted it for 1–0.

For Romania a sickening blow was coming as the Croats were appearing finally to flag. They never recovered. The goal serving to galvanize them, Croatia pressed determinedly, seeking a second goal to secure their passage to the quarter-finals. Boban almost provided it from Suker's cross before Suker himself brushed aside Popescu to shoot against Stelea's flailing legs. At the end the goalkeeper capped his heroic performance by denying Boban and then Krpan, but his team would go home. Overwhelmed in midfield and thoroughly outplayed throughout, they appeared strangely undermotivated and had paid the price for their lethargy. Croatia would go on to Lyons.

England and Argentina faced one another in St Etienne that evening, a contest of quite breathtaking drama and extraordinary courage in adversity of almost epic proportion. England, as they had in Lens against the Colombians, started with a swagger, forcing the game. Although this time their opponents had the undoubted firepower to go with ability, it still came as a surprise when the Argentineans took an early lead. Escaping his marker, Diego Simeone darted toward goal; Seaman's advance forced him wide, but the goalkeeper's subsequent dive for the ball succeeded only in bringing down the Argentinean captain. Thus a penalty kick was awarded. Batistuta duly obliged. If England were shocked by the goal, they refused to show it, and Michael Owen, at eighteen a human dynamo, brought them back almost immediately. Running at and threatening to pass Ayala, Argentina's sweeper, he was sent crashing down. Another penalty, another goal, Shearer this time stepping up to thunder the ball into the net. For the South Americans bad turned to worse. Beckham in sublime form struck an exquisite lofted pass into the path of the rampaging Owen – raw pace did the rest. Resisting Chamot's determined challenge, the diminutive striker simply accelerated away, and confronted by Ayala en route to goal, ran around the hapless defender before striking a bullet-like shot into the startled Roa's net. At 2–1 England might have made it 3–1 before half-time, Scholes failing negligently to hit the target from close range. Instead it became 2–2. Awarded a free kick seconds before the interval, Batistuta shaped to shoot but Veron in a well-rehearsed drill instead slipped the ball precisely into Zanetti's run, his touch assured and the shot explosive. As the second half began, there seemed little doubt that England were the likelier winners. They were largely dominant for 45 minutes and had in Owen the key to open Argentina's much vaunted defence with apparent ease. Two minutes later and a moment of madness, crass stupidity, swung the game's flow decisively back in Argentina's favour. So far a revelation, Beckham proved now to be a weakness. Clattered roughly from behind by Simeone, the Manchester United player fell forward and then as he lay prone, flicked out a boot at the perpetrator. Simeone collapsed disgracefully as if pole-axed. Danish referee Mr Nielson sought out the red card and England were condemned to play the remainder of the game with ten men. Argentina pressed with increasing vigour to the final whistle whilst England, rarely seen as an attacking force, resisted in depth. Vivas prompted, Ortega a pocket size ball juggler wriggling this way and that. But all avenues were closed. Remarkably England held on amidst unbearable tension and may have won it, Campbell's late header ruled out for a foul by Shearer. In extra time for the ten, heroes everywhere, there was the towering Adams a rock in defence, Shearer, little Owen and Ince simply awesome in his handling of the Argentine midfield

And so to penalties and an opportunity for England to complete their mission impossible. Sadly for the romantics it was not to be. David Batty stepped up to take the last of the regulation kicks. Crespo for Argentina and Ince had already missed. Batty could not. But he did, striking the ball firmly but too close to the athletic Roa. England were out, yet they had snarled defiance to the bitterest of ends. Hoddle, the coach, summed up the feeling in the England camp, a curious mixture of distress and pride: 'There is so much hurt in there, I don't know where to start. Everyone involved can walk with their heads held high because it was a magnificent performance. We defended like lions. To hold out that long against a side like Argentina is incredible. We were so near to one of the most historic wins ever.' And of Beckham later to be castigated for his petulance? 'The sending off cost us dearly? I can't deny that it cost us the game. The whole incident was very disappointing because with eleven men we would have won the game. I've been around the dressing room and shaken hands with everybody but I have not said anything to David. He is still too upset to speak.'

Round of Sixteen

Italy (1) **1, Norway** (0) **0**
27.6.98 MARSEILLES
Italy: Pagliuca, Costacurta, Bergomi, Cannavaro, Moriero (Di Livio), Albertini (Pessotto), Di Biagio, Baggio, Maldini, Vieri (1), Del Piero, Chiesa
Norway: Grodås, Berg, Eggen, Johnsen, Bjørnebye, Flo H (Solskjaer), Mykland, Rekdal, Leonhardsen (Strand, Solbakken), Riseth, Flo T A
Referee: Heynemann (Germany)

Brazil (3) **4, Chile** (0) **1**
27.6.98 PARIS
Brazil: Taffarel, Cafu, Junior Baiano, Aldair (Goncalves), Roberto Carlos, Cesar Sampaio (2), Dunga, Leonardo, Rivaldo, Bebeto (Denilson) Ronaldo (2,1 pen)
Chile: Tapia, Reyes, Fuentes, Margas, Cornejo, Acuña (Musrri), Ramirez (Estay), Aros, Sierra (Estay), Salas (1), Zamorano
Referee: Batta (France)

France (0) **1, Paraguay** (0) **0** (aet, 0–0 after 90 mins) (Golden Goal)
28.6.98 LENS
France: Barthez, Thuram, Blanc (1), Desailly, Lizarazu, Deschamps, Petit (Boghossian), Henry (Pires), Djorkaeff, Diomede (Guivarc'h), Trezeguet
Paraguay: Chilavert, Gamarra, Ayala, Sarabia, Arce, Acuña, Enciso, Paredes (Caniza), Campos (Yegros), Benitez, Cardoza (Rojas)
Referee: Bujsaim (UAE)

Nigeria (0) **1, Denmark** (2) **4**
28.6.98 PARIS
Nigeria: Rufai, Adepoju, Okechukwu, West, Babayaro, Finidi, Okocha, Lawal (Babangida (1)), Kanu (Yekini), Ikpeba, Oliseh
Denmark: Schmeichel, Colding, Rieper, Høgh, Heintze, Jørgensen, Helveg (1), Nielsen, Laudrup B (1) (Wieghorst), Laudrup M (Frandsen), Möller (1) (Sand (1))
Referee: Meier (Switzerland)

Germany (0) **2, Mexico** (0) **1**
29.6.98 MONTPELLIER
Germany: Köpke, Matthäus, Wörns, Babbel, Heinrich (Möller), Hamann, Helmer (Ziege), Tarnat, Hässler (Kirsten), Klinsmann (1), Bierhoff (1)
Mexico: Campos, Pardo, Davino, Suarez, Garcia Aspe (Pelaez), Villa, Bernal (Carmona), Lara, Blanco, Hernandez (1), Palencia (Arellano)
Referee: Pereira (Portugal)

Holland (1) **2, Yugoslavia** (0) **1**
29.6.98 TOULOUSE
Holland: Van Der Saar, Reiziger, De Boer F, Stam, Numan, De Boer R, Seedorf, Davids (1), Overmars, Bergkamp (1), Cocu
Yugoslavia: Kralj, Mirkovic, Djorovic, Mihajlovic (Saveljic), Komljenovic (1), Petrovic, Jokanovic, Brnovic, Jugovic, Stojkovic (Savicevic), Mijatovic
Referee: Garcia-Aranda (Spain)

Romania (0) **0, Croatia** (1) **1**
30.6.98 BORDEAUX
Romania: Stelea, Popescu, Ciubotariu, Filipescu, Petrescu (Marinescu), Galca, Munteanu, Hagi (Craioveanu), Gabriel Popescu (Niculescu), Moldovan, Ilie
Croatia: Ladic, Stimac, Bilic, Simic, Stanic (Tudor), Jurcic, Asanovic, Boban, Suker (1 pen), Vlaovic (Krpan)
Referee: Castrilli (Argentina)

Argentina (2) **2, England** (2) **2** (aet, 2–2 after 90 mins, Argentina win 4–3 on penalties)
30.6.98 ST ETIENNE
Argentina: Roa, Chamot, Ayala, Vivas, Zanetti (1), Almeyda, Simeone (Berti), Veron, Ortega, Batistuta (1 pen) (Crespo), Lopez (Gallardo)
England: Seaman, Neville, Adams, Campbell, Anderton (Batty), Ince, Beckham, Scholes (Merson), Le Saux (Southgate), Shearer (1 pen), Owen (1)
Referee: Nielsen (Denmark)

The Quarter-Finals

Italy v France
Brazil v Denmark
Croatia v Germany
Holland v Argentina

THE QUARTER-FINALS

In Paris, Italy now stood between the French and further progress. Their objective was clear from the very beginning: stifle, spoil and seek, if at all possible, to plunder a goal on the counter-attack. For the vast crowd assembled, the majority supporting the hosts, it was another day of tortuous tension and fraying nerves. France began in irresistible mode, their opening surge threatening at once to overwhelm the retreating Italians. Zidane, their mercurial midfield player, was twice off target, and Petit was spectacularly denied, his overhead kick touched to safety by Pagliuca. Five minutes had passed and the Italians, by nature cautious, had food for thought. Until half-time it remained one-way traffic. If Italy had chosen to break free from their carefully organized defensive fortress, it was difficult to see how they might have managed it; with Desailly and Thuram launching attacks and Lizarazu raking their right flank, the crosses poured in. However, there were no goals, and for France regret only that for all their superiority a natural goalscorer had not been found to capitalize on opportunities. Djorkaeff, so gifted as a provider, illustrated their Achilles heel. Running on to Deschamps' inviting pass, he fired miserably wide. A suspicion almost, a dread lurked, could Italy, the 'Artful Dodger' of world football, pick the French pocket, steal a goal and bundle them undeservedly out of the Tournament?

It proved beyond them. Introducing Trezeguet and Henry, if anything France increased the tempo, their swift passing and movement utterly bewildering Italy's more workmanlike approach. Still lacking a goal, at the end of extra time there was the distinct possibility that for all of their obvious supremacy, the heartbreak of defeat by penalty shoot-out would be their destiny.

In the event the French victory was richly deserved. At 4–3 Di Biagio stepped forward. With monumental pressure on him to bring Italy level, he could not manage it, his kick firmly rebounding to safety off the crossbar. France's team were moving forward ever more purposefully, their ambition nothing less than the World Cup Trophy itself. For poor Luigi Di Biagio, so influential in an Italian team somewhat short of its own lofty standard, there was only devastation. Could it be right to allow one the burden of failure felt by an entire nation? 'A penalty shoot-out is a lottery,' said coach Cesare Maldini in the aftermath, conveniently forgetting his team's negative approach. 'This is the third time Italy has been eliminated from the Tournament in this manner. It seems as though we are cursed.'

In Nantes a thrilling prospect awaited: the free flowing Brazilians facing Denmark, whose remarkable demolition of Nigeria had caused raised eyebrows. If drama had been expected, it took little time to arrive. Almost immediately the inventive Danes took the lead with a goal of stunning simplicity. A free kick taken quickly by Michael Laudrup to his brother Brian caught the Brazilians in disarray. The younger Laudrup galloped to the line before drilling the ball across goal. Jørgensen, alert to the situation, arrived on cue, his left-foot shot leaving Taffarel hopelessly beaten. The 1–0 score to Denmark lasted less than ten minutes. Ronaldo, receiving the ball in midfield and spotting Bebeto's run, struck the ball gloriously into the veteran's path. Much criticized beforehand for his indifferent form, Bebeto held off Helveg before driving low and hard beyond the reach of Schmeichel to bring Brazil level.

Still the pattern continued, as fluent and open as before. Brazil on 26 minutes took the lead, it being Rivaldo's turn to beat Schmeichel as he advanced, this time with the deftest of touches. At 2–1 to Brazil, Peter Möller courtesy of woeful marking could and should have equalized before the interval. The second half began as had the first, within moments a goal for Denmark, this time perhaps less to do with Danish creativity and more to do with Brazilian eccentricity. Jørgensen, ploughing forward, ran directly at Taffarel's goal. His way was blocked, the ball flew up and towards the left-hand side of Brazil's penalty area. Roberto Carlos tracking back attempted a scissor kick clearance, failed to make any contact and Brian Laudrup, scarcely believing his luck, needed no second invitation, his shot tearing into Taffarel's net. At 2–2, ten minutes later another goal arrived as the relentless attacking continued. Rivaldo, allowed space, surged into it. Marc Rieper sensing the danger tried desperately to avert it, but to no avail. Thirty yards out and on the point of Rieper's intervention, Rivaldo pulled the trigger, his sweetly struck shot flashing beyond Schmeichel. Denmark, admirably brave, fought to the bitter end and in their final onslaught their best chances fell to Rieper, the first from a cross by Helveg charged down, the second more typically from the big centre half a header that struck the bar with Taffarel hopelessly beaten. At the whistle the world of football bade farewell to the magical Michael Laudrup, retired from international competition. His finale had been a glorious adventure in which, with brother Brian as the sorcerer's apprentice, a conjuring trick of improbable proportions had almost been achieved.

In Marseilles, Holland and their team of many talents faced Argentina, survivors of the epic contest in St Etienne and a tough rugged team with aspirations of being the World Champions. The opening moments on a warm and muggy afternoon saw from both teams a declaration of intent. Jonk was almost the first beneficiary of the game's free flowing play, his shot from Bergkamp's swivel and cross rebounding off the goalpost. Then Ronald De Boer on five minutes powered forward and picked out Bergkamp stealing space in the Argentine penalty area; the striker deadened the ball, dropping it cleverly into Kluivert. Quick as a flash, the striker marked his reintroduction after suspension by carrying the ball forward towards Roa before slipping the ball into the net. However, if the Dutch felt secure for a moment, they were in for the rudest of awakenings. Barely 12 minutes had passed since their goal when Argentina drew level. Juan Veron, so instrumental in their progress, demonstrated his vision again, a long pass searching out little Claudio Lopez who ran in to utterly bemuse Van Der Sar, his shot driven between the goalkeeper's flailing legs. For all of their polish, the cunning of the Argentineans almost caught the Dutch again before the break, though this time it was Ortega who held his head in anguish as his swerving shot came back off Van Der Sar's goalpost.

Threatened, Dutch coach Guus Hiddink sent on Marc Overmars, risking his injured winger, and the game swung back and forth, the tension growing as the game wore on. Numan in the 76th minute became the first casualty of pressure: an ill-judged challenge on Simeone – the same Simeone who had proved Beckham's nemesis in the previous round – earned a second fatal yellow card and subsequent dismissal. If Argentina had learned anything from their experience of playing ten men, Ortega rashly denied them the chance to demonstrate it. Diving outrageously to claim a foul, he rose frustrated to seek retribution, his head butt aimed at Van Der Sar. Foolish in the extreme, his dismissal was inevitable and devastating to the chances of his team. As extra time beckoned there was a goal, breathtaking in its creation and execution as any yet seen. Frank De Boer delivered an exquisite pass of seventy yards, Bergkamp on the right controlled it with one touch, beat Ayala with a second and swept the ball almost arrogantly beyond the bewildered Roa and into Argentina's net. Holland at the death had triumphed, while the vanquished Argentineans left to reflect on their defeat. Passarella, their coach, afterwards would blame the schedule and the demands physically and emotionally of his team's two-hour battle with England.

Croatia, perhaps surpassing even their own expectations, faced Germany, a country of magnificent World Cup pedigree in an emotional quarter-final played in Lyons that evening. In a tense opening period the teams sparred, Croatian wile against German power, with the Germans launching a series of crosses towards the heads of Klinsmann and Bierhoff. It was Bierhoff who came closest to breaking the deadlock, thumping Heinrich's cross goalward on half an hour; Ladic scrambling along his line kept it out.

The defining moment came when Wörns raced across to stifle Davor Suker and blatantly obstructed him. Referee Pedersen reached into his pocket and produced a red card. Germany would play the remaining 50 minutes with ten men. Legendary though German resilience is, the hill they needed to climb proved far too steep for this elderly team. Suker almost immediately took advantage of their disorganization, finding room to fire in but wastefully wide. If Germany hoped for parity at the interval and the opportunity to regroup, Robert Jarni denied it to them. The wing back sauntering forward received Stanic's pass and rifled his shot home from twenty-five yards. Had Germany drawn level through Bierhoff against the run of play, it might have been different, but Ladic again frustrated the big Udinese striker, shovelling his close-range effort to safety. Instead Croatia, growing increasingly assured and thriving on the extra space, dominated: Stimac and Boban at the heart of their intricate passing game, Suker again wide just before the hour, Boban with a fierce dipping volley touched over by Köpke. The onslaught continued on the German goal, Vlaovic and Boban again going close before Vlaovic finally settled it, his driven shot crashing past Köpke for 2–0. Germany – never say die – persisted, but spirit was no substitute for style. Davor Suker, an immense and elusive talent, put the lid on it five minutes from the end, weaving forward to smash a third quite unstoppable shot into Köpke's net. Germany thus went out and for them the rebuilding would begin. 'I thank my players for their commitment,' said coach Berti Vogts. While Croatia would advance, the liveliest of outsiders, France in the semi-final in Paris would underestimate them at their peril.

Quarter-Finals

Italy (0) **0, France** (0) **0** (aet, 0–0 after 90 mins, France win 4–3 on penalties)
3.7.98 PARIS
Italy: Pagliuca, Cannavaro, Bergomi, Costacurta, Pessotto (Di Livio), Moriero, Baggio D (Albertini) Di Biagio, Maldini, Del Piero (Baggio R), Vieri
France: Barthez, Thuram, Blanc, Desailly, Karembeu (Henry), Deschamps, Petit, Lizarazu, Zidane, Djorkaeff, Guivarc'h (Trezeguet)
Referee: Dallas (Scotland)

Brazil (2) **3, Denmark** (1) **2**
3.7.98 NANTES
Brazil: Taffarel, Cafu, Junior Baiano, Aldair, Roberto Carlos, Dunga, Leonardo (Emerson), Cesar Sampaio, Rivaldo (2), Ronaldo (Se Roberto), Bebeto (1) (Denilson)
Denmark: Schmeichel, Colding, Rieper, Høgh, Heintze, Jørgensen (1), Helveg (Schonberg), Nielsen (Tøfting), Laudrup M, Laudrup B (1), Möller (Sand)
Referee: Ghandour (Egypt)

Holland (1) **2, Argentina** (1) **1**
4.7.98 MARSEILLES
Holland: Van Der Sar, Reiziger, Stam, De Boer F, Numan, De Boer R (Overmars) Davids, Jonk, Cocu, Bergkamp (1), Kluivert (1)
Argentina: Roa, Sensini, Ayala, Chamot, Zanetti, Almeyda, Veron, Simeone, Ortega, Lopez (1), Batistuta
Referee: Carter (Mexico)

Germany (0) **0, Croatia** (1) **3**
4.7.98 LYONS
Germany: Köpke, Wörns, Matthäus, Kohler, Heinrich, Hamann (Marschall), Jeremies, Tarnat, Hässler (Kirsten), Klinsmann, Bierhoff
Croatia: Ladic, Bilic, Stimac, Simic, Stanic, Soldo, Asanovic, Boban, Jarni (1), Suker (1), Vlaovic (1) (Maric)
Referee: Pedersen (Norway)

THE SEMI-FINALS

The prospect in Marseilles was an exhilarating one. Two teams, masters of open football, had come to compete for a place in the World Cup final. Brazil, the favourites, were fluent and incisive; Holland, their opponents, upholding the magnificent traditions of their nation's past.

The game began more cautiously than might have been expected: two heavyweights sparring, searching constantly for the opportunity to strike, fearful always of an opponent's counter, both Bergkamp and Ronaldo firmly shackled. For Holland, Edgar Davids chose this night to stamp an indelible impression on all that watched. Seeming inexhaustible, fearless in the tackle, his inspiration gave the Dutch an edge for most of the evening, Kluivert for them twice going close with headers whilst Ronaldo, hounded and harassed, could only watch, envious of the service from the other end. If the first half had been dour, the second instantly exploded into life. Rivaldo from the kick off picked out Ronaldo, who beat Van Der Sar with ease. Dominant thus far, Holland were behind, punished for their lack of concentration. Frank De Boer almost brought them level: arriving to meet Kluivert's neatly flicked header, he volleyed fiercely. Taffarel beat it out and Roberto Carlos, reacting quickest, cleared the loose ball. On 64 minutes Ronaldo powered through to be denied by Van Der Sar, and then as Bebeto moved in on the loose ball, the big goalkeeper frustrated him. Another ten minutes and Ronaldo again found himself free. This time it was the wonderful, energetic Davids who dispossessed him. Significantly though, as Holland's need for an equalizer grew desperate, Brazil had wrested control of the game. Twelve minutes from the end Rivaldo should have settled it. Denilson swept by Winter and whipped in a cross, while Rivaldo, legs-a-tangle, could not control the ball properly and his shot from only six yards dug out of the ground had not the power to trouble Van Der Sar. It would be another eight minutes, four from the end, before his error would be compounded, Ronald De Boer delivering a cross, and Kluivert taking full advantage of slack marking to beat Taffarel at his near post. In extra time hard as both teams tried, there were no further goals. Ronaldo might twice have won it for the Brazilians but Kluivert came closest of all with a drive that shaved Taffarel's goalpost. Cruelly it would be the pain of elimination by penalty shoot-out, and when poor Ronald De Boer stepped forward to take his team's fourth, the equation was simple: score or go home. Under such intolerable pressure greater players than he had succumbed, and whilst his shot was firmly struck, it proved within reach of Taffarel. Brazil were through; Taffarel, their artisan amongst artists, was the hero.

Hiddink, the devastated Dutch coach, praised his team's courage and commitment, refusing to discuss contributory reasons for defeat. 'I do not search for excuses in the injuries and suspensions that affected team selection,' he said. Zagallo, for his part, looked only towards his ultimate goal. 'I will not celebrate yet. We can only do that if we win the final on Sunday. Holland played very well against us. They were far more difficult than Denmark had been in the last round. I thought we were good tactically and physically, but we were defensive towards the end of normal time because we had to try and stop Holland scoring.'

If Croatia had exceeded themselves, now their ambitions knew no bounds, their clever, thoughtful approach standing in the path of France and a Parisian crowd at last recognizing their team's enormous potential. From Zidane, as ever the fulcrum of all that was good, came the inspiration, and it was he who almost opened the scoring during the opening exchanges, Guivarc'h back heeling the ball into his path, but the shot was a disappointing one straight at Ladic. On ten minutes came another chance, this time from Petit's teasing cross, Zidane's header firm but too high. Zidane, so elegant and effective, appeared likeliest to break the deadlock for the French, but Ladic stretched to save his raking drive on 23 minutes, and then for good measure beat out Deschamps' free kick. The tension in the stadium mounted, the men in blue shirts clearly feeling the strain. As the half progressed and the initial French storm subsided, Croatia thus far content to contain and wait patiently came forward with purpose, fuelling anxieties. First Simic played in Asanovic, his shot weak and wide. Then Bilic lifted an effort over the bar. Just as half-time approached, Suker, cunning and deadly, stretched to reach an Asanovic pass. To the relief of the vast majority in the stadium he failed by a whisker.

Any French delusions were shattered, however, within a minute of the restart, all the time Croatia needed to score through Suker. Again Asanovic swept forward from midfield but this time Suker collected his pass and drove the ball with great certainty beyond Barthez and into the net. How France responded. Had Croatia settled on their lead it might have proven difficult. That they did not for even a minute owed everything to the determination of Lillian Thuram. Winning the ball from Boban, the full back played a one-two on the edge of the area. Ploughing on he received the return and whipped his shot past Ladic for 1–1. Zidane saw a shot blocked by Bilic, and Vlaovic for Croatia through on goal saw the ball swept to safety by Thuram's last ditch challenge.

The winner came on 70 minutes from Thuram once more, the unlikeliest of heroes. With another powerful run and exchange of passes, this time with Trezeguet, he surged forward, beating Ladic this time with a curling half volley struck across the goalkeeper and inside his right-hand post. The score was 2–1. That could and should have been the platform for France to win at a canter. But Bilic's theatrical collapse saw Blanc, however foolishly, dismissed for a push in the face, reducing them to ten men before the end, and condemning the home crowd, collectively suffering frayed nerves, to further uncertainty until the final whistle. For France there was huge and joyous celebration, but in the dressing room the feeling was of relief tempered with regret. Lauren Blanc would not play in the final.

Semi-Finals

Brazil (0) **1, Holland** (0) **1** (aet, 1–1 after 90 mins, Brazil win 4–3 on pens)
7.7.98 MARSEILLES
Brazil: Taffarel, Ze Carlos, Aldair, Junior Baiano, Roberto Carlos, Cesar Sampaio, Leonardo (Emerson), Dunga, Rivaldo, Ronaldo (1), Bebeto (Denilson)
Holland: Van Der Sar, Reiziger (Winter), Stam, De Boer F, Cocu, De Boer R, Davids, Jonk (Seedorf), Zenden (Van Hooijdonk), Kluivert (1), Bergkamp
Referee: Bujsaim (UAE)

France (0) **2, Croatia** (0) **1**
8.7.98 PARIS
France: Barthez, Thuram (2), Blanc, Desailly, Lizarazu, Karembeu (Henry), Deschamps, Petit, Zidane, Djorkaeff (Leboeuf), Guivarc'h, (Trezeguet)
Croatia: Ladic, Bilic, Stimac, Simic, Stanic (Prosinecki), Soldo, Asanovic, Jarni, Boban (Mario), Vlaovic, Suker (1)
Referee: Garcia-Aranda (Spain)

PLAY-OFF FOR THIRD PLACE

In the third and fourth place play-off were Holland and Croatia at the Parc de Princes. For once two teams, though undoubtedly tired, were willing to compete for one final victory. During an outstanding first half, Robert Prosinecki gave Croatia an early lead, applying an unerring finish to a typically incisive run and cross from Robert Jarni. Zenden brought the Dutch level in the 20th minute, cutting inside from the right wing to shoot spectacularly past Ladic from twenty-five yards for 1–1. Throughout, chances came and went, Kluivert twice breaking through but denied by Ladic, Jonk shooting from distance whenever in range. Suker, however, showed the striker's touch in 36 minutes, receiving Boban's pass to sweep the ball easily into Van Der Sar's net. It was a remarkable achievement, for in putting his team back into the lead, Davor Suker had scored his sixth goal of the Tournament. With little more than pride at stake, Holland to their credit fought hard for an equalizer. Kluivert continued to be frustrated by Ladic, and Seedorf might have scored, but the athleticism and elasticity of the goalkeeper again saved the day. Suker could have added to his personal tally but failed narrowly to make contact with Prosinecki's free kick, and it was over. Croatia, full of the burning pride of a new nation, had claimed third spot, while Holland at the finish appeared scarcely to notice. They had cried their tears in Marseilles.

Match for Third Place

Holland (1) **1, Croatia** (2) **2**
11.7.98 PARIS
Holland: Van Der Sar, Stam, De Boer F, Numan, Zenden (1), Seedorf, Jonk, Davids, Cocu (Overmars), Bergkamp (Van Hooijdonk)
Croatia: Ladic, Bilic, Stimac, Soldo, Stanic, Asanovic, Prosinecki (1) (Vlaovic), Jurcic, Jarni, Boban (Tudor), Suker (1)
Referee: Chavez (Paraguay)

THE FINAL

'We have spectators here in France, but we need fans, we need the nation to show its support,' said the French camp, expressing concern at the lack of passion filtering down from the stands during the Paraguay match. Here at the Stade de France on 12 July something quite different was happening. On this World Cup final day there was an outpouring of emotion, a cauldron of tumultuous sound. The French public had come to will their heroes to triumph; the prayer of 'Team France' had been answered.

Even before the kick off there had been confusion and controversy. The Brazilian team sheet indicated that Ronaldo would not be among those to start the match. Had Mario Zagallo taken leave of his senses and replaced the golden boy of Brazilian football with the sullen, volatile figure of Edmundo? Journalists scrambled around searching for the truth. What had happened in the Champions' dressing room? Then, 15 minutes later, a second and revised sheet appeared – Ronaldo was now in and Edmundo out. In the event it would hardly matter.

At kick off any uncertainty in the minds of the South Americans was swiftly and ruthlessly exploited by France, always the aggressors, always controlling the pace of the game's flow. Within seconds Guivarc'h pounded towards goal before lifting the ball over Taffarel and the Brazilian crossbar. If Brazil had been warned, they hardly heeded it. Four minutes had passed when Zidane – already commanding in midfield – and Djorkaeff conspired to free Guivarc'h again; this time, however, the striker's shot was a wretched one. France were noticeably driving Brazil back. In another three minutes there was another glorious chance – again it was Zidane in the thick of things who delivered the telling ball, a swinging near-post free kick, Djorkaeff this time the target, his header mistimed and misdirected. Brazil thus far as an attacking force had seldom been seen, their nervous and suspect defence peering fearfully over the parapet as the French onslaught continued. Ronaldo, so admired, was a lonely forlorn figure, his service weak and erratic. Just before the half-hour a richly deserved goal was gained by both team and scorer. Petit fired in a corner, Zidane rose with Leonardo and met the ball cleanly, his header bulleting down-wards and past the helpless Taffarel. At last Brazil rallied. Ronaldo burst through to be denied by Barthez. Bebeto headed miserably into the French goalkeeper's hands. No matter, France simply increased their momentum. Petit could not score, his volley flying wide; nor could the unfortunate Guivarc'h, bullish but scarcely reliable, his effort in first-half injury time his best, saved with difficulty by Taffarel. Never mind, for on this day France had their hero, and from the resultant corner he stepped forward again. This time Djorkaeff sent the ball over, and Zidane, as if protected by some invisible force-field, rose quite unchallenged in the congested penalty area to steer his header home.

There is an aura with all Brazilian teams, real or imagined, where the impos-sible is never far from achievable. Here the evidence of one's own eyes, of undoubted French supremacy, was in question. Outplayed? Certainly. Overwhelmed? Almost. Yet France's apparently unassailable position could still be threatened by a fresh Brazilian approach. Sadly for the South Americans, while they woke from lethargy it was not to be. In truth, only when France were reduced to ten men did they gain any semblance of com-mand. The introduction of the lithe Denilson, on for the culpable Leonardo, galvanized Brazil. Ronaldo at last found himself in on goal, put there by Roberto Carlos beating Guivarc'h. He thumped the ball goalwards. Barthez, with good fortune, in precisely the right place, clasped the ball gratefully to his chest.

On the hour Barthez once more appeared to come to the rescue of his team, but in galloping from his line to win the race with Bebeto, the goalkeeper suc-ceeded only in losing his balance and possession. Here, fleetingly, came Brazil's chance: Bebeto drove the ball goalwards, but Desailly, a rock in the French defence, scrambled back to thump it to safety.

If Desailly had enjoyed a moment of glory, it would not last. Only ten minutes later and with twenty left to play, he crashed into the back of Cafu as the Brazilian sought to launch a counter-attack, and was promptly given a red card. Ten Frenchmen would need to hold out against eleven Brazilians. By now Guivarc'h, having a difficult day in front of goal, had almost sealed it, but one on one with Taffarel his shot flew high. Brazil, for all of the drive of Dunga, numerical superiority and possession, were impotent. Zidane's quick thinking worried them to the end. Didier Deschamps' swaggering, diminutive general harried remorselessly. Then in injury time as realization of success dawned even on their most pessimistic supporter, Petit put the lid on it, running through a dispirited Brazilian defence to fire a left-footed angled drive beyond the dive of Taffarel. Ending 3–0, the delirious celebrations could begin.

A little later the mystery surrounding Ronaldo and his original non-selection was explained. The twenty-one-year-old, under the enormous strain and expectation, had suffered convulsions, later described as an emotional fit. Under such circumstances Zagallo's decision to exclude him was a perfectly justified one. Less than an hour before kick off and 30 minutes after the team sheet had been circulated, Ronaldo arrived declaring himself fit to play. In the bizarre dressing room debate that ensued, Zagallo assented to play Ronaldo, a decision that enraged the temperamental Edmundo to a point where punches were exchanged between players. It can hardly have helped. An ill-prepared, distracted team replete with a physically and mentally exhausted striker were thrust out beneath the floodlights to face clever and powerful opponents fuelled with desire and willed on by the huge throng in the stadium. It was not a contest. France had won because they deserved to. A nation so cruelly deprived in 1982 and 1986 sat on top of the world. The right team playing the right way were the Champions.

Final

Brazil (0) **0, France** (2) **3**
12.7.98 PARIS
Brazil: Taffarel, Cafu, Aldair, Junior Baiano, Roberto Carlos, Leonardo (Denilson), Cesar Sampaio (Edmundo), Dunga, Rivaldo, Ronaldo, Bebeto
France: Barthez, Thuram, Desailly, Leboeuf, Lizarazu, Karembeu (Boghossian), Deschamps, Petit (1), Zidane (1), Djorkaeff (Vieira), Guivarc'h (Dugarry)
Referee: Belqola (Morocco)

CHAPTER 17

JAPAN AND

SOUTH KOREA

2002

Qualifying Tournament
198 Entries
France qualify as holders, South Korea/Japan qualify as co-hosts

Europe (51): Albania, Andorra, Austria, Armenia, Azerbaijan, Belarus, Belgium, Bosnia-Herzegovina, Bulgaria, Croatia, Cyprus, Czech Republic, Denmark, England, Estonia, Faroe Islands, Finland, France, Georgia, Germany, Greece, Holland, Hungary, Iceland, Israel, Italy, Latvia, Liechtenstein, Lithuania, Luxembourg, Macedonia, Malta, Moldova, Northern Ireland, Norway, Poland, Portugal, Republic of Ireland, Romania, Russia, San Marino, Scotland, Slovakia, Slovenia, Spain, Sweden, Switzerland, Turkey, Ukraine, Wales, Yugoslavia

South America (10): Argentina, Bolivia, Brazil, Chile, Colombia, Ecuador, Paraguay, Peru, Uruguay, Venezuela

CONCACAF (35): Anguilla, Antigua and Barbuda, Aruba, Bahamas, Barbados, Belize, Bermuda, British Virgin Islands, Canada, Cayman Islands, Costa Rica, Cuba, Dominica, Dominican Republic, Dutch Antilles, El Salvador, Ghana, Grenada, Guatemala, Haiti, Honduras, Jamaica, Mexico, Monserrat, Nicaragua, Panama, Puerto Rico, St Kitts, St Lucia, St Vincent, Surinam, Trinidad and Caicos Islands, USA, US Virgin Islands

Asia (42): Bangladesh, Bahrain, Brunei, China, Cambodia, Guam, Hong Kong, India, Indonesia, Iran, Iraq, Japan, Jordan, Kazakhstan, Kyrgyzstan, Kuwait, Laos, Lebanon, Macao, Malaysia, Maldives, Mongolia, Myanmar, Nepal, Oman, Pakistan, Palestine, Philippines, Qatar, Saudi Arabia, Singapore, South Korea, Sri Lanka, Syria, Taiwan, Tajikistan, Thailand, Turkmenistan, United Arab Emirates, Uzbekistan, Vietnam, Yemen

Africa (50): Algeria, Angola, Benin, Botswana, Burkina Faso, Cameroon, Cape Verde Islands, Central African Republic, Chad, Congo, Djibouti, DR Congo, Egypt, Equatorial Guinea, Eritrea, Ethiopia, Gabon, Gambia, Ghana, Guinea, Guinea-Bissau, Ivory Coast, Kenya, Lesotho, Liberia, Libya, Madagascar, Malawi, Mali, Mauritania, Mauritius, Morocco, Mozambique, Namibia, Nigeria, Rwanda, Sao Tome E Principe, Senegal, Seychelles, Sierra Leone, Somalia, South Africa, Sudan, Swaziland, Tanzania, Togo, Tunisia, Uganda, Zambia, Zimbabwe

Oceania (10): American Samoa, Australia, Cook Islands, Fiji, New Zealand, Samoa, Solomon Islands, Tahiti, Tonga, Vanuatu

Europe

Group 1

Switzerland v Russia 0–1, Faroe Islands v Slovenia 2–2, Luxembourg v Yugoslavia 0–2, Luxembourg v Slovenia 1–2, Switzerland v Faroe Islands 5–1, Russia v Luxembourg 3–0, Slovenia v Switzerland 2–2, Luxembourg v Faroe Islands 0–2, Russia v Slovenia 1–1, Yugoslavia v Switzerland 1–1, Russia v Faroe Islands 1–0, Slovenia v Yugoslavia 1–1, Switzerland v Luxembourg 5–0, Yugoslavia v Russia 0–1, Faroe Islands v Switzerland 0–1, Russia v Yugoslavia 1–1, Slovenia v Luxembourg 2–0, Faroe Islands v Yugoslavia 0–6, Luxembourg v Russia 1–2, Switzerland v Slovenia 0–1, Yugoslavia v Faroe Islands 2–0, Faroe Islands v Luxembourg 1–0, Slovenia v Russia 2–1, Switzerland v Yugoslavia 1–2, Faroe Islands v Russia 0–3, Luxembourg v Switzerland 0–3, Yugoslavia v Slovenia 1–1, Russia v Switzerland 4–0, Slovenia v Faroe Islands 3–0, Yugoslavia v Luxembourg 6–2

	P	W	D	L	F	A	Pts
Russia	10	7	2	1	18	5	23
Slovenia	10	5	5	0	17	9	20
Yugoslavia	10	5	4	1	22	8	19
Switzerland	10	4	2	4	18	12	14
Faroe Islands	10	2	1	7	6	23	7
Luxembourg	10	0	0	10	4	28	0

Russia qualify for finals
Slovenia to play-offs

Group 2

Estonia v Andorra 1–0, Andorra v Cyprus 2–3, Holland v Republic of Ireland 2–2, Estonia v Portugal 1–3, Andorra v Estonia 1–2, Cyprus v Holland 0–4, Portugal v Republic of Ireland 1–1, Holland v Portugal 0–2, Republic of Ireland v Estonia 2–0, Cyprus v Andorra 5–0, Portugal v Andorra 3–0, Andorra v Holland 0–5, Cyprus v Republic of Ireland 0–4, Andorra v Republic of Ireland 0–3, Cyprus v Estonia 2–2, Portugal v Holland 2–2, Holland v Cyprus 4–0, Republic of Ireland v Andorra 3–1, Estonia v Holland 2–4, Republic of Ireland v Portugal 1–1, Estonia v Republic of Ireland 0–2, Portugal v Cyprus 6–0, Estonia v Cyprus 2–2, Andorra v Portugal 1–7, Republic of Ireland v Holland 1–0, Cyprus v Portugal 1–3, Holland v Estonia 5–0, Holland v Andorra 4–0, Portugal v Estonia 5–0, Republic of Ireland v Cyprus 4–0

	P	W	D	L	F	A	Pts
Portugal	10	7	3	0	33	7	24
Republic of Ireland	10	7	3	0	23	5	24
Holland	10	6	2	2	30	9	20
Estonia	10	2	2	6	10	26	8
Cyprus	10	2	2	6	13	31	8
Andorra	10	0	0	10	5	36	0

Portugal qualify for finals
Republic of Ireland to play-offs

Group 3

Bulgaria v Czech Republic 0–1, Iceland v Denmark 1–2, Northern Ireland v Malta 1–0, Bulgaria v Malta 3–0, Czech Republic v Iceland 4–0, Northern Ireland v Denmark 1–1, Denmark v Bulgaria 1–1, Iceland v Northern Ireland 1–0, Malta v Czech Republic 0–0, Bulgaria v Iceland 2–1, Malta v Denmark 0–5, Northern Ireland v Czech Republic 0–1, Bulgaria v Northern Ireland 4–3, Czech Republic v Denmark 0–0, Malta v Iceland 1–4, Denmark v Czech Republic 2–1, Iceland v Malta 3–0, Northern Ireland v Bulgaria 0–1, Czech Republic v Northern Ireland 3–1, Denmark v Malta 2–1, Iceland v Bulgaria 1–1, Denmark v Northern Ireland 1–1, Iceland v Czech Republic 3–1, Malta v Bulgaria 0–2, Bulgaria v Denmark 0–2, Czech Republic v Malta 3–2, Northern Ireland v Iceland 3–0, Czech Republic v Bulgaria 6–0, Denmark v Iceland 6–0, Malta v Northern Ireland 0–1

	P	W	D	L	F	A	Pts
Denmark	10	6	4	0	22	6	22
Czech Republic	10	6	2	2	20	8	20
Bulgaria	10	5	2	3	14	15	17
Iceland	10	4	1	5	14	20	13
Northern Ireland	10	3	2	5	11	12	11
Malta	10	0	1	9	4	24	1

Denmark qualify for finals
Czech Republic to play-offs

Group 4

Azerbaijan v Sweden 0–1, Turkey v Moldova 2–0, Slovakia v Macedonia 2–0, Macedonia v Azerbaijan 3–0, Moldova v Slovakia 0–1, Sweden v Turkey 1–1, Azerbaijan v Turkey 0–1, Moldova v Macedonia 0–0, Slovakia v Sweden 0–0, Azerbaijan v Moldova 0–0, Sweden v Macedonia 1–0, Turkey v Slovakia 1–1, Macedonia v Turkey 1–2, Moldova v Sweden 0–2, Slovakia v Azerbaijan 3–1, Macedonia v Moldova 2–2, Sweden v Slovakia 2–0, Turkey v Azerbaijan 3–0,

Azerbaijan v Slovakia 2–0, Sweden v Moldova 6–0, Turkey v Macedonia 3–3, Macedonia v Sweden 1–2, Moldova v Azerbaijan 2–0, Slovakia v Turkey 0–1, Azerbaijan v Macedonia 1 –1, Slovakia v Moldova 4–2, Turkey v Sweden 1–2, Moldova v Turkey 0–3, Macedonia v Slovakia 0–5, Sweden v Azerbaijan 3–0

	P	W	D	L	F	A	Pts
Sweden	10	8	2	0	20	3	26
Turkey	10	6	3	1	18	8	21
Slovakia	10	5	2	3	16	9	17
Macedonia	10	1	4	5	11	18	7
Moldova	10	1	3	6	6	20	6
Azerbaijan	10	1	2	7	4	17	5

Sweden qualify for finals
Turkey to play-offs

Group 5
Belarus v Wales 2–1, Norway v Armenia 0–0, Ukraine v Poland 1–3, Armenia v Ukraine 2–3, Poland v Belarus 3–1, Wales v Norway 1–1, Belarus v Armenia 2–1, Norway v Ukraine 0–1, Poland v Wales 0–0, Armenia v Wales 2–2, Norway v Poland 2–3, Ukraine v Belarus 0–0, Belarus v Norway 2–1, Poland v Armenia 4–0, Wales v Ukraine 1–1, Armenia v Belarus 0–0, Ukraine v Norway 0–0, Wales v Poland 1–2, Armenia v Poland 1–1, Norway v Belarus 1–1, Ukraine v Wales 1–1, Belarus v Ukraine 0–2, Poland v Norway 3–0, Wales v Armenia 0–0, Belarus v Poland 4–1, Norway v Wales 3–2, Ukraine v Armenia 3–0, Armenia v Norway 1–4, Poland v Ukraine 1–1, Wales v Belarus 1–0

	P	W	D	L	F	A	Pts
Poland	10	6	3	1	21	11	21
Ukraine	10	4	5	1	13	8	17
Belarus	10	4	3	3	12	11	15
Norway	10	2	4	4	12	14	10
Wales	10	1	6	3	10	12	9
Armenia	10	0	5	5	7	19	5

Poland qualify for finals
Ukraine to play-offs

Group 6
Belgium v Croatia 0–0, Latvia v Scotland 0–1, Latvia v Belgium 0–4, San Marino v Scotland 0–2, Croatia v Scotland 1–1, San Marino v Latvia 0–1, Belgium v San Marino 10–1, Croatia v Latvia 4–1, Scotland v Belgium 2–2, Scotland v San Marino 4–0, Latvia v San Marino 1–1, Belgium v Latvia 3–1, Croatia v San Marino 4–0, Latvia v Croatia 0–1, San Marino v Belgium 1–4, Scotland v Croatia

0–0, Belgium v Scotland 2–0, San Marino v Croatia 0–4, Croatia v Belgium 1–0, Scotland v Latvia 2–1

	P	W	D	L	F	A	Pts
Croatia	8	5	3	0	15	2	18
Belgium	8	5	2	1	25	6	17
Scotland	8	4	3	1	12	6	12
Latvia	8	1	1	6	7	17	4
San Marino	8	0	1	7	3	30	1

Croatia qualify for finals
Belgium to play-offs

Group 7

Bosnia-Herzegovina v Spain 1–2, Israel v Liechtenstein 2–0, Liechtenstein v Austria 0–1, Spain v Israel 2–0, Austria v Spain 1–1, Israel v Bosnia-Herzegovina 3–1, Bosnia-Herzegovina v Austria 1–1, Spain v Liechtenstein 5–0, Austria v Israel 2–1, Liechtenstein v Bosnia-Herzegovina 0–3, Austria v Liechtenstein 2–0, Liechtenstein v Israel 0–3, Spain v Bosnia-Herzegovina 4–1, Israel v Spain 1–1, Bosnia-Herzegovina v Israel 0–0, Spain v Austria 4–0, Austria v Bosnia-Herzegovina 2–0, Liechtenstein v Spain 0–2, Bosnia-Herzegovina v Liechtenstein 5–0, Israel v Austria 1–1

	P	W	D	L	F	A	Pts
Spain	8	6	2	0	21	4	20
Austria	8	4	3	1	10	8	15
Israel	8	3	3	2	11	7	12
Bosnia-Herzegovina	8	2	2	4	12	12	8
Liechtenstein	8	0	0	8	0	23	0

Spain qualify for finals
Austria to play-offs

Group 8

Hungary v Italy 2–2, Romania v Lithuania 1–0, Italy v Romania 3–0, Lithuania v Georgia 0–4, Italy v Georgia 2–0, Lithuania v Hungary 1–6, Hungary v Lithuania 1–1, Romania v Italy 0–2, Georgia v Romania 0–2, Italy v Lithuania 4–0, Georgia v Italy 1–2, Romania v Hungary 2–0, Hungary v Georgia 4–1, Lithuania v Romania 1–2, Georgia v Hungary 3–1, Lithuania v Italy 0–0, Georgia v Lithuania 2–0, Hungary v Romania 0–2, Italy v Hungary 1–0, Romania v Georgia 1–1

	P	W	D	L	F	A	Pts
Italy	8	6	2	0	16	3	20
Romania	8	5	1	2	10	7	16
Georgia	8	3	1	4	12	12	10
Hungary	8	2	2	4	14	13	8
Lithuania	8	0	2	6	3	20	2

Italy qualify for finals
Romania to play-offs

Group 9

Finland v Albania 2–1, Germany v Greece 2–0, England v Germany 0–1, Greece v Finland 1–0, Albania v Greece 2–0, Finland v England 0–0, England v Finland 2–1, Germany v Albania 2–1, Albania v England 1–3, Greece v Germany 2–4, Finland v Germany 2–2, Greece v Albania 1–0, Albania v Germany 0–2, Greece v England 0–2, Albania v Finland 0–2, Germany v England 1–5, England v Albania 2–0, Finland v Greece 5–1, England v Greece 2–2, Germany v Finland 0–0

	P	W	D	L	F	A	Pts
England	8	5	2	1	16	6	17
Germany	8	5	2	1	14	10	17
Finland	8	3	3	2	12	7	12
Greece	8	2	1	5	7	17	7
Albania	8	1	0	7	5	14	3

England qualify for finals
Germany to play-offs

South America

Colombia v Brazil 0–0, Argentina v Chile 4–1, Ecuador v Venezuela 2–0, Peru v Paraguay 2–0, Uruguay v Bolivia 1–0, Bolivia v Colombia 1–1, Brazil v Ecuador 3–2, Chile v Peru 1–1, Paraguay v Uruguay 1–0, Venezuela v Argentina 0–4, Paraguay v Ecuador 3–1, Uruguay v Chile 2–1, Argentina v Bolivia 1–0, Colombia v Venezuela 3–0, Peru v Brazil 0–1, Brazil v Uruguay 1–1, Venezuela v Bolivia 4–2, Chile v Paraguay 3–1, Colombia v Argentina 1–3, Ecuador v Peru 2–1, Paraguay v Brazil 2–1, Uruguay v Venezuela 3–1, Argentina v Ecuador 2–0, Bolivia v Chile 1–0, Peru v Colombia 0–1, Ecuador v Colombia 0–0, Venezuela v Chile 0–2, Brazil v Argentina 3–1, Uruguay v Peru 0–0, Bolivia v Paraguay 0–0, Chile v Brazil 3–0, Colombia v Uruguay 1–0, Argentina v Paraguay 1–1, Ecuador v Bolivia 2–0, Peru v Venezuela 1–0, Chile v Colombia 0–1, Paraguay v Venezuela 3–0, Brazil v Bolivia 5–0, Peru v Argentina 1–2, Uruguay v Ecuador 4–0, Colombia v Paraguay 0–2, Argentina v Uruguay 2–1, Bolivia v Peru 1–0, Ecuador v Chile 1–0, Venezuela v Brazil 0–6, Bolivia v Uruguay 0–0, Brazil v Colombia 1–0, Chile v Argentina 0–2, Paraguay v Peru 5–1, Venezuela v Ecuador 1–2, Colombia v Bolivia 2–0, Peru v Chile 3–1, Argentina v Venezuela 5–0, Ecuador v Brazil 1–0, Uruguay v Paraguay 0–1, Chile v Uruguay 0–1, Ecuador v Paraguay 2–1, Venezuela v Colombia 2–2, Bolivia v Argentina 3–3, Brazil v Peru 1–1, Paraguay v Chile 1–0, Peru v Ecuador 1–2, Argentina v Colombia 3–0, Bolivia v Venezuela 5–0, Uruguay v Brazil 1–0, Chile v Bolivia 2–2, Venezuela v Uruguay 2–0, Brazil v Paraguay 2–0, Ecuador v Argentina 0–2, Colombia v Peru 0–1, Chile v Venezuela 0–2, Peru v Uruguay 0–2, Argentina v Brazil 2–1, Colombia v Ecuador 0–0, Paraguay v Bolivia 5–1, Bolivia v Ecuador 1–5, Venezuela v Peru 3–0, Brazil v Chile 2–0, Paraguay v Argentina 2–2, Uruguay v Colombia 1–1, Bolivia v Brazil 3–1, Colombia v Chile 3–1, Ecuador v Uruguay 1–1, Argentina v Peru 2–0, Venezuela v Paraguay 3–1, Brazil v Venezuela 3–0, Chile v Ecuador 0–0, Paraguay v Colombia 0–4, Peru v Bolivia 1–1, Uruguay v Argentina 1–1

	P	W	D	L	F	A	Pts
Argentina	18	13	4	1	42	15	43
Ecuador	18	9	4	5	23	20	31
Brazil	18	9	3	6	31	17	30
Paraguay	18	9	3	6	29	23	30
Uruguay	18	7	6	5	19	13	27
Colombia	18	7	6	5	20	15	27
Bolivia	18	4	6	8	21	33	18
Peru	18	4	4	10	14	25	16
Venezuela	18	5	1	12	18	44	16
Chile	18	3	3	12	15	27	12

Argentina, Brazil, Ecuador and Paraguay qualify for the finals.
Uruguay play-off home and away with Oceania winner.

CONCACAF

Preliminary Phase
Central American Zone Group A
El Salvador v Belize 5–0, *Belize v Guatemala 1–2, Guatemala v El Salvador 0–1, Belize v El Salvador 1–3, El Salvador v Guatemala 1–1, **Guatemala v Belize 0–0

	P	W	D	L	F	A	Pts
El Salvador	4	3	1	0	10	2	10
Guatemala	4	1	2	1	3	3	5
Belize	4	0	1	3	2	10	1

*In Panama City
**In Tegucigalpa, Honduras

Central American Zone Group B

Honduras v Nicaragua 3–0, Nicaragua v Panama 0–2, Panama v Honduras 1–0, Nicaragua v Honduras 0–1, Honduras v Panama 3–1, Panama v Nicaragua 4–0

	P	W	D	L	F	A	Pts
Panama	4	3	0	1	8	3	9
Honduras	4	3	0	1	7	2	9
Nicaragua	4	0	0	4	0	10	0

Group winners qualified for the overall confederation semi-final round. A runners-up played off against Caribbean Zone Group 2 runners-up for a semi-final round place, Group B runners-up played off against Caribbean Zone Group 3 runners-up for a semi-final round place.

Caribbean Zone First Round
Group 1

Cuba v Cayman Islands 4–0, Cayman Islands v Cuba 0–0 (Cuba 4–0 on agg), St Lucia v Surinam 1–0, Surinam v St Lucia (aet) 1–0 (Agg 1–1. Surinam 3–1 on pens), Barbados v Grenada 2–2, Grenada v Barbados 2–3 (Barbados 5–4 on agg), Aruba v Puerto Rico 4–2, Puerto Rico v Aruba 2–2 (Aruba 6–4 on agg)

Group 2

St Vincent v US Virgin Islands 9–0, US Virgin Islands v St Vincent 1–5 (St Vincent 14–1 on agg), British Virgin Islands v Bermuda 1–5, Bermuda v British Virgin Islands 9–0 (Bermuda 14–1 on agg), St Kitts v Turks & Caicos Islands 8–0, Turks & Caicos Islands v St Kitts* 0–6 (St Kitts 14–0 on agg)
Guyana v Antigua & Barbuda–Guyana suspended by FIFA, Antigua & Barbuda went through to second round.
*2nd leg also played in St Kitts

Group 3

Trinidad & Tobago–Dutch Antilles 5–0, Dutch Antilles v Trinidad & Tobago 1–1 (Trinidad & Tobago 6–1 on agg), Anguilla v Bahamas 1–3, Bahamas v Anguilla 2–1 (Bahamas 5–2 on agg), Dominican Republic v Montserrat 3–0, Montserrat v Dominican Republic 1–3 (Dominican Republic 6–1 on agg), Haiti v Dominica 4–0, Dominica v Haiti 1–3 (Haiti 7–1 on agg)

Caribbean Zone Second Round
Group 1
Aruba v Barbados 1–3, Barbados v Aruba 4–0 (Barbados 7–1 on agg), Cuba v Surinam 1–0, Surinam v Cuba 0–0 (Cuba 1–0 on agg),

Group 2
Antigua & Barbuda v Bermuda 0–0, Bermuda v Antigua & Barbuda 1–1 (Agg 1–1. Antigua & Barbuda on away goals), St Vincent v St Kitts 1–0, St Kitts v St Vincent 1–2 (St Vincent 3–1 on agg)

Group 3
Haiti v Bahamas 9–0, Bahamas v Haiti 0–4 (Haiti 13–0 on agg), Trinidad & Tobago v Dominican Republic 3–0, Dominican Republic v Trinidad & Tobago 0–1 (Trinidad & Tobago 4–0 on agg)

Caribbean Zone Finals
Group 1
Cuba v Barbados 1–1, Barbados v Cuba 1–1 (agg 2–2. Barbados 5–4 on pens)

Group 2
Antigua & Barbuda v St Vincent 2–1, St Vincent v Antigua & Barbuda 4–0 (St Vincent 5–2 on agg)

Group 3
Trinidad & Tobago v Haiti 3–1, Haiti v Trinidad & Tobago 1–1 (Trinidad & Tobago 4–2 on agg)

The three finals winners qualified for the overall confederation semi-final round.

Group 1 runners-up played off against Canada for a semi-final round place, Group 2 runners-up played off against Central American Zone Group A runners-up for a semi-final round place, Group 3 runners-up played off against Central American Zone Group B runners-up for a semi-final round place.

Inter-zone Play-offs
Cuba v Canada 0–1, Canada v Cuba 0–0 (Canada 1–0 on agg), Antigua & Barbuda v Guatemala 0–1, Guatemala v Antigua & Barbuda 8–1 (Guatemala 9–1 on agg), Honduras v Haiti 4–0, Haiti v Honduras 1–3 (Honduras 7–1 on agg)

Semi-Final Round

Cost Rica, Jamaica, Mexico and the United States qualified directly for the semi-final round.

Group C

Canada v Trinidad & Tobago 0–2, Panama v Mexico 0–1, Panama v Canada 0–0, Trinidad & Tobago v Mexico 1–0, Mexico v Canada 2–0, Trinidad & Tobago v Panama 6–0, Mexico v Panama 7–1, Trinidad & Tobago v Canada 4–0, Mexico v Trinidad & Tobago 7–0, Canada v Panama 1–0, Canada v Mexico 0–0, Panama v Trinidad & Tobago* 0–1
*Tie played in Port-of-Spain, Trinidad

	P	W	D	L	F	A	Pts
Trinidad & Tobago	6	5	0	1	14	7	15
Mexico	6	4	1	1	17	2	13
Canada	6	1	2	3	1	8	5
Panama	6	0	1	5	1	16	1

Group D

El Salvador v Honduras 2–5, St Vincent v Jamaica 0–1, El Salvador v St Vincent 7–1, Jamaica v Honduras 3–1, Honduras v St Vincent 6–0, Jamaica v El Salvador 1–0, Honduras v El Salvador 5–0, Jamaica v St Vincent 2–0, Honduras v Jamaica 1–0, St Vincent v El Salvador 1–2, St Vincent v Honduras 0–7, El Salvador v Jamaica 2–0

	P	W	D	L	F	A	Pts
Honduras	6	5	0	1	25	5	15
Jamaica	6	4	0	2	7	4	12
El Salvador	6	3	0	3	13	13	9
St Vincent	6	0	0	6	2	25	0

Group E

Barbados v Costa Rica 2–1, Guatemala v Unites States 1–1, Guatemala v Barbados 2–0, Costa Rica v United States 2–1, Costa Rica v Guatemala 2–1, United States v Barbados 7–0, Costa Rica v Barbados 3–0, United States v Guatemala 1–0, Barbados v Guatemala 1–3, United States v Costa Rica 0–0, Barbados v United States 0–4, Guatemala v Costa Rica 2–1

	P	W	D	L	F	A	Pts
United States	6	3	2	1	14	3	11
Costa Rica**	6	3	1	2	9	6	10
Guatemala**	6	3	1	2	9	6	10
Barbados	6	1	0	5	3	20	3

The top two from each group qualified for the final round group of six.
**Play-off required because head-to-head and overall group records were identical.

Semi-Final Round Play-off
Costa Rica v Guatemala 5–2
Tie played in Miami

Final Round (Costa Rica, Honduras, Jamaica, Mexico, Trinidad & Tobago, United States)
Costa Rica v Honduras 2–2, Jamaica v Trinidad & Tobago 1–0, United States v Mexico 2–0, Mexico v Jamaica 4–0, Costa Rica v Trinidad & Tobago 3–0, Honduras v United States 1–2, Jamaica v Honduras 1–1, Trinidad & Tobago v Mexico 1–1, United States v Costa Rica 1–0, Jamaica v United States 0–0, Mexico v Costa Rica 1–2, Trinidad & Tobago v Honduras 2–4, Costa Rica v Jamaica 2–1, Honduras v Mexico 3–1, United States v Trinidad & Tobago 2–0, Trinidad & Tobago v Jamaica 1–2, Honduras v Costa Rica 2–3, Mexico v United States 1–0, Trinidad & Tobago v Costa Rica 0–2, United States v Honduras 2–3, Jamaica v Mexico 1–2, Costa Rica v United States 2–0, Honduras v Jamaica 1–0, Mexico v Trinidad & Tobago 3–0, Costa Rica v Mexico 0–0, Honduras v Trinidad & Tobago 0–1, United States v Jamaica 2–1, Jamaica v Costa Rica 0–1, Mexico v Honduras 3–0, Trinidad & Tobago v United States 0–0

	P	W	D	L	F	A	Pts
Costa Rica	10	7	2	1	17	7	23
Mexico	10	5	2	3	16	9	17
United States	10	5	2	3	11	8	17
Honduras	10	4	2	4	17	17	14
Jamaica	10	2	2	6	7	14	8
Trinidad & Tobago	10	1	2	7	5	18	5

Costa Rica, Mexico and USA qualify for the finals.

Asia

First Round
Group 1
Oman v Laos 12–0, Syria v Philippines 12–0, Laos v Oman* 0–7, Philippines v Syria 1–5, Oman v Philippines 7–0, Syria v Laos 11–0, Laos v Syria** 0–9, Philippines v Oman* 0–2, Syria v Oman 3–3, Laos v Philippines 2–0, Oman v Syria 2–0, Philippines v Laos 1–1
Ties played on a home and away basis

*Played in Muscat, Laos and Philippines waived right to stage game. **Played in Aleppo, Laos waived right to stage game

	P	W	D	L	F	A	Pts
Oman	6	5	1	0	33	3	16
Syria	6	4	1	1	40	6	13
Laos	6	1	1	4	3	40	4
Philippines	6	0	1	5	2	29	1

Group 2
Iran v Guam 19–0, Tajikistan v Guam 16–0, Iran v Tajikistan 2–0
All ties played in Tabriz, Iran

	P	W	D	L	F	A	Pts
Iran	2	2	0	0	21	0	6
Tajikistan	2	1	0	1	16	2	3
Guam	2	0	0	2	0	35	0

Myanmar withdrew

Group 3
Qatar v Malaysia 5–1, Hong Kong v Palestine 1 –1, Palestine v Qatar 1–2, Malaysia v Hong Kong 2–0, Palestine v Malaysia 1–0, Qatar v Hong Kong 2–0
Ties played in Hong Kong

Palestine v Hong Kong 1–0, Malaysia v Qatar 0–0, Qatar v Palestine 2–1, Hong Kong v Malaysia 2–1, Hong Kong v Qatar 0–3, Malaysia v Palestine 4–3
Ties played in Doha, Qatar

	P	W	D	L	F	A	Pts
Qatar*	6	5	1	0	14	3	16
Palestine	6	2	1	3	8	9	7
Malaysia	6	2	1	3	8	11	7
Hong Kong	6	1	1	4	3	10	4

Group 4
Bahrain v Kuwait 1–2, Singapore v Kyrgyzstan 0–1, Bahrain v Kyrgyzstan 1–0, Kuwait v Singapore 1–1, Kyrgyzstan v Kuwait 0–3, Singapore v Bahrain 1–2
Ties played in Singapore

Kyrgyzstan v Bahrain 1–2, Singapore v Kuwait 0–1, Kuwait v Kyrgyzstan 2–0, Bahrain v Singapore 2–0, Kyrgyzstan v Singapore 1–1, Kuwait v Bahrain 0–1
Ties played in Kuwait City

	P	W	D	L	F	A	Pts
Bahrain	6	5	0	1	9	4	15
Kuwait	6	4	1	1	9	3	13
Kyrgyzstan	6	1	1	4	3	9	4
Singapore	6	0	2	4	3	8	2

Group 5
Thailand v Sri Lanak 4–2, Lebanon v Pakistan 6–0, Thailand v Pakistan 3–0, Lebanon v Sri Lanka 4–0, Pakistan v Sri Lanka 3–3, Lebanon v Thailand 1–2
Ties played in Beirut, Lebanon

Pakistan v Lebanon 1–8, Sri Lanka v Thailand 0–3, Sri Lanka v Lebanon 0–5, Pakistan v Thailand 0–6, Sri Lanka v Pakistan 3–1, Thailand v Lebanon 2–2
Ties played in Bangkok, Thailand

	P	W	D	L	F	A	Pts
Thailand	6	5	1	0	20	5	16
Lebanon	6	4	1	1	26	5	13
Sri Lanka	6	1	1	4	8	20	4
Pakistan	6	0	1	5	5	29	1

Group 6
Nepal v Kazakhstan 0–6, Iraq v Macao 8–0, Kazakhstan v Macao 3–0, Nepal v Iraq 1–9, Nepal v Macao 4–1, Kazakhstan v Iraq 1–1
Ties played in Baghdad, Iraq

Kazakhstan v Nepal 4–0, Macao v Iraq 0–5, Macao v Kazakhstan 0–5, Iraq v Nepal 4–2, Macao v Nepal 1–6, Iraq v Kazakhstan 1–1
Ties played in Almaty, Kazakhstan

	P	W	D	L	F	A	Pts
Iraq	6	4	2	0	28	5	14
Kazakhstan	6	4	2	0	20	2	14
Nepal	6	2	0	4	13	25	6
Macao	6	0	0	6	2	31	0

Group 7

Turkmenistan v Jordan 2–0, Uzbekistan v Taiwan 7–0, Taiwan v Jordan 0–2, Uzbekistan v Turkmenistan 1–0, Taiwan v Turkmenistan 0–5, Uzbekistan v Jordan 2–2
Ties played in Tashkent, Uzbekistan

Jordan v Taiwan 6–0, Turkmenistan v Uzbekistan 2–5, Taiwan v Uzbekistan 0–4, Jordan v Turkmenistan 1–2, Turkmenistan v Taiwan 1–0, Jordan v Uzbekistan 1 –1
Ties played in Amman, Jordan

	P	W	D	L	F	A	Pts
Uzbekistan	6	4	2	0	20	5	14
Turkmenistan	6	4	0	2	12	7	12
Jordan	6	2	2	2	12	7	8
Taiwan	6	0	0	6	0	25	0

Group 8

Brunei v Yemen 0–5, India v United Arab Emirates 1–0, Brunei v United Arab Emirates 0–12, India v Yemen 1–1, United Arab Emirates v India 1–0, Yemen v Brunei 1–0, United Arab Emirates v Brunei 4–0, Yemen v India 3–3, Yemen v United Arab Emirates 2–1, Brunei v India 0–1, United Arab Emirates v Yemen 3–2, India v Brunei 5–0

Ties played on a home and away basis

	P	W	D	L	F	A	Pts
United Arab Emirates	6	4	0	2	21	5	12
Yemen	6	3	2	1	14	8	11
India	6	3	2	1	11	5	11
Brunei	6	0	0	6	0	28	0

Group 9

Maldives v Cambodia 6–0, Indonesia v Maldives 5–0, Cambodia v Maldives 1–1, China v Maldives 10–1, Indonesia v Cambodia 6–0, Maldives v China 0–1, Cambodia v Indonesia 0–2, Cambodia v China 0–4, Maldives v Indonesia 0–2, China v Indonesia 5–1, China v Cambodia 3–1, Indonesia v China 0–2

Ties played on a home and away basis

	P	W	D	L	F	A	Pts
China	6	6	0	0	25	3	18
Indonesia	6	4	0	2	16	7	12
Maldives	6	1	1	4	8	19	4
Cambodia	6	0	1	5	2	22	1

Group 10

Vietnam v Bangladesh 0–0, Saudi Arabia v Mongolia 6–0, Mongolia v Vietnam 0–1, Bangladesh v Saudi Arabia 0–3, Mongolia v Bangladesh 0–3, Saudi Arabia v Vietnam 5–0, Mongolia v Saudi Arabia 0–6, Bangladesh v Vietnam 0–4, Vietnam v Mongolia 4–0, Saudi Arabia v Bangladesh 6–0, Bangladesh v Mongolia 2–2, Vietnam v Saudi Arabia 0–4

All ties played in Dammam, Saudi Arabia

	P	W	D	L	F	A	Pts
Saudi Arabia	6	6	0	0	30	0	18
Vietnam	6	3	1	2	9	9	10
Bangladesh	6	1	2	3	5	15	5
Mongolia	6	0	1	5	2	22	1

Second Round
Group A

Iraq v Thailand 4–0, Saudi Arabia v Bahrain 1 –1, Bahrain v Iraq 2–0, Iran v Saudi Arabia 2–0, Saudi Arabia v Iraq 1–0, Thailand v Iran 0–0, Bahrain v Thailand 1–1, Iraq v Iran 1–2, Iran v Bahrain 0–0, Thailand v Saudi Arabia 1–3, Bahrain v Saudi Arabia 0–4, Thailand v Iraq 1–1, Iraq v Bahrain 1–0, Saudi Arabia v Iran 2–2, Iran v Thailand 1–0, Iraq v Saudi Arabia 1–2, Iran v Iraq 2–1, Thailand v Bahrain 1–1, Bahrain v Iran 3–1, Saudi Arabia v Thailand 4–1

	P	W	D	L	F	A	Pts
Saudi Arabia	8	5	2	1	17	8	17
Iran	8	4	3	1	10	7	15
Bahrain	8	2	4	2	8	9	10
Iraq	8	2	1	5	9	10	7
Thailand	8	0	4	4	5	15	4

Saudi Arabia qualify for the finals

Group B

Qatar v Oman 0–0, United Arab Emirates v Uzbekistan 4–1, China v United Arab Emirates 3–0, Uzbekistan v Qatar 2–1, United Arab Emirates v Qatar 0–2, Oman v China 0–2, Qatar v China 1 –1, Uzbekistan v Oman 5–0, Oman v United Arab Emirates 1–1, China v Uzbekistan 2–0, Oman v Qatar 0–3, Uzbekistan v United Arab Emirates 0–1, United Arab Emirates v China 0–1, Qatar v Uzbekistan 2–2, Qatar v United Arab Emirates 1–2, China v Oman 1–0, Oman v Uzbekistan 4–2, China v Qatar 3–0, United Arab Emirates v Oman 2–2, Uzbekistan v China 1–0

	P	W	D	L	F	A	Pts
China	8	6	1	1	13	2	19
United Arab Emirates	8	3	2	3	10	11	11
Uzbekistan	8	3	1	4	13	14	10
Qatar	8	2	3	3	10	10	9
Oman	8	1	3	4	7	16	6

Ties played on a home and away basis. The two group winners qualify directly for the finals. The two runners-up entered the play-off.

China qualify for the finals

Asian Runners-up Play-off

Iran v United Arab Emirates 1–0, United Arab Emirates v Iran 0–3 (Iran 4–0 on agg)

Iran entered the Asian/European play-off

Africa

First Round

Djibouti v DR Congo 1–1, DR Congo v Djibouti 9–1 (DR Congo 10–2 on agg), Mauritania v Tunisia 1–2, Tunisia v Mauritania 3–0 (Tunisia 5–1 on agg), Botswana v Zambia 0–1, Zambia v Botswana 1–0 (Zambia 2–0 on agg), Guinea-Bissau v

Togo 0–0, Togo v Guinea-Bissau 3–0 (Togo 3–0 on agg), Madagascar v Gabon 2–0, Gabon v Madagascar 1–0 (Madagascar 2–1 on agg), Malawi v Kenya 2–0, Kenya v Malawi 0–0 (2nd leg abandoned after 88mins–result stood. Malawi 2–0 on agg), Sao Tome e Principe v Sierra Leone 2–0, Sierra Leone v Sao Tome e Principe 4–0 (Sierra Leone 4–2 on agg), Seychelles v Namibia 1–1, Namibia v Seychelles 3–0 (Namibia 4–1 on agg), Tanzania v Ghana 0–1, Ghana v Tanzania 3–2 (Ghana 4–2 on agg), Uganda v Guinea 4–4, Guinea v Uganda 3–0 (Guinea 7–4 on agg), Benin v Senegal 1–1, Senegal v Benin 1–0 (Senegal 2–1 on agg), Cape Verde Islands v Algeria 0–0, Algeria v Cape Verde Islands 2–0 (Algeria 2–0 on agg), Central African Republic v Zimbabwe 0–1, Zimbabwe v Central African Republic 3–1 (Zimbabwe 4–1 on agg), Chad v Liberia 0–1, Liberia v Chad 0–0 (Liberia 1–0 on agg), Equatorial Guinea v Congo 1–3, Congo v Equatorial Guinea 2–1 (Congo 5–2 on agg), Eritrea v Nigeria 0–0, Nigeria v Eritrea 4–0 (Nigeria 4–0 on agg), Ethiopia v Burkina Faso 2–1, Burkina Faso v Ethiopia 3–0 (Burkina Faso 4–2 on agg), Gambia v Morocco 0–1, Morocco v Gambia 2–0 (Morocco 3–0 on agg), Lesotho v South Africa 0–2, South Africa v Lesotho 1–0 (South Africa 3–0 on agg), Libya v Mali 3–0, Mali v Libya 3–1 (Libya 4–3 on agg), Rwanda v Ivory Coast 2–2, Ivory Coast v Rwanda 2–0 (Ivory Coast 4–2 on agg), Sudan v Mozambique 1–0, Mozambique v Sudan 2–1 (Agg 2–2. Sudan on away goals), Swaziland v Angola 0–1, Angola v Swaziland 7–1 (Angola 8–1 on agg), *Somalia v Cameroon 0–3, Cameroon v Somalia 3–0 (Cameroon 6–0 on agg), *Mauritius v Egypt 0–2, Egypt v Mauritius 4–2 (Egypt 6–2 on agg)

Winners qualified for second round.
*Somalia and Mauritius forfeited the right to stage the first leg at home.

Second Round
Group A
Angola v Zambia 2–1, Libya v Cameroon 0–3, Zambia v Togo 2–0, Cameroon v Angola 3–0, Angola v Libya 3–1, Togo v Cameroon 0–2, Libya v Togo 3–3, Cameroon v Zambia 1–0, Zambia v Libya 2–0, Togo v Angola 1–1, Zambia v Angola 1–1, Cameroon v Libya 1–0, Angola v Cameroon 2–0, Togo v Zambia 3–2, Libya v Angola 1–1, Cameroon v Togo 2–0, Zambia v Cameroon 2–2, Togo v Libya 2–0, Libya v Zambia 2–4, Angola v Togo 1–1

	P	W	D	L	F	A	Pts
Cameroon	8	6	1	1	14	4	19
Angola	8	3	4	1	11	9	13
Zambia	8	3	2	3	14	11	11
Togo	8	2	3	3	10	13	9
Libya	8	0	2	6	7	19	2

Cameroon qualify for the finals

Group B

Nigeria v Sierra Leone 2–0, Sudan v Liberia 2–0, Ghana v Sierra Leone 5–0, Liberia v Nigeria 2–1, Nigeria v Sudan 3–0, Ghana v Liberia 1–3, Liberia v Sierra Leone 1–0, Sudan v Ghana 1–0, Ghana v Nigeria 0–0, Sierra Leone v Sudan 0–2, Sierra Leone v Nigeria 1–0, Liberia v Sudan 2–0, Nigeria v Liberia 2–0, Sierra Leone v Ghana 1–1, Liberia v Ghana 1–2, Sudan v Nigeria 0–4, Sierra Leone v Liberia 0–1, Ghana v Sudan 1–0, Nigeria v Ghana 3–0, Sudan v Sierra Leone 3–0

	P	W	D	L	F	A	Pts
Nigeria	8	5	1	2	15	3	16
Liberia	8	5	0	3	10	8	15
Sudan	8	4	0	4	8	10	12
Ghana	8	3	2	3	10	9	11
Sierra Leone	8	1	1	6	2	15	4

Nigeria qualify for the finals

Group C

Algeria v Senegal 1–1, Namibia v Morocco 0–0, Morocco v Algeria 2–1, Senegal v Egypt 0–0, Algeria v Namibia 1–0, Egypt v Morocco 0–0, Morocco v Senegal 0–0, Namibia v Egypt 1–1, Senegal v Namibia 4–0, Egypt v Algeria 5–2, Morocco v Namibia 3–0, Senegal v Algeria 3–0, Algeria v Morocco 1–2, Egypt v Senegal 1–0, Morocco v Egypt 1–0, Namibia v Algeria 0–4, Egypt v Namibia 8–2, Senegal v Morocco 1–0, Algeria v Egypt 1–1, Namibia v Senegal 0–5

	P	W	D	L	F	A	Pts
Senegal	8	4	3	1	14	2	15
Morocco	8	4	3	1	8	3	15
Egypt	8	3	4	1	16	7	13
Algeria	8	2	2	4	11	14	8
Namibia	8	0	2	6	3	26	2

Senegal qualify for the finals

Group D

Ivory Coast v Tunisia 2–2, Madagascar v DR Congo 3–0, Tunisia v Madagascar 1–0, DR Congo v Congo 2–0, Congo v Tunisia 1–2, Madagascar v Ivory Coast 1–3, Tunisia v DR Congo 6–0, DR Congo v Ivory Coast 1–2, DR Congo v Madagascar 1–0, Ivory Coast v Congo 2–0, Congo v Madagascar 2–0, Madagascar v Tunisia 0–2, Congo v DR Congo 1–1, Tunisia v Ivory Coast 1–1, Ivory Coast v Madagascar 6–0, Tunisia v Congo 6–0, Congo v Ivory Coast 1–1, DR Congo v Tunisia 0–3, Madagascar v Congo 1–0, Ivory Coast v DR Congo 1–2

	P	W	D	L	F	A	Pts
Tunisia	8	6	2	0	23	4	20
Ivory Coast	8	4	3	1	18	8	15
DR Congo	8	3	1	4	7	16	10
Madagascar	8	2	0	6	5	15	6
Congo	8	1	2	5	5	15	5

Tunisia qualify for the finals

Group E

Malawi v Burkina Faso 1–1, Guinea v Zimbabwe 3–0 (annulled), Burkina Faso v Guinea 2–3 (annulled), Zimbabwe v South Africa** 0–2, South Africa v Burkina Faso 1–0, Guinea v Malawi 1–1 (annulled), Burkina Faso v Zimbabwe 1–2, Malawi v South Africa 1–2, Zimbabwe v Malawi 2–0, Burkina Faso v Malawi 4–2, South Africa v Zimbabwe 2–1, Burkina Faso v South Africa 1–1, South Africa v Malawi 2–0, Zimbabwe v Burkina Faso 1–0, Malawi v Zimbabwe 0–1

**Match abandoned after 82 minutes, result stood

	P	W	D	L	F	A	Pts
South Africa	6	5	1	0	10	3	16
Zimbabwe	6	4	0	2	7	5	12
Burkina Faso	6	1	2	3	7	8	5
Malawi	6	0	1	5	4	12	1

South Africa qualify for the finals

Oceania

First Round

Group 1 (American Samoa, Australia, Fiji, Samoa, Tonga)

Samoa v Tonga 0–1, Fiji v American Samoa 13–0, Tonga v Australia 0–22, American Samoa v Samoa 0–8, Samoa v Fiji 1–6, Australia v American Samoa 31–0, Fiji v Australia 0–2, American Samoa v Tonga 0–5, Australia v Samoa 11–0, Tonga v Fiji 1–8

All ties played in Coffs Harbour, Australia

	P	W	D	L	F	A	Pts
Australia	4	4	0	0	66	0	12
Fiji	4	3	0	1	27	4	9
Tonga	4	2	0	2	7	30	6
Samoa	4	1	0	3	9	18	3
American Samoa	4	0	0	4	0	57	0

Australia qualified for Oceania play-off

Group 2 (Cook Islands, New Zealand, Solomon Islands, Tahiti, Vanuatu)

Vanuatu v Tahiti 1–6, Solomon Islands v Cook Islands 9–1, Tahiti v New Zealand 0–5, Cook Islands v Vanuatu 1–8, Vanuatu v Solomon Islands 2–7, New Zealand v Cook Islands 2–0, Solomon Islands v New Zealand 1–5, Cook Islands v Tahiti 0–6, New Zealand v Vanuatu 7–0, Tahiti v Solomon Islands 2–0
All ties played in Auckland, New Zealand

	P	W	D	L	F	A	Pts
New Zealand	4	4	0	0	19	1	12
Tahiti	4	3	0	1	14	6	9
Solomon Islands	4	2	0	2	17	10	6
Vanuatu	4	1	0	3	11	21	3
Cook Islands	4	0	0	4	2	25	0

New Zealand qualified for Oceania play-off

Oceania Play-off

New Zealand v Australia 0–2, Australia v New Zealand 4–1 (Australia 6–1 on agg)
Australia play home and away against the fifth-placed South American team for a place in the finals.

European and Euro/Asian Play-offs

1st legs

Slovenia v Romania 2–1, Ukraine v Germany 1–1, Belgium v Czech Republic 1–0, Austria v Turkey 0–1, Republic of Ireland v Iran 2–0

2nd legs

Romania v Slovenia 1–1, Germany v Ukraine 4–1, Czech Republic v Belgium 0–1, Turkey v Austria 5–0, Iran v Republic of Ireland 1–0

Qualifiers
Slovenia
Germany
Belgium
Turkey
Republic of Ireland

South American/Oceania Play-off
Australia v Uruguay 1–0, Uruguay v Australia 3–0 (Uruguay won 3–1 on agg)

2002 JAPAN AND SOUTH KOREA 31 May–30 June

QUALIFIERS

Argentina	Germany	Senegal
Belgium	Italy	Slovenia
Brazil	Japan	South Africa
Cameroon	Mexico	South Korea
China	Nigeria	Spain
Costa Rica	Paraguay	Sweden
Croatia	Poland	Tunisia
Denmark	Portugal	Turkey
Ecuador	Republic of Ireland	Uruguay
England	Russia	USA
France	Saudi Arabia	

On 1 December the eagerly awaited draw finally took place before an expectant gathering. Sadly, the ludicrous method of seeding top sides served only to be highlighted when the favourites, and South America's best qualifiers, Argentina were 'rewarded' with Group F. England, another of the favourites, and Sweden – UEFA Group winners both – plus Nigeria's 'Super Eagles' faced a competition for two places. Worse, one of those qualifiers would be asked in all probability to overcome France in the round of sixteen. Joining France in Group A would be Senegal, Denmark and, intriguingly, Uruguay, whose volatile temperament might be sorely tested by the French at their very best. Brazil and Germany, unconvincing and late qualifiers, meantime enjoyed undeserved good fortune after their dismal form, Brazil particularly, drawn bizarrely in Group C with UEFA play-off winner Turkey, debutants China and Costa Rica (featuring in their second championship). Winners here faced the runners-up in Group H where they should once again prosper.

Germany faced Ireland and by no means relished the prospect. The silver lining for the Germans, however, was in their other opponents in Group E. Certainly Cameroon and Saudi Arabia were no pushover, but Argentina would cast envious eyes towards both Germany and Brazil. Qualifiers from Group E would face those from Group B, where Spain were the team to avoid. Slovenia, Paraguay (of whom Spain had few fond memories) and South Africa, the 'Bafana, Bafana', completed another frankly undistinguished grouping. South Korea's task of qualification was to a degree aided by Group D, where Poland and the USA needed to be beaten. Nonetheless, Portugal offered a monumental obstacle to their pretensions as they looked to win their Group and so miss the Italians. Japan, too, drawn in Group H, faced two European opponents: surprise play-off winners Belgium and Russia with whom the nation had shared an often uneasy history. Tunisia completed the Group, one of whose qualifiers might face the enticing prospect of an encounter with Brazil.

While Italy's task in Group G looked hardly daunting, its three remaining members might at least offer the prospect of competitive fixtures. Ecuador, Mexico and Croatia, semi-finalists in 1998, would face the 'Azzurri', with the runner-up coming up against the winner of Group D.

Group A

(Venue: Korea)
France
Senegal
Uruguay
Denmark

Group B

(Venue: Korea)
Spain
South Africa
Paraguay
Slovenia

Group C

(Venue: Korea)
Brazil
Turkey
China
Costa Rica

Group E

(Venue: Japan)
Germany
Cameroon
Ireland
Saudi Arabia

Group F

(Venue: Japan)
Argentina
Nigeria
England
Sweden

Group G

(Venue: Japan)
Italy
Croatia
Ecuador
Mexico

Group D	Group H
(Venue: Korea)	**(Venue: Japan)**
South Korea	Japan
Poland	Tunisia
Portugal	Belgium
USA	Russia

THE FIRST SERIES

France opened the championships and opened them without their brightest star, the incomparable Zinedine Zidane, but their seemingly routine fixture with debutants Senegal proved anything but a formality.

Throughout a game dominated territorially by the holders, *Les Bleus* moved the ball too slowly around the field, perhaps wary of the heat or humidity. Senegal, by contrast, were quick and incisive and threatened to make more from less by harrying an ageing back four – El Hadji Diouf, their tormentor in chief. The 21-year-old's directness caused them great discomfort and on 30 minutes the upstarts were rewarded. Diouf, who had earlier waltzed by Desailly, now isolated Frank Leboeuf and accelerated towards goal with the bald defender trailing in his wake. His near-post cross confounded Petit and Barthez, allowing Bouba Diop to arrive on cue and give the Africans the lead. France were shocked and, though seven minutes earlier David Trezeguet had struck the post, chances were few and fleeting. Cisse had proved a commanding and inspirational first-half leader for Senegal.

After half-time the French steadily applied pressure if not a higher tempo. Trezeguet and the subdued Henry might have scored, Vieira should have but planted his header straight at Sylva. Senegal absorbed and struck back when Khalilou Fadiga attacked the hapless Leboeuf before zipping a shot onto the crossbar. One minute later Dugarry set up Henry but his shot only beat the goalkeeper, not the woodwork.

If France did not know it then they surely knew it at the very end. It would not be their day; Tony Sylva again denied Henry at the death. France, for all their pressure (they had ten corners to Senegal's zero) and illustrious players, had been beaten. As the jubilant Senegalese began their wild celebrations, the city of Seoul rose to acclaim a gallant underdog.

The following day at Ulsan, Denmark faced Uruguay; two qualifiers with a glorious past whose expectations must have grown after the previous day's events.

Uruguay, abandoning the sterile approach of recent tournaments, attacked from the outset using three forwards, the wonderfully gifted Alvaro Recoba, in particular, menacing the Danes. Denmark, neat and powerful, enjoyed good early moments but Ebbe Sand squandered the best chance, meeting Thomas Helveg's accurate cross with a thumping header which bounced into the turf, beat Carini but flew up onto the crossbar. Slowly, surely the Danes took control with Gronkjaer and Rommedahl raking the flanks and Sand and Gravesen, a combative pairing, physically dominant. Uruguay, though, thanks largely to the talent of Recoba, possessed threat and the Internazionale man had already come close to a goal when his curling free kick forced an excellent save from Thomas Sorensen.

Denmark punished the error as half-time approached. Gronkjaer, thundering down the left wing, drove his cross low and hard into the path of Jon Dahl Tomasson who finished with great aplomb from ten yards.

If Uruguay's resolve was tested at all, it was but for a short while. Within moments of the re-start they had their equaliser. Denmark, under pressure, cleared their lines and the long ball fell out of the sky and into the path of full back Dario Rodriguez twenty-five yards out. Without hesitation, he struck a ferocious curling volley past the perplexed Sorensen and into the roof of the net to make it 1–1.

The game became an absorbing contest, with thrust and counter thrust; Sand saw an effort beaten away while Recoba again found Sorensen in top form when his on-target effort was thwarted. It fell ultimately to the predatory Tomasson to settle it, meeting Jorgensen's cross with an exquisite header which struck the underside of the bar before settling in Carini's net.

For Ireland, at least their tournament opener against Cameroon ensured football, and not the furore surrounding Roy Keane's departure, would at last make the headlines. Their opponents were the Indomitable Lions of Cameroon, a team fancied by many as the darkest horses of all. Ireland, in spite of their disrupted preparations, began brightly in a half that see-sawed to and fro. Kilbane, finding space out on the wing, swung the ball into the path of Robbie Keane whose header flashed wide. Mboma and Eto'o, though, were proving a handful and the pair worked a neat opening before Eto'o forced Given into action. Thus warned, the Irish were forced onto the defensive by Cameroon pressure and were soon undone. Eto'o, escaping Staunton, crossed and Mboma smashed the ball in. Irish spirit, though, was not punctured and Alioum had to dive to prevent an equaliser after Harte's driven free kick deflected off Rigobert Song.

Encouraged, the Republic, driven by Holland and the mercurial Duff, seized the initiative after the break. Holland, having seen Geremi shoot wide at the other end, snatched a deserved equaliser by latching on to a poorly timed clearance to shoot with power beyond the flailing goalkeeper. The inspired Irish continued to pursue the winner to the finish. Keane was frustrated by the goal post but then conjured up a shot which Alioum fingertipped to safety.

Ireland were the better side on balance and had much to be satisfied with, not least their show of team unity in the absence of their sulky, exiled leader.

The German's prospects were held to be modest following their humiliating qualification defeat at the hands of England but they produced an astonishing performance in the demolition of hapless Saudi Arabia. The German side, led with distinction from the outset by the tall rangy Jancker, controlled the game from the start, the striker shooting narrowly wide in the opening minute before having a goal disallowed six minutes later. The Saudis, horribly outclassed, chased and ran but their fate was all but sealed when Miroslav Klose arrived to meet the ball with a low header which gave Al Daeyea no chance at all. A second followed swiftly, with Klose again heading beyond the floundering goalkeeper, this time from Michael Ballack's swinging cross.

Worse followed when Ballack, a dynamic presence throughout, leapt to meet Christian Ziege's cross and then, before half-time, Jancker slotted home a fourth to send the Asian qualifiers scurrying to the dressing room in disarray, fearful of further mauling from their rampant and thrillingly revitalised opponents. Unable to keep possession or pose a threat after the restart, the Saudis could do little but resist. Germany swaggered and were dominant. Klose added a fifth, his hat trick another header with twenty minutes remaining, then Thomas Linke joined the scorers three minutes later. If 6–0 was an embarrassment for Asia's coach of the year, Nasser Al Jehar, his team's pounding was not yet complete. Veteran substitute, Oliver Bierhoff, rapped in a seventh before Schneider arrived on cue to complete the rout. Afterwards Rudi Voeller reflected with masterly understatement on the Saudis' inadequacies, saying: 'We have to keep our feet on the ground because we know our opponent wasn't that strong.' Germany, though, seemed ready for the sterner challenges ahead.

Paraguay at Bulsan appeared to have beaten South Africa with something to spare, though were left only with disappointment as the 'Bafana Bafana' showed great strength of character. Santa Cruz, the gifted young Bayern Munich striker, threatened from the outset and was unfortunate, perhaps, when his collision with goalkeeper Arendse went unpunished. Still, while the Africans struggled to establish a rhythm, Santa Cruz sought to put the game beyond them; first the watchful Lucas Radebe denied him with a last-ditch tackle, then, on the half hour, Arendse came to his team's rescue with an outstanding save after Santa Cruz had directed a low header towards the South Africa goal. South Africa were floundering and Paraguay finally got their reward. Arce fired in a wicked curling free kick and this time Santa Cruz on the far post made certain.

If the application of the South Africans was greater after the interval, their opponents' sharper cutting edge threatened to overwhelm them. Arce, a wizard with the dead ball, had already forced Arendse into a spectacular save in the first half and had a second opportunity on 55 minutes. This time his shot whistled past Arendse, striking the underside of the bar as it flew into the net. 2–0, but remarkably Jomo Sono's team began to find belief and pressed a Paraguay now electing unwisely to defend. Mokoena struck a shot which flew past Tavarelli deflected off Struway and, in a desperately tense finale, Sibusiso Zuma was brought down by Tavarelli's clumsy challenge and Quinton Fortune stepped up to convert the last minute penalty. South Africa celebrated joyously while the Paraguyans trudged off distraught.

At Gwangju, Spain, the great underachievers, met Slovenia, perhaps already the great over-achiever solely by dint of their qualification. The team led by their talented talisman, Zlatko Zahovic, showed no fear and produced an early threat, forcing Casillas into action after Zahovic had sent over a perfect corner for Knavs' header to test the goalkeeper. Soon, though, a sense of order prevailed and Spain began to dictate. Valeron was at the hub of every Spain attack and Slovenia became absorbed with trying to stop him, looking only to counter-attack through Rudonja if an opportunity presented itself. The deadlock was broken by Raul, the darling of the Bernabeu, when he swivelled to shoot home after Luis Enrique's pass had caused confusion in Slovenia's penalty area. The goal presented Slovenia with a conundrum: the positive approach that was now required would leave them open to the Spaniards' clever and precise attacking play. Still, Srecko Katanec sent on Cimirotic to galvanize his team and the substitute's presence did at least initially have the desired effect. Slovenia's robust physical football and a less negative gameplan brought parity, at least territorially. Spain, though, on 74 minutes effectively put the lid on it. De Pedro, another of Spain's star performers on the day, crossed sumptuously for Valeron to control the ball and crack a shot past Simeunovic for 2–0. To their credit Slovenia continued to look for a way back and Cimirotic, exchanging passes with Acimovic, scored to renew their hopes, and caused Spanish hearts to flutter albeit briefly. It fell to Hierro to win the game and he delivered, sweeping a penalty, given for a foul on Fernando Morientes, decisively beyond Simeunovic two minutes from time.

Argentina kicked off against Nigeria in the aptly named 'group of death', and entered a fixture where defeat might prove disastrous without Ayala and preferring the veteran Batistuta to Hernan Crespo. Nevertheless, with Veron influential in midfield the South Americans began in smooth, rhythmic fashion, dominating their opponents with patient probing passes. Nigeria's Shorunmu saved from Ariel Ortega on the half hour in a move that epitomised Argentina's dominance, but then on the counter-attack Jay-Jay Okocha produced a stunning left-footed drive which Cavallero scrambled to safety. At half-time Argentina had created little and converted nothing despite their mastery of possession.

The second-half introduction of Kily Gonzalez, though, brought about a more urgent dynamic approach and within moments Batistuta had contrived to miss when offered time and space while Sorin and Pochettino both spurned opportunities created by Veron's accurate crosses. Nigeria toiled and chased in the sunshine, offering little in return and then, almost inevitably, the goal the South Americans richly deserved arrived, provided by the leaping Batistuta with a header driven powered beyond Shorunmu on 63 minutes.

By the end it might have been worse for the Super Eagles; their muscular approach had little effect on faster, sharper opponents and their players, collectively and individually, proved a disappointment. Aimar replaced the captain Veron and the substitute teased the Nigerian defence but neither Batistuta nor Gonzalez could convert chances into the second goal their superiority merited. But it did not matter – with the three points safe they could turn their attention to Sapporo and the little matter of a game with England.

England's tournament began with what had always appeared a difficult fixture against Eriksson's native Sweden: Europe's perennial over-achievers were organized, robust and enjoying an unbeaten run against the English dating back to 1968. England began the better, though. Faster and surprisingly direct from the start, Eriksson's charges dominated, pushing Sweden onto the back foot, and took the lead when Sol Campbell's sweetly timed header from a Beckham free kick slammed past Magnus Hedman. But both sides' conspicuous endeavour apart, few chances were forthcoming and only the impressive Ashley Cole's busy forays seemed to trouble the Scandinavians.

Whatever Lars Lagerback said to his team at the interval energized the Swedes and their positive response turned the tide. Allback felt aggrieved when felled heavily by the excellent Rio Ferdinand but the referee, Carlos Simon, did not deem the challenge worthy of a penalty. Now the pressure mounted and England began to show signs of distress, most notably the captain Beckham, whose fitness worries had overshadowed Eriksson's preparations. Southampton's Anders Svensson, a substitute running against heavy-legged opponents, started to discomfort England and on the hour his side's persistence paid off. Danny Mills, failing to deal effectively with a hopeful ball, gave it back to the Swedes instead and the beneficiary of his largesse, Niclas Alexandersson, struck the ball past David Seaman.

Beckham, not before time, was replaced by Dyer but the Swedes, exerting pressure by harrying England's players, now looked the likelier winners. Seaman twice saved from Teddy Lucic and though Michael Owen did fashion one shooting opportunity – missing narrowly – England had wilted in the heat and altitude of Saitama by the end and there could be no doubt that the Swedes, physically superior, had the edge. In his post-match interview Eriksson claimed to a sceptical press corps that 'a draw was a fair result'. Argentina in Sapporo awaited.

Croatia, facing Mexico in Niigata, began brightly, taking the game to the

Central Americans with their veteran playmaker, Robert Prosinecki, influential in the early stages. Indeed, early on, the goalkeeper Oscar Perez resembled a man under siege and had to claw away a Simunic header in acrobatic fashion and then watched a Soldo shot flash over his bar. But as the half wore on, the men in green grew in stature and began to wrestle control away from the Croats – Blanco escaped his marker at a corner but headed straight at Pletikosa then Borgetti's outstretched boot failed to guide Morales's cross goalwards from close range. Although it was stalemate at the interval and Mexico had the upper hand, Croatia, as in the first, began the second half in the ascendancy. Disaster lurked on their horizon, though. Blanco, a constant nuisance to the Croats, isolated then dribbled past Zivkovic whose rustic, ill-judged tackle sent him crashing and earned Mexico a penalty and a red card for himself. Blanco dusted himself down and converted the spot kick to give Mexico the lead.

Though Croatia toiled, fruitlessly, in the sunshine their task, with ten men, looked a hopeless one. And so it proved, yet Simunic could still have saved it but his powerful header was beaten away by Oscar Perez and Mexico, in a game that for an hour at least looked destined for a draw, had all three points.

Brazil's qualification had been less than imperious and, consequently, their campaign began with less expectation than normal. Their first opponents, Turkey, surprised them with slick, inventive passing, looking ever more threatening as they grew in confidence. But Ronaldinho had the first scoring chance when he lifted the ball neatly over Rustu only to see his chip clear the crossbar. Turkey, busy in midfield and organized in defence, worked tirelessly to close the four-times winners down and then, on 20 minutes, Tugay fired goalwards, his shot deflecting off Gilberto Silva to leave Marcos stranded, but the ball clipped the bar. The game developed into the most absorbing of the tournament so far, with thrust and counter thrust. Brazil, as one would expect, set the tempo but Turkey looked assured and measured, first frustrating and then menacing the favourites. Rustu, again called into action, thwarted Rivaldo's sharp header and then had to beat away Ronaldinho's effort with his legs as the Brazilian playmaker found time and space. Then, not unexpectedly given their performance, Turkish guile crafted a goal; Basturk, clever and composed, sought out Hakan Sas and the striker outwitted his markers and beat Marcos with ease.

Typically, Brazil's response was furious and unrelenting. Five minutes into an eventful second half, the portly but still mercurial Ronaldo guided home Rivaldo's neat cross for 1–1 and the siege began in earnest. Ronaldo, Roberto Carlos, Lucio and Rivaldo all failed to extend Brazil's lead and Rivaldo was adjudged offside after netting another header. Turkey hung on and still posed danger, Hakan Unsal's sharp free kick testing Marcos, but their attacking thrusts petered out as the half continued. Brazil persisted and Rivaldo went close before the Turks' resistance was finally undone: Alpay's indiscipline in dragging down Luizao was compounded by Kim Young-Joo's error in award-ing a penalty kick for an offence a yard outside Rustu's area. Alpay was sent off and Rivaldo slotted home from twelve yards depriving the brave Turks of a point with just four minutes' pressure left to withstand. There was still time, though, for Rivaldo to sully his reputation in front of a worldwide audience by collapsing with hammily unconvincing theatricality after Unsal's aimless kick at the ball had struck him. It brought the Turk a red card but the Brazilian dis-grace and embarrassment.

At Sapporo Italy took on Ecuador, a clash between tournament stalwarts and newcomers. The South Americans, seemingly overawed by their oppo-nents and the occasion, quickly fell behind, undone by the quality of Totti and Vieri. Keeper Cevallos, already called upon to smother Vieri's shot desper-ately on seven minutes, was left floundering as the deadly duo combined for Vieri's fierce strike to put the Italians ahead. Their self-belief and nerves shred-ded, Ecuador, outplayed and outthought, retreated. Totti tested Cevallos again on 15 minutes and Italy were 2–0 up before the half hour when Di Biagio took advantage of Ecuador's careless passing to send Vieri off on a run at goal. Ivan Hurtado, trying to intervene, was brushed aside and though the Italian's goalbound effort struck Cevallos, the ball ran free and Vieri gleefully took advantage. Ecuador could not disrupt the Italians, sincerely though they tried by throwing themselves bodily into challenges. Tommasi shot over the bar then Vieri, for once, found Cevallos too good before Doni beat the overworked goalkeeper but crashed his shot onto the bar. Agustin Delgado, Ecuador's great hope, should have brought his disappointed and disappointing team some consolation at the death but Buffon's save denied them even that small consolation. At the final whistle, Ecuador could at least say that they had made their tournament bow but for Italy, in truth, it was little more than a stroll in the sun.

In Busan, Poland faced South Korea – not just the team but an entire nation, it seemed, as an outpouring of emotion and expectation greeted the co-hosts' first match. The Europeans began well enough with the determined and pacy African-born Emmanuel Olisadebe worrying the hosts by putting through Krzynowek, whose shot had power but not accuracy. Olisadebe continued to cause trouble and was prevented from scoring by a last-ditch tackle from Choi Jin-Cheul. After these early scares, South Korea slowly found their rhythm and Yoo Sang-Chul marked their growing confidence by sending Dudek flying across his goal. Dudek could do nothing on 26 minutes as Lee Eul-Yong scuttled down Poland's right-hand side to cross accurately for Hwang Sun-Hong to meet the ball with his flashing boot and send the city into an eruption of joy. Poland, palpably deflated, withered in the remorse-lessly frenzied and partisan atmosphere. After the interval, the Koreans' high-energy football looked likely to overwhelm the Poles. First Dudek had to react acrobatically to deny Park Ji-Sung but he was then left exposed on 53 minutes as Yoo Sang-Chul let fly from the edge of the area and his despairing dive almost but not quite saved his team. 2–0, and bedlam. Poland, fortunate not to be further embarrassed when Ahn Jung-Hwan stole in to force a fine save from the beleaguered Dudek, laboured gamely but to no effect. So South Korea, whose previous World Cup adventures had bordered on national humiliation, finally had their win and ambitious eyes turned to Daegu and the United States.

As the excitement in Korea began to subside, their co-hosts in Japan faced another European opponent, Belgium, in their opening fixture. Neat and tidy as they were, the Japanese appeared quite unable to threaten a strong organized defence and Belgium instead began to exploit their aerial advantage. Verheyen missed when presented with an excellent chance before the outstanding Wilmots forced Narazaki into a save on the half hour. Belgium were enjoying themselves but without reward and, before the interval, Goor joined the list of those who might have scored yet shot wide after Wilmots' drive had been scrambled away.

The home team's disappointment continued into the second half as Belgium continued to dominate and, just before the hour, the goal they had searched for duly arrived. Van Meir retrieved a Japanese clearance, returned the ball to the heart of the penalty area where Wilmots waited and the captain this time gave Narazaki no chance as his acrobatic bicycle kick flew in. Crestfallen and outplayed, fortune came to the rescue of the humbled hosts as Peeters allowed Suzuki to capitalize on his mistimed intervention and the striker raced on to shoot past De Vlieger. Japan now found belief and the stadium reverberated to the sound of new-found optimism. Thus encouraged, their team responded. Geert de Vlieger, almost superfluous for an hour, found himself leaping to prevent Ono's free kick from swinging inside his post. Then, within ten minutes of falling behind, Japan snatched the lead. Again Belgium played a part in their own downfall as Inamoto capitalized on poor passing to snatch the ball, race goalwards and beat Vlieger emphatically. Belgium, for all their effort, appeared beaten, but justice was done when Van der Heyden strode through a static defence to lift the ball expertly over Narazaki's head to make it 2–2.

China, the world's most populated nation, at last made their finals bow at Gwangju. Their opponents were Costa Rica, a country dwarfed in comparison but an equal on this stage. The Central Americans began well, stifling Chinese momentum with their hustle and bustle. Fonseca was a handful throughout and forced Li Weifeng into a save. Possession was even but Costa Rica conspired to make much more from it than their admirably energetic but less creative opponents. Solis fashioned an opportunity that he spurned and then Wallace fizzed over a cross that the much-travelled Paulo Wanchope squandered.

In the second half the Asian qualifiers lifted themselves and attacked lustily, testing Costa Rica's resolve, but for all of their effort only Wu Chengying's wicked cross threatened and even then Yang Chen could only shoot horribly wide. Costa Rica patiently waited for the breakthrough and finally struck when Gomez's back-heeled flick fell into the path of Wanchope and, though the striker's attempt was blocked, it rebounded for Gomez to score. A second followed soon after to confound the Chinese further. Gomez was again the architect, picking out Mauricio Wright's near-post dart at a short corner and the defender's header thumped into Jiang Jin's net. China persisted but were thoroughly beaten; their tremendous workrate and no little luck spared them from greater embarrassment.

At Kobe, Russia ultimately overcame Tunisia but the African qualifiers made them work hard in the unrelenting heat. Beginning in positive fashion, the Russians sought to capitalize on a string of half chances, the best of which fell to Pimenov, but the striker, launching himself into an overhead kick, could manage only to pick out Ali Boumnijel, who saved effortlessly. For all their pressure and possession, though, the Russians could not break Tunisian resistance and very nearly fell behind when Nikiforov's hurried clearance struck team mate Yuri Kovtun and rebounded narrowly wide of his own goal. Tunisia, resolute in defence and composed in possession, continued to seek a way to open up their opponents, looking for an incisive through ball. Badra almost stole onto a pass from Jaziri but Nigmatullin, alert to the danger, was a fraction quicker. Titov might have scored just before half-time with a powerful shot but 14 minutes into the second half he made no mistake, drilling the ball past Ali Boumnijel for 1–0. Five minutes later it became 2–0; Sychev threatened, bursting into the Tunisian penalty area, and the otherwise outstanding Jaidi committed the rashest of challenges. Karpin scored from the spot to seal Russia's victory.

Portugal's vaunted 'golden generation' took on the unfancied Americans in Group D at Suwon and promptly fell apart in bewildering fashion. Victor Baia's fumble presented John O'Brien with the first goal and calamitous defending allowed Landon Donovan to steal the ball from Costa and drive in a second courtesy of a deflection. 2–0 down and in disarray but worse was to follow for the Portuguese on 36 minutes when the fallibility of Baia and his defenders was demonstrated again as Ernie Stewart's simple cross eluded them all and Kevin McBride completed the simplest of tasks with a neat header to go 3–0 up. The Americans, organized and efficient against an opponent who was not, had an unassailable lead. Portugal improved but their substantial efforts after the interval, doubtless inspired by Beto's 39th-minute goal, proved too little too late. An own goal by Agoos, diverting Pauleta's cross past his own goalkeeper with 20 minutes remaining, was scant consolation as the USA deservedly held out for a memorable victory.

THE SECOND SERIES

In Ibaraki, the Republic of Ireland met a German side rejuvenated by their triumphant opening game. The Irish, as compelling as ever, tore into their opponents from the start, pushing them back onto the defensive in their search for an opening. Typically patient, the Germans waited and the chance, when it finally came, fell their way; Ballack, instrumental in all their better moments, crossed and Klose, allowed room, rose to direct his header beyond Shay Given. Stung, the Irish responded furiously; Matt Holland seized on an indecisive clearance to fire narrowly wide. Ireland persisted, dominating possession at times, and Duff and Kilbane caused great discomfort with their surging runs while Germany contented themselves with counter attacking. From one such surge forward, Ballack forced Given to leap across his goal to save. Irish hearts looked set for breaking, but then, as the final seconds ticked by, Niall Quinn rose to head the ball into the run of Robbie Keane and the striker fired it emphatically beyond Oliver Kahn's reach.

In a poor game at Saitama Cameroon put paid to Saudi Arabia with a 1–0 victory made difficult by profligate finishing. The Saudis, savaged so ruthlessly by the Germans, began cautiously, survived an early penalty appeal and sought to catch the Indomitable Lions on the break. Al Dossari almost managed it but his header flew too high. Cameroon dictated play and the Saudis, determined not to suffer further humiliation, concentrated largely on defending. Twice the Africans had the ball in the net, first Mboma and then Lauren, though neither escaped the referee's assistant's flag. Occasional raids from the Saudis and prolonged Cameroon attacks were the order of this day. Eto'o, given a golden opportunity, fired wastefully wide and an improbable draw seemed possible until Eto'o atoned. On 64 minutes Geremi played a ball in behind the Saudi defenders, Eto'o latched onto it in a flash, took careful aim and struck his shot fiercely past Al Daeyea. The Saudis, obviously disappointed but frankly ill-equipped to play at the highest level this time, had deservedly lost.

Denmark versus Senegal in Daegu was at times tedious in the oppressive heat. The Danes, ignoring the conditions, started fast with Gravesen and the combative Tofting establishing control of the midfield. Some ill-tempered shenanigans preceded any football when Diao, trying to escape Sand, was disgracefully hacked down, prompting protracted pushing and shoving from both teams. Fadiga, principal amongst the protagonists, joined Sand in the referee's notebook. Diao's day was set to be an eventful one and shortly afterwards he knocked Jon Dahl Tomasson to the ground to concede a penalty. The victim of the clumsy challenge calmly shot past Sylva for a 1–0 lead. Senegal were rocked and, though Diao leapt to head a corner goalward only to be denied by Sorensen's acrobatics, the Danes, neat and incisive, retained control. Tomasson beat Sylva again, bringing the ball down and shooting home, but his effort was disallowed by Mr Batres who remarkably saw a handball that no one else did. The Senegalese, who had looked such a force against France, were exposed by the busy Danes. Senegal grew stronger after the interval; either that or the Danes, playing in such unfamiliar strength-sapping conditions, began to weaken. Fired by their two substitutes, Henri and Souleymane Kamara, the Africans significantly improved and seven minutes in had an equaliser made by football of speed and precision, again with the industrious Diao at its hub. The ball zipped from player to player before falling into his path; picking his spot he swept the ball beyond Sorensen. Galvanized, Senegal pressed and Denmark subsided. Souleymane Camara and El Hadji Diouf both wasted decent openings before Diao completed his memorable day by collecting a red card for his disgraceful lunge at Henriksen.

France, so disappointed by defeat on the opening day, sought redemption against Uruguay in Busan. Beginning confidently, the French built up momentum. Uruguay waited patiently, watchful of Henry and Trezeguet. Both escaped defenders in the early going but neither could beat the offside trap. At the other end, the irrepressible Alvaro Recoba threatened, though Barthez, reacting quickly, saved comfortably. For Roger Lemerre, the beleaguered French coach, matters beyond his control were about to influence proceedings. France's great hope, Thierry Henry, all subtlety, style and speed, condemned them to a desperate struggle when his clumsy challenge on Romero resulted in a red card, leaving ten Frenchmen to face eleven Uruguayans. Still France persisted, Emmanuel Petit's driven free kick crashing against the post with Carini a spectator. That, though, was that as the half petered out in the balmy conditions. The second period predictably showed no great improvement, both sides looking to steal victory. Recoba might have managed just that for Uruguay, forcing Barthez into a fine stop. Then, exploiting Barthez's eccentric decision-making, he beat the goalkeeper to the ball but, forced wide, was unable to control his shot. Micoud went close and, at the death, Wiltord snatched at a presentable opportunity but, for all their industry, victory always seemed beyond France's grasp. Worse still, Frederico Magallanes might have condemned them to defeat but the alert Barthez did just enough to thwart him.

Spain met Paraguay as they had in 1998 and the South Americans, who so upset their rivals four years earlier, began with the same intent. Slicker and quicker to the ball, they pressurized the Spaniards and snatched a bizarre goal. Awarded a free kick, up stepped Chilavert, goalkeeper and eternal maverick, whose long punt down field was met by Carlos Puyol but the defender's header fell into the path of Arce, who shot powerfully at goal. Casillas proved good enough, just, to beat the ball away, but to no avail as it struck poor Puyol and flew back into the net.

Spain, to their credit, knuckled down and began slowly to take control. Raul, elusive and enigmatic as ever, created a series of half chances but took none and then, as the half closed, Paraguay threatened again. Ilker Casillas pursued an aimless cross-field ball and found himself in no man's land giving Roque Santa Cruz the opportunity to capitalize as the ball fell to him but Puyol, a commanding figure in spite of his earlier misfortune, did just enough to deny the striker.

Duly warned, in the second half Camacho made the substitution that unlocked the Paraguayan door. On came Morientes for the ineffective Tristan and Spanish dominance was finally converted into goals, Morientes himself, on 53 minutes, thumping a head past Chilavert. Paraguay's rare forays forward seldom suggested menace though Casillas, this time wisely, left his goal to foil Santa Cruz. Spain looked favourites and Morientes, perhaps eager to cement his place in the starting line up, proved a handful for an increasingly ragged Paraguay defence. The Real Madrid striker seized on to a through ball, advanced and lifted his shot wastefully high of Chilavert's goal but then, with 20 minutes left, took a golden chance presented by the goalkeeper as the Paraguayan captain left his line to intercept De Pedro's cross and missed it. It was 2–1 but not quite game over as Raul tricked his way into the area and went down for a penalty. Up stepped Hierro, calmly slotting home, and Spain had won and won well.

Back in the group of death, Sweden faced Nigeria in Kobo. Punished for a sluggish first half against England, here the Swedes stormed out of the blocks, their opponents appearing to wilt under the onslaught. Two chances fell their way, both missed, and it was Nigeria who took the lead on 27 minutes. Joseph Yobo carried the ball forward swiftly before picking out the run of Junior Aghahowa and a simple header was all that was required to pick Sweden's pocket.

In perhaps the most eagerly anticipated fixture of the entire group stages England met Argentina with national pride and a fierce rivalry on the line. England began the better, controlling the early stages, with Beckham, who had been so out of sorts against the Swedes, prominent this time. Michael Owen too, a player the South Americans had good reason to be wary of, worried them with clever movement and on 24 minutes almost gave his team the lead when he collected a pass from Butt before squeezing his shot beneath Cavallero onto the upright and off to safety. Argentina, largely outplayed, contained but showed little momentum going forward. England stuck to their task, bullying in midfield, probing, and then, just a minute from half time, had their reward. Owen, wriggling into the area, was felled by Pochettino and Beckham, to wild acclaim, thumped home the penalty kick.

After the interval there was more of the same but opportunities for Owen, Beckham, Scholes and Sheringham all failed to add to the English tally and slowly, remorselessly, the Argentinians began to take control as England tired. Pochettino, hoping to make amends, came closest of all but his shot was brilliantly saved by Seaman. England, undoubtedly the better side, had the win they fully deserved.

If Italy's first win had bred overconfidence, then Croatia in Ibaraki quickly dispelled them of it, as the Croatians won, somewhat controversially, by 2–1. Typically, the Italians sat back, inviting Croatia to attack them and the resulting opening half proved a dull, sterile affair with just one goalscoring opportunity – Rapaic's shot wonderfully saved by Buffon.

But the second half began in scintillating fashion when Vieri powered a header into the net only to be judged offside. Four minutes later, though, the striker made amends, out-jumping Croatian defenders to meet Doni's cross and beat Pletikosa. As is their wont, the Azzuri then contented themselves with the cautious preservation of their 1–0 lead and this time paid the price. Seventeen minutes remained when Robert Jarni fired the ball into Buffon's area and Olic, sharper than the defenders, reacted fastest to slot home the equaliser. Three minutes later, Rapaic, perhaps the game's outstanding performer, snatched what proved the winner, his speculative effort striking Materazzi to deflect past the unfortunate Buffon. Italy's response, predictably frenetic, saw Totti strike a post from a free kick, then hit the back of the net only for the goal to be disallowed for Inzaghi's sly foul. Italy had no way back and only themselves to blame – they had contributed to the manner of their defeat by their perplexing negativity.

For China, the disappointment of defeat at the hands of Costa Rica left them facing Brazil knowing failure would mean almost certain elimination. As if inspired, they began brightly, testing Marcos in the early stages and causing their celebrated opponents some discomfort. Brazil waited for their opportunity and, when it came on 15 minutes, struck in devastating fashion. Ronaldinho broke forward purposefully, only to be bundled off the ball and Roberto Carlos stepped up to take the free kick, twenty-five yards out. The squat, muscular full back, deadly or dreadful from set pieces, this time elected to be the former, drilling the ball fiercely beyond the reach of Jiang Jin. The lead curbed China's enthusiasm and Brazil began to run the men in red ragged. Cafu broke through, driving the ball at Jiang Jin, while Ronaldo, waiting for a Roberto Carlos pass, saw Wu Chengying intervene. Brazil persevered despite dogged resistance then Du Wei, heading the ball away, placed it into the path of Ronaldinho, whose cross picked out Rivaldo's run to double their lead. Mightily though they tried, China fell further behind by the interval; Ronaldo was impeded by both Lei Weifeng and Du Wei in the penalty area and Ronaldinho converted the spot kick. Trailing 3–0 going into the second half, China's commitment was admirable but they continued to be picked apart, not least by the craft of Ronaldinho and the bustling power of Ronaldo. The big centre forward had bided his time until Cafu finally gave him his chance when the captain danced away from two defenders before sliding the ball into his path and Ronaldo finished with aplomb.

The suspicion during the last 30 minutes was that the South Americans, sated by a four-goal lead, had relaxed but China enjoyed their best moments as the clock ran down – Junzhe struck a post, and then Shao Jiayi forced Marcos into a flying save. By full time China, though goalless, had salvaged pride and Brazil had predictably claimed their place in the knock out stages.

In Group B Slovenia conceded a goal within three minutes, showed little stomach for the fight thereafter, and went down to a second defeat, this time to South Africa, in Daegu. Siyabonga Nomvethe gave Bafana Bafana the lead when he bundled in Fortune's deep penetrating cross. Fortune, involved in much of his team's better work, went close himself from a free kick after a foul on Benni McCarthy but, in truth, the fare on offer was mediocre at best.

Internal shenanigans, including the sending home of captain Zlatko Zahovic for a Roy Keanesque breach of discipline, had hampered Slovenian morale, and their performance was further handicapped by the expulsion from the dug out of coach Katanec. It was not their day. McCarthy continued to threaten, first shooting sharply on the turn to force Simeunovic to save, then leaping to head against the woodwork with the goalkeeper beaten. It hardly mattered; like a boxer unable to deliver a knockout punch against an opponent who cannot fight, the Africans laboured for a second goal that would not come. Again McCarthy, inside the penalty area, shot straight at Simeunovic who saved without difficulty. Slovenia did manufacture one chance, a good one, when Ceh's header was kept out by Arendse, but their overall effort had been feeble. South Africa's coach, Jomo Sono, declared afterwards: 'It was not a nice game, but we didn't come here to play a nice game, we came to win.' That, at least, had been achieved.

In Group H a fiercely determined Japan did just enough to edge out Russia, helped by an astonishingly frenzied atmosphere at Yokohama. The co-hosts started at a furious pace, Inamoto surging upfield and lashing his shot narrowly wide of Nigmatullin's goal. Russia, briefly unsettled, slowly found their way into the game and might have snatched the lead when Marat Izmailov sent his shot screaming by Narazaki's post with the goalkeeper beaten on 15 minutes. Russia's attacking ambition, though, was thwarted by the willingness of the Japanese to commit numbers up front. Hidetoshi Nakata, the country's most famous footballer, shot wastefully high after Koji had skipped by Solomatin. For all their determination, though, Japan were vulnerable to Russia's thoughtful tactics – Narazaki was twice called into desperate action, first to dive at the feet of Pimenov and then to cut out Nikiforov's incisive pass. Miyamoto, in a protective mask, and Matsuda were working hard to plug the gaps. After the interval, Japan roared on and continued their frantic assault on the Russian goal; six minutes in they gained their reward. Koji Nakata, a thorn in Russia's side, swept another cross into their penalty area where Yanagisawa won it and knocked the ball into the path of Inamoto who thwacked his shot into the net. Russia did not wilt but were eventually ground down by a team running on adrenaline. True, Beschastnykh could and should have equalized before the hour yet misdirected his shot after weaving around the goalkeeper, but Japan had the upper hand. Nakata set up Yanagisawa, who fired hopelessly high, and then the playmaker tried himself, crashing a raking shot against the cross bar with Nigmatullin helpless. It didn't matter; Japan had their win and one foot in the knock-out stages.

Costa Rica's game against Turkey in Incheon was a tense, tight encounter whose result satisfied neither team. Costa Rica created the first opportunity, Wanchope given room to strike a volley, but the ball flew just high. The Turks looked neat and imaginative going forward and Hakan Sas was a menacing presence but their defending was less than adequate at times. Much huffing and puffing ensued without a genuine goal-scoring opportunity until Centeno found himself through on Recber's goal on the half-hour but blasted over the bar. The second half began with a quicker tempo; Hakan Sas twice threatened and, at the other end, Gomez caused further anxiety to the static Turkish defenders but his shot curled wide. It fell to one of the game's more influential players to break the deadlock: Emre, so composed in his World Cup finals' debut, found room to shoot and, seeing the ball cannon back to him off Martinez, swiftly controlled the rebound then steered it past Lonnis in Costa Rica's goal. The hitherto positive Turks foolishly elected to defend once ahead and the Central Americans duly accepted the invitation to take the initiative. Wilmer Lopez first blazed wildly over the bar, and then forced Rustu Recber into a diving save but his team's persistence finally got the reward it deserved. Again poor defending helped and Winston Park took full advantage from close range. Just five minutes remained and Turkey, who should have had it wrapped up by now, came close to losing as Park missed from a testing angle with the keeper beaten. It ended at 1–1 but why a team who did not appear able to defend sought to do so was a conundrum only Senol Gunes, the Turkish coach, could answer.

To Miyagi where Mexico, looking an impressive outfit at times, accounted for Ecuador. The South Americans, though, started in fine fashion, rocking the Mexicans in the fifth minute. Agustin Delgado, Ecuador's talisman, leapt to meet De la Cruz's cross and beat Oscar Perez with a powerful header. Once ahead, Ecuador were content to contain, stifling Mexican creativity and retreating in numbers. Mexico floundered, their flowing passing breaking down before disciplined defending, but just before the half hour they found a way back: Morales crossed from the left for Borgetti to control and volley a shot past Cevallos at the far post. Parity restored, Mexico were rampant but could not score. Blanco, with the best opportunity, found the ball trapped beneath him and hurried his shot tamely goalward. After the interval, Mexico dominated and 12 minutes in Torrado scored superbly as he collected Borgetti's pass, ran at the defence at pace and fired beyond Cevallos. Ecuador tried to rally but their efforts left them vulnerable to the counter; Borgetti twice failed to punish them but his wastefulness had no impact on the result. Mexico were easily the better team and deserved their victory.

It is arguable that the USA, in Daegu, played in front of the most intimidating crowd in the tournament's rich history. Sixty thousand partisan supporters clad in South Korean red created a wall of sound that threatened to engulf the Americans. Against the odds, however, the States produced a performance full of self-belief and courage. It was no great surprise to anyone that the Koreans started at a blistering pace, forcing the USA to do little more than hold out. Their staunchness in the face of such pressure was rewarded when, to the chagrin of the co-hosts, they took a 24th-minute lead through Mathis. The Asians, noticeably stunned, almost fell further behind but Landon Donovan was swiftly crowded out. Then, having failed to craft a single significant chance, Korea were gifted one as half-time approached when Hwang Sun-Hong moved into the area and Agoos clattered into him. A penalty was awarded and pandemonium broke out in the stands. Lee Eul-Yong, a man under almost intolerable pressure, bravely stepped forward and struck his shot well but Friedel clawed the ball away and Nam-il missed the parried rebound. After the interval South Korea cranked up the pressure, feeling for a way through. Friedel first produced a stunning save from Ki-Hyeon and then, as Korea turned the screw, pulled off another to frustrate Yong-Soo. America were closing in on the three points when, with 12 minutes left, Friedel was finally beaten. Jung-Hwan leapt to direct a header beyond the big goalkeeper's reach and spark a huge celebration, part joy, part relief. At the end Yong-Soo found himself alone with the opportunity to be a hero but he was not up to the task, shooting horribly high and wide. Korea probably deserved more but Friedel and his gallant team-mates had won their point.

Poland had the misfortune in Jeonju to meet a determined, vastly improved Portugal who were eager to make amends for their embarrassing defeat by the USA. In appalling conditions, Portugal set about the Poles and had the lead on the quarter hour. Pauleta received Pinto's pass with little sign of imminent danger, dismissed his marker with a nimble turn and fired past Jerzy Dudek for 1–0. But, hindered by torrential rain, neither side impressed, though Portugal looked the stronger, better-organized unit while Poland were as humdrum as they had been against South Korea. In the second half, Portugal showed greater desire and took their chances; Pauleta snatched his second on 65 minutes, finishing off a cross from Luis Figo, forcing Poland, dismal in all areas, to fall apart. The star of the show waltzed past desperate defenders to score his hat-trick 12 minutes later and Rui Costa made it 4–0 three minutes from time as Jerzy Dudek was left exposed by shamelessly inept defending again. Third in the competition twice, it was difficult to accept that Poland with such a good pedigree could be so feeble here.

Belgium were clear favourites before their Group H encounter with Tunisia but, having taken the lead, lost it and, in spite of their best efforts, were forced to settle for a draw. Tunisia began with surprising confidence, taking the game to their opponents throughout a first half they shaded. For all their neatness, though, they conceded early when Marc Wilmots lashed in an inviting pass from Strupar on thirteen minutes. To their credit, the Tunisian reply was immediate and impressive, Bouzaine beating de Vlieger emphatically with a driven, curling free kick to equalize. The goal galvanized the Africans, who then produced their best moments in their quest to take the lead, but Jaziri, their industrious attacker, failed disappointingly to put them ahead having worked an opening. The pace of the game in oppressive heat and humidity dropped in the second half and the Tunisians surrendered the initiative. Belgium pressed and probed to no benefit and then, exhausted, almost lost it at the finish when de Vlieger had to move smartly to save from Ghodbane in the last minute.

THE THIRD SERIES

In a quite remarkable match in Group A, a compelling story unfolded as Senegal, dismissed by most as no hopers, clung on to qualify by the skin of their teeth for the round of sixteen while Uruguay, twice world champions, were sent home. The South Americans needed a win to guarantee their progress and laid siege to the Senegal goal in the opening period but without success. The Africans again proved obstinate foes and regrouped to strike back through Diouf, whose surge towards goal was impeded by the goalkeeper Carini. The referee awarded a penalty amid furious protests from Uruguay and Khalilou Fadiga stepped up to give Senegal the lead. Once bitten, Uruguay proceeded to be mauled again seven minutes later when Camara, leading the counter attack, stormed forward and passed to Diop, who blasted into Carini's goal. Worse misfortune was to befall Uruguay in the 38th minute as Diop scored Senegal's third with a fierce shot which the Uruguayans protested had been struck from an off-side position. Their plight seemingly desperate, Morales brought Uruguay some hope with a simple finish early in the second half. The goal encouraged Uruguay to go for the improbable win at full pelt but only 20 minutes remained when Diego Forlan, from what looked an innocuous position, struck a quite wonderful shot past Sylva. Now 3–2, Senegal slowly, almost imperceptibly, began to wilt under the pressure and tension. Then, with three minutes left, another penalty added to the drama. Recoba scored from the spot and his team began their desperate pursuit of a winner. They should have snatched it too but, right at the death,

Morales failed miserably from point-blank range with a header that should have bought glory and not ignominy. Of course Uruguay had been unfortunate, but most neutrals chose instead to celebrate the achievement of Senegal, the most gallant of underdogs.

Although France, the reigning champions, introduced a half-fit Zinedine Zidane at Incheon, Denmark, thoroughly efficient, dispatched them 2–0 to move into the last sixteen. The French started in spritely fashion with Zidane prominent and Trezeguet profligate, shooting wildly wide when Wiltord was free on 18 minutes. The thought lingered that as Denmark at first pressured and ultimately shackled Zidane, French confidence might be fragile and, on 22 minutes, their resolve was put to the test when Tofting floated a ball in to Rommedahl whose instant shot left Barthez groping. Once behind France responded, forcing Sorensen into a succession of saves, notably from Cisse and Trezeguet. Zidane too went close, reminding the Danes of the folly of giving him room in the 38th minute, and his instant control and exquisite chip almost brought the equaliser his team deserved. But it was not to be. France continued to press, Denmark countered; Marcel Desailly, ambling upfield, struck a post with a fierce shot but then the Danes wrapped it up when Jon Dahl Tomasson's emphatic finish made it 2–0 with 20 minutes left. There was still time for Trezeguet to hit the woodwork but, lacking form and fortune, the champions were eliminated on the final whistle.

Germany looked uncomfortable against a spirited Cameroon side but still did enough to claim all three points and a place in the last sixteen. Cameroon seemed inspired by their precarious position in the group and Alioum almost gave them the lead but was thwarted by the quick-thinking Kahn. The Africans' gung-ho approach unsettled the Germans, forcing Linke, following a scramble, to threaten his own goal. Song too might have scored when left unmarked at a corner before Germany added to their own problems. Ramelow, left for dead by Eto'o, tripped the striker and received the red card following an earlier yellow. Cameroon had their chances to exploit their superiority in numbers but it swiftly deserted them when Germany sent on Bode. Only four minutes of the second half had been played when the substitute galloped onto Klose's pass to slide the ball past Alioum. The goal galvanized the men in white and though Cameroon attacked, their best attempts came to little and frustration grew. Suffo, who was only on the field for 24 minutes as substitute before he received a red card for two yellows, left the field a symbol of the Indomitable Lions' despair. Then, to confirm their elimination, Klose rose to meet Ballack's cross and headed home emphatically for 2–0.

Ireland, as expected, easily overcame Saudi Arabia, winning 3–0 in Yokohama and progressed through to the knock-out stage. Needing to win by two goals, Ireland understandably attacked from the off and their policy reaped rewards, Gary Kelly, the least likely of scorers, galloping onto Steve

Staunton's clever pass and rifling the ball into the net. Instead of collapsing as they had against Germany, the Saudis demonstrated new-found resolve and resisted and could have snatched an equaliser before half-time but Shay Given reacted quickly to deny Al-Jahani.

After the interval the game of cat and mouse continued as the Irish pursued the second goal that would guarantee qualification and their patient probing eventually paid dividends. Staunton was again the provider when he delivered an accurate cross from a free kick for Gary Breen to apply the simplest finish. A third followed through Damien Duff, a raiding tormentor all evening, but it barely mattered.

Argentina, South American's finest or so it had once seemed, failed to beat the muscular, organized Swedes at Miyagi and thus were sent packing. The Argentinians at last displayed real purpose and drive but were undone by their inability to take the numerous chances created. Hedman was pressed into action as early as the 14th minute by Sorin and Sweden's goalkeeper saw the diminutive Claudio Lopez take aim three times but shoot wide as the South Americans ended the first half in control but without reward. Sweden, perhaps astonished to be level at the break, must have anticipated a furious second-half onslaught. They were not to be disappointed as Argentina quickened the tempo, desperately striving for a goal to save themselves; Batistuta might have scored, sending a header narrowly wide, and Sorin had a chance beaten away. Then, wholly against the run of play, the Scandinavians snatched the lead when Anders Svensson was fouled by Almeyda and took the resulting free kick, beating Cavallero from thirty yards with a swinging, dipping shot that crashed into the net. It was cruel but Argentina courageously continued to redress the set-back; first Aimar's shot was saved then Zanetti was denied by the big goalkeeper. At the other end Anders Andersson, benefiting from Argentina's total commitment to attack, found himself alone but unable to hit the target. Just when it seemed over, the champions of 1978 and '86 almost found salvation at the death when Jonson fouled Ortega and the little man picked himself up to take the penalty kick. His shot was kept out by Hedman but Crespo, on for Batistuta, slotted in the rebound for 1–1. Two minutes remained for a frantic assault but their efforts proved in vain. At the end the Swedes celebrated joyously while the group favourites were left in despair.

In a group that had hardly sent the pulses racing, Paraguay emerged as qualifiers behind Spain courtesy of a resilient effort against Slovenia in Seogwipo. There could hardly have been a worse possible start for the South Americans when an edgy opening period culminated in Carlos Paredes's red card for a reckless lunge at Acimovic. Sensing an opportunity, Slovenia pressed their advantage methodically but their goal, when it came on the stroke of half-time, owed more to Chilavert's generous goalkeeping than invention as Acimovic fired home from a tight angle. Immediately after the interval

Acimovic came close again with Chilavert beaten but a second goal eluded them. Paraguay clung on and then struck back. First Cuevas strode forward, cut inside and shot left-footed past Dabanovic then, five minutes later, Campos, given time and space, fired a low, fierce shot into the net from twenty yards. Slovenia's disappointment manifested itself in Nastja Ceh's ugly tackle and his subsequent red card and three minutes later Cuevas capped Paraguay's come-back by skipping past two defenders before beating Dabanovic all ends up with a shot that flew in off the underside of the cross bar. 3–1 was good enough for the South Americans and there was better news still from Daegu where South Africa were playing Spain.

There, South Africa went out, having failed to take the point they needed against Spain to finish the group ahead of Paraguay. Their performance, though, had been admirably brave. That silky predator Raul scored in the fourth minute, capitalizing on a simple handling error by Arendse to put the ball into an empty net. The keeper redeemed himself, though, with a spectacular save to deny Morientes and South Africa, suitably inspired, were level within a minute as McCarthy, put through by Nomvethe, rifled his shot past Casillas. Bafana Bafana kept up the pace, their sorties often prompted by Fortune's energetic surges, and troubled Spain. But, as half-time approached, the Africans fell behind again when Morientes scored direct from a free kick. Undeterred at 2–1 down, South Africa rallied in the 53rd minute when Lucas Radebe smashed in a header from a corner. But Spain's quality had long threatened to be the decisive factor and so it proved when, just three minutes later at another corner, Raul stole in and headed emphatically beyond Arendse. South Africa strived to the end to get the point to secure their progress but the more they threw caution to the wind, the more vulnerable they were to Spain's cunning. Their disappointment at the end was multiplied swiftly by news of Paraguay's victory that had sent them home.

In Osaka England faced Nigeria in a tame draw between one team – England – needing a point and the other content with one. Nigeria initially showed ambition, constantly trying to thread the ball through to the hard-running Aghahowa, but England, curiously lethargic after their blood and thunder encounter with Argentina, eventually shook themselves awake and took control. Heskey had a chance smothered by Enyeama, Okocha and Beckham traded free kicks and Owen shot wide of the target. As half-time approached Nicky Butt's dominance of midfield had put England in the ascendancy and they became progressively stronger in the second half. But the goal to settle their nerves proved elusive: Beckham wasted a free-kick and twice Teddy Sheringham ghosted into good positions without troubling Enyeama. Meanwhile Nigeria, their World Cup over long before, sat back, happy to escape with a draw that was easily achieved once England's energy and enthu-siasm expired in the heat towards the end. For Sven-Goran Eriksson's team, consolation for this drab affair came in their qualification for the last sixteen.

In Group D at Incheon, South Korea, again setting a blistering pace, destroyed the World Cup ambitions of fragile, disappointing Portugal. Under pressure early-on and facing the home nation's fanatical support, Portugal were forced onto the defensive right from the start. After four minutes Yong-Pyo went close with a fiercely struck effort that set the tone for a half marked by a Korean barrage of crosses and through balls. Portugal's tricky task looked hopeless when Joao Pinto was red-carded on 26 minutes for a filthy challenge on Park Ji-Sung, a symbol perhaps of Portugal's exasperation. With their ten men visibly wilting, Portugal were relieved to see Ki-Hyeon's goal ruled out for a foul but, as the half closed, Pauleta, lethal against the Poles, spurned a great chance to mug South Korea by firing miserably wide from Figo's exquisite pass. The second half brought the Europeans little respite as Korea surged forward. Ki-Hyeon, Sang-Chul and Nam-il all went close before Portugal's indiscipline betrayed them again and handed the match to their hosts. Beto joined Joao Pinto in the showers by dragging down Young-Pyo leaving the already run-ragged Portuguese nine men to hold out. Korea, though, would not allow them to and on 70 minutes Ji-Sung controlled a cross, beat Couto and shot past Baia to take the lead. Having endured a dismal tournament with their talisman Figo an anonymous, frustrated passenger, Portugal now, and to their great credit, finally sprang into life and fought bravely for World Cup survival. Figo shot wide from a free kick, Conceicao struck the inside of the post only to see it run away to safety and then brought Woon-Jae into action with a rasping shot. Their belated response was a case of too little too late; lacking composure and confidence, the Portuguese were out. But South Korea's adventure had only just begun.

Brazil in Suwon predictably accounted for the bold Costa Ricans, who attacked at every opportunity but were found too often to be vulnerable to swift counter-attacks. It might have been different had Mauricio Wright taken advantage of a ninth-minute chance from six yards but his header flew too high and within five minutes Brazil had a two-goal lead. Ronaldo, the tormentor, first hit a deflected shot past Lonnis and then, allowed room inside the penalty area, advanced to beat him again from close range. The shaken Costa Ricans tried to respond and Martin wasted an excellent cross with a misdirected header. But then Brazil had their third after Edmilson nonchalantly beat poor Lonnis with an acrobatic overhead kick from twenty yards out. It looked like humiliation was on the horizon for the Central Americans but Wanchope's goal a minute later, neatly moving onto Wright's pass to beat Marcos, gave them hope. In the second half Brazil gave the impression they might score at will but Costa Rica continued to throw men forward and they were rewarded with a second goal as Gomez, diving acrobatically, met Centeno's cross to punish Marcos. But if Brazil had doubts, it did not show; Rivaldo scored a fourth from ten yards six minutes later, then Junior made it 5–2. Costa Rica had done their best, commendably so, but had been ruthlessly exposed and the news from Seoul where Turkey were playing China was even more depressing.

Needing to beat China in Seoul, the Turks did so and, to their great delight, advanced at the expense of Costa Rica. They began in perfect fashion too, as the clever, crafty Hakan Sas took advantage of dire communication in the Chinese defence to steal the ball and beat goalkeeper Jiang Jin with ease. Three minutes later, Sas escaped down the touchline and his driven cross was met by Bulent Korkmaz and, in spite of Li Xiaopeng's attentions, his header looped into the net. China fought back as Turkey complacently sat on their lead but eagerly though they pressed, Yang Chen's snap shot against the foot of the post was as good as it got.

Turkey's response to China's pressure came after the break. More urgent now, they regrouped and began to resume control of the game. Umit Davala almost decided matters, his header cleared off the line, before substitute Shao Jiayi did, his clattering challenge on Emre earning a red card. China's tiny glimmer of hope went with him. At ten men versus eleven, Turkey's showboaters indulged themselves, moving the ball around with ease. Jiang Jin did manage to keep out Hakan Sur's close range header but five minutes from time Davala added a third, sweeping Sas's inviting past into the net. Turkey, given their chance, had taken it with glee. In contrast, China were a turgid disappointment.

Croatia had aspirations of another extended run in the tournament but were outplayed and eliminated by the vibrant Ecuador in Yokohama. In truth, Croatia's lacklustre performance still produced enough first half chances to beat the South Americans but Alen Boksic's ill-fortune in front of goal doomed his team. First he swivelled and struck a hard, accurate shot onto the goal post, and then Hurtado robbed him with the goalkeeper beaten. Ecuador's neatness led to good spells of possession but they created little to concern Pletikosa and, as the interval approached, Boksic again failed to give Croatia the lead when his shot once more beat Cevallos but not the defender, this time Poroso, who scrambled to head clear. Lethargic but still the more likely team to score, Croatia were shaken from their slumbers after the break as Delgado climbed to flick on to Mendez, who struck the ball past Pletikosa to steal the lead. With almost 45 minutes to hold out, Ecuador must have feared a siege. Instead, though anxiety brought a higher tempo, Croatia produced less in terms of goal threats and in spite of Olic's header being beaten away in the final moments, Ecuador held out in relative comfort.

Italy, playing Mexico in Oita, left it late but avoided the abyss as both teams celebrated qualification for the last sixteen at the end. With uncharacteristically attacking tactics, the Italians pressed hard against their skilful opponents and would have taken an early lead had the linesman's flag been as accurate as Totti's pass to Inzaghi; the striker's shot was precise but the offside flag was not. Although Italy were the more forceful side, the Mexican's delightfully intricate passing kept them at bay. Vieri could have scored twice but he misdirected one shot and the other was well saved. Totti, too, spurned a decent chance. Having survived this onslaught, the Mexicans added to Italy's frustration by sweeping the ball into the path of Blanco whose delightful cross found the head of Borghetti to put his team ahead. Italy ratcheted up the pressure in the second half while Mexico were content to hit on the break. Then Italy were again denied by a poor off-side decision as Montella beat Perez. When the same player shot wide with seven minutes remaining they were cursing the fates that seemed to have conspired to deny them. They were deliriously relieved, then, when Del Piero arrived to meet Montella's cross two minutes later and sent a header flashing past Perez and into Mexico's net.

Over in Osaka, Japan's incessant adrenaline-fuelled attacking play predictably accounted for Tunisia, who surrendered meekly, perhaps intimidated by their opponents' remarkable supporters. The Africans looked intent on riding out Japan's storm and adopted a siege mentality, inviting their rivals to take territorial advantage and dominate. Japan, prompted by Nakata, were happy to oblige and attacked as Tunisia defended throughout the first half. This they achieved to good effect, stifling and frustrating their hyped-up hosts. Then, to everyone's surprise including, possibly, their own, they almost scavenged a good goal when Khaled Badra leapt to head a corner but it lacked aim. Japan changed personnel in the second half as coach Philippe Troussier replaced Yanagisawa and, more curiously, the crafty Junichi Inamoto and his substitutes swiftly rewarded his gamble. Morishima had been on for just three minutes and scarcely been noticed when he arrived in the penalty area to drive his shot past Ali Boumnijel and into Tunisia's net. Given little to cheer before, the sell-out crowd were sent into frenzied hysteria by the goal. Tunisia, facing elimination, tried to be more positive but to little effect and Hidetoshi Nakata, Japanese football's poster boy, put the lid on it with a header to make it 2–0. Japan were through and a nation celebrated with wild abandon.

Belgium and Russia were both intent on qualification from Group H in Shizuoka but, by the narrowest of margins, it was Les Diables who celebrated at the final whistle. Belgium, beneath Russia in the table before kick-off, began the better and had the lead within seven minutes, Walem capitalizing on a clumsy foul by Solomatin on the buccaneering Wilmots by curling a beautiful free kick into Nigmatullin's net. Shaken, Russia found themselves in danger of being overrun with Wilmots and Mpenza hounding them. Solomatin, culpable for the Belgian goal, almost made amends but saw his goalbound shot charged down. Yet Russia were relieved at the interval to be trailing by just the one goal and they had the profligate Verheyen to thank as he twice missed simple chances. For the second half a bolder, better Russia surfaced, galvanized, arguably, by the knowledge that Belgium might already have done for them. Sychev, stealing in, might have equalized but De Vlieger's save instead rebounded to Beschastnykh who blasted the ball into the net to level it. The scorer might have given Russia the lead moments later but his header flew wide. At 1–1 the Belgians were on the precipice, but a four-minute passage, late in the second half, changed everything. On 78 minutes substitute Wesley Sonck leapt to head past Nigmatullin and then, as Russia reeled, the unselfish, outstanding Marc Wilmots grabbed a Belgian third. There was time left for Sychev to take it to 3–2 with a well-taken consolation goal but Belgium qualified to go on to Kobe where Brazil awaited them.

At last, and far too late, poor Poland found their form, dismissing the USA without difficulty and leaving their supporters to wonder at their two prior inept displays. Here at Daejeon, freed from the pressures of qualification, they sparkled. Within five minutes they had a decisive lead: first Olisadebe smashed a loose ball in off the cross bar after three minutes and then, in a blistering opening, Kryszalowicz swept a second in, arriving in perfect time to meet Krzynowek's cross. Though behind, the USA largely dictated matters throughout the first half and had a scrappy Donovan goal disallowed for a foul, but they could not legitimately breach the normally porous Polish defence. Indeed, only the athleticism of Brad Friedel denied the Poles a third as he brilliantly saved from Krzynowek and then watched helplessly as Zurawski hammered the rebound against the goal post. This pattern continued into the second half with the Americans straining for a way back but threatened continuously by the raiding Poles. Twenty minutes in, Zewlakow, just on as a substitute, settled it, his header beating Friedel from close range. Next Zurawski failed with a penalty kick before the US finally got a goal as Landon Donovan struck. Although they had been embarrassed, the USA advanced and Poland's tournament was over.

Final Tournament – Japan and South Korea
First Round

Group A

France (0) **0**, **Senegal** (1) **1**
31.5.02 SEOUL
France: Barthez, Thuram, Leboeuf, Desailly, Lizarazu, Wiltord (Cisse), Petit, Djorkaeff (Dugarry), Vieira, Henry, Trezeguet
Senegal: Sylva, Daf, Coly, Diao, Diouf, Pape Bouba Diop (1), Cisse, Diatta, Pape Malick Diop, Moussa N'diaye, Fadiga
Referee: Bujsaim (United Arab Emirates)

Uruguay (0) **1, Denmark** (1) **2**
1.6.02 ULSAN
Uruguay: Carini, Mendez, Sorondo, Montero, Rodriguez (1) (Magallanes), Garcia, Guigou, Varela, Silva, Abreu (Morales), Recoba (Regueiro)
Denmark: Sorensen, Henriksen, Laursen, Heintze (Niclas Jensen), Helveg, Tofting, Gravesen, Gronkjaer (Jorgensen), Tomasson (2), Sand (Poulsen), Rommedahl
Referee: Mane (Kuwait)

Denmark (1) **1, Senegal** (0) **1**
6.6.02 DAEGU
Denmark: Sorensen, Henriksen, Laursen, Heintze, Helveg, Gronkjaer (Jorgensen), Gravesen (Poulsen), Tofting, Rommedahl (Lovenkrands), Tomasson (1), Sand
Senegal: Sylva, Coly, Daf, Sarr (Henri Camara), Diao (1), Diouf, Pape Malick Diop, Diatta, Papa Bouba Diop, Fadiga, Moussa N'Diaye (Souleymayne Camara), (Beye)
Referee: Batres (Guatemala)

France (0) **0, Uruguay** (0) **0**
6.6.02 BUSAN
France: Barthez, Thuram, Leboeuf (Candela), Desailly, Lizarazu, Vieira, Petit, Micoud, Wiltord (Dugarry), Henry, Trezeguet (Cisse)
Uruguay: Carini, Lembo, Sorondo, Montero, Romero (De Los Santos), Garcia, Varela, Rodriguez (Guigou), Recoba, Silva (Magallanes), Abreu
Referee: Rizo (Mexico)

Denmark (1) **2, France** (0) **0**
11.6.02 INCHEON
Denmark: Sorensen, Helveg, Henriksen, Laursen, Niclas Jensen, Rommedahl (1), Gravesen, Tofting (Nielsen), Jorgensen (Gronkjaer), Poulsen (Bogelund), Tomasson (1)
France: Barthez, Candela, Thuram, Desailly, Lizarazu, Vieira (Micoud), Makelele, Wiltord (Djorkaeff), Zidane, Dugarry (Cisse), Trezeguet
Referee: Pereira (Portugal)

Senegal (3) **3, Uruguay** (0) **3**
11.6.02 SUWON
Senegal: Sylva, Coly (Beye), Pape Malik Diop, Diatta, Daf, Ndour (Faye), Aliou
Cisse, Pape Bouba Diop (2), Fadiga (1), Henri Camara (Moussa N'Diaye 67),
Diouf
Uruguay: Carini, Lembo, Sorondo (Regueiro), Montero, Romero (Forlan (1)),
Garcia, Varela, Rodriguez, Recoba (1), Silva, Abreu (Morales (1))
Referee: Wegereef (Holland)

	P	W	D	L	F	A	Pts
Denmark	3	2	1	0	5	2	7
Senegal	3	1	2	0	5	4	5
Uruguay	3	0	2	1	4	5	2
France	3	0	1	2	0	3	1

Group B

Paraguay (1) **2, South Africa** (0) **2**
2.6.02 BUSAN
Paraguay: Tavarelli, Arce (1), Gamarra, Ayala, Caceres, Caniza, Alvarenga
(Gavilan), Acuna, Campos (Morinigo), Struway (1o.g.) (Franco), Santa Cruz (1)
South Africa: Arendse, Nzama, Carnell, Aaron Mokoena, Radebe, Fortune(1),
Sibaya, Tebeho Mokoena, Zuma, Issa (Mukasi), McCarthy (Koumantarakis)
Referee: Michel (Slovakia)

Spain (1) **3, Slovenia** (0) **1**
2.6.02 GWANGJU
Spain: Casillas, Juanfran (Romero), Puyol, Hierro (1), Nadal, Baraja, Luis
Enrique (Helguera), De Pedro, Valeron (1), Raul (1), Tristan (Morientes)
Slovenia: Simeunovic, Milinovic, Galic, Knavs, Novak (Gajser), Ales Ceh,
Karic, Zahovic (Acimovic), Pavlin, Osterc (Cimirotic (1)), Rudonja
Referee: Guezzaz (Morocco)

Spain (0) **3, Paraguay** (1) **1**
7.6.02 JEONJU
Spain: Casillas, Puyol (1o.g.), Nadal, Hierro (1), Juanfran, Baraja, Luis Enrique
(Helguera), Valeron (Xavi), De Pedro, Tristan (Morientes (2)), Raul
Paraguay: Chilavert, Arce, Gamarra, Ayala, Caceres, Caniza (Struway),
Paredes, Gavilan, Acuna, Cardozo (Campos), Santa Cruz
Referee: Ghandour (Egypt)

South Africa (1) **1, Slovenia** (0) **0**
8.6.02 DAEGU
South Africa: Arendse, Nzama, Radebe, Mokoena, Carnell, Zuma, Sibaya, Mokoena, Fortune (Pule), Nomvethe (1) (Buckley), McCarthy (Koumantarakis)
Slovenia: Simeunovic, Milinovic, Vugdalic, Knavs (Bulajic), Novak, Ceh, Pavlin, Karic, Acimovic (Ceh), Rudonja, Cimirotic (Osterc)
Referee: Sanchez Ruzafa (Argentina)

Slovenia (1) **1, Paraguay** (0) **3**
12.6.02 SEOGWIPO
Slovenia: Dabanovic, Milinovic, Novak, Ceh, Osterc (Tiganj), Pavlin (Rudonja), Tavcar, Acimovic (1) (Ceh), Karic, Cimirotic, Bulajic
Paraguay: Chilavert, Arce, Gamarra, Ayala, Alvarenga (Campos (1)), Santa Cruz, Acuna, Paredes, Caceres, Cardozo (Cuevas (2) (Franco)), Caniza
Referee: Rizo (Mexico)

South Africa (1) **2, Spain** (2) **3**
12.6.02 DAEJEON
South Africa: Arendse, Zama, Mokoena, Radebe (1), Carnell, Sibaya, Mokoena, Fortune (Lekgetho), Zuma, Nomvethe (Koumantarakis), McCarthy (1)
Spain: Casillas, Torres, Helguera, Nadal, Romero, Mendieta, Xavi, Albelda (Sergio), Joaquin, Raul (2) (Luis Enrique), Morientes (1) (Luque)
Referee: Mane (Kuwait)

	P	W	D	L	F	A	Pts
Spain	3	3	0	0	9	4	9
Paraguay	3	1	1	1	6	6	4
South Africa	3	1	1	1	5	5	4
Slovenia	3	0	0	3	2	7	0

Group C

Brazil (0) **2, Turkey** (1) **1**
3.6.02 ULSAN
Brazil: Marcos, Cafu, Lucio, Roque Junior, Carlos, Edmilson, Juninho Paulista (Vampeta), Gilberto, Ronaldinho (Denilson), Rivaldo (1), Ronaldo (1) (Luizao)
Turkey: Rustu, Korkmaz (Mansiz), Akyel, Alpay, Unsal, Ozat, Basturk (Davala), Emre, Tugay (Erdem), Sukur, Sas (1)
Referee: Joo Kim (Korea)

China (0) **0, Costa Rica** (0) **2**
4.6.02 GWANGJU
China: Jiang Jin, Wu Chengying, Li Weifeng, Fan Zhiyi (Yu Genwei), Sun Jihai (Qu Bo), Xu Yunlong, Li Tie, Ma Mingyu, Li Xiaopeng, Yang Chen (Su Maozhen), Hao Haidong
Costa Rica: Lonnis, Marin, Wright (1), Martinez, Castro, Wallace (Bryce 70), Solis, Centeno, Fonseca (Medford), Wanchope (Lopez), Gomez (1)
Referee: Vassaras (Greece)

Brazil (3) **4, China** (0) **0**
8.6.02 SEOGWIPO
Brazil: Marcos, Cafu, Lucio, Roque Junior, Roberto Carlos (1), Gilberto, Ronaldo (1) (Edilson), Rivaldo (1), Ronaldinho (1) (Denilson), Juninho (Ricardinho), Polga
China: Jiang Jin, Wu Chengying, Li Tie, Ma Mingyu (Pu Yang), Hao Haidong (Qu Bo), Li Weifeng, Zhao Junze, Du Wei, Li Xiaopeng, Qi Hong (Zhao Junzhe), Xu Yunlong
Referee: Frisk (Sweden)

Costa Rica (0) **1, Turkey** (0) **1**
9.6.02 INCHEON
Costa Rica: Lonnis, Marin, Wright, Martinez, Castro, Solis, Lopez (Parks (1)), Wallace (Bryce), Centeno (Medford), Gomez, Wanchope
Turkey: Rustu, Asik, Akyel, Ergun, Ozat, Davala, Tugay (Erdem), Basturk (Nihat), Emre (1), Sas, Sukur (Mansiz)
Referee: Codjia (Benin)

Brazil (3) **5, Costa Rica** (1) **2**
13.6.02 SUWON
Brazil: Marcos, Cafu, Lucio, Edmilson (1), Polga, Junior (1), Juninho Paulista (Ricardinho), Gilberto, Rivaldo (1) (Kaka), Ronaldo (2), Edilson (Kleberson)
Costa Rica: Lonnis, Marin, Wright, Martinez (Parks), Castro, Wallace (Bryce), Lopez, Solis (Fonseca), Centeno, Gomez (1), Wanchope (1)
Referee: Ghandour (Egypt)

Turkey (2) **3, China** (0) **0**
13.6.02 SEOUL
Turkey: Rustu (Omar), Asik, Korkmaz (1), Unsal, Akyel, Tugay (Tayfur), Basturk (Mansiz), Emre, Davala (1), Sukur, Sas (1)
China: Jiang Jing, Pu Yang, Wu Chengying (Shao), Weifeng Li, Du Wei, Xu Yunlong, Li Tie, Zhao Junzue, Li Xiaopeng, Hao Haidong (Qu Bo), Chen Yang (Yu Genwei)
Referee: Ruiz (Colombia)

	P	W	D	L	F	A	Pts
Brazil	3	3	0	0	11	3	9
Turkey	3	1	1	1	5	3	4
Costa Rica	3	1	1	1	5	6	4
China	3	0	0	3	0	9	0

Group D

South Korea (1) **2, Poland** (0) **0**
4.6.02 BUSAN
South Korea: Woon-Jae Lee, Tae-Young Kim, Jin-Cheul Choi, Hong, Nam-Il Kim, Yoo Sang-Chul (1) (Chun-Soo Lee), Eul-Young Lee, Song Chong-Gug, Park Ji-Sung, Seol Ki-Hyeon (Cha Doo-Ri), Hwang Sun-Hong (1) (Ahn Jung-Hwan)
Poland: Dudek, Zewlakow, Hajto, Swierczewski, Kaluzny (Zewlakow), Olisadebe, Waldoch, Krzynowek, Zurawski (Kryszalowicz), Bak (Klos), Kozminski
Referee: Ruiz (Colombia)

USA (3) **3, Portugal** (1) **2**
5.6.02 SUWON
USA: Friedel, Mastroeni, Sanneh, Pope (Llamosa), Agoos (1o.g.), O'Brien (1), Hejduk, Beasley, McBride (1), Donovan (Moore), Stewart (Jones)
Portugal: Baia, Costa (1o.g.) (Andrade), Couto, Beto (1), Jorge (Bento), Rui Costa (Nuno Gomes), Petit, Sergio Conceicao, Figo, Pauleta, Pinto
Referee: Moreno (Ecuador)

South Korea (0) **1, USA** (1) **1**
10.6.02 DAEGU
South Korea: Lee Woon-Jae, Choi JinCheul, Kim Nam-il, Yoo Sang-Chul (Choi Yong-Soo), Kim Tae-Young, Seol KiHyeon, Lee Eul-Yong, Hwang Sun-Hong (Ahn Jung-Hwan (1)), Hong Myung-Bo, Park Ji-Sung (Lee Chun-Soo), Song Chong-Gug
USA: Friedel, Hejduk, O'Brien, Reyna, Mathis (1) (Wolff), Agoos, Beasley (Lewis), McBride, Donovan, Sanneh, Pope
Referee: Meier (Swi)

Portugal (1) **4, Poland** (0) **0**
10.6.02 JEONJU
Portugal: Baia, Costa, Couto, Jorge, Figo, Petit, Bento, Frechaut (Beto), Sergio Conceicao (Capucho), Pauleta (3), Pinto (Rui Costa (1))
Poland: Dudek, Kozminski, Waldoch, Hajto, Michal Zewlakow (Rzasa), Kryszalowicz, Swierczewski, Kaluzny (Arkadiusz Bak), Krzynowek, Olisadebe, Zurawski (Marcin Zewlakow)
Referee: Dallas (Scotland)

Poland (2) **3, USA** (0) **1**
14.6.02 DAEJEON
Poland: Majdan, Klos (Waldoch), Zielinski, Glowacki, Krzynowek, Zurawski, Murawski, Kucharski (Zewlakow (1)), Olisadebe (1) (Sibik), Kryszalowicz (1), Kozminski
USA: Friedel, Hejduk, Agoos (Beasley), Pope, Sanneh, O'Brien, Reyna, Stewart (Jones), Mathis, McBride (Moore), Donovan (1)
Referee: Lu Jun (China)

Portugal (0) **0, South Korea** (0) **1**
14.6.02 INCHEON
Portugal: Baia, Costa, Couto, Figo, Pinto, Pauleta, Bento, Conceicao, Petit, Beto, Rui Jorge
South Korea: Lee Woon-Jae, Choi Jin-Cheul, Kim Nam-il, Yoo Sang-Chul, Kim Tae-Young, Seol Ki-Hyeon, Lee Young-pyo, Ahn Jung-Hwan, Hong Myung-Bo, Park Ji-Sung (1), Song Chong-Gug
Referee: Sanchez (Argentina)

	P	W	D	L	F	A	Pts
South Korea	3	2	1	0	4	1	7
USA	3	1	1	1	5	6	4
Portugal	3	1	0	2	6	4	3
Poland	3	1	0	2	3	7	3

Group E

Republic of Ireland (0) **1, Cameroon** (1) **1**
1.6.02 NIIGATA
Republic of Ireland: Given, Gary Kelly, Breen, Staunton, Harte (Reid), McAteer (Finnan), Holland (1), Kilbane, Kinsella, Duff, Robbie Keane
Cameroon: Alioum, Kalla, Wome, Song, Lauren, Geremi, Eto'o, Foe, Olembe, Tchato, Mboma (1) (Suffo)
Referee: Kamikawa (Japan)

Germany (4) **8, Saudi Arabia** (0) **0**
1.6.02 SAPPORO
Germany: Kahn, Frings, Linke (1), Metzelder, Ziege, Schneider (1), Ramelow (Jeremies), Hamann, Ballack (1), Jancker (1) (Bierhoff (1)), Klose (3) (Neuville)
Saudi Arabia: Al Daeyea, Tukar, Ahmed Al Dossari, Zubromawi, Sulimani, Noor, Al Owairan (Ibrahim Al Shahrani), Abdallah Al Shahrani, Al Temyat (Al Khathran), Al Jaber, Al Yami (Abdallah Al Dossari)
Referee: Aquino (Paraguay)

Germany (1) **1, Republic of Ireland** (0) **1**
5.6.02 IBARAKI
Germany: Kahn, Linke, Ramelow, Metzelder, Frings, Hamann, Ballack, Schneider (Jeremies), Ziege, Jancker (Bierhoff), Klose (1) (Bode)
Republic of Ireland: Given, Finnan, Breen, Staunton (Cunningham), Harte (Reid), Kelly (Quinn), Holland, Kinsella, Kilbane, Keane (1), Duff
Referee: Nielsen (Denmark)

Cameroon (0) **1, Saudi Arabia** (0) **0**
6.6.02 SAITAMA
Cameroon: Alioum, Wome (Njanka), Tchato, Song, Kalla, Lauren, Foe, Kome (Olembe), Geremi, Eto'o (1), Mboma (N'Diefi)
Saudi Arabia: Al Daeyea, Al Jahani, Tukar, Zubromawi (Abdallah Al Dossari), Al Shehri, Sulimani, Al Khathran (Noor), Abdallah Al Shahrani, Ibrahim Al Shahrani, Al Temyat, Obeid Al Dossari (Al Yami)
Referee: Hauge (Norway)

Saudi Arabia (0) **0, Republic of Ireland** (1) **3**
11.6.02 YOKOHAMA
Saudi Arabia: Al-Daeyea, Al-Jahani (Al Dossari), Tokar, Suleiman Al-Zubromawi (Al Dossari), Al-Shehri, Al-Shahrani, Al-Sulimani, Al Khathran (Al Shlhoub), Al Owairan Al Dossari, Al-Temyat, Al-Yami
Rep of Ireland: Given, Finnan, Staunton, Breen (1), Harte (Quinn), Kelly (McAteer), Kinsella (Carsley), Holland, Kilbane, Keane (1), Duff (1)
Referee: Ndoye (Senegal)

Cameroon (0) **0, Germany** (0) **2**
11.6.02 SHIZUOKA
Cameroon: Alioum, Tchato (Suffo 53), Kalla, Song, Wome, Geremi, Olembe (Kome), Foe, Lauren, Mboma (Job), Eto'o
Germany: Kahn, Linke, Ramelow, Metzelder, Frings, Schneider (Jeremies), Hamann, Ballack, Ziege, Klose (1) (Neuville), Jancker (Bode (1))
Referee: Lopez Nieto (Spain)

	P	W	D	L	F	A	Pts
Germany	3	2	1	0	11	1	7
Rep of Ireland	3	1	2	0	5	2	5
Cameroon	3	1	1	1	2	3	4
Saudi Arabia	3	0	0	3	0	12	0

Group F

Argentina (0) **1, Nigeria** (0) **0**
2.6.02 IBARAKI
Argentina: Cavallero, Placente, Sorin, Pocchettino, Samuel, Zanetti, Simeone, Veron (Aimar), Ortega, Claudio Lopez (Gonzalez), Batistuta (1) (Crespo)
Nigeria: Shorunmu, Yobo, Babayaro, Okoronkwo, West, Sodje (Christopher), Ogbeche, Okocha, Lawal, Kanu (Ikedia), Aghahowa
Referee: Veissiere (France)

England (1) **1, Sweden** (0) **1**
2.6.02 SAITAMA
England: Seaman, Mills, Ashley Cole, Ferdinand, Campbell (1), Beckham (Dyer), Scholes, Hargreaves, Heskey, Vassell (Joe Cole), Owen
Sweden: Hedman, Mellberg, Mjallby, Jakobsson, Lucic, Linderoth, Alexandersson (1), Ljungberg, Magnus Svensson (Anders Svensson), Allback (Andreas Andersson), Larsson
Referee: Simon (Brazil)

Sweden (1) **2, Nigeria** (1) **1**
7.6.02 KOBE
Sweden: Hedman, Mellberg, Mjallby, Lucic, Jakobsson, Anders Svensson (Magnus Svensson), Linderoth, Alexandersson, Ljungberg, Allback (Andreas Andersson), Larsson (2)
Nigeria: Shorunmu, Yobo, Christopher, Okoronkwo, West, Babayaro (Kanu), Okocha, Ogbeche (Ikedia), Udeze, Aghahowa (1), Utaka
Referee: Ortube (Bolivia)

Argentina (0) **0, England** (1) **1**
7.6.02 SAPPORO
Argentina: Cavallero, Pochettino, Samuel, Placente, Zanetti, Simeone, Veron (Aimar), Sorin, Ortega, Batistuta (Crespo), Gonzalez (Lopez)
England: Seaman, Mills, Ashley Cole, Ferdinand, Campbell, Beckham (1), Scholes, Butt, Hargreaves (Sinclair), Owen (Bridge), Heskey (Sheringham)
Referee: Collina (Italy)

Sweden (0) **1, Argentina** (0) **1**
12.6.02 MIYAGI
Sweden: Hedman, Mellberg, Mjallby, Jakobsson, Lucic, Alexandersson, Linderoth, Anders Svensson (1) (Jonson), Magnus Svensson, Larsson (Ibrahimovic), Allback (Andreas Andersson)
Argentina: Cavallero, Zanetti, Samuel, Pocchettino, Chamot, Ortega, Almeyda (Veron), Sorin (Gonzalez), Aimar, Claudio Lopez, Batistuta (Crespo (1))
Referee: Bujsaim (United Arab Emirates)

Nigeria (0) **0, England** (0) **0**
12.6.02 OSAKA
England: Seaman, Mills, Ferdinand, Campbell, Ashley Cole (Bridge), Beckham, Butt, Scholes, Sinclair, Heskey (Sheringham), Owen (Vassell)
Nigeria: Enyeama, Yobo, Okoronkwo, Udeze, Sodje, Christopher, Okocha, Obiorah, Aghahowa, Akwuegbu, Opabunmi (Ikedia)
Referee: Hall (USA)

	P	W	D	L	F	A	Pts
Sweden	3	1	2	0	4	3	5
England	3	1	2	0	2	1	5
Argentina	3	1	1	1	2	2	4
Nigeria	3	0	1	2	1	3	1

Group G

Croatia (0) **0, Mexico** (0) **1**
3.6.02 NIIGATA
Croatia: Pletikosa, Simunic, Tomas, Zivkovic, Robert Kovac, Jarni, Niko Kovac, Prosinecki (Rapaic), Soldo, Boksic (Stanic), Suker (Saric)
Mexico: Perez, Vidrio, Marquez, Carmona, Morales, Torrado, Caballero, Luna, Mercado, Borguetti (Hernandez), Blanco (1) (Palencia)
Referee: Jun Lu (China)

Italy (2) **2, Ecuador** (0) **0**
3.6.02 SAPPORO
Italy: Buffon, Panucci, Nesta, Cannavaro, Maldini, Zambrotta, Doni (Di Livio), Di Biagio (Gattuso), Tommasi, Totti (Del Piero), Vieri (2)
Ecuador: Cevallos, De la Cruz, Hurtado, Guerron, Poroso, Obregon, Mendez, Edwin Tenorio (Marion Ayovi), Chala (Ascensio), Aguinaga (Carlos Tenorio), Delgado
Referee: Hall (USA)

Italy (0) **1, Croatia** (0) **2**
8.6.02 IBARAKI
Italy: Buffon, Panucci, Nesta (Materazzi), Cannavaro, Maldini, Zambrotta, Zanetti, Tommasi, Doni (Inzaghi), Totti, Vieri (1)
Croatia: Pletikosa, Robert Kovac, Simunic, Saric, Jarni, Tomas, Rapaic (1) (Simic), Niko Kovac, Soldo (Vranjes), Vugrinec (Olic (1)), Boksic
Referee: Poll (England)

Mexico (1) **2, Ecuador** (1) **1**
9.6.02 MIYAGI
Mexico: Perez, Marquez, Vidrio, Torrado (1), Morales, Borgetti (1) (Hernandez), Blanco (Mercado), Luna, Carmona, Rodriguez (Caballero), Arellano
Ecuador: Cevallos, Poroso, Hurtado, De la Cruz, Obregon (Aguinaga), Guerron, Kaviedes (Tenorio), Delgado (1), Chala, Mendez, Tenorio (Ayovi)
Referee: Daami (Tunisia)

Ecuador (0) **1, Croatia** (0) **0**
13.6.02 YOKOHAMA
Ecuador: Cevallos, De la Cruz, Hurtado, Guerron, Marlon Ayovi, Mendez (1), Obregon (Aguinaga), Poroso, Carlos Tenorio (Kaviedes), Chala, Delgado
Croatia: Pletikosa, Simunic, Tomas, Simic (Vugrinec), Robert Kovac, Jarni, Niko Kovac (Vranjes), Saric (Stanic), Rapaic, Olic, Boksic
Referee: Mattus Vega (Costa Rica)

Mexico (1) **1, Italy** (0) **1**
13.6.02 OITA
Mexico: Perez, Marquez, Vidrio, Carmona, Morales (Garcia), Arellano, Johan Rodriguez (Caballero), Luna, Torrado, Blanco, Borguetti (1) (Palencia)
Italy: Buffon, Panucci (Coco), Cannavaro, Nesta, Maldini, Inzaghi (Montella), Zambrotta, Zanetti, Tommasi, Totti (Del Piero (1)), Vieri
Referee: Simon (Brazil)

	P	W	D	L	F	A	Pts
Mexico	3	2	1	0	4	2	7
Italy	3	1	1	1	4	3	4
Croatia	3	1	0	2	2	3	3
Ecuador	3	1	0	2	2	4	3

Group H

Japan (0) **2, Belgium** (0) **2**
4.6.02 SAITAMA
Japan: Narazaki, Matsuda, Morioka (Miyamoto), Koji Nakata, Inamoto (1), Hidetoshi Nakata, Ono (Alex), Toda, Ichikawa, Suzuki (1) (Morishima), Yanagisawa
Belgium: de Vlieger, van Meir, Simons, Peeters, van der Heyden (1), van Buyten, Walem (Sonck), Verheyen (Strupar), Vanderhaeghe, Goor, Wilmots (1)
Referee: Mattus Vega (Costa Rica)

Russia (0) **2, Tunisia** (0) **0**
5.6.02 KOBE
Russia: Nigmatullin, Kovtun, Nikiforov, Solomatin, Semshov (Kokhlov), Onopko, Karpin (1), Titov (1), Beschastnykh (Sychyov), Pimenov, Izmailov (Alenichev)
Tunisia: Boumnijel, Badra (Zitouni), Mkacher, Jaziri, Trabelsi, Gabsi (Beya), Sellimi (Mhadhebi), Bouzaiene, Bouazizi, Jaidi, Ben Achour
Referee: Prendergast (Jamaica)

Japan (0) **1, Russia** (0) **0**
9.6.02 YOKOHAMA
Japan: Narazaki, Matsuda, Miyamoto, Koji Nakata, Myojin, Inamoto (1), Toda, Hidetoshi Nakata, Ono, Suzuki, Yanagisawa
Russia: Nigmatullin, Kovtun, Nikiforov, Onopko, Solomatin, Karpin, Titov, Smertin, Semshov, Izmailov, Pimenov
Referee: Merk (Germany)

Tunisia (1) **1, Belgium** (1) **1**
10.6.02 OITA
Tunisia: Boumnijel, Badra, Jaidi, Gabsi (Sellimi), Bouzaine (1), Ghodbane, Trabelsi, Bouazizi, Melki (Beya), Ben Achour, Jaziri (Zitouni)
Belgium: de Vlieger, Deflandre, De Boeck, Van Buyten, Van Der Heyden, Simons (Mpenza), Verheyen (Sonck), Wilmots (1), Vanderhaeghe, Goor, Strupar (Vermant)
Referee: Shield (Australia)

Belgium (1) **3, Russia** (0) **2**
14.6.02 SHIZUOKA
Belgium: De Vlieger, De Boeck (van Meir), van Kerckhoven, Peeters, van Buyten, Goor, Walem (1), Verheyen (Simons), Vanderhaeghe, Wilmots (1), Mpenza (Sonck (1))
Russia: Nigmatullin, Kovtun, Nikiforov (Sennikov), Onopko, Smertin (Sychev (1)), Solomatin, Karpin (Kerzhakov), Titov, Alenichev, Khokhlov, Beschastnykh
Referee: Milton Nielsen (Den)

Tunisia (0) **0, Japan** (0) **2**
14.6.02 OSAKA
Tunisia: Boumnijel, Badra, Trabelsi, Bouzaiene (Zitouni), Jaidi, Clayton (Mhadhebi), Bouazizi, Ben Achour, Ghodhbane, Melki (Baya), Jaziri
Japan: Narazaki, Matsuda, Miyamoto, Koji Nakata, Myojin, Inamoto (Ichikawa), Toda, Hidetoshi Nakata (1) (Ogasawara), Ono, Suzuki, Yanagisawa (Morishima (1))
Referee: Veissiere (France)

	P	W	D	L	F	A	Pts
Japan	3	2	1	0	5	2	7
Belgium	3	1	2	0	6	5	5
Russia	3	1	0	2	4	4	3
Tunisia	3	0	1	2	1	5	1

THE ROUND OF SIXTEEN

Though dull and uninspired, the Germans nevertheless overcame Paraguay whose timidity hinted – as it had against France in 1998 – at an inferiority complex. Neither side seized the initiative during a tepid first half. Although Germany had enjoyed more possession, it was Oliver Kahn who was forced to make the first half's only real save when he pounced to deflect Campos's shot. The second half was an improvement. Driven by Ballack, Germany began to take charge and Bernd Schneider might have given them the lead but his shot was well saved by Chilavert. Having seen Ayala fire hopelessly high of Kahn's goal, Campos then forced a save from the blond keeper but, all in all, while the belatedly emboldened South Americans demonstrated a more enterprising approach, the Germans looked likelier winners. Soon Neuville, galloping forward before cutting inside, had his shot held by the goalkeeper, then Frings, put through by Schneider, wasted a chance. Extra time beckoned and, as so often before, Germany seized the day through Neuville's effortless conversion of Schneider's cross. Two minutes remained and, though they tried, Paraguay couldn't get off the canvas. Still, Acuna took the opportunity to disgrace himself, sent off for clattering Ballack. Germany's win sent them to Ulsan to wait for Mexico or the United States.

England had been hit and miss thus far, their usual tournament impression of Dr Jekyll and Mr Hyde rolled out once again, but found their best form to dispatch Denmark in a cakewalk at Nigata. It could not have started better for the English, nor worse for the Danes. Within five minutes, Beckham's belted corner was caught then dropped by the mortified Sorensen who watched the ball cross the goal line. Thus encouraged, England began to dominate – chances for Owen and Heskey came and went, and, though the Danes threatened sporadically with pace on the break, the Scandinavians struggled to contain their rampant opponents. On 22 minutes, Owen, the beneficiary of Sinclair's hard work and a neat touch from Butt, drove home a second to underline England's superiority. Ebbe Sand might have brought Denmark back into it but he missed the target and seconds later they were three down when Beckham picked out Heskey to spank a shot past Sorensen. The second half, understandably, was an anticlimax: England, patient in possession in the withering heat, continued to probe for chances and Beckham and Fowler might have furthered the anguish of the demoralised Danes but they celebrated a comfortable victory at the end, giving their hugely vocal and colourful support a quarter final against either Belgium or Brazil to savour.

Few would have chosen Senegal as prospective quarter-finalists but, having already knocked out Uruguay and France, they surprised us again in Oita when they grittily rallied to eject Sweden after conceding an early goal. The Swedes moved ahead on 11 minutes, Larsson, that most predatory of European strikers, capping their dominance by reacting first to meet a cross at the near post to beat Tony Sylva with a close-range header. Senegal's response was immediate with Pape Bouba Diop and El Hadji Diouf to the fore and eager to test Sweden's defenders for pace. Diouf, in particular, mesmerized, appearing here and there and one of his better moments appeared to have brought the Africans back, but his cross bundled in by Bouba Diop was disallowed for offside. The Europeans' respite, though, was shortlived as Camara soon after pulled the ball down, deceived his markers and beat Hedman with an accurate low shot. Level at half-time, Sweden, clearly roused to greater effort at the interval, came out in determined manner. Both Allback and Svensson went close and Andersson should have hit the target. Still, Senegal carried an air of menace with their waves of fleet-footed counter attacks but there was no breakthrough. In the first period of extra-time, Svensson, having created a space, struck a fierce shot but saw it rebound off Tony Sylva's goal-post. Their disappointment was followed swiftly by despair when Camara, again reacting sharply, seized on Thiaw's backheel, glided around the stationary Mjallby and cracked a shot past Hedman and in off the keeper's right-hand post. The golden goal ended the game cruelly for Sweden and Senegal were through.

Spain broke Irish hearts in Suwon, scoring early and resisting a momentous fight back to edge out their courageous opponents on penalty kicks. Ireland could not cope with Spain's early, slick passing and movement and Morientes's goal on eight minutes, a steered header from Puyol's cross, surprised no one. Outplayed, the Irish hung on and rode their luck as Raul, Luis Enrique and Valeron tormented them. Surviving until half-time, Ireland introduced the tall, gangling Quinn shortly after the restart and the striker's presence rejuvenated his team-mates. Duff, restored to the wing, attacked the Spanish flanks and the game's momentum was emphatically changed. One of the Blackburn winger's weaving runs drew Juanfran's clumsy foul but Harte's penalty kick, struck firmly but not accurately, was beaten into the path of Kilbane by Casillas and the midfielder blazed it wide. It seemed all over for the men in green in spite of their increasing dominance as Duff and Keane went close but not close enough but, right at the death, Quinn, so troublesome to a discomforted defence, tempted Hierro to tug his shirt. Ireland's second penalty was taken by Keane and the Leeds United forward reprieved his club colleague Harte with an accurate shot to seal a last-minute, dramatic and thoroughly deserved equaliser. Suitably encouraged, Ireland carried the game to the deflated Spaniards and, when injury reduced Spain to ten men, Ireland's bombardment seemed relentless. Robbie Keane again came closest to the decisive golden goal but neither side could find the net. The road to Gwangju and the quarter-finals would be settled by penalties. There was no happy ending for the brave Irish, their penalties (specifically those of the otherwise excellent Holland, Connolly and Kilbane) were wasted and it fell to Mendieta to beat Given and send tired, lucky Spain into the last eight.

Mexico, neat, controlled and expecting to win, became another victim of the organised, resilient USA, crumbling in miserable fashion at Jeonju. At the beginning, two opponents, well acquainted with one another, sparred for openings with Mexico, slick and inventive, dominant. But in lightning fast fashion the USA broke the shackles when Reyna scampered past defenders, raced goalwards and got the ball to McBride via Wolff and he smashed the ball into the net. The Mexicans were shaken but redoubled their effort, vulnerable though they clearly were to the counter attack. Still, Torrado and Blanco twice threatened the reliable Friedel without success in an eventful half whilst, at the other end, McBride's lay-off to Wolff was squandered by the youngster. Mexico upped the tempo and intensity as the second half progressed, calling on Friedel to tip away Luna's free kick but then, as before, the USA struck swiftly. This time Lewis beat his man on the left, and crossed for Donovan to head sweetly on the run to double their lead. Mexico were undone. Frustrated and demoralized, Mexican disappointment manifested itself and the USA, now very much on top, sought to punish them further. O'Brien, Stewart and Donovan all went close, though it hardly mattered. Mexico were beaten and Marquez's red card for his reckless lunge on Jones merely added to their woe.

Brazil, as anticipated, beat Belgium in Kobe but failed to impress and were flattered by the 2–0 scoreline. Belgium hounded their opponents from the whistle, denying Brazil the time to be effective. Early on Mpenza worried Marcos with a delicate, lofted shot which the goalkeeper had to stretch for to help over the bar. Well organized and quick to attack when given the opportunity, the Belgians thought they had the lead on 36 minutes when Wilmots headed home, but the Jamaican referee, Peter Prendergast, thought otherwise, awarding a free kick to Brazil for a push. For all their hard work in containment strategies, Belgium still faced a creative force far greater than their own and chances for Brazil inevitably came. And went, as Ronaldo, thrice, Juninho, Rivaldo and Roberto Carlos all went close in a frenetic first half. In the second, no doubt encouraged by their excellent performance, the Belgians went for the jugular but Marcos, twice saving from Wilmots whose troublesome presence worried the Brazilian backline throughout, kept them at bay. Quickly, the glory Belgium had sought was snatched from them when Rivaldo smashed a shot which clipped Van Buyten and flew past De Vlieger. The Europeans had 25 minutes to save the match and, undeterred, responded with an inspirational onslaught, laying siege to Brazil's goal. But their efforts were unrewarded and they were undeservedly beaten again on the break at the death. Ronaldo, taking advantage of Belgium's imperative to throw men forward, found time and space in the penalty area to drive home the second and decisive goal and schedule a date in Shizuoka with England.

Japan had intimidated their three previous opponents with their fanatical home support but fell behind to Turkey in the early stages and, surprisingly and in truth tamely, bowed out of the tournament. The Turks ignored the wall of sound and settled to their task. Basturk, surging forward in the early moments, found the barrier of Narazaki just too much. But Japan did not heed their warning and fell behind on 12 minutes once Ergun's corner was headed home powerfully by Davala. Ahead, Turkey, grimly determined to hold onto their advantage, played carefully, neat in possession though cautious. Japan, gaining momentum, attacked in their familiar way, committed, seeking to overwhelm their opponents. Alex, their adopted Brazilian, might have brought them level but his shot rebounded off the goal frame and the Turks stood firm throughout a second-half bombardment. Towards the end, and as if the Miyagi crowd's anxiety had transmitted itself to the Japanese players on the pitch, their efforts became increasingly desperate and less threatening, too much sweat and not quite enough guile. At the end a collective national despair swept through the stadium: Japan, the hosts, were out and Turkey, against the odds, would meet Senegal in an unlikely quarter-final.

For Korea, remarkably, the adventure at Daejeon rolled on as Italy, World Cup heavyweights, were put to the sword. The Koreans, knowing no other way, took the game to Italy in the feistiest fashion and sought to ruffle their illustrious opponents. Within four minutes Italian nerves had been frayed. Panucci, adjudged to have fouled Ki-Hyeon, gave Korea a penalty. Buffon, though, and not for the last time, guessed right and saved his team with a wonderful dive low to his left. Handed a chance and squandering it, the hosts were soon to regret their largesse. Vieri, that accomplished poacher, lurked and 15 minutes later he reacted quickest as Totti's corner kick floated into a crowded goal mouth to make it 1–0 to Italy. It brought the typical, frenetic response from South Korea whilst Italy, masters of defence, resisted comfortably with the veteran Maldini, their inspiration, to the fore. True, Jung-Hwan, busy and troublesome, forced Buffon to make another athletic save but, like their co-hosts Japan, Korea looked to be going down to frustrating defeat, suffocated by Italian efficiency. Then, two minutes from time, salvation came. Panucci, the penalty-kick villain, was again at fault when his misdirected clearance fell to Ki-Hyeon who drove the ball back past the startled Buffon. With relief pulsating in the stands, Italy were forced to play the remainder of the tie in a cauldron of emotion. That might not have been so long had Vieri taken his chance as the Italians sought to snatch it; he shot wide of an open goal and the game went to extra time. Superior in terms of technique though they were, Italy were engulfed by Korean passion on and off the pitch. First Totti's dismissal further handicapped his team and then, as penalties loomed, came a glorious winning goal from a new national hero, Jung-Hwan, who eluded Maldini to power Young-Pyo's cross home. The golden goal was a golden moment for South Korea but a dark day indeed for sad Italy.

The Round of Sixteen

Germany (0) **1, Paraguay** (0) **0**
15.6.02 SEOGWIPO
Germany: Kahn, Linke, Metzelder (Baumann), Frings, Rehmer (Kehl), Ballack, Jeremies, Schneider, Neuville (1) (Asamoah), Bode, Klose
Paraguay: Chilavert, Caniza, Arce, Gamarra, Ayala, Struway (Cuevas), Acuna, Bonet (Gavilan), Caceres, Santa Cruz (Campos), Cardozo
Referee: Batres (Guatemala)

Denmark (0) **0, England** (3) **3**
15.6.02 NIIGATA
Denmark: Sorensen (1 0G), Helveg (Bogelund), Niclas Jensen, Henriksen, Laursen, Rommedahl, Gravesen, Tofting (Claus Jensen), Gronkjaer, Sand, Tomasson
England: Seaman, Mills, Ferdinand, Campbell, Cole, Beckham, Scholes (Dyer), Butt, Sinclair, Heskey (1) (Sheringham), Owen (1) (Fowler)
Referee: Merk (Germany)

Sweden (1) **1, Senegal** (1) **2** (aet, 1–1 after 90 mins)
16.6.02 OITA
Sweden: Hedman, Jakobsson, Mellberg, Mjallby, Lucic, Alexandersson (Ibrahimovic), Magnus Svensson (Jonson), Anders Svensson, Linderoth, Larsson (1), Allback (Andreas Andersson)
Senegal: Sylva, Daf, Coly, Pape Malick Diop (Beye), Henri Camara (2), Pape Bouba Diop, Cisse, Faye, Diatta, Thiaw, Diouf
Referee: Aquino (Paraguay)

Spain (1) **1, Republic of Ireland** (0) **1** (aet, 1–1 after 90 mins, Spain win 3–2 on penalties)
16.6.02 SUWON
Spain: Casillas, Puyol, Helguera, Hierro, Juanfran, Baraja, Valeron, De Pedro (Mendieta), Luis Enrique, Raul (Luque), Morientes (1) (Albelda)
Rep. of Ireland: Given, Kelly (Quinn), Staunton (Cunningham), Breen, Harte (Connolly), Finnan, Kinsella, Holland, Kilbane, Duff, Keane (1)
Referee: Frisk (Sweden)

Mexico (0) **0, USA** (1) **2**
17.6.02 JEONJU
Mexico: Perez, Marquez, Carmona, Vidrio (Mercado), Torrado (Garcia Aspe), Morales (Hernandez), Luna, Johan Rodriguez, Arellano, Borguetti, Blanco
USA: Friedel, Berhalter, Sanneh, Pope, Mastroeni (Lamosa), O'Brien, Lewis, Reyna, Wolff (Stewart), McBride (1) (Jones), Donovan (1)
Referee: Pereira (Portugal)

Brazil (0) **2, Belgium** (0) **0**
17.6.02 KOBE
Brazil: Marcos, Cafu, Lucio, Roque Junior, Edmilson, Carlos, Gilberto, Juninho Paulista (Denilson), Rivaldo (1) (Ricardinho), Ronaldinho (Kleberson), Ronaldo (1)
Belgium: De Vlieger, Van Kerckhoven, Van Buyten, Peeters (Sonck), Simons, Wilmots, Goor, Verheyen, Vanderhaeghe, Walem, Mpenza
Referee: Prendergast (Jamaica)

Japan (0) **0, Turkey** (1) **1**
18.6.02 MIYAGI
Japan: Narazaki, Matsuda, Miyamoto, Nakata, Myojin, Inamoto (Ichikawa), Nakata, Toda, Ono, Alex (Suzuki), Nishizawa (Morishima)
Turkey: Rustu, Akyel, Korkmaz, Alpay, Unsal, Davala (1) (Nihat), Tugay, Basturk (Mansiz), Ergun, Sas (Tayfur), Sukur
Referee: Collina (Italy)

South Korea (0) **2, Italy** (1) **1** (aet, 1–1 after 90 mins)
18.6.02 DAEJEON
South Korea: Lee Woon-Jae, Choi Jin-Chul, Hong Myung-Bo (Cha Doo-Ri), Kim Tae-Young (Hwang Sun-Hong); Kim Nam-Il (Lee Chun-Soo), Yoo Sang-Chul, Lee Young-Pyo, Park Ji-Sung, Song Chong-Gug; Seol Ki-Hyeon (1), Ahn Jung-Hwan (1)
Italy: Buffon, Panucci, Iuliano, Coco, Maldini, Zanetti, Zambrotta (Di Livio), Tommasi, Totti, Del Piero (Gattuso), Vieri (1)
Referee: Moreno (Ecuador)

THE QUARTER-FINALS

The England team that showed up at Shizuoka played poorly, without the freedom and self-belief that had accounted for Denmark, and surrendered meekly to ten-man Brazil and an astonishing goal from their play-maker Ronaldinho. The South Americans began in their accustomed manner, moving the ball easily but scarcely troubling the England goal where Campbell, in particular, was a tower of strength. For the main part, England resorted to faster, often more direct, routes to goal and, on 23 minutes, they took the lead when Heskey's pass, intended for Owen, landed at Lucio's feet. But, as the big defender dithered he was robbed of the ball, and Owen advanced to loft the ball over Marcos and into the net. Brazil's media had warned about the diminutive striker pre-match and now those fears were realized. England, enjoying a 1–0 lead and parity at least in playing terms, made no further chances, but Brazil had been rocked, their rhythm disrupted. Almost on half-time disaster struck for Eriksson and his team when Scholes lunged and missed a challenge and Beckham, still patently unfit, committed himself. Ronaldinho, the conjurer, was away and running at the heart of the English rearguard whilst Rivaldo loitered in the space he had worked to the right. When the ball was slipped effortlessly into his path, he shot across Seaman and in at his far post. Disappointed, England's hopes took another monumental blow five minutes into the second half as Ronaldinho launched a forty-yard free kick goalwards from the right-hand touchline. Seaman, anticipating a cross and caught off his line, could only watch aghast as the ball sailed over his head to make it 2–1. Was it genius or good fortune? The debate raged on for weeks. Ronaldinho understandably claimed the former, though a mishit cross seemed more plausible. England's response was as bafflingly lethargic as their overall performance, as if they were cowed by Brazil's reputation. Referee Ramos Rizo improved their chances by dismissing Ronaldinho for an innocuous-looking challenge on Mills but the eleven men could not pressure the ten even though they had 30 minutes to make the extra man count. Moreover, shackled by the muddled and conservative thinking of their head coach and a batch of bewildering substitutions, they went out in feeble fashion, failing to manage a single shot on target against a depleted but delighted Brazil.

Germany advanced to no great surprise in Ulsan, though the manner of their victory over a battling, perhaps over-achieving USA was not particularly impressive. The Americans played positively, attacking from the off through Donovan and the robust McBride. Donovan forced Oliver Kahn into a smart save on the quarter hour, his fierce drive just kept out, and then the ever-alert Kahn stopped him again as he bore down on goal. The Germans, organized but overly cautious, found themselves threatened again by the same man on 36 minutes. This time, though, he made the chance for Eddie Lewis, who struck his shot crisply and on target, but Kahn yet again denied America. Subdued and thus far displaying little to concern their buoyant opponents, Germany, like a coiled snake, momentarily snapped and struck the deadly blow. Michael Ballack once more found the goal, applying the simplest header from Ziege's inviting cross. The USA, winded by the blow, almost suffered the indignity of conceding a second but Klose's shot thumped against the post with Friedel beaten. Intent on conserving energy and concentrating on defending to preserve their 1–0 lead, the Germans settled for containment. The USA's best shout came when they thought Frings had prevented Berhalter's effort from crossing the line with his hand but the referee, Hugh Dallas, did not agree. Oliver Kahn was equal to everything thrown at him, including another shot from Landon Donovan, and Germany eased through to the semi-final. There was no doubt that the unheralded USA, the more enterprising and adventurous team, had been a little unlucky but Kahn's astounding performance merited Germany's progress.

To general astonishment at Gwangju, thoroughbreds Spain were derailed by the plucky, fully committed South Koreans. Ironically, the Europeans were undone in the same heartbreaking manner that they themselves had inflicted on Ireland in the previous round. Dull and sterile, due in part to Spain's caution, the first half petered out in uneventful fashion, Korean vim breaking down on Spain's organized back line whilst Joaquin, Raul and Morientes, quiet for long spells, still posed a huge threat to their hosts when they managed to venture forward. There was little, though, for either goalkeeper to worry about as the tepid encounter began its second period. Now at least, and to the final moments of extra time, Spain found ambition and urgency and their greater quality created opportunities. At the other end, Korea's vigour, combined with Spain's more aggressive approach, allowed them to threaten. On 50 minutes Helguera looked to have broken the deadlock, his towering header powered emphatically beyond Lee Woon-Jae, but it was disallowed for a foul. As full-time approached both sides raised the tempo and Park Ji Sung, striking a volley goalwards, was denied by Casillas's acrobatic save. In extra time Spain continued to press and stretched their hosts' resolve to near breaking point. Again Ghandour came to South Korea's rescue, scratching off Morientes's header from Joaquin's superb cross, this time believing the ball had swung out of play. Amid the protests and anger, Spain must have begun to recognize that the day was not to be theirs, even more so when Morientes hit the post with a rasping shot eight minutes later. And so it proved as Korea, scoring from each of their five penalties, saw Joaquin – the game's most influential performer – miss to put them through and leave Spain's livid players to pursue the referee from the pitch.

In perhaps the World Cup's most unlikely quarter-final ever, substitute Ilhan Manziz pounced in the early moments of extra time to grab a golden goal to send Senegal home and all of Turkey into rapture. Senegal's glorious adventure fizzled out in disappointing fashion as their team, so uninhibited in the early rounds, were affected by the magnitude of the occasion and unable to play with their customary zest. Their best effort came on 20 minutes, Henri

Camara putting the ball in the net from point blank range after Fadiga's goal-bound effort had struck him, but it was ruled offside. Turkey then began to dictate the flow in their tidy way and Senegal's threat evaporated. Hakan Sas set Hakan Sukur up with the simplest of chances but the big striker fluffed his lines, miscontrolling and failing to trouble Tony Sylva; then Sas, directing operations, menaced the Africans. Basturk too was a lively outlet as the Turks went in a search of a goal. But Sukur, so often their saviour, this day failed them. Goalless at the interval, Senegal retreated afterwards, out-played and out-thought. Their defenders, though, continued to protect the goalkeeper and, when Basturk found himself with time and space to shoot, Diatta's athletic intervention denied him. Finally the out-of-sorts Sukur was withdrawn and his replacement, Manziz, almost immediately made an impact but his chip was just kept out by Sylva. In stalemate at ninety minutes, the match went into extra time, but not much. Only four minutes had passed when Davala's run along the touchline resulted in a long cross into the path of Manziz and his assured finish put Turkey into the semi-final and a return match with Brazil.

Quarter-Finals

Brazil (1) **2, England** (1) **1**
21.6.02 SHIZUOKA
England: Seaman, Mills, Campbell, Ferdinand, Ashley Cole (Sheringham), Beckham, Scholes, Butt, Sinclair (Dyer), Owen (1) (Vassell), Heskey
Brazil: Marcos, Roque Junior, Lucio, Edmilson, Cafu, Gilberto, Ronaldinho (1), Kleberson, Carlos, Ronaldo (Edilson), Rivaldo (1)
Referee: Ramos Rizo (Mexico)

Germany (1) **1, USA** (0) **0**
21.6.02 ULSAN
Germany: Kahn, Linke, Kehl, Metzelder, Frings, Hamann, Ballack (1), Schneider (Jeremies), Ziege, Neuville (Bode), Klose (Bierhoff)
USA: Friedel, Sanneh, Mastroeni (Stewart), Pope, Berhalter, Hajduk (Jones), O'Brien, Reyna, Lewis, Donovan, McBride (Mathis)
Referee: Dallas (Scotland)

Spain (0) **0, South Korea** (0) **0** (aet, 0–0 after 90 mins, South Korea win 5–3 on penalties)
22.6.02 GWANGJU
Spain: Casillas, Puyol, Nadal, Hierro, Romero, Joaquin, Helguera (Xavi), Baraja, De Pedro (Mendieta), Valeron (Luis Enrique), Morientes

South Korea: Lee Woon-Jae, Choi Jin-Cheul, Hongmyong-Bo, Kim Tae-Young, (Hwang Sun-Hong), Yoo Sang-Chul, (Lee Chun-Soo) Park Ji Sung, Lee Yong-Pyo, Song Chong-Gug, Kimnam-Ill, (Lee Chong Eul) Seol Ki-Hyeon, Ahn Jung-Hwan
Referee: Ghandour (Egypt)

Senegal (0) **0, Turkey** (0) **1** (aet, 0–0 after 90 mins)
22.6.02 OSAKA
Senegal: Sylva, Coly, Diatta, Cisse, Daf, Henri Camara, Pape Bouba Diop, Pape Malick Diop, Diao, Fadiga, Diouf
Turkey: Rustu, Korkmaz, Akyel, Alpay, Ergun, Davala, Basturk, Tugay, Emre (Erdem), Sukur (Mansiz (1)), Sas
Referee: Ruiz (Colombia)

THE SEMI-FINALS

South Korea's remarkable run finally came to a shuddering halt in Seoul where German steel and big tournament experience proved too much for them. The hosts, as ever supported by a frenzied full house, launched themselves at the Germans from the start. It was Ramelow though, who was first to shoot meaningfully but his shot went straight into the goalkeeper's grasp. The red tide, though, did not faze the Germans: Cha Doo Ri and Lee Chun Soo combined for the latter to hammer the ball goalward but Kahn, an inspiration throughout the tournament, produced another flying save. The Korean strikers, causing problems with pace and movement, were well marshalled and Ballack began to exert influence as the match progressed. Sensing opportunities to attack on the flanks, the Germans slowly turned the screw. Klose, Bode and Ballack all unsettled the co-hosts as they tried to meet a barrage of crosses swung into the penalty area. Korea had been vibrant, imaginative and hugely energetic throughout the competition but could do little to undermine Germany's greater organization and extra quality. Ballack, alongside Kahn as one of only two Germans of truly world-class ability, provided the decisive moment though not before personal disaster befell him when his ugly foul on Lee Chun-Soo brought him a yellow card and suspension from the final match. Yet, 15 minutes from time, he scored the goal, rifling his shot low to the goalkeeper's left to ensure that the match he missed would be the final and not the third-place play-off. Germany ultimately had deservedly won but their glee was tempered by the knowledge that they would face either Brazil or Turkey without their playmaker and leader. Korea, unable to mesmerize an opponent with pace, fanaticism and a frenzied onslaught for the first time in the tournament, were out, though their achievement in getting this far had been extraordinary.

Brazil predictably overcame Turkey in Saitama to book a place in their seventh World Cup final though the Turks, once again playing with considerable verve and skill, tested them fully. Taking the game to their opponents in the opening exchanges, the Turks troubled Brazil, attacking on the flanks and mastering possession. On 19 minutes, Alpay might have given them the lead but his header from Akyels' cross was saved well by Marcos. The underdog's cleverness and the menace of Sas, in particular, always kept them in it but slowly and surely the pendulum swung Brazil's way. Rivaldo, exerting huge influence in front of retreating Turkish defenders, began to create the chances and even forced Rustu to an instinctive block after the goalkeeper had first beaten away an effort from Ronaldo. Rustu then stopped Cafu after Rivaldo and Ronaldo had combined to set him up and it said much for the game's shift in momentum that by the interval the keeper was by some distance Turkey's best player. Formidable barrier though he had been, Rustu was beaten just four minutes into the second half as Ronaldo surged through onto Gilberto's pass and rolled the ball under the keeper. They kept going manfully to the end, but Turkey were outplayed and Brazil's speed and invention threatened to overrun them. Akyel, another to have a fine match, had to stretch to take the ball off Edilson's toe when the Brazilian was set to make it two and Rustu and his hard-working defenders managed, just, to keep their rampant opponents at bay. Turkey went out of the tournament by 1–0 but had emerged with enormous credit. Their fans were left to reflect on the marvellous performances of Rustu, Basturk and Sas and wonder quite what might have been achieved had the curiously isolated and ineffective Sukur been at his best.

Semi-Finals

Germany (0) **1, South Korea** (0) **0**
25.6.02 SEOUL
Germany: Kahn, Linke, Metzelder, Frings, Ramelow, Hamann, Ballack (1), Schneider (Jeremies), Klose (Bierhoff), Neuville (Asamoah), Bode
South Korea: Lee Woon-Jae, Choi Jin-Cheul (Lee Min-Sung), Yoo Sang-Chul, Kim Tae-Young, Lee Chun-Soo, Lee Young-Pyo, Hong Myung-Bo (Seol Ki-Hyeon), Hwang Sun-Hong (Ahn Jung-Hwan), Park Ji-Sung, Song Chong-Gug, Cha Du-Ri
Referee: Meier (Swi)

Brazil (0) **1, Turkey** (0) **0**
26.6.02 SAITAMA
Brazil: Marcos, Cafu, Lucio, Roque Junior, Edmilson, Roberto Carlos, Gilberto Silva, Ronaldo (1) (Luizao), Rivaldo, Kleberson (Belleti), Edilson (Denilson)
Turkey: Rustu, Korkmaz, Akyel, Alpay, Tugay, Sukur, Basturk (Erdem), Sas, Ergun, Emre (Mansiz), Davala (Izzet)
Referee: Nielsen (Denmark)

PLAY-OFF FOR THIRD PLACE

The third and fourth place match for once was between two teams willing to play fast open football. That was no surprise, perhaps, given the participants, particularly South Korea, nor indeed a start that set the tempo for what was to follow. Eleven seconds had passed – a championship record – when Manziz robbed the veteran captain Myung-Bo and played the ball into the path of Sukur for the Internazionale forward to score his first of a personally dreadful competition. Korea dusted themselves down and roared back. From a free kick eight minutes later, Lee Eul-Young sent a swinging, dipping shot, up and over the defensive wall and crashing into Rustu's net to make it 1–1 and Korea's spirit, thus re-ignited, drove them on for more. But Rustu proved equal to their best effort when Lee Chung-Soo bore down on him, then Sukur, having his best day, combined on 13 minutes with Manziz and his co-striker advanced to beat Lee Woon-Jae comprehensively. For all their commitment to attack, Korea's vulnerability was evident. Turkey stood up to the hosts' surging raids and again exposed them on 32 minutes, Sukur again involved, Manziz this time lifting the ball delicately over the goalkeeper. There was huff and puff from the home team during a frenetic second half whilst Turkey worked diligently to plug gaps. At the death, perhaps tiring, Turkey began to wither. South Korea, pressing hard, finally had their chances: Ahn Jung-Hwang shot narrowly wide but Rustu dealt with the rest, his presence once more a formidable barrier. Korea, deep into time, added a deserved consolation as Song Chong-Gug's heavily deflected strike flew past Rustu but Turkey won 3–2 and underlined that their success throughout had been achieved through talent, organization and no little grit.

Match for Third Place

South Korea (1) **2, Turkey** (3) **3**
29.6.02 DAEGU
South Korea: Lee Woon-Jae, Hong Myong-Bo (Kim Tae-Young), Lee Min-Sung, Yoo Sang-Chul, Lee Yong-Pyo, Lee Eul-Young (1) (Cha Doo-Ri), Lee Chun Soo, Park Ji-Sung, Song Chong-Gug (1), Ahn Jung-Hwan, Seol Ki-Hyeon (Choi Tae-Uk)
Turkey: Rustu, Akyel, Korkmaz, Alpay, Ergun, Davala (Okan), Basturk (Tayfur), Tugay, Emre (Unsal), Sukur (1), Manziz (2)
Referee: Saad Kameel Mane (Kuwait)

THE FINAL

The final in Yokohama was a game to relish. Brazil and Germany, each playing their seventh final, faced each other for the first time at this stage. Germany's journey to this decisive match had been far more conservative than their exuberant opponents but they discarded the patient approach that had served them so well hitherto and opted for an open, aggressive contest. In the absence of Michael Ballack, Bernd Schneider organized the German midfield and his slick passing helped them enjoy a little more possession than the South Americans. But Brazil created far more from less ball, their movement and imagination always a threat. Germany lacked the cutting edge which, in Ronaldo, Rivaldo and Ronaldinho, Brazil had in abundance. Ronaldinho, mercurial as ever, tore holes in the normally solid Germany defence and Ronaldo ran at them but his best efforts were thwarted twice by the brilliance of the redoubtable Oliver Kahn and once by his own unusually profligate finishing. Kleberson, too, strode forward to drive his shot past the outstretched fingers of Kahn but saw the ball thump against the bar. Undeterred by Brazil's excellence around Kahn's penalty area, the Germans continued the second half in positive fashion. Jens Jeremies, right at the start, leapt to direct a header goalward but Edmilson rescued his goalkeeper with a timely clearance. Encouraged, the Germans had another chance moments later through Neuville's curling free-kick, which hit the post. Now Germany appeared to have the edge for the first time in the match and were making goalscoring opportunities. Sadly it proved to be an illusion; though fiercely competitive in midfield, Brazil's attacking qualities always seemed likely to settle matters. Twenty-two minutes remained when Rivaldo's speculative shot travelled apparently harmlessly towards Kahn. Horribly and unexpectedly though, the big goalkeeper, a firm contender for player of the tournament, fumbled the ball into the turf and Ronaldo, following up, lashed it beyond him in an instant. Poor Kahn, a man who had done more than anyone to take his country to the final, had sabotaged their chance to win it. Worse followed on 79 minutes when Rivaldo's step over deceived Germany's defenders and Ronaldo, with time to pick his spot, fizzed his shot into the net. Brazil had won, their transformation from qualification strugglers to champions a tribute to their blunt-talking coach Scolari. As for Germany, given their shocking thrashing in Munich at the hands of England, their recovery had been magnificent but despite performing over and above everyone's expectations, they fell at the final hurdle.

Final

Brazil (0) **2**, **Germany** (0) **0**
30.6.02 YOKOHAMA
Brazil: Marcos, Edmilson, Lucio, Roque Junior, Cafu, Kleberson, Gilberto, Carlos, Ronaldinho (Juninho Paulista), Rivaldo, Ronaldo (2) (Denilson)
Germany: Kahn, Linke, Ramelow, Metzelder, Frings, Schneider, Jeremies (Asamoah), Hamann, Bode (Ziege), Neuville, Klose (Bierhoff)
Referee: Collina (Italy)

CHAPTER 18

GERMANY

2006

Qualifying Tournament
194 entries
Germany qualify as hosts

Europe (51): Albania, Andorra, Austria, Armenia, Azerbaijan, Belarus, Belgium, Bosnia-Herzegovina, Bulgaria, Croatia, Cyprus, Czech Republic, Denmark, England, Estonia, Faroe Islands, Finland, France, Georgia, Germany, Greece, Holland, Hungary, Iceland, Israel, Italy, Latvia, Liechtenstein, Lithuania, Luxembourg, Macedonia, Malta, Moldova, Northern Ireland, Norway, Poland, Portugal, Republic of Ireland, Romania, Russia, San Marino, Scotland, Slovakia, Slovenia, Spain, Sweden, Switzerland, Turkey, Ukraine, Wales, Serbia and Montenegro

South America (10): Argentina, Bolivia, Brazil, Chile, Colombia, Ecuador, Paraguay, Peru, Uruguay, Venezuela

CONCACAF (34): Anguilla, Antigua & Barbuda, Aruba, Bahamas, Barbados, Belize, Bermuda, British Virgin Islands, Canada, Cayman Islands, Costa Rica, Cuba, Dominica, Dominican Republic, El Salvador, Grenada, Guatemala, Haiti, Honduras, Jamaica, Mexico, Montserrat, Netherlands Antilles, Nicaragua, Panama, Puerto Rico, St Kitts & Nevis Islands, St Lucia, St Vincent & Grenadines, Surinam, Trinidad & Tobago, Turks & Caicos Islands, US Virgin Islands, United States of America

Asia (42): Bangladesh, Bahrain, Brunei, China, Cambodia, Guam, Hong Kong, India, Indonesia, Iran, Iraq, Japan, Jordan, Kazakhstan, Kyrgyzstan, Kuwait, Laos, Lebanon, Macao, Malaysia, Maldives, Mongolia, Myanmar, Nepal, Oman, Pakistan, Palestine, Philippines, Qatar, Saudi Arabia, Singapore, South Korea, Sri Lanka, Syria, Taiwan, Tajikistan, Thailand, Turkmenistan, United Arab Emirates, Uzbekistan, Vietnam, Yemen

Africa (51): Algeria, Angola, Benin, Botswana, Burkino Faso, Burundi, Cameroon, Cape Verde Islands, Central African Republic, Chad, Congo, D.R. Congo, Egypt, Equatorial Guinea, Eritrea, Ethiopia, Gabon, Gambia, Guana, Guinea, Guinea Bissau, Ivory Coast, Kenya, Lesotho, Liberia, Libya, Madagascar, Malawi, Mali, Mauritania, Mauritius, Morocco, Mozambique, Namibia, Niger, Nigeria, Rwanda, São Tomé e Princípe, Senegal, Seychelles, Sierra Leone, Somalia, South Africa, Sudan, Swaziland, Tanzania, Togo, Tunisia, Uganda, Zambia, Zimbabwe

Oceania (12): American Samoa, Australia, Cook Islands, Fiji, New Caledonia, New Zealand, Papua New Guinea, Samoa, Solomon Islands, Tahiti, Tonga, Vanuatu

Europe

Group 1

Macedonia v Armenia 3–0, Romania v Finland 2–1, Finland v Andorra 3–0, Romania v Macedonia 2–1, Andorra v Romania 1–5, Armenia v Finland 0–2, Holland v Czech Republic 2–0, Czech Republic v Romania 1–0, Finland v Armenia 3–1, Macedonia v Holland 2–2, Andorra v Macedonia 1–0, Armenia v Czech Republic 0–3, Holland v Finland 3–1, Andorra v Holland 0–3, Armenia v Romania 1–1, Macedonia v Czech Republic 0–2, Macedonia v Andorra 0–0, Armenia v Andorra 2–1, Czech Republic v Finland 4–3, Romania v Holland 0–2, Andorra v Czech Republic 0–4, Holland v Armenia 2–0, Macedonia v Romania 1–2, Armenia v Macedonia 1–2, Czech Republic v Andorra 8–1, Holland v Romania 2–0, Czech Republic v Macedonia 6–1, Finland v Holland 0–4, Romania v Armenia 3–0, Macedonia v Finland 0–3, Romania v Andorra 2–0, Andorra v Finland 0–0, Armenia v Holland 0–1, Romania v Czech Republic 2–0, Czech Republic v Armenia 4–1, Finland v Macedonia 5–1, Holland v Andorra 4–0, Czech Republic v Holland 0–2, Finland v Romania 0–1, Andorra v Armenia 0–3, Finland v Czech Republic 0–3, Holland v Macedonia 0–0

	P	W	D	L	F	A	Pts
Holland	12	10	2	0	27	3	32
Czech Republic	12	9	0	3	35	12	27
Romania	12	8	1	3	20	10	25
Finland	12	5	1	6	21	19	16
Macedonia	12	2	3	7	11	24	9
Armenia	12	2	1	9	9	25	7
Andorra	12	1	2	9	4	34	5

Holland qualify for finals
Czech Republic to play-offs

Group 2

Albania v Greece 2–1, Denmark v Ukraine 1–1, Turkey v Georgia 1–1, Georgia v Albania 2–0, Greece v Turkey 0–0, Kazakhstan v Ukraine 1–2, Albania v Denmark 0–2, Turkey v Kazakhstan 4–0, Ukraine v Greece 1–1, Denmark v Turkey 1–1, Kazakhstan v Albania 0–1, Ukraine v Georgia 2–0, Georgia v Denmark 2–2, Greece v Kazakhstan 3–1, Turkey v Ukraine 0–3, Albania v Ukraine 0–2, Greece v Denmark 2–1, Denmark v Kazakhstan 3–0, Georgia v

Greece 1–3, Turkey v Albania 2–0, Georgia v Turkey 2–5, Greece v Albania 2–0, Ukraine v Denmark 1–0, Albania v Georgia 3–2, Turkey v Greece 0–0, Ukraine v Kazakhstan 2–0, Denmark v Albania 3–1, Greece v Ukraine 0–1, Kazakhstan v Turkey 0–6, Kazakhstan v Georgia 1–2, Albania v Kazakhstan 2–1, Georgia v Ukraine 1–1, Turkey v Denmark 2–2, Denmark v Georgia 6–1, Kazakhstan v Greece 1–2, Ukraine v Turkey 0–1, Denmark v Greece 1–0, Georgia v Kazakhstan 0–0, Ukraine v Albania 2–2, Albania v Turkey 0–1, Greece v Georgia 1–0, Kazakhstan v Denmark 1–2

	P	W	D	L	F	A	Pts
Ukraine	12	7	4	1	18	7	25
Turkey	12	6	5	1	23	9	23
Denmark	12	6	4	2	24	12	22
Greece	12	6	3	3	15	9	21
Albania	12	4	1	7	11	20	13
Georgia	12	2	4	6	14	25	10
Kazakhstan	12	0	1	11	6	29	1

Ukraine qualify for finals
Turkey to play-offs

Group 3

Liechtenstein v Estonia 1–2, Slovakia v Luxembourg 3–1, Estonia v Luxembourg 4–0, Latvia v Portugal 0–2, Russia v Slovakia 1–1, Luxembourg v Latvia 3–4, Portugal v Estonia 4–0, Slovakia v Liechtenstein 7–0, Liechtenstein v Portugal 2–2, Luxembourg v Russia 0–4, Slovakia v Latvia 4–1, Latvia v Estonia 2–2, Luxembourg v Liechtenstein 0–4, Portugal v Russia 7–1, Liechtenstein v Latvia 1–3, Luxembourg v Portugal 0–5, Russia v Estonia 4–0, Estonia v Slovakia 1–2, Liechtenstein v Russia 1–2, Estonia v Russia 1–1, Latvia v Luxembourg 4–0, Slovakia v Portugal 1–1, Estonia v Liechtenstein 2–0, Portugal v Slovakia 2–0, Russia v Latvia 2–0, Estonia v Portugal 0–1, Latvia v Liechtenstein 1–0, Luxembourg v Slovakia 0–4, Latvia v Russia 1–1, Liechtenstein v Slovakia 0–0, Estonia v Latvia 2–1, Portugal v Luxembourg 6–0, Russia v Liechtenstein 2–0, Latvia v Slovakia 1–1, Liechtenstein v Luxembourg 3–0, Russia v Portugal 0–0, Portugal v Liechtenstein 2–1, Russia v Luxembourg 5–1, Slovakia v Estonia 1–0, Luxembourg v Estonia 0–2, Portugal v Latvia 3–0, Slovakia v Russia 0–0

	P	W	D	L	F	A	Pts
Portugal	12	9	3	0	35	5	30
Slovakia	12	6	5	1	24	8	23
Russia	12	6	5	1	23	12	23
Estonia	12	5	2	5	16	17	17
Latvia	12	4	3	5	18	21	15
Liechtenstein	12	2	2	8	13	23	8
Luxembourg	12	0	0	12	5	48	0

Portugal qualify for final
Slovakia to play-offs

Group 4

France v Israel 0–0, Ireland v Cyprus 3–0, Switzerland v Faroe Islands 6–0, Faroe Islands v France 0–2, Israel v Cyprus 2–1, Switzerland v Ireland 1–1, Cyprus v Faroe Islands 2–2, France v Ireland 0–0, Israel v Switzerland 2–2, Cyprus v France 0–2, Ireland v Faroe Islands 2–0, Cyprus v Israel 1–2, France v Switzerland 0–0, Israel v Ireland 1–1, Israel v France 1–1, Switzerland v Cyprus 1–0, Faroe Islands v Switzerland 1–3, Ireland v Israel 2–2, Faroe Islands v Ireland 0–2, Faroe Islands v Cyprus 0–3, France v Faroe Islands 3–0, Switzerland v Israel 1–1, Cyprus v Switzerland 1–3, Faroe Islands v Israel 0–2, Rep Ireland v France 0–1, Cyprus v Ireland 0–1, Israel v Faroe Islands 2–1, Switzerland v France 1–1, France v Cyprus 4–0, Ireland v Switzerland 0–0

	P	W	D	L	F	A	Pts
France	10	5	5	0	14	2	20
Switzerland	10	4	6	0	18	7	18
Israel	10	4	6	0	15	10	18
Ireland	10	4	5	1	12	5	17
Cyprus	10	1	1	8	8	20	4
Faroe Islands	10	0	1	9	4	27	1

France qualify for finals
Switzerland to play-offs

Group 5

Italy v Norway 2–1, Slovenia v Moldova 3–0, Moldova v Italy 0–1, Norway v Belarus 1–1, Scotland v Slovenia 0–0, Belarus v Moldova 4–0, Scotland v Norway 0–1, Slovenia v Italy 1–0, Italy v Belarus 4–3, Moldova v Scotland 1–1, Norway v Slovenia 3–0, Italy v Scotland 2–0, Moldova v Norway 0–0, Slovenia v Belarus 1–1, Belarus v Slovenia 1–1, Norway v Italy 0–0, Scotland v Moldova 2–0, Belarus v Scotland 0–0, Moldova v Belarus 2–0, Scotland v Italy 1–1, Slovenia v Norway 2–3, Belarus v Italy 1–4, Moldova v Slovenia 1–2, Norway v Scotland 1–2, Italy v Slovenia 1–0, Norway v Moldova 1–0, Scotland v Belarus 0–1, Belarus v Norway 0–1, Italy v Moldova 2–1, Slovenia v Scotland 0–3

	P	W	D	L	F	A	Pts
Italy	10	7	2	1	17	8	23
Norway	10	5	3	2	12	7	18
Scotland	10	3	4	3	9	7	13
Slovenia	10	3	3	4	10	13	12
Belarus	10	2	4	4	12	14	10
Moldova	10	1	2	7	5	16	5

Italy qualify for the finals
Norway to play-offs

Group 6
Austria v England 2–2, Azerbaijan v Wales 1–1, Northern Ireland v Poland 0–3, Austria v Azerbaijan 2–0, Poland v England 1–2, Wales v Northern Ireland 2–2, Austria v Poland 1–3, Azerbaijan v Northern Ireland 0–0, England v Wales 2–0, Azerbaijan v England 0–1, Northern Ireland v Austria 3–3, Wales v Poland 2–3, England v Northern Ireland 4–0, Poland v Azerbaijan 8–0, Wales v Austria 0–2, Austria v Wales 1–0, England v Azerbaijan 2–0, Poland v Northern Ireland 1–0, Azerbaijan v Poland 0–3, Northern Ireland v Azerbaijan 2–0, Poland v Austria 3–2, Wales v England 0–1, Azerbaijan v Austria 0–0, Northern Ireland v England 1–0, Poland v Wales 1–0, England v Austria 1–0, Northern Ireland v Wales 2–3, Austria v Northern Ireland 2–0, England v Poland 2–1, Wales v Azerbaijan 2–0

	P	W	D	L	F	A	Pts
England	10	8	1	1	17	5	25
Poland	10	8	0	2	27	9	24
Austria	10	4	3	3	15	12	15
N Ireland	10	2	3	5	10	18	9
Wales	10	2	2	6	10	15	8
Azerbaijan	10	0	3	7	1	21	3

England and Poland qualify for finals

Group 7
Belgium v Lithuania1–1, San Marino v Serbia & M'negro 0–3, Bosnia-Herz v Spain 1–1, Lithuania v San Marino 4–0, Bosnia-Herz v Serbia & M'negro 0–0, Spain v Belgium 2–0, Lithuania v Spain 0–0, Serbia & M'negro v San Marino 5–0, Belgium v Serbia & M'negro 0–2, San Marino v Lithuania 0–1, Spain v San Marino 5–0, Belgium v Bosnia-Herz 4–1, Bosnia-Herz v Lithuania 1–1, San Marino v Belgium 1–2, Serbia & M'negro v Spain 0–0, San Marino v Bosnia-Herz

1–3, Serbia & M'negro v Belgium 0–0, Spain v Lithuania 1–0, Spain v Bosnia-Herz 1–1, Bosnia-Herz v Belgium 1–0, Serbia & M'negro v Lithuania 2–0, Belgium v San Marino 8–0, Lithuania v Bosnia-Herz 0–1, Spain v Serbia & M'negro 1–1, Belgium v Spain 0–2, Bosnia-Herz v San Marino 3–0, Lithuania v Serbia & M'negro 0–2, Lithuania v Belgium 1–1, San Marino v Spain 0–6, Serbia & M'negro v Bosnia-Herz 1–0

	P	W	D	L	F	A	Pts
Serbia & M	10	6	4	0	16	1	22
Spain	10	5	5	0	19	3	20
Bosnia-Herz	10	4	4	2	12	9	16
Belgium	10	3	3	4	16	11	12
Lithuania	10	2	4	4	8	9	10
San Marino	10	0	0	10	2	40	0

Serbia & Montenegro qualify for finals
Spain to play-offs

Group 8

Croatia v Hungary 3–0, Iceland v Bulgaria 1–3, Malta v Sweden 0–7, Hungary v Iceland 3–2, Sweden v Croatia 0–1, Croatia v Bulgaria 2–2, Malta v Iceland 0–0, Sweden v Hungary 3–0, Bulgaria v Malta 4–1, Iceland v Sweden 1–4, Malta v Hungary 0–2, Bulgaria v Sweden 0–3, Croatia v Iceland 4–0, Croatia v Malta 3–0, Hungary v Bulgaria 1–1, Bulgaria v Croatia 1–3, Iceland v Hungary 2–3, Sweden v Malta 6–0, Iceland v Malta 4–1, Hungary v Malta 4–0, Iceland v Croatia 1–3, Sweden v Bulgaria 3–0, Bulgaria v Iceland 3–2, Hungary v Sweden 0–1, Malta v Croatia 1–1, Bulgaria v Hungary 2–0, Croatia v Sweden 1–0, Hungary v Croatia 0–0, Malta v Bulgaria 1–1, Sweden v Iceland 3–1

	P	W	D	L	F	A	Pts
Croatia	10	7	3	0	21	5	24
Sweden	10	8	0	2	30	4	24
Bulgaria	10	4	3	3	17	17	15
Hungary	10	4	2	4	13	14	14
Iceland	10	11	8	1	4	27	4
Malta	10	0	3	7	4	32	3

Croatia and Sweden qualify for finals

Group winners and the two best runners-up qualify for finals. The other six runners-up are paired in three two-leg play-off matches.

South America

Argentina v Chile 2–2, Ecuador v Venezuela 2–0, Peru v Paraguay 4–1, Colombia v Brazil 1–2, Uruguay v Bolivia 5–0, Chile v Peru 2–1, Venezuela v Argentina 0–3, Bolivia v Colombia 4–0, Brazil v Ecuador 1–0, Paraguay v Uruguay 4–1, Argentina v Bolivia 3–0, Colombia v Venezuela 0–1, Paraguay v Ecuador 2–1, Uruguay v Chile 2–1, Peru v Brazil 1–1, Chile v Paraguay 0–1, Venezuela v Bolivia 2–1, Brazil v Uruguay 3–3, Colombia v Argentina 1–1, Ecuador v Peru 0–0, Argentina v Ecuador 1–0, Bolivia v Chile 0–2, Paraguay v Brazil 0–0, Peru v Colombia 0–2, Uruguay v Venezuela 0–3, Bolivia v Paraguay 2–1, Uruguay v Peru 1–3, Venezuela v Chile 0–1, Brazil v Argentina 3–1, Ecuador v Colombia 2–1, Ecuador v Bolivia 3–2, Argentina v Paraguay 0–0, Chile v Brazil 1–1, Colombia v Uruguay 5–0, Peru v Venezuela 0–0, Peru v Argentina 1–3, Brazil v Bolivia 3–1, Chile v Colombia 0–0, Paraguay v Venezuela 1–0, Uruguay v Ecuador 1–0, Argentina v Uruguay 4–2, Bolivia v Peru 1–0, Colombia v Paraguay 1–1, Venezuela v Brazil 2–5, Ecuador v Chile 2–0, Bolivia v Uruguay 0–0, Brazil v Colombia 0–0, Chile v Argentina 0–0, Paraguay v Peru 1–1, Venezuela v Ecuador 3–1, Argentina v Venezuela 3–2, Colombia v Bolivia 1–0, Ecuador v Brazil 1–0, Peru v Chile 2–1, Uruguay v Paraguay 1–0, Bolivia v Argentina 1–2, Chile v Uruguay 1–1, Venezuela v Colombia 0–0, Brazil v Peru 1–0, Ecuador v Paraguay 5–2, Bolivia v Venezuela 3–1, Argentina v Colombia 1–0, Paraguay v Chile 2–1, Peru v Ecuador 2–2, Uruguay v Brazil 1–1, Chile v Bolivia 3–1, Colombia v Peru 5–0, Ecuador v Argentina 2–0, Venezuela v Uruguay 1–1, Brazil v Paraguay 4–1, Peru v Uruguay 0–0, Argentina v Brazil 3–1, Chile v Venezuela 2–1, Colombia v Ecuador 3–0, Paraguay v Bolivia 4–1, Bolivia v Ecuador 1–2, Paraguay v Argentina 1–0, Venezuela v Peru 4–1, Brazil v Chile 5–0, Uruguay v Colombia 3–2, Colombia v Chile 1–1, Ecuador v Uruguay 0–0, Venezuela v Paraguay 0–1, Argentina v Peru 2–0, Bolivia v Brazil 1–1, Brazil v Venezuela 3–0, Chile v Ecuador 0–0, Paraguay v Colombia 0–1, Peru v Bolivia 4–1, Uruguay v Argentina 1–0

	P	W	D	L	F	A	Pts
Brazil	18	9	7	2	35	17	34
Argentina	18	10	4	4	29	17	34
Ecuador	18	8	4	6	23	19	28
Paraguay	18	8	4	6	23	23	28
Uruguay	18	6	7	5	23	28	25
Colombia	18	6	6	6	24	16	24
Chile	18	5	7	6	18	22	22
Venezuela	18	5	3	10	20	28	18
Peru	18	4	6	8	20	28	18
Bolivia	18	4	2	12	20	37	14

Brazil, Argentina, Ecuador and Paraguay qualify for finals

Uruguay meet Australia, the Oceania section winners, in the Oceania-South America play-off

CONCACAF

Round 1

Group 1
Grenada v Guyana 5–0; Guyana v Grenada 1–3
United States v Grenada 3–0; Grenada v United States 2–3
United States advanced to Round 2.

Group 2
Bermuda v Montserrat 13–0; Montserrat v Bermuda 0–7
El Salvador v Bermuda 2–1; Bermuda v El Salvador 2–2
El Salvador advanced to Round 2.

Group 3
Haiti v Turks and Caicos Islands 5–0; Turks and Caicos Islands v Haiti 0–2
Haiti v Jamaica 1–1; Jamaica v Haiti 3–0
Jamaica advanced to Round 2.

Group 4
British Virgin Islands v St Lucia 0–1; St Lucia v British Virgin Islands 9–0
Panama v St Lucia 4–0; St Lucia v Panama 0–3
Panama advanced to Round 2.

Group 5
Cayman Islands v Cuba 1–2; Cuba v Cayman Islands 3–0
Cuba v Costa Rica 2–2; Costa Rica v Cuba 1–1
Costa Rica advanced to Round 2.

Group 6
Aruba v Surinam 1–2; Surinam v Aruba 8–1
Surinam v Guatemala 1–1; Guatemala v Surinam 3–1
Guatemala advanced to Round 2.

Group 7
Antigua and Barbuda v Netherlands Antilles 2–0; Netherlands Antilles v Antigua and Barbuda 3–0
Netherlands Antilles v Honduras 1–2; Honduras v Netherlands Antilles 4–0
Honduras advanced to Round 2.

Group 8
Canada v Belize 4–0; Belize v Canada 0–4
Canada advanced to Round 2.

Group 9
Dominica v Bahamas 1–1; Bahamas v Dominica 1–3
Dominica v Mexico 0–10; Mexico v Dominica 8–0
Mexico advanced to Round 2.

Group 10
U.S. Virgin Islands v St Kitts and Nevis 0–4; St Kitts and Nevis v U.S. Virgin
Islands 7–0
Barbados v St Kitts and Nevis 0–2; St Kitts and Nevis v Barbados 3–2
St Kitts and Nevis advanced to Round 2.

Group 11
Dominican Republic v Anguilla 0–0; Anguilla v Dominican Republic 0–6
Dominican Republic v Trinidad & Tobago 0–2; Trinidad & Tobago v Dominican
Republic 4–0
Trinidad and Tobago advanced to Round 2.

Group 12
Nicaragua v St Vincent and the Grenadines 2–2; St Vincent and the Grenadines
v Nicaragua 4–1
St Vincent and the Grenadines advanced to Round 2.

Round 2

Group 1
El Salvador v Panama 2–1, Jamaica v United States 1–1, Jamaica v Panama 1–2,
United States v El Salvador 2–0, Panama v United States 1–1, El Salvador v
Jamaica 0–3, El Salvador v United States 0–2, Panama v Jamaica 1–1, United
States v Panama 6–0, Jamaica v El Salvador 0–0, United States v Jamaica 1–1,
Panama v El Salvador 3–0

	P	W	D	L	F	A	Pts
United States	6	3	3	0	13	3	12
Panama	6	2	2	2	8	11	8
Jamaica	6	1	4	1	7	5	7
El Salvador	6	1	1	4	2	11	4

United States and Panama advance to Round 3

Group 2

Costa Rica v Honduras 2–5, Canada v Guatemala 0–2, Canada v Honduras 1–1, Guatemala v Costa Rica 2–1, Costa Rica v Canada 1–0, Honduras v Guatemala 2–2, Honduras v Canada 1–1, Costa Rica v Guatemala 5–0, Guatemala v Honduras 1–0, Canada v Costa Rica 1–3, Guatemala v Canada 0–1, Honduras v Costa Rica 0–0

	P	W	D	L	F	A	Pts
Costa Rica	6	3	1	2	12	8	10
Guatemala	6	3	1	2	7	9	10
Honduras	6	1	4	1	9	7	7
Canada	6	1	2	3	4	8	5

Costa Rica and Guatemala advance to Round 3

Group 3

St Vincent and the Grenadines v Trinidad & Tobago 0–2, St Kitts and Nevis v Trinidad & Tobago 1–2, Trinidad & Tobago v Mexico 1–3, St Vincent and the Grenadines v St Kitts and Nevis 1–0, Mexico v St Vincent and the Grenadines 7–0, St Vincent and the Grenadines v Mexico 0–1, Trinidad & Tobago v St Kitts and Nevis 5–1, Mexico v Trinidad & Tobago 3–0, St Kitts and Nevis v St Vincent and the Grenadines 0–3, St Kitts and Nevis v Mexico 0–5, Mexico v St Kitts and Nevis 8–0, Trinidad & Tobago v St Vincent and the Grenadines 2–1

	P	W	D	L	F	A	Pts
Mexico	6	6	0	0	2	7	18
Trinidad & Tobago	6	4	0	2	12	9	12
St Vincent and the Grenadines	6	2	0	4	5	12	6
St Kitts and Nevis	6	0	0	6	2	24	0

Mexico and Trinidad & Tobago advance to Round 3

Round 3

Costa Rica v Mexico 1–2, Panama v Guatemala 0–0, Trinidad & Tobago v United States 1–2, Costa Rica v Panama 2–1, Guatemala v Trinidad & Tobago 5–1, Mexico v United States 2–1, Panama v Mexico 1–1, Trinidad & Tobago v Costa Rica 0–0, United States v Guatemala2–0, Guatemala v Mexico 0–2, Trinidad & Tobago v Panama 2–0, United States v Costa Rica 3–0, Costa Rica v Guatemala 3–2, Mexico v Trinidad & Tobago 2–0, Panama v United States 0–3, Guatemala v Panama 2–1, Mexico v Costa Rica 2–0, United States v Trinidad & Tobago 1–0, Panama v Costa Rica 1–3, Trinidad & Tobago v Guatemala 3–2, United States v Mexico 2–0, Costa Rica v Trinidad & Tobago 2–0, Guatemala v United States 0–0, Mexico v Panama 5–0, Costa Rica v United States 3–0,

Mexico v Guatemala 5–2, Panama v Trinidad & Tobago 0–1, Guatemala v Costa Rica 3–1, Trinidad & Tobago v Mexico 2–1, United States v Panama 2–0

	P	W	D	L	F	A	Pts
United States	10	7	1	2	16	6	22
Mexico	10	7	1	2	22	9	22
Costa Rica	10	5	1	4	15	14	16
Trinidad & Tob	10	4	1	5	10	15	13
Guatemala	10	3	2	5	16	18	11
Panama	10	0	2	8	4	2	12

United States, Mexico and Costa Rica qualify for finals
Trinidad & Tobago meet Bahrain, the winners of the Asian play-off, in the Asia-CONCACAF play-off

Asia

Round 1

Turkmenistan 11–0 Afghanistan, Afghanistan 0–2 Turkmenistan; Chinese Taipei 3–0 Macau, Macau 1–3 Chinese Taipei; Bangladesh 0–2 Tajikistan, Tajikistan 2–0 Bangladesh; Laos 0–0 Sri Lanka, Sri Lanka 3–0 Laos; Mongolia 0–1 Maldives, Maldives 12–0 Mongolia; Pakistan 0–2 Kyrgyzstan, Kyrgyzstan 4–0 Pakistan

Round 2

Group 1
Jordan v Laos 5–0, Iran v Qatar 3–1, Jordan v Qatar 1–0, Laos v Iran 0–7, Iran v Jordan 0–1, Qatar v Laos 5–0, Laos v Qatar 1–6, Jordan v Iran 0–2, Laos v Jordan 2–3, Qatar v Iran 2–3, Qatar v Jordan 2–0, Iran v Laos 7–0

	P	W	D	L	F	A	Pts
Iran	6	5	0	1	22	4	15
Jordan	6	4	0	2	10	6	12
Qatar	6	3	0	3	16	8	9
Laos	6	0	0	6	3	33	0

Group 2
Uzbekistan v Iraq 1–1, Palestine v Chinese Taipei 8–0, Chinese Taipei v Uzbekistan 0–1, Palestine v Iraq 1–1, Iraq v Chinese Taipei 6–1, Uzbekistan v Palestine 3–0, Palestine v Uzbekistan 0–3, Chinese Taipei v Iraq 1–4, Iraq v Uzbekistan 1–2, Chinese Taipei v Palestine 0–1, Iraq v Palestine 4–1, Uzbekistan v Chinese Taipei 6–1

	P	W	D	L	F	A	Pts
Uzbekistan	6	5	1	0	16	3	16
Iraq	6	3	2	1	17	7	11
Palestine	6	2	1	3	11	11	7
Chinese Taipei	6	0	0	6	3	26	0

Group 3

India v Singapore 1–0, Japan v Oman 1–0, India v Oman 1–5, Singapore v Japan 1–2, Japan v India 7–0, Oman v Singapore 7–0, India v Japan 0–4, Singapore v Oman 0–2, Oman v Japan 0–1, Singapore v India 2–0, Oman v India 0–0, Japan v Singapore 1–0

	P	W	D	L	F	A	Pts
Japan	6	6	0	0	16	1	18
Oman	6	3	1	2	14	3	10
India	6	1	1	4	2	18	4
Singapore	6	1	0	5	3	13	3

Group 4

China v Kuwait 1–0, Malaysia v Hong Kong 1–3, Hong Kong v China 0–1, Malaysia v Kuwait 0–2, China v Malaysia 4–0, Kuwait v Hong Kong 4–0, Hong Kong v Kuwait 0–2, Malaysia v China 0–1, Kuwait v China 1–0, Hong Kong v Malaysia 2–0, Kuwait v Malaysia 6–1, China v Hong Kong 7–0

	P	W	D	L	F	A	Pts
Kuwait	6	5	0	1	15	2	15
China	6	5	0	1	14	1	15
Hong Kong	6	2	0	4	5	15	6
Malaysia	6	0	0	6	2	18	0

Group 5

Yemen v North Korea 1–1, UAE v Thailand 1–0, Yemen v Thailand 0–3, North Korea v UAE 0–0, Thailand v North Korea 1–4, UAE v Yemen 3–0, North Korea v Thailand 4–1, Yemen v UAE 3–1, North Korea v Yemen 2–1, Thailand v UAE 3–0, UAE v North Korea 1–0, Thailand v Yemen 1–1

	P	W	D	L	F	A	Pts
North Korea	6	3	2	1	11	5	11
UAE	6	3	1	2	6	6	10
Thailand	6	2	1	3	9	10	7
Yemen	6	1	2	3	6	11	5

Group 6
Kyrgyzstan v Tajikistan 1–2, Bahrain v Syria 2–1, Kyrgyzstan v Syria 1–1, Tajikistan v Bahrain 0–0, Bahrain v Kyrgyzstan 5–0, Syria v Tajikistan 2–1, Tajikistan v Syria 0–1, Kyrgyzstan v Bahrain 1–2, Tajikistan v Kyrgyzstan 2–1, Syria v Bahrain 2–2, Syria v Kyrgyzstan 0–1, Bahrain v Tajikistan 4–0

	P	W	D	L	F	A	Pts
Bahrain	6	4	2	0	15	4	14
UAE	6	2	2	2	7	7	8
Thailand	6	2	1	3	5	9	7
Yemen	6	1	1	4	5	12	4

Group 7
Vietnam v Maldives 4–0, South Korea v Lebanon 2–0, Maldives v South Korea 0–0, Vietnam v Lebanon 0–2, South Korea v Vietnam 2–0, Lebanon v Maldives 3–0, Maldives v Lebanon 2–5, Vietnam v South Korea 1–2, Maldives v Vietnam 3–0, Lebanon v South Korea 1–1, Lebanon v Vietnam 0–0, South Korea v Maldives 2–0

	P	W	D	L	F	A	Pts
South Korea	6	4	2	0	9	2	14
Lebanon	6	3	2	1	11	5	11
Vietnam	6	1	1	4	5	9	4
Maldives	6	1	1	4	5	14	4

Group 8
Turkmenistan v Sri Lanka 2–0, Saudi Arabia v Indonesia 3–0, Sri Lanka v Saudi Arabia 0–1, Turkmenistan v Indonesia 3–1, Indonesia v Sri Lanka 1–0, Saudi Arabia v Turkmenistan 3–0, Sri Lanka v Indonesia 2–2, Turkmenistan v Saudi Arabia 0–1, Sri Lanka v Turkmenistan 2–2, Indonesia v Saudi Arabia 1–3, Indonesia v Turkmenistan 3–1, Saudi Arabia v Sri Lanka 3–0

	P	W	D	L	F	A	Pts
Saudi Arabia	6	6	0	0	14	1	18
Turkmenistan	6	2	1	3	8	10	7
Indonesia	6	2	1	3	8	12	7
Sri Lanka	6	0	2	4	4	11	2

Round 3

Group A
South Korea v Kuwait 2–0, Uzbekistan v Saudi Arabia 1–1, Kuwait v Uzbekistan 2–1, Saudi Arabia v South Korea 2–0, Kuwait v Saudi Arabia 0–0,

South Korea v Uzbekistan 2–1, Saudi Arabia v Kuwait 3–0, Uzbekistan v South Korea 1–1, Kuwait v South Korea 0–4, Saudi Arabia v Uzbekistan 3–0, South Korea v Saudi Arabia 0–1, Uzbekistan v Kuwait 3–2

	P	W	D	L	F	A	Pts
Saudi Arabia	6	4	2	0	10	1	14
South Korea	6	3	1	2	9	5	10
Uzbekistan	6	1	2	3	7	11	5
Kuwait	6	1	1	4	4	13	4

Saudi Arabia and South Korea qualify for finals
Uzbekistan to play-offs

Group B

Bahrain v Iran 0–0, Japan v North Korea 2–1, Iran v Japan 2–1, North Korea v Bahrain 1–2, Japan v Bahrain 1–0, North Korea v Iran 0–2, Iran v North Korea 1–0, Bahrain v Japan 0–1, Iran v Bahrain 1–0, North Korea v Japan 0–2, Bahrain v North Korea 2–3, Japan v Iran 2–1

	P	W	D	L	F	A	Pts
Japan	6	5	0	1	9	4	15
Iran	6	4	1	1	7	3	13
Bahrain	6	1	1	4	4	7	4
North Korea	6	1	0	5	5	11	3

Japan and Iran qualify for finals
Bahrain to play-offs

Play-off

Uzbekistan v Bahrain 1–1, Bahrain v Uzbekistan 0–0

Bahrain win on away goals and meet Trinidad & Tobago in Asia-Concacaf play off.

Africa

Round 1

Burkina Faso w/o Central African Republic (withdrawn); Equatorial Guinea 1–0 Togo, Togo 2–0 Equatorial Guinea; Zimbabwe 3–0 Mauritania, Mauritania 2–1 Zimbabwe; Somalia 0–5 Ghana, Ghana 2–0 Somalia; Seychelles 0–4 Zambia, Zambia 1–1 Seychelles; Chad 3–1 Angola, Angola 2–0 Chad; Guinea–Bissau 1–2 Mali, Mali 2–0 Guinea–Bissau; São Tomé e Príncipe 0–1 Libya, Libya 8–0 São Tomé e Príncipe; Niger 0–1 Algeria, Algeria 6–0 Niger;

Tanzania 0–0 Kenya, Kenya 3–0 Tanzania; Madagascar 1–1 Benin, Benin 3–2 Madagascar; Ethiopia 1–3 Malawi, Malawi 0–0 Ethiopia; Guinea 1–0 Mozambique, Mozambique 3–4 Guinea; Botswana 4–1 Lesotho, Lesotho 0–0 Botswana; Congo 1–0 Sierra Leone, Sierra Leone 1–1 Congo; Sudan 3–0 Eritrea, Eritrea 0–0 Sudan; Swaziland 1–1 Cape Verde Islands, Cape Verde Islands 3–0 Swaziland; Uganda 3–0 Mauritius, Mauritius 3–1 AET Uganda; Rwanda 3–0 Namibia, Namibia 1–1 Rwanda; Gambia 2–0 Liberia, Liberia 3–0 Gambia; Burundi 0–0 Gabon, Gabon 4–1 Burundi

Aggregate winners join Tunisia, Cameroon, South Africa, Senegal, Nigeria, Congo DR, Ivory Coast, Egypt and Morocco for the next round.

Round 2

Group 1
Senegal v Congo 2–0, Zambia v Togo 1–0, Liberia v Mali 1–0, Mali v Zambia 1–1, Congo v Liberia 3–0, Togo v Senegal 3–1, Senegal v Zambia 1–0, Congo v Mali 1–0, Liberia v Togo 0–0, Zambia v Liberia 1–0, Mali v Senegal 2–2, Togo v Congo 2–0, Congo v Zambia 2–3, Liberia v Senegal 0–3, Togo v Mali 1–0, Senegal v Liberia 6–1, Zambia v Congo 2–0, Mali v Togo 1–2, Congo v Senegal 0–0, Mali v Liberia 4–1, Togo v Zambia 4–1, Senegal v Togo 2–2, Zambia v Mali 2–1, Liberia v Congo 0–2, Mali v Congo 2–0, Zambia v Senegal 0–1, Togo v Liberia 3–0, Liberia v Zambia 0–5, Congo v Togo 2–3, Senegal v Mali 3–0

	P	W	D	L	F	A	Pts
Togo	10	7	2	1	20	8	23
Senegal	10	6	3	1	21	8	21
Zambia	10	6	1	3	16	10	19
Congo	10	3	1	6	10	14	10
Mali	10	2	2	6	11	14	8
Liberia	10	1	1	8	3	27	4

Togo qualify for the finals

Group 2
Burkina Faso v Ghana 1–0, South Africa v Cape Verde Is 2–1, Uganda v DR Congo 1–0, Cape Verde Is v Uganda 1–0, DR Congo v Burkina Faso 3–2, Ghana v South Africa 3–0, Cape Verde Is v DR Congo 1–1, South Africa v Burkina Faso 2–0, Uganda v Ghana 1–1, Burkina Faso v Uganda 2–0, DR Congo v South Africa 1–0, Ghana v Cape Verde Is 2–0, Cape Verde Is v Burkina Faso 1–0, Ghana v DR Congo 0–0, Uganda v South Africa 0–1, Burkina Faso v Cape Verde Is 1–2, South Africa v Uganda 2–1, DR Congo v Ghana 1–1, Cape Verde

Is v South Africa 1–2, DR Congo v Uganda 4–0, Ghana v Burkina Faso 2–1, Burkina Faso v DR Congo 2–0, South Africa v Ghana 0–2, Uganda v Cape Verde Is 1–0, Burkina Faso v South Africa 3–1, DR Congo v Cape Verde Is 2–1, Ghana v Uganda 2–0, Cape Verde Is v Ghana 0–4, South Africa v DR Congo 2–2, Uganda v Burkina Faso 2–2

	P	W	D	L	F	A	Pts
Ghana	10	6	3	1	17	4	21
DR Congo	10	4	4	2	14	10	16
South Africa	10	5	1	4	12	14	16
Burkina Faso	10	4	1	5	14	13	13
Cape Verde Is	10	3	1	6	8	15	10
Uganda	10	2	2	6	6	15	8

Ghana qualify for the finals

Group 3
Cameroon v Benin 2–1, Ivory Coast v Libya 2–0, Sudan v Egypt 0–3, Libya v Cameroon 0–0, Benin v Sudan 1–1, Egypt v Ivory Coast 1–2, Sudan v Libya 0–1, Benin v Egypt 3–3, Cameroon v Ivory Coast 2–0, Libya v Benin 4–1, Egypt v Cameroon 3–2, Ivory Coast v Sudan 5–0, Libya v Egypt 2–1, Sudan v Cameroon 1–1, Benin v Ivory Coast 0–1, Cameroon v Sudan 2–1, Egypt v Libya 4–1, Ivory Coast v Benin 3–0, Libya v Ivory Coast 0–0, Benin v Cameroon 1–4, Egypt v Sudan 6–1, Cameroon v Libya 1–0, Ivory Coast v Egypt 2–0, Sudan v Benin 1–0, Libya v Sudan 0–0, Egypt v Benin 4–1, Ivory Coast v Cameroon 2–3, Cameroon v Egypt 1–1, Sudan v Ivory Coast 1–3, Benin v Libya 1–0

	P	W	D	L	F	A	Pts
Ivory Coast	10	7	1	2	20	7	22
Cameroon	10	6	3	1	18	10	21
Egypt	10	5	2	3	26	15	17
Libya	10	3	3	4	8	10	12
Sudan	10	1	3	6	6	22	6
Benin	10	1	2	7	9	23	5

Ivory Coast qualify for the finals

Group 4
Algeria v Angola 0–0, Gabon v Zimbabwe 1–1, Nigeria v Rwanda 2–0, Rwanda v Gabon 3–1, Angola v Nigeria 1–0, Zimbabwe v Algeria 1–1, Gabon v Angola 2–2, Rwanda v Zimbabwe 0–2, Zimbabwe v Nigeria 0–3, Algeria v Gabon 0–3, Angola v Rwanda 1–0, Gabon v Nigeria 1–1, Rwanda v Algeria 1–1, Angola v Zimbabwe 1–0, Nigeria v Gabon 2–0, Algeria v Rwanda 1–0, Zimbabwe v

Angola 2–0, Angola v Algeria 2–1, Rwanda v Nigeria 1–1, Zimbabwe v Gabon 1–0, Gabon v Rwanda 3–0, Nigeria v Angola 1–1, Algeria v Zimbabwe 2–2, Algeria v Nigeria 2–5, Angola v Gabon 3–0, Zimbabwe v Rwanda 3–1, Gabon v Algeria 0–0, Nigeria v Zimbabwe 5–1, Rwanda v Angola 0–1

	P	W	D	L	F	A	Pts
Angola	10	6	3	1	12	6	21
Nigeria	10	6	3	1	21	7	21
Zimbabwe	10	4	3	3	13	14	15
Gabon	10	2	4	4	11	13	10
Algeria	10	1	5	4	8	15	8
Rwanda	10	1	2	7	6	16	5

Angola qualify for the finals

Group 5
Malawi v Morocco 1–1, Tunisia v Botswana 4–1, Botswana v Malawi 2–0, Guinea v Tunisia 2–1, Botswana v Morocco 0–1, Malawi v Guinea 1–1, Kenya v Malawi 3–2, Morocco v Tunisia 1–1, Guinea v Botswana 4–0, Botswana v Kenya 2–1, Malawi v Tunisia 2–2, Guinea v Morocco 1–1, Kenya v Guinea 2–1, Morocco v Kenya 5–1, Kenya v Botswana 1–0, Morocco v Guinea 1–0, Tunisia v Malawi 7–0, Botswana v Tunisia 1–3, Morocco v Malawi 4–1, Guinea v Kenya 1–0, Tunisia v Guinea 2–0, Kenya v Morocco 0–0, Malawi v Botswana 1–3, Tunisia v Kenya 1–0, Kenya v Tunisia 0–2, Morocco v Botswana 1–0, Guinea v Malawi 3–1, Botswana v Guinea 1–2, Malawi v Kenya 3–0, Tunisia v Morocco 2–2

	P	W	D	L	F	A	Pts
Tunisia	10	6	3	1	25	9	21
Morocco	10	5	5	0	17	7	20
Guinea	10	5	2	3	15	10	17
Kenya	10	3	1	6	8	17	10
Botswana	10	3	0	7	10	18	9
Malawi	10	1	3	6	12	26	6

Tunisia qualify for the finals

Oceania

Round 1

Group 1
All matches played in Solomon Islands

Solomon Islands v Tonga 6–0, Tahiti v Cook Islands 2–0, Solomon Islands v Cook Islands 5–0, Tahiti v New Caledonia 0–0, Solomon Islands v New Caledonia 2–0, Tonga v Cook Islands 2–1, New Caledonia v Cook Islands 8–0, Tahiti v Tonga 2–0, New Caledonia v Tonga 8–0, Solomon Islands v Tahiti 1–1

	P	W	D	L	F	A	Pts
Solomon Islands	4	3	1	0	14	1	10
Tahiti	4	2	2	0	5	1	8
New Caledonia	4	2	1	1	16	2	7
Tonga	4	1	0	3	2	17	3
Cook Islands	4	0	0	4	1	17	0

Group 2
All matches played in Samoa

Papua New Guinea v Vanuatu 1–1, Samoa v American Samoa 4–0, American Samoa v Vanuatu 1–9, Fiji v Papua New Guinea 4–2, Fiji v American Samoa 11–0, Samoa v Vanuatu 0–3, American Samoa v Papua New Guinea 0–10, Samoa v Fiji 0–4, Fiji v Vanuatu 0–3, Samoa v Papua New Guinea 1–4

	P	W	D	L	F	A	Pts
Vanuatu	4	3	1	0	16	2	10
Fiji	4	3	0	1	19	5	9
Papua New Guinea	4	2	1	1	17	6	7
Samoa	4	1	0	3	5	11	3
American Samoa	4	0	0	4	1	34	0

Round 2

Australia and New Zealand qualified automatically
All matches played in Australia

Australia v New Zealand 1–0, Solomon Islands v Vanuatu 1–0, Tahiti v Fiji 0–0, Australia v Tahiti 9–0, New Zealand v Solomon Islands 3–0, Vanuatu v Fiji 0–1, Australia v Fiji 6–1, New Zealand v Vanuatu 2–4, Solomon Islands v Tahiti 4–0, Australia v Vanuatu 3–0, New Zealand v Tahiti 10–0, Solomon Islands v Fiji 2–1, Australia v Solomon Islands 2–2, New Zealand v Fiji 2–0, Vanuatu v Tahiti 1–2

	P	W	D	L	F	A	Pts
Australia	5	4	1	0	21	3	13
Solomon Islands	5	3	1	1	9	6	10
New Zealand	5	3	0	2	17	5	9
Fiji	5	1	1	3	3	10	4
Tahiti	5	1	1	3	2	24	4
Vanuatu	5	1	0	4	5	9	3

Australia and Solomon Islands qualified for the third round and for 2004 Oceania Cup Final.

Play-off

Australia v Solomon Islands 7–0
Solomon Islands v Australia 1–2

Australia advance to meet fifth-placed South American team

THE PLAY-OFFS

CONCACAF–Asia

Trinidad & Tobago v Bahrain 1–1; Bahrain v Trinidad & Tobago 0–1
Trinidad & Tobago win 2–1 on aggregate

South America–Oceania

Uruguay v Australia 1–0; Australia v Uruguay 1–0
1–1 on aggregate; Australia win 4–2 on penalties

Europe

Switzerland v Turkey 2–0; Turkey v Switzerland 4–2
4–4 on aggregate; Switzerland win on away goals

Spain v Slovakia 5–1; Slovakia v Spain 1–1
Spain win 6–2 on aggregate

Norway v Czech Republic 0–1; Czech Republic v Norway 1–0
Czech Republic win 2–0 on aggregate

2006 GERMANY 9 June–9 July

QUALIFIERS

Angola	Ghana	Serbia and Montenegro
Argentina	Holland	South Korea
Australia	Iran	Spain
Brazil	Italy	Sweden
Costa Rica	Ivory Coast	Switzerland
Croatia	Japan	Togo
Czech Republic	Mexico	Trinidad & Tobago
Ecuador	Paraguay	Tunisia
England	Poland	Ukraine
France	Portugal	United States
Germany	Saudi Arabia	

With the 2010 World Cup finals designated to South Africa, and FIFA committed to seeing the subsequent tournament hosted in South America, Germany's World Cup was to be the last finals hosted in Europe for at least twelve years. In winning the right to stage the tournament, the German bid team – headed by Franz Beckenbauer – had seen off the challenges of England and South Africa in a bitterly fought contest. Beckenbauer, who had won the World Cup as a player and manager, now headed its organizing committee and promised the 'greatest football party ever seen'. This was no hyperbole, and with its new generation of world-class stadia packed to the rafters, its enthusiastically attended fan parks, and the warmth afforded by the hosts to some two million visiting supporters, Germany would be an outstanding event. In fulfilling Beckenbauer's promise, the world's perception of a country still tainted by memories of the two world wars and sometimes considered fusty and uptight was also radically altered.

Again thirty-two countries made up the tournament, including eight debutants, four of which came from Africa. But in an age of multicultural club teams and satellite television, with foreign leagues and international games available at the flick of a remote control, football was becoming more cosmopolitan by the year and there were fewer unknown faces than ever before. Of 736 players, 102 played in English leagues, 74 in Germany, and 61 played their football in Italy. The days when a Florian Albert or Roger Milla could emerge from seemingly nowhere and steal the hearts of the world were apparently over.

Hosts Germany entered the tournament facing the same sort of vitriolic press their English cousins were more accustomed to. Their results in the year leading up to the tournament included a defeat to Slovakia, unimpressive displays against China and Australia, and a 4–1 hammering by Italy in Florence. Their manager, Jürgen Klinsmann, an idol as a player during the 1980s and early 1990s, faced stringent criticism not only for his results, but for his decision to manage Germany while keeping his family home in California, a thirteen-hour flight away. 'They gave us a lesson,' Klinsmann said after the Italy debacle, 'but I'd rather we had it now than in the World Cup.' Germany were Group A top seeds in a line-up that offered an easy passage to the second round: neither Costa Rica, Ecuador nor Poland offered a serious threat even to a German team in a state – by their own methodical standards – of disarray.

Group B was headed by England, who, on paper at least, possessed one of the strongest teams in the tournament. The country's so-called 'Golden Generation' – David Beckham, Steven Gerrard, Frank Lampard, Wayne Rooney, John Terry, Rio Ferdinand, Michael Owen and Ashley Cole – provided a world-class spine to the squad, but unrelenting expectation and a malevolent domestic media had already seriously undermined the squad in the tournament's build-up.

Earlier in the year, it was announced that the country's manager, Sven-Göran Eriksson, would depart post-tournament. Eriksson, so often cautious in his tactical mantra, was otherwise governed by a sense of recklessness that would prove his undoing. When selecting his squad, he picked just four forwards, two of whom – Michael Owen and Wayne Rooney – had been troubled by long-term injury, and a third – the seventeen-year-old tyro, Theo Walcott – was without even a Premier League appearance, never mind a full cap, to his name.

Group C represented 2006's 'Group of Death'. Holland, by virtue of not qualifying in 2002, and debutants Ivory Coast found themselves low down in the seedings and so up against the mighty Argentina. Serbia and Montenegro, appearing for the first time without the vestiges of the old Yugoslavia applied to its name, were unfancied, but had topped their qualifying group ahead of Spain.

Holland, so poor in failing to qualify in 2002 and underwhelming at the 2004 European Championships in Portugal, had shed most of the 1990s generation of stars, whose origins usually lay with Ajax's outstanding European Cup-winning team of the middle of that decade. Now managed by Marco Van Basten they were lacking in the star quality of the teams once dominated by Dennis Bergkamp, Marc Overmars, the De Boer brothers and Patrick Kluivert. But they were a more cohesive unit for these absences, and with such young stars as Arjen Robben, Rafael Van der Vaart and Robin Van Persie possessed the sort of pace and imagination in attack that marked them out as a threat.

The Ivorians had finished runners-up to Egypt in January's African Cup of Nations and were unfortunate to miss out on that title to a wily and experienced Egypt team. In Didier Drogba they possessed one of the world's most outstanding centre forwards, and with the Touré brothers – Arsenal's Kolo, and Yaya of Olympiakos (and later Barcelona) – Didier Zokora and a complement of stars who mostly played in France's Ligue 1 they were Africa's strongest qualifiers.

And then there was Argentina, a team whose core played their football with the elite clubs of Italy, Spain and England. Diego Maradona was, of course, long gone, but in Lionel Messi, the diminutive and brilliant eighteen-year-old Barcelona forward, his rightful heir had – perhaps – finally been found. Such other 'new Maradonas' as Pablo Aimar, Javier Saviola and Carlos Tevez lined up alongside the prodigy, but it was Villareal's Juan Roman Riquelme who provided the creative heartbeat of this team. Tall, slim, gloomy in appearance, one-footed and single-paced, yet possessing an acute footballing brain capable of controlling the tempo of any game, he was in many ways a throwback to a slower, more civilized footballing era: a connoisseur's player, and compelling to watch. The team had grown up under coach José Pekerman, who managed Argentina to FIFA World Youth Championship success in 1995, 1997 and 2001, before taking the national team on in 2004. Impressive qualifiers, they were tipped among the favourites.

Group D offered a few intriguing match-ups. Portugal, with a former World Player of the Year in the veteran winger Luis Figo and a future one in Manchester United's Cristiano Ronaldo, had been unfortunate to miss out on the European Championship crown when they hosted the tournament two years previously and were among the strongest European qualifiers, with a 7–1 annihilation of Russia among their qualifying results. Mexico and Iran, powerhouses in regional qualification but usually underwhelming on the biggest stage, both had realistic chances of progressing from the group. Portugal's former colonial subject, the war-torn diamond-rich state of Angola, made up the group, appearing in the finals for the first time.

Italy came to Germany with its domestic game in disarray as the largest football scandal in a generation came to light. Investigators made public taped conversations, centring on Juventus's powerful general-manager Luciano Moggi, which unveiled at play the complex relationships between top clubs and referees. What emerged was the *Calciopoli* scandal, or *Calciogate* (*calcio* is Italian for football), a complicated network of match-fixing dating back several years, which entirely destroyed Serie A's credibility as a competition. As the World Cup kicked off, revelations were still surfacing on a daily basis, but at the time of Italy's first game against Ghana on 12 June, it seemed likely that Juventus would be stripped of their 2006 title and relegated, along with AC Milan, Lazio, Fiorentina and Reggina. Thirteen of Italy's squad hailed from those clubs.

The troubled Italians were drawn in Group E with Ghana, the United States and the Czech Republic. In qualifying for their first World Cup finals, the Ghanaians had put years of underperforming behind them. They possessed in Sulley Muntari, Stephen Appiah and Michael Essien one of the most talented midfields in the tournament, but lacked the strength in depth of fellow African qualifiers, Ivory Coast. With players like Tomas Rosicky, who had joined Arsenal on the eve of the tournament, Chelsea's goalkeeping colossus Petr Cech and Juventus's Pavel Nedved, the 2003 European Footballer of the Year, the Czech Republic claimed a world-class complement, but they were mostly backed up by journeymen of the European game. The United States were an experienced and cohesive unit, but looked set to struggle in such a tough group.

Holders Brazil, as is seemingly routine, started the tournament as favourites. Because of the increasing clamour for places in the finals, for the first time the previous winners had had to qualify along with everyone else; Brazil topped the South American group, finishing strongly to pip Argentina on goal difference. Rivaldo, now aged thirty-four and playing out his career in Greece, was gone from the national team, but Ronaldo – still not yet thirty – had overcome his chronic injury problems to merit inclusion, alongside Ronaldinho. The creative force behind the 2002 win was now rivalled as the world's best player by Kaka, Milan's powerful, fleet-footed forward. With their most solid defence in years, by any reckoning Brazil were formidable contenders.

They were joined in Group F by Australia, Japan and Croatia. The latter were considered among Europe's best up-and-coming teams, but their time was still, perhaps, to come. Australia, qualifiers for the first time since 1974, were astutely managed by Guus Hiddink – genius of South Korea's march to the 2002 semi-finals – and highly motivated, resilient and spirited contenders. Japan, appearing for the third time, had impressed in flashes when co-hosting the tournament four years earlier, but needed to match the passion of its devoted fans at crucial times on the field.

The ghosts of once great France took top billing in Group G. Managed by Raymond Domenech, a much-mocked individual as well known for his love of astrology and amateur dramatics as any great pedigree as a football manager, he had risen from his position as long-standing France under-21 coach to national coach after Euro 2004. A spluttering qualification campaign, that ultimately saw France lead a group whose top four were separated by just three points, was only brought back on track when he persuaded Zinedine Zidane, Lilian Thuram and Claude Makélélé out of retirement. With players like Patrick Viera, Franck Ribéry and Thierry Henry to call upon they should have been doing much better; the French nation saw it as an indictment of Domenech that they weren't.

Switzerland, South Korea and Togo made up Group G. The African first timers – spearheaded by Arsenal forward Emmanuel Adebayor – were the most intriguing entrants to the tournament. Their inclusion was only guaranteed at the last moment after a player boycott was averted by FIFA agreeing to circumvent the country's dysfunctional Football Association and pay the players directly. South Korea were now managed by Hiddink's compatriot, Dick Advocaat, but even their most ardent fan must surely have been convinced that the country's run of luck had been exhausted four years earlier.

Of the European heavyweights, Spain were given the easiest draw, in Group H, where they were up against Ukraine, Saudi Arabia and Tunisia. With La Liga in the ascendancy and Spanish players also starting to make a deep impression on the English Premier League, there were clear signs that Spain were emerging as European football's next great power. Ukraine, once the footballing heartland of the former USSR, had qualified for the first time as an independent nation. Although most of their squad was an uninspiring assembly of journeymen from the Russian and German leagues, in Andriy Shevchenko – the prolific AC Milan striker, who was Chelsea-bound that summer for a British record transfer fee of £30 million – they possessed one of the finest forwards of the era. Tunisia and Saudi Arabia, so often formidable at regional level, were still to make their presence felt on the world stage.

Venues: Munich, Stuttgart, Nuremburg, Leipzig, Kaiserslautern, Cologne, Hamburg, Hanover, Gelsenkirchen, Frankfurt, Berlin, Dortmund

Group A

Germany
Costa Rica
Poland
Ecuador

Group D

Mexico
Iran
Angola
Portugal

Group B

England
Paraguay
Trinidad & Tobago
Sweden

Group E

Italy
Ghana
United States
Czech Republic

Group C

Argentina
Ivory Coast
Serbia and Montenegro
Holland

Group F

Brazil
Croatia
Australia
Japan

Group G

France
Switzerland
South Korea
Togo

Group H

Spain
Ukraine
Tunisia
Saudi Arabia

THE FIRST SERIES

Derided by their own supporters, missing through injury their influential captain Michael Ballack, lacking the experience that had once been their hallmark, it was still, nevertheless, difficult to dismiss Germany's chances on home soil. They opened the 2006 World Cup against Costa Rica in Munich, and it took just six minutes for some of the self-doubt to evaporate. Philip Lahm, Germany's roving left back who would prove among his country's most potent attackers, strode past a Costa Rica defender on the edge of the area before curling a thunderous right-footed shot off the underside of the crossbar. Six minutes later all the edginess returned when Paolo Wanchope caught the Germany defence asleep, beating the offside trap and goalkeeper to level the scores. A brace from Miroslaw Klose – a naturalized German who, with Lukas Podolski, formed a Polish-born forward pairing – and a late goal by Torsten Frings ensured the victory Germany's play deserved. It had been a vibrant, attacking performance – the highest scoring opening game in World Cup history – that was so unlike the mechanical and defensive German teams of its 1980s and 1990s heyday. But there were lapses too, not least when the sleeping defence allowed Wanchope to grab a second goal on 73 minutes. Germany would be facing far more formidable centre forwards than the Premier League journeyman.

England promised so much on paper but had desperately struggled for cohesion and form since a friendly victory over Argentina the previous November. They opened Group B in Frankfurt, against Paraguay. Eriksson had come under intense criticism for persisting under all circumstances with his captain David Beckham. Once the golden boy of English football, aged thirty-one his pace and influence had diminished and he was a ripe scapegoat for a country that loves making villains out of heroes. But the reality was that with Frank Lampard and Steven Gerrard unable to combine their formidable abilities into a cohesive midfield partnership, Beckham's right boot remained England's most potent creative force. Just three minutes into the Paraguay game, Beckham whipped in a teasing cross-shot from the left, which touched off Carlos Gamarra's head for the game's only goal.

Group C – the group of death – opened in Hamburg between Argentina and Ivory Coast, arguably the best teams in South America and Africa. The Ivorian

'Elephants' threatened to stampede their opponents in the early stages, with a fusillade of attacks. But Argentina withstood the barrage and Juan Roman Riquelme seized control of the game. On 15 minutes he showed the world his potency when his pinpoint corner was crisply volleyed home by Robert Ayala, but the Belgium referee failed to see it cross the line.

The reprieve was only temporary. Nine minutes later Riquelme's viciously whipped free kick from the left found Hernan Crespo, who prodded home through the melee. Riquelme was in the thick of things soon after. On 38 minutes he cut in through the left and his sumptuously weighted through pass found Javier Saviola, who nudged the ball past Tizié and into the back of the net.

The Ivorians were still, nevertheless, very much alive. Didier Drogba pulled a second-half goal back, and his pace and power was testing for the Argentines all afternoon. The South Americans held on for the victory, their speed and élan on the break serving an early warning to the other contenders.

A day later in Leipzig, Holland faced Serbia and Montenegro in Group C's second match, but the Balkan dark horses proved anaemic. Inspired by their lightning winger Arjen Robben – whose quicksilver performance inspired 'Flying Dutchman' headlines the world over – Holland ran out easy winners, Robben's solitary goal flattering their Balkan opponents.

With Portugal overwhelming favourites to progress as Group D winners, the key game was arguably the group's opening match between Mexico and Iran in Nuremburg. The winners of the encounter stood an excellent chance of qualification. Iran took the early initative and only an early outstanding sprawling save by Oswaldo Sanchez in the Mexican goal repelled Vahid Hashemian's powerful header. Omar Bravo gave Mexico a lead on 28 minutes, but Iran refused to give up. Eight minutes later Yahya Golmohammadi deservedly brought the scores level and in a tightly balanced game, Iran held the edge.

Had they possessed a little more adventure instead of trying to hold out for a draw they may have taken three points. Instead they left Nuremburg with none, self-destructing in the final 15 minutes. On 76 minutes Iran's goalkeeper, Ebrahim Mirzapour, miskicked a clearance which found its way to Zinha. His perfectly weighted pass left Bravo with an easy finish. Three minutes later the Mexican victory was assured when Zinha appeared unmarked in the penalty area to head past Mirzapour.

Later that day Angola faced former colonial masters Portugal in Cologne. Their previous two encounters had ended in a thrashing and a farce. In 1989 Portugal won 6–0, and in 2002 were leading 5–1 when the referee abandoned the game after the Africans had four players sent off. A repeat of previous humiliations seemed on the cards early on: Portugal might have scored after just twelve seconds, and did so after four minutes. But they laboured against obstinate defending and failed to add to Pauleta's early strike.

Bruised by the unfolding *calciopoli* scandal back home and with some domestic pundits even urging fans to back their opponents, Italy kicked off Group E in Hanover, against Ghana. Often sluggish starters, Italy defied the form book as well as the prevailing sense of crisis against tricky opponents. Andrea Pirlo's first-half goal brought some light, and Luca Toni – who, for Fiorentina, had scored a staggering 31 Serie A goals against ordinarily parsimonious Italian defences the previous season – spurned three good chances to kill Ghana off in the first half.

Although the West Africans were full of industry, they ultimately lacked guile and a bit of luck. Unfortunate to not be awarded an 80th minute penalty after Cristian Zaccardo's lunge on Asamoah Gyan, with seven minutes remaining Ghana committed defensive suicide. Vincenzo Iaquinta latched onto Sammy Kuffour's underhit back-pass before rounding Richard Kingson and slotting into the empty net.

That evening in Gelsenkirchen, the Czech Republic showed the sort of impressive and incisive football that saw them reach the semi-finals of the European Championships two years earlier, summarily dismissing the United States 3–0. Jan Koller, the Czech's giant centre forward, opened the scoring after just five minutes with a powerful header. The Americans held much possession, but had little cutting edge and when Claudio Reyna struck the post on 28 minutes it represented their best chance.

Eight minutes later, the effervescent Tomas Rosicky – a recent signing for Arsenal who had previously illuminated this corner of Germany with former club Borussia Dortmund – doubled the score with a 35-yard drive that swerved past the grasp of Kasey Keller. He almost repeated the trick in the second half with a dipping shot from the same distance, but it crashed off the American crossbar and to safety. Rosicky's second goal, and the Czech's third, came after a one-two with Pavel Nedved; he dipped his shoulder and accelerated clear of the American defence before clipping home a fine shot to seal a resounding win.

Australia and Japan opened Group F in Kaiserslautern, and it was the Japanese that took a first-half lead in controversial circumstances. On 26 minutes Shunsuke Nakamura chipped in a left-footed cross, which Mark Schwarzer, the Australian goalkeeper, rose to collect, but he was clearly impeded by Naohiro Takahara as the ball flew into the net. No foul said the Egyptian referee, as the Australian players protested first in bewilderment, then anger.

Japan retained their lead until the closing stages when Tim Cahill, Everton's talismanic midfielder who had only started as a substitute and was still recovering from knee ligament damage, intervened. On 83 minutes, Lucas Neill's long throw-in caused panic in the Japan penalty area and Cahill stabbed home through a chaos of flailing legs, before running to the corner flag to carry out the kangaroo-boxing celebration that is his trademark. Five minutes after scoring his country's first ever World Cup goal, Cahill scored Australia's second, letting fly from the edge of Japan's area to send a shot in off the inside of each post. Moments later, Cahill threaded the ball through to John Aloisi, who kept his composure to complete the tournament's most memorable turnaround and some of its biggest celebrations.

Given such excitement, when Brazil faced Croatia in Group F's second match in Berlin a day later, it seemed destined to be anticlimactic. It proved a less dramatic encounter, but was nevertheless a compelling advert for football. Brazil were sumptuous in possession, but sometimes too casual; Croatia, afforded four sights of goal, failed to take any of their chances. Kaka made such profligacy pay with his 44th minute drive, a goal that proved the difference between the two countries.

Group G kicked off in Stuttgart, where France faced Switzerland. The frailties of Raymond Domenech's team were all too apparent as they toiled to a goalless bore draw; Thierry Henry provided the game's best chance shortly before half-time when latching onto Zinedine Zidane's through ball, but he was unable to beat the Swiss goalkeeper Pascal Zuberbühler.

In Frankfurt, Togo, put turbulent preparations behind them to make an impressive start. Otto Pfister, the country's German coach, had quit a week earlier following the players' pay dispute which had so undermined the build-up to their first World Cup. He made a surprise return to his post the day before their opening match against South Korea, and oversaw a good first-half performance in which Mohamed Kader's goal put the Africans ahead against the 2002 semi-finalists.

But the old frailties were still there, and Togo's propensity to self-destruct was never far from the surface. On 53 minutes the captain Jean-Paul Abalo was sent off for bringing down Park Ji-Sung on the edge of the penalty area. Lee Chun-Soo curled the ball home from the resulting free kick. The substitute Ahn Jung-Hwan then netted the winner in the 72nd minute.

Spain's new forward pairing of Fernando Torres and David Villa, a coalminer's son from Asturias who reputedly wanted to follow his father down the pit, gave evidence of their potency in Group H's opening match against Ukraine in Leipzig. Villa scored twice, Torres another in a 4–0 thrashing that was a tough lesson for ten-man Ukraine in their first ever finals match.

In the group's other game, between Tunisia and Saudi Arabia in Munich, the North Africans looked good with a half-time lead through Ziad Jaziri. The Saudis fought back and second-half goals from Yasser Al-Kahtani and substitute Sami Al-Jaber, appearing in his fourth consecutive finals, looked to have won it. But a stoppage-time header from Bolton's Radhi Jaidi meant the spoils were shared and neither country could truly prosper from Ukraine's collapse.

THE SECOND SERIES

With the two best Polish players of their generation – Klose and Podolski – naturalised Germans, it was always going to be a big ask for Poland to progress to the second round, particularly after they limped to a 2–0 defeat against the impressive Ecuador in their opening Group A match. When they faced Germany in Dortmund, Poland were banking on a shock to stay in the tournament. Prior to the match one Polish paper asserted that anything was possible by printing a picture of the former East Germany's Trabant car with the headline 'The Germans Don't Get Everything Right'.

Quickly they demonstrated that they were far from overawed by the occasion. Feisty and energetic, but badly missing the guile a Klose or Podolski might have brought, they held their own until stoppage time, when one substitute, David Odonkor, crossed for another, Oliver Neuville, to score the game's only goal and send Poland home. In Hamburg a day later, Ecuador dismantled a torpid Costa Rica, to qualify alongside the Germans.

In Group B, World Cup debutants Trinidad & Tobago had provided an early shock in holding Sweden to a 0–0 draw. Astutely managed by the veteran Dutch coach Leo Beenhaker, they combined a mixture of Premier League veterans, such as Dwight Yorke and Shaka Hislop, and lower league journeymen, like Port Vale's Chris Birchall and Wrexham's Dennis Lawrence. Up against England's superstars, they were stoic and committed, but ultimately unable to last the duration. On 83 minutes Beckham crossed from the right and Peter Crouch, England's 6 feet 7 inch centre forward, rose above Brent Sancho – possibly with a tug of his opponent's dreadlocks – to head England in front. Steven Gerrard added a late second that added gloss to England's laboured performance.

Every good World Cup produces at least one footballing annihiliation, but punters would surely have put money on the minnows of Angola or Togo to provide 2006's whipping boys, not the hitherto doughty Serbia and Montenegro. But in Gelsenkirchen, when faced with a rampant Argentina, this is what passed. Both in terms of possession, with the South Americans seemingly holding on to the ball at will, and clinical dispatch of chances, this was a footballing master class, and triumph of total football; a piece-by-piece dissection of a footballing power.

Orchestrated by the magnificent Riquelme, Argentina surged into a 3–0 half-time lead, and by full time had doubled it. Maxi Rodriguez scored twice, Crespo, Carlos Tevez and Lionel Messi all found the scoresheet, but the goal everyone would remember came not from one of Argentina's many attackers, but Esteban Cambiasso, a defensive midfielder. It followed a twenty-four-man passing movement, the crucial touch an instinctive back-heel from Saviola that found Cambiasso unmarked on the penalty spot, who fired home with aplomb.

Having witnessed Argentina crush their Balkan opponents, it became imperative for Holland to render their final group match against the South Americans meaningless. To do so, they needed a victory over Ivory Coast, no small matter given the talent at the Africans' disposal.

Yet within 27 minutes the Dutch had a two-goal advantage. First Robin Van Persie scored directly from a ferociously taken free kick on the edge of the Ivorian penalty area, having himself been crudely fouled moments earlier. Four minutes later, Mark Van Bommel's reverse pass found Ruud Van Nistelrooy in space on the edge of the Ivorian penalty area, and his cleanly struck shot found the back of the net.

Against Argentina, Ivory Coast played their best football when trailing by two goals, and in Stuttgart it was the same. Edwin Van der Sar's post had scarcely stopped reverberating from Didier Zokora's thirty-yard drive, when Bakary Koné brought his side back into the game on 38 minutes. His run and angled shot from the edge of the Holland penalty area evaded the reach of the mighty Van der Sar to give the Africans a chance. The game ebbed and flowed in the second half, but chances were few. On 77 minutes Van Persie chested from his own line Drogba's header and so Ivory Coast's best chance passed.

The Ivorians were spirited and full of attacking verve; in an easier group they would surely have progressed, instead of having their dreams ended after just two games. But facing footballing aristocrats on their World Cup debut meant the odds were stacked against them, and where they showed promise, the Dutch, like Argentina, showed experience and ruthlessness.

Against Angola in Hanover, Mexico virtually assured their progress to the last sixteen, despite a frustrating 0–0 draw. Their captain Rafael Marquez struck the outside of the goal post direct from a first-half free kick, and Omar Bravo did the same with two minutes remaining. But Angola, marshalled one way or another by their eccentric goalkeeper Joao Ricardo, a veteran of the Portuguese lower leagues but in Germany without a club, held on.

Portugal, so underwhelming in their opening match against Angola, had much to prove against Iran. Their manager, Luis Felipe Scolari, who had managed Brazil to success four years earlier, resisted calls from sections of the Portuguese media to drop the country's golden boy, Cristiano Ronaldo. Ronaldo would score Portugal's second from the penalty spot after Deco's 63rd minute strike had put them in front. Iran, for their part, offered little invention. But it would be difficult to argue that any of Portugal's talented attackers lived up to their billing. A win is nevertheless a win, and it ensured their first progression beyond the World Cup's first stage in forty years, when Eusebio illuminated the 1966 tournament.

When Italy met the United States in Kaiserslautern for the first of Group E's second phase of matches, the World Cup, hitherto defined by its large, exuberant crowds and made memorable by such moments as Cambiasso's wonder goal, took on a new complexion. Indeed, this ugly encounter seemed to personify many of Italian football's emerging ills, although Italy were by no means wholly culpable for what followed.

The United States, still smarting from their humiliation against the Czech Republic, were fitter, more hungry than their European opponents. There was ceaseless, spirited running and pride in their shirt that should, ultimately, have brought victory.

But it was Italy that took a 22nd minute lead through Alberto Gilardino's diving header from Pirlo's right-wing free kick. Five minutes later, the US drew level when Cristian Zaccardo sliced Bobby Convey's free kick past his own goalkeeper. A minute later the game bubbled over in an ugly manner, Daniele De Rossi brutally elbowing the US centre forward Brian McBride, who, with a black eye and gashed cheek, somehow found the resolve to play the full 90 minutes. De Rossi's game was brought to an abrupt end by the red card shown by the Uruguayan referee, Jorge Larrionda.

By half-time, however, it was ten v ten, when Pablo Mastroeni was dismissed for a crude, studs-up challenge on Pirlo. Afterwards the American coach, Bruce Arena, implied that Larrionda was trying to even up the two teams, but the decision was correct. Two minutes after the interval Larrionda was reaching for the red card again, when Eddie Pope received his second yellow card of the night for a tackle from behind.

Given the American collapse against the Czechs, one might have expected the Italians to march on to victory. Carlos Bocanegra headed against his own crossbar and Keller saved acrobatically from Del Piero. But it was the US that found the net again, through DaMarcus Beasley's fierce shot, disallowed only after McBride was adjudged to be in an offside position and interfering with play.

The United States were given a fighting chance for their third game, when Ghana conquered the Czech Republic. As Chelsea goalkeeper in 2005/06, Petr Cech stood behind one of the meanest defences in world football, conceding just twenty-two league goals through the season. Scarcely could he have envisaged an afternoon at Stamford Bridge like the one he endured in Cologne against Ghana. On 70 seconds, Stephen Appiah's through ball found Asamoah Gyan, whose first touch split the Czech defence and whose second put them a goal to the good.

For the next 90 minutes the Africans attacked the Czechs, only their unusual profligacy, particularly in the second half, sparing the Europeans a thrashing. Appiah dragged a shot wide from thirty yards after Gyan's pass found him in acres of space; Gyan took on three men, but his piercing drive from the edge of the penalty area was repelled by Cech; Amoah was fouled for a 65th minute penalty, for which Tomas Ujfalusi was sent off, but Gyan missed the spot kick; Cech brilliantly beat down Amoah's near-post shot; Cech then saved low from Sulley Muntari.

With Ghana cutting through the Czechs at will, in the 82nd minute Muntari lashed home a shot into the top corner from twelve yards to make it 2–0. Libor Sionko and Jan Polak might have brought some redemption for the Czech's late on, but Ghana's goalkeeper Richard Kingson was equal to their efforts, and soon after the Argentinean referee brought an end to Cech's ordeal.

In Brazil's opening match against Croatia, the favourites had scarcely slipped out of first gear. Up against the spirited Australians five days later they still played within themselves, but ultimately did enough to progress to the last sixteen. Suffocated in the first half by Australia's five-man midfield, neither country had much chance to breathe, let alone create chances. On 49 minutes Adriano was offered a brief glimpse of goal and fired a low shot from the edge of the penalty area through Scott Chipperfield's lunge to put Brazil in front.

The game opened up, and Harry Kewell should have brought the scores level when Dida dropped an easy cross at his feet, but the Australian shot high and wide. Ten minutes later, Kewell sent a long-range effort narrowly over the crossbar, with Dida stranded, and the Socceroos began to believe. Dida punched Bresciano's scissor-kick wide; earlier the same player procrastinated fatally when played in by Mark Viduka. At the other end, Kaka's header from a corner struck the crossbar, before Fred sealed it in the last minute, striking home the rebound after Ronaldinho's shot cannoned off a post. The old hands had won the day without particularly impressing, but it was Australia that seized the moment, seeming to grow as a team.

For the abysmal French, who faced South Korea in their second Group G match, things briefly promised to improve when Thierry Henry gave them a ninth minute opener. But through the first half they failed to make their superiority count and in the second they were overcome by the sort of listlessness that had defined Domenech's reign as manager. On 81 minutes Park Ji-Sung reacted quickest to a penalty area melee and brought the scores level.

In Dortmund, the Togo players called off another threatened strike to face the Swiss in the group's other game. The subject of the dispute was supposedly win and draw bonuses, but the Togolese might have saved their breath. With more commitment and more incisiveness they may have seen off mediocre European opponents, but the Swiss – often second best – withstood any threat. Alex Frei scored on 16 minutes and Tranquillio Barnetta with two minutes left to send the Africans home.

In Group H, Spain, so blistering in their first match against Ukraine, seemed asleep in the first half of their second tie, against Tunisia in Stuttgart. Jaouhar Mnari gave the North Africans an eighth minute lead, which they held for more than an hour. But then Spain seemed to click into action and when Raul opened their scoring with a poacher's goal in the 71st minute, there was only ever likely to be one winner. Five minutes later, Fernando Torres ran clear and slotted home, and in the final minute he went to ground easily and dispatched the resultant penalty.

Ukraine, so woeful against the Spaniards in Leipzig, were given an immediate opportunity to bounce back against Saudi Arabia in Hamburg. They took the opportunity with relish, bringing their goal difference back into neutral with a 4–0 thrashing of the pallid Saudis.

THE THIRD SERIES

By the time the shadow teams of Germany and Ecuador met in Berlin, the main business of Group A had been concluded, with both countries already qualified for the second round. Germany were stronger and faster than their South American opponents and won 3–0 at a canter, their goals again coming from their Polish-born forwards, Klose and Podolski. Poland, for their part, finally scored goals of their own – their first of the tournament. A 2–1 win over Costa Rica in a dead rubber of a match was too little, too late.

Group A's outcome meant that England faced Sweden in Cologne needing to avoid defeat in order to avert a second-round tie with old enemies Germany. Sweden, for their part, were banking on bettering Trinidad's result against Paraguay to qualify for the last sixteen.

England got off to a nightmare start: on three minutes Michael Owen was stretchered off with a cruciate ligament injury from which he would never properly recover. In his absence his team-mates put in their most effective 45 minutes of the tournament, Joe Cole's sumptuous thirty-yard volley providing a deserved half-time advantage. Sweden in the second half were a different proposition, however, and after regrouping adopted a far more direct approach. England looked hideously vulnerable from set pieces and Marcus Allbäck quickly brought the scores level.

Sweden may have taken a lead on several occasions, but on 85 minutes Gerrard made it 2–1. Still there was time for another twist. In the final minute a long throw-in bounced over John Terry, Sol Campbell swung a boot at the ball and missed and Henrik Larrsson prodded home an equalizer from close range. In Kaiserslautern Sweden's progress was in any case ensured when Paraguay beat Trinidad & Tobago 2–0.

Group C's outcome had already been decided ahead of the final round of matches, but even if it counted for little Argentina v Holland in Frankfurt still offered the mouth-watering prospect of two of the World Cup's early pace setters coming face to face. Both countries made significant changes, mostly to avert injuries or suspensions, and while the young Dutch team defended well, it was clear that their opponents kept much in reserve. Tevez hit a post and drew a fine second-half save from Van der Sar, but Argentina's vibrant passing game lacked the incision of previous outings and produced few clear chances as the game petered to a goalless stalemate.

In Munich the dispirited Ivory Coast met the hapless Serbia and Montenegro in another nothing encounter that would emerge as one of the tournament's most exciting games. Shocking defending gifted Serbia a two-goal lead within 20 minutes but, as witnessed previously, the Africans only started to play after giving their opponents a head start. Wave after wave of Ivorian attacks followed. On 36 minutes Dindane scored a retaken penalty, after Milan Dudic bizarrely handled in his own area. On 43 minutes the Serbs were reduced to ten men after Albert Nadj was sent off for a two-footed lunge on Zokora. Dindane brought the scores level with a well-taken header 20 minutes from full time, but the game could still have gone either way. With five minutes remaining, the hopeless Dudic handled in his area for the second time and Bonaventure Kalou scored Ivory Coast's winner.

Much was still to play for in Group D, where the winner was still to be decided between Mexico and Portugal. Angola, who faced Iran in Leipzig, also stood a chance of overtaking the Mexicans in second place.

Portugal's manager, Luis Felipe Scolari, rested four of his regular starters from the team that faced Mexico. After just six minutes, a rapier-like break saw the ball squared to Maniche on the penalty spot, who sidefooted into the top-right corner. Sixteen minutes later Simao, deputising for Ronaldo, doubled the score from the penalty spot.

Mexico battled back immediately and might ultimately have taken something from the game. On 29 minutes Ricardo's outstanding save with his legs stopped Omar Bravo's close-range volley and from the resultant corner José Fonseca headed a goal back. From then on the attacking impetus passed into Mexico's favour, but an equalizing goal was elusive. Bravo sent a 57th minute penalty into the sky, and four minutes later Luis Perez received a second yellow card for diving his way to try and win a second chance from twelve yards.

In Leipzig, it was Iran – already eliminated after straight defeats to Portugal and Mexico – that set the early pace when they faced Angola. They dominated the first half and should have taken the lead in the 24th minute, when Ali Daei rose unmarked at the back post, but the thirty-seven-year-old Iranian football icon sent a wild header over. Soon after the Angola midfielder Mendonca blocked a powerful header from Vahid Hashemian on the line.

Yet it was the Africans that took the lead on the hour mark. Flavio, a second-half substitute, kept his composure to head a deep cross from the right wing past Mirzapour. Hopes of progress were, however, soon dulled. With 15 minutes remaining, Iran won a corner, the Angola defence went to sleep and Sohrab Bakhtiarizadeh headed a deserved equalizer.

Group E was even more replete with possibilities, all four countries entering the third phase with a chance of progression. Italy faced the Czech Republic in Hamburg. The Czechs, ranked second in the world by FIFA, had opened with a demolition of the United States, before themselves being dismantled by Ghana. Which side would the world see in Hamburg? On nine minutes Nedved's glorious through ball, curled with the outside of his boot, played in Milan Baros. But his compatriot's first touch was leaden and thereafter the Czechs struggled to find openings.

Soon after, Italy's centre half Alessandro Nesta limped off with the recurrence of a thigh injury to be replaced by Marco Materazzi. The arrival of the Internazionale colossus – a tattooed, niggling hulk of a man – was to be one of the defining moments of the tournament. Within ten minutes of coming on, Materazzi had made his mark, heading home from a corner.

The Czechs' cause was hampered by the dismissal of Jan Polak for a needless second booking on the stroke of half-time. Although Buffon reacted sharply to Nedved's fierce drive, it was Italy that were the most dangerous threat through the second half. Felippo Inzaghi missed two gilt-edged close-range chances before breaking the Czechs' offside trap with three minutes remaining and rounding Cech to deliver the killer blow.

The Czechs' demise meant that the game simultaneously played between Ghana and the United States in Nuremberg assumed a winner-takes-all complexion. The Africans seized the initiative. Midway through the first half Haminu Draman robbed Reyna, the American captain, on the edge of his own area and bounded through to dispatch the ball past Keller.

On 43 minutes, DaMarcus Beasley repeated the trick, stealing a loose ball on the left wing before sending over a sweeping cross from the angle of the penalty box. The ball eluded Ghana's defence, and Clint Dempsey met it on the half-volley with a thumping shot that swelled the back of Kingson's net.

If the Americans thought that they would enter the second half on level terms, such hopes were soon shattered by the fussy German referee, Marcus Merk. Oguchi Onyewu rose with Razak Pimpong on the edge of the US penalty area to try and clear a high ball, but Merk inexplicably awarded a penalty against the Americans. Despite howls of boos from the American supporters, Stephen Appiah converted the resultant kick.

The US chased and harried, desperate for redemption. Brian McBride headed against a post, Onyewu headed narrowly over from a corner and Kingson was continually alert to further threats. At the other end, Ghana remained a perpetual threat on the break, but no further goals came for either side.

Afterwards, the US coach Bruce Arena raged about Merk's decision to penalise Onyewu. But if he had been dealt a bad hand by the German referee, Merk's display paled into insignificance when compared to that of his English counterpart, Graham Poll, officiating between Croatia and Australia in Stuttgart later that day.

Poll was the most divisive English referee of his generation. He had forged his refereeing reputation as a no-nonsense stickler, but infuriated fans, players and managers with the way he laid down football's law. A frequent accusation, that Poll always denied, was that he liked to be at the centre of attention. Many memories of him are defined by maddening incidents, such as when he scuppered an Everton Merseyside derby victory by prematurely blowing the final whistle as the winning goal sailed into the Liverpool net.

Although Australia seemed to have irresistible momentum after two impressive displays against Japan and Brazil, it was Croatia that took the early initiative. Darijo Srna opened the scoring after just two minutes, crashing home his country's first goal of the tournament with a thirty-yard free kick that arrowed into the top corner of Zeljko Kalac's net. The goalkeeper, called up to replace Mark Schwarzer, was one of several Australia players with Croatian antecedents.

In a tense, feisty encounter, Poll's first big call came on 38 minutes when he correctly adjudged Stjepan Tomas to have handled in his own penalty area. Craig Moore scored the resultant penalty, but equilibrium was brief. On 56 minutes Niko Kovac twisted right then left before firing a low drive that slipped under the hapless Kalac's body.

The spirited Socceroos were, however, indomitable and surged forward in search of an equalizer. Correct in spotting Tomas's first-half handling of the ball, Poll missed an identical scenario with the same player on 74 minutes, only awarding a corner. Four minutes later some natural justice was restored when his linesman missed Kewell in a marginally offside position as the Liverpool forward fired home Australia's equalizer.

The game then veered out of control, as Poll began to hand out a flurry of cards. Brett Emerton was harshly booked, then Dario Simic was given a second yellow, but Srna, who shoved Poll in the chest, escaped punishment. Two minutes later it was ten v ten when Emerton received a harsh second yellow card after the ball was kicked into his hand. Then in injury time Josip Simunic, already booked 30 minutes previously, was given a second yellow but Poll, seemingly oblivious to his earlier booking, failed to bring out his third red card of the night. Simunic played on, but when Australia had a third goal disallowed, the Croat was booked a third time for dissent and finally sent on his way. Immediately after Poll blew his final whistle, signalling Australia's progress and also the end of his international refereeing career. The Socceroos celebrated, the Croats hissed with indignation, and Poll's critics basked in the sense of *schadenfreude* that accompanied his inevitable demise.

Given such dramas, the other Group F game between Japan and Brazil was overshadowed. Despite falling behind to Keiji Tamada's 34th minute opener, the Brazilians put in their best performance of the tournament, running riot in the second half as a 4–1 win was secured. Ronaldo's brace brought him level with Gerd Müller as the World Cup's all-time leading goalscorer.

France entered the final round of Group G matches in danger of falling at the first hurdle once more. Facing Togo should have promised an easy route to advancement and France had so many chances against the Africans' porous defence that they should have run up a cricket score. Trézéguet, Henry, Ribéry and Malouda were all profligate – sometimes wildly so – before Patrick Viera marked his thirtieth birthday with a turn and shot on the penalty spot that finally found the back of the net on 55 minutes. Six minutes later his former Arsenal team-mate, Thierry Henry, doubled the score, settling French nerves and ensuring their first finals' win since beating Brazil in the final eight years earlier.

French progress meant that Switzerland needed to avoid defeat to South Korea to qualify alongside them. Phillipe Senderos bravely opened the scoring with a 23rd minute header, his head catching both the ball and his Korean opponent, leaving him bloodied. The Swiss remained in control and Alex Frei sealed the Koreans' fate with a controversial 77th minute goal. Flagged offside by the Argentine official, as some Korean players stood still, the linesman, realising his mistake, lowered his flag while Frei kept playing, rounding the goalkeeper to score. With memories of Korea's dubious passage to the semi-finals in 2002, a perverse sense of justice prevailed in some minds.

In Group H Spain played their reserve team, but still had too much class for a woeful Saudi Arabia, winning 1–0. For the third tournament in succession the Saudis returned to their desert kingdom without recording a win.

The Saudis' demise left Ukraine and Tunisia to fight it out for the last of the sixteen second-round places. The east Europeans were the least feeble of two poor teams, but still required Andrei Shevchenko's tumble in the penalty area and subsequent penalty to proceed to the knockout stage of the tournament.

Final Tournament – Germany
First Round

Group A

Germany (2) **4, Costa Rica** (1) **2**
9.6.06 MUNICH
Germany: Lehmann, Friedrich, Mertesacker, Metzelder, Lahm (1), Schweinsteiger, Frings (1), Borowski (Kehl), Schneider (Odonkor), Podolski, Klose (2) (Neuville)

Costa Rica: Porras, Marin, Umaña, Gonzalez, Martinez (Drummond), Fonseca, Solis (Bolaños), Centeno, Sequeira, Gomez (Azofeifa), Wanchope (2)
Referee: Elizondo (Argentina)

Ecuador (1) **2, Poland** (0) **0**
9.6.06 GELSENKIRCHEN
Ecuador: Mora, De la Cruz, Hurtado (Guagua), Espinoza, Reasco, Mendez, Castillo, Valencia, Edwin Tenorio, Delgado (1) (Urrutia), Carlos Tenorio (1) (Kaviedes)
Poland: Boruc, Jop, Baszczynski, Bak, Zewlakow, Sobolewski (Jelen), Krzynowek (Kosowski), Szymkowiak, Smolarek, Radomski, Zurawski (Brozek)
Referee: Kamikawa (Japan)

Germany (0) **1, Poland** (0) **0**
14.6.06 DORTMUND
Germany: Lehmann, Friedrich (Odonkor), Mertesacker, Metzelder, Lahm, Schweinsteiger (Borowski), Ballack, Frings, Schneider, Podolski (Neuville (1)), Klose
Poland: Boruc, Bosacki, Baszczynski, Bak, Zewlakow (Dudka), Sobolewski, Krzynowek (Lewandowski), Smolarek, Radomski, Zurawski, Jelen (Brozek)
Referee: Cantalejo (Spain)

Ecuador (1) **3, Costa Rica** (0) **0**
15.6.06 HAMBURG
Ecuador: Mora, De la Cruz, Hurtado, Espinoza (Guagua), Reasco, Mendez, Edwin Tenorio, Castillo, Valencia (Urrutia), Delgado (1), Carlos Tenorio (1) (Kaviedes (1))
Costa Rica: Porras, Marin, Umaña, Wallace, Gonzalez (Hernandez), Solis, Centeno (Bernard), Sequeira, Fonseca (Saborio), Gomez, Wanchope.
Referee: Codjia (Benin)

Germany (2) **3, Ecuador** (0) **0**
20.6.06 BERLIN
Germany: Lehmann, Friedrich, Huth, Mertesacker, Lahm, Schneider (Asamoah), Frings (Borowski), Ballack, Schweinsteiger, Podolski (1), Klose (2) (Neuville)
Ecuador: Mora, De la Cruz, Guagua, Espinoza, Ambrossi, Mendez, Edwin Tenorio, Ayovi (Urrutia), Valencia (Lara), Borja (Benitez), Kaviedes
Referee: Ivanov (Russia)

Poland (1) **2, Costa Rica** (1) **1**
20.6.06 HANOVER
Poland: Boruc, Baszczynski, Bak, Bosacki (2), Zewlakow, Krzynowek, Szymkowiak, Radomski (Lewandowski), Jelen, Smolarek (Rasiak), Zurawski (Brozek)
Costa Rica: Porras, Drummond (Wallace), Marin, Umaña, Gonzalez, Badilla, Bolaños (Saborio), Solis, Centeno, Gomez (1) (Hernandez), Wanchope
Referee: Maidin (Singapore)

	P	W	D	L	F	A	Pts
Germany	3	3	0	0	8	2	9
Ecuador	3	2	0	1	5	3	6
Poland	3	1	0	2	2	4	3
Costa Rica	3	0	0	3	3	9	0

Group B

England (1) **1, Paraguay** (0) **0**
10.6.06 FRANKFURT
England: Robinson, Neville, Ferdinand, Terry, Ashley Cole, Beckham, Lampard, Gerrard, Joe Cole (Hargreaves), Owen (Downing), Crouch
Paraguay: Villar (Bobadilla), Caniza, Gamarra (o.g.), Caceres, Toledo (Nuñez), Bonet (Cuevas), Acuña, Paredes, Riveros, Valdez, Santa Cruz
Referee: Rodriguez (Mexico)

Trinidad & Tobago (0) **0, Sweden** (0) **0**
10.6.06 DORTMUND
Trinidad & Tobago: Hislop, Avery John, Sancho, Lawrence, Gray, Birchall, Edwards, Theobald (Whitley), Samuel (Glen), Stern John, Yorke
Sweden: Shaaban, Linderoth (Källström), Mellberg, Lucic, Edman, Ljungberg, Alexandersson, Anders Svensson (Allbäck), Wilhelmsson (Jonson), Ibrahimovic, Larsson.
Referee: Maidin (Singapore)

England (0) **2, Trinidad & Tobago** (0) **0**
15.6.06 NUREMBURG
England: Robinson, Carragher (Lennon), Terry, Ferdinand, Ashley Cole, Beckham, Lampard, Gerrard, Joe Cole (Downing), Owen (Rooney), Crouch (2)
Trinidad & Tobago: Hislop, Edwards, Sancho, Lawrence, Gray, Birchall, Whitley, Yorke, Theobald (Wise), Stern John, Jones (Glen)
Referee: Kamikawa (Japan)

Sweden (0) **1, Paraguay** (0) **0**
15.6.06 BERLIN
Sweden: Isaksson, Mellberg, Lucic, Edman, Linderoth, Alexandersson, Ljungberg (1), Wilhelmsson (Jonson), Källström (Elmander), Ibrahimovic (Allbäck), Larsson
Paraguay: Bobadilla, Caniza, Caceres, Gamarra, Nuñez, Bonet (Barreto), Acuña, Paredes, Riveros (Dos Santos), Santa Cruz (Lopez), Valdez
Referee: Michel (Slovakia)

England (1) **2, Sweden** (0) **2**
20.6.06 COLOGNE
England: Robinson, Carragher, Ferdinand (Campbell), Terry, Ashley Cole, Beckham, Lampard, Hargreaves, Joe Cole (1), Owen (Crouch), Rooney (Gerrard (1))
Sweden: Isaksson, Mellberg, Lucic, Edman, Alexandersson, Jonson (Wilhelmsson), Linderoth (Andersson), Källström, Ljungberg, Allbäck (1) (Elmander), Larsson (1)
Referee: Busacca (Switzerland)

Paraguay (1) **2, Trinidad & Tobago** (0) **0**
20.6.06 KAISERSLAUTERN
Paraguay: Bobadilla, Nuñez, Gamarra, Caceres (Manzur), Caniza (Da Silva), Barreto, Acuña, Paredes, Dos Santos, Santa Cruz, Valdez (Cuevas (1))
Trinidad & Tobago: Jack, Avery John (Jones), Sancho (o.g.), Lawrence, Birchall, Whitley (Lapaty), Edwards, Theobald, Glen (Wise), Stern John, Yorke
Referee: Rosetti (Italy)

	P	W	D	L	F	A	Pts
England	3	2	1	0	5	2	7
Sweden	3	1	2	0	3	2	5
Paraguay	3	1	0	2	2	2	3
Trinidad & Tobago	3	0	1	2	0	4	1

Group C

Argentina (2) **2, Ivory Coast** (0) **1**
10.6.06 HAMBURG
Argentina: Abbondanzieri, Burdisso, Ayala, Heinze, Sorin, Maxi, Mascherano, Cambiasso, Riquelme (Aimar), Saviola (1) (Gonzalez), Crespo (1) (Palacio)
Ivory Coast: Tizié, Eboué, Kolo Touré, Meité, Boka, Akale (Bakary Koné), Zokora, Kalou (Dindane), Keita (Arouna Koné), Yaya Touré, Drogba (1)
Referee: De Bleeckere (Belgium)

Holland (1) **1, Serbia and Montenegro** (0) **0**
11.6.06 LEIPZIG
Holland: Van der Sar, Heitinga, Mathijsen (Boulahrouz), Ooijer, Van Bronckhorst, Sneijder, Van Bommel (Landzaat), Cocu, Van Persie, Van Nistelrooy (Kuyt), Robben (1)
Serbia and Montenegro: Jevric, Dragutinovic, Gavrancic, Nenad Djordjevic (Koroman), Krstajic, Duljaj, Stankovic, Predrag Djordjevic, Nadj, Kezman (Ljuboja), Milosevic (Zigic)
Referee: Merk (Germany)

Argentina (3) **6, Serbia and Montenegro** (0) **0**
16.6.06 GELSENKIRCHEN
Argentina: Abbondanzieri, Burdisso, Ayala, Heinze, Sorin, Gonzalez (Cambiasso (1)), Mascherano, Rodriguez (2) (Messi (1)), Riquelme, Saviola (Tevez (1)), Crespo (1)
Serbia and Montenegro: Jevric, Duljaj, Gavrancic, Krstajic, Dragutinovic, Nadj (Ergic), Stankovic, Predrag Djordjevic, Koroman (Ljuboja), Milosevic (Vukic), Kezman
Referee: Rosetti (Italy)

Holland (2) **2, Ivory Coast** (1) **1**
16.6.06 STUTTGART
Holland: Van der Sar, Heitinga (Boulahrouz), Ooijer, Mathijsen, Van Bronckhorst, Van Bommel, Sneijder (Van der Vaart), Cocu, Van Persie (1), Van Nistelrooy (1) (Landzaat), Robben
Ivory Coast: Tizié, Eboué, Kolo Touré, Meité, Yaya Touré, Boka, Arouna Koné (Akale), Zokora, Romaric (Yapi Yapo), Drogba, Bakary Koné (1) (Dindane)
Referee: Ruiz (Colombia)

Holland (0) **0, Argentina** (0) **0**
21.6.06 FRANKFURT
Holland: Van der Sar, Jaliens, Boulahrouz, Ooijer, De Cler, Sneijder (Maduro), Cocu, Van der Vaart, Van Persie (Landzaat), Van Nistelrooy (Babel), Kuyt
Argentina: Abbondanzieri, Burdisso (Coloccini), Ayala, Milito, Cufré, Cambiasso, Mascherano, Rodriguez, Riquelme (Aimar), Tevez, Messi (Cruz)
Referee: Cantalejo (Spain)

Ivory Coast (1) **3, Serbia and Montenegro** (2) **2**
21.6.06 MUNICH
Ivory Coast: Barry, Eboué, Domoraud, Boka, Kouassi, Zokora, Yaya Touré, Akale (Bakary Koné (1 pen)), Keita (Kalou), Arouna Koné, Dindane (2, 1 pen)
Serbia and Montenegro: Jevric, Nenad Djordjevic, Gavrancic, Krstajic (Nadj), Dudic, Ergic, Duljaj, Stankovic, Predrag Djordjevic, Ilic (1), Zigic (1) (Milosevic)
Referee: Rodriguez (Mexico)

	P	W	D	L	F	A	Pts
Argentina	3	2	1	0	8	1	7
Holland	3	2	1	0	3	1	7
Ivory Coast	3	1	0	2	5	6	3
Serbia and Montenegro	3	0	0	3	2	10	0

Group D

Mexico (1) **3, Iran** (1) **1**
11.6.06 NUREMBURG
Mexico: Sanchez, Salcido, Mendez, Osorio, Pineda, Marquez, Torrado (Perez), Pardo, Franco (Zinha (1)), Borgetti (Fonseca), Bravo(1)
Iran: Mirzapour, Golmohammadi (1), Rezaei, Kaabi, Nosrati (Borhani), Mahdavikia, Nekounam, Karimi (Mandachini), Teymourian, Hashemian, Daei
Referee: Rosetti (Italy)

Portugal (1) **1, Angola** (0) **0**
11.6.06 COLOGNE
Portugal: Ricardo, Meira, Miguel, Nuno Valente, Ricardo Carvalho, Petit (Maniche), Tiago (Viano), Figo, Ronaldo (Costinha), Pauleta (1), Simao
Angola: Joao Ricardo, Jamba, Kali, Loco, Delgado, Figueiredo (Miloy), Macanga, Mateus, Mendonca, Ze Kalanga (Edson), Akwa (Mantorras)
Referee: Larrionda (Uruguay)

Mexico (0) **0, Angola** (0) **0**
16.6.06 HANOVER
Mexico: Sanchez, Salcido, Marquez, Osorio, Pineda (Morales), Torrado, Zinha (Arellano), Pardo, Mendez, Franco (Fonseca), Bravo
Angola: Joao Ricardo, Jamba, Kali, Delgado, Loco, Figueiredo (Rui Marques), Macanga, Mateus (Mantorras), Mendonca, Ze Kalanga (Miloy), Akwa
Referee: Maidin (Singapore)

Portugal (0) **2, Iran** (0) **0**
17.6.06 FRANKFURT
Portugal: Ricardo, Miguel, Valente, Carvalho, Meira, Maniche (Petit), Costinha, Deco (1) (Tiago), Figo (Simao), Ronaldo (1 pen), Pauleta
Iran: Mirzapour, Golmohammadi (Bakhtiarizadeh), Rezaei, Nosrati, Teymourian, Nekounam, Mahdavikia, Hashemian, Karimi (Zandi), Madanchi (Khatibi), Kaabi
Referee: Poulat (France)

Portugal (2) **2, Mexico** (1) **1**
21.6.06 GELSENKIRCHEN
Portugal: Ricardo, Miguel, Ricardo Carvalho, Meira, Caneira, Petit, Maniche (1), Tiago, Figo (Boa Morte), Simao (1 pen), Postiga (Gomes)
Mexico: Sanchez, Pineda (Castro), Marquez, Osorio, Salcido, Rodriguez (Zinha), Pardo, Perez, Mendez (Franco), Fonseca (1), Bravo
Referee: Michel (Slovakia)

Iran (0) **1, Angola** (0) **1**
21.6.06 LEIPZIG
Iran: Mirzapour, Kaabi (Bohrani), Rezaei, Bakhtiarizadeh (1), Nosrati (Shojaei), Mahdavikia, Zandi, Madanchi, Taymoorian, Hashemian (Khatibi), Daei
Angola: Joao Ricardo, Jamba, Kali, Delgado, Loco, Ze Kalanga, Miloy, Figueiredo (Rui Marques), Mateus (Love), Mendonca, Akwa (Flavio (1))
Referee: Shield (Australia)

	P	W	D	L	F	A	Pts
Portugal	3	3	0	0	5	1	9
Mexico	3	1	1	1	4	3	4
Angola	3	0	2	1	1	2	2
Iran	3	0	1	2	2	6	1

Group E

Italy (1) **2, Ghana** (0) **0**
12.6.06 HANOVER
Italy: Buffon, Zaccardo, Nesta, Cannavaro, Grosso, Totti (Camoranesi), Perrotta, Pirlo (1), De Rossi, Toni (Del Piero), Gilardino (Iaquinta (1))
Ghana: Kingson, Pantsil, Kuffour, Mensah, Pappoe (Shilla), Muntari,Essien, Appiah, Eric Addo, Gyan (Tachie-Mensah), Amoah (Pimpong)
Referee: Simon (Brazil)

Czech Republic (2) **3, United States** (0) **0**
12.6.06 GELSENKIRCHEN
Czech Republic: Cech, Grygera, Rozehnal, Ujfalusi, Jankulovski, Poborsky (Polak), Galasek, Rosicky (2) (Stajner), Nedved, Plasil, Koller (1) (Lokvenc)
United States: Keller, Cherundolo (O'Brien), Onyewu, Pope, Lewis, Donovan, Reyna, Convey, Mastroeni (Johnson), Beasley, McBride (Wolff)
Referee: Amarilla (Paraguay)

Italy (1) **1, United States** (1) **1**
17.6.06 KAISERSLAUTERN
Italy: Buffon, Zaccardo (o.g.) (Del Piero), Nesta, Cannavaro, Zambrotta, Perrotta, Pirlo, De Rossi, Totti (Gattuso), Toni (Iaquinto), Gilardino (1)
United States: Keller, Cherundolo, Onyewu, Pope, Bocanegra, Dempsey (Beasley), Mastroeni, Reyna, Convey (Conrad), McBride, Donovan
Referee: Larrionda (Uruguay)

Ghana (1) **2, Czech Republic** (0) **0**
17.6.06 COLOGNE
Ghana: Kingson, Pantsil, Kuffour, Mensah, Shilla, Muntari (1), Essien, Appiah, Otto Addo (Boateng), Gyan (1) (Pimpong), Amoah (Eric Addo)
Czech Republic: Cech, Grygera, Jankulovski, Rozehnal, Ujfalusi, Galase (Polak), Nedved, Poborsky (Stajner), Rosicky, Plasil (Sionko), Lokvenc
Referee: Elizondo (Argentina)

Italy (1) **2, Czech Republic** (0) **0**
22.6.06 HAMBURG
Italy: Buffon, Zambrotta, Cannavaro, Nesta (Materazzi (1)), Grosso, Camoranesi (Barone), Pirlo, Perrotta, Gattuso, Totti, Gilardino (Inzaghi (1))
Czech Republic: Cech, Grygera, Kovac (Heinz), Rozehnal, Jankulovski, Plasil, Polak, Nedved, Poborsky (Stajner), Rosicky, Baros (Jarolim)
Referee: Archundia (Mexico)

Ghana (2) **2, United States** (1) **1**
22.6.06 NUREMBERG
Ghana: Kingson, Mensah, Pantsil, Shilla, Mohamed, Appiah (1 pen), Essien, Draman (1) (Tachie-Mensah), Boateng (Otto Addo), Amoah (Eric Addo), Pimpong
United States: Keller, Onyewu, Conrad, Cherundolo (Johnson), Bocanegra, Dempsey (1), Reyna (Olson), Lewis (Convey), Beasley, Donovan, McBride
Referee: Merk (Germany)

	P	W	D	L	F	A	Pts
Italy	3	2	1	0	5	1	7
Ghana	3	2	0	1	4	3	6
Czech Republic	3	1	0	2	3	4	3
United States	3	0	1	2	2	6	1

Group F

Australia (0) **3, Japan** (1) **1**
12.6.06 KAISERSLAUTERN
Australia: Schwarzer, Neill, Moore (Kennedy), Culina, Wilkshire (Aloisi (1)), Emerton, Grella, Bresciano (Cahill (2)), Chipperfield, Kewell, Viduka
Japan: Kawaguchi, Komano, Miyamoto, Santos, Tsuboi (Moniwa) (Oguro), Nakazawa, Fukunishi, Hidetoshi Nakata, Nakamura, Takahara, Yanagisawa (Ono)
Referee: El Fatah (Egypt)

Brazil (1) **1, Croatia** (0) **0**
13.6.06 BERLIN
Brazil: Dida, Cafu, Lucio, Juan, Roberto Carlos, Zé Roberto, Emerson, Ronaldinho, Kaka (1), Adriano, Ronaldo (Robinho)
Croatia: Pletikosa, Simunic, Robert Kovac, Tudor, Simic, Srna, Babic, Nico Kovac (Leko), Kranjcar, Prso, Klasnic (Olic)
Referee: Tellez (Mexico)

Brazil (0) **2, Australia** (0) **0**
18.6.06 MUNICH
Brazil: Dida, Cafu, Lucio, Juan, Roberto Carlos, Emerson (Gilberto Silva), Zé Roberto, Kaka, Ronaldinho, Ronaldo (Robinho), Adriano (1) (Fred (1))
Australia: Schwarzer, Neill, Moore (Aloisi), Popovic (Bresciano), Culina, Emerton, Chipperfield, Grella, Cahill (Kewell), Sterjovski, Viduka
Referee: Merk (Germany)

Japan (0) **0, Croatia** (0) **0**
18.6.06 NUREMBURG
Japan: Kawaguchi, Miyamoto, Kaji, Nakazawa, Santos, Ogasawara, Hidetoshi Nakata, Nakamura, Fukunishi (Inamoto), Takahara (Oguro), Yanagisawa (Tamada)
Croatia: Pletikosa, Robert Kovac, Simunic, Tudor (Olic), Simic, Srna (Bosnjak), Babic, Nico Kovac, Kranjcar (Modric), Prso, Klasnic
Referee: De Bleeckere (Belgium)

Brazil (1) **4, Japan** (1) **1**
22.6.06 DORTMUND
Brazil: Dida (Rogerio Ceni), Lucio, Juan, Cicinho, Gilberto (1), Kaka (Zé Roberto), Ronaldinho (Ricardinho), Gilberto Silva, Juninho (1), Ronaldo (2), Robinho
Japan: Kawaguchi, Santos, Tsuboi, Kaji, Nakazawa, Hidetoshi Nakata, Ogasawara (Koji Nakata), Nakamura, Inamoto, Maki (Takahara) (Oguro), Tamada (1)
Referee: Poulat (France)

Croatia (1) **2, Australia** (1) **2**
22.6.06 STUTTGART
Croatia: Pletikosa, Simic, Tudor, Tomas (Klasnic), Simunic, Srna (1), Nico Kovac (1), Babic, Kranjcar (Jerko Leko), Prso, Olic (Modric)
Australia: Kalac, Neill, Moore (1 pen), Chipperfield (Kennedy), Emerton, Grella (Aloisi), Culina, Cahill, Sterjovski (Bresciano), Kewell (1), Viduka
Referee: Poll (England)

	P	W	D	L	F	A	Pts
Brazil	3	3	0	0	7	1	9
Australia	3	1	1	1	5	5	4
Croatia	3	0	2	1	2	3	2
Japan	3	0	1	2	2	7	1

Group G

France (0) **0, Switzerland** (0) **0**
13.6.06 STUTTGART
France: Barthez, Thuram, Sagnol, Gallas, Abidal, Wiltord (Dhorasoo), Vieira, Makélélé, Zidane, Ribéry (Saha), Henry
Switzerland: Zuberbühler, Philipp Degen, Müller (Djourou), Senderos, Magnin, Cabanas, Wicky (Margairaz), Vogel, Barnetta, Frei, Streller (Gygax)
Referee: Ivanov (Russia)

South Korea (0) **2, Togo** (1) **1**
13.6.06 FRANKFURT
South Korea: Lee Woon-Jae, Young-Pyo Lee, Choi Jin-Cheul, Kim Young-Chul, Kim Jin-Kyu (Ahn Jung-Hwan (1)), Song Chong-Gug, Lee Eul-Yong (Kim Nam Il), Park Ji-Sung, Lee Ho, Cho Jae-Jin (Kim Sang Sik), Lee Chun-Soo (1)
Togo: Agassa, Nibombé, Abalo, Tchangai, Salifou (Aziawonou), Mamam, Romao, Mohamed Kader (1), Senaya (Touré), Assemoassa (Forson), Adebayor
Referee: Poll (England)

France (1) **1, South Korea** (0) **1**
18.6.06 LEIPZIG
France: Barthez, Sagnol, Thuram, Gallas, Abidal, Vieira, Makélélé, Malouda (Dhorasoo), Zidane (Trézéguet), Wiltord (Ribéry), Henry (1)
South Korea: Lee Woon-Jae, Kim Young-Chul, Kim Dong-Jin, Choi Jin-Cheul, Lee Young-Pyo, Kim Nam-Il, Lee Ho (Kim Sang-Sik), Lee Eul-Yong (Seol Ki-Hyeon), Lee Chun-Soo (Ahn Jung-Hwan), Cho Jae-Jin, Park Ji-Sung (1)
Referee: Archundia (Mexico)

Switzerland (1) **2, Togo** (0) **0**
19.6.06 DORTMUND
Switzerland: Zuberbühler, Magnin, Senderos, Müller, Degen, Raphael Wicky, Vogel, Cabanas (Streller), Barnetta (1), Gygax (Yakin), Frei (1) (Lustrinelli)
Togo: Agassa, Nibombé, Touré, Tchangai, Agboh (Salifou), Dossevi (Senaya), Mamam (Malm), Romao, Mohamed Kader, Forson, Adebayor
Referee: Amarilla (Paraguay)

France (0) **2, Togo** (0) **0**
23.6.06 COLOGNE
France: Barthez, Gallas, Silvestre, Thuram, Sagnol, Malouda (Wiltord), Makélélé, Vieira (1) (Diarra), Ribéry (Govou), Trézéguet, Henry (1)
Togo: Agassa, Nibombé, Abalo, Tchangai, Aziawonou, Mamam (Olufadé), Senaya, Salifou, Forson, Mohamed Kader, Adebayor (Dossevi)
Referee: Larrionda (Uruguay)

Switzerland (1) **2, South Korea** (0) **0**
23.6.06 HANOVER
Switzerland: Zuberbühler, Degen, Senderos (1) (Djourou), Müller, Spycher, Barnetta, Vogel, Cabanas, Yakin (Margairaz), Wicky (Behrami), Frei (1)
South Korea: Lee Woon-Jae, Lee Young-Pyo (Ahn Jung-Hwan), Kim Jin-Kyu, Choi Jin-Cheul, Kim Dong-Jin, Park Ji-Sung, Kim Nam-Il, Lee Ho, Lee Chun-Soo, Cho Jae-Jin, Park Chu-Young (Seol Ki-Hyeon)
Referee: Elizondo (Argentina)

	P	W	D	L	F	A	Pts
Switzerland	3	2	1	0	4	0	7
France	3	1	2	0	3	1	5
South Korea	3	1	1	1	3	4	4
Togo	3	0	0	3	1	6	0

Group H

Spain (2) **4, Ukraine** (0) **0**
14.6.06 LEIPZIG
Spain: Casillas, Pernia, Puyol, Ramos, Pablo, Garcia (Fabregas), Alonso (1) (Albelda), Xavi, Senna, Torres (1), Villa (2, 1 pen) (Raul)
Ukraine: Shovkovskyi, Nesmachnyi, Rusol, Vashchuk, Yezerskyi, Gusev (Shelayev), Gusin (Vorobey), Tymoshchuk, Rotan (Rebrov), Voronin, Shevchenko
Referee: Busacca (Switzerland)

Tunisia (1) **2, Saudi Arabia** (0) **2**
14.6.06 MUNICH
Tunisia: Boumnijel, Trabelsi, Jemmali, Haggui, Jaidi (1), Namouchi, Bouazizi (Nafti), Mnari, Chedli (Ghodhbane), Chikhaoui (Essediri), Jaziri (1)
Saudi Arabia: Zaid, Dokhi, Tukar, Al-Montashari, Sulaimani, Al-Ghamdi, Noor (Ameen), Aziz, Al-Temyat (Al-Hawsawi), Khariri, Al-Khatani (1), (Al-Jaber (1))
Referee: Shield (Australia)

Spain (0) **3, Tunisia** (1) **1**
19.6.06 STUTTGART
Spain: Casillas, Sergio Ramos, Puyol, Pablo, Pernia, Xavi, Alonso, Senna (Fabregas), Garcia (Raul (1)), Torres (2, 1 pen), Villa (Joaquin)
Tunisia: Boumnijel, Haggui, Jaidi, Ayari (Yahia), Trabelsi, Mnari (1), Bouazizi (Ghodhbane), Chedli (Guemadia), Namouchi, Nafti, Jaziri
Referee: Simon (Brazil)

Ukraine (2) **4, Saudi Arabia** (0) **0**
19.6.06 HAMBURG
Ukraine: Shovkovskyi, Rusol (1), Nesmachnyi, Svidersky, Gusev, Tymoshchyuk, Shelayev, Kalinichenko (1), Rebrov (1) (Rotan), Shevchenko (1) (Milevskyi), Voronin (Gusin)
Saudi Arabia: Zaid, Dokhi (Al-Khathran), Sulaimani, Al-Montashari, Tukar, Saud Al-Khariri, Al-Ghamdi, Noor (Al-Jaber), Ameen (Al-Hawsawi), Aziz, Al-Qahtani
Referee: Poll (England)

Spain (1) **1, Saudi Arabia** (0) **0**

23.6.06 KAISERSLAUTERN

Spain: Cañizares, Salgado, Marchena, Albelda, Raul (Villa), Reyes (Torres), Lopez, Iniesta, Joaquin, Fabregas (Xavi), Juanito (1)

Saudi Arabia: Zaid, Dokhi, Tukar, Al-Montashari, Noor, Al-Jaber (Al-Hawsawi), Al-Harthi, Khathran, Sulimani (Massad), Kariri, Aziz (Al-Temyat)

Referee: Codjia (Benin)

Ukraine (0) **1, Tunisia** (0) **0**

23.6.06 BERLIN

Ukraine: Shovkovskyi, Nesmachnyi, Rusol, Sviderskyi, Tymoschuk, Shelayev, Gusev, Rebrov (Vorobey), Kalinichenko (Gusin), Shevchenko (1 pen) (Milevskyi), Voronin

Tunisia: Boumnijel, Haggui, Jaidi, Ayari, Trabelsi, Mnari, Bouazizi (Santos), Chedli (Ben Saada), Namouchi, Nafti (Ghodhbane), Jaziri

Referee: Amarilla (Paraguay)

	P	W	D	L	F	A	Pts
Spain	3	3	0	0	8	1	9
Ukraine	3	2	0	1	5	4	6
Tunisia	3	0	1	2	3	6	1
Saudi Arabia	3	0	1	2	2	7	1

THE ROUND OF SIXTEEN

The round of sixteen kicked off on 24 June, with two of the tournament's form teams – hosts Germany and trailblazers Argentina – vying for the chance to meet each other in the quarter-finals.

In Munich, the Germans faced Sweden, whose directness had so unsettled England in the group stage. Germany – a people so often perceived by the outside world as uptight and reserved – had already surprised everyone by throwing what was widely reckoned the greatest football party ever witnessed, and no atmosphere was more highly charged than when Germany themselves played. Against the Swedes the mood was raucous, loud, *electric*.

It was an intimidating challenge and would have been even for more accomplished opponents than the spirited but ultimately limited Scandinavians. Within just four minutes their defence crumbled, and within twelve the game was over. First from Michael Ballack's pass, Miroslav Klose took out the Swedish defence with an impeccable first touch; Isaksson raced from his line to deny him, but Podolski fired home the rebound via Mellberg's head. Eight minutes later, Klose held up the ball on the edge of the Sweden area and, encircled by his opponents, played a cute reverse pass into Podolski's path for him to fire in Germany's second with a first-time left-foot shot from fourteen yards.

Germany at times threatened to run away with the game, but Isaksson's outstanding goalkeeping staved off a rout. Hopes of a Swedish revival died on 35 minutes, when Teddy Lucic was sent off for a second bookable offence. A miserable afternoon was ensured eight minutes after half-time, when Henrik Larsson sent a penalty kick crashing into the heavens.

Later that day, Argentina – so invincible in the group stages – showed a glimmer of fallibility when they faced Mexico. The World Cup's perennial underachievers had been underwhelming in the first round, but started against Argentina in terrific fashion. Jared Borgetti headed narrowly over from a corner in the first minute, and on six minutes the breakthrough came. A free kick from the right wing was flicked on by Mendez, and Mexico's captain, Rafael Marquez, slid in unmarked at the back post to send the ball into the roof of the Argentina net. Mexico's huge travelling support celebrated ecstatically.

These celebrations were abruptly cut short. On ten minutes, Riquelme whipped in a devilish corner kick from the right. Borgetti stooped to block Crespo, but succeeded only in heading the ball into his own net, although the Argentine claimed – and was subsequently awarded – the goal as his own.

The following 110 minutes witnessed some of the tournament's best football as a mini classic unfolded. Reminiscent of the great Brazil v France clash in the quarter-finals of the 1986 tournament, both teams showed technical excellence, composure and élan as they swaggered around, masters of sublime, intricate play in tight spaces, footballing equals in virtually every respect. Crespo lobbed narrowly wide and Abbondanzieri tipped Borgetti's twenty-five-yard drive over the Argentine bar. On the stroke of half-time Gabriel Heinze was fortunate to evade a red card after cynically wrestling Francisco Fonseca to the ground when he was through on goal.

In the second half, Borgetti found himself unmarked and in space six yards from goal after Fonseca's cross, but Sorin's lunge prevented a near-certain goal. Then Riquelme played in Javier Saviola, who brought a smart save from Sanchez in the Mexican goal.

Night fell, a plethora of substitutions came, and still the unrelenting pace of the game was maintained. Nothing divided the two countries until Lionel Messi stroked home Pablo Aimar's square ball in stoppage time – only to see the goal wrongly disallowed for offside.

With extra time's arrival, the momentum was suddenly with Argentina, who began to throw forward wave after wave of attacks. Mexico proved indomitable until the 98th minute. With his chest, Maxi Rodriguez took Sorin's cross on the right corner of the Mexico area and then unleashed a fabulous, dipping, curling left-footed shot past Sanchez. It was the goal of the tournament and a worthy decider to one of 2006's outstanding encounters.

A day later, the spluttering, underwhelming English took centre stage, now depleted of the injured Michael Owen, but with Wayne Rooney – the bullish and brilliant tyro – returning to fitness after a metatarsal injury that had originally threatened his participation in the tournament. In Stuttgart they faced Ecuador, one of the most impressive first-round dark horses, but who seemingly offered England a straightforward passage to the quarter-finals.

But nothing could be taken for granted with the misfiring English. On 11 minutes, John Terry completely misjudged a simple blocking header thirty yards from his own goal, blasting the ball into the air instead of to safety. Carlos Tenorio raced through, composed himself and, one-on-one with Paul Robinson, seemed certain to score until Ashley Cole's desperate block deflected the ball onto the England crossbar and to safety.

England continued to look hideously vulnerable in defence, particularly from set pieces. But on the hour mark, they broke the deadlock from a free kick of their own. The maligned David Beckham rode to his country's rescue yet again, sending a superb, swerving free kick dipping over the Ecuador wall and into the bottom corner of the goal. They might have scored again when Rooney broke in from the left, and cut the ball back for Lampard who was lurking on the penalty spot. So often deadly for his club, Chelsea, he proved hopeless in front of goal throughout the tournament, and sent his shot high over the crossbar, his erraticness seeming to symbolise England's form.

If England's match was insipid, the encounter between Portugal and Holland in Nuremburg later that evening was anything but. Holland were the better attacking team, and had the best chances: Van Persie single-handedly weaved through the Portugal defence, before curling a shot across the face of goal; Cocu almost snapped the Portugal crossbar with a fierce close-range volley that deflected down and to safety; and Dirk Kuyt was profligate when played in one-on-one, but the teams were ultimately separated by Maniche's 23rd minute goal. The game will nevertheless be remembered less for Portugal's victory than the petulance and spite that defined it.

The sixteen yellow cards and four reds that accompanied Maniche's goal represented a World Cup record in an unpleasant encounter that defied the tournament's logo – 'A Time to Make Friends'. It wasn't helped by the Russian referee, Valentin Ivanov, who entirely lost control of the game, but both sides crudely weighed into each other.

Khalid Boulahrouz set the tone in the seventh minute with a high foot that found its way into Ronaldo's groin. Costinha crudely scythed down Cocu, then received a second yellow on half-time for handball. In truth this was the least of the crimes committed all evening. Luis Figo head-butted Mark Van Bommel, but escaped with a booking. Boulahrouz then received a second yellow after Figo made a meal out of a stray – but seemingly unintentional – elbow; the two benches then came together in a display of posturing and shoving. Deco hacked down Heitinga, but received only a yellow – and another brawl ensued with Sneijder shoving over Petit. On 78 minutes Ivanov gave Deco the red card his earlier hack deserved, but this time for the innocuous offence of holding on to the ball too long. Deep into stoppage time the Russian made it nine v nine by dismissing Van Bronckhurst for a second yellow, bringing the game to its sordid conclusion.

A day later in Kaiserslautern – 26 June – where Italy faced Australia, there was more opprobrium directed towards referees. This time it was a Spaniard, Luis Medina Cantalejo. Three minutes into stoppage time and with the scores goalless, the Italy left back, Fabio Grosso, cut into his opponents' penalty area. As he neared the edge of the six-yard box, Lucas Neill lunged in with a sliding tackle, but Grosso cut the ball back and tried to go around Neill's prostrate body, in the process tripping over him. There was neither an attempt to foul nor make an illegal obstruction but Cantalejo pointed to the spot anyway, and Francesco Totti sent the Australians packing.

Before Cantalejo's decisive call the game had been an evenly matched encounter, with the rag-bag Australians threatening to be the second underdogs to humiliate the thoroughbred Italians in successive tournaments. Australia had the edge on first-half possession, but Italy looked likelier to score. Mark Schwarzer thrice denied Luca Toni with fine saves.

On 50 minutes Marco Materazzi was harshly sent off for a hack on Marco Bresciano and the initiative passed firmly to Australia. Scott Chipperfield brought a good low save from Gianluigi Buffon; Tim Cahill headed over from eight yards; and Bresciano and Mark Viduka both went close late on, but Cantalejo's generosity saw Italy's progress secured with the game's last kick.

Fortune was clearly favouring Italy, who faced the winners of Switzerland v Ukraine, played later that day. Switzerland had been impressive qualifiers from Group G, defying all odds to outstrip France. Ukraine, on the other hand, had scraped through their group, losing their first match 4–0 to Spain. What followed in Cologne – an abysmal encounter – when the two countries met, had Italy confident of a straightforward passage to the last four.

In the worst game of 2006, both teams showed an entire paucity of quality over the course of 120 goalless minutes. Andrei Shevchenko struck the Swiss crossbar in the first half, and Alexander Frei repeated the trick at the other end, direct from a free kick. But little else of note followed, and when the game reached its inevitable scoreless conclusion no greater aptitude was shown during the penalty shoot-out. Four of the seven penalties were missed, and Ukraine prevailed 3–0, despite Shevchenko seeing his country's first spot kick saved. Switzerland returned home despite not conceding a goal in six-and-a-half hours of World Cup football.

Brazil, in the tournament's group stage, had barely moved up from second gear, but still shown the world their deadly potential, brushing off all challengers without breaking a sweat. Their round of sixteen opponents, Ghana, had been impressive on their World Cup debut, dismantling the highly rated Czechs, but were missing through suspension their best player, Michael Essien, Chelsea's midfield powerhouse.

Ghana were enthusiastic and provided Brazil a stern challenge, but ultimately fell down by fulfilling the old cliché about African defending. On five minutes Kaka cut the Ghanaian defence in two with a superlative through ball that found Ronaldo one-on-one with Kingson. Excellent in such situations, even approaching his veteran years, he shimmied past the Ghana goalkeeper and slotted home Brazil's opener, in the process surpassing Gerd Müller's World Cup scoring record, which he had equalled a week earlier.

Ghana enjoyed more possession and pressure and John Mensah might have equalized with a powerful header, but Dida kept the ball out with a flailing foot. None of this advantage was made to count and in first-half injury time Adriano doubled Brazil's lead by stroking Cafu's right-wing cross home with his thigh.

The Africans kept plugging away through the second half, Asamoah Gyan forcing a fine, low save from Dida on 69 minutes. The striker turned villain 12 minutes later, however, receiving a second yellow card for a ludicrous dive inside the Brazil penalty area. Ghana then fell to pieces. Ricardinho split the Ghana defence and Zé Roberto, finding himself without a defender in sight, tipped the ball over Kingson and then rolled it home for Brazil's third. Kingson's heroics in the final stages ensured Brazil were not flattered any further by the scoreline.

The round of sixteen concluded with Europe's great form team – Spain – up against France, a country so out of sorts that they made England's performances look impressive. But time and again Spain had proven frail when in the knockout stages of a tournament, and despite their earlier, often mesmerising displays, would prove so again.

After a cagey opening, the first real action came on 22 minutes. Thierry Henry cut down the right wing and sent a delicious cross straight across the Spain six-yard box. Ribéry mistimed his run and Viera, expecting the shot, missed the ball with the goal at his mercy. Six minutes later the breakthrough came when Thuram went through the back of Pablo with a crude tackle and the Italian referee pointed to the spot. David Villa made no mistake and put Spain in front.

It was Zinedine Zidane, for a decade the heartbeat of the French team, that reawakened France from their slumber. Back from suspension, he tormented Spain all night with simple passes and expansive ones, his feet like a wand casting magic across the Hanover pitch. As half-time approached, Zidane increased pressure on the Spaniards and on 41 minutes they finally cracked.

Ribéry played a one-two with Viera, who sprung the offside trap with a deft through ball, and the forward was suddenly away from the defence, rounding the goalkeeper and levelling the scores.

The second half saw France ascendant, but the game could still have gone either way. Malouda chipped just over after being sumptuously played in by Zidane, while Joaquin hit the side netting at the other end. Then with seven minutes remaining, Zidane took a free kick from the right, midway through the Spain half; Henry headed on and Viera stole in at the back post to head the ball home via Ramos's leg and put France in front.

Deep into injury time Zidane scored the goal his performance merited. Spain lost possession near the halfway line and ball was played forward to Wiltord, who put Zidane through thirty-five yards from goal. He cut inside Puyol with ease, then sent Casillas the wrong way with a low drive into the bottom corner to prolong his illustrious career by at least another 90 minutes.

The Round of Sixteen

Germany (2) **2, Sweden** (0) **0**
24.6.06 MUNICH
Germany: Lehmann, Friedrich, Metzelder, Mertesacker, Lahm, Schneider, Frings (Kehl), Ballack, Schweinsteiger (Borowski), Podolski (2) (Neuville), Klose
Sweden: Isaksson, Mellberg, Lucic, Edman, Alexandersson, Linderoth, Ljungberg, Jonson (Wilhelmsson), Källström (Hansson), Ibrahimovic (Allbäck), Larsson
Referee: Simon (Brazil)

Argentina (1) **2, Mexico** (1) **1** (aet, 1–1 after 90 mins)
24.6.06 LEIPZIG
Argentina: Abbondanzieri, Ayala, Heinze, Scaloni, Sorin, Cambiasso (Aimar), Riquelme, Maxi Rodriguez (1), Mascherano, Saviola (Messi), Crespo (1) (Tevez)
Mexico: Sanchez, Salcido, Marquez (1), Guardado (Pineda), Osorio, Castro, Mendez, Pardo (Torrado), Borgetti, Morales (Zinha), Fonseca
Referee: Busacca (Switzerland)

England (0) **1, Ecuador** (0) **0**
25.6.06 STUTTGART
England: Robinson, Hargreaves, Terry, Ferdinand, Ashley Cole, Beckham (1) (Lennon), Carrick, Gerrard (Downing), Lampard, Joe Cole (Carragher), Rooney
Ecuador: Mora, De la Cruz, Hurtado, Espinoza, Reasco, Valencia, Edwin Tenorio (Lara), Castillo, Mendez, Delgado, Carlos Tenorio (Kaviedes)
Referee: De Bleeckere (Belgium)

Portugal (1) **1, Holland** (0) **0**
25.6.06 NUREMBERG
Portugal: Ricardo, Miguel, Carvalho, Meira, Valente, Costinha, Maniche (1), Figo (Tiago), Deco, Ronaldo (Simao), Pauleta (Petit)
Holland: Van der Sar, Boulahrouz, Ooijer, Mathijsen (Van der Vaart), Van Bronckhorst, Van Bommel (Heitinga), Sneijder, Cocu (Vennegoor of Hesselink), Van Persie, Kuyt, Robben
Referee: Ivanov (Russia)

Italy (0) **1, Australia** (0) **0**
26.6.06 KAISERSLAUTERN
Italy: Buffon, Zambrotta, Materazzi, Cannavaro, Grosso, Perrotta, Pirlo, Gattuso, Del Piero (Totti (1 pen)), Toni (Barzagli), Gilardino (Iaquinto)
Australia: Schwarzer, Bresciano, Neill, Moore, Chipperfield, Grella, Culina, Cahill, Sterjovski (Aloisi), Wilkshire, Viduka
Referee: Cantalejo (Spain)

Switzerland (0) **0, Ukraine** (0) **0** (aet, Ukraine won 3–0 on penalties)
26.6.06 COLOGNE
Switzerland: Zuberbühler, Djourou (Grichting), Magnin, Müller, Philipp Degen, Vogel, Cabanas, Wicky, Barnetta, Yakin (Streller), Frei (Lustrinelli)
Ukraine: Shovkovskyi, Vashchuk, Nesmachnyi, Tymoschuk, Shelayev, Gusev, Gusin, Kalinichenko (Rotan), Voronin (Milevskyi), Vorobey (Rebrov), Shevchenko
Referee: Archundia (Mexico)

Brazil (2) **3, Ghana** (0) **0**
27.6.06 DORTMUND
Brazil: Dida, Cafu, Lucio, Juan, Roberto Carlos, Emerson (Gilberto Silva), Zé Roberto (1), Kaka (Ricardinho), Ronaldinho, Ronaldo (1), Adriano (1) (Juninho)
Ghana: Kingson, Pantsil, Pappoe, Mensah, Illiasu, Eric Addo (Boateng), Appiah, Dramani, Muntari, Amoah (Tachie-Mensah), Gyan
Referee: Michel (Slovakia)

France (1) **3, Spain** (1) **1**
27.6.06 HANOVER
France: Barthez, Sagnol, Thuram, Gallas, Abidal, Ribéry (1), Zidane (1), Makélélé, Vieira (1), Malouda (Govou), Henry (Wiltord)
Spain: Casillas, Pablo, Puyol, Sergio Ramos, Pernia, Fabregas, Xavi (Senna), Alonso, Villa (1 pen) (Joaquin), Torres, Raul (Garcia)
Referee: Rosetti (Italy)

THE QUARTER-FINALS

The quarter-finals opened in Berlin with tournament hosts, Germany, facing its pacesetters, Argentina, who had so impressed in its opening stage. Yet the World Cup's history is littered with the carcasses of footballing teams who have fallen before their time – often the victims of German organisation over their own exuberance. England in 1970 and 1990, Holland in 1974, France in 1982 and 1986 had each had their lights extinguished by occasionally brutal Teutonic organisation.

Germany's class of 2006 were different from the cynical teams of the 1980s and 1990s, however, bringing élan and panache to the workmanlike structure that traditionally provided the core to German success. While the Germans were less expansive than in previous games, the quarter-final was nevertheless a fascinating encounter, full of individual battles and intricate interplay. Goalscoring opportunities, however, remained rare. Michael Ballack had the best first-half chance, heading over from twelve yards. Shortly after the interval, Robert Ayala put Argentina in front, heading home a corner after Crespo's dummy run wreaked momentary confusion in the German penalty area. Germany pressed hard, but Argentina had the clearest chance to score when Jens Lehman pushed Rodriguez's 73rd minute shot around his post.

The game, however, hinged on three substitutions over the course of four minutes. On 71 minutes the Argentine goalkeeper Abbondanzieri limped off injured after a collision with Klose. A minute later Riquelme, the talisman, was replaced by Cambiasso, a far more defensive player. On 74 minutes, Tim Borowski entered as a substitute and he would make several decisive inputs to the game's destiny.

Riquelme's withdrawal handed some of the attacking initiative back to Germany. On 80 minutes Ballack crossed from the left, Borowski's flick header played in Klose and his pinpoint header from eight yards saw an equalizer.

The game seemed headed for penalties from there on, with both teams limited to long-range shots. When they eventually came, Germany's colourful goalkeeper, Jens Lehman, previously a spectator for much of the game, rose to the challenge, outshining Franco, the Argentine substitute. Lehman saved Argentina's second penalty from Ayala, handing the advantage to his ruthless compatriots. Borowski made the score 4–2, then indicated that the Argentineans – provoking their opponents where they stood watching from the halfway line – should shut up. This lit the torch-paper of Argentine indignation, and it fully ignited when Lehman stooped to stop Cambiasso's penalty and send Germany through. As the Germans celebrated, Argentine players led by Gabriel Heinze attacked the victors. Leandro Cufré, an unused substitute, was eventually shown a red card for an assault on Germany defender Per Mertesacker, who was kicked in the groin and had his legs raked by Argentine studs. Afterwards FIFA President Sepp Blatter declared himself 'furious' and Alf Ramsey's forty-year-old 'animals' jibe – which José Pekerman's managerial reign had done so much to diminish – reared its head again.

The crisis engulfing Italian football reached its apogee on 27 June – three days before the country's quarter-final with Ukraine – when Gianluca Pessotto, the Juventus team manager, threw himself out of a fourth-storey window at the *Bianconeri*'s training ground, clutching a set of rosary beads. Pessotto, who had also played for Juventus during the 2005/06 season alongside the likes of Alessandro Del Piero and Gianluca Zambrotta, survived the suicide attempt, but remained in a coma when Del Piero and Zambrotta flew back to Italy to visit him on the eve of the game.

Rather than further upsetting the fractious Italians, Italy's domestic dramas served to unify the squad over the coming weeks. They were also helped by a fortuitous draw that pitted them against the uninspiring Ukrainians. After just six minutes Zambrotta took possession on the halfway line; surging forward he played a one-two with Totti and from thirty yards fired in a low shot to put Italy ahead. Woeful against Switzerland, Ukraine showed surprising resilience, and in the early part of the second half rallied strongly: Buffon pushed Gusin's header onto his right post, then made an outstanding save low to his left from Gusev. The ball was then played to Kalinichenko and Zambrotta blocked his shot on the line.

After weathering this storm, Italy immediately killed off Ukrainian hopes. From a short corner, Totti's cross found Toni unmarked in the six-yard box, and he headed Italy into a 2–0 lead. Kalinichenko was then denied by the crossbar, but soon after Italy showed their ruthlessness. Grosso rampaged down the left side of the Ukraine penalty area, cut the ball back to the edge of the six-yard box, and Toni side-footed Italy into the semi-finals.

The following afternoon in Gelsenkirchen, England came up against their great nemesis, Portugal's Brazilian manager, Luis Felipe Scolari. Twice – as Brazil manager at the 2002 World Cup, then with Portugal two years later at the European Championships – he had denied English progress at the quarter-final stage. Two months before the meeting in Germany, he rubbed English noses in the mud when he turned down the England manager's job after the FA chief executive, Brian Barwick, made an excruciatingly high-profile trip to Lisbon to secure his services. Notwithstanding Scolari, England had a poor record against Portugal and had beaten them just once in ten games.

England stuck with a five-man midfield – Sven-Göran Eriksson resisting calls to promote the lively winger Aaron Lennon in place of Beckham – while Ronaldo overcame injury to start for Portugal. A tepid first half saw both countries limited to long-range efforts. Shortly into the second half Beckham shot the ball against Nuno Valente's hand, but the Argentinean referee was oblivious to the incident. This was Beckham's last meaningful action and on 52 minutes he limped off tearfully with a leg injury, his World Cup over. His replacement, Aaron Lennon, almost immediately brought England a goal when his mazy run down the right carried him into the penalty area. However, he was slow in providing a pass, Rooney missed his cut-back and Joe Cole stabbed over from eight yards. Soon after, Rooney's World Cup was also brought to an early end when he was sent off for stamping on Ricardo Carvalho's groin. The intent was nevertheless questionable and the referee, who had missed a blatant penalty appeal by England ten minutes earlier, proved strangely vigilant. Ronaldo's knowing wink to the Portugal bench suggested the most was made of the incident.

Ten-man England were forced to defend deeply, hitting Portugal on the counter-attack. Their best chance came on 81 minutes when Ricardo spilled Lampard's free kick to the feet of Lennon, but the winger's low shot lacked potency. Oddly, England played the best they had all tournament with reduced numbers, limiting Portugal to half chances and a goal that was disallowed for offside. But the game always seemed destined for penalties and England's dire record from twelve yards continued – despite both countries missing two of their first three kicks. Lampard and Gerrard – lethal for their clubs, yet mystifyingly impotent for their country – missed their penalties and when Jamie Carragher also saw his retaken spot kick saved by Ricardo it was left to Ronaldo to seal their fate.

Later that evening in Frankfurt, two of the World Cup's greats – Zinedine Zidane and Ronaldo – came face to face in the knowledge that one of their careers would draw to a close that night. The thirty-four-year-old Frenchman was quitting the game altogether at the end of the tournament, while the striker was planning to hang up his Brazil shirt for the final time.

An intriguing if slightly one-paced encounter followed with chances at a premium, but it was elevated into a spectacle by the excellence of Zidane. Even more so than when France met Spain in the round of sixteen, Zidane dominated proceedings, his tricks and shimmies ensuring that his genius would be remembered long after the evening had passed. Invariably he was involved in the game's deciding moment, lofting a left-wing free kick to Brazil's back post where a gleeful Henry – entirely unmarked – volleyed a 57th minute winner into the roof of the Brazil net. France could have added more – Ribéry's ball across the face of goal narrowly evaded Zidane's lunge, Dida was quick to save at Ribéry's feet, and also saved well from Saha late on. Ronaldo, a podgy, pallid shadow of his former self, added little to the occasion until the final minute when, perhaps finally realising his international career was nearly over, he let fly with a fierce, low drive from thirty yards that was beaten away by Barthez. Moments later the Spanish referee's whistle called time on the Brazilian's illustrious career. Zidane's, on the other hand, would go on for another two matches.

Quarter-Finals

Germany (0) **1, Argentina** (0) **1** (aet, 1–1 at 90 mins, Germany won 4–2 on penalties)
30.6.06 BERLIN
Germany: Lehmann, Friedrich, Mertesacker, Metzelder, Lahm, Schweinsteiger (Borowski), Frings, Ballack, Schneider (Odonkor), Klose (1) (Neuville), Podolski
Argentina: Abbondanzieri (Franco), Sorin, Ayala (1), Coloccini, Heinze, Maxi Rodriguez, Gonzalez, Riquelme (Cambiasso), Mascherano, Crespo (Cruz), Tevez
Referee: Michel (Slovakia)

Italy (1) **3, Ukraine** (0) **0**
30.6.06 HAMBURG
Italy: Buffon, Zambrotta (1), Barzagli, Cannavaro, Grosso, Perrotta, Pirlo (Oddo), Gattuso (Zaccardo), Camoranesi (Barone), Totti, Toni (2)
Ukraine: Shovkovskyi, Rusol (Vashchuk), Svidersky (Vorobey), Nesmachnyi, Gusev, Tymoshchyuk, Shelayev, Kalinichenko, Gusin, Shevchenko, Milevskyi (Belik)
Referee: De Bleeckere (Belgium)

England (0) **0, Portugal** (0) **0** (aet, Portugal won 3–1 on penalties)
1.7.06 GELSENKIRCHEN
England: Robinson, Neville, Ferdinand, Terry, Ashley Cole, Beckham (Lennon) (Carragher), Lampard, Hargreaves, Gerrard, Joe Cole (Crouch), Rooney
Portugal: Ricardo, Miguel, Carvalho, Meira, Valente, Petit, Maniche, Tiago (Viano), Figo (Postiga), Ronaldo, Pauleta (Simao)
Referee: Elizondo (Argentina)

Brazil (0) **0, France** (0) **1**
1.7.06 FRANKFURT
Brazil: Dida, Cafu (Cicinho), Lucio, Juan, Carlos, Juninho (Adriano), Silva, Zé Roberto, Kaka (Robinho), Ronaldinho, Ronaldo
France: Barthez, Sagnol, Thuram, Gallas, Abidal, Ribéry (Govou), Makélélé, Vieira, Zidane, Malouda (Wiltord), Henry (1) (Saha)
Referee: Cantalejo (Spain)

THE SEMI-FINALS

Four months before Germany faced Italy in the World Cup semi-final in Dortmund, the Italians had humbled them 4–1 in Florence. Germany despaired, Jürgen Klinsmann became a figure of fun, and Italian football briefly seemed invincible. How quickly times had changed. Germany was now a swaggering, vibrant footballing force again, the highest scorers in the World Cup. Italian football, by contrast, was a mess, although the scourge of *Calciopoli* had still to infect its national team. In Dortmund's Westfalenstadion the noise was enormous, the stands a sea of white bellowing 'Deutschland, Deutschland' and whistling every Italian touch. With an incessant racket and relentless, frenetic play, this was to be 2006's most compelling encounter.

The first half was tight, but the pace unrelenting even if chances were few. On 14 minutes Pirlo picked up Perotta's run from deep and suddenly he was through on goal. Lehman, however, was quick to react, racing off his line and blocking the shot. At the other end, Klose played in Schneider who blazed his shot high and over. There was a slickness and efficiency to Italy's play that was more befitting of the German footballing tradition. Italy's previous encounter against the Ukraine had been a case in point: from just five attacks they scored three goals. All tournament the only goal they had conceded was when Cristian Zaccardo put through his own net against the United States.

As the game progressed into the second half, the pace picked up and so – if it were possible – did the noise. Klose dribbled through the Italian defence and was only denied by the onrushing Buffon. Immediately the ball was played upfield and Pirlo – the Italians' irrepressible schemer – played in Grosso. Surging from the left-back position to the edge of the German area, and one-on-one with Lehman, he too was denied by an outcoming goalkeeper and, belatedly, a linesman's flag. Elaborate wing play by Schneider found Podolski and he span and shot from the edge of the six-yard area, but was denied by Buffon. For 25 minutes it was all Germany, but Italy soaked up everything that was thrown at them, while the Germans lacked the incisive touch in front of goal that was once the hallmark of their manager, Klinsmann.

Extra time came and, as the Italians increased their attacking tempo, slowly the realization dawned that the Germans had played above themselves throughout the tournament, that their best chance of progress now perhaps lay from the penalty spot. Gilardino cut in from the German by-line, went past Ballack and fired a near-post shot that wrong-footed Lehman but cannoned off the post. Zambrotta let fly from the edge of the German penalty area, but it crashed off the crossbar. Yet it could still have gone either way. Against the run of play Odonkor broke down the right and crossed early; Podolski, unmarked and usually lethal from such distances, headed wide from ten yards. Shortly into the second half of extra time, Podolski was played in to the left channel of the Italy penalty area and his fierce drive towards the top corner was palmed clear by Buffon.

The game seemed headed for penalties, but such a destiny would be no lottery. Italy had never won a World Cup penalty shoot-out, Germany had never lost one. In fact Germany hadn't even missed a World Cup penalty since 1982 – a record that extended to twenty-two consecutively scored spot kicks. For the Italians penalties were a disaster waiting to happen. But as they loomed, the breakthrough finally came.

Two minutes from full time, Pirlo stung the palms of Lehman from thirty yards and the ball went for a corner. Del Piero took it and Germany could only clear as far as Pirlo on the outside of the penalty area. He ghosted around the edge of the German area and found Grosso, the left back, unmarked at the right angle of the six-yard box. His first-time shot arrowed past Lehman and into the far corner of the German goal. Germany piled everybody forward in a desperate attempt to rescue the game, but Cannavaro broke up play and Gilardino was played in. He seemed happy to hold up the ball and waste time but then, spotting Del Piero overlapping on the left, he rolled the ball through and the Juventus captain sumptuously chipped Lehman with the last kick of a long, tense, memorable evening.

The other semi-final, in Munich, saw the master of world football – the soon-to-be-retired Zidane – come up against his most likely successor, Cristiano Ronaldo. Eyed by Real Madrid as the *Galactico*'s replacement, the Portuguese star largely outshone the veteran. Booed throughout for his perceived role in Rooney's dismissal in the quarter-final, his long runs from deep on the left set up early long-range efforts from Maniche and Deco, and deep into the second half his free kick should have yielded a goal. But the final killer ball remained elusive.

That golden touch remained the preserve of the older man. For two matches, Zidane's sorcery lifted France above the abyss, but in the semi-final against Portugal they reverted to type – dull, uninspiring, edging through a turgid encounter. Zidane – who else? – had the decisive say on the game's destiny, striking home a 32nd minute penalty after a customary two-step run-up following Carvalho's trip of Henry.

The standard of football in the second half remained scrappy and uninspiring. As France sat back on their lead a long ball was played up to Henry, who held it up, and when support was slow in coming took on the Portugal defence on his own. His bold run eventually brought a fine low save from Ricardo, who almost spilled the shot into his own goal. Ricardo then made a meal of Ribéry's turn and shot from the edge of the area after Zidane had slipped him through, making it seem less straightforward than it actually was. At the other end, Barthez had his own crazy moment, throwing into the air Ronaldo's long-range free kick. The ball fell to Figo on the edge of the six-yard box, but with the goal at his mercy the former World Player of the Year could only head over the crossbar. Portugal rallied in the closing stages, but nothing could overcome the stubborn, methodical defending of the French players, who progressed to their second final in three tournaments.

Semi-Finals

Italy (0) **2**, **Germany** (0) **0** (aet, 0–0 at 90 mins)
4.7.06 DORTMUND
Italy: Buffon, Zambrotta, Cannavaro, Materazzi, Grosso (1), Camoranesi (Iaquinta), Perrotta (Del Piero (1)), Gattuso, Pirlo, Totti, Toni (Gilardino)
Germany: Lehmann, Friedrich, Metzelder, Mertesacker, Lahm, Borowski (Schweinsteiger), Ballack, Kehl, Schneider (Odonkor), Klose (Neuville), Podolski
Referee: Archundia (Mexico)

France (1) **1**, **Portugal** (0) **0**
5.7.06 MUNICH
France: Barthez, Sagnol, Thuram, Gallas, Abidal, Vieira, Makélélé, Ribéry (Govou), Zidane (1 pen), Malouda (Wiltord), Henry (Saha)
Portugal: Ricardo, Miguel (Ferreira), Carvalho, Meira, Valente, Costinha (Postiga), Maniche, Deco, Figo, Ronaldo, Pauleta (Simao)
Referee: Larrionda (Uruguay)

PLAY-OFF FOR THIRD PLACE

In Stuttgart, Klinsmann's home patch, Germany faced Portugal for the unheralded distinction of third place. They say the playoff is the game no one remembers, but contrary to its billing this was a free-flowing attractive game, full of chances, most by Germany, who dominated but failed to score in the first half. For Portugal, the niggardliness and cynicism that had been a feature of their play throughout the tournament did not eviscerate with the pressure largely off.

In the second half, Bastian Schweinsteiger, Germany's livewire young winger who was overlooked for the semi-final, brought the tie alive. On 56 minutes a meandering run down the Portuguese left suddenly gained purpose when he was forced to cut inside two defenders. Afforded a moment, he unleashed a fierce, dipping shot from the angle of the penalty area that moved in the air in front of Ricardo and buried itself into the top of the net. Four minutes later his left-wing free kick was deflected into his own net by Petit. On

78 minutes Schweinsteiger added a second and Germany's third: taking the ball forty yards from goal, he marched forward with purpose and from the edge of the 'D' unleashed an unstoppable drive that curled into the right of the net. Nuno Gomes grabbed a late consolation with a diving header from Figo's cross, but it was too late to change the outcome of the match.

Somehow Portugal were awarded 'the most entertaining team of the tournament', which seemed particularly perverse given the diving, dissent and general unpleasantness that defined much of their play. Whether the 'entertaining' encompassed the disgrace witnessed against Holland, the gamesmanship against England or the insipid semi-final display against France we will never know. Germany, on the other hand, left the tournament with their heads held high, both in the way they played and in the party they had thrown. Klinsmann, a laughing stock before the tournament started, emerged at its end a national hero again, the Stuttgart crowd reverberating to the chants of 'Klinsmann must stay!' But in the city where his career started as a player, it ended as the national manager.

The outside world's perception of Germany – for so long dominated by tired World War Two stereotyping – was also radically changed by its hosting of the tournament. 'We did not win the World Cup, but it gave us so much. Foreign visitors and television audiences saw a cheerful, confident and hospitable country,' said German President Horst Koehler. 'I believe that this soccer festival also gave us as Germans a new window onto ourselves and our country.'

Match for Third Place

Germany (0) **3, Portugal** (0) **1**
8.7.06 STUTTGART
Germany: Kahn, Lahm, Metzelder, Huth, Jansen, Schneider, Kehl, Frings, Schweinsteiger (2) (Hitzlsperger), Podolski (Hanke), Klose (Neuville)
Portugal: Ricardo, Ferreira, Meira, Costa, Valente (Gomes (1)), Costinha (Petit (o.g.)), Maniche, Simao, Deco, Ronaldo, Pauleta (Figo)
Referee: Kamikawa (Japan)

THE FINAL

Italy had built a head of steam through the tournament and, seemingly unimpeded by the country's domestic footballing crises – which left question marks over many players' futures – were slight favourites for the final against France. How much of a favourite depended on which France turned up in Berlin – the insipid, dreary team that was reliant on victory over Togo to qualify for the round of sixteen, or the brilliant conquerors of Brazil, orchestrated by the majestic Zidane.

Italy knew to take nothing for granted. The match was a reprise of the 2000 European Championship Final and Italy had seemed destined to win that match, leading 1–0 until the very death, when France led a blitzkrieg assault against them, equalizing deep into stoppage time, then killing them with a 'Golden Goal'. Five of the players who started for France that night in Rotterdam also started in Berlin. Ominously for Italy, France's two substitute scorers that night – Sylvain Wiltord and David Trézéguet – also took places on the bench in Germany.

An entire generation had passed since a World Cup final of rousing quality had been witnessed, and 2006's affair was no better than previous finals – niggly, tense, often untidy, certainly not an advert for the very summit of global football. Drab would be the wrong word, however, and 20 minutes of high drama at each end of the game sandwiched the mediocrity.

France took first blood, taking just seven minutes to breach an Italy defence that had not conceded a goal to an opposition player all tournament. Malouda chased a long ball into the left channel of the Italy penalty area and Materazzi, wildly charging across to cut out his run, could not stop himself from colliding with the French winger. Zidane, invariably, claimed the resultant penalty. But even this straightforward task was executed with an outrageous flourish. After a two-step approach, Buffon moved early and Zidane chipped the ball delicately off the underside of the crossbar and it rebounded a foot over the goal line and back into play. Few players in football history would ever have dared – much less pulled off – so bold a trick on so high a stage.

Three minutes later, Materazzi was in the thick of the action again, backward-heading a cross and forcing Buffon to save in order to avert an own goal. On 19 minutes his contribution was rather more meaningful for Italy. From a right-wing corner, the statuesque defender rose like a basketball player and headed into the back of the France net for his country's equalizer. Seventeen minutes later Italy might have taken the lead from the same scenario, but this time Toni's header cannoned off the France crossbar.

Clear chances beyond this were at a premium as the game progressed into the second half. Henry dribbled into the Italy area but shot tamely at Buffon. The same player then pirouetted a path through the right of the Italy area, but his cut-back to the unmarked Malouda was snuffed out. At the other end Toni headed a left-wing free kick into the net, but the goal was adjudged offside. Buffon saved low from Henry's drive and Pirlo's free kick curled narrowly wide. But as night fell extra time was inevitable.

In the first half of extra time France were in the ascendancy. Neat interplay by Ribéry and Malouda on the edge of the area gave the former a sight of goal, but he placed his shot just wide of Buffon's far post. Then from Sagnol's right-wing cross Zidane crashed a powerful header goalwards that required his former Juventus team-mate, Buffon, to tip over the crossbar.

But it was for using his head in the wrong way that the game achieved notoriety in the second phase of extra time. All night Materazzi – an in-the-face, intimidating giant, the latest in a long tradition of Italian hard men – had shadowed Zidane, doing his utmost to suffocate his play. The Frenchman, who combined his genius as a player with a fearsome, occasionally violent temper, finally snapped ten minutes from the end. After exchanging words with the Italian, Zidane launched an extraordinary head-butt into the centre of Materazzi's chest. The Argentinean referee missed the incident, but his assistant spotted it. A red card was produced and Zidane's World Cup – and career – ended in disgrace.

So shocked were the other players – and, indeed, the entire world – that no meaningful chances followed, and for only the second time the World Cup final went to penalties. Italy, defeated from twelve yards four times before, including the 1994 final, finally had to face their hoodoo.

Pirlo sent his shot straight down the middle; Wiltord sent Buffon the wrong way; Materazzi, who had been in the thick of everything throughout, was sufficiently recovered from Zidane's assault to make it 2–1 to Italy. Next was David Trézéguet, who had so broken Italian hearts with his golden goal in Rotterdam in 2000. Up against his Juventus team-mate Buffon, he sent the goalkeeper the wrong way, but his shot crashed off the underside of the bar and rebounded away without crossing the line. He cut a distraught, solitary figure on the halfway line as De Rossi buried his penalty into the roof of the net to make it 3–1. Abidal gave France hope, as did Sagnol after Del Piero made it 4–3. The deciding kick then fell to Fabio Grosso, the tall, lithe Palermo left back who had already played a crucial role in the eliminations of Australia and Germany. Faced with the biggest challenge of his life, he seized it with gusto – sending Barthez the wrong way to complete a perfect set of penalties. Under a rain of ticker-tape and streamers, Fabio Cannavaro lifted Italy's fourth World Cup, the worries and disgrace of the country's domestic game, for one night at least, forgotten.

Final

Italy (1) **1, France** (1) **1** (aet, 1–1 at 90 mins, Italy won 5–3 on penalties
9.7.06 BERLIN
Italy: Buffon, Zambrotta, Materazzi (1), Cannavaro, Grosso, Pirlo, Gattuso, Camoranesi (Del Piero), Totti (Iaquinta), Perrotta (De Rossi), Toni
France: Barthez, Sagnol, Thuram, Gallas, Abidal, Vieira (Diarra), Makélélé, Ribéry (Trézéguet), Zidane (1 pen), Malouda, Henry (Wiltord)
Referee: Elizondo (Argentina)

CHAPTER 19

SOUTH AFRICA

2010

Qualifying Tournament
205 entries
South Africa qualify as holders

Europe (53): Albania, Andorra, Armenia, Austria, Azerbaijan, Belarus, Belgium, Bosnia-Herzegovina, Bulgaria, Croatia, Cyprus, Czech Republic, Denmark, England, Estonia, Faroe Islands, Finland, France, FYR Macedonia, Georgia, Germany, Greece, Holland, Hungary, Iceland, Israel, Italy, Kazakhstan, Latvia, Liechtenstein, Lithuania, Luxembourg, Malta, Moldova, Montenegro, Northern Ireland, Norway, Poland, Portugal, Republic of Ireland, Romania, Russia, San Marino, Scotland, Serbia, Slovakia, Slovenia, Spain, Sweden, Switzerland, Turkey, Ukraine, Wales

South America (10): Argentina, Bolivia, Brazil, Chile, Colombia, Ecuador, Paraguay, Peru, Uruguay, Venezuela

CONCACAF (35): Anguilla, Antigua & Barbuda, Aruba, Bahamas, Barbados, Belize, Bermuda, British Virgin Islands, Canada, Cayman Islands, Costa Rica, Cuba, Dominica, Dominican Republic, El Salvador, Grenada, Guatemala, Guyana, Haiti, Honduras, Jamaica, Mexico, Montserrat, Netherlands Antilles, Nicaragua, Panama, Puerto Rico, St Kitts & Nevis, St Lucia, St Vincent & Grenadines, Surinam, Trinidad & Tobago, Turks & Caicos Islands, US Virgin Islands, USA

Asia (43): Afghanistan, Australia, Bahrain, Bangladesh, Bhutan, Cambodia, China, East Timor, Guam, Hong Kong, India, Indonesia, Iran, Iraq, Japan, Jordan, Kuwait, Kyrgyzstan, Lebanon, Macau, Malaysia, Maldives, Mongolia, Myanmar, Nepal, North Korea, Oman, Pakistan, Palestine, Qatar, Saudi Arabia, Singapore, South Korea, Sri Lanka, Syria, Taiwan, Tajikistan, Thailand, Turkmenistan, United Arab Emirates, Uzbekistan, Vietnam, Yemen

Africa (51): Algeria, Angola, Benin, Botswana, Burkina Faso, Burundi, Cameroon, Cape Verde Islands, Chad, Comoros, Congo, DR Congo, Djibouti, Egypt, Equatorial Guinea, Eritrea, Ethiopia, Gabon, Gambia, Ghana, Guinea, Guinea-Bissau, Ivory Coast, Kenya, Lesotho, Liberia, Libya, Madagascar, Malawi, Mali, Mauritania, Mauritius, Morocco, Mozambique, Namibia, Niger, Nigeria, Rwanda, Senegal, Seychelles, Sierra Leone, Somalia, South Africa, Sudan, Swaziland, Tanzania, Togo, Tunisia, Uganda, Zambia, Zimbabwe

Oceania (11): American Samoa, Cook Islands, Fiji, New Caledonia, New Zealand, Samoa, Solomon Islands, Tahiti, Tonga, Tuvalu, Vanuatu

Europe
53 entries, 13 qualify

Eight groups of six and one of five made up the European qualifying round, with those topping the group guaranteed a place at the finals and the runners-up given a second chance via the play-offs. Ultimately, by belatedly seeding this last round, FIFA ensured there were few great shocks, with none of the great powers – barring perhaps Russia – failing to make the tournament.

Scandinavia's two principal powers, Sweden and Denmark, were given a difficult challenge when pitted against Portugal in Group 1. Denmark gained an early advantage when they travelled to Lisbon in September 2008; trailing 2–1 in the final minute, they dramatically turned the game on its head, with Christian Poulsen and Daniel Jensen scoring injury-time goals to seize a 3–2 victory. The Danes' advantage was heightened when Portugal could only manage goalless draws at home to Albania and Sweden, and they took hold of the group with home and away wins over their Swedish neighbours. Portugal rose from fourth to the runners-up spot with wins in their last four games, but even with World Player of the Year Cristiano Ronaldo they looked unimpressive throughout.

From the six nations that made up Group 2, only Switzerland had managed to qualify for any of the previous three finals. It included 2004 European Champions Greece – who subsequently finished fourth in their 2006 World Cup qualifying group then lost all their matches when defending their European crown in 2008 – Latvia, who had qualified for Euro 2004; and Israel, who had threatened to make a major tournament on several occasions but not yet managed it. The Swiss edged the group by a point, with Greece making the play-offs, but as with Group 1 just five points separated the top four countries.

Group 3 would see a mockery made of FIFA's seedings, with the fourth and fifth ranked nations – Slovakia and Slovenia – defying all odds to top the group. A resurgent Northern Ireland also briefly threatened to upset the balance of power, failing to lose against either of the top two seeds, Poland and the Czech Republic – beating the former in Belfast – before slipping out of the running. The Czechs, now shorn of the retired Pavel Nedved, a former European Footballer of the Year, wilted without their creative heartbeat and seemed doomed to finish behind their neighbours from the moment Slovakia beat them with a late goal in Prague in April 2009. Despite putting ten goals past San Marino, Poland endured a miserable qualification campaign, finishing fifth.

The key battle in Group 4 was between one of Europe's established football powers, Germany, and one of its emergent forces, Russia. At the 2008 European Championships the Russians, now managed by Guus Hiddink, wowed with brilliant free–flowing football inspired by their playmaker and captain Andrei Arshavin. But the Germans were ultimately too good. In the group's crucial encounter in Moscow in October 2009, Russia played with real verve but ultimately lacked a cutting edge against experienced opponents. Germany won 1–0 and Russia were left with a play-off.

Spain, imperious since their shock exit at the previous World Cup to France, between November 2006 and June 2009 embarked upon an international football record-equalling run of 35 undefeated games. The sequence included a dazzling European Championship Finals victory in 2008 and by the time it was ended by the United States in the 2009 Confederations Cup they were virtually assured of a return to South Africa. Eventually they qualified with a 100 per cent record. They were followed by Bosnia-Herzegovina, who, managed by Miroslav Blazevic, a veteran coach with forty years of experience who had taken Croatia to third at the 1998 Finals, upset Belgium and Turkey to comfortably take the runners-up berth.

England faced a tough draw in Group 6 with Croatia and Ukraine, both finalists in 2006, also vying for a place in South Africa. There was an added edge to England versus Croatia as the Croats had inflicted English football's most recent humiliation. In qualifying for the 2008 European Championships, the Croats had humbled England, outplaying them at home and then making a mockery of them at Wembley, thus ending Steve McLaren's dire – but mercifully brief – international managerial career. Now managed by Fabio Capello, one of the great club managers of his era, England were more disciplined and possessed a consistency in selection and a winning ethic in playing that was reminiscent of the Alf Ramsey era. Croatia were crushed 4–1 in Zagreb then 5–1 at Wembley, and only a narrow defeat to Ukraine, with qualification already assured, prevented England from matching the 100 per cent record of Spain and Holland. Their thirty-four goals was nevertheless six better than the Spaniards.

For France, so dismal until Zinedine Zidane had elevated them from the mire at World Cup 2006, things had got scarcely better. After finishing bottom of their group at the European Championship Finals, they lost their opening World Cup qualifying match 3–1 to Austria. The failure of Raymond Domenech – who somehow kept his job through these lean times – to introduce young talent when the Zidanes and Thurams were still supreme meant there was a lost generation of French footballers that struggled to assume the lofty legacy left them. France stuttered through to the runners-up spot in Group 7, beaten by Serbia, who were impressive in their first qualifying campaign as a single nation.

Italy had also struggled since lifting the 2006 World Cup and were underwhelming at both the 2008 European Championships and the Confederations Cup a year later. Marcello Lippi, the World Cup-winning manager, was recalled for a second spell, but his problems were similar to Domenech's earlier in the decade, namely replacing a once successful but aging squad. Throughout

Group 8 Italy desperately struggled for form, squeaking victories against Montenegro and Georgia, but ultimately they outclassed runners-up Ireland. Like Italy they finished the group unbeaten, but drew too many games to go through automatically.

Holland were simply too good for a weak Group 9, winning all their matches and conceding just two goals. For Scotland, who qualified for every World Cup finals bar one between 1974 and 1998, it was a familiar tale of woe for a football nation in decline. A 4–0 defeat to Norway in August 2009 highlighted the malaise facing Scottish football, but even this resounding win wasn't enough to make the Norwegians one of the eight best runners-up and ensure a play-off place.

Group 1 (Albania, Denmark, Hungary, Malta, Portugal, Sweden)

Albania v Sweden 0–0, Malta v Portugal 0–4, Hungary v Denmark 0–0, Sweden v Hungary 2–1, Albania v Malta 3–0, Portugal v Denmark 2–3, Hungary v Albania 2–0, Denmark v Malta 3–0, Sweden v Portugal 0–0, Malta v Hungary 0–1, Portugal v Albania 0–0, Malta v Albania 0–0, Malta v Denmark 0–3, Albania v Hungary 0–1, Portugal v Sweden 0–0, Hungary v Malta 3–0, Denmark v Albania 3–0, Sweden v Denmark 0–1, Albania v Portugal 1–2, Sweden v Malta 4–0, Denmark v Portugal 1–1, Hungary v Sweden 1–2, Malta v Sweden 0–1, Albania v Denmark 1–1, Hungary v Portugal 0–1, Portugal v Hungary 3–0, Denmark v Sweden 1–0, Portugal v Malta 4–0, Sweden v Albania 4–1, Denmark v Hungary 0–1

	P	W	D	L	F	A	Pts
Denmark	10	6	3	1	16	5	21
Portugal	10	5	4	1	17	5	19
Sweden	10	5	3	2	13	5	18
Hungary	10	5	1	4	10	8	16
Albania	10	1	4	5	6	13	7
Malta	10	0	1	9	0	26	1

Denmark qualify for finals
Portugal to play-offs

Group 2 (Greece, Israel, Latvia, Luxembourg, Moldova, Switzerland)

Moldova v Latvia 1–2, Israel v Switzerland 2–2, Luxembourg v Greece 0–3, Moldova v Israel 1–2, Latvia v Greece 0–2, Switzerland v Luxembourg 1–2, Switzerland v Latvia 2–1, Greece v Moldova 3–0, Luxembourg v Israel 1–3, Latvia v Israel 1–1, Luxembourg v Moldova 0–0, Greece v Switzerland 1–2, Luxembourg v Latvia 0–4, Moldova v Switzerland 0–2, Israel v Greece 1–1, Latvia v Luxembourg 2–0, Greece v Israel 2–1, Switzerland v Moldova 2–0, Moldova v Luxembourg 0–0, Israel v Latvia 0–1, Switzerland v Greece 2–0,

Israel v Luxembourg 7–0, Latvia v Switzerland 2–2, Moldova v Greece 1–1, Greece v Latvia 5–2, Israel v Moldova 3–1, Luxembourg v Switzerland 0–3, Greece v Luxembourg 2–1, Latvia v Moldova 3–2, Switzerland v Israel 0–0

	P	W	D	L	F	A	Pts
Switzerland	10	6	3	1	18	8	21
Greece	10	6	2	2	20	10	20
Latvia	10	5	2	3	18	15	17
Israel	10	4	4	2	20	10	16
Luxembourg	10	1	2	7	4	25	5
Moldova	10	0	3	7	6	18	3

Switzerland qualify for finals
Greece to play-offs

Group 3 (Czech Republic, Northern Ireland, Poland, San Marino, Slovakia, Slovenia)

Slovakia v Northern Ireland 2–1, Poland v Slovenia 1–1, San Marino v Poland 0–2, Northern Ireland v Czech Republic 0–0, Slovenia v Slovakia 2–1, Poland v Czech Republic 2–1, San Marino v Slovakia 1–3, Slovenia v Northern Ireland 2–0, Czech Republic v Slovenia 1–0, Slovakia v Poland 2–1, Northern Ireland v San Marino 4–0, San Marino v Czech Republic 0–3, San Marino v Northern Ireland 0–3, Northern Ireland v Poland 3–2, Slovenia v Czech Republic 0–0, Czech Republic v Slovakia 1–2, Poland v San Marino 10–0, Northern Ireland v Slovenia 1–0, Slovakia v San Marino 7–0, Slovenia v San Marino 5–0, Poland v Northern Ireland 1–1, Slovakia v Czech Republic 2–2, Czech Republic v San Marino 7–0, Slovenia v Poland 3–0, Northern Ireland v Slovakia 0–2, Czech Republic v Poland 2–0, Slovakia v Slovenia 0–2, Czech Republic v Northern Ireland 0–0, Poland v Slovakia 0–1, San Marino v Slovenia 0–3

	P	W	L	D	F	A	Pts
Slovakia	10	7	1	2	22	10	22
Slovenia	10	6	2	2	18	4	20
Czech Republic	10	4	4	2	17	6	16
Northern Ireland	10	4	3	3	13	9	15
Poland	10	3	2	5	19	14	11
San Marino	10	0	0	10	1	47	0

Slovakia qualify for finals
Slovenia to play-offs

Group 4 (Azerbaijan, Finland, Germany, Liechtenstein, Russia, Wales)

Wales v Azerbaijan 1–0, Liechtenstein v Germany 0–6, Russia v Wales 2–1, Azerbaijan v Liechtenstein 0–0, Finland v Germany 3–3, Finland v Azerbaijan

1–0, Wales v Liechtenstein 2–0, Germany v Russia 2–1, Russia v Finland 3–0, Germany v Wales 1–0, Russia v Azerbaijan 2–0, Wales v Finland 0–2, Germany v Liechtenstein 4–0, Liechtenstein v Russia 0–1, Wales v Germany 0–2, Finland v Liechtenstein 2–1, Azerbaijan v Wales 0–1, Finland v Russia 0–3, Azerbaijan v Germany 0–2, Azerbaijan v Finland 1–2, Russia v Liechtenstein 3–0, Liechtenstein v Finland 1–1, Germany v Azerbaijan 4–0, Wales v Russia 1–3, Finland v Wales 2–1, Liechtenstein v Azerbaijan 0–2, Russia v Germany 0–1, Azerbaijan v Russia 1–1, Germany v Finland 1–1, Liechtenstein v Wales 0–2

	P	W	D	L	F	A	Pts
Germany	10	8	2	0	26	5	26
Russia	10	7	1	2	19	6	22
Finland	10	5	3	2	14	14	18
Wales	10	4	0	6	9	12	12
Azerbaijan	10	1	2	7	4	14	5
Liechtenstein	10	0	2	8	2	23	2

Germany qualify for finals
Russia to play-offs

Group 5 (Armenia, Belgium, Bosnia-Herzegovina, Estonia, Spain, Turkey)

Armenia v Turkey 0–2, Belgium v Estonia 3–2, Spain v Bosnia-Herzegovina 1–0, Turkey v Belgium 1–1, Bosnia-Herzegovina v Estonia 7–0, Spain v Armenia 4–0, Turkey v Bosnia-Herzegovina 2–1, Belgium v Armenia 2–0, Estonia v Spain 0–3, Bosnia-Herzegovina v Armenia 4–1, Estonia v Turkey 0–0, Belgium v Spain 1–2, Armenia v Estonia 2–2, Belgium v Bosnia-Herzegovina 2–4, Spain v Turkey 1–0, Estonia v Armenia 1–0, Turkey v Spain 1–2, Bosnia-Herzegovina v Belgium 2–1, Armenia v Bosnia-Herzegovina 0–2, Turkey v Estonia 4–2, Spain v Belgium 5–0, Armenia v Belgium 2–1, Bosnia-Herzegovina v Turkey 1–1, Spain v Estonia 3–0, Armenia v Spain 1–2, Belgium v Turkey 2–0, Estonia v Bosnia-Herzegovina 0–2, Bosnia-Herzegovina v Spain 2–5, Estonia v Belgium 2–0, Turkey v Armenia 2–0

	P	W	D	L	F	A	Pts
Spain	10	10	0	0	28	5	30
Bosnia-Herzegovina	10	6	1	3	25	13	19
Turkey	10	4	3	3	13	10	15
Belgium	10	3	1	6	13	20	10
Estonia	10	2	2	6	9	24	8
Armenia	10	1	1	8	6	22	4

Spain qualify for finals
Bosnia-Herzegovina to play-offs

Group 6 (Andorra, Belarus, Croatia, England, Kazakhstan, Ukraine)

Kazakhstan v Andorra 3–0, Ukraine v Belarus 1–0, Croatia v Kazakhstan 3–0, Andorra v England 0–2, Kazakhstan v Ukraine 1–3, Andorra v Belarus 1–3, Croatia v England 1–4, England v Kazakhstan 5–1, Ukraine v Croatia 0–0, Croatia v Andorra 4–0, Belarus v England 1–3, Kazakhstan v Belarus 1–5, Andorra v Croatia 0–2, England v Ukraine 2–1, Belarus v Andorra 5–1, Croatia v Ukraine 2–2, Kazakhstan v England 0–4, Ukraine v Kazakhstan 2–1, England v Andorra 6–0, Belarus v Croatia 1–3, Ukraine v Andorra 5–0, Croatia v Belarus 1–0, Belarus v Ukraine 0–0, Andorra v Kazakhstan 1–3, England v Croatia 5–1, Belarus v Kazakhstan 4–0, Ukraine v England 1–0, Andorra v Ukraine 0–6, England v Belarus 3–0, Kazakhstan v Croatia 1–2

	P	W	D	L	F	A	Pts
England	10	9	0	1	34	6	27
Ukraine	10	6	3	1	21	6	21
Croatia	10	6	2	2	19	13	20
Belarus	10	4	1	5	19	14	13
Kazakhstan	10	2	0	8	11	29	6
Andorra	10	0	0	10	3	39	0

England qualify for finals
Ukraine to play-offs

Group 7 (Austria, Faroe Islands, France, Lithuania, Romania, Serbia)

Austria v France 3–1, Serbia v Faroe Islands 2–0, Romania v Lithuania 0–3 , Faroe Islands v Romania 0–1, Lithuania v Austria 2–0, France v Serbia 2–1, Faroe Islands v Austria 1–1, Serbia v Lithuania 3–0, Romania v France 2–2, Lithuania v Faroe Islands 1–0, Austria v Serbia 1–3, Romania v Serbia 2–3, Lithuania v France 0–1, Austria v Romania 2–1, France v Lithuania 1–0, Serbia v Austria 1–0, Lithuania v Romania 0–1, Faroe Islands v Serbia 0–2, Faroe Islands v France 0–1, Austria v Faroe Islands 3–1, France v Romania 1–1, Faroe Islands v Lithuania 2–1, Romania v Austria 1–1, Serbia v France 1–1, Austria v Lithuania 2–1, Serbia v Romania 5–0, France v Faroe Islands 5–0, France v Austria 3–1, Lithuania v Serbia 2–1, Romania v Faroe Islands 3–1

	P	W	D	L	F	A	Pts
Serbia	10	7	1	2	22	8	22
France	10	6	3	1	18	9	21
Austria	10	4	2	4	14	15	14
Lithuania	10	4	0	6	10	11	12
Romania	10	3	3	4	12	18	12
Faroe Islands	10	1	1	8	5	20	4

Serbia qualify for finals
France to play-offs

Group 8 (Georgia, Bulgaria, Cyprus, Ireland, Italy, Montenegro)
Georgia v Ireland 1–2, Cyprus v Italy 1–2, Montenegro v Bulgaria 2–2, Montenegro v Ireland 0–0, Italy v Georgia 2–0, Georgia v Cyprus 1–1, Bulgaria v Italy 0–0, Georgia v Bulgaria 0–0, Ireland v Cyprus 1–0, Italy v Montenegro 2–1, Ireland v Georgia 2–1, Cyprus v Georgia 2–1, Montenegro v Italy 0–2, Ireland v Bulgaria 1–1, Bulgaria v Cyprus 2–0, Georgia v Montenegro 0–0, Italy v Ireland 1–1, Cyprus v Montenegro 2–2, Bulgaria v Ireland 1–1, Bulgaria v Montenegro 4–1, Georgia v Italy 0–2, Cyprus v Ireland 1–2, Montenegro v Cyprus 1–1, Italy v Bulgaria 2–0, Cyprus v Bulgaria 4–1, Montenegro v Georgia 2–1, Ireland v Italy 2–2, Bulgaria v Georgia 6–2, Italy v Cyprus 3–2, Ireland v Montenegro 0–0

	P	W	D	L	F	A	Pts
Italy	10	7	3	0	18	7	24
Ireland	10	4	6	0	12	8	18
Bulgaria	10	3	5	2	17	13	14
Cyprus	10	2	3	5	14	16	9
Montenegro	10	1	6	3	9	14	9
Georgia	10	0	3	7	7	19	3

Italy qualify for finals
Ireland to play-offs

Group 9 (Holland, Iceland, Macedonia, Norway, Scotland)
Norway v Iceland 2–2, Macedonia v Scotland 1–0, Macedonia v Holland 1–2, Iceland v Scotland 1–2, Scotland v Norway 0–0, Holland v Iceland 2–0, Norway v Holland 0–1, Iceland v Macedonia 1–0, Holland v Scotland 3–0, Holland v Macedonia 4–0, Scotland v Iceland 2–1, Macedonia v Norway 0–0, Iceland v Holland 1–2, Holland v Norway 2–0, Macedonia v Iceland 2–0, Norway v Scotland 4–0, Scotland v Macedonia 2–0, Iceland v Norway 1–1, Norway v Macedonia 2–1, Scotland v Holland 0–1

	P	W	D	L	F	A	Pts
Holland	8	8	0	0	17	2	24
Norway	8	2	4	2	9	7	10
Scotland	8	3	1	4	6	11	10
Macedonia	8	2	1	5	5	11	7
Iceland	8	1	2	5	7	13	5

Holland qualify for finals

South America
10 countries, 4 to qualify, 1 to South America/CONCACAF play-off

It had been almost an entire generation since he last graced top-class football, and during that period he had been to hell and back. Doping scandals, drug addiction, a firearms offence, allegations of tax evasion and links to the Naples mafia, a massive heart attack, an operation to staple his stomach and stop the chronic overeating that threatened to kill him – the life of Diego Armando Maradona since he ended one of the greatest playing careers ever witnessed in the mid-1990s had been an unending drama that saw him lurch from one tabloid front page to another.

Invariably, following his unexpected recall to the top of international football when he was made Argentina manager in place of Alfredo Basile in November 2008, he dominated the two-year-long South American qualifying group's narrative. Indeed at times Argentina under Maradona seemed to mirror the personality of its manager, jumping from crisis to crisis, with the stench of disaster never far away.

It began positively enough, with a resounding 4–0 win over Ecuador in Buenos Aries in March 2009. But then came annihilation in La Paz – a 6–1 defeat to Bolivia, which even allowing for altitude represented a national disgrace. Further defeats to Ecuador and Brazil followed, which left Argentina needing to beat Peru in their penultimate game to stave off the threat of a play-off or even outright elimination. On a night of high drama and torrential rain, Maradona's edgy team – with several bizarre inclusions in the line-up – looked to have done enough to seize a 1–0 win when in the final minute Peru equalized from a corner. Argentina piled forward and deep into stoppage time the veteran forward Martin Palermo – hitherto considered an eccentric call-up by Maradona following a ten-year absence from the national team – scored from close range to bring salvation. Even then, Argentina almost self-destructed when Peru hit the crossbar straight from the kick-off.

It left a winner-takes-all final match against Uruguay in Montevideo, with the winner assured of qualification and the loser left with a play-off, or even elimination should Ecuador have beaten Chile (which they failed to do). Argentina squeaked through, but rather than celebrate Maradona faced his critics in the press box and let rip. 'You lot take it up the arse,' he announced to journalists afterwards, 'if the ladies will pardon the expression.' His attempt at an apology did nothing to lessen the ire of FIFA, which handed him a two-month ban that included his exclusion from the World Cup finals draw in Cape Town.

Given such dramas and controversies, the rest of the South American qualifying group seemed a mere footnote to the unfolding Maradona show. Brazil qualified as group winners but, now managed by their former captain, Dunga, they were more restrained than the exuberant winners of 2002. Combining the sort of work ethic Dunga once brought to the Brazil team as a player, the tactical discipline of their European rivals, and the flair of players like Kaka and Nilmar, their qualification was never in doubt.

Chile and Paraguay both nevertheless won more games than Brazil to qualify for South Africa alongside them. The former, brought tactical organization by their Argentine manager Marcelo Bielsa, and fire power by their free-scoring striker Humberto Suazo, were the qualifying round's surprise package. Paraguay may well have topped the group had they not lost impetus at the end, winless in their last four matches but still finishing within a point of Brazil. Twice winners Uruguay qualified for the play-off, despite their final match-day defeat to Maradona's Argentina.

Uruguay v Bolivia 5–0, Argentina v Chile 2–0, Ecuador v Venezuela 0–1, Peru v Paraguay 0–0, Colombia v Brazil 0–0, Venezuela v Argentina 0–2, Bolivia v Colombia 0–0, Chile v Peru 2–0, Paraguay v Uruguay 1–0, Brazil v Ecuador 5–0, Argentina v Bolivia 3–0, Colombia v Venezuela 1–0, Paraguay v Ecuador 5–1, Uruguay v Chile 2–2, Peru v Brazil 1–1, Colombia v Argentina 2–1, Venezuela v Bolivia 5–3, Ecuador v Peru 5–1, Brazil v Uruguay 2–1, Chile v Paraguay 0–3, Uruguay v Venezuela 1–1, Peru v Colombia 1–1, Paraguay v Brazil 2–0, Argentina v Ecuador 1–1, Bolivia v Chile 0–2, Uruguay v Peru 6–0, Bolivia v Paraguay 4–2, Ecuador v Colombia 0–0, Brazil v Argentina 0–0, Venezuela v Chile 2–3, Argentina v Paraguay 1–1, Colombia v Uruguay 0–1, Ecuador v Bolivia 3–1, Peru v Venezuela 1–0, Chile v Brazil 0–3, Paraguay v Venezuela 2–0, Brazil v Bolivia 0–0, Chile v Colombia 4–0, Peru v Argentina 1–1, Uruguay v Ecuador 0–0, Argentina v Uruguay 2–1, Bolivia v Peru 3–0, Colombia v Paraguay 0–1, Ecuador v Chile 1–0, Venezuela v Brazil 0–4, Bolivia v Uruguay 2–2, Brazil v Colombia 0–0, Chile v Argentina 1–0, Paraguay v Peru 1–0, Venezuela v Ecuador 3–1, Argentina v Venezuela 4–0, Colombia v Bolivia 2–0, Uruguay v Paraguay 2–0, Ecuador v Brazil 1–1, Peru v Chile 1–3,

Venezuela v Colombia 2–0, Bolivia v Argentina 6–1, Brazil v Peru 3–0, Chile v Uruguay 0–0, Ecuador v Paraguay 1–1, Argentina v Colombia 1–0, Bolivia v Venezuela 0–1, Paraguay v Chile 0–2, Uruguay v Brazil 0–4, Peru v Ecuador 1–2, Ecuador v Argentina 2–0, Brazil v Paraguay 2–1, Chile v Bolivia 4–0, Colombia v Peru 1–0, Venezuela v Uruguay 2–2, Argentina v Brazil 1–3, Chile v Venezuela 2–2, Colombia v Ecuador 2–0, Paraguay v Bolivia 1–0, Peru v Uruguay 1–0, Bolivia v Ecuador 1–3, Brazil v Chile 4–2, Paraguay v Argentina 1–0, Uruguay v Colombia 3–1, Venezuela v Peru 3–1, Argentina v Peru 2–1, Colombia v Chile 2–4, Ecuador v Uruguay 1–2, Venezuela v Paraguay 1–2, Bolivia v Brazil 2–1, Brazil v Venezuela 0–0, Chile v Ecuador 1–0, Paraguay v Colombia 0–2, Peru v Bolivia 1–0, Uruguay v Argentina 0–1

	P	W	D	L	F	A	Pts
Brazil	18	9	7	2	33	11	34
Chile	18	10	3	5	32	22	33
Paraguay	18	10	3	5	24	16	33
Argentina	18	8	4	6	23	20	28
Uruguay	18	6	6	6	28	20	24
Ecuador	18	6	5	7	22	26	23
Colombia	18	6	5	7	14	18	23
Venezuela	18	6	4	8	23	29	22
Bolivia	18	4	3	11	22	36	15
Peru	18	3	4	11	11	34	13

Brazil, Chile, Paraguay and Argentina qualify for finals
Uruguay to play off with fourth–placed CONCACAF nation, Costa Rica

CONCACAF
35 countries, 3 to qualify, 1 to South America/CONCACAF play-off

CONCACAF's final qualifying group was dominated by the two regional powers, the United States and Mexico. The former had been ever-present at World Cups since Italia '90, the latter since 1994, and they ultimately formed a familiar one-two at its top – although Mexico's passage was far from assured. Managed for the first half of the campaign by Sven-Göran Eriksson, the Swede who was so underwhelming in his two finals appearances with England, Mexico had already suffered semi-final-stage defeats to Honduras and Jamaica when they suffered further indignities at the hands of Honduras (again) and, even worse in the eyes of its demanding public, lowly El Salvador. In April 2009 the Mexican public and FA finally lost patience with Eriksson, and he went off to a bizarre but potentially lucrative tenure at Notts County in England's fourth division. His replacement, old coach Javier Aguirre, steered Mexico to their usual place at the finals.

Honduras were the group's surprise package, and their powerful and energetic team pipped Costa Rica to the third automatic qualifying spot. Costa Rica, looking to qualify for their third straight tournament, were left to face Uruguay in a play-off.

First Stage
(Single-leg matches)
Grenada v US Virgin Islands 10–0, Montserrat v Surinam 1–7, Puerto Rico v Dominican Republic 1–0 (aet)

(Two-leg matches)
Bermuda v Cayman Islands 1–1, Cayman Islands v Bermuda 1–3, Aruba v Antigua & Barbuda 0–3, Antigua & Barbuda v Aruba 1–0, Belize v St Kitts & Nevis 3–1, St Kitts & Nevis v Belize 1–1, Dominica v Barbados 1–1, Barbados v Dominica 1–0, El Salvador v Anguilla 12–0, Anguilla v El Salvador 0–4, Nicaragua v Netherlands Antilles 0–1, Netherlands Antilles v Nicaragua 2–0, Turks & Caicos Islands v St Lucia 2–1, St Lucia v Turks & Caicos Islands 2–0, Bahamas v British Virgin Islands 1–1, British Virgin Islands v Bahamas 2–2

Second stage
Honduras v Puerto Rico 4–0, Puerto Rico v Honduras 2–2, Surinam v Guyana 1–0, Guyana v Surinam 1–2, Grenada v Costa Rica 2–2, Costa Rica v Grenada 3–0, Jamaica v Bahamas 7–0, Bahamas v Jamaica 0–6, Guatemala v St Lucia 6–0, St Lucia v Guatemala 1–3, USA v Barbados 8–0, Barbados v USA 0–1, St Vincent & Grenadines v Canada 0–3, Canada v St Vincent & Grenadines 4–1, Haiti v Netherlands Antilles 0–0, Netherlands Antilles v Haiti 0–1, Belize v Mexico 0–2, Mexico v Belize 7–0, Trinidad & Tobago v Bermuda 1–2, Bermuda v Trinidad & Tobago 0–2, Panama v El Salvador 1–0, El Salvador v Panama 3–1, Antigua & Barbuda v Cuba 3–4, Cuba v Antigua & Barbuda 4–0

Semi-final Stage

Group A (Cuba, Guatemala, Trinidad & Tobago, USA)
Cuba v Trinidad & Tobago 1–3, Guatemala v USA 0–1, Trinidad & Tobago v Guatemala 1–1, Cuba v USA 0–1, USA v Trinidad & Tobago 3–0, Guatemala v Cuba 4–1, USA v Cuba 6–1, Guatemala v Trinidad & Tobago 0–0, Cuba v Guatemala 2–1, Trinidad & Tobago v USA 2–1, Trinidad & Tobago v Cuba 3–0, USA v Guatemala 2–0

	P	W	D	L	F	A	Pts
USA	6	5	0	1	14	3	15
Trinidad & Tobago	6	3	2	1	9	6	11
Guatemala	6	1	2	3	6	7	5
Cuba	6	1	0	5	5	18	3

USA and Trinidad & Tobago to final stage

Group B (Canada, Honduras, Jamaica, Mexico)
Canada v Jamaica 1–1, Mexico v Honduras 2–1, Mexico v Jamaica 3–0, Canada v Honduras 1–2, Mexico v Canada 2–1, Honduras v Jamaica 2–0, Jamaica v Mexico 1–0, Honduras v Canada 3–1, Jamaica v Honduras 1–0, Canada v Mexico 2–2, Honduras v Mexico 1–0, Jamaica v Canada 3–0

	P	W	D	L	F	A	Pts
Honduras	6	4	0	2	9	5	12
Mexico	6	3	1	2	9	6	10
Jamaica	6	3	1	2	6	6	10
Canada	6	0	2	4	6	13	2

Honduras and Mexico to final stage

Group C (Costa Rica, El Salvador, Haiti, Surinam)
Costa Rica v El Salvador 1–0, Haiti v Surinam 2–2, El Salvador v Haiti 5–0, Costa Rica v Surinam 7–0, Surinam v El Salvador 0–2, Haiti v Costa Rica 1–3, Surinam v Costa Rica 1–4, Haiti v El Salvador 0–0, Costa Rica v Haiti 2–0, El Salvador v Surinam 3–0, Surinam v Haiti 1–1, El Salvador v Costa Rica 1–3

	P	W	D	L	F	A	Pts
Costa Rica	6	6	0	0	20	3	18
El Salvador	6	3	1	2	11	4	10
Haiti	6	0	3	3	4	13	3
Surinam	6	0	2	4	4	19	2

Costa Rica and El Salvador to final stage

Final Stage (Costa Rica, El Salvador, Honduras, Mexico, Trinidad & Tobago, USA)
USA v Mexico 2–0, El Salvador v Trinidad & Tobago 2–2, Costa Rica v Honduras 2–0, Mexico v Costa Rica 2–0, Trinidad & Tobago v Honduras 1–1, El Salvador v USA 2–2, USA v Trinidad & Tobago 3–0, Honduras v Mexico 3–1, Costa Rica v El Salvador 1–0, Costa Rica v USA 3–1, El Salvador v Mexico 2–1, Trinidad & Tobago v Costa Rica 2–3, USA v Honduras 2–1, Mexico v Trinidad & Tobago 2–1, Honduras v El Salvador 1–0, Mexico v USA 2–1, Trinidad &

Tobago v El Salvador 1–0, Honduras v Costa Rica 4–0, USA v El Salvador 2–1, Honduras v Trinidad & Tobago 4–1, Costa Rica v Mexico 0–3, El Salvador v Costa Rica 1–0, Mexico v Honduras 1–0, Trinidad & Tobago v USA 0–1, Mexico v El Salvador 4–1, Costa Rica v Trinidad & Tobago 4–0, Honduras v USA 2–3, El Salvador v Honduras 0–1, Trinidad & Tobago v Mexico 2–2, USA v Costa Rica 2–2

	P	W	D	L	F	A	Pts
USA	10	6	2	2	19	13	20
Mexico	10	6	1	3	18	12	19
Honduras	10	5	1	4	17	11	16
Costa Rica	10	5	1	4	15	15	16
El Salvador	10	2	2	6	9	15	8
Trinidad & Tobago	10	1	3	6	10	22	6

USA, Mexico and Honduras qualify for finals
Costa Rica to CONCACAF/South America play-off

Asia
43 countries, 4 to qualify plus 1 to Asia/Oceania play-off

Asia continued to represent the most eclectic of the six qualifying zones, a continent where population size and economic development of a country had little bearing on its national football team's progress towards the World Cup finals. Take Indonesia, the football-mad archipelago of 230 million people, which was humbled 11–1 on aggregate by Syria – never before or subsequently noted as a football power – in the second round. China, given a bye to the third round, won just one game and finished bottom of their group, yet the tiny Gulf kingdoms of Qatar and Bahrain each made the last stage. India, the world's second most populous nation, were crushed by tiny war–torn Lebanon in the opening round.

Without question the story of the Asian qualifiers was North Korea's entirely unforeseen progress to the finals for the first time since 1966. With a stout, resolute defence and indomitable team spirit they went all the way from the first to the fourth round, where they overcame regular finalists Saudi Arabia and Iran to make it into the finals draw alongside South Korea. 'Our spirit became the unifying force of the team and inspired the players, and these were the biggest advantages we enjoyed throughout the qualifying campaign,' said the North Korea coach, Kim Jong–Hun. 'The players' qualities ensured they can cope with any difficult games and achieve satisfying results.'

The quality of Asia's qualifying zone was boosted with the addition of Australia, who left the Oceania Confederation following their successful qualification to the 2006 finals. They repeated the trick, finishing top of their fourth-round group, with Japan qualifying alongside them.

Bahrain and Saudi Arabia, the third-placed teams in each group, faced each other in a play-off for the right to face Oceania winners New Zealand, with the winners of that match going through to the finals. After a goalless first leg in Bahrain, Saudi Arabia led 2–1 deep into stoppage time. But at a Bahrain corner their defence went asleep and Ismaeel Latif crashed home a late, late equalizer to send his country through to the play-off on away goals.

Round One

Bangladesh v Tajikistan 1–1, Tajikistan v Bangladesh 5–0, Thailand v Macau 6–1, Macau v Thailand 1–7, Lebanon v India 4–1, India v Lebanon 2–2, Vietnam v UAE 0–1, UAE v Vietnam 5–0, Syria v Afghanistan 3–0, Afghanistan v Syria 1–2, Palestine v Singapore 0–4, Singapore v Palestine not played (Palestine did not show, Singapore awarded a 3–0 win by FIFA), Oman v Nepal 2–0, Nepal v Oman 0–2, Yemen v Maldives 3–0, Maldives v Yemen 2–0, Cambodia v Turkmenistan 0–1, Turkmenistan v Cambodia 4–1, Uzbekistan v Taiwan 9–0, Taiwan v Uzbekistan 0–2, Kyrgyzstan v Jordan 2–0, Jordan v Kyrgyzstan 2–0 (aet, Jordan won 6–5 on penalties), Mongolia v North Korea 1–4, North Korea v Mongolia 5–1, East Timor v Hong Kong 2–3, Hong Kong v East Timor 8–1, Sri Lanka v Qatar 0–1, Qatar v Sri Lanka 5–0, Bahrain v Malaysia 4–1, Malaysia v Bahrain 0–0, China v Myanmar 7–0, Myanmar v China 0–4, Pakistan v Iraq 0–7, Iraq v Pakistan 0–0, Kuwait walkover Bhutan (Bhutan withdrew), Indonesia walkover Guam (Guam withdrew)

Eight highest-ranking Round One qualifiers (Bahrain, China, Iraq, Jordan, Kuwait, Jordan, North Korea, Oman, Qatar, UAE, Uzbekistan) given a bye to Round Three. Eight lowest-ranking winners (Hong Kong, Indonesia, Singapore, Syria, Tajikistan, Thailand, Turkmenistan, Yemen) play off against each other in Round Two for the right to join them.

Round Two

Yemen v Thailand 1–1, Thailand v Yemen 1–0, Singapore v Tajikistan 2–0, Tajikistan v Singapore 1–1, Indonesia v Syria 1–4, Syria v Indonesia 7–0, Hong Kong v Turkmenistan 0–0, Turkmenistan v Hong Kong 3–0

Round Three

Group 1 (Australia, China, Iraq, Qatar)
Australia v Qatar 3–0, Iraq v China 1–1, China v Australia 0–0, Qatar v Iraq 2–0, Australia v Iraq 1–0, Qatar v China 0–0, China v Qatar 0–1, Iraq v Australia 1–0, China v Iraq 1–2, Qatar v Australia 1–3, Australia v China 0–1, Iraq v Qatar 0–1

	P	W	D	L	F	A	Pts
Australia	6	3	1	2	7	3	10
Qatar	6	3	1	2	5	6	10
Iraq	6	2	1	3	4	6	7
China	6	1	3	2	3	4	6

Australia and Qatar qualify for Round Four

Group 2 (Bahrain, Japan, Oman, Thailand)
Japan v Thailand 4–1, Oman v Bahrain 0–1, Thailand v Oman 0–1, Bahrain v Japan 1–0, Japan v Oman 3–0, Thailand v Bahrain 2–3, Oman v Japan 1–1, Bahrain v Thailand 1–1, Thailand v Japan 0–3, Bahrain v Oman 1–1, Japan v Bahrain 1–0, Oman v Thailand 2–1

	P	W	D	L	F	A	Pts
Japan	6	4	1	1	12	3	13
Bahrain	6	3	2	1	7	5	11
Oman	6	2	2	2	5	7	8
Thailand	6	0	1	5	5	14	1

Japan and Bahrain qualify for Round Four

Group 3 (Jordan, North Korea, South Korea, Turkmenistan)
South Korea v Turkmenistan 4–0, Jordan v North Korea 0–1, North Korea v South Korea 0–0, Turkmenistan v Jordan 0–2, South Korea v Jordan 2–2, Turkmenistan v North Korea 0–0, North Korea v Turkmenistan 1–0, Jordan v South Korea 0–1, North Korea v Jordan 2–0, Turkmenistan v South Korea 1–3, South Korea v North Korea 0–0, Jordan v Turkmenistan 2–0

	P	W	D	L	F	A	Pts
South Korea	6	3	3	0	10	3	12
North Korea	6	3	3	0	4	0	12
Jordan	6	2	1	3	6	6	7
Turkmenistan	6	0	1	5	1	12	1

South Korea and North Korea qualify for Round Four

Group 4 (Lebanon, Saudi Arabia, Singapore, Uzbekistan)

Lebanon v Uzbekistan 0–1, Saudi Arabia v Singapore 2–0, Uzbekistan v Saudi Arabia 3–0, Singapore v Lebanon 2–0, Singapore v Uzbekistan 3–7, Saudi Arabia v Lebanon 4–1, Uzbekistan v Singapore 1–0, Lebanon v Saudi Arabia 1–2, Singapore v Saudi Arabia 0–2, Uzbekistan v Lebanon 3–0, Lebanon v Singapore 1–2, Saudi Arabia v Uzbekistan 4–0

	P	W	D	L	F	A	Pts
Saudi Arabia	6	5	0	1	14	5	15
Uzbekistan	6	5	0	1	15	7	15
Singapore	6	2	0	4	7	13	6
Lebanon	6	0	0	6	3	14	0

Saudi Arabia and Uzbekistan qualify for Round Four

Group 5 (Iran, Kuwait, Syria, UAE)

Iran v Syria 0–0, UAE v Kuwait 2–0, Syria v UAE 1–1, Kuwait v Iran 2–2, Iran v UAE 0–0, Syria v Kuwait 1–0, UAE v Iran 0–1, Kuwait v Syria 4–2, Syria v Iran 0–2, Kuwait v UAE 2–3, Iran v Kuwait 2–0, UAE v Syria 1–3

	P	W	D	L	F	A	Pts
Iran	6	3	3	0	7	2	12
UAE	6	2	2	2	7	7	8
Syria	6	2	2	2	7	8	8
Kuwait	6	1	1	4	8	12	4

Iran and UAE qualify for Round Four

Round Four

Group 1 (Australia, Bahrain, Japan, Qatar, Uzbekistan)

Bahrain v Japan 2–3, Qatar v Uzbekistan 3–0, Uzbekistan v Australia 0–1, Qatar v Bahrain 1–1, Australia v Qatar 4–0, Japan v Uzbekistan 1–1, Qatar v Japan 0–3, Bahrain v Australia 0–1, Japan v Australia 0–0, Uzbekistan v Bahrain 0–1, Japan v Bahrain 1–0, Uzbekistan v Qatar 4–0, Australia v Uzbekistan 2–0, Bahrain v Qatar 1–0, Uzbekistan v Japan 0–1, Qatar v Australia 0–0, Australia v Bahrain 2–0, Japan v Qatar 1–1, Australia v Japan 2–1, Bahrain v Uzbekistan 1–0

	P	W	D	L	F	A	Pts
Australia	8	6	2	0	12	1	20
Japan	8	4	3	1	11	6	15
Bahrain	8	3	1	4	6	8	10
Qatar	8	1	3	4	5	14	6
Uzbekistan	8	1	1	6	5	10	4

Australia and Japan qualify for finals
Bahrain to fifth place play-off

Group 2 (Iran, North Korea, Saudi Arabia, South Korea, UAE)

Saudi Arabia v Iran 1–1, UAE v North Korea 1–2, North Korea v South Korea 1–1, UAE v Saudi Arabia 1–2, South Korea v UAE 4–1, Iran v North Korea 2–1, UAE v Iran 1–1, Saudi Arabia v South Korea 0–2, North Korea v Saudi Arabia 1–0, Iran v South Korea 1–1, North Korea v UAE 2–0, Iran v Saudi Arabia 1–2, South Korea v North Korea 1–0, Saudi Arabia v UAE 3–2, North Korea v Iran 0–0, UAE v South Korea 0–2, South Korea v Saudi Arabia 0–0, Iran v UAE 1–0, South Korea v Iran 1–1, Saudi Arabia v North Korea 0–0

	P	W	D	L	F	A	Pts
South Korea	8	4	4	0	12	4	16
North Korea	8	3	3	2	7	5	12
Saudi Arabia	8	3	3	2	8	8	12
Iran	8	2	5	1	8	7	11
UAE	8	0	1	7	6	17	1

South Korea and North Korea qualify for finals
Saudi Arabia to fifth place play-off

Fifth place play-off

Bahrain v Saudi Arabia 0–0, Saudi Arabia v Bahrain 2–2 (Bahrain win on away goals)

Bahrain to play off v Oceania winners (New Zealand)

Africa
53 countries, 5 qualify plus hosts South Africa

World Cup 2010 offered African nations not just a place on football's highest stage, but a chance to play on 'home soil'. For according to Danny Jordaan, head of South Africa's World Cup organizing committee, his country's was a tournament not just for South Africans but 'all Africans'.

In a qualifying contest that spanned twenty-five months and also doubled as the qualifying round of the 2010 African Cup of Nations in Angola, West African nations proved the continent's dominant forces once more, with Cameroon, Nigeria, Ghana and Ivory Coast joining hosts South Africa in qualifying for the 2010 finals. They were belatedly joined by Algeria, who qualified for the first time in a generation.

Led by a resurgent Didier Drogba, Ivory Coast progressed through their two group stages in emphatic fashion, going undefeated through twelve matches. Ghana, inspired by Drogba's Chelsea team-mate Michael Essien, likewise topped their group impressively.

Cameroon and Nigeria's passages were rather less seamless, however. Cameroon started their second qualifying group sluggishly, losing to Togo and drawing at home to Morocco. The country switched managers, replacing Otto Pfister, a veteran African national coach, with Paul Le Guen, a former Rangers and Paris St Germain manager, who had tasted success with Lyon earlier in the decade. He saw a dramatic turnaround, and the country won its last four matches to top Group A. Nigeria, likewise, started poorly, drawing games they needed to win. In their penultimate match against Mozambique, only a late winner by substitute Victor Obinna kept them in the competition, and they entered the final weekend two points behind Tunisia. Even against group underdogs Kenya, Nigeria needed to come back from behind to win 3–2, while Tunisia fell at the last, unexpectedly losing to Mozambique.

The most closely fought and intriguing group – arguably in the entire qualifying competition – was Group C, which pitted Algeria and Egypt together. Bitter memories still lingered of 1989, when Egypt beat Algeria to qualify for Italia '90. Then Algeria had gone ballistic at the final whistle, causing a near riot; in the post–match scramble the Egyptian team doctor was bottled by an Algerian player and blinded in one eye. The earlier encounter overshadowed Group C's final game in Cairo, which Egypt needed to win by more than two goals to stay in the competition. As Algeria made their way to the stadium, Egyptian fans – apparently with police looking the other way – threw bricks at the team bus and smashed in most of its windows. That set the tone for the tie, with a raucous, bitter atmosphere. Amr Zaki opened the scoring on just three minutes, but it took Emad Meteab until the fifth minute of stoppage time to get Egypt the goal they needed for salvation. Afterwards, Egypt and the Egyptian diaspora went wild in celebration, while in Algiers locals attacked Egyptian businesses.

The win left the two countries exactly level in their group and necessitated a play-off in Sudan the following week. Under the shadow of a massive police presence, Antar Yahia's brilliant 40th minute goal was enough to separate the two nations and send Algeria through to the finals for the first time since 1986.

Preliminary stage
(Single-leg match, due to civil war in Somalia)
Djibouti v Somalia 1–0

(Two-leg matches)
Madagascar v Comoros 6–2, Comoros v Madagascar 0–4, Sierra Leone v Guinea Bissau 1–0, Guinea Bissau v Sierra Leone 0–0

Djibouti, Madagascar and Sierra Leone qualify for first stage

Stage One
(World Cup qualifying tournament doubled as qualifying for 2010 African Cup of Nations. South Africa entered but only as part of African Cup of Nations qualifying process.)

Group 1 (Cameroon, Cape Verde, Mauritius, Tanzania)
Tanzania v Mauritius 1–1, Cameroon v Cape Verde 2–0, Cape Verde v Tanzania 1–0, Mauritius v Cameroon 0–3, Tanzania v Cameroon 0–0, Mauritius v Cape Verde 0–1, Cameroon v Tanzania 2–1, Cape Verde v Mauritius 3–1, Mauritius v Tanzania 1–4, Cape Verde v Cameroon 1–2, Tanzania v Cape Verde 3–1, Cameroon v Mauritius 5–0

	P	W	D	L	F	A	Pts
Cameroon	6	5	1	0	14	2	16
Cape Verde	6	3	0	3	7	8	9
Tanzania	6	2	2	2	9	6	8
Mauritius	6	0	1	5	3	17	1

Group 2 (Guinea, Kenya, Namibia, Zimbabwe)
Namibia v Kenya 2–1, Guinea v Zimbabwe 0–0, Kenya v Guinea 2–0, Zimbabwe v Namibia 2–0, Kenya v Zimbabwe 2–0, Namibia v Guinea 1–2, Zimbabwe v Kenya 0–0, Guinea v Namibia 4–0, Kenya v Namibia 1–0, Zimbabwe v Guinea 0–0, Namibia v Zimbabwe 4–2, Guinea v Kenya 3–2

	P	W	D	L	F	A	Pts
Guinea	6	3	2	1	9	5	11
Kenya	6	3	1	2	8	5	10
Zimbabwe	6	1	3	2	4	6	6
Namibia	6	2	0	4	7	12	6

Group 3 (Angola, Benin, Niger, Uganda)

Uganda v Niger 1–0, Angola v Benin 3–0, Benin v Uganda 4–1, Niger v Angola 1–2, Uganda v Angola 3–1, Niger v Benin 0–2, Benin v Niger 2–0, Angola v Uganda 0–0, Niger v Uganda 3–1, Benin v Angola 3–2, Angola v Niger 3–1, Uganda v Benin 2–1

	P	W	D	L	F	A	Pts
Benin	6	4	0	2	12	8	12
Angola	6	3	1	2	11	8	10
Uganda	6	3	1	2	8	9	10
Niger	6	1	0	5	5	11	3

Group 4 (Equatorial Guinea, Nigeria, Sierra Leone, South Africa)

Equatorial Guinea v Sierra Leone 2–0, Nigeria v South Africa 2–0, South Africa v Equatorial Guinea 4–1, Sierra Leone v Nigeria 0–1, Sierra Leone v South Africa 1–0, Equatorial Guinea v Nigeria 0–1, South Africa v Sierra Leone 0–0, Nigeria v Equatorial Guinea 2–0, Sierra Leone v Equatorial Guinea 2–1, South Africa v Nigeria 0–1, Equatorial Guinea v South Africa 0–1, Nigeria v Sierra Leone 4–1

	P	W	D	L	F	A	Pts
Nigeria	6	6	0	0	11	1	18
South Africa	6	2	1	3	5	5	7
Sierra Leone	6	2	1	3	4	8	7
Equatorial Guinea	6	1	0	5	4	10	3

Group 5 (Gabon, Ghana, Lesotho, Libya)

Ghana v Libya 3–0, Libya v Gabon 1–0, Lesotho v Ghana 2–3, Gabon v Ghana 2–0, Lesotho v Libya 0–1, Libya v Lesotho 4–0, Ghana v Gabon 2–0, Gabon v Lesotho 2–0, Libya v Ghana 1–0, Lesotho v Gabon 0–3, Gabon v Libya 1–0, Ghana v Lesotho 3–0

	P	W	D	L	F	A	Pts
Ghana	6	4	0	2	11	5	12
Gabon	6	4	0	2	8	3	12
Libya	6	4	0	2	7	4	12
Lesotho	6	0	0	6	2	16	0

Group 6 (Algeria, Gambia, Liberia, Senegal)

Senegal v Algeria 1–0, Liberia v Gambia 1–1, Algeria v Liberia 3–0, Gambia v Senegal 0–0, Gambia v Algeria 1–0, Liberia v Senegal 2–2, Algeria v Gambia 1–0, Senegal v Liberia 3–1, Algeria v Senegal 3–2, Gambia v Liberia 3–0, Senegal v Gambia 1–1, Liberia v Algeria 0–0

	P	W	D	L	F	A	Pts
Algeria	6	3	1	2	7	4	10
Gambia	6	2	3	1	6	3	9
Senegal	6	2	3	1	9	7	9
Liberia	6	0	3	3	4	12	3

Group 7 (Botswana, Ivory Coast, Madagascar, Mozambique)

Botswana v Madagascar 0–0, Ivory Coast v Mozambique 1–0, Madagascar v Ivory Coast 0–0, Mozambique v Botswana 1–2, Botswana v Ivory Coast 1–1, Madagascar v Mozambique 1–1, Mozambique v Madagascar 3–0, Ivory Coast v Botswana 4–0, Mozambique v Ivory Coast 1–1, Madagascar v Botswana 1–0, Ivory Coast v Madagascar 3–0, Botswana v Mozambique 0–1

	P	W	D	L	F	A	Pts
Ivory Coast	6	3	3	0	10	2	12
Mozambique	6	2	2	2	7	5	8
Madagascar	6	1	3	2	2	7	6
Botswana	6	1	2	3	3	8	5

Group 8 (Ethiopia, Mauritania, Morocco, Rwanda)

Rwanda v Mauritania 3–0, Morocco v Ethiopia 3–0*, Mauritania v Morocco 1–4, Ethiopia v Rwanda 1–2*, Mauritania v Ethiopia 0–1*, Rwanda v Morocco 3–1, Morocco v Rwanda 2–0, Ethiopia v Mauritania 6–1*, Mauritania v Rwanda 0–1, Ethiopia v Morocco not played, Morocco v Mauritania 4–1, Rwanda v Ethiopia not played

*Results annulled

Ethiopia were excluded from the qualifying tournament by FIFA on 12 September 2008, after the Ethiopian FA reneged on an earlier agreement to 'normalize the situation of the federation'.

	P	W	D	L	F	A	Pts
Morocco	4	3	0	1	11	5	9
Rwanda	4	3	0	1	7	3	9
Mauritania	4	0	0	4	2	12	0
Ethiopia	disqualified						
(match record:	4	2	0	2	8	6	6)

Group 9 (Burkina Faso, Burundi, Seychelles, Tunisia)

Burundi v Seychelles 1–0, Tunisia v Burkina Faso 1–2, Seychelles v Tunisia 0–2, Burkina Faso v Burundi 2–0, Seychelles v Burkina Faso 2–3, Burundi v Tunisia 0–1, Burkina Faso v Seychelles 4–1, Tunisia v Burundi 2–1, Seychelles v Burundi 1–2, Burkina Faso v Tunisia 0–0, Tunisia v Seychelles 5–0, Burundi v Burkina Faso 1–3

	P	W	D	L	F	A	Pts
Burkina Faso	6	5	1	0	14	5	16
Tunisia	6	4	1	1	11	3	13
Burundi	6	2	0	4	5	9	6
Seychelles	6	0	0	6	4	17	0

Group 10 (Chad, Congo, Mali, Sudan)

Mali v Congo 4–2, Chad v Mali 1–2, Congo v Sudan 1–0, Chad v Congo 2–1, Sudan v Mali 3–2, Congo v Chad 2–0, Mali v Sudan 3–0, Sudan v Chad 1–2, Congo v Mali 1–0, Chad v Sudan 1–3, Sudan v Congo 2–0, Mali v Chad 2–1

	P	W	D	L	F	A	Pts
Mali	6	4	0	2	13	8	12
Sudan	6	3	0	3	9	9	9
Congo	6	3	0	3	7	8	9
Chad	6	2	0	4	7	11	6 *

*Chad disqualified from the African Cup of Nations but their results allowed to stand towards World Cup qualifying.

Group 11 (Eritrea, Swaziland, Togo, Zambia)

Togo v Zambia 1–0, Swaziland v Togo 2–1, Swaziland v Zambia 0–0, Zambia v Swaziland 1–0, Zambia v Togo 1–0, Togo v Swaziland 6–0

	P	W	D	L	F	A	Pts
Zambia	4	2	1	1	2	1	7
Togo	4	2	0	2	8	3	6
Swaziland	4	1	1	2	2	8	4
Eritrea	Withdrew						

Eritrea withdrew from qualifying on 25 March 2008, before Group 11 kicked off.

Group 12 (DR Congo, Djibouti, Egypt, Malawi)

Malawi v Djibouti 8–1, Egypt v DR Congo 2–1, Djibouti v Egypt 0–4, DR Congo v Malawi 1–0, Djibouti v DR Congo 0–6, Malawi v Egypt 1–0, DR Congo v Djibouti 5–1, Egypt v Malawi 2–0, Djibouti v Malawi 0–3, DR Congo v Egypt 0–1, Malawi v DR Congo 2–1, Egypt v Djibouti 4–0

	P	W	D	L	F	A	Pts
Egypt	6	5	0	1	13	2	15
Malawi	6	4	0	2	14	5	12
DR Congo	6	3	0	3	14	6	9
Djibouti	6	0	0	6	2	30	0

Best runners-up Rwanda, Kenya, Tunisia, Togo, Gabon, Sudan, Malawi and Mozambique qualified for final stage along with the twelve group winners, Gambia, Angola and Cape Verde eliminated, South Africa failed to qualify for African Cup of Nations.

Stage Two

Group A (Cameroon, Gabon, Morocco, Togo)

Togo v Cameroon 1–0, Morocco v Gabon 1–2, Gabon v Togo 3–0, Cameroon v Morocco 0–0, Morocco v Togo 0–0, Gabon v Cameroon 0–2, Togo v Morocco 1–1, Cameroon v Gabon 2–1, Cameroon v Togo 3–0, Gabon v Morocco 3–1, Morocco v Cameroon 0–2, Togo v Gabon 1–0

	P	W	D	L	F	A	Pts
Cameroon	6	4	1	1	9	2	13
Gabon	6	3	0	3	9	7	9
Togo	6	2	2	2	3	7	8
Morocco	6	0	3	3	3	8	3

Cameroon qualify for finals

Group B (Kenya, Mozambique, Nigeria, Tunisia)
Kenya v Tunisia 1–2, Mozambique v Nigeria 0–0, Tunisia v Mozambique 2–0, Nigeria v Kenya 3–0, Kenya v Mozambique 2–1, Tunisia v Nigeria 0–0, Mozambique v Kenya 1–0, Nigeria v Tunisia 2–2, Nigeria v Mozambique 1–0, Tunisia v Kenya 1–0, Kenya v Nigeria 2–3, Mozambique v Tunisia 1–0

	P	W	D	L	F	A	Pts
Nigeria	6	3	3	0	9	4	12
Tunisia	6	3	2	1	7	4	11
Mozambique	6	2	1	3	3	5	7
Kenya	6	1	0	5	5	11	3

Nigeria qualify for finals

Group C (Algeria, Egypt, Rwanda, Zambia)
Rwanda v Algeria 0–0, Egypt v Zambia 1–1, Zambia v Rwanda 1–0, Algeria v Egypt 3–1, Zambia v Algeria 0–2, Egypt v Rwanda 3–0, Rwanda v Egypt 0–1, Algeria v Zambia 1–0, Zambia v Egypt 0–1, Algeria v Rwanda 3–1, Egypt v Algeria 2–0, Rwanda v Zambia 0–0

	P	W	D	L	F	A	Pts
Algeria	6	4	1	1	9	4	13
Egypt	6	4	1	1	9	4	13
Zambia	6	1	2	3	2	5	5
Rwanda	6	0	2	4	1	8	2

Play-off
Omdurman (Sudan) Algeria v Egypt 1–0

Algeria qualify for finals

Group D (Benin, Ghana, Mali, Sudan)
Sudan v Mali 1–1, Ghana v Benin 1–0, Benin v Sudan 1–0, Mali v Ghana 0–2, Sudan v Ghana 0–2, Mali v Benin 3–1, Benin v Mali 1–1, Ghana v Sudan 2–0, Mali v Sudan 1–0, Benin v Ghana 1–0, Sudan v Benin 1–2, Ghana v Mali 2–2

	P	W	D	L	F	A	Pts
Ghana	6	4	1	1	9	3	13
Benin	6	3	1	2	6	6	10
Mali	6	2	3	1	8	7	9
Sudan	6	0	1	5	2	9	1

Ghana qualify for finals

Group E (Burkina Faso, Guinea, Ivory Coast, Malawi)

Burkina Faso v Guinea 4–2, Ivory Coast v Malawi 5–0, Malawi v Burkina Faso 0–1, Guinea v Ivory Coast 1–2, Burkina Faso v Ivory Coast 2–3, Guinea v Malawi 2–1, Malawi v Guinea 2–1, Ivory Coast v Burkina Faso 5–0, Malawi v Ivory Coast 1–1, Guinea v Burkina Faso 1–2, Burkina Faso v Malawi 1–0, Ivory Coast v Guinea 3–0

	P	W	D	L	F	A	Pts
Ivory Coast	6	5	1	0	19	4	16
Burkina Faso	6	4	0	2	10	11	12
Malawi	6	1	1	4	4	11	4
Guinea	6	1	0	5	7	14	3

Ivory Coast qualify for finals

Oceania
11 countries, 1 to qualify for Asia/Oceania play-off

In a part of the world more synonymous with its passion for rugby, it was fitting that the Oceania qualifying round kicked off with score-lines more reminiscent of the oval-ball game. The South Pacific Games doubled up as the preliminary round, and Fiji kicked it off in resounding fashion, defeating Tuvalu 16–0, while the Solomon Islands started with a 12–1 win over American Samoa. The latter were the qualifying tournament's whipping boys, with a record of 'played 4, lost 4, scored 1, conceded 38'. Quite how Papua New Guinea, somehow ranked beneath American Samoa in the FIFA rankings, would have fared had they entered remains to be seen.

New Caledonia, Fiji and Vanuatu eventually qualified for the final round-robin series, in which they were joined by New Zealand, now Oceania's regional power following Australia's defection to the Asian Federation. The previous World Cup qualifying tournament had witnessed a new low in the history of New Zealand football, when they were trounced 4–2 by Vanuatu. But the new generation of the 'All Whites' were a different class, and this time they made no mistake in progressing to the Asia/Oceania play-off, where they would come up against Bahrain.

Preliminary stage (all games played in Apia, Samoa)

Group A (Cook Islands, Fiji, New Caledonia, Tahiti, Tuvalu)

Fiji v Tuvalu 16–0, Tahiti v New Caledonia 0–1, Tuvalu v New Caledonia 0–1,

Fiji v Cook Islands 4–0, Tuvalu v Tahiti 1–1, New Caledonia v Cook Islands 3–0, Cook Islands v Tuvalu 4–1, Tahiti v Fiji 0–4, New Caledonia v Fiji 1–1, Cook Islands v Tahiti 0–1

	P	W	D	L	F	A	Pts
Fiji	4	3	1	0	25	1	10
New Caledonia	4	3	1	0	6	1	10
Tahiti	4	1	1	2	2	6	4
Cook Islands	4	1	0	3	4	9	3
Tuvalu	4	0	1	3	2	22	1

Group B (American Samoa, Samoa, Solomon Islands, Tonga, Vanuatu)
Solomon Islands v American Samoa 12–1, Vanuatu v Samoa 4–0, Solomon Islands v Tonga 4–0, American Samoa v Samoa 0–7, American Samoa v Vanuatu 0–15, Samoa v Tonga 2–1, Tonga v American Samoa 4–0, Vanuatu 0–2 Solomon Islands, Samoa 0–3 Solomon Islands, Tonga v Vanuatu 1–4

	P	W	D	L	F	A	Pts
Solomon Islands	4	4	0	0	21	1	12
Vanuatu	4	3	0	1	23	3	9
Samoa	4	2	0	2	9	8	6
Tonga	4	1	0	3	6	10	3
American Samoa	4	0	0	4	1	38	0

Semi-finals
Solomon Islands v New Caledonia 2–3, Fiji v Vanuatu 3–0

Third place match
Solomon Islands 0–2 Vanuatu

Final
Fiji 0–1 New Caledonia

New Caledonia, Fiji and Vanuatu qualify for the qualifying stage

Qualifying stage (Fiji, New Caledonia, New Zealand, Vanuatu)
Fiji v New Zealand 0–2, Vanuatu v New Zealand 1–2, Fiji v New Caledonia 3–3, New Zealand v Vanuatu 4–1, New Caledonia v Fiji 4–0, Vanuatu v New Caledonia 1–1, New Caledonia v Vanuatu 3–0, Fiji v Vanuatu 2–0, New Caledonia v New Zealand 1–3, Vanuatu v Fiji 2–1, New Zealand v New Caledonia 3–0, New Zealand v Fiji 0–2

	P	W	D	L	F	A	Pts
New Zealand	6	5	0	1	14	5	15
New Caledonia	6	2	2	2	12	10	8
Fiji	6	2	1	3	8	11	7
Vanuatu	6	1	1	4	5	13	4

New Zealand qualify to Asia–Oceania play-off (v Bahrain)

THE PLAY-OFFS

Consternation dominated the European play-offs before a ball was even kicked. After a session of the FIFA Executive Committee in Rio de Janeiro in September 2009, President Sepp Blatter let slip – without adequately explaining the rationale – that they would in fact be seeded. No mention had been made of this before and it took no time for conspiracy theories to abound. In reality the reasoning was simple. At the time France, Germany, Italy, Portugal and Russia all faced the prospect of a play-off. The prospect of two or possibly four of these giants, including the holders and the previous runners-up, being drawn against one another, leading to the certain elimination of a major contender, was simply too unedifying for FIFA to contemplate. France, Greece, Portugal and Russia were the eventual seeds, to rightful howls of indignation from their opponents.

Given their poor form under Raymond Domenech's management, many fans viewed France as the weak link among the seeds. Ireland were drawn against them and had been undefeated in a group that included Italy, whom they briefly threatened to overhaul. Thet were managed by Italian Giovanni Trapattoni, who had moulded the weakest selection of Irish players in years into a formidably organized unit that, like Jack Charlton's famous sides, played to its strengths. This wasn't always pretty, but with their spirit, discipline and commitment they were an effective force. On a pulsating night at Dublin's giant Croke Park they were not quite effective enough, missing the best of a limited number of chances, while Nicolas Anelka's goal gave France the edge for the second leg in Paris.

Stade de France four days later was a sea of Irish shirts and noise, while the French whistled their own team and booed Domenech when his face appeared on a big screen. Many French fans had sold their tickets to Irish supporters, who descended on the city in their droves. Encouraged by their fervent support, Ireland dominated the game, going ahead through Robbie Keane's first-half goal. John O'Shea and Damien Duff should each have put the game beyond reach in the second half, but the game went to extra time. Here it entered infamy. In the 103rd minute Thierry Henry controlled a cross in the

Ireland area with his hand not once, but twice, then crossed for William Gallas to head what proved an aggregate winner. Henry, once an icon of European football, became a global villain for failing to own up to his crime, while Ireland desperately and unsuccessfully pleaded with Blatter to let them into South Africa as the '33rd team'.

Less drama hung over the other European play-offs. Portugal defeated Bosnia-Herzegovina home and away, ending one of the tournament's fairy tales. Workmanlike Greece overcame the equally unspectacular Ukraine 1–0 in Kiev, having been held to a goalless draw in the first leg. When Russia, so fresh and lively under Guus Hiddink's management, went 2–0 up through a Diniyar Bilyaletdinov brace against Slovenia, it looked as if FIFA's seedings machinations were paying a full dividend. But two minutes from the end of the first leg, substitute Nejc Pecnik silenced the Moscow crowd with a late consolation goal. Four days later in Maribor Zlatko Dedic's winner sent Slovenia – fifth out of six seeds in their qualifying group – through to their second finals.

In Manama, Bahrain, vying for their first finals appearance, were distinctly unlucky against New Zealand, who held them to a goalless draw in the Asia–Oceania play off, despite the host nation dominating proceedings. Four days and nine thousand miles later the two countries met again in Wellington. On a night of high drama Rory Fallon, a former England Youth international who had carved out a journeyman's career in the English lower leagues, headed a 44th minute winner. Before the All Whites progress was assured, New Zealand had to rely on a second-half penalty save from Mark Paston to send the 35,000 crowd – the largest football attendance in the country's history – wild.

Uruguay, in their third successive play-off, sought to erase memories of their painful exit in 2005, when Australia eliminated them in a penalty shoot-out. Facing Costa Rica in the South America–CONCACAF play-off, they closed out a 1–0 victory in San Jose with ruthlessness and close defending that had been their hallmark in their distant glory years. Yet in Montevideo, Costa Rica may well have won the return leg, the South Americans eventually doing enough to hold out for a 1–1 draw and become the 32nd and final qualifier for South Africa.

Europe
Ireland v France 0–1, France v Ireland 1–1 (aet, 0–1 after 90 mins)
France win 2–1 on aggregate

Portugal v Bosnia-Herzegovina 1–0, Bosnia-Herzegovina v Portugal 0–1
Portugal win 2–0 on aggregate

Greece v Ukraine 0–0, Ukraine v Greece 0–1
Greece win 1–0 on aggregate

Russia v Slovenia 2–1, Slovenia v Russia 1–0
2–2 on aggregate, Slovenia win on away goals

CONCACAF/South America
Costa Rica v Uruguay 0–1, Uruguay v Costa Rica 1–1
Uruguay win 2–1 on aggregate

Asia/Oceania
Bahrain v New Zealand 0–0, New Zealand v Bahrain 1–0
New Zealand win 1–0 on aggregate

The Venues
Capacities will fluctuate due to viewing restrictions and security
arrangements, figures therefore are approximate

Durban Stadium – 70,000
Durban

Ellis Park – 61,000
Johannesburg

Green Point – 70,000
Cape Town

Free State Stadium – 48,000
Bloemfontein

Loftus Versfeld Stadium – 50,000
Pretoria

Mbombela Stadium – 46,000
Nelspruit

Nelson Mandela Bay Stadium – 48,000
Port Elizabeth

Peter Mokaba Stadium – 46,000
Polokwane

Royal Bafokeng Stadium – 42,000
Rustenburg

Soccer City – 94,700
Johannesburg

The Draw

The draw, on 4 December 2009, brought Cape Town to a standstill. The city had been building up for it all week, and proceedings were kicked off by a recorded message from a frail-looking Nelson Mandela. 'We must ensure a lasting benefit to all our people,' he said. 'Let us prove that the long wait for a World Cup on African soil is worth it.' South African President Jacob Zuma appeared and said that he wanted the world to be 'surprised' and 'at the end of the World Cup, it stays on African soil'. His hope for an African winner drew one of the loudest cheers of the evening.

Zuma was joined on stage by FIFA President Sepp Blatter, in exuberant form, describing the female compere as 'a love story' and then forgetting that the tournament kicked off in Johannesburg. 'The World Cup will not only bring the best players in the world to South Africa, it will bring a recognition of Africa,' he said. 'Africa has waited so long for the World Cup, and now it has the World Cup.'

Giancarlo Aliberti, Italy Football Federation President, then handed the trophy back to Sepp Blatter and proceedings, overseen by actress Charlize Theron, dressed in brilliant pink and resembling a young Farrah Fawcett, got under way. She was joined by FIFA Secretary-General Jerome Valcke, the runner Haile Gebrselassie, South African rugby player John Smit, South African fast bowler Makhaya Ntini, Bafana Bafana player Matthew Booth, women's player Simphiwe Dludlu and David Beckham.

England manager Fabio Capello was one of the happiest of the thirty-two coaches afterwards, after what looked like an easy draw for his team. The United States, Algeria and Slovenia joined them in Group C, but they were left with the prospect of coming face to face with old rivals Germany in the round of sixteen.

Italy, the country of Capello's birth, also looked certain to qualify from Group F, with New Zealand, Paraguay and Slovakia standing in their way.

Favourites Brazil had the toughest draw and found themselves in the dreaded 'group of death' with North Korea, Portugal and Ivory Coast – the latter once more unfortunate, having come up against Argentina and Holland four years earlier.

The draw was also unkind to Germany, who face Australia, Ghana and Serbia, competing in a finals for the first time as a single nation.

World Cup hosts South Africa are likely to struggle to qualify from Group A; they will have to overcome the challenge posed by Mexico, France and Uruguay. Group B sees Argentina and Nigeria reunited, after the two countries faced each other in 2002. They are joined by South Korea and Greece.

Holland face Japan, Cameroon and Denmark in Group E, while Group H sees second–favourites Spain joined by Switzerland, Honduras and Chile.

Group A

South Africa
Mexico
Uruguay
France

Group B

Argentina
South Korea
Nigeria
Greece

Group C

England
USA
Algeria
Slovenia

Group D

Germany
Australia
Ghana
Serbia

Group E

Holland
Japan
Cameroon
Denmark

Group F

Italy
New Zealand
Paraguay
Slovakia

Group G

Brazil
North Korea
Ivory Coast
Portugal

Group H

Spain
Honduras
Chile
Switzerland

The Candidates

Staged in the middle of an African winter, where temperatures at night – particularly in Johannesburg, setting of two venues – can drop below freezing in June, the tournament is well suited to European nations, who are still to record a World Cup win outside their own continent. Among the giants of the European game, Spain are the outstanding candidates. Resounding winners at the 2008 European Championships, they have lost just a solitary match since November 2006, an incredible run heightened by the country's breathtaking football. The quality of Spain's players is reflected not so much in who starts every game – Andrés Iniesta, Xavi, Ikar Casillas, David Villa and so on – but who isn't guaranteed a place – Arsenal's captain and playmaker, Cesc Fabregas being one such player – and even those still yet to even make the national squad, such as Everton's outstanding playmaker, Mikel Arteta. But at the same time, Spain have a poor finals record and a tradition of choking at the big occasion. For all their exuberant football in 2006, they still fell to the sclerotic French, and will need to be tougher this time in the knockout stages.

Saved by Zidane in 2006 and eventually promoted to the final beyond their abilities, it seems difficult to argue a case for France's class of 2010. Even a favourable first-round draw after they went unseeded may not be enough. Their best chances rest with Thierry Henry, an aging but still potent threat, and Franck Ribéry, who must overcome an injury-ridden 2009/10 season to again show the world his supreme pace and power. Yet the defensive and midfield solidity that once formed the basis of their success has diminished and they lack natural leaders, particularly in the dugout – where the unpopular Raymond Domenech is almost certainly going to preside when France start their World Cup campaign against Uruguay.

England, by contrast, have in the recent past boasted excellent squads, but weak managers. Now, in Fabio Capello, a winner in every sense of the word, they boast one of the outstanding managers of the era, but a patchy squad. They have both a good midfield and defence – some of whom, such as Steven Gerrard, John Terry and Frank Lampard, can claim world-class credentials – and a sense that it's the last chance of this so–called golden generation. But will it be enough? Lacking an outstanding goalkeeper or forwards beyond Wayne Rooney is a serious problem for Capello. So, too are the personal foibles of his squad. Four months before the tournament kicked off, Terry was stripped of his captaincy after it was revealed he had an extra-marital affair with the mother of one of his team-mates' children. So much for esprit de corps! But the Italian coach seems to have restored the winning mentality and consistency of selection so lacking since the 1960s. With luck England could go far.

Holland, likewise, lack the thoroughbreds of their footballing past, but in an era when individual technique counts for so much, the ability of their well-rounded players to retain possession and dominate the middle of the pitch stands them in good stead. Moreover the pace and panache of players like Arjen Robben, Robin Van Persie and Rafael Van der Vaart means that the small lowland nation still punches above its weight and can count itself among the elite of world football.

Germany, like their Dutch neighbours, no longer seem to have the big individual names that once illuminated European football, but should never be discounted. Written off in 2002 after their 5–1 obliteration on home soil by England in qualifying, Germany reached the final. Four years later, when hosting the tournament, they overcame their own public's scepticism to reach the semi-finals, and were arguably the tournament's best team. They possess an experience and understanding of the big occasion that is almost without parallel in world football, while the country's best young players – such as the elegant winger Mesut Özil – seem to have slipped beneath the notice of many of their rivals.

Reigning champions Italy have endured a precarious few years since their moment of glory in Berlin. The *Calciopoli* scandal heightened the malaise of the world's once most powerful domestic league, and an aging international squad has not been benefited by its clubs' reluctance to invest in youth. A poor showing at Euro 2008, which included the country's biggest defeat – 3–0 – in twenty-five years to Holland in its opening game, saw Roberto Donadoni sacked as manager, and a return for World Cup-winning coach Marcello Lippi. But although he qualified for the finals, there has been little sense of progress. Italy were again shown up in the 2009 Confederations Cup, when Brazil tore through their aging defence and repeated the 3–0 beating handed out by the Dutch a year earlier. A 1–0 defeat to Egypt compounded the country's misery. They will, nevertheless, benefit from a straightforward group stage and could belatedly grow as a team, as they did when they won the competition last time.

It would be difficult to consider any of the other European nations for much beyond a round of sixteen place. Portugal, now without Luis Felipe Scolari and Luis Figo, may even struggle to get out of a tough group, which includes Brazil and Ivory Coast. Much depends on the form of Cristiano Ronaldo, although as France showed in 2006, one man blessed with footballing genius can make a nation go far. Neither Greece, Slovenia, Serbia, Denmark, Slovakia nor Switzerland possess the sort of magic needed to illuminate the latter stages of the tournament.

The chaos that has so far accompanied Diego Maradona's reign as Argentina manager diminishes the chances of one of the most talented squads in the tournament. This is a shame, for not even Brazil can boast such strength in depth in attack as their neighbours and rivals. Argentina's forwards include

Lionel Messi, the diminutive and brilliant FIFA World Player of the Year; Atlético Madrid's Sergio Aguero, who combines the burden of being one of the hottest properties in the world game with being Maradona's son-in-law; Carlos Tevez; and Real Madrid's young tyro, Gonzalo Higuain. But memories of the glorious football witnessed in Germany may just be that. One thing is nevertheless for sure; there will never be a dull moment with El Diego around.

His Brazilian counterpart Dunga was, as a player, everything that Maradona was not – steady, efficient, dependable, dour – and as managers their differences are equally similar. Brazil bear the imprint of Dunga, resembling in many ways the side that lifted the World Cup in 1994. Despite boasting such flair players as Kaka, Robhino and Nilmar, Dunga's Brazil are defined by their tactical discipline, their almost European way of play; there is frequently a sense that they play within themselves, but conversely they are more efficient and deadly for it.

Pelé's famous maxim about an African nation winning the World Cup by the end of the last century was, of course, never fulfilled, but will 2010 be their year? South Africa, the lowest ranked of all thirty-two finalists, can be immediately discounted and, having received a tough draw, may well become the first hosts to fall in the opening stage. In the African Cup of Nations Algeria showed little of the spirit that saw them through to their first finals in a generation, and they too might struggle. Nigeria are less of the force they were in the 1990s, and only qualified for South Africa in dramatic circumstances. But they have a fairly straightforward group and may well click in the knockout stages. Paul Le Guen, who enjoyed great success as Lyon coach, looks to have brought the sort of tactical discipline to Cameroon's 'Indomitable Lions' so often lacking in African teams. Their performance in January's African Cup of Nations was nevertheless underwhelming.

Ghana progressed the furthest of African nations in 2006, but despite a spirited show against Brazil in the round of sixteen their tactical naivety was exposed and they were clinically dismantled. With the benefit of more experience and a fairly generous draw, they could make the quarter-finals; their powerful midfielder Michael Essien often promises to be among the world's best, and South Africa could be his stage.

Who would want the luck of the Ivory Coast? They possess the best squad of Africa's qualifiers and the potential to go far. But last time they were drawn with Argentina and Holland and dismissed by their third game; in 2010 they meet Portugal and Brazil in their first two games, and may well be finished by the time they meet North Korea in their third. If they can overcome their group, things scarcely improve in the second round. Awaiting Drogba and company there may well be Spain.

South American dark horses have fallen before. In 1994 Columbia were rated among the favourites, but returned home after the first round having been humbled by Romania and unexpectedly beaten by the United States. But Chile, in only their second finals in a quarter of a century, possess verve and panache as well as something of the unknown, which could see them land a knockout blow. Without Guus Hiddink in charge, the spirited Australians may struggle to repeat the heroics of 2006; much rests on their second group match with Ghana, and victory in that encounter could be crucial. As for their fellow Asian qualifiers, South Korea might benefit from mediocre group opponents, but for North Korea the group of death looks too much for them to overcome.

South Africa was a controversial choice to host the World Cup finals, with concerns over its high crime rate, infrastructure and ability to pay and adequately prepare for the tournament dominating many outsiders' minds. Yet many of these attitudes were misplaced and remained rooted in outmoded colonial attitudes, ignorance and casual racism. South Africa 2010's CEO Danny Jordaan had made it his life's work to see a World Cup on his country's soil and, once vested with the authority to host the tournament, was not prepared to see the country's doubters proved right. A thoughtful man, who kept South African football alive during its apartheid era, Jordaan has spent many of the last few years biting his lip as misconceptions about his country have been presented to him by the rest of the world. The world's media, he said six months before the big kick-off, had 'misrepresented' South Africa and 'the core of who we are as South Africans'. He urged the world to ignore scare stories and experience 'the warmth' of the South African people. Anyone lucky enough to visit the country will find out just what he means.

It is true that South Africa will lack the gloss of recent World Cups, but it will also be missing the cynical current of commercialism that increasingly defines it. As Jordaan often says, it will be a tournament not just for South Africa, but all Africans, and they can take justifiable pride in enjoying a good news story about what many outsiders still consider a 'hopeless' continent. South Africa's finals will be vibrant, colourful and a little edgy; there will be a prevailing sense that anything can happen – it will be a little like the World Cups we used to know.

Above all, though, it will be an outstanding celebration of a misunderstood but wonderful country. And, of course, of world football.

LEADING

SCORERS

THE LEADING SCORERS
The 'Golden Boot' Award

1930	Stabile **Argentina**	8
1934	Nejedly **Czechoslovakia**	4
	Schiavio **Italy**	4
	Conen **Germany**	4
1938	Leonidas **Brazil**	8
1950	Ademir **Brazil**	9
1954	Kocsis **Hungary**	11
1958	Fontaine **France**	13
1962	Garrincha **Brazil**	4
	Vava **Brazil**	4
	Sanchez **Chile**	4
	Jerkovic **Yugoslavia**	4
	Albert **Hungary**	4
	Ivanov **USSR**	4
1966	Eusebio **Portugal**	9
1970	Muller **West Germany**	9
1974	Lato **Poland**	7
1978	Kempes **Argentina**	6
1982	Rossi **Italy**	6
1986	Lineker **England**	6
1990	Schillaci **Italy**	6
1994	Salenko **Russia**	6
	Stoichkov **Bulgaria**	6
1998	Suker **Croatia**	6
2002	Ronaldo **Brazil**	8
2006	Klose **Germany**	5